The Audit Committee Handbook

Fourth Edition

THE AUDIT COMMITTEE HANDBOOK

Fourth Edition

LOUIS BRAIOTTA, JR., C.P.A.
School of Management
State University of New York at Binghamton

WILEY

New York • Chichester • Brisbane • Toronto • Singapore

Published by John Wiley & Sons, Inc., Hoboken, New Jersey
Published simultaneously in Canada

For general information on our other products and services, or technical support, please
contact our Customer Care Department within the United States at 800-762-2974, outside
the United States at 317-572-3993 or fax 317-572-4002.

Wiley also publishes its books in a variety of electronic formats. Some content that appears in print may not be available in electronic books.

ISBN: 0-471-48884-4

Printed in the United States of America

10 9 8 7 6 5 4 3 2 1

To the Adopters of the third edition
and dedicated to my mother,
Frances Braiotta.

From the Forewords of the First Two Editions . . .

Excerpt from the foreword to the second edition:

Members of audit committees will find this second edition an invaluable resource in meeting their oversight responsibilities and give them an increasing awareness of their current duties as well as an insight into future developments.

—Richard S. Hickok, CPA
Chairman, Hickok Associates, Inc.,
and Chairman Emeritus of KMG/Main Hurdman
(now KPMG Peat Marwick)

Excerpt from the foreword of the first edition:

Audit committee members will find this book a useful reference in performing their oversight responsibilities. It should also help them develop a constructive relationship between their function and the activities of the full corporate board, management, and internal and external auditors.

—John C. Biegler, CPA
Chairman Emeritus, Price Waterhouse International
(now PricewaterhouseCoopers)

About the Website

As a purchaser of *Audit Committee Handbook, Fourth Edition,* you have access to the companion website. The website contains a Glossary and other Appendices that provide valuable perspective and key legislation to interested readers. To access the website, go to *www.wiley.com/go/auditcommittee.*

Website Contents

C   Glossary

D   Historical Perspective on Audit Committees

E   Foreign Corrupt Practices Act Amendments

F   Federal Deposit Insurance Corporation Improvement Act

G   Excerpt from *The Code of Best Practice*

H   Model Business Corporation Act—Chapter 8: Directors and Officers

I   Committee of Sponsoring Organizations of the Treadway Commission, *Internal Control-Integrated Framework—Volume 1, Executive Summary*

J   Example of a Code of Business Conduct—Some Broad Guidelines

Contents

APPENDIXES

Appendixes C–J are available on *The Audit Committee Handbook* website at *www.wiley.com/go/auditcommittee*.

Preface

Since the publication of the third edition of *The Audit Committee Handbook* in 1999, a number of major accounting scandals (e.g., Enron, WorldCom, and others) as well as the demise of the international accounting firm of Anderson LLP have shaken the global capital markets. As a result, the U.S. Congress enacted the Sarbanes-Oxley Act of 2002 and the Securities and Exchange Commission adopted final rules amending the securities laws. Likewise, the Self-Regulatory Organizations set forth a number of amendments to their listing standards with respect to corporate governance and accountability. The major thrust of these reforms is to create a new regulatory and legal environment and corporate accountability framework, which, in turn, provides an effective financial reporting system with relevant and reliable financial information. The primary goal is to restore investor confidence through an efficient securities market system.

Historically, the role and responsibilities of the audit committee as a key institution in corporate governance has been accepted as an important oversight mechanism to help the board of directors discharge its fiduciary financial responsibility and stewardship accountability to the shareholders. However, the aforementioned events have caused a reexamination of the audit committee's role in the context of corporate governance. In fact, these events have caused a number of best practices for the audit committee to become federal statute. Given these mandates, members of audit committees must adhere to higher standards in corporate accountability to ensure the quality of financial information and investor protection against accounting scandals. Audit committees in a global securities marketplace continue to respond to the investing public's demand for oversight protection. (See Appendix D on this book's website.) As noted, such committees not only help engender a high degree of integrity in both the internal and external audit processes and financial reporting process, but they also help provide for an efficient and transparent securities market. For example, many countries with developed equity markets or emerging markets have adopted audit committees through public and/or private sector initiatives to ensure price protection of their securities to investors. Moreover, the recent initiatives to develop and adopt harmonized international accounting and auditing standards accentuate the need to achieve uniformity in oversight protection to investors. It should be noted that companies will use the endorsement of these standards by the International Organization of Securities Commissions in their stock offering documents to raise capital in a global securities marketplace.

Although many countries have recognized that the establishment and benefits of audit committees help to ensure integrity in the corporate accountability process, it is imperative that such committees conduct their activities in an efficient and effective manner to help their boards of directors discharge their financial and fiduciary responsibilities to stockholders. As noted in the text, the recent enactment of the Sarbanes-Oxley Act of 2002 will influence significantly how boards of directors through their audit committees can meet their oversight responsibilities in both the auditing and financial reporting areas. This fourth edition provides comprehensive guidance to all functions, duties, and responsibilities of audit committees as well as their direction in the corporate governance context. It retains the thrust of the third edition, focusing on current trends and developments that maximize the effectiveness of audit committees. Numerous references are made to the pronouncements of leading organizations in both the public and private sectors to bring an element of authority to the handbook.

Recognizing that audit committees interact with the internal auditor, independent auditor, chief financial officer, internal legal counsel, and independent legal counsel, the fourth edition continues to offer practical guidance in developing a constructive relationship between the committees' jurisdictional responsibilities and the activities of these executives. This revised professional reference work enables the aforementioned parties to help audit committees plan their agendas and achieve their mission in corporate governance. It provides a perspective that will help the members of the audit committee develop the appropriate requisite knowledge with respect to such matters as:

- Understanding the role and responsibilities of the audit committee with a general update and reality check on auditing cycle activities.
- Identifying the developments that impact audit committee practices and the latest techniques and strategies for committee meetings.
- Understanding the latest authoritative sources that enable audit committee members to develop a repertoire of effective strategies to help the board of directors discharge its fiduciary responsibility to the stockholders.
- Developing a comprehensive professional development program that enables committee members to prepare a periodic assessment of their activities and an informed review of both audit processes and financial reporting process.
- Understanding the legal aspects of the audit committee and role of legal counsel as well as fraudulent financial reporting.

The book is divided into four parts. Part 1 includes a discussion on corporate accountability, the audit committee's basic roles and responsibilities, the external users of accounting information, and the legal position of the audit committee. In addition, the broad framework of generally accepted auditing standards and their integration with generally accepted accounting principles are dealt with in one chapter to show their interrelationship.

Part 2 covers the planning function of the audit committee. An initial overview of the concept of audit planning is presented and followed with a discussion of the audit director's role in planning the audit. This part includes a discussion of the selection or reappointment of the public accounting firm.

Part 3 describes the monitoring and reviewing functions of the audit committee. Here the book focuses on the system of internal control, the internal audit function, accounting policy disclosures, fraud and the auditor, and sensitive business practices.

Part 4 covers the reporting function of the audit committee. Special attention initially is given to an overview of the independent auditor's opinions and reports. The final chapter explains the purpose of the audit committee's report and discusses the guidelines for preparing it.

This book seeks to provide useful information and guidance for the audit committee and to point out opportunities for auditors and management to better serve the audit committee.

LOUIS BRAIOTTA, JR., C.P.A.
Binghamton, New York

Acknowledgments

I want to express my appreciation to Dr. Upinder Dhillon, dean of the School of Management of Binghamton University (State University of New York), for his encouragement in the preparation of the manuscript. Also, I want to thank my faculty colleagues, accounting practitioners, and students for their encouragement and support.

I am grateful to the American Institute of Certified Public Accountants, the Institute of Internal Auditors, the American Bar Association, and the Association of Certified Fraud Examiners for their permission to use certain materials subject to their copyrights.

My sincere thanks to Bernie Cencetti for her fine typing work and to Colleen Hailey, associate librarian. My thanks to the people at John Wiley & Sons for their production and editorial assistance.

Part One

Getting Acquainted with Your Responsibilities

Corporate Accountability: The New Environment

To properly understand the importance of the corporate director's position on the audit committee, one must understand the nature and importance of the concept of corporate accountability in the new legal and regulatory framework under statutory law. Therefore, the major objectives of this chapter are: first, to revisit the meaning and significance of corporate accountability; second, to explain the significance of major audit committee developments in the context of corporate accountability with special emphasis on those of the past five years; and third, to show the impact of corporate accountability on the audit committee and its corporate relationships.

Although the recent failures of major corporations, such as Enron, WorldCom, and others, have accelerated the need for legal and regulatory reforms, the concept and meaning of corporate accountability in relation to the institution of the audit committee remains the same both before and after accounting scandals. However, with the enactment of the Sarbanes-Oxley Act of 2002, the substantive meaning of corporate accountability has caused many best practices for audit committees to become statutory law. Moreover, the new legislation has caused an institutional restructuring of the accounting profession as well as additional resources for the Securities and Exchange Commission (SEC) to curb abuses of fraudulent financial reporting.

THE NATURE AND IMPORTANCE OF CORPORATE ACCOUNTABILITY

The Meaning of Corporate Accountability

With the recent establishment of the Public Company Accounting Oversight Board (PCAOB) with its oversight and enforcement authority over the independent audit process and the concomitant effect on strengthening the institution of the audit committee, it is reasonable to expect that shareholders and other constituencies of corporations will receive relevant and reliable financial information. Thus, such congressional legislative action will help to ensure an efficient capital market system. As James S. Turley, chairman and chief executive officer of Ernst & Young LLP, points out;

> The biggest problem today is the loss of confidence, in not just our profession, but in financial management, executive management. audit committees and boards.

[While] I see no silver bullet to turn that around, I think it is going to be turned around by sustained, outstanding performance, high quality [and] high integrity by all parties—management, audit committees, audit firms.[1]

Strictly speaking, the concept of corporate accountability may be stated in this way:

The board of directors is charged with safeguarding and advancing the interest of the stockholders, acting as their representatives in establishing corporate policies, and reviewing management's execution of those policies. Accordingly, the directors have a fiduciary responsibility to the stockholders. They have an obligation to inform themselves about the company's affairs and to act diligently and capably in fulfilling their responsibilities.[2]

The board of directors is charged with protecting the interests of the stockholders because the position of the board is determined by state laws. The powers and responsibilities of the board are defined in the corporate charter and the corporate bylaws. Therefore, from a legal point of view, the basic purpose of corporate accountability is to provide a legal framework within which the directors must discharge their stewardship accountability to the stockholders. Furthermore, the board is directly answerable to the stockholders because the stockholders, as the owners of the enterprise, have entrusted their capital resources to the management of the corporation. (See Appendix H on this book's website.)

The Business Roundtable described corporate accountability in this way:

The board of directors is ultimately accountable to the shareholders for the long-term successful economic performance of the corporation consistent with its underlying public purpose. Directors are held accountable for their performance in a variety of ways.

First, there is the powerful accountability imposed by markets. The impact of consumer dissatisfaction with products and services is quick and visible. Financial markets also quickly reflect their evaluation of the quality of accountability through the price of equity and debt.

Accountability is also imposed through the numerous statutes and regulations enacted by governmental bodies to limit and control corporate action. Directors are held accountable to regulatory mechanisms.

There is also a body of law—part statutory, part court-made—which defines the duties of directors and the principles and boundaries within which they must keep their decisions. If they overstep, their decisions are subject to reversal by the courts. Directors can also be held personally liable, without limitation, to the extent of their personal assets if they violate their duty of loyalty to the corporation.

A final form of board accountability comes through the election of directors by the shareholders at the corporation's annual meeting. Annual meetings may also include shareholder resolutions which are a form of governance by referendum.

---

[1]James S. Turley, "The Future of Corporate Reporting: From the Top," *Financial Executive* 70 (December 2002), p. 2.
[2]American Institute of Certified Public Accountants, *Audit Committees, Answers to Typical Questions about Their Organization and Operations* (New York: AICPA, 1978), p. 7.

Each of these forms of accountability is dynamic, not static. The developing specifics of each form of accountability must be judged as to its overall potential to contribute to the successful long-term performance of the corporation. Each specific new item of accountability carries with it the potential for harm as well as good.[3]

More recently, the Business Roundtable restated its guiding principles of corporate governance:

First, the paramount duty of the board of directors of a public corporation is to select a chief executive officer and to oversee the CEO and other senior management in the competent and ethical operation of the corporation on a day-to-day basis.

Second, it is the responsibility of management to operate the corporation in an effective and ethical manner in order to produce value for stockholders. Senior management is expected to know how the corporation earns its income and what risks the corporation is undertaking in the course of carrying out its business. Management should never put personal interests ahead of or in conflict with the interests of the corporation.

Third, it is the responsiblity of management, under the oversight of the board and its audit committee, to produce financial statements that fairly present the financial condition and results of operations of the corporation, and to make the timely disclosures investors need to permit them to assess the financial and business soundness and risks of the corporation.

Fourth, it is the responsibility of the board and its audit committee to engage an independent accounting firm to audit the financial statements prepared by management and to issue an opinion on those statements based on Generally Accepted Accounting Principles. The board, its audit committee, and management must be vigilant to ensure that no actions are taken by the corporation or its employees that compromise the independence of the outside auditor.

Fifth, it is the responsibility of the independent accounting firm to ensure that it is in fact independent, is without conflicts of interest, employs highly competent staff, and carries out its work in accordance with Generally Accepted Auditing Standards. It is also the responsibility of the independent accounting firm to inform the board, through the audit committee, of any concerns the auditor may have about the appropriateness or quality of significant accounting treatments, business transactions that affect the fair presentation of the corporation's financial condition and results of operations, and weaknesses in internal control systems. The auditor should do so in a forthright manner and on a timely basis, whether or not management has also communicated with the board or the audit committee on these matters.

Sixth, the corporation has a responsibility to deal with its employees in a fair and equitable manner.

These responsibilities, and others, are critical to the functioning of the modern public corporation and the integrity of the public markets. No law or regulation alone can be a substitute for the voluntary adherence to these principles by corporate directors and management and by the accounting firms retained to serve American corporations.

The Business Roundtable continues to believe that the most effective way to enhance corporate governance is through conscientious and forward-looking action by a

---

[3]The Business Roundtable, *Corporate Governance and American Competitiveness* (New York: The Business Roundtable, 1990), pp. 15–16.

business community that focuses on generating long-term stockholder value with the highest degree of integrity.

The principles discussed here are intended to assist corporate management and boards of directors in their individual efforts to implement best practices of corporate governance, and also to serve as guideposts for the public dialogue on evolving governance standards.[4]

With respect to establishing and maintaining corporate policies, the board of directors is responsible to the stockholders for ensuring that management fulfills its responsibilities in the execution of the corporate policies. For example, the board can authorize the establishment of an audit committee to assist the board with the development of the financial accounting policies. In addition, the audit committee can be authorized to review the preparation of the financial statements as well as to select the independent auditors. Although the board has the power to delegate authority to the various standing committees, such as the audit committee or the executive committee, the board must render an accountability to the stockholders. In short, the board has a fiduciary relationship with the stockholders and, as a result, must report periodically on the status of the corporation's economic resources.

As John Shandor points out:

Audit committees have become crucial to the audit process. Also, the audit committee has been considered essential in an organizational approach to making boards of directors more effective in their interaction with financial management and chief executive officers as well as with internal audit staff and independent auditors.[5]

In addition to the directors' fiduciary responsibility, they are expected to attend board meetings and their appropriate standing committee meetings. A director must keep informed on the affairs of the corporation and use reasonable care and diligence in the performance of his or her duties. It is imperative that the director keep abreast of the corporate developments since he or she is directly responsible for participating in the decisions that affect the management of the corporation. Thus the director may be held liable for losses sustained by the corporation as a result of his or her neglect.

Practically speaking, the concept of corporate accountability extends not only to the stockholders but also to the other constituencies of the board of directors, such as credit grantors and governmental agencies. The extension of corporate accountability to the other constituencies is evidenced by a meeting of the American Assembly. The discussion leaders focused their attention on questions central to running the corporation vis-à-vis its many constituencies. With respect to a framework for corporate accountability, the participants generally agreed on this:

Boards of directors have a primary role in interpreting society's expectations and standards for management.

---

[4]The Business Roundtable, *Principles of Corporate Governance* (Washington, DC: The Business Roundtable, May 2002), pp. iv–vi.

[5]John Shandor, "Audit Committees Take a Broader Role in Corporate Policy," *Corporate Controller* 2 (November/December 1989), pp. 46–48.

The five key board functions are:

(a) Appraisal of management performance and provision for management and board succession;

(b) Determination of significant policies and actions with respect to present and future profitability and strategic direction of the enterprise;

(c) Determination of policies and actions with a potential for significant financial, economic, and social impact;

(d) Establishment of policies and procedures designed to obtain compliance with the law; and

(e) Responsibility for monitoring the totality of corporate performance.

Boards should continue to be the central focus in improving the way corporations are governed.[6]

In addition to the American Assembly's recommendations, to establish and maintain a successful program of corporate accountability, the following three prerequisites are necessary:

1. The board of directors and the officers must assume prime responsibility for corporate accountability as well as define and clarify the objectives and responsibilities concerning the different levels of the organization. Therefore, the individuals who are assigned responsibility at the middle and lower management levels should be held accountable for their activities.

2. The organization chart of the corporation is central to establishing corporate accountability since the jurisdiction for each area within the corporation must be defined. Also, the extent of authority should not only be clearly outlined but also commensurate with the individual's responsibilities.

3. Executive management should create a management environment whereby the middle and lower management levels understand the nature of corporate accountability. Thus management should maintain an effective communications network within the organizational structure.

As a case in point, Bruce W. McCuaig and Paul G. Makosz report that Gulf Canada Resources, Ltd., has developed a new approach to corporate governance through the use of an internal control assessment strategy. Such a strategy was developed based on a clear definition of internal control as a combination of (1) organization controls, (2) systems development and change controls, (3) authorization and reporting controls, (4) accounting systems controls, (5) safeguarding controls, (6) management supervisory controls, and (7) documentation controls. With the implementation of a management-by-objectives framework and related control mechanisms, the authors observed that the board of directors and senior management are far better informed.[7]

---

[6]The American Assembly, *Corporate Governance in America*, Pamphlet 54 (New York: Columbia University, April 1978), p. 6.

[7]Bruce W. McCuaig and Paul G. Makosz, "Is Everything Under Control? A New Approach to Corporate Governance," *Financial Executive* 6, No. 1 (January/February 1990), p. 25.

The subject of corporate accountability is a dynamic concept in the governance of the corporation. It is dynamic because the directors not only must assess the changing needs of their constituencies but also render a stewardship accountability based on legal pressures from their constituencies.

The Need for Corporate Accountability

In view of the size and scope of modern corporations as well as the increasing demands in the legal and regulatory environment, the need for corporate accountability has become very important in the evaluation of the performance of the board of directors. For example, the sales figures of these corporations amount to billions of dollars, which far exceed the gross national product of several countries. In addition, large corporations have control over the major economic resources of society. Furthermore, the board of directors is subject to numerous public laws, such as the Environmental Protection Act, the Occupational Safety and Health Act, federal securities laws, and antitrust laws. Thus many of these corporate enterprises play a significant role in the future of our society, since the decisions of corporate management have a direct impact on the economy.

Unfortunately, corporations are confronted with the problem of a lack of credibility because they often have been subject to corporate self-interest as opposed to the public interest. As one former executive partner of Price Waterhouse International asserts:

> We have all been stunned by the shocking disclosures of alleged improper payments and similar activities, not by funny fly-by-night firms nobody ever heard of, but by some of the finest names on the roster of American enterprise. . . . As one inevitable result, reinforced by uneasy business conditions, public confidence in American business has plunged to its lowest level since the great depression. It is as if these events simply confirmed a gathering suspicion that such transgressions are not exceptional—a suspicion that American business is built on bribery and deceit.[8]

Samuel A. DiPiazza, Jr., CEO, PricewaterhouseCoopers LLP, and Robert G. Eccles, president, Advisory Capital Partners, echo that observation:

> Public trust has shaken in the institutions on which this value creation depends. These institutions share a collective responsibility for producing the information on which people of many levels—investors, lenders, trading partners, customers, employees—depend to make a wide range of economic decisions. The challenge now is to institute the necessary reforms to ensure that public trust does not disappear, and the foundation for those reforms lies in corporate reporting.[9]

In an effort to close the credibility gap or the expectation gap with respect corporate accounting scandals, the U.S. Congress passed the Sarbanes-Oxley Act on

---

[8]John C. Biegler, "Rebuilding Public Trust in Business," *Financial Executive* 45 (June 1977), p. 28.
[9]Samuel A. DiPiazza and Robert Eccles, *Building Public Trust: The Future of Corporate Reporting* (New York: John Wiley & Sons, 2002), p. 2. See also John Morrissey, Securities and Exchange Commission, "Corporate Responsibility and the Audit Committee," March 21, 2000, *www.sec.gov/news/ speech/spch357.htm.*

July 25, 2002, and President George W. Bush signed the bill into law on July 30, 2002.[10] Now the standards of corporate accountability have been enacted into statutory law, including securities laws and self-regulatory organizations' listing standards. Such legislation will provide a framework that can be used to measure the performance of audit committee members, independent auditors, chief executive officers, and chief financial officers. Consequently, directors of publicly help corporations may be more vulnerable to lawsuits as well as to the increased risk of liability. As a result, many qualified persons may be reluctant to accept a position on a board of directors.

Although the standards of corporate accountability have been addressed recently in the U.S. Congress, the call for higher standards in corporate governance and financial reporting has remained a top priority, as evidenced by these observations.

The need to resolve the credibility gap is evident. Corporate management must adopt standards of corporate accountability. As one proponent points out:

> Every corporation's business is conducted by some standard. If it is not formulated systematically at the top, it will be formulated haphazardly and impulsively in the field. And top management will be called on to defend practices that were unnecessary and unintended.[11]

Consequently, the need for corporate accountability is not only apparent but essential in shaping and projecting a corporate image to the public.

Shaun F. O'Malley, former co-chairman of Price Waterhouse World Firm (now PricewaterhouseCoopers), points out that dramatic changes have occurred in the roles of boards of directors, auditors, and management and in the relationships between these groups. Corporate accountability is a question of balance among the three groups as well as between government and the private sector. Shareholders and other constituencies of the company will continue their demands for protecting the company from fraud along with communicating warning signals of possible business failures.[12]

Daniel J. McCauley and John C. Burton comment on the changing expectations of director responsibility and audit committees:

> The limited responsibility of the directors for financial matters, as it formerly existed, has been significantly changed in recent years. The public's loss of confidence in the business community has been accompanied by a correlative demand for greater director vigilance over company financial integrity. This oversight function of the board has been promoted as one of the means for restoring business's image.[13]

---

[10]Sarbanes-Oxley Act of 2002, H.R. Rep. No. 107-610, July 25, 2002, and Title 1 of Public Law No. 107-204, July 30, 2002.

[11]Biegler, "Rebuilding Public Trust in Business," p. 29.

[12]Shaun F. O'Malley, "Auditing, Directors, and Management: Promoting Accountability," *Internal Auditing* 5, No. 3 (Winter 1990), p. 3.

[13]Daniel J. McCauley and John C. Burton, *Audit Committees,* C.P.S. No. 49 (Washington, DC: The Bureau of National Affairs, 1986), p. A–3.

RECENT DEVELOPMENTS IN CORPORATE ACCOUNTABILITY

As previously discussed, during the late 1990s, unprecedented public attention was focused on the role and responsibility of audit committees in promoting corporate accountability and investor confidence in the integrity of the audit processes and financial reporting process. Although the concept and practices of audit committees were recognized and accepted over the past 20 years, unexpected failures of major corporations and disclosures of questionable financial reporting practices diluted investors' confidence in the capital marketplace. Notwithstanding, the common question asked by investors was "Where were the auditors?" Another question was "Where was the audit committee?" As a result, a number of public and private sector initiatives were undertaken in the late 1990s and the post–Enron, post–WorldCom period in response to high-profile accounting scandals and the demise of a large accounting firm.

This time line provides a chronology of the important developments and/or studies related to audit committees. (The time line presents major developments; the reader may wish to visit the websites noted parenthetically for further reading.)

1998   SEC chairman Arthur Levitt's speech, "The Numbers Game" (Remarks at New York University's Center for Law and Business and the SEC's Nine-Point Action Plan)

1999   Blue Ribbon Committee on Improving the Effectiveness of Corporate Audit Committees,
        Report and Recommendations of the Blue Ribbon Committee on Improving the Effectiveness of Corporate Audit Committees
        Securities and Exchange Commission,
        Final Rules, Audit Committee Disclosure, and approval of the New York Stock Exchange, Nasdaq, and American Stock Exchange
        American Institute of Certified Public Accountants' Auditing Standards Board
        Statement on Auditing Standards No. 90, "Audit Committee Communication"
        National Association of Corporate Directors (NACD) *Blue Ribbon Commission on Audit Committees,*
        Report of the NACD Blue Ribbon Commission on Audit Committees (visit the NACD website, *www.nacdonline.org.*)
        Committee of Sponsoring Organizations of the Treadway Commission,
        Fraudulent Financial Reporting: 1987–1997 An Analysis of U.S. Public Companies (visit the AICPA website, *www.aicpa.org.*)
        Independence Standards Board
        No. 1 "Independence Discussion with Audit Committees" (Visit the ISB website, *www.cpaindependence.org*; see also Appendix D on this book's website.)

2000   Public Oversight Board
        Panel on Audit Effectiveness (O'Malley Panel),
        The Panel on Audit Effectiveness,
        Report and Recommendations

2001   Chairman Arthur Levitt's Letter to Audit Committees
        Public Oversight Board, Final Annual Report
        (May 1, 2002 the POB terminated its existence; visit the POB website,
        www.POB.org.)

2002   *The Business Roundtable*
        Principles of Corporate Governance
        NYSE Corporate Accountability and Listing Standards Committee,
        Report on Proposed Changes to the Corporate Governance Listing
        Standards
        Nasdaq Listing and Hearing Review Council, *Letter of recommendations*
        proposing corporate governance reforms (Visit the NASD website,
        www.nasdaqnewsroom.com.)
        U.S. Congress, *Corporate Responsibility Act and the Public Company*
        Accountability Public Oversight Board
        (Sarbanes-Oxley Act of 2002)
        CEO/CFO Certification Statement Day
        (Visit the SEC website, *www.sec.gov.*)
        Public Company Accounting Oversight Board
        (Visit the SEC website, *www.sec.gov.*)

2003   Implementation of the sections of the Sarbanes-Oxley Act of 2002
        through amendments to Sec. 10A of the Securities Exchange of 1934

Public and Private Sector Initiatives

Securities and Exchange Commission   In September 1998, Arthur Levitt,
chairman of the Securities and Exchange Commission and now chairman emeritus, expressed his concerns about "hocus pocus accounting" in a keynote speech
entitled "The Numbers Game." In addition to his remarks regarding the decline in
the quality of financial reporting (e.g., earnings management strategies to meet
analyst and market quarterly expectations via creative acquisition accounting, premature revenue recognition, restructuring charges, "cookie jar reserves," and materiality judgments) as well as the related decline in market capitalization, Levitt
stated that with respect to audit committees:

> qualified, committed, independent and toughminded audit committees represent the
> most reliable guardians of the public interest. Sadly, stories abound of audit com-
> mittees whose members lack expertise in the basic principles of financial reporting
> as well as the mandate to ask probing questions.[14]

Recognizing the problem with respect to the decline in the integrity and credibility of financial reporting, Levitt set forth the SEC's nine-point action plan (see
Exhibit 1.1). Strengthening the audit committee process was number 8 of the action items. As a result, the SEC, the New York Stock Exchange (NYSE), and the

---

[14]See remarks by Chairman Arthur Levitt, Securities and Exchange Commission, "The Numbers
Game," NYU Center for Law and Business, New York, September 28, 1998, (*www.sec.gov/news/*
speeches/spch220.txt).

Exhibit 1.1 Summary of the Securities and Exchange's Nine-Point Action Plan

---

First, I have instructed the SEC staff to require well-detailed disclosures about the impact of changes in accounting assumptions. This should include a supplement to the financial statement showing beginning and ending balances as well as activity in between, including any adjustments. This will, I believe, enable the market to better understand the nature and effects of the restructuring liabilites and other loss accruals.

Second, we are challenging the profession, through the AICPA, to clarify the ground rules for auditing of purchased R&D. We also are requesting that they augment existing guidance on restructurings, large acquisition write-offs, and revenue recognition practices. It's time for the accounting profession to better qualify for auditors what's acceptable and what's not.

Third, I reject the notion that the concept of materiality can be used to excuse deliberate misstatements of performance. I know of one Fortune 500 company who had recorded a significant accounting error, and whose auditors told them so. But they still used a materiality ceiling of six percent earnings to justify the error. I have asked the SEC staff to focus on this problem and publish guidance that emphasizes the need to consider qualitative, not just quantitative factors of earnings. Materiality is not a bright line cutoff of three or five percent. It requires consideration of all relevant factors that could impact an investor's decision.

Fourth, SEC staff will immediately consider interpretive accounting guidance on the do's and don'ts of revenue recognition. The staff will also determine whether recently published standards for the software industry can be applied to other service companies.

Fifth, I am asking private sector standard setters to take action where current standards and guidance are inadequate. I encourage a prompt resolution of the FASB's projects, currently underway, that should bring greater clarity to the definition of a liability.

Sixth, the SEC's review and enforcement teams will reinforce these regulatory initiatives. We will formally target reviews of public companies that announce restructuring liability reserves, major write-offs or other practices that appear to manage earnings. Likewise, our enforcement team will continue to root out and aggressively act on abuses of the financial reporting process.

Improved Outside Auditing in the Financial Reporting Process
Seventh, I don't think it should surprise anyone here that recent headlines of accounting failures have led some people to question the thoroughness of audits. I need not remind auditors they are the public's watchdog in the financial reporting process. We rely on auditors to put something like the good housekeeping seal of approval on the information investors receive. The integrity of that information must take priority over a desire for cost efficiencies or competitive advantage in the audit process. High quality auditing requires well-trained, well-focused and well-supervised auditors.

As I look at some of the failures today, I can't help but wonder if the staff in the trenches of the profession have the training and supervision they need to ensure that audits are being done right. We cannot permit thorough audits to be sacrificed for re-engineered approaches that are efficient, but less effective. I have just proposed that the Public Oversight Board form a group of all the major constituencies to review the way audits are performed and assess the impact of recent trends on the public interest.

Strengthening the Audit Committee Process
And, finally, qualified, committed, independent and tough-minded audit committees represent the most reliable guardians of the public interest. Sadly, stories abound of audit committees whose members lack expertise in the basic principles of financial reporting as well as the mandate to ask probing questions. In fact, I've heard of one audit committee that convenes only twice a year before the regular board meeting for 15 minutes and whose duties are limited to a perfunctory presentation.

Compare that situation with the audit committee which meets twelve times a year before each board meeting; where every member has a financial background; where there are no personal ties to the chairman or the company; where they have their own advisers; where they ask tough questions of management and outside auditors; and where, ultimately, the investor interest is being served.

The SEC stands ready to take appropriate action if that interest is not protected. But, a private sector response that empowers audit committtees and obviates the need for public sector dictates seems the wisest choice. I am pleased to announce that the financial community has agreed to accept this challenge.

As part eight of this comprehensive effort to address earnings management, the New York Stock Exchange and the National Association of Securities Dealers have agreed to sponsor a "blue-ribbon" panel to be headed by John Whitehead, former Deputy Secretary of State and retired senior partner of Goldman, Sachs, and Ira Millstein, a lawyer and noted corporate governance expert. Within the next 90 days, this distinguished group will develop a series of far-ranging recommendations intended to empower audit committees and function as the ultimate guardian of investor interests and corporate accountability. They are going to examine how we can get the right people to do the right things and ask the right questions.

Need for a Cultural Change
Finally, I'm challenging corporate management and Wall Street to re-examine our current environment. I believe we need to embrace nothing less than a cultural change. For corporate managers, remember, the integrity of the numbers in the financial reporting system is directly related to the long-term interests of a corporation. While the temptations are great, and the pressures strong, illusions in numbers are only that— ephemeral, and ultimately self-destructive.

To Wall Street, I say, look beyond the latest quarter. Punish those who rely on deception, rather than the practice of openness and transparency.

Source: See remarks by Chairman Arthur Levitt, Securites and Exchange Commission, "The Numbers Game," NYU Center for Law and Business, New York, September 28, 1998, *www.sec.gov/news/speeches/spch220.txt.*

National Association of Securities Dealers agreed that both self-regulatory organizations sponsor a Blue Ribbon Committee (BRC) called Improving the Effectiveness of Corporate Audit Committees. In September 1998, the BRC was formed. It issued its final report and recommendations in February 1999. The BRC's primary goal was to produce a report "geared toward effecting pragmatic, progressive changes in the functions and expectations placed on corporate boards, audit committees, senior and financial management, the internal audit, and the outside auditors regarding financial reporting and the oversight process."[15] Furthermore, the BRC noted that its final recommendations were based on two essentials: "First, an audit committee, with actual practice and overall performance that reflects the professionalism embodied by the full board of which it is a part, and second, a legal, regulatory, and self-regulating framework that emphasizes disclosure and transparency and accountability."[16] (See Exhibit 1.2 for a summary of the BRC's recommendations.)

During the period between February and December 1999, boards of directors and their audit committees studied the BRC's recommendations and reevaluated the responsibilities of their audit committees.[17] Additionally, the SEC and

---

Exhibit 1.2   Summary of Recommendations of the Blue Ribbon Committee on Improving the Effectiveness of Corporate Audit Committees

---

The first two recommendations are aimed at strengthing the independence of the audit committee:

Recommendation 1
The Committee recommends that both the New York Stock Exchange (NYSE) and the National Association of Securities Dealers (NASD) adopt the following definitions of independence for purposes of service on the audit committee for listed companies with a market capitalization above $200 million (or a more appropriate measure for identifying smaller-sized companies as determined jointly by the NYSE and the NASD):

Members of the audit committee shall be considered independent if they have no relationship to the corporation that may interfere with the exercise of their independence from management and the corporation. Examples of such relationships include:

- a director being employed by the corporation or any of its affiliates for the current year or any of the past five years;
- a director accepting any compensation from the corporation or any of its affiliates other than compensation for board service or benefits under a tax-qualified retirement plan;
- a director being a member of the immediate family of an individual who is, or has been in any of the past five years, employed by the corporation or any of its affiliates as an executive officer;

(continued)

---

[15]The report is available on the Internet at *www.nyse.com* and *www.nasd.com*.
[16]Ibid., p. 8.
[17]See for example, *Report of the NACD Blue Ribbon Commission on Audit Committees* (Washington, DC: NACD, 1999); see also Financial Executives Institute and Arthur Andersen, "The Audit Symposium: A Balanced Reponsibility" (Morristown, NJ: Financial Executives Institute); *Fraudulent Financial Reporting: 1987–1997, An Analysis of U.S. Public Companies* (New York: COSO of the Treadway Commission, 1999).

- a director being a partner in, or a controlling shareholder or an executive officer of, any for-profit business organizations to which the corporation made, or from which the corporation received, payments that are or have been significant* to the corporation or business organization in any of the past five years;
- a director being employed as an executive of another company where any of the corporation's executives serves on that company's compensation committee.

A director who has one or more of these relationships may be appointed to the audit committee, if the board, under exceptional and limited circumstances, determines that membership on the committee by the individual is required by the best interests of the corporation and its shareholders, and the board discloses, in the next annual proxy statement subsequent to such determination, the nature of the relationship and the reasons for that determination.

Recommendation 2

The Committee recommends that in addition to adopting and complying with the definition of independence set forth above for purposes of service on the audit committee, the NYSE and the NASD require that listed companies with a market capitalization above $200 million (or a more appropriate measure for identifying smaller-sized companies as determined jointly by the NYSE and the NASD) have an audit committee comprised solely of independent directors.

The Committee recommends that the NYSE and the NASD maintain their respective current audit committee independence requirements as well as their respective definitions of independence for listed companies with a market capitalization of $200 million or below (or a more appropriate measure for identifying smaller-sized companies as determined jointly by the NYSE and the NASD).

Our second set of recommendations is aimed at making the audit committee more effective:

Recommendation 3

The Committee recommends that the NYSE and the NASD require listed companies with a market capitalization above $200 million (or a more appropriate measure for identifying smaller-sized companies as determined jointly by the NYSE and the NASD) to have an audit committee comprised of a minimum of three directors, each of whom is financially literate (as described in the section of this report entitled "Financial Literacy") or becomes financially literate within a reasonable period of time after his or her appointment to the audit committee, and further that at least one member of the audit committee have accounting or related financial management expertise.

The Committee recommends that the NYSE and the NASD maintain their respective current audit committee size and membership requirements for companies with a market capitalization of $200 million or below (or a more appropriate measure for identifying smaller-sized companies as determined jointly by the NYSE and the NASD).

Recommendation 4

The Committee recommends that the NYSE and the NASD require the audit committee of each listed company to (i) adopt a formal written charter that is approved by the full board of directors and that specifies the scope of the committee's responsibilities, and how it

---

*The committee views the term "significant" in the spirit of Section 1.34(a)(4) of the American Law Institute Principles of Corporate Governance and the accompanying commentary to that section.

(continued)

Exhibit 1.2   (*Continued*)

carries out those responsibilities, including structure, processes, and membership requirements, and (ii) review and reassess the adequacy of the audit committee charter on an annual basis.

Recommendation 5
The Committee recommends that the Securities and Exchange Commission (SEC) promulgate rules that require the audit committee for each reporting company to disclose in
the company's proxy statement for its annual meeting of shareholders whether the audit
committee has adopted a formal written charter, and, if so, whether the audit committee
satisfied its responsibilities during the prior year in compliance with its charter, which
charter shall be disclosed at least triennially in the annual report to shareholders or proxy
statement and in the next annual report to shareholders or proxy statement after any significant amendment to that charter.
    The Committee further recommends that the SEC adopt a "safe harbor" applicable to
all disclosure referenced in the Recommendation 5.

**Our final group of recommendations addresses mechanisms for accountability
among the audit committee, the outside auditors, and management:**

Recommendation 6
The Committee recommends that the listing rules for both the NYSE and the NASD require that the audit committee charter for every listed company specifiy that the oustide auditor is ultimately accountable to the board of directors and the audit committee, as
representatives of shareholders, and that these shareholder representatives have the ultimate authority and responsibility to select, evaluate, and, where appropriate, replace the
outside auditor (or to nominate the outside auditor to be proposed for shareholder approval
in any proxy statement).

Recommendation 7
The Committee recommends that the listing rules for both the NYSE and the NASD
require that the audit committee charter for every listed company specify that the audit
committee is responsible for ensuring its receipt from the outside auditors of a formal
written statement delineating all relationships between the auditor and the company,
consistent with Independence Standards Board Standard 1, and that the audit committee
is also responsible for actively engaging in a dialogue with the auditor with respect to
any disclosed relationships or services that may impact the objectivity and independence
of the auditor and for taking, or recommending that the full board take, appropriate
action to ensure the independence of the outside auditor.

Recommendation 8
The Committee recommends that Generally Accepted Auditing Standards (GAAS) require that a company's outside auditor discuss with the audit committee the auditor's
judgments about the quality, not just the acceptability, of the company's accounting principles as applied in its financial reporting; the discussion should include such issues as the
clarity of the company's financial disclosures and degree of aggressiveness or conser-
vatism of the company's accounting principles and underlying estimates and other significant decisions made by management in preparing the financial disclosure and reviewed by

the outside auditors. This requirement should be written in a way to encourage open, frank discussion and to avoid boilerplate.

Recommendation 9
The Committee recommends that the SEC require all reporting companies to include a letter from the audit committee in the company's annual report to shareholders and Form 10-K Annual Report disclosing whether or not, with respect to the prior fiscal year: (i) management has reviewed the audited financial statements with the audit committee, including a discussion of the quality of the accounting principles as applied and significant judgments affecting the company's financial statements; (ii) the outside auditors have discussed with the audit committee the outside auditors' judgments of the quality of those principles as applied and judgments referenced in (i) above under the circumstances; (iii) the members of the audit committee have discussed among themselves, without management or the outside auditors present, the information disclosed to the audit committee described in (i) and (ii) above; and (iv) the audit committee, in reliance on the review and discussions conducted with management and the outside auditors pursuant to (i) and (ii) above, believes that the company's financial statements are fairly presented in conformity with Generally Accepted Accounting Principles (GAAP) in all material aspects.

The Committee further recommends that the SEC adopt a "safe harbor" applicable to any disclosure referenced in this Recommendation 9.

Recommendation 10
The Committee recommends that the SEC require that a reporting company's outside auditor conduct a SAS 71 Interim Financial Review prior to the company's filing of its Form 10-Q.

The Committee further recommends that SAS 71 be amended to require that a reporting company's outside auditor discuss with the audit committee, or at least its chairman, and a representative of financial management, in person, or by telephone conference call, the matters described in AU Section 380, Communications With the Audit Committee, prior to the filing of the Form 10-Q (and preferably prior to any public announcement of financial results), including significant adjustments, management judgments and accounting estimates, significant new accounting policies, and disagreements with management.

Source: Blue Ribbon Committee on Improving the Effectiveness of Corporate Audit Committees, *Report and Recommendations of the Blue Ribbon Committee on Improving the Effectiveness of Corporate Audit Committees* (New York: The Blue Ribbon Committee on Improving the Effectiveness of Corporate Audit Committees, 1999), pp. 10–16.

self-regulatory organizations (SROs) issued proposed rules and changes to the SRO's listing standards. Finally, in December 1999, the SEC, the SRO's, and the AICPA's Auditing Standards Board adopted new rules, listing standards, and auditing standards for improving the effectiveness of audit committees. Exhibit 1.3 contains a flow chart that delineates the items to meet the new SEC disclosure rules, the SRO's listing standards, and professional auditing standards.

Exhibit 1.3 New Requirements and Disclosure Rules for Audit Committees: A Flow Chart

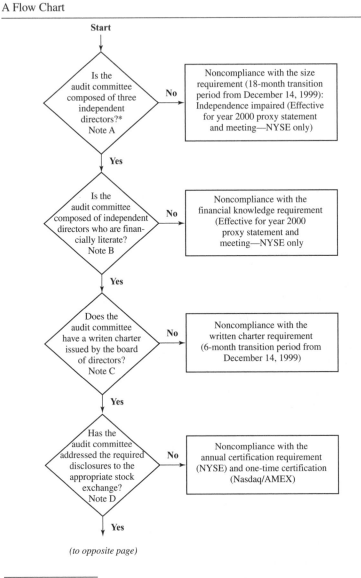

(to opposite page)

Notes: A. If the board of directors determines in its business judgment that the relationship (e.g., certain business relationships and/or one nonindependent member relationship) does not interfere with the director's exercise of independent judgment, then independence is not impaired.

B. The board of directors determines in its business judgment whether each member of the audit committee is financially literate. Based on the board's business judgment, at least one member must have accounting or related financial management expertise.

C. Each listed company must have an audit committee charter that guides its activities.

D. Each listed company (NYSE) is required to furnish a written certification letter, submitted annually, affirming the aforementioned points in A, B, and C. Nasdaq/AMEX listed companies require a one-time certification with respect to A, B, and C above.

E. After December 15, 2000, the SEC requires proxy statement disclosure of a report from the audit committee indicating whether the committee: (1) reviewed and discussed financial statements with management and the external auditors; (2) discussed with the external auditors matters required by SAS No. 61;

(from preceding page)

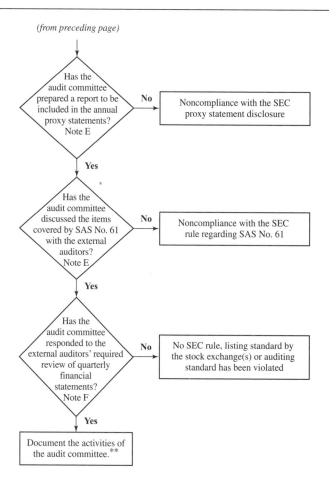

Has the audit committee prepared a report to be included in the annual proxy statements? Note E

No → Noncompliance with the SEC proxy statement disclosure

Yes

Has the audit committee discussed the items covered by SAS No. 61 with the external auditors? Note E

No → Noncompliance with the SEC rule regarding SAS No. 61

Yes

Has the audit committee responded to the external auditors' required review of quarterly financial statements? Note F

No → No SEC rule, listing standard by the stock exchange(s) or auditing standard has been violated

Yes

Document the activities of the audit committee.**

(3) received a written letter from the external auditors required by ISBS No. 1 and discussed independence issues; and (4) based on the aforementioned review and discussions, recommended to the board that the audited financial statements be included in the company's annual SEC 10-K report. Additionally, after December 15, 2000, the SEC requires proxy statement disclosures of whether the audit committee is governed by a written charter, and if it is, each registrant must attach a copy to the proxy statement once every three years. Finally, each SEC registrant is required to disclose in its proxy statements whether audit committee members are independent and provide information about members that are not. (See Note A above).

F. Starting with the fiscal quarter ending on or after March 15, 2000, SEC rules mandate that the external auditors review the quarterly financial statements prior to the filing of Form 10-Q or 10-QSB. In its 1987 report, the National Commission on Fraudulent Financial Reporting (NCFFR) recommended that "the audit committee oversight responsibilites undertaken on behalf of the board of directors extend to the quarterly reporting process. The audit committee should review the controls that management has established to protect the integrity of the quarterly reporting process. This review should be ongoing" (p. 48). In February 1999, the Blue Ribbon Committee reaffirmed the NCFFR's position (p. 16).

*The SEC approved amendments to the NYSE, NASD, and AMEX listing standards that require all audit committee members to be independent; however, one nonindependent member can serve on the committee. See Order Approving Proposed Rule Change SEC Release No. NYSE 34-42233, SEC Release No. NASD 34-42231, and SEC Release No. AMEX 34-42232.

Source: This flow chart, prepared by Louis Braiotta, Jr., is included and adopted from an article by Robert W. Rouse and Mark R. Borrelli, "Audit Committees in an Era of Increased Scrutiny." *CPA Journal* 70, No. 6 (June 2000), pp. 30–31. Copyright © 2000 by the New York State Society of Certified Public Accountants, 530 Fifth Avenue, New York, NY 10036-5101. All rights reserved.

**It may be advisable to have in-house general counsel review the above documentation as well as a review by outside legal counsel.

In January 1999, the Public Oversight Board agreed to sponsor the Panel on Audit Effectiveness. The major objective of the panel was to review and evaluate ways to improve independent audits in the financial reporting process and to assess the impact of recent trends on the public interest. In August 2000, the panel issued its report and recommendations. With respect to audit committees, the panel made these recommendations:

2.88 The Panel recommends that audit committees increase the time and attention they devote to discussions of internal control with management and both the internal and external auditors. Specifically, audit committees should:

- Obtain a written report from management on the effectiveness of internal control over financial reporting (ordinarily using the criteria in the 1992 report of the Committee of Sponsoring Organizations of the Treadway Commission [COSO]). Annual reporting by management on internal control to the audit committee is necessary for the effective discharge of the audit committee's responsibilities and will serve as a catalyst for its more substantive involvement in the area of internal control and a more meaningful dialogue with the internal and external auditors about controls. It also should provide a basis for discussions about the degree of the external auditor's involvement with internal control during the financial statement audit.

- Establish specific expectations with management and the internal and external auditors about the qualitative information needs of the committee related to internal control. Particular emphasis should be given to understanding management's and the auditors' views on (1) the control environment and (2) the controls (or lack thereof) over financial reporting, with particular attention to controls in higher-risk areas of the company's information systems. In addition, these discussions should include the effects of technology on current and future information systems. [pp. 32–33]

2.164 The Panel recommends that audit committees evaluate the nature of entities' reserves and review activity in them with both management and the auditors. [p. 55]

2.219 The Panel recommends that audit committees:

- Specify in their charters and reflect in their actions, as recommended by the Blue Ribbon Committee, "that the outside auditor is ultimately accountable to the board of directors and the audit committee, as representatives of the shareholders, and that these shareholder representatives have the ultimate authority and responsibility to select, evaluate, and where appropriate, replace the outside auditors (or to nominate the outside auditors to be proposed for shareholder approval in any proxy statement)."

- Develop a formal calendar of activities related to those areas of responsibility prescribed in the committee charter, including a meeting plan that is reviewed and agreed to by the entire board. The meeting plan should include communications between the committee chair or full committee and the auditor before the release of interim or year-end financial data. In addition, the Panel recommends a minimum of two face-to-face meetings during the year with the external auditor and at least one executive session with the internal and external auditors without management's presence.

- Take charge of their agenda and ensure, in particular, that it focuses on, among other matters, risks directly affecting the financial statements, key controls, interim financial information, policies and practices for management's communications with analysts, and the qualitative aspects of financial reporting.

- Inquire about time pressures on the auditor, including pressures on the timing of audit procedures; the degree of management's cooperation with the auditor; and their potential effects on audit effectiveness.

- Review the internal and external auditors' performance on an annual basis; exercise responsibility, as the external auditor's primary client, to assess the auditor's responsiveness to the committee's and board of directors' expections; and be satisfied that the auditor is appropriately compensated for performing a thorough audit.

- Require the auditor and management to advise the committee of the entity's plans to hire any of the audit firm's personnel into high-level positions, and the actions, if any, that the auditor and management intend to take to ensure that the auditor maintains independence. [pp. 68–69]

3.54 The Panel recommends that audit committees:

- Request management to report on the control environment within the entity and how that environment and the entity's policies and procedures (including management's monitoring activities) serve to prevent and detect financial statement fraud. Such reporting should acknowledge, in explicit terms, that fraud prevention and detection are primarily the responsibility of management. It also should help audit committees assess the strength of management's commitment to a culture of intolerance for improper conduct. Furthermore, audit committees should seek the views of auditors on their assessment of the risks of financial statement fraud and their understanding of the controls designed to mitigate such risks.

- Accept responsibility for ascertaining that the auditors receive the necessary cooperation from management to carry out their duties in accordance with the strengthened auditing standards to be developed by the ASB [Accouting Standards Board]. [p. 94]

5.30 The Panel recommends that audit committees pre-approve non-audit services that exceed a threshold determined by the committee. This recommendation is consistent with the recommendations of the Blue Ribbon Committee on Improving the Effectiveness of Corporate Audit Committees regarding auditors' services. The threshold should be at a level that ensures that significant services are pre-approved, but not so low that the committee assumes a management function.

When audit committees determine whether to approve specific non-audit services, the Panel recommends that they consider the same guiding principle and the factors suggested above for use by the ISB. [p. 117][18]

   In addition to the panel's recommendations, Arthur Levitt issued a letter to the chairmen of audit committees of the top 5,000 corporations. The letter is shown in Exhibit 1.4.

   In May 2002, the Business Roundtable issued a white paper, *Principles of Corporate Governance*, with respect to how boards of directors perform their oversight function through the audit committee. The Business Roundtable provides these guidelines:

- Every publicly owned corporation should have an audit committee comprised solely of independent directors.

---

[18]Panel on Audit Effectiveness, *Panel on Audit Effectiveness Report and Recommendations* (Stanford, CT: POB, 2000).

Exhibit 1.4   Chairman Arthur Levitt's Letter to Audit Committees

Washington, DC, January 5, 2001—Securities and Exchange Commission Chairman Arthur Levitt today sent the following letter to the audit committee chairmen of the top 5,000 public companies.

Dear Members of the Audit Committee:

Almost a year ago, the Commission, our major markets and standard setters—building on the work of the Blue Ribbon Committee on Audit Committee Effectiveness—adopted rules that strengthen the audit committee's independence, and give its members the tools and the wherewithal to fulfill their duty to the investing public. In addition, the rules improve communications, through greater disclosure, among the board, outside auditors and management.

When auditors and the board engage in frank and meaningful discussions about the significant, but sometimes gray areas of accounting, both the company's and its shareholders' interests are served. In this way, the board, including the audit committee, management, and outside auditors, form a "three-legged stool" of responsible disclosure and active oversight.

In recent months, the Commission and the accounting profession have been engaged in a discussion on the vital issue of auditor independence. Among other reasons, increased economic pressures on the profession, coupled with greater competition and consolidation, mandated that we modernize and further clarify independence requirements. This discussion has led to a combination of rules and disclosures that establish clear guidelines on the non-audit services an auditor may provide to an audit client, as well as the meaningful involvement of the audit committee in consideration of consulting services that may impair independence. More specifically, the Commission's rules require companies to state in their proxy statement whether the audit committee has considered whether the provision of non-audit services is compatible with maintaining the auditor's independence.

In August, the Panel on Audit Effectiveness issued its final report recommending that, among other things, audit committees obtain annual reports from mangement assessing the company's internal controls, specify in their charters that the outside auditor is ultimately accountable to the board of directors and audit committee, inquire about time pressures on the auditor, and pre-approve non-audit services provided by the auditor.

The Panel, more specifically, provided guidance an audit committee can use to determine the appropriateness of a service. This guidance includes:

1. Whether the service is being performed principally for the audit committee.
2. The effects of the service, if any, on audit effectiveness or on the quality and timeliness of the entity's financial reporting process.
3. Whether the service would be performed by specialists (e.g., technology specialists) who ordinarily also provide recurring audit support.
4. Whether the service would be performed by audit personnel, and if so, whether it will enhance their knowledge of the entity's business and operations.
5. Whether the role of those performing the service would be inconsistent with the auditors' role (e.g., a role where neutrality, impartiality, and auditor skepticism are likely to be subverted).
6. Whether the audit firm personnel would be assuming a management role or creating a mutual or conflicting interest with management.
7. Whether the auditors, in effect, would be "auditing their own numbers."
8. Whether the project must be started and completed very quickly.
9. Whether the audit firm has unique expertise in the service.
10. The size of the fee(s) for the non-audit service(s).

I encourage your audit committee to discuss the Panel's recommendations as well as these ten factors and consider them in relevant discussions with your auditor. The Panel's report can be found at *www.pobauditpanel.org/*. I also encourage you to read the Commission's rule release at *www.sec.gov.rules/final/33-7919.htm*.

During my almost eight years at the Commission, I have come to believe that one of the most reliable guardians of the public interest is a competent, committed, independent and tough-minded audit committee. The audit committee stands to protect and preserve the integrity of America's financial reporting process. I encourage your committee to take every step possible to ensure that the integrity of the financial statements, and by extension, the interest of shareholders, remains second to none.

Sincerely,

Arthur Levitt

Source: www.sec.gov/news.htm.

- Audit committees typically consist of three to five members. The listing standards of the major securities markets require audit committees and require that an audit committee have at least three members and that all members of the audit committee qualify as independent under the applicable listing standards, subject to limited exceptions.

- Audit committee members should meet minimum financial literacy standards, and at least one of the committee members should have accounting or financial management expertise, as required by the listing standards of the major securities markets. However, more important than financial expertise is the ability of audit committee members, as with all directors, to understand the corporation's business and risk profile and to apply their business experience and judgment to the issues for which the committee is responsible with an independent and critical eye.

- The audit committee is responsible for oversight of the corporation's financial reporting process. The primary functions of the audit committee are the following:

  - *Risk profile.* The audit committee should understand the corporation's risk profile and oversee the corporation's risk assessment and management practices.

  - *Outside auditor.* The audit committee is responsible for supervising the corporation's relationship with its outside auditor, including recommending to the full board the firm to be engaged as the outside auditor, evaluating the auditor's performance, and considering whether it would be appropriate to rotate senior audit personnel or for the corporation periodically to change its outside auditor. The selection of an outside auditor should involve an annual due diligence process in which the audit committee reviews the qualifications, work product, independence, and reputation of the proposed outside auditor. The audit committee should base its decisions about selecting and possibly changing the outside auditor on its assessment of what is likely to lead to more effective audits. Based on its due diligence, the audit committee should make an annual recommendation to the full board about the selection of the outside auditor.

- *Auditor independence.* The audit committee should consider the independence of the outside auditor and should develop policies concerning the provision of nonaudit services by the outside auditor. The provision of some types of audit-related and consulting services by the outside auditor may not be inconsistent with independence or the attestation function. In considering whether the outside auditor should provide certain types of nonaudit services, the audit committee should consider the degree of review and oversight that may be appropriate for new and existing services. When making independence judgments, the audit committee should consider the nature and dollar amount of all services provided by the outside auditor.

- *Critical accounting policies, judgments, and estimates.* The audit committee should review and discuss with management and the outside auditor the corporation's critical accounting policies and the quality of accounting judgments and estimates made by management.

- *Internal controls.* The audit committee should understand and be familiar with the corporation's system of internal controls and on a periodic basis should review with both internal and outside auditors the adequacy of this system.

- *Compliance.* Unless the full board or another committee does so, the audit committee should review the corporation's procedures addressing compliance with the law and important corporate policies, including the corporation's code of ethics or code of conduct.

- *Financial statements.* The audit committee should review and discuss the corporation's annual financial statements with management and the outside auditor and, based on these discussions, recommend that the board approve the financial statements for publication and filing. Most audit committees also find it advisable to implement processes for the committee or its designee to review the corporation's quarterly financial statements prior to release.

- *Internal audit function.* The audit committee should oversee the corporation's internal audit function, including review of reports submitted by the internal audit staff, and should review the appointment and replacement of the senior internal auditing executive.

- *Communication.* The audit committee should provide a channel of communication to the board for the outside auditor and internal auditors and may also meet with and receive reports from finance officers, compliance officers, and the general counsel.

- *Hiring auditor personnel.* Under audit committee supervision, some corporations have implemented "revolving door" policies covering the hiring of auditor personnel. For example, these policies may impose "cooling off" periods prohibiting the corporation from employing members of the audit engagement team in senior financial management positions for some period of time after their work as auditors for the corporation. The audit committee should consider whether to adopt such a policy. Any policy on the hiring of auditor personnel should be flexible enough to allow exceptions, but only when specifically approved by the audit committee.

- Audit committee meetings should be held frequently enough to allow the committee to appropriately monitor the annual and quarterly financial reports. For many corporations, this means four or more meetings a year. Meetings should be scheduled with enough time to permit and encourage active discussions with management and the internal and outside auditors. The audit committee should meet with the internal and outside auditors, without management present, at every meeting and communicate with them between meetings as necessary. Some audit committees may decide that specific functions, such as quarterly review meetings with the outside auditor or management, can be delegated to the audit committee chairman or other members of the audit committee.[19]

In addition to the Business Roundtable's *Principles of Corporate Governance*, both the NYSE and Nasdaq proposed new changes to their corporate governance listing standards. The NYSE's proposed rule changes are:

6. Add to the "independence" requirement for audit committee membership the requirements of Rule 10A-3(b)(1) under the Exchange Act, subject to the exemptions provided for in Rule 10A-3(c).

Commentary Applicable to All Companies: While it is not the audit committee's responsibility to certify the company's financial statements or to guarantee the auditor's report, the committee stands at the crucial intersection of management, independent auditors, internal auditors and the board of directors. The Exchange supports additional directors' fees to compensate audit committee members for the significant time and effort they expend to fulfill their duties as audit committee members, but does not believe that any member of the audit committee should receive any compensation other than such director's fees from the company. If a director satisfies the definition of "independent director" set out in Section 303A(2), then his or her receipt of a pension or other form of deferred compensation from the company for prior service (provided such compensation is not contingent in any way on continued service) will not preclude him or her from satisfying the requirement that director's fees are the only form of compensation he or she receives from the company.

An audit committee member may receive his or her fee in cash and/or company stock or options or other in-kind consideration ordinarily available to directors, as well as all of the regular benefits that other directors receive. Because of the significantly greater commitment of audit committee members, they may receive reasonable compensation greater than that paid to the other directors (as may other directors for other committee work). Disallowed compensation for an audit committee member includes fees paid directly or indirectly for services as a consultant or a legal or financial advisor, regardless of the amount. Disallowed compensation also includes compensation paid to such a director's firm for such consulting or advisory services even if the director is not the actual service provider. Disallowed compensation is not intended to include ordinary compensation paid in another customer or supplier or business relationship that the board has already determined to be immaterial for purposes of its basic director independence analysis. To avoid any confusion, note that this requirement pertains only to audit committee qualification and not to the independence determinations that the board must make for other directors.

Commentary Applicable to All Companies Other than Foreign Private Issuers: Each member of the committee must be financially literate, as such qualification is interpreted by the company's board in its business judgment, or must become financially literate within a reasonable period of time after his or her appointment to the audit

---

[19]The Business Roundtable, *Principles of Corporate Governance* (Washington, DC: The Business Roundtable, May 2002), pp. 12–16.

committee. In addition, at least one member of the audit committee must have accounting or related financial management expertise, as the company's board interprets such qualification in its business judgment. A board may presume that a person who satisfies the definition of audit committee financial expert set out in Item 401(e) of Regulation S-K has accounting or related financial management expertise.

Because of the audit committee's demanding role and responsibilities, and the time commitment attendant to committee membership, each prospective audit committee member should evaluate carefully the existing demands on his or her time before accepting this important assignment. Additionally, if an audit committee member simultaneously serves on the audit committee of more than three public companies, and the listed company does not limit the number of audit committees on which its audit committee members serve, then in each case, the board must determine that such simultaneous service would not impair the ability of such member to effectively serve on the listed company's audit committee and disclose such determination in the annual proxy statement or, if the company does not file an annual proxy statement, in the company's annual report on Form 10-K filed with the SEC.

7. *(a) Each company is required to have a minimum three person audit committee composed entirely of independent directors that meet the requirements of Section 303A(6).*

   (b) The audit committee must have a written charter that addresses:

   (i) the committee's purpose—which, at minimum, must be to:

   (A) assist board oversight of (1) the integrity of the company's financial statements, (2) the company's compliance with legal and regulatory requirements, (3) the independent auditor's qualifications and independence, and (4) the performance of the company's internal audit function and independent auditors; and

   (B) prepare the report required by the SEC's proxy rules to be included in the company's annual proxy statement, or, if the company does not file a proxy statement, in the company's annual report filed on Form 10-K with the SEC;

   (ii) the duties and responsibilities of the audit committee set out in Section 303A (7)(c) and (d); and

   (iii) an annual performance evaluation of the audit committee.

   (c) As required by Rule 10A-3(b)(2), (3), (4) and (5) of the Securities Exchange Act of 1934, and subject to the exemptions provided for in Rule 10A-3(c), the audit committee must:

   (i) directly appoint, retain, compensate, evaluate and terminate the company's independent auditors;

Commentary: In connection with this requirement, the audit committee must have the sole authority to approve all audit engagement fees and terms, as well as all significant non-audit engagements with the independent auditors. In addition, the independent auditor must report directly to the audit committee. This requirement does not preclude the committee from obtaining the input of management, but these responsibilities may not be delegated to management. The audit committee must be directly responsible for oversight of the independent auditors, including resolution of disagreements between management and the independent auditor and pre-approval of all non-audit services.

(ii) establish procedures for the receipt, retention and treatment of complaints from listed company employees on accounting, internal accounting controls or auditing matters, as well as for confidential, anonymous submissions by listed company employees of concerns regarding questionable accounting or auditing matters;

(iii) obtain advice and assistance from outside legal, accounting or other advisors as the audit committee deems necessary to carry out its duties; and

Commentary: In the course of fulfilling its duties, the audit committee may wish to consult with independent counsel and other advisors. The audit committee must be empowered to retain and compensate these advisors without seeking board approval.

(iv) receive appropriate funding, as determined by the audit committee, from the listed company for payment of compensation to the ouside legal, accounting or other advisors employed by the audit committee.

(d) In addition to the duties set out in Section 303(A)(7)(c), the duties of the audit committee must be, at a minimum, to:

(i) at least annually, obtain and review a report by the independent auditor describing: the firm's internal quality-control procedures; any material issues raised by the most recent internal quality-control review, or peer review, of the firm, or by any inquiry or investigation by governmental or professional authorities, within the preceding five years, respecting one or more independent audits carried out by the firm, and any steps taken to deal with any such issues; and (to assess the auditor's independence) all relationships between the independent auditor and the company;

Commentary: After reviewing the foregoing report and the independent auditor's work throughout the year, the audit committee will be in a position to evaluate the auditor's qualifications, performance and independence. This evaluation should include the review and evaluation of the lead partner of the independent auditor. In making its evaluation, the audit committee should take into account the opinions of management and the company's internal auditors (or other personnel responsible for the internal audit function). In addition to assuring the regular rotation of the lead audit partner as required by law, the audit committee should further consider whether, in order to assure continuing auditor independence, there should be regular rotation of the audit firm itself. The audit committee should present its conclusions with respect to the independent auditor to the full board.

(ii) discuss the annual audited financial statements and quarterly financial statements with management and the independent auditor, including the company's disclosures under "Management's Discussion and Analysis of Financial Condition and Results of Operations";

(iii) discuss earnings press releases, as well as financial information and earnings guidance provided to analysts and rating agencies;

Commentary: The audit committee's responsibility to discuss earnings releases as well as financial information and earnings guidance may be done generally (i.e., discussion of the types of information to be disclosed and the type of presentation to be made). The audit committee need not discuss in advance each earnings release or each instance in which a company may provide earnings guidance.

(iv) discuss policies with respect to risk assessment and risk management;

Commentary: While it is the job of the CEO and senior management to assess and manage the company's exposure to risk, the audit committee must discuss guidelines and policies to govern the process by which this is handled. The audit committee should discuss the company's major financial risk exposures and the steps management has taken to monitor and control such exposures. The audit committee is not required to be the sole body responsible for risk assessment and management, but, as stated above, the committee must discuss guidelines and policies to govern the process by which risk assessment and management is undertaken. Many companies, particularly financial companies, manage and assess their risk through mechanisms other than the audit committee. The processes these companies have in place should be reviewed in a general manner by the audit committee, but they need not be replaced by the audit committee.

(v) meet separately, periodically, with management, with internal auditors (or other personnel responsible for the internal audit function) and with independent auditors

Commentary: To perform its oversight functions most effectively, the audit committee must have the benefit of separate sessions with management, the independent auditors and those responsible for the internal audit function. As noted herein, all listed companies must have an internal audit function. These separate sessions may be more productive than joint sessions in surfacing issues warranting committee attention.

(vi) review with the independent auditor any audit problems or difficulties and management's response;

Commentary: The audit committee must regularly review with the independent auditor any difficulties the auditor encountered in the course of the audit work, including any restrictions on the scope of the independent auditor's activities or on access to requested information, and any significant disagreements with management. Among the items the audit committee may want to review with the auditor are: any accounting adjustments that were noted or proposed by the auditor but were "passed" (as immaterial or otherwise); any communications between the audit team and the audit firm's national office respecting auditing or accounting issues presented by the engagement; and any "management" or "internal control" letter issued, or proposed to be issued, by the audit firm to the company. The review should also include discussion of the responsibilities, budget and staffing of the company's internal audit function.

(vii) set clear hiring policies for employees or former employees of the independent auditors; and

Commentary: Employees or former employees of the independent auditor are often valuable additions to corporate management. Such individuals' familiarity with the business, and personal rapport with the employees, may be attractive qualities when filling a key opening. However, the audit committee should set hiring policies taking into account the pressures that may exist for auditors consciously or subconsciously seeking a job with the company they audit.

(viii) report regularly to the board of directors.

Commentary: The audit committee should review with the full board any issues that arise with respect to the quality or integrity of the company's financial statements, the company's compliance with legal or regulatory requirements, the performance and independence of the company's independent auditors, or the performance of the internal audit function.

General Commentary to Section 303A(7)(d): While the fundamental responsibility for the company's financial statements and disclosures rests with management and the independent auditor, the audit committee must review: (A) major issues regarding accounting principles and financial statement presentations, including any significant changes in the company's selection or application of accounting principles, and major issues as to the adequacy of the company's internal controls and any special audit steps adopted in light of material control deficiencies; (B) analyses prepared by management and/or the independent auditor setting forth significant financial reporting issues and judgments made in connection with the preparation of the financial statements, including analyses of the effects of alternative GAAP methods on the financial statements; (C) the effect of regulatory and accounting initiatives, as well as off-balance sheet structures, on the financial statements of the company; and (D) the type and presentation of information to be included in earnings press releases (paying particular attention to any use of "pro forma," or "adjusted" non-GAAP, information), as well as review any financial information and earnings guidance provided to analysts and rating agencies.

General Commentary to Section 303A(7): To avoid any confusion, note that the audit committee functions specified in Section 303A(7) are the sole responsibility of the audit committee and may not be allocated to a different committee.

(e) Each listed company must have an internal audit function.

Commentary: Listed companies must maintain an internal audit function to provide management and the audit committee with ongoing assessments of the company's risk management processes and system of internal control. A company may choose to outsource this function to a firm other than its independent auditor.[20]

CORPORATE ACCOUNTABILITY AND THE AUDIT COMMITTEE

The Role of the Audit Committee

The audit committee has a critical role within the framework of corporate accountability since the jurisdiction of the committee is to oversee and monitor the activities of the corporation's financial reporting system and the internal and external audit processes. The audit committee assists the board of directors with the development and maintenance of the corporate accountability framework, because the committee compels the board to be accountable for its stewardship accountability. Thus the audit committee helps create an environment in which the activities of corporate management are subject to scrutiny.

As Harold M. Williams, former chairman of the SEC, asserted:

It should be evident, but perhaps bears repeating, that integrity in reporting financial data is vital both to an efficient and effective securities market and to capital formation. One key to increasing public confidence in that data long advocated by many segments of the financial community, including public accounting firms, is more direct involvement by boards of directors in the auditing process and the integrity of reported financial information. The vehicle which the Securities and Exchange

---

[20]Securities and Exchange Commission Release No. 34-47672, File No. SR-NYSE-2002-33, *Proposed Rule Change Relating to Corporate Governance* (Washington DC: April 11, 2003). See also SEC Release No. 34-47672, File No. SR-NASD-2002-141, for the NASD, *Proposed Rule Change Relating to Corporate Governance.*

Commission, the New York Stock Exchange and an increasing number of public corporations have turned to has been the independent audit committee.[21]

As a standing committee appointed by the board of directors, the audit committee is directly accountable for its actions to the board. The audit committee operates in an advisory capacity. Thus the audit committee has limited authority, because a final decision concerning its recommendations is made by the board. The board seeks guidance from the audit committee in formulating or amending the financial accounting policies to service properly the needs of its various constituencies.

With respect to the expectations of the various constituencies, Russell E. Palmer, former managing partner of Touche Ross and Co. (now Deloitte and Touche), stated:

> Every audit committee will be expected to weigh the appropriateness of the corporation's accounting policies as they apply to the corporation and its industry. It seems reasonable that committee members will be expected to assess and be satisfied with the corporation's entire disclosure system—the financial statements, the published stockholders' reports, and even discussions between management and the financial media.[22]

To further illustrate the role of the audit committee, Exhibit 1.5 diagrams the direct relationship between the committee and its constituencies in the internal corporate environment.

Important Surveys

In their survey of audit committees, Joseph F. Castellano, Harper A. Roehm, and Albert A. Vondra found that the corporate community is building a strong case for self-regulation by complying with the recommendation of the Treadway Commission. Such compliance has improved the quality of financial reporting.[23] Their survey results are further supported by Ivan Bull. He found that in a survey of 13 chairpersons of publicly held corporations in Illinois, "most boards were either already following or have since implemented the Treadway Commission recommendations" to prevent fraudulent misstatements in their financial statements. "Audit committee chairpeople generally believe their committees are 'informed, vigilant, and effective overseers' described in the Treadway report."[24]

In another survey of audit partners, directors of internal auditing, and chief financial officers associated with audit committees of 90 U.S. corporations, Lawrence P. Kalbers and Timothy J. Fogarty investigated the relationship between audit committee effectiveness and the types and extent of the committee's power. They concluded:

---

[21]Harold M. Williams, "Audit Committees—The Public Sector's View," *Journal of Accountancy* 144, No. 3 (September 1977), p. 71.

[22]Russell E. Palmer, "Audit Committees—Are They Effective? An Auditor's View," *Journal of Accountancy* 144, No. 3 (September 1977), p. 77.

[23]Joseph F. Castellano, Harper A. Roehm, and Albert A. Vondra, "Audit Committee Compliance with the Treadway Commission Report: A Survey," *OHIO CPA Journal* 48, No. 4 (Winter 1989), p. 42.

[24]Ivan Bull, "Board of Director Acceptance of Treadway Responsibilities," *Journal of Accountancy* 171, No. 2 (February 1991), p. 67.

Exhibit 1.5   The Audit Committee's Accountability Relationship

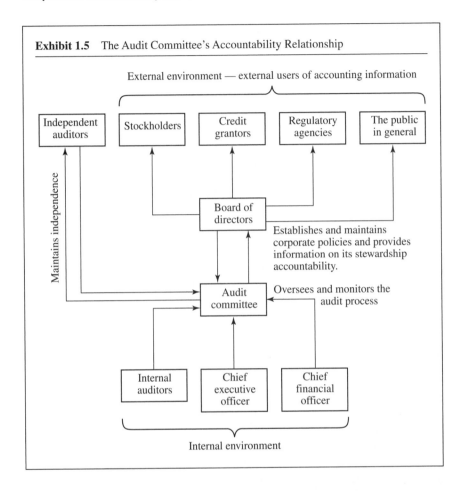

This study suggests that the fundamental types of power needed by audit committees to perform effectively are (1) institutional support, (2) actual authority (written and implied), and (3) diligence. With the possible exception of written mandates (such as audit committee charters), these factors are especially difficult to evaluate with any traditional means of regulation. Perhaps more effective regulation should aim for more substantive reviews of power within the organization.[25]

---

[25]Lawrence P. Kalbers and Timothy J. Fogarty, "Audit Committee Effectiveness: An Empirical Investigation of the Contribution of Power," *Auditing: A Journal of Practice & Theory* 12, No. 1 (Spring 1993), p. 45. For additional information, consult Dana Wechsler, "Giving the Watchdog Fangs," *Forbes* 144 (November 13, 1989), pp. 130, 132–133; Nelson Luscombe, "More Power to Audit Committees" *CA Magazine* 122, No. 5 (May 1989), pp. 26–37; Dorothy A. McMullen, "Audit Committee Performance: An Investigation of the Consequences Associated with Audit Committees," *Auditing: A Journal of Practice & Theory* 15, No. 1 (Spring 1996), pp. 87–103; Donald J. Kirk and Arthur Siegel, "How Directors and Auditors Can Improve Corporate Governance," *Journal of Accountancy* 181, No. 1 (January 1996), pp. 53–57; Zabihollah Rezaee, "Corporate Governance and Accountability: The Role of Audit Committees," *Internal Auditing* 13, No. 1 (Summer 1997), pp. 27–41; and Michael A. Mackenzie, "The Evolving Board: The Mechanism of Board Oversight," *Canadian Business Law Journal* 26 (1996), pp. 140–144. Also see additional suggested readings.

The Audit Committee and the Chief Executive Officer   The chief executive officer has an obligation not only to the board but also to the standing committees of the board. The chief CEO is responsible primarily for recommending major policy decisions to the board of directors. Since the CEO participates in the decisions concerning the financial accounting policies, he or she should have direct communication with the audit committee.

However, it is essential that the audit committee be totally independent from the CEO because he or she is a "managing director." As a managing director, the CEO participates in the general administration of the corporation as well as assuming ultimate responsibility for the decisions.

Based on a close examination of the audit committees of 13 corporations listed on the NYSE, Michael L. Lovdal found that:

> Effective audit committees permit the chief executive to attend by invitation only. . . . After all, he is the best source concerning questions related to the business and he can ensure quick action on committee requests. In achieving the appropriate relationship with the chief executive, a key ingredient is the quality of the audit committee chairman. He must have both the sensitivity to know when to bring the CEO into the group's deliberations and the strength to stand up to him when the committee wants to pursue an inquiry or change policy.[26]

In short, the audit committee should determine its own agenda items, which should not be based on the chief executive officer's prerogatives. As Ivan Bull observed:

> Concern about other environmental factors, such as legal liability, also may have influenced board agendas and operating practices. The board's practice of allowing and listening to dissent and advice from outside members is healthier than the popular belief that CEOs dominate passive boards.[27]

The Audit Committee and the Chief Financial Officer[28]   In most corporations, the chief financial officer (CFO) is responsible for the functions of the controller. In turn, the CFO is accountable to the president for the conduct of the various administrative functions of the controller. Although the controller is responsible for the general administration and supervision of the accounting operations, the CFO has executive responsibility for the financial accounting policies.

Since the audit committee is responsible for assuring that management fulfills its responsibilities in the preparation of the financial statements, the CFO should

---

[26]Michael L. Lovdal, "Making the Audit Committee Work," *Harvard Business Review* 55 (March–April 1977), p. 110.

[27]Bull, "Board of Director Acceptance," p. 71. Also see J. Michael Cook, "The CEO and the Audit Committee," *Chief Executive,* No. 76 (April 1993), pp. 44–47.

[28]For further discussion, see Louis Braiotta, Jr., and Jay R. Olson, "Guiding the Audit Committee: A CFO's Concern," *Financial Executive* 51, No. 9 (September 1983), pp. 52–54. See also Chapter 13 for a discussion of the audit committee's review of the quarterly reporting process.

consult with the committee in order to coordinate the financial accounting activities. Thus the audit committee should have a dialogue with the CFO to consider any questions concerning the financial reporting practices. For example, if the CFO has certain reservations or exceptions to certain accounting policies and practices, the audit committee would recommend the necessary course of action subsequent to its consultation with the independent auditors.

The Audit Committee and the Internal Audit Group   The internal audit executive is essentially responsible for the establishment and maintenance of an effective and efficient system of internal auditing. With respect to the audit committee's involvement with the internal audit group, Lovdal points out:

> The internal audit group can be an avenue for the committee in reaching the source of a variety of problems. One committee I examined uses internal auditors regularly for investigations in such areas as computer security, transfer pricing, and capital budgeting. For these activities, the committee should deal directly with the head of internal audit, rather than solely through other finance or control executives, and should make itself knowledgeable about the organization, staffing, and budgets of the internal audit department.[29]

The reporting responsibility of the internal audit group varies from one organization to the next. For example, the director of internal auditing may report to the controller or CFO and meet with the audit committee on a separate or joint basis. However, the director of internal auditing should have access to the audit committee to provide for a forum whereby the internal audit group can resolve questionable matters between the audit staff and corporate management. (See Chapter 9.)

Exhibit 1.6 presents more recent academic research studies. To the extent that the audit committee maintains an independent posture in the corporate environment, the committee will represent a check on the corporate management with respect to its corporate power and stewardship accountability. The primary objective is to foster the accountability relationship between the audit committee and the representatives of management and thereby create an environment in which management will be responsive to its constituencies.

Subsequent to the aforementioned proxy statement seasons, a number of accounting scandals and the demise of a large international accounting firm provided the impetus for the Sarbanes-Oxley Act of 2002 and proposed amendments to the SRO's listing standards. Exhibit 1.7 presents a summary of selected sections and titles of the act. Each section is presented in Chapter 2. Also, Exhibit 1.8 summarizes the SEC releases to implement the sections of the Sarbanes-Oxley Act available at the time of this writing. Exhibit 1.9 contains a corporate accountability self-assessment checklist.

---

[29]Lovdal, "Making the Audit Committee Work," p. 111.

Exhibit 1.6   Summaries of Recent Research Studies

DeZoort, F. Todd, Dana R. Hermanson, and Richard W. Houston, "Audit Committee Support for Auditors: The Effects of Materiality Justification and Accounting Precision." *Journal of Accounting and Public Policy* 22, (2003), pp. 175–199.

> Summary: The authors find that, in the context of auditor-management disagreements, independent auditors and audit committees need to discuss the qualitative aspects of materiality with respect to undrecorded adjustments. Additionally, the authors conclude that both accounting and auditing standard setters should consider approaches to enhance accounting estimates in the financial reporting process, including communications with audit committees. Finally, they find that audit committees with CPAs provide greater support for independent auditors.

Klein, April, "Audit Committees, Board of Director Characteristics, and Earnings Management." *Journal of Accounting & Economics* 33 (2002), pp. 375–400.

> Summary: Klein concludes that reductions in the independence of boards of directors or audit committees cause large increases in abnormal accruals. The results suggest that boards of directors that are more independent of the CEO are more effective in monitoring earnings management in the financial reporting process.

Beasley, Mark S. and Steven E. Salterio, "The Relationship between Board Characteristics and Voluntary Improvements in Audit Committee Composition and Experience." *Contemporary Accounting Research* 18, No. 4 (Winter 2001), pp. 539–570.

> Summary: Beasley and Salterio find that Canadian firms that voluntarily include more outside directors on the audit committee than the minimum mandated by Canadian corporate law have larger boards of directors with more outside directors and thus are more likely to segregate the board chair and CEO/president positions. Likewise, audit committees with financial reporting knowledge and experience and larger boards with outside members are less likely to be chaired by the CEO/president. Thus the researchers conclude that one person serving as both chairman and CEO/president increases the potential for less effective monitoring by the audit committee.

Klein, April, "Economic Determinants of Audit Committee Independence." *Accounting Review* 77, No. 2 (April 2002), pp. 435–452.

> Summary: Klein reports that audit committee independence increases with board size and the percentage of outsiders on the board of directors. However, audit committee independence decreases with an increase in a firm's growth opportunities or when a firm reports net losses. Klein confirms the findings of the Blue Ribbon Committee on Improving the Effectiveness of Corporate Audit Committees that "one size doesn't fill all" when it comes to audit committees. The results suggest that the stock exchanges should allow boards flexibility with respect to audit committee composition.

Carcello, Joseph V. and Terry L. Neal, "Audit Committee Composition and Auditor Reporting." *Accounting Review* 75, No. 4 (October 2000), pp. 453–467.

> Summary: Carcello and Neal find that the greater the percentage of affiliated directors on the audit committee, the lower the probability the auditor will issue a going-concern report. Thus their evidence supports the proposition that the audit committee should be composed of independent, outside directors.

Beasley, Mark S., Joseph V. Carcello, Dana R. Hermanson, and Paul D. Lapides, "Fraudulent Financial Reporting: Consideration of Industry Traits and Corporate Governance Mechanisms." *Accounting Horizons* 14, No. 4 (December 2000), pp. 441–454.

Summary: The authors confirm earlier findings that fraudulent firms and no-fraud firms differ to the extent that audit committees exist and such committees are independent, including the board's independence from management. With the identification of no-fraud industry benchmarks (e.g., number of audit committee meetings and internal audit experience), they find that the sample fraud firms have weak governance mechanisms. Moreover, independent auditors should consider the industry context with respect to their fraud risk assessment on client audit engagements.

Abbott, Lawrence J. and Susan Parker, "Auditor Selection and Audit Committee Characteristics." *Auditing: A Journal of Practice and Theory* 19, No. 2 (Fall 2000), pp. 47–66.

Summary: The authors conclude that the requirement for financial experts on audit committees is more likely to change the structure and focus of audit committee discussions about the quality of the financial reporting process. Their results suggest that audit committee members who are financially literate are more likely to focus on reporting treatments that are prominent in the press and nonrecurring, while financial experts are more likely to focus on the relevance of reporting treatments as well as recurring activities.

Abbott, Lawrence J. and Susan Parker, "Auditor Selection and Audit Committee Characteristics." *Auditing: A Journal of Practice and Theory* 19, No. 2 (Fall 2000), pp. 47–66.

Summary: Abbott and Parker find that independent and active audit committee members are more likely to select an industry-specialist auditor because they demand a high level of audit quality. Their results suggest that an industry-specialist auditor helps minimize the client's reputational or monetary losses.

McDaniel, Linda, Roger D. Martin, and Laureen A. Maines, "Evaluating Financial Reporting Quality: The Effects of Financial Expertise vs. Financial Literacy." *Accounting Review* 77 (Supplement 2002), pp. 139–167.

Summary: The authors conclude that the requirement for financial experts on audit committees is more likely to change the structure and focus of audit committee discussions about the quality of the financial reporting process. Their results suggest that audit committee members who are financially literate are more likely to focus on reporting treatments that are prominent in the press and nonrecurring, while financial experts are more likely to focus on the relevance of reporting treatments as well as recurring activities.

Carcello, Joseph V., and Terry L. Neal, "Audit Committee Characteristics and Auditor Dismissals Following 'New' Going-Concern Reports." *Accounting Review* 78, No. 1 (January 2003), pp. 95–117.

Summary: Carcello and Neal find as a follow-on to their 2000 study that the higher the percentage of affiliated directors on the audit committee, the more likely a client will dismiss its independent auditors because of a going-concern audit report. Moreover, they report that the probability of client dismissal of the independent auditors subsequent to the going-concern report increases as audit committee ownership of client stock increases. In contrast, audit committee members with more governance expertise are less likely to dismiss their independent auditors after receiving a going-concern report. Likewise, the turnover rate of independent audit committee members who retain their independent auditors is less significant compared to audit committee members who dismiss their independent auditors.

Exhibit 1.7 Summary of Sections of the Sarbanes-Oxley Act of 2002 Impacting
Audit Committees

Sections	Title
2	Definitions
101	Public Company Accounting Oversight Board
201	Services Outside the Scope of Practice of Auditors
202	Preapproval Requirements (audit and nonaudit services)
203	Audit Partner Rotation (5-year rotation period)
204	Auditor Reports to Audit Committees
206	Conflicts of Interest (1-year cooling-off period)
207	Study of Mandatory Rotation of Registered Public Accounting Firms
301	Public Company Audit Committees
302	Corporate Responsibility for Financial Reports
303	Improper Influence on Conduct of Audits
307	Rules of Professional Responsibility for Attorneys
401	Disclosure in Periodic Reports
402	Enhanced Conflict of Interest Provisions (Personal Loans to Executives)
403	Disclosures of Transactions Involving Management and Principlal Stockholders
404	Management Assessment of Internal Controls
406	Code of Ethics for Senior Financial Officers
407	Disclosure of Audit Committee Financial Expert
409	Real Time Issues Disclosures
906	Corporate Responsibility for Financial Reports (Failure of Corporate Officers to Certify Financial Reports and Criminal Penalties)

Source: The act is contained in Public Law No. 107-204, July 30, 2002.

Exhibit 1.8   Summary of SEC Releases Issued to Implement the Provisions of the Sarbanes-Oxley Act of 2002, Relating to Audit Committees (as of June 2003)

Release No.	Date	Title
34-46421	August 27, 2002	Ownership Reports and Trading by Officers, Directors and Principal Security Holders
33-8124	August 28, 2002	Certification of Disclosures in Companies' Quarterly and Annual Reports
33-46685	October 18, 2002	Proposals Regarding Improper Influence on Conduct of Audits
33-8138	October 22, 2002	Proposals Regarding Internal Control Reports
33-8176	January 22, 2003	Conditions for Use on Non-GAAP Financial Information
34-47225	January 22, 2003	Insider Traders During Pension Plan Blackout Periods
33-8177	January 23, 2003	Disclosure Regarding Audit Committee Financial Experts and Company Codes of Ethics
33-8180	January 24, 2003	Retention of Records Relevant to Audits and Reviews
33-8182	January 28, 2003	Disclosure About Off-Balance Sheet Arrangements
33-8183	January 28, 2003	Strengthening the Commission's Requirements Regarding Auditor Independence
33-8185	January 29, 2003	Implementation of Standards of Professional Conduct for Attorneys
33-8212	March 21, 2003	Certification of Disclosure in Certain Exchange Act Reports
33-8177a	March 26, 2003	Disclosure Required by Sections 406 and 407 of Sarbanes-Oxley Act of 2002
33-8220	April 9, 2003	Standards Relating to Listed Company Audit Committees
34-47672	April 11, 2003	Self-Regulating Organizations; Notice of Filing of Proposed Rule Changes and Amendment No. 1 thereto by the NYSE Relating to Corporate Governance
2003-66	May 27, 2003	SEC Implements Internal Control Provisions of Sarbanes-Oxley Act
33-8238	June 5, 2003	Management's Reports on Internal Control Over Financial Reporting and Certification of Disclosure in Exchange Act Periodic Reports

Source: www.sec.gov/rules/final/htm; www.sec.gov/new/press/htm; and www.sec.gov/rules/proposed/htm.

Exhibit 1.9   Corporate Accountability: Self-Assessment Checklist

Audit Committee Practice Area	Management	Internal Auditors	External Auditors	Legal counsel	Board of Directors	Sarbanes-Oxley Act	SEC	SROs	ASB	Comments
Legal liabilities under, State statutes										
Fiduciary liability				✔						
Business judgment rule				✔						
Standards of conduct				✔						
Federal Statutes*										
Sarbanes-Oxley Act of 2002				✔		✔	✔			
Private Securities Litigation Reform Act of 1995				✔			✔			
Securities Act of 1933				✔			✔			
Securities Exchange Act of 1934				✔			✔			
Legal Cases				✔						
Corporate Governance Principles and Rules					✔	✔	✔	✔		
Formation†						✔	✔			
Membership										
Number of members (size)						✔	✔			
Appointments						✔				
Term of Service						✔				
Qualifications						✔	✔			
Composition						✔	✔			
Meetings, frequency and type							✔			
Knowledge Areas										
Type of business and industry	✔									
Internal audit process		✔								
External audit process			✔							
Internal control concepts‡		✔	✔							
Management's risk assessment	✔	✔	✔							
Industry accounting practices	✔	✔	✔							
Complex business transactions	✔	✔	✔	✔						
Financial reporting process	✔	✔	✔							
Internal communication process§	✔	✔	✔	✔	✔	✔	✔	✔	✔	
External communication process					✔	✔	✔	✔	✔	

---

*See Chapter 4 and Appendix D in this book's website for other acts.
†Board resolution or corporate bylaws and a format written charter.
‡Includes conflicts of interest (e.g., code of conduct, related party transactions).
§Related to the above areas.

SOURCES AND SUGGESTED READINGS

American Assembly, *Corporate Governance in America,* Pamphlet 54 (New York: Columbia University, April 1978).

American Institute of Certified Public Accountants, *Audit Committees, Answers to Typical Questions about Their Organization and Operations* (New York: AICPA, 1978).

Barlas, Stephen, "Blue Ribbon Panel Focus: Audit Committees." *Management Accounting* 80, No. 6 (December 1998), p. 10.

Bean, James W., "The Audit Committee's Readings." *Journal of Accountancy* 187, No. 1 (January 1999), pp. 47–54.

Beresford, Dennis R., "After Enron: Let's Not Throw Out the Baby," *CPA Journal* 72, No. 7 (July 2002), pp. 10–13.

Biegler, John C., "Rebuilding Public Trust in Business." *Financial Executive* 45 (June 1977), pp. 23–31.

Bishop, William G., Dana R. Hermanson, Paul D. Lapides, and Larry E. Rittenberg, "The Year of the Audit Committee." *Internal Auditor* 57, No. 2 (April 2000), pp. 46–51.

Blue Ribbon Committee on Improving the Effectiveness of Corporate Audit Committees, *Report and Recommendations of the Blue Ribbon Committee on Improving the Effectiveness of Corporate Audit Committees* (New York: NYSE and Washington DC: National Association of Securities Dealers, 1999).

Braiotta, Louis, and Jay R. Olson, "Guiding the Audit Committee: A CFO's Concern." *Financial Executive* 51, No. 9 (September 1983), pp. 52–54.

Bull, Ivan, "Board of Directors Acceptance of Treadway Responsibilities." *Journal of Accountancy* 171, No. 2 (February 1991), pp. 67–72, 74.

The Business Roundtable, *Corporate Governance and American Competitiveness* (New York: The Business Roundtable, 1990, 2002).

The Business Roundtable, *Principles of Corporate Governance* (Washington, DC: The Business Roundtable, 2002).

Castellano, Joseph F., Harper A. Roehm, and Albert A. Vondra, "Audit Committee Compliance with the Treadway Commission Report: A Survey." *Ohio CPA Journal* 48, No. 4 (Winter 1989), pp. 37–42.

DiPiazza, Samuel A., and Robert G. Eccles, *Building Public Trust: The Future of Corporate Reporting* (New York: John Wiley & Sons, 2002).

Estey, John S., and David W. Marston, "Pitfalls (and Loopholes) in the Foreign Bribery Law." *Fortune* (October 1978), pp. 182–188.

Fleming, John M., "Audit Committees: Roles, Responsibilities, and Performance." *Pennsylvania CPA Journal* 73, No. 2 (Summer 2002), pp. 29–32.

Goodman, Amy L., and Michael J. Scanlon, "Enhanced Audit Committee Responsibilities." *Insights, The Corporate & Securities Law Advisor* 15, No. 2 (February 2001), pp. 12–17.

Hermanson, Dana R., "Does Corporate Governance Really Matter? What the Research Tells Us." *Internal Auditing* 18, No. 2 (March/April 2003), pp. 44–45.

Hills, Roderick M., "Restoring Faith with Audit Process." *Directors & Boards* 26, No. 3 (Spring 2002), pp. 26–37.

Hnatt, Kelly M., "Forge the Right Relationship." *Journal of Accountancy* 191, No. 5 (May 2001), pp. 49–54.

Kalbers, Lawrence P., and Timothy J. Fogarty, "Audit Committee Effectiveness: An Empirical Investigation of the Contribution of Power." *Auditing: A Journal of Practice & Theory* 12, No. 1 (Spring 1993), pp. 24–49.

Kirk, Donald J., "Experiences with the Public Oversight Board and Corporate Audit Committees." *Accounting Horizons* 14, No. 1 (March 2000), pp. 103–111.

Lear, Robert W., "Auditing the Audit Committee." *Chief Executive* 139 (November 1998), pp. 16–17.

Levitt, Arthur, "The Numbers Game," speech presented at the NYU Center for Law and Business (Washington, DC: SEC, September 28, 1998).

Levitt, Arthur, "Letter to Audit Committees Chairmen of the Top 5000 Public Companies" (Washington, DC: SEC, January 5, 2001).

Lovdal, Michael L., "Making the Audit Committee Work." *Harvard Business Review* 55 (March–April 1977), pp. 108–114.

Luscombe, Nelson, "More Power to Audit Committees." *CA Magazine* 122, No. 5 (May 1989), pp. 26–37.

McCauley, Daniel J., and John C. Burton, *Audit Committees*. C.P.S. No. 49 (Washington, DC: The Bureau of National Affairs, Inc., 1986).

McCuaig, Bruce W. and Paul G. Makosz, "Is Everything Under Control? A New Approach to Corporate Governance." *Financial Executive* 6, No. 1 (January/February 1990), pp. 24–29.

Miller, Richard I., and Paul H. Pashkoff, "Regulations under the Sarbanes-Oxley Act." *Journal of Accountancy* 194, No. 4 (October 2002), pp. 33–36.

Morrissey, John, "Corporate Responsibility and the Audit Committee," speech presented at the General Audit Management Conference (Washington, DC: SEC, March 21, 2000).

Olson, John F., Ronald O. Mueller, Stephanie Tsacoumis, and Amy L. Goodman, "After Enron: Issues for Boards and Audit Committees to Consider." *Insights* 16, No. 4 (April 2002), pp. 2–8.

O'Malley, Shaun F., "Auditing, Directors, and Management: Promoting Accountability." *Internal Auditing* 5, No. 3 (Winter 1990), pp. 3–9.

Palmer, Russell E., "Audit Committees—Are They Effective? An Auditor's View." *Journal of Accountancy* 144, No. 3 (September 1977), pp. 76–79.

Panel on Audit Effectiveness, *Panel on Audit Effectiveness Report and Recommendations* (Stamford, CT: POB, 2000).

Pearson, Mark W., "Where Was the Audit Committee?" *Financial Executive* 17, No. 8 (November 2001), pp. 44–47.

Read, William J., and Kannass Raghunandan, "The State of Audit Committees." *Journal of Accountancy* 191, No. 5 (May 2001), pp. 57–60.

Rouse, Robert W., and Mark R. Borrelli, "Audit Committees in an Era of Increased Scrutiny," *CPA Journal* 70, No. 6 (June 2000), pp. 26–32.

Sarbanes-Oxley Act of 2002, H.R. Rep. No. 107-610, July 25, 2002. Title 1 of Public Law No. 107-204, July 30, 2002.

Securities and Exchange Commission Release No. 34-47672, File No. SR-NYSE-2002-03, *Proposed Rule Changes Relating to Corporate Governance* (Washington, DC: April 11, 2003).

Shandor, John, "Audit Committees Take a Broader Role in Corporate Policy." *Corporate Controller* 2 (November/December 1989), pp. 46–48.

Sweeney, Paul, "Audit Committees Bracing for Shakeys." *Financial Executive* 18, No. 9, (December 2002), pp. 16–18.

Terrill, Mark C., and Timothy J. Zanni, "CFOs and Audit Committees: Mutual Expectations." *CPA Journal* 72, No. 2 (February 2002), p. 54.

Turley, James S., "The Future of Corporate Reporting: From the Top." *Financial Executive* 70 (December 2002), p. 2.

Turner, Lynn E., "Audit Committees: A Roadway for Establishing Accountability." *Insights, the Corporate & Securities Law Advisor* 15, No. 5 (May 2001), pp. 17–24.

Wechsler, Dana, "Giving the Watchdog Fangs." *Forbes* 144 (November 13, 1989), pp. 130, 132–133.

Whitehead, John C., "A Healthy 'Self-Cleaning': What Can and Should Be Done Now to Restore Confidence in the System." *Directors & Boards* 26, No. 3 (Spring 2002), pp. 88–91.

Williams, Harold M., "Audit Committees—The Public Sector's View." *Journal of Accountancy* 144 No. 3 (September 1977), pp. 71–74.

Chapter 2

Audit Committees: Basic Roles and Responsibilities

The major purpose of this chapter is not only to examine the organizational and functional characteristics of the audit committee but also to introduce the nature and importance of the external and internal auditing processes. Conceptually, one should understand the following:

- The basic considerations in forming the audit committee
- The basic audit committee functions
- The role of the audit committee with respect to the external and internal auditing processes

ORGANIZATION OF THE AUDIT COMMITTEE

Nature of the Audit Committee

In view of the complexity of the modern corporation and the increased demands for corporate accountability, the audit committee's role has become an increasingly important consideration in the conduct of corporate affairs.[1] As defined by the American Institute of Certified Public Accounts (AICPA), "An audit committee should be organized as a standing committee of the board composed mainly

---

[1]With respect to critical issues, Korn/Ferry International found in its annual survey of 327 chief executive officers that:

> According to our respondents, chief executive officers believe their attention should focus on financial results, followed by maximizing shareholder value and executive leadership. Eighty-five percent ranked financial results as most deserving of their time and 83 percent ranked maximizing shareholder value as most important. Executive leadership was seen as the most important issue by 81 percent of responding CEOs. (p. 12)

In another survey of 1,020 directors, Korn/Ferry International found that among the greatest challenges facing boards of directors are "board independence, shareholder value and effective strategic planning" along with two dominant challenges, namely, "management succession and recruiting good directors" (p. 5). As Richard M. Ferry, chairman of Korn/Ferry International, points out:

> Two overwhelming trends are cited as the most important developments during the past 25 years in board policy and structure—the emerging independence of the audit, compensation

of nonofficer directors."[2] In Section 2 (a) (3) of the Sarbanes-Oxley Act of 2002, the U.S. Congress reaffirmed the AICPA's definition of the audit committee, stating:

> (3) AUDIT COMMITTEE—The term "audit committee" means—
>
> (A) a committee (or equivalent body) established by and amongst the board of directors of an issuer for the purpose of overseeing the accounting and financial reporting processes of the issuer and audits of the financial statements of the issuer; and
>
> (B) if no such committee exists with respect to an issuer, the entire board of directors of the issuer.[3]

In contrast to the other standing committees of the board, such as the executive or finance committees, the audit committee is unique because it consists of outside or independent directors. Independent directors are individuals who are not directly involved in managing the corporation. For example, the chief executive officer and chief financial officer are considered management directors because not only are they immediately involved in managing corporate affairs, they are also employees of the corporation. Thus the independent audit committee is composed of individuals who are nonmanagement directors.

The Corporate Organization Policy Committee of The Business Roundtable concluded that the board of directors should be served by an audit committee because it would allow committee members to focus their attention on corporate matters in greater depth than would be practical for the full board. Moreover, a Conference Board study on audit committees found that "93 percent of the surveyed companies have such a committee. The recent action of the New York Stock Exchange requiring the 1,200 or so listed companies to establish by mid-1978 such a committee made up solely of directors independent of management reinforces this development."[4] (See also Appendix D on the book's website.)

In a subsequent survey of 692 companies (628 companies compared with 1978), the Conference Board found a significant increase in the audit committee's involvement in such activities as reviewing the internal audit function and the independent status of the outside auditors, approving both audit and nonaudit

---

and nominating committees and the presence of fewer inside directors. Other major changes are the rise in formal evaluations of CEO [chief executive officer] performance, the increased strictness regarding directors with conflicting interests, the increasing popularity of corporate governance committees, the increasing diversity of board composition and, somewhat surprisingly, the trend toward paying directors in stock. (p. 9)

See Korn/Ferry International, *Twentieth Annual Board of Directors Study*, and *Twenty-fifth Annual Board of Directors Study* (New York: Korn/Ferry International, 1993 and 1998).

[2]American Institute of Certified Public Accountants, *Audit Committees, Answers to Typical Questions About Their Organization and Operations* (New York: AICPA, 1978), p. 11.

[3]The act is contained in Title 1 of Public Law No. 107-204, July 30, 2002.

[4]The Business Roundtable, *The Role and Composition of the Board of Directors of the Large Publicly Owned Corporation* (New York: The Business Roundtable, 1978), pp. 21–22.

services and related fees, and preparing a written agenda in advance of the meetings. They concluded that:

> Audit committees are larger: median sizes are now 4 members for manufacturing and nonfinancial services companies—up from 3 in 1978—and 4.5 for financial firms, up from 4.

> Their members include fewer directors with relationships that might interfere with the exercise of independent judgment, especially former executives of the company and directors affiliated with banks serving the company. Ninety percent of the committees have *no* members with such a potential conflict of interest.[5]

Notwithstanding the Conference Board survey results, the National Commission on Fraudulent Financial Reporting (NCFFR) endorsed the principle that "the board of directors of all public companies should be required by SEC rule to establish audit committees composed solely of independent directors."[6] The Commission recommended that senior management set the tone for the corporation's control environment, which includes an effective audit committee of the board of directors. The Commission asserted that "Audit Committees should be informed, vigilant, and effective overseers of the financial reporting process and the company's internal controls."[7]

Ray Bromark and Ralph Hoffman note that the role of the audit committee is expanding because of its value to the board of directors and to management and because of the need to meet the challenges of constantly changing business conditions. They point out that the audit committee has the following primary responsibilities:

> Assisting the board to fulfill its oversight responsibilities as they relate to the financial reporting process and the internal structure

> Maintaining, by way of regularly scheduled meetings, direct lines of communication between the board, financial management, the independent accountant, and internal audit

Additional responsibilities include:

> Reviewing corporate policies relating to compliance with laws and regulations, ethics, conflict of interests, and the investigation of misconduct and fraud

> Conducting periodic reviews of current pending litigation of regulatory proceedings bearing on corporate governance in which the corporation is a party

---

[5]Jeremy Bacon, *The Audit Committee: A Broader Mandate*, Report No. 914 (New York: The Conference Board, 1988), p. vii.

[6]National Commission on Fraudulent Financial Reporting, *Report of the National Commission on Fraudulent Financial Reporting* (Washington, DC: NCFFR, 1987), p. 40. This principle has become statutory law under the Sarbanes-Oxley Act and the federal securities laws.

Moreover, a recent American Society of Corporate Secretaries study on current board practices found in a survey of 804 companies that most respondents (85.6 percent) have no management director on the audit committee (p. 12). In a subsequent survey of 648 companies, they found that such a board practice continued to rank high among the most commonly adopted practices (p. 14). See ASCS, *Current Board Practices* (New York: ASCS, 1996), and *Current Board Practices, Second Study* (New York: ASCS, 1998).

[7]NCFFR *Report*, p. 41.

Coordinating annual reviews of compliance with corporate governance policies through internal audit or the company's independent accountants

Performing or supervising special investigations

Reviewing executive expenses

Reviewing policies on sensitive payments

Reviewing past or proposed transactions between the corporation and members of management

Reviewing the corporation's benefits programs

Assessing the performance of financial management[8]

Making the Audit Committee Effective

To organize an effective and efficient audit committee, consideration should be given to the proper delegation of responsibility and authority as well as to its written charter, membership, and size.

Delegation of Responsibility and Authority   As a prerequisite to the effective performance of the committee, the board of directors should formulate a clear definition of the committee's responsibilities and authority. Moreover, the board should either pass a formal resolution or amend the bylaws of the corporation in order to document the establishment of the committee. Wayne Zetzman reports that an audit committee can best serve a corporation when "it is a viable, independent group with a definite mission and it has full access to the company's financial information."[9] One study noted that 51 companies with financial reporting problems, namely Securities and Exchange Commission (SEC) enforcement actions and/or material misstatements of quarterly earnings, were much less likely to have audit committees consisting solely of outside directors. Additionally, the researchers found that accounting and finance knowledge as well as frequent meetings are minimum steps needed to improve the quality in financial reporting.[10] In addition to both the internal and external auditors' guidance and assistance, Zetzman notes that the chief financial officer must educate and guide the audit committee to enable it to serve the company effectively.[11]

---

[8]Ray Bromark and Ralph Hoffman, "An Audit Committee for Dynamic Times," *Directors and Boards* 16, No. 3 (Spring 1992), pp. 52, 53, 60.

[9]Wayne Zetzman, "How to Organize and Use the Audit Committee," *Financial Executive* 5, No. 4 (July/August 1989), p. 54.

[10]See Dorothy A. McMullen and K. Raghunandan, "Enhancing Audit Committee Effectiveness," *Journal of Accountancy* 182, No. 2 (August 1996), pp. 79–81. Also see Eugene M. Katz, "Keys to an Effective Audit Committee," *Credit World* 86, No. 4 (March/April 1998), pp. 21–23; Krishnagopal Menon and Joanne D. Williams, "The Use of Audit Committees for Monitoring," *Journal of Accounting & Public Policy* 13, No. 2 (Summer 1994), pp. 121–139; F. Todd De Zoort, "An Investigation of Audit Committees' Oversight Responsibilities," *Abacus* 33, No. 2 (September 1997), pp. 208–227; Robert Lear, "The Decline of the Audit Committee," *Chief Executive,* No. 111 (March 1996), p. 10; William W. Warrick and Duncan J. Galloway, "The Governance Audit: How Can We Make Sure We Don't Get Surprised?" *Directorship* 22, No. 5 (May 1996), pp. 1–4.

[11]Zetzman, "How to Organize and Use the Audit Committee," p. 57.

An example of the board's delegation of responsibility and authority to the audit committee is that of Wal-Mart Stores, Inc.:

BOARD COMMITTEES

Committee	Members	Functions and Additional Information
Audit	Stanley C. Gault Roland A. Hernandez J. Paul Reason	• Reviews financial reporting, policies, procedures, and internal controls of Wal-Mart • Recommends appointment of outside auditors • Reviews related party transactions • The Board has determined that the members are "independent" as defined by the current listing standards of the New York Stock Exchange and • The Board has adopted a written charter for the Audit Committee[12]

In addition, the activities of the audit committee are further disclosed in the annual stockholders' report, which states in part:

Wal-Mart's Audit Committee consists of three directors, each of whom is "independent" as defined by the current listing standards of the New York Stock Exchange. The members of the Committee are Stanley C. Gault, Roland A. Hernandez, who is the Committee's chairperson, and J. Paul Reason. The Audit Committee is governed by a written charter adopted by the Board. Given the current trends in corporate governance, recent legislation by Congress, and the proposed New York Stock Exchange corporate governance listing standards, the Audit Committee and the Board recently adopted a revised Audit Committee charter in March 2003. A copy of the revised charter is available on our website at *www.walmartstores.com*.

Wal-Mart's management is responsible for Wal-Mart's internal controls and financial reporting, including the preparation of Wal-Mart's consolidated financial statements. Wal-Mart's independent auditors are responsible for auditing Wal-Mart's annual consolidated financial statements in accordance with generally accepted auditing standards and ensuring that the financial statements fairly present Wal-Mart's results of operations and financial position. The independent auditors also are responsible for issuing a report on those financial statements. The Audit Committee monitors and oversees these processes. The Audit Committee annually recommends to the Board for its approval an independent accounting firm to be Wal-Mart's independent auditors. Beginning with the June 6, 2003 shareholders' meeting, ratification of the Board's approval of the independent auditors is being sought. Ernst & Young LLP is Wal-Mart's current independent auditor.

As part of the oversight process, the Audit Committee regularly meets with management, the outside auditors, and Wal-Mart's internal auditors. The Audit Committee often meets with these groups in closed sessions. Throughout the year, the

---

[12]Wal-Mart Stores, Inc., *Notice of Annual Meeting of Shareholders and Proxy Statement*, (June 6, 2003), pp. 4–6.

Audit Committee had full access to management, and the outside and internal auditors for the Company. To fulfill its responsibilities, the Audit Committee did the following:

- reviewed and discussed with Wal-Mart's management and the independent auditors Wal-Mart's consolidated financial statements for the fiscal year ended January 31, 2003;

- reviewed management's representations that those consolidated financial statements were prepared in accordance with generally accepted accounting principles and fairly present the results of operations and financial positions of the Company;

- discussed with the independent auditors the matters required by Statement on Auditing Standards 61, including matters related to the conduct of the audit of Wal-Mart's consolidated financial statements;

- received written disclosures and the letter from the independent auditors required by Independence Standards Board Standard No. 1 relating to their independence from Wal-Mart, and discussed with Ernst & Young LLP their independence from Wal-Mart;

- based on the discussions with management and the independent auditors, the independent auditors' disclosures and letter to the Audit Committee, the representations of management to the Audit Committee and the report of the independent auditors, the Audit Committee recommended to the board that Wal-Mart's audited annual consolidated financial statements for fiscal year 2003 be included in Wal-Mart's Annual Report on Form 10-K for the fiscal year ended January 31, 2003, for filing with the Securities and Exchange Commission;

- reviewed all non-audit services performed for Wal-Mart by Ernst & Young LLP and considered whether Ernst & Young LLP's provision of non-audit services was compatible with maintaining its independence from Wal-Mart;

- recommended that the Board select Ernst & Young LLP as Wal-Mart's independent auditors to audit and report on the annual consolidated financial statements of Wal-Mart filed with the Securities and Exchange Commission prior to Wal-Mart's annual shareholders meeting to be held in calendar year 2004; and

- consulted with advisors regarding the Sarbanes-Oxley Act of 2002, the New York Stock Exchange's proposed corporate governance listing standards and the corporate governance environment in general and considered any additional requirements placed on the Audit Committee as well as additional procedures or matters that the Audit Committee should consider.

The Audit Committee submits this report:

Stanley C. Gault
Roland A. Hernandez, Chairperson
J. Paul Reason

The Board of Directors, through the activities of its Audit Committee consisting solely of outside directors, provides oversight of the process of reporting financial information. The Committee stays informed of the financial condition of the Company and regularly reviews its financial policies and procedures, the independence of the Company's independent auditors, its internal accounting controls and the objectivity of its financial reporting. Both the Company's independent auditors and the internal auditors have free access to the Audit Committee and meet with the Committee periodically, both with and without management present.

H. Lee Scott	Thomas M. Schoewe
President and Chief	Executive Vice President and Chief
Executive Officer	Financial Officer[13]

Audit Committee Charter

As noted in Chapter 1, both the SEC and SROs require that the audit committee adopt and annually reassess its written charter, which describes the scope of the committee's responsibilities and how it fulfills these responsibilities. Moreover, the rules require that the audit committee charter be included in the proxy statement at least every three years.

Exhibit 2.1 presents the audit committee charter of Wal-Mart Stores, Inc.

Membership and Size of the Audit Committee   The effectiveness of the audit committee depends on the backgrounds of the members and of the chairman.

Audit Committee Independence

Under Section 301 of the Sarbanes-Oxley Act of 2002, Section 10A of the Securities Exchange Act of 1934 is amended by adding (m) Standards Relating to Audit Committees, which states in part:

(2) RESPONSIBILITIES RELATING TO REGISTERED PUBLIC ACCOUNT-
ING FIRMS—The audit committee of each issuer, in its capacity as a committee of
the board of directors, shall be directly responsible for the appointment, compensation, and oversight of the work of any registered public accounting firm employed by
that issuer (including resolution of disagreements between management and the auditor regarding financial reporting) for the purpose of preparing or issuing an audit
report or related work, and each such registered public accounting firm shall report
directly to the audit committee.

(3) INDEPENDENCE—

(A) IN GENERAL—Each member of the audit committee of the issuer shall
be a member of the board of directors of the issuer, and shall otherwise be
independent.

(B) CRITERIA—In order to be considered to be independent for purposes of
this paragraph, a member of an audit committee of an issuer may not, other than
in his or her capacity as a member of the audit committee, the board of directors,
or any other board committee—

(i) accept any consulting, advisory, or other compensatory fee from the
issuer; or

(ii) be an affiliated person of the issuer or any subsidiary thereof.

---

[13]Wal-Mart Stores, Inc., *2003 Annual Report,* p. 52.

Exhibit 2.1 Wal-Mart Stores, Inc., Audit Committee Charter

WAL-MART STORES, INC.
AUDIT COMMITTEE CHARTER

Purpose

The Audit Committee is appointed by the Board to: (1) assist the Board in monitoring (a) the integrity of the financial reporting process, systems of internal controls and financial statements and reports of the Company, (b) the performance of the Company's internal audit function, and (c) the compliance by the Company with legal and regulatory requirements; and (2) be directly responsible for the appointment, compensation and oversight of the Company's independent auditor employed by the Company for the purpose of preparing or issuing an audit report or related work (the "Outside Auditor").

Committee Membership

The Audit Committee shall consist of no fewer than three members, as determined annually by the Board on the recommendation of the Compensation, Nominating and Governance Committee. The members of the Audit Committee shall meet the independence and expertise requirements of the New York Stock Exchange, any other exchange on which the Company's securities are traded, Section 10A(m)(3) of the Securities Exchange Act of 1934 (the "Exchange Act") and the rules and regulations of the Securities and Exchange Commission (the "Commission"). Audit Committee members shall not serve simultaneously on the audit committees of more than two other public companies without the approval of the full Board.

The members of the Audit Committee shall be appointed annually by the Board on the recommendation of the Compensation, Nominating and Governance Committee. Audit Committee members may be replaced by the Board at any time. The Board shall designate the Chairman or Chairwoman ("Chairperson") of the Audit Committee.

Committee Authority and Responsibilities

The basic responsibility of the members of the Audit Committee is to exercise their business judgment to act in what they reasonably believe to be in the best interests of the Company and its shareholders. In discharging that obligation, members should be entitled to rely on the honesty and integrity of the Company's senior executives and its outside advisors and auditors, to the fullest extent permitted by law.

The Audit Committee shall prepare the report required by the rules of the Commission to be included in the Company's annual proxy statement.

The Audit Committee shall be responsible directly for the appointment (subject, if applicable, to shareholder ratification), retention, termination, compensation and terms of engagement, evaluation, and oversight of the work of the Outside Auditor (including resolution of disagreements between management and the Outside Auditor regarding financial reporting). The Outside Auditor shall report directly to the Audit Committee.

The Audit Committee shall oversee the integrity of the audit process, financial reporting and internal accounting controls of the Company, oversee the work of the Company's management, internal auditors (the "Internal Auditors") and the Outside Auditor in these areas, oversee management's development of, and adherence to, a sound system of internal accounting and financial controls, review whether the Internal Auditors and the Outside Auditor objectively assess the Company's financial reporting, accounting practices and internal

(continued)

Exhibit 2.1 *(Continued)*

controls, and provide an open avenue of communication among the Outside Auditor, the Internal Auditors and the Board. It is the responsibility of: (i) management of the Company and the Outside Auditor, under the oversight of the Audit Committee and the Board, to plan and conduct financial audits and to determine that the Company's financial statements and disclosures are complete and accurate in accordance with generally accepted accounting principles ("GAAP") and applicable rules and regulations and fairly present, in all material respects, the financial condition of the Company; (ii) management of the Company, under the oversight of the Audit Committee and the Board, to assure compliance by the Company with applicable legal and regulatory requirements; and (iii) the Internal Auditors, under the oversight of the Audit Committee and the Board, to review the Company's internal transactions and accounting which do not require involvement in the detailed presentation of the Company's financial statements.

The Audit Committee shall pre-approve all audit services and non-audit services (including the fees and terms thereof) to be performed for the Company by the Outside Auditor to the extent required by and in a manner consistent with the applicable law.

The Audit Committee shall meet as often as it determines necessary or appropriate, but not less frequently than quarterly. The Chairperson shall preside at each meeting and, in the absence of the Chairperson, one of the other members of the Audit Committee shall be designated as the acting chair of the meeting. The Chairperson (or acting chair) may direct appropriate members of management and staff to prepare draft agendas and related background information for each Audit Committee meeting. The draft agenda shall be reviewed and approved by the Audit Committee Chairperson (or acting chair) in advance of distribution to the other Audit Committee members. Any background materials, together with the agenda, should be distributed to the Audit Committee members in advance of the meeting. All meetings of the Audit Committee shall be held pursuant to the by-laws of the Company with regard to notice and waiver thereof, and written minutes of each meeting, in the form approved by the Audit Committee, shall be duly filed in the Company records. Reports of meetings of the Audit Committee shall be made to the Board at its next regularly scheduled meeting following the Audit Committee meeting accompanied by any recommendations to the Board approved by the Audit Committee.

The Audit Committee may form and delegate authority to subcommittees consisting of one or more members when appropriate.

The Audit Committee shall have the authority, to the extent it deems necessary or appropriate, to retain independent legal, accounting or other advisers. The Company shall provide for appropriate funding, as determined by the Audit Committee, for payment of compensation to the Outside Auditor for the purpose of rendering or issuing an audit report and to any advisers employed by the Audit Committee, subject only to any limitations imposed by applicable rules and regulations. The Audit Committee may request any officer or associate of the Company or the Company's outside counsel or Outside Auditor to attend a meeting of the Audit Committee or to meet with any members of, or consultants to, the Audit Committee. The Audit Committee shall meet with management, the Internal Auditors and the Outside Auditor in separate executive sessions at least quarterly to discuss matters for which the Audit Committee has responsibility.

The Audit Committee shall make regular reports to the Board. The Audit Committee shall review and reassess the adequacy of this Charter annually and recommend any proposed changes to the Board for approval. The Audit Committee shall annually review its own performance.

In performing its functions, the Audit Committee shall undertake those tasks and responsibilities that, in its judgment, would contribute most effectively to and implement the purposes of the Audit Committee. In addition to the general tasks and responsibilities noted above, the following are the specific functions of the Audit Committee:

Financial Statement and Disclosure Matters

1.   Review and discuss with management, and to the extent the Audit Committee deems necessary or appropriate, the Internal Auditors and the Outside Auditor, the Company's disclosure controls and procedures that are designed to ensure that the reports the Company files with the Commission comply with the Commission's rules and forms.

2.   Review and discuss with management, the Internal Auditors and the Outside Auditor the annual audited financial statements, including disclosures made in management's discussion and analysis, and recommend to the Board whether the audited financial statements should be included in the Company's Form 10-K.

3.   Review and discuss with management, the Internal Auditors and the Outside Auditor the Company's quarterly financial statements, including disclosures made in management's discussion and analysis, prior to the filing of its Form 10-K, including the results of the Outside Auditor's reviews of the quarterly financial statements.

4.   Review and discuss quarterly reports from the Outside Auditor on:
    (a) All critical accounting policies and practices to be used;
    (b) All alternative treatments within GAAP for policies and practices related to material items that have been discussed with management, including ramifications of the use of such alternative disclosures and treatments, and the treatment preferred by the Outside Auditor;
    (c) The internal controls adhered to by the Company, management, and the Company's financial, accounting and internal auditing personnel, and the impact of each on the quality and reliability of the Company's financial reporting; and
    (d) Other material written communications between the Outside Auditor and management, such as any management letter or schedule of unadjusted differences.

5.   Discuss in advance with management the Company's practice with respect to the types of information to be disclosed and the types of presentations to be made in earnings press releases, including the use, if any, of "pro forma" or "adjusted" non-GAAP information, as well as financial information and earnings guidance provided to analysts and rating agencies.

6.   Review and discuss with management, the Internal Auditors and the Outside Auditor:
    (a) Significant financial reporting issues and judgments made in connection with the preparation of the Company's financial statements;
    (b) The clarity of the financial disclosures made by the Company;
    (c) The development, selection and disclosure of critical accounting estimates and the analyses of alternative assumptions or estimates, and the effect of such estimates on the Company's financial statements;
    (d) Potential changes in GAAP and the effect such changes would have on the Company's financial statements;
    (e) Significant changes in accounting principles, financial reporting policies and internal controls implemented by the Company;
    (f) Significant litigation, contingencies and claims against the Company and material accounting issues that require disclosure in the Company's financial statements;
    (g) Information regarding any "second" opinions sought by management from an independent auditor with respect to the accounting treatment of a particular

(continued)

Exhibit 2.1 *(Continued)*

> event or transaction;
> (h) Management's compliance with the Company's processes, procedures and internal controls;
> (i) The adequacy and effectiveness of the Company's internal accounting and financial controls and the recommendations of management, the Internal Auditors and the Outside Auditor for the improvement of accounting practices and internal controls; and
> (j) Any difficulties encountered by the Outside Auditor or the Internal Auditors in the course of their audit work, including any restrictions on the scope of activities or access to requested information, and any significant disagreements with management.

7. Discuss with management and the Outside Auditor the effect of regulatory and accounting initiatives as well as off-balance sheet structures and aggregate contractual obligations on the Company's financial statements.

8. Discuss with management the Company's major financial risk exposures and the steps management has taken to monitor and control such exposures, including the Company's risk assessment and risk management policies.

9. Discuss with the Outside Auditor the matters required to be discussed by Statement on Auditing Standards ("SAS") No. 61 relating to the conduct of the audit. In particular, discuss:
   > (a) The adoption of, or changes to, the Company's significant internal auditing and accounting principles and practices as suggested by the Outside Auditor, Internal Auditors or management; and
   > (b) The management letter provided by the Outside Auditor and the Company's response to that letter.

10. Receive and review disclosures made to the Audit Committee by the Company's Chief Executive Officer and Chief Financial Officer during their certification process for the Company's Form 10-K and Form 10-Q about (a) any significant deficiencies in the design or operation of internal controls or material weakness therein, (b) any fraud involving management or other associates who have a significant role in the Company's internal controls and (c) any significant changes in internal controls or in other factors that could significantly affect internal controls subsequent to the date of their evaluation.

Oversight of the Company's Relationship with the Outside Auditor

11. Review the experience and qualifications of the senior members of the Outside Auditor team.

12. Obtain and review a report from the Outside Auditor at least annually regarding (a) the Outside Auditor's internal quality-control procedures, (b) any material issues raised by the most recent internal quality-control review, or peer review, of the firm, or by any inquiry or investigation by governmental or professional authorities, within the preceding five years respecting one or more independent audits carried out by the firm, (c) any steps taken to deal with any such issues, and (d) all relationships between the Outside Auditor and the Company, including the written disclosures and the letter required by Independence Standards Board Standard 1, as that standard may be modified or supplemented from time to time.

13. Evaluate the qualifications, performance and independence of the Outside Auditor, including considering whether the Outside Auditor's quality controls are adequate and the provision of non-audit services is compatible with maintaining the Outside Auditor's independence, and taking into account the opinions of management and the

Internal Auditor. The Audit Committee shall present its conclusions to the Board.

14. Oversee the rotation of the lead (or coordinating) audit partner having primary responsibility for the audit and the audit partner responsible for reviewing the audit at least once every five years, and oversee the rotation of other audit partners, in accordance with the rules of the Commission.
15. Recommend to the Board policies for the Company's hiring of present and former associates of the Outside Auditor who have participated in any capacity in the audit of the Company, in accordance with the rules of the Commission.
16. To the extent the Audit Committee deems necessary or appropriate, discuss with the national office of the Outside Auditor issues on which they were consulted by the Company's audit team and matters of audit quality and consistency.
17. Discuss with management, the Internal Auditors and the Outside Auditor any accounting adjustments that were noted or proposed by the Outside Auditor, but were not adopted or reflected.
18. Meet with management, the Internal Auditors and the Outside Auditor prior to the audit to discuss and review the scope, planning and staffing of the audit.
19. Obtain from the Outside Auditor the information required to be disclosed to the Company by generally accepted auditing standards in connection with the conduct of an audit, including topics covered by SAS 54, 60, 61 and 82.
20. Require the Outside Auditor to review the financial information included in the Company's Form 10-Q in accordance with Rule 10-01(d) of Regulation S-X of the Commission prior to the Company filing such reports with the Commission and to provide to the Company for inclusion in the Company's Form 10-Q any reports of the Outside Auditor required by Rule 10-01(d).

Oversight of the Company's Internal Audit Function

21. Ensure that the Company has an internal audit function.
22. Review and concur in the appointment, replacement, reassignment or dismissal of the senior auditing executive, and the compensation package for such person.
23. Review the significant reports to management prepared by the internal auditing department and management's responses.
24. Communicate with management and the Internal Auditors to obtain information concerning internal audits, accounting principles adopted by the Company, internal controls of the Company, management, and the Company's financial and accounting personnel, and review the impact of each on the quality and reliability of the Company's financial statements.
25. Evaluate the internal auditing department and its impact on the accounting practices, internal controls and financial reporting of the Company.
26. Discuss with the Outside Auditor the internal audit department's responsibilities, budget and staffing and any recommended changes in the planned scope of the internal audit.

Compliance Oversight Responsibilities

27. Obtain from the Outside Auditor the reports required to be furnished to the Audit Committee under Section 10A of the Exchange Act and obtain from the Outside Auditor any information with respect to illegal acts in accordance with Section 10A.
28. Obtain reports from management, the Company's senior internal auditing executive and the Outside Auditor concerning whether the Company and its subsidiary/foreign affiliated entities are in compliance with applicable legal requirements and the Statement of Ethics. Obtain and review reports and disclosures of insider and

(continued)

Exhibit 2.1 *(Continued)*

---

affiliated party transactions. Advise the Board with respect to the Company's policies and procedures regarding compliance with applicable laws and regulations and the Statement of Ethics.

29. Establish procedures for (a) the receipt, retention and treatment of complaints received by the Company regarding accounting, internal accounting controls or auditing matters, and (b) the confidential, anonymous submission by associates of the Company of concerns regarding questionable accounting or auditing matters.

30. Discuss with management and the Outside Auditor any correspondence between the Company and regulators or governmental agencies and any associate complaints or published reports that raise material issues regarding the Company's financial statements or accounting policies.

31. Discuss with the Company's Chief Legal Officer legal matters that may have a material impact on the financial statements or the Company's compliance policies.

Additional Responsibilities

32. Prepare annually a report for inclusion in the Company's proxy statement relating to its annual shareholders meeting. In that report, the Audit Committee will state whether it has: (a) reviewed and discussed the audited financial statements with management; (b) discussed with the Outside Auditor the matters required to be discussed by SAS No. 61, as that statement may be modified or supplemented from time to time; (c) received from the Outside Auditor the written disclosures and the letter required by Independence Standards Board Standard 1, as that standard may be modified or supplemented from time to time, and has discussed with the Outside Auditor, the Outside Auditor's independence; and (d) based on the review and discussions referred to in clauses (a), (b) and (c) above, recommended to the Board that the audited financial statements be included in the Company's Annual Report on Form 10-K for the last fiscal year for filing with the Commission.

33. Conduct or authorize investigations into any matters within the Audit Committee's scope of responsibilities.

34. Review the Company's Related-Party Transaction Policy and recommend any changes to the Compensation, Nominating and Governance Committee and then to the Board for approval. Review and determine whether to approve or ratify transactions covered by such policy, as appropriate.

Source: Wal-Mart Stores, Inc., Notice of Annual Meeting of Shareholders, June 6, 2003 (Bentonville, Arkansas: Wal-Mart Stores, Inc., April 15, 2003); *www.walmartstores.com.*

(C) EXEMPTION AUTHORITY—The Commission may exempt from the requirements of subparagraph (B) a particular relationship with respect to audit committee members, as the Commission determines appropriate in light of the circumstances.

(4) COMPLAINTS—Each audit committee shall establish procedures for—

(A) the receipt, retention, and treatment of complaints received by the issuer regarding accounting, internal accounting controls, or auditing matters; and

(B) the confidential, anonymous submission by employees of the issuer of concerns regarding questionable accounting or auditing matters.

(5) AUTHORITY TO ENGAGE ADVISERS—Each audit committee shall have the authority to engage independent counsel and other advisers, as it determines necessary to carry out its duties.

(6) FUNDING—Each issuer shall provide for appropriate funding, as determined by the audit committee, in its capacity as a committee of the board of directors, for payment of compensation—

> (A) to the registered public accounting firm employed by the issuer for the purpose of rendering or issuing an audit report; and

> (B) to any advisers employed by the audit committee under paragraph (5).[14]

The standard of independence is also disclosed in the Federal Deposit Insurance Corporation Improvement Act (FDICIA) as noted in the historical perspective. See Appendixes D and F on this book's website.

With respect to additional SEC and SRO audit committee independence requirements, the next section of this chapter contains the Standards Relating to Listing Company Audit Committees.

One academic study provides empirical evidence on the status of the standard of independence and demonstrates the need for regulatory reforms. Recognizing the importance of the standard of independence rules, David Vicknair, Kent Hickman, and Kay C. Carnes investigated proxy statement data from the period 1980 to 1987 of 100 New York Stock Exchange companies to determine "grey" area director representation on audit committees. Proxy statements report such grey areas as interlocking directorships, related-party transactions, affiliations with the firm's bank, lawyers receiving fee income, service by retirees of corporation, consulting fees, and kinship relationships. They found that "approximately one-third of the 418 audit committee members could be classified as 'grey' area directors. Interlocking directorships (12 percent) and other related-party transactions (11.5 percent) individually account for more than ten percent of the directors." The remaining categories individually account for approximately 3 percent or less. They concluded that such directors may be a potential source of violations of audit committee independence.[15]

In addition to those outlined in the Sarbanes-Oxley Act, other basic qualifications of the audit committee are:

- A general understanding of the company's industry and the social, political, economic, and legal forces that affect the industry
- A knowledge of the company with respect to its history, organization, and operational policies
- An understanding of the fundamental problems of planning and control, as well as the fundamentals of the functional aspects of the company

---

[14]Sarbanes-Oxley Act of 2002, H.R. Rep. No. 107-610, July 25, 2002. See also remarks by Commissioner Paul S. Atkins, Securities and Exchange Commission, "The Sarbanes-Oxley Act of 2002: Goals, Content, and Status of Implementation," University of Cologne, Germany, February 5, 2003 (*www.sec.gov/news/speech/spch020503psa.htm*).

[15]David Vicknair, Kent Hickman, and Kay C. Carnes, "A Note on Audit Committee Independence: Evidence from the NYSE on 'Grey' Area Directors," *Accounting Horizons* 7, No. 1 (March 1993), pp. 55–56.

In short, the membership of the committee should consist of both financial and nonfinancial people so that the board can draw on members from various professions, such as accounting, economics, education, psychology, and sociology. As Richard T. Baker, retired managing partner of E&W (now E&Y) and now a member of several audit committees, points out:

> Having one or two nonfinancial people can make a committee more effective. They bring a different and useful perspective. Over the years I have come to greatly respect these people. . . . They add balance to a committee.[16]

Thus, a committee that has members with diverse backgrounds is advantageous since it provides the audit committee with the kind of perspective and experience desirable in assessing both the internal and external audit functions.

Equally important, the chairman has a critical role in coordinating the committee's task. The success or failure of the operation could depend on the chairman, and therefore such an individual should be chosen with great care. Specifically, the chairman should possess the same basic qualifications listed earlier as well as:

- The ability to stimulate the audit directors' thinking without dominating the meeting
- The ability to retain not only each member's personal interest in the work of the committee but also the willingness to contribute to its objectives
- A general understanding of the objectives and jurisdictional aspects
- The ability to plan the agenda and to coordinate and disseminate information to the committee and the board members

In a study of 42 publicly held companies dealing with leadership styles of audit committee effectiveness, William D. Spangler and Louis Braiotta, Jr., report that transformational leadership and active management by exception have a substantial impact on the performance of audit committees. They found that "correlations of transformational leadership (charisma, intellectual stimulation, and individualized considerations), contingent rewards, and active management by exception with effectiveness were significant in the predicted positive direction and passive management by exception was nonstatistically related to audit committee effectiveness as predicted."[17] Their findings and conclusions were based on Bernard M. Bass's theoretical leadership perspective, which states: "Transformational leadership is somewhat independent of organizational structure and relies on the personality, beliefs, and behavior of leaders and subordinates. Indeed, transformational leaders are likely to emerge in times of crises when traditional organizational and social structures and values are weak."[18]

---

[16]Ernst & Whinney, *E&W People* Booklet No. 46302, Cleveland, OH. (1980), p. 7.

[17]William D. Spangler and Louis Braiotta, Jr., "Leadership and Audit Committee Effectiveness," *Group and Organization Studies* 15, No. 2 (June 1990), p. 134. See also Lawrence Kalbers and Timothy J. Fogarty, "Organizational and Economic Explanations of Audit Committee Oversight," *Journal of Managerial Issues* 10, No. 2 (Summer 1998), pp. 129–150.

[18]Bernard M. Bass, *Leadership and Performance Beyond Expectations* (New York: Free Press, 1985), p. 37.

With respect to the size of the audit committee, the American Institute of Certified Public Accountants indicates that:

> A survey of corporations with audit committees revealed that nearly 90 percent had audit committees of three to five members. In general, the audit committee should be large enough to have members with a good mix of business judgment and experience, but not so large as to be unwieldy.[19]

This survey is further supported by the Conference Board survey, which reports that the median sizes are now 4 members for manufacturing and nonfinancial service companies and 4.5 for financial firms.[20]

Although there is general consensus regarding the size, obviously, the number of members will vary from corporation to corporation. The number of members depends not only on the committee's responsibility and authority but also on the size of both the board of directors and the corporation. For example, Wal-Mart Stores, Inc., has 14 members on the board of directors. Ten are nonemployee directors, including three who are members of the audit committee. Furthermore, Wal-Mart's audit committee members are individuals from the fields of communications and industry.[21]

Financial Expert

Section 407 of the Sarbanes-Oxley Act provides that:

> (a) RULES DEFINING "FINANCIAL EXPERT"—The Commission shall issue rules, as necessary or appropriate in the public interest and consistent with the protection of investors, to require each issuer, together with periodic reports required pursuant to sections 13(a) and 15(d) of the Securities Exchange Act of 1934, to disclose whether or not, and if not, the reasons therefor, the audit committee of that issuer is comprised of at least 1 member who is a financial expert, as such term is defined by the Commission.
>
> (b) CONSIDERATIONS—In defining the term "financial expert" for purposes of subsection (a), the Commission shall consider whether a person has, through education and experience as a public accountant or auditor or a principal financial officer, comptroller, or principle accounting officer of an issuer, of from a position involving the performance of similar functions—
>
>> (1) an understanding of generally accepted accounting principles and financial statements;
>>
>> (2) experience in—
>>
>>> (A) the preparation or auditing of financial statements of generally comparable issuers; and
>>>
>>> (B) the application of such principles in connection with the accounting for estimates, accruals, and reserves;

[19]American Institute of Certified Public Accountants, *Audit Committees*, p. 12.
[20]Bacon, *The Audit Committee: A Broader Mandate*, p. 5.
[21]Wal-Mart Stores, Inc., *Notice of Annual Meeting of Stockholders*, June 6, 3003, pp. 2–3.

(3) experience with internal accounting controls; and

(4) an understanding of audit committee functions.[22]

Audit Committee Meetings

Although the Sarbanes-Oxley Act does not address audit committee meetings, the New York Stock Exchange issued a proposed rule change that states:

> Meet separately, periodically, with management, with internal Auditors (or other personnel responsible for the internal audit Function) and with independent auditors.[23]

Furthermore, the National Commission on Fraudulent Financial Reporting recommended the "audit committee oversight responsibilities undertakes on behalf of the board of directors extend to the quarterly reporting process. The audit committee should review the controls that management has established to protect the integrity of the quarterly reporting process. This review should be ongoing."[24]

THE AUDIT COMMITTEE FUNCTIONS

Audit Committee Functions as Defined by the American Bar Association

The Committee on Corporate Laws of the American Bar Association has defined the functions of the audit committee in this way:

> In its capacity as the communication link between the board of directors as representative of stockholders, on the one hand, and the independent auditors, on the other hand, the audit committee should have prime responsibility for the discharge of at least the following four functions:
>
> **1.** To recommend the particular persons or firm to be employed by the corporation as its independent auditors;
>
> **2.** To consult with the persons so chosen to be the independent auditors with regard to the plan of audit;
>
> **3.** To review, in consultation with the independent auditors, their report of audit, or proposed report of audit, and the accompanying management letter, if any; and
>
> **4.** To consult with the independent auditors (periodically, as appropriate, out of the presence of management) with regard to the adequacy of internal controls, and if need be, to consult also with the internal auditors (since their product has a strong influence on the quality and integrity of the resulting independent audit).[25]

---

[22]Sarbanes-Oxley Act of 2002, H.R. Rep. No. 107-610, July 25, 2002. See also SEC Release No. 33-8177, January 23, 2003.

[23]Securities and Exchange Commission Release No. 34-47672, File No. SR-NYSE-2002-33 Proposed Rule Change Relating to Corporate Governance (April 11, 2003), p. 13.

[24] National Commission on Fraudulent Financial Reporting, *Report of the National Commission on Fraudulent Reporting* (Washington, DC: NCFFR, 1987), p. 48.

[25]American Bar Association, *Corporate Director's Guidebook* (Chicago: ABA, 1978), pp. 32–33.

Subsequently, the Committee on Corporate Laws expanded its definitions to include in substantial part the American Law Institute's Principles of Corporate Governances:

1. Recommend which firm to engage as the corporation's external auditor and whether to terminate that relationship.

2. Review the external auditor's compensation, the proposed terms of its engagement, and its independence.

3. Review the appointment and replacement of the senior internal auditing executive, if any.

4. Serve as a channel of communication between the external auditor and the board and between the senior internal auditing executive, if any, and the board.

5. Review the results of each external audit, including any qualifications in the external auditor's opinion, any related management letter, management's responses to recommendations made by the external auditor in connection with the audit, reports submitted to the Audit Committee by the internal auditing department that are material to the corporation as a whole, and management's responses to those reports.

6. Review the corporation's annual financial statements and any significant disputes between management and the external auditor that arose in connection with the preparation of those financial statements.

7. Consider, in consultation with the external auditor and the senior internal auditing executive, if any, the adequacy of the corporation's internal financial controls. Among other things, these controls must be designed to provide reasonable assurance that the corporation's publicly reported financial statements are presented fairly in conformity with generally accepted accounting principles.

8. Consider major changes and other major questions of choice regarding the appropriate auditing and accounting principles and practices to be followed when preparing the corporation's financial statements.

9. Review the procedures employed by the corporation in preparing published financial statements and related management commentaries.

10. Meet periodically with management to review the corporation's major financial risk exposures.[26]

In addition to the American Bar Association's definition on the function of the audit committee, the National Commission on Fraudulent Financial Reporting recommends these functions:

As part of its ongoing oversight of the effectiveness of internal controls, a company's audit committee should review annually the program management establishes to monitor compliance with the code of conduct. (p. 35)

All public companies should develop a written charter setting forth the duties and responsibilities of the audit committee. The board of directors should approve the charter, review it periodically, and modify it as necessary. (p. 42)

---

[26]American Bar Association, *Corporate Director's Guidebook* (Chicago: ABA, 1994), pp. 28–29.

Audit committees should have adequate resources and authority to discharge their responsibilities. (p. 43)

Audit committees should oversee the quarterly reporting process. (p. 47)

Management and the audit committee should ensure that the internal auditors' involvement in the audit of the financial reporting process is appropriate and properly
coordinated with the independent public accountant. (p. 39)

The audit committee should review management's evaluation of factors related to the
independence of the company's public accountant. Both the audit committee and management should assist the public accountant in preserving his independence. (p. 43)

Before the beginning of each year, the audit committee should review management's
plans for engaging the company's independent public accountant to perform management advisory services during the coming year, considering both the types of services that may be rendered and the projected fees. (p. 43)

All public companies should be required by SEC rule to include in their annual report to stockholders a letter signed by the chairman of the audit committee describing the committee's responsibilities and activities during the year. (p. 46)

Management should advise the audit committee when it seeks a second opinion on
a significant accounting issue. (p. 47)[27]

Basic Audit Committee Functions

In addition to the preceding conclusions on the functions of the audit committee,
the basic functions should include:

- The planning function
- The monitoring function
- The reporting function

The Planning Function   Since the primary objective of the committee is to
oversee and monitor the financial accounting and auditing processes, it should
adopt its own coordinated plan of administration that is consistent with this objective. Such a plan should be designed to provide assurance to the full board of
directors that both the internal and external resources allocated to the audit function are adequate and used effectively. The Committee on Corporate Organization
Policy of The Business Roundtable agreed on two core functions of the board that
are directly related to the committee's planning function:

1. Although the board cannot effectively conduct day-to-day operations, the board
   does have a major role in, and a major accountability for, the financial performance of the enterprise. This clearly requires a continuing check on corporate financial results and prospects.

---

[27]NCFFR, *Report of the National Commission on Fraudulent Financial Reporting,* 1987. For further
discussion, see the Committee of Sponsoring Organizations of the Treadway Commission (COSO),
International Control-Integrated Framework 4, COSO of the Treadway Commission (1992), pp.
8–10.

2. Directors and top management cannot be the guarantors of the lawful conduct of every employee or manager in a large organization. . . . Policies and procedures should be designed to promote corporate law compliance.[28]

Thus, in view of the committee's oversight and advisory capacity, its plan should include:

- A review and appraisal of the overall purpose, objectives, and resources available for the entity's overall audit plan in accordance with the committee's charter as well as the committee's recommendation of the audit goals and objectives to the board for its approval
- A review and consolidation of the audit plans of the internal and external auditing groups
- An appraisal of the corporate audit plan annually[29]

Furthermore, the committee should consider an integrated approach whereby its plan is oriented toward the segments of the auditing cycle, which are: (1) initial planning segment, (2) preaudit segment, and (3) postaudit segment. For example, during the initial planning segment, it should develop a basic understanding of the entity's business and its industry. Such an understanding of the qualitative characteristics of the entity and its position in the industry will enhance the committee's ability to discharge its responsibilities more effectively. In addition, during the preaudit and postaudit segments, it should develop an understanding of management's business risk assessment process and the audit risk assessment process related to financial reporting risk as well as the analytical review process with respect to the financial statements.

New Responsibilities under Sarbanes-Oxley (S-Ox) Act of 2002

S-Ox Section 201—Services Outside the Scope of Practice of Auditors

(a) PROHIBITED ACTIVITIES—Section 10A of the Securities Exchange Act of 1934 (15 U.S.C. 78j-1) is amended by adding at the end the following:

(g) PROHIBITED ACTIVITIES—Except as provided in subsection (h), it shall be unlawful for a registered public accounting firm (and any associated person of that firm, to the extent determined appropriate by the Commission) that performs for any issuer any audit required by this title or the rules of the Commission under this title or, beginning 180 days after the date of commencement of the operations of the Public Company Accounting Oversight Board established under section 101 of the

---

[28]The Business Roundtable, *The Role and Composition of the Board of Directors of the Large Publicly Owned Corporations*, pp. 10–13.

[29]See Chapters 6 and 7 for more information on the committee's role in the planning function. It should be noted that the chairman of the audit committee usually will ask the audit engagement partner, the director of internal audit, and the chief financial officer to suggest agenda items for the committee meetings. These individuals are a major source of guidance and information to the committee. In addition, it is essential that agenda and supporting documents are prepared and distributed in advance for each meeting.

Sarbanes-Oxley Act of 2002 (in this section referred to as the "Board"), the rules of the Board, to provide to that issuer, contemporaneously with the audit, any non-audit service, including—

(1) bookkeeping or other services related to the accounting records or financial statements of the audit client;

(2) financial information systems design and implementation;

(3) appraisal or valuation services, fairness opinions, or contribution-in-kind reports;

(4) actuarial services;

(5) internal audit outsourcing services;

(6) management functions or human resources;

(7) broker or dealer, investment adviser, or investment banking services;

(8) legal services and expert services unrelated to the audit; and

(9) any other service that the Board determines, by regulation, is impermissible.

(h) PREAPPROVAL REQUIRED FOR NON-AUDIT SERVICES—A registered public accounting firm may engage in any non-audit service, including tax services, that is not described in any of paragraphs (1) through (9) of subsection (g) for an audit client, only if the activity is approved in advance by the audit committee of the issuer, in accordance with subsection (i).

(b) EXEMPTION AUTHORITY—The Board may, on a case-by-case basis, exempt any person, issuer, public accounting firm, or transaction from the prohibition on the provision of services under section 10A(g) of the Securities Exchange Act of 1934 (as added by this section), to the extent that such exemption is necessary or appropriate in the public interest and is consistent with the protection of investors, and subject to review by the Commission in the same manner as for rules of the Board under section 107.[30]

S-Ox Section 202—Preapproval of Audit and Non-Audit Services

Section 10A of the Securities Exchange Act of 1934 (15 U.S.C. 78j-1), as amended by this Act, is amended by adding at the end the following:

(i) PREAPPROVAL REQUIREMENTS—

(1) IN GENERAL—

(A) AUDIT COMMITTEE ACTION—All auditing services (which may entail providing comfort letters in connection with securities underwritings or statutory audits required for insurance companies for purposes of State law) and non-audit services, other than as provided in subparagraph (B), provided to an issuer by the auditor of the issuer shall be preapproved by the audit committee of the issuer.

(B) DE MINIMUS EXCEPTION—The preapproval requirement under subparagraph (A) is waived with respect to the provision of non-audit services for an issuer, if—

(i) the aggregate amount of all such non-audit services provided to the issuer constitutes not more than 5 percent of the total amount of rev-

---

[30]Sarbanes-Oxley Act of 2002, H.R. Rep. No. 107-610, July 25, 2002.

enues paid by the issuer to its auditor during the fiscal year in which the nonaudit services are provided;

(ii) such services were not recognized by the issuer at the time of the engagement to be non-audit services; and

(iii) such services are promptly brought to the attention of the audit committee of the issuer and approved prior to the completion of the audit by the audit committee or by 1 or more members of the audit committee who are members of the board of directors to whom authority to grant such approvals has been delegated by the audit committee.

(2) DISCLOSURE TO INVESTORS—Approval by an audit committee of an issuer under this subsection of a non-audit service to be performed by the auditor of the issuer shall be disclosed to investors in periodic reports required by section 13(a).

(3) DELEGATION AUTHORITY—The audit committee of an issuer may delegate to 1 or more designated members of the audit committee who are independent directors of the board of directors, the authority to grant preapprovals required by this subsection. The decisions of any member to whom authority is delegated under this paragraph to preapprove an activity under this subsection shall be presented to the full audit committee at each of its scheduled meetings.

(4) APPROVAL OF AUDIT SERVICES FOR OTHER PURPOSES—In carrying out its duties under subsection (m)(2), if the audit committee of an issuer approves an audit service within the scope of the engagement of the auditor, such audit service shall be deemed to have been preapproved for purposes of this subsection.[31]

S-Ox Section 203—Audit Partner Rotation

Section 10A of the Securities Exchange Act of 1934 (15 U.S.C. 78j-1), as amended by this Act, is amended by adding at the end the following:

(j) AUDIT PARTNER ROTATION—It shall be unlawful for a registered public accounting firm to provide audit services to an issuer if the lead (or coordinating) audit partner (having primary responsibility for the audit), or the audit partner responsible for reviewing the audit, has performed audit services for that issuer in each of the 5 previous fiscal years of that issuer.[32]

S-Ox Section 204—Auditors' Reports to Audit Committees

Section 10A of the Securities Exchange Act of 1934 (15 U.S.C. 78j-1), as amended by this Act, is amended by adding at the end the following:

(k) REPORTS TO AUDIT COMMITTEES—Each registered public accounting firm that performs for any issuer any audit required by this title shall timely report to the audit committee of the issuer—

(1) all critical accounting policies and practices to be used;

(2) all alternative treatments of financial information within generally accepted accounting principles that have been discussed with management officials of the

---

[31]Ibid., Sec. 202.
[32]Ibid., Sec. 203.

issuer, ramifications of the use of such alternative disclosures and treatments, and the treatment preferred by the registered public accounting firm; and

(3) other material written communications between the registered public accounting firm and the management of the issuer, such as any management letter or schedule of unadjusted differences.[33]

S-Ox Section 206—Conflicts of Interest

Section 10A of the Securities Exchange Act of 1934 (15 U.S.C. 78j-1), as amended by this Act, is amended by adding at the end the following:

(l) CONFLICTS OF INTEREST—It shall be unlawful for a registered public accounting firm to perform for an issuer any audit service required by this title, if a chief executive officer, controller, chief financial officer, chief accounting officer, or any person serving in an equivalent position for the issuer, was employed by that registered independent public accounting firm and participated in any capacity in the audit of that issuer during the 1-year period preceding the date of the initiation of the audit.[34]

S-Ox Section 403—Disclosure of Transactions Involving Management and Principal Stockholders

(a) AMENDMENT—Section 16 of the Securities Exchange Act of 1934 (15 U.S.C. 78p) is amended by striking the heading of such section and subsection (a) and inserting the following:

SEC. 16. DIRECTORS, OFFICERS, AND PRINCIPAL STOCKHOLDERS.

(a) DISCLOSURES REQUIRED—

(1) DIRECTORS, OFFICERS, AND PRINCIPAL STOCKHOLDERS REQUIRED TO FILE—Every person who is directly or indirectly the beneficial owner of more than 10 percent of any class of any equity security (other than an exempted security) which is registered pursuant to section 12, or who is a director or an officer of the issuer of such security, shall file the statements required by this subsection with the Commission (and, if such security is registered on a national securities exchange, also with the exchange).

(2) TIME OF FILING—The statements required by this subsection shall be filed—

(A) at the time of the registration of such security on a national securities exchange or by the effective date of a registration statement filed pursuant to section 12(g);

(B) within 10 days after he or she becomes such beneficial owner, director, or officer;

(C) if there has been a change in such ownership, or if such person shall have purchased or sold a security-based swap agreement (as defined in section 206(b) of the Gramm-Leach-Bliley Act (15 U.S.C. 78c note)) involving such equity security, before the end of the second business day following the day on which the subject transaction has been executed, or at such other time as

---

[33]Ibid., Sec. 204.
[34]Ibid., Sec. 206.

the Commission shall establish, by rule, in any case in which the Commission determines that such 2-day period is not feasible.

(3) CONTENTS OF STATEMENTS—A statement filed—

(A) under subparagraph (A) or (B) of paragraph (2) shall contain a statement of the amount of all equity securities of such issuer of which the filing person is the beneficial owner; and

(B) under subparagraph (C) of such paragraph shall indicate ownership by the filing person at the date of filing, any such changes in such ownership, and such purchases and sales of the security-based swap agreements as have occurred since the most recent filing under such subparagraph.

(4) ELECTRONIC FILING AND AVAILABILITY—Beginning not later than 1 year after the date of enactment of the Sarbanes-Oxley Act of 2002—

(A) a statement filed under subparagraph (C) of paragraph (2) shall be filed electronically;

(B) the Commission shall provide each such statement on a publicly accessible Internet site not later than the end of the business day following that filing; and

(C) the issuer (if the issuer maintains a corporate website) shall provide that statements on that corporate website, not later than the end of the business day following that filing.

(b) EFFECTIVE DATE—The amendment made by this section shall be effective 30 days after the date of the enactment of this Act.[35]

S-Ox Section 404—Management Assessment of Internal Controls

(a) RULES REQUIRED—The Commission shall prescribe rules requiring each annual report required by section 13(a) or 15(d) of the Securities Exchange Act of 1934 (15 U.S.C. 78m or 78o(d)) to contain an internal control report, which shall—

(1) state the responsibility of management for establishing and maintaining an adequate internal control structure and procedures for financial reporting; and

(2) contain an assessment, as of the end of the most recent fiscal year of the issuer, of the effectiveness of the internal control structure and procedures of the issuer for financial reporting.

(b) INTERNAL CONTROL EVALUATION AND REPORTING—With respect to the internal control assessment required by subsection (a), each registered public accounting firm that prepares or issues the audit report for the issuer shall attest to, and report on, the assessment made by the management of the issuer. An attestation made under this subsection shall be made in accordance with standards for attestation engagements issued or adopted by the Board. Any such attestation shall not be the subject of a separate engagement.[36]

S-Ox Section 406—Code of Ethics for Senior Financial Officers

(a) CODE OF ETHICS DISCLOSURE—The Commission shall issue rules to require each issuer, together with periodic reports required pursuant to section 13(a) or

---

[35]Ibid., Sec. 403.
[36]Ibid., Sec. 404.

15(d) of the Securities Exchange Act of 1934, to disclose whether or not, and if not, the reason therefor, such issuer has adopted a code of ethics for senior financial officers, applicable to its principal financial officer and comptroller or principal accounting officer, or persons performing similar functions.

(b) CHANGES IN CODES OF ETHICS—The Commission shall revise its regulations concerning matters requiring prompt disclosure on Form 8-K (or any successor thereto) to require the immediate disclosure, by means of the filing of such form, dissemination by the Internet or by other electronic means, by any issuer of any change in or waiver of the code of ethics for senior financial officers.

(c) DEFINITION—In this section, the term "code of ethics" means such standards as are reasonably necessary to promote—

(1) honest and ethical conduct, including the ethical handling of actual or apparent conflicts of interest between personal and professional relationships;

(2) full, fair, accurate, timely, and understandable disclosure in the periodic reports required to be filed by the issuer; and

(3) compliance with applicable governmental rules and regulations.

(d) DEADLINE FOR RULEMAKING—The Commission shall—

(1) propose rules to implement this section, not later than 90 days after the date of enactment of this Act; and

(2) issue final rules to implement this section, not later than 180 days after that date of enactment.[37]

The Monitoring Function   Obviously, the audit committee cannot participate in the accounting and auditing functions on a day-to-day basis, because such a task is contrary to its overall purpose. However, since the board of directors has the ultimate responsibility for these functions, the audit directors should monitor the corporation's activities based on their jurisdiction. The monitoring function should be administered so that the planning function is accomplished. Consequently, the committee can assist the board by obtaining information from the accounting and auditing executives in order to discharge the board's responsibility. The consensus seems to be that the audit directors should monitor:

- The internal auditing function
- The internal control system and related business risks
- The financial reporting disclosures
- Conflicts of interest, ethics audit, and fraud audit activities
- Corporate perquisites
- Corporate contributions[38]
- Information technology systems
- Other tasks as requested by the board

---

[37]Ibid., Sec. 406.

[38]The board of directors may request that the audit committee review corporate contributions to ensure compliance with the corporate giving policy.

In administering the monitoring function, it may be advisable for the committee to retain the necessary professional expertise, such as the corporation's outside legal counsel or outside data processing experts.

S-Ox Section 806—Protection for Employees of Publicly Traded Companies Who Provide Evidence of Fraud

(a) IN GENERAL—Chapter 73 of title 18, United States Code, is amended by inserting after section 1514 the following:

Sec. 1514A. Civil action to protect against retaliation in fraud cases

(a) WHISTLEBLOWER PROTECTION FOR EMPLOYEES OF PUBLICLY TRADED COMPANIES—No company with a class of securities registered under section 12 of the Securities Exchange Act of 1934 (15 U.S.C 78l), or that is required to file reports under section 15(d) of the Securities Exchange Act of 1934 (15 U.S.C. 78o(d))), or any officer, employee, contractor, subcontractor, or agent of such company, may discharge, demote, suspend, threaten, harass, or in any other manner discriminate against an employee in the terms and conditions of employment because of any lawful act done by the employee—

(1) to provide information, cause information to be provided, or otherwise assist in an investigation regarding any conduct which the employee reasonably believes constitutes a violation of section 1341, 1343, 1344, or 1348, any rule or regulation of the Securities and Exchange Commission, or any provision of Federal law relating to fraud against shareholders, when the information or assistance is provided to or the investigation conducted by—

(A) a Federal regulatory or law enforcement agency;

(B) any Member of Congress or any committee of Congress; or

(C) a person with supervisory authority over the employee (or such other person working for the employer who has the authority to investigate, discover, or terminate misconduct); or

(2) to file, cause to be filed, testify, participate in, or otherwise assist in a proceeding filed or about to be filed (with any knowledge of the employer) relating to an alleged violation of section 1341, 1343, 1344, or 1348, any rule or regulation of the Securities and Exchange Commission, or any provision of Federal law relating to fraud against shareholders.

(b) ENFORCEMENT ACTION—

(1) IN GENERAL—A person who alleges discharge or other discrimination by any person in violation of subsection (a) may seek relief under subsection (c), by—

(A) filing a complaint with the Secretary of Labor; or

(B) if the Secretary has not issued a final decision within 180 days of the filing of the complaint and there is no showing that such delay is due to the bad faith of the claimant, bringing an action at law or equity for de novo review in the appropriate district court of the United States, which shall have jurisdiction over such an action without regard to the amount in controversy.

(2) PROCEDURE—

(A) IN GENERAL—An action under paragraph (1)(A) shall be governed under the rules and procedures set forth in section 42121(b) of title 49, United States Code.

(B) EXCEPTION—Notification made under section 42121(b)(1) of title 49, United States Code, shall be made to the person named in the complaint and to the employer.

(C) BURDENS OF PROOF—An action brought under paragraph (1)(B) shall be governed by the legal burdens of proof set forth in section 42121(b) of title 49, United States Code.

(D) STATUTE OF LIMITATIONS—An action under paragraph (1) shall be commenced not later than 90 days after the date on which the violation occurs.

(c) REMEDIES—

(1) IN GENERAL—An employee prevailing in any action under subsection (b)(1) shall be entitled to all relief necessary to make the employee whole.

(2) COMPENSATORY DAMAGES—Relief for any action under paragraph (1) shall include—

(A) reinstatement with the same seniority status that the employee would have had, but for the discrimination;

(B) the amount of back pay, with interest; and

(C) compensation for any special damages sustained as a result of the discrimination, including litigation costs, expert witness fees, and reasonable attorney fees.

(d) RIGHTS RETAINED BY EMPLOYEE—Nothing in this section shall be deemed to diminish the rights, privileges, or remedies of any employee under any Federal or State law, or under any collective bargaining agreement.

(b) CLERICAL AMENDMENT—The table of sections at the beginning of chapter 73 of title 18, United States Code, is amended by inserting after the item relating to section 1514 the following new item:

"1514A. Civil action to protect against retaliation in fraud cases."[39]

S-Ox Section 303—Improper Influence on Conducts of Audits

(a) RULES TO PROHIBIT—It shall be unlawful, in contravention of such rules or regulations as the Commission shall prescribe as necessary and appropriate in the public interest or for the protection of investors, for any officer or director of an issuer, or any other person acting under the direction thereof, to take any action to fraudulently influence, coerce, manipulate, or mislead any independent public or certified accountant engaged in the performance of an audit of the financial statements of that issuer for the purpose of rendering such financial statements materially misleading.

(b) ENFORCEMENT—In any civil proceeding, the Commission shall have exclusive authority to enforce this section and any rule or regulation issued under this section.

(c) NO PREEMPTION OF OTHER LAW—The provisions of subsection (a) shall be in addition to, and shall not supersede or preempt, any other provision of law or any rule or regulation issued thereunder.

(d) DEADLINE FOR RULEMAKING—The Commission shall—

---

[39]Ibid., Sec. 806.

(1) propose the rules or regulations required by this section, not later than 90 days after the date of enactment of this Act; and

(2) issue final rules or regulations required by this section, not later than 270 days after that date of enactment.[40]

S-Ox Section 402—Enhanced Conflict of Interest Provisions

(a) PROHIBITION ON PERSONAL LOANS TO EXECUTIVES—Section 13 of the Securities Exchange Act of 1934 (15 U.S.C. 78m), as amended by this Act, is amended by adding at the end the following:

(k) PROHIBITION ON PERSONAL LOANS TO EXECUTIVES—

(1) IN GENERAL—It shall be unlawful for any issuer (as defined in section 2 of the Sarbanes-Oxley Act of 2002), directly or indirectly, including through any subsidiary, to extend or maintain credit, to arrange for the extension of credit, or to renew an extension of credit, in the form of a personal loan to or for any director or executive officer (or equivalent thereof) of that issuer. An extension of credit maintained by the issuer on the date of enactment of this subsection shall not be subject to the provisions of this subsection, provided that there is no material modification to any term of any such extension of credit or any renewal of any such extension of credit on or after that date of enactment.

(2) LIMITATION—Paragraph (1) does not preclude any home improvement and manufactured home loans (as that term is defined in section 5 of the Home Owners' Loan Act (12 U.S.C. 1464)), consumer credit (as defined in section 103 of the Truth in Lending Act (15 U.S.C. 1602)), or any extension of credit under an open end credit plan (as defined in section 127(c)(4)(e) of the Truth in Lending Act (15 U.S.C. 1637(c)(4)(e)), or any extension of credit by a broker or dealer registered under section 15 of this title to an employee of that broker or dealer to buy, trade, or carry securities, that is permitted under rules or regulations of the Board of Governors of the Federal Reserve System pursuant to section 7 of this title (other than an extension of credit that would be used to purchase stock of that issuer), that is—

(A) made or provided in the ordinary course of the consumer credit business of such issuer;

(B) of a type that is generally made available by such issuer to the public; and

(C) made by such issuer on market terms, or terms that are no more favorable than those offered by the issuer to the general public for such extensions of credit.

(3) RULE OF CONSTRUCTION FOR CERTAIN LOANS—Paragraph (1) does not apply to any loan made or maintained by an insured depository institution (as defined in section 3 of the Federal Deposit Insurance Act (12 U.S.C. 1813)), if the loan is subject to the insider lending restrictions of section 22(h) of the Federal Reserve Act (12 U.S.C. 375b)."[41]

---

[40]Ibid., Sec. 303.
[41]Ibid., Sec. 402.

With respect to the internal audit function, the NYSE's proposed listing standards (Section 303A(7)(e) provides that:

> Each listed company must have an internal audit function.
>
> Commentary: Listed companies must maintain an internal audit function to provide management and the audit committee with ongoing assessments of the company's risk management processes and system of internal control. A company may choose to outsource this function to a firm other than its independent auditor.[42]

The Reporting Function[43] The audit committee should report directly to the board of directors and not to the chief executive officer. Since the members are independent or nonmanagement directors, they provide an objective appraisal of management's accounting and auditing performance. Furthermore, the reporting function is directly related to both the planning and monitoring functions. The general content of the audit directors' report should be based on the review programs regarding the planning function. Although the minutes of the committee meetings are a record of the proceedings, the nature of its function warrants a formal report. The report should contain a summary of its findings and recommendations with the appropriate figures and narrative remarks. In developing the reports for the board, the committee should focus its attention on the board's interests in such matters as:

- The financial accounting policies and the related industry accounting practices (e.g., depreciation methods, inventory pricing, basis for consolidation)
- The reports of the independent auditors and the internal auditors (e.g., the auditors' opinion on the system of internal control)
- The reports of legal counsel with respect to significant commitments, contingencies, and governmental compliance
- The reports of a special investigation concerning the review of the corporation's financial affairs, such as political contributions

In short, the report of the audit committee may vary in form; however, the committee should render a concise report that fulfills the needs and interests of the board.

S-Ox Section 302—Corporate Responsibility for Financial Reports

> (a) REGULATIONS REQUIRED—The Commission shall, by rule, require, for each company filing periodic reports under section 13(a) or 15(d) of the Securities Exchange Act of 1934 (15 U.S.C. 78m, 78o(d)), that the principal executive officer or officers and the principal financial officer or officers, or persons performing similar functions, certify in each annual or quarterly report filed or submitted under either such section of such Act that—

---

[42]Securities and Exchange Commission, Release No. 34-47672; File No. SR-NYSE-2002-33, *Proposed Rule Change Relating to Corporate Governance* (Washington, DC: SEC, April 11, 2003), p. 13.
[43]For further discussion, see Chapter 14.

(1) the signing officer has reviewed the report;

(2) based on the officer's knowledge, the report does not contain any untrue statement of a material fact or omit to state a material fact necessary in order to make the statements made, in light of the circumstances under which such statements were made, not misleading;

(3) based on such officer's knowledge, the financial statements, and other financial information included in the report, fairly present in all material respects the financial condition and results of operations of the issuer as of, and for, the periods presented in the report;

(4) the signing officers—

    (A) are responsible for establishing and maintaining internal controls;

    (B) have designed such internal controls to ensure that material information relating to the issuer and its consolidated subsidiaries is made known to such officers by others within those entities, particularly during the period in which the periodic reports are being prepared;

    (C) have evaluated the effectiveness of the issuer's internal controls as of a date within 90 days prior to the report; and

    (D) have presented in the report their conclusions about the effectiveness of their internal controls based on their evaluation as of that date;

(5) the signing officers have disclosed to the issuer's auditors and the audit committee of the board of directors (or persons fulfilling the equivalent function)—

    (A) all significant deficiencies in the design or operation of internal controls which could adversely affect the issuer's ability to record, process, summarize, and report financial data and have identified for the issuer's auditors any material weaknesses in internal controls; and

    (B) any fraud, whether or not material, that involves management or other employees who have a significant role in the issuer's internal controls; and

(6) the signing officers have indicated in the report whether or not there were significant changes in internal controls or in other factors that could significantly affect internal controls subsequent to the date of their evaluation, including any corrective actions with regard to significant deficiencies and material weaknesses.

(b) FOREIGN REINCORPORATIONS HAVE NO EFFECT—Nothing in this section 302 shall be interpreted or applied in any way to allow any issuer to lessen the legal force of the statement required under this section 302, by an issuer having reincorporated or having engaged in any other transaction that resulted in the transfer of the corporate domicile or offices of the issuer from inside the United States to outside of the United States.

(c) DEADLINE—The rules required by subsection (a) shall be effective not later than 30 days after the date of enactment of this act.[44]

S-Ox Section 906—Corporate Responsibility for Financial Reports

(a) IN GENERAL—Chapter 63 of title 18, United States Code, is amended by inserting after section 1349, as created by this Act, the following:

---

[44]Sarbanes-Oxley Act of 2002, H.R. Rep. No. 107-610, July 25, 2002.

Sec. 1350. Failure of corporate officers to certify financial reports

(a) CERTIFICATION OF PERIODIC FINANCIAL REPORTS—Each periodic report containing financial statements filed by an issuer with the Securities Exchange Commission pursuant to section 13(a) or 15(d) of the Securities Exchange Act of 1934 (15 U.S.C. 78m(a) or 78o(d)) shall be accompanied by a written statement by the chief executive officer and chief financial officer (or equivalent thereof) of the issuer.

(b) CONTENT—The statement required under subsection (a) shall certify that the periodic report containing the financial statements fully complies with the requirements of section 13(a) or 15(d) of the Securities Exchange Act of 1934 (15 U.S.C. 78m or 78o(d)) and that information contained in the periodic report fairly presents, in all material respects, the financial condition and results of operations of the issuer.

(c) CRIMINAL PENALTIES—Whoever—

(1) certifies any statement as set forth in subsections (a) and (b) of this section knowing that the periodic report accompanying the statement does not comport with all the requirements set forth in this section shall be fined not more than $1,000,000 or imprisoned not more than 10 years, or both; or

(2) willfully certifies any statement as set forth in subsections (a) and (b) of this section knowing that the periodic report accompanying the statement does not comport with all the requirements set forth in this section shall be fined not more than $5,000,000, or imprisoned not more than 20 years, or both.

(b) CLERICAL AMENDMENT—The table of sections at the beginning of chapter 63 of title 18, United States Code, is amended by adding at the end the following:

1350. Failure of corporate officers to certify financial reports.[45]

An example of the CEO and CFO certification in the annual SEC 10-K report by Wal-Mart Stores, Inc., is shown in Exhibits 2.2 and 2.3.

S-Ox Section 401: Disclosure of Periodic Reports

(a) DISCLOSURES REQUIRED—Section 13 of the Securities Exchange Act of 1934 (15 U.S.C. 78m) is amended by adding at the end the following:

(i) ACCURACY OF FINANCIAL REPORTS—Each financial report that contains financial statements, and that is required to be prepared in accordance with (or reconciled to) generally accepted accounting principles under this title and filed with the Commission shall reflect all material correcting adjustments that have been identified by a registered public accounting firm in accordance with generally accepted accounting principles and the rules and regulations of the Commission.

(j) OFF-BALANCE SHEET TRANSACTIONS—Not later than 180 days after the date of enactment of the Sarbanes-Oxley Act of 2002, the Commission shall issue final rules providing that each annual and quarterly financial report required to be filed with the Commission shall disclose all material off-balance sheet transactions, arrangements, obligations (including contingent obligations), and other relationships of the issuer with unconsolidated entities or other persons, that may have a material current or future effect on financial condition,

---

[45]Ibid., Sec. 906.

Exhibit 2.2. CEO and CFO Certification (Sarbanes-Oxley Act of 2002, Section 302)

CERTIFICATIONS

I, H. Lee Scott, Jr., certify that:

1. I have reviewed this annual report on Form 10-K of Wal-Mart Stores, Inc. (the "registrant");
2. Based on my knowledge, this annual report does not contain any untrue statement of a material fact or omit to state a material fact necessary to make the statements made, in light of the circumstances under which such statements were made, not misleading with respect to the period covered by this annual report;
3. Based on my knowledge, the financial statements, and other financial information included in this annual report, fairly present in all material respects the financial condition, results of operations and cash flows of the registrant as of, and for, the periods presented in this annual report;
4. The registrant's other certifying officers and I are responsible for establishing and maintaining disclosure controls and procedures (as defined in Exchange Act Rules 13a-14 and 15d-14) for the registrant and have:
    a) Designed such disclosure controls and procedures to ensure that material information relating to the registrant, including its consolidated subsidiaries, is made known to us by others within those entries, particularly during the period in which this annual report is being prepared;
    b) Evaluated the effectiveness of the registrant's disclosure controls and procedures as of a date within 90 days prior to the filing date of this annual report (the "Evaluation Date"); and
    c) Presented in this annual report our conclusions about the effectiveness of the disclosure controls and procedures based on our evaluation as of the Evaluation Date;
5. The registrant's other certifying officers and I have disclosed, based on our most recent evaluation, to the registrant's auditors and the audit committee of the registrant's board of directors (or persons performing the equivalent function):
    a) All significant deficiencies in the design or operation of internal controls which could adversely affect the registrant's ability to record, process, summarize and report financial data and have identified for the registrant's auditors any material weaknesses in internal controls; and
    b) Any fraud, whether or not material, that involves management or other employees who have a significant role in the registrant's internal controls; and
6. The registrant's other certifying officers and I have indicated in this annual report whether or not there were significant changes in internal controls or in other factors that could significantly affect internal controls subsequent to the date of our most recent evaluation, including any corrective actions with regard to significant deficiencies and material weaknesses.

Date: April 15, 2003

/s/H. Lee Scott, Jr.
H. Lee Scott, Jr.
President and
Chief Executive Officer

(continued)

Exhibit 2.2   *(Continued)*

I, Thomas M. Schoewe, certify that:

1. I have reviewed this annual report on Form 10-K of Wal-Mart Stores, Inc. (the "registrant");
2. Based on my knowledge, this annual report does not contain any untrue statement of a material fact or omit to state a material fact necessary to make the statements made, in light of the circumstances under which such statements were made, not misleading with respect to the period covered by this annual report;
3. Based on my knowledge, the financial statements, and other financial information included in this annual report, fairly present in all material respects the financial condition, results of operations and cash flows of the registrant as of, and for, the periods presented in this annual report;
4. The registrant's other certifying officers and I are responsible for establishing and maintaining disclosure controls and procedures (as defined in Exchange Act Rules 13a-14 and 15d-14) for the registrant and have:
   a) Designed such disclosure controls and procedures to ensure that material information relating to the registrant, including its consolidated subsidiaries, is made known to us by others within those entries, particularly during the period in which this annual report is being prepared;
   b) Evaluated the effectiveness of the registrant's disclosure controls and procedures as of a date within 90 days prior to the filing date of this annual report (the "Evaluation Date"); and
   c) Presented in this annual report our conclusions about the effectiveness of the disclosure controls and procedures based on our evaluation as of the Evaluation Date;
5. The registrant's other certifying officers and I have disclosed, based on our most recent evaluation, to the registrant's auditors and the audit committee of the registrant's board of directors (or persons performing the equivalent function):
   a) All significant deficiencies in the design or operation of internal controls which could adversely affect the registrant's ability to record, process, summarize and report financial data and have identified for the registrant's auditors any material weaknesses in internal controls; and
   b) Any fraud, whether or not material, that involves management or other employees who have a significant role in the registrant's internal controls; and
6. The registrant's other certifying officers and I have indicated in this annual report whether or not there were significant changes in internal controls or in other factors that could significantly affect internal controls subsequent to the date of our most recent evaluation, including any corrective actions with regard to significant deficiencies and material weaknesses.

Date: April 15, 2003

/s/Thomas M. Schoewe
Thomas M. Schoewe
Executive Vice President
and Chief Financial Officer

Source: Wal-Mart Stores, Inc., *SEC Form 10-K Report*, April 15, 2003, pp. 25–26.

Exhibit 2.3   CEO and CFO Certification

CERTIFICATION PURSUANT TO
18 U.S.C. SECTION 1350 (AS ADOPTED PURSUANT TO SECTION 906
OF THE SARBANES-OXLEY ACT OF 2002)

In connection with the Annual Report of Wal-Mart Stores, Inc. (the "Company") on Form 10-K for the period ending January 31, 2003, as filed with the Securities and Exchange Commission on the date hereof (the "Report"), I, H. Lee Scott, Jr., President and Chief Executive Officer of the Company, certify to my knowledge and in my capacity as an officer of the company, pursuant to 18 U.S.C. 1350, as adopted pursuant to Section 906 of the Sarbanes-Oxley Act of 2002, that:

1. The Report fully complies with the requirements of Section 13(a) or 15(d) of the Securities Exchange Act of 1934, as amended; and
2. The information contained in the Report fairly presents, in all material respects, the financial condition and results of operations of the Company as of the dates and for the periods expressed in the Report.

IN WITNESS WHEREOF, the undersigned has executed this Certificate, effective as of April 15, 2003

H. Lee Scott, Jr.
President and Chief Executive Officer

A signed original of this written statement required by Section 906 has been provided to Wal-Mart Stores, Inc. and will be retained by Wal-Mart Stores, Inc. and furnished to the Securities and Exchange Commission or its staff upon request.

CERTIFICATION PURSUANT TO
18 U.S.C. SECTION 1350 (AS ADOPTED PURSUANT TO SECTION 906
OF THE SARBANES-OXLEY ACT OF 2002)

In connection with the Annual Report of Wal-Mart Stores, Inc. (the "Company") on Form 10-K for the period ending January 31, 2003, as filed with the Securities and Exchange Commission on the date hereof (the "Report"), I, Thomas M. Schoewe, Executive Vice President and Chief Financial Officer of the Company, certify to my knowledge and in my capacity as an officer of the company, pursuant to 18 U.S.C. 1350, as adopted pursuant to Section 906 of the Sarbanes-Oxley Act of 2002, that:

1. The Report fully complies with the requirements of Section 13(a) or 15(d) of the Securities Exchange Act of 1934, as amended; and
2. The information contained in the Report fairly presents, in all material respects, the financial condition and results of operations of the Company as of the dates and for the periods expressed in the Report.

IN WITNESS WHEREOF, the undersigned has executed this Certificate, effective as of April 15, 2003

Thomas M. Schoewe
Executive Vice President and Chief Financial Officer

A signed original of this written statement required by Section 906 has been provided to Wal-Mart Stores, Inc. and will be retained by Wal-Mart Stores, Inc. and furnished to the Securities and Exchange Commission or its staff upon request.

Source: Wal-Mart Stores, Inc., *SEC Form 10-K Report*, April 15, 2003, Exhibit 99.1.

changes in financial condition, results of operations, liquidity, capital expenditures, capital resources, or significant components of revenues or expenses.

(b) COMMISSION RULES ON PRO FORMA FIGURES—Not later than 180 days
after the date of enactment of the Sarbanes-Oxley Act of 2002, the Commission shall
issue final rules providing that pro forma financial information included in any periodic or other report filed with the Commission pursuant to the securities laws, or in
any public disclosure or press or other release, shall be presented in a manner that—

(1) does not contain an untrue statement of a material fact or omit to state a material fact necessary in order to make the pro forma financial information, in light
of the circumstances under which it is presented, not misleading; and

(2) reconciles it with the financial condition and results of operation of the issuer
under generally accepted accounting principles.

(c) STUDY AND REPORT ON SPECIAL PURPOSES ENTITIES—

(1) STUDY REQUIRED—The Commission shall, not later than 1 year after the
effective date of adoption of off-balance sheet disclosure rules required by section
13(j) of the Securities Exchange Act of 1934, as added by this section, completes
a study of filings by issuers and their disclosures to determine—

(A) the extent of off-balance sheet transactions, including assets, liabilities,
leases, losses, and the use of special purpose entities; and

(B) whether generally accepted accounting rules result in financial statements of issuers reflecting the economics of such off-balance sheet transactions to investors in a transparent fashion.

(2) REPORT AND RECOMMENDATIONS—Not later than 6 months after the
date of completion of the study required by paragraph (1), the Commission shall
submit a report to the President, the Committee on Banking, Housing, and Urban
Affairs of the Senate, and the Committee on Financial Services of the House of
Representatives, setting forth—

(A) the amount or an estimate of the amount of off-balance sheet transactions, including assets, liabilities, leases, and losses of, and the use of special
purpose entities by, issuers filing periodic reports pursuant to section 13 or 15
of the Securities Exchange Act of 1934;

(B) the extent to which special purpose entities are used to facilitate off-balance sheet transactions;

(C) whether generally accepted accounting principles or the rules of the
Commission result in financial statements of issuers reflecting the economics of such transactions to investors in a transparent fashion;

(D) whether generally accepted accounting principles specifically result in
the consolidation of special purpose entities sponsored by an issuer in cases
in which the issuer has the majority of the risks and rewards of the special
purpose entity; and

(E) any recommendations of the Commission for improving the transparency and quality of reporting off-balance sheet transactions in the financial statements and disclosures required to be filed by an issuer with the
Commission.[46]

---

[46]Ibid., Sec. 401.

S-Ox Section 409—Real Time Issuer Disclosures

Section 13 of the Securities Exchange Act of 1934 (15 U.S.C. 78m), as amended by this Act is amended by adding at the end the following:

(l) REAL TIME ISSUER DISCLOSURES—Each issuer reporting under section 13(a) or 15(d) shall disclose to the public on a rapid and current basis such additional information concerning material changes in the financial condition or operations of the issuer, in plain English, which may include trend and qualitative information and graphic presentations, as the Commission determines, by rule, is necessary or useful for the protection of investors and in the public interest.[47]

SEC Final Rules—Standards Relating to Listing Company Audit Committee On April 9, 2003, the SEC issued a release that mandates changes in the SROs listing standards. As directed by the Sarbanes-Oxley Act of 2002, the SEC issued a directive to the SROs to prohibit the listing of any security of an issuer that is not in compliance with the audit committee requirements mandated by the Sarbanes-Oxley Act. These requirements relate to:

* The independence of audit committee members
* The audit committee's responsibility to select and oversee the issuer's independent accountant
* Procedures for handling complaints regarding the issuer's accounting practices
* The authority of the audit committee to engage advisors
* Funding for the independent auditor and any outside advisors engaged by the audit committee[48]

Audit Committee Member Independence In an effort to tighten the independence requirements for audit committee members, the SEC final rules contained two criteria:[49]

1. Audit committee members are barred from accepting any consulting, advisory or other compensatory fee from the issuer or any subsidiary thereof, other than in the member's capacity as a member of the board of directors and any board committees;[50] and
2. Audit committee members of an issuer that are not an investment company may not be an affiliated person of the issuer or any subsidiary of the issuer

---

[47]Ibid., Sec. 409.

[48]Securities and Exchange Commission, Release No. 38-8220, *Standards Relating to Listing Company Audit Committee* (Washington, DC: SEC, April 9, 2003).

[49]For further information regarding the SRO's proposed additional standards, see SEC Release No. 34-47672.

[50]More specifically, disallowed payments to an audit committee member include payments made directly or indirectly. See SEC Release No. 33-8220 for examples of relationships. Also, de minimis exception for independence is non-existent and will be removed from the listing requirements.

apart from his or her capacity as a member of the board and any board committee.[51]

Responsibilities Relating to Registered Public Accounting Firms   To increase investor confidence in the audit process, the SEC adopted the requirement that the audit committee of a listed issuer will be directly responsible for the appointment, compensation, retention, and oversight of the work of any registered public accounting firm engaged for the purpose of preparing or issuing an audit report or performing other audits, or review or attest services. The independent auditor will report directly to the audit committee.[52]

Procedures for Handling Complaints   Each audit committee must establish procedure for:

- The receipt, retention, and treatment of complaints received by the issuer regarding accounting, internal controls or auditing matters
- The confidential, anonymous submission by employees of the issuer of concerns regarding questionable accounting or auditing matters

The SEC pointed out that audit committees should be provided with flexibility to develop and utilize procedures appropriate for their circumstances.

Authority to Engage Advisors   The SEC's final rule requires audit committees to have authority to engage outside advisors, including accounting and legal experts. Hence this rule supports the SEC's position that the audit committee must have the necessary resources to fulfill its function.

Funding   The SEC's final rule on funding requires the issuer to provide for payment of compensation to:

- Any registered public accounting firm engaged for the purpose of preparing or issuing an audit report or performing other audit, review, or attest services
- Any advisor employed by the audit committee

The final rule does not set funding limits. Finally, the final rule provides that the issuer must provide funding for the ordinary administrative expenses of the audit committee.

---

[51]The SEC defines "affiliate" and "affiliated person" as a person that directly or indirectly, through one or more intermediaries, controls, or is controlled by, or is under common control with, the person specified. Under the final rule, only executive officers, directors who are also employees of an affiliate, general partner, and managing members of an affiliate, will be deemed to be affiliates. Moreover, the limitation on directors will exclude outside directors of an affiliate as well as individuals with passive, noncontrol positions, and non-policymaking functions. For further information on investment company issuers and new issuers, see the aforementioned release number.

[52]With respect to clarifications regarding possible conflicts with other requirements, see the release for such matters as the application of noncountry laws or listing requirements for the appointment of laws or listing requirements for the appointment of the independent auditors. However, if the issuer provides a recommendation or nomination for the independent auditors, then the audit committee (or body performing similar functions) must be responsible for making the recommendation on nomination.

Compliance and Curing Defects In addition to the listing or delisting requirement, for issuers not in compliance with the standards, the SEC adopted a final rule stating that the SROs must require a listed issuer to notify the applicable SRO of any material noncompliance with the audit committee requirements.

With respect to the SEC's final rule on curing defects, the SROs are required to establish procedures before they prohibit the listing of or delist any security of an issuer. The SEC believes that the SRO's existing continued listing procedures will suffice.[53]

Disclosure Changes Regarding Audit Committees—Disclosure Regarding Exemptions The SEC requires issuers to disclose their reliance on an exemption and their assessment of whether, and if so, how such reliance will materially adversely affect the ability of their audit committee to act independently and to satisfy the other requirements. Such disclosure will need to appear in, or be incorporated by reference into, annual reports filed with the Commission. The disclosure also will need to appear in proxy statements or information statements for shareholders' meetings at which elections for directors are held.[54]

Identification of the Audit Committee in Annual Reports In an effort to readily determine basic information about the composition of a listed issuer's audit committee, the SEC requires that disclosure of audit committee members be included or incorporated by reference in the issuer's annual report. Additionally, if a listed issuer does not have an audit committee, then it must disclose that the entire board of directors is acting as the audit committee.

Updates to Existing Audit Committee Disclosure Regarding the independence disclosure for audit committees, all national exchanges and national securities associations will need to have independence standards for audit committee members, not just the NYSE, AMEX, and Nasdaq.

Nonlisted issuers that have separately designated audit committees still will be required to disclose whether their audit committee members are independent. Such issuers may choose any definition for audit committee independence of a national securities exchange or national securities association that has been approved by the Commission.

Audit Committee Financial Expert Disclosures for Foreign Private Issuers[55] A foreign private listed issuer must disclose whether its audit committee's financial expert is independent, as defined by the SRO listing standard applicable to that issuer, the issuer may choose one of the SRO definitions of audit

---

[53]See the text of the release regarding rare situations that may occur when the audit committee member ceases to be independent as well as SRO implanting rules.

[54]The SEC's final rule on listed issuers that are not required to provide disclosure on their reliance on one of the exemptions to the rule, such as a subsidiary relying on multiple listing exemption, a foreign government issuer, or an asset-backed issuer are excluded from the requirement to disclose, whether they have a separate audit committee or not.

[55]For additional information regarding proposed rule changes by the New York Stock Exchange, see SEC Release No. 34-47672, Sections 303A (6) and 303 A (7).

committee independence (SEC approval) to determine whether its audit committee financial expert, if it has one, is independent.

THE EXTERNAL AND INTERNAL AUDITING PROCESS

The Nature of External Auditing

External auditing is the process not only of examining the financial statements but also of testing the underlying accounting records of the company. The examination is conducted by the independent auditors, who express an objective opinion regarding the fairness of presentation of the financial statements. The audit examination is conducted within a predetermined set of generally accepted auditing standards that are promulgated by the Auditing Standards Board, formerly named the Auditing Standards Executive Committee of the American Institute of Certified Public Accountants (AICPA).[56] Since the audit examination is performed by certified public accountants who are independent of the company's management, the objective opinion of the independent auditing firm strengthens the reliability and credibility of the company's financial reporting practices.

More specifically, corporate management has full responsibility for the financial statements because such statements represent a report on management's stewardship accountability to its outside constituencies. The Auditing Standards Board of the AICPA asserts:

> The financial statements are management's responsibility. The auditor's responsibility is to express an opinion on the financial statements. Management is responsible for adopting sound accounting policies and for establishing and maintaining internal control that will, among other things, record, process, summarize, and report transactions (as well as events and conditions) consistent with management's assertions embodied in the financial statements. The entity's transactions and the related assets, liabilities, and equity are within the direct knowledge and control of management. The auditor's knowledge of these matters and internal control is limited to that acquired through the audit. Thus, the fair presentation of financial statements in conformity with generally accepted accounting principles is an implicit and integral part of management's responsibility. The independent auditor may make suggestions about the form or content of the financial statements or draft them, in whole or in part, based on information from management during the performance of the audit. However, the auditor's responsibility for the financial statements he or she has audited is confined to the expression of his or her opinion on them.[57]

Increasingly, management's responsibilities for financial statements are typically acknowledged in a Report of Management in the annual stockholders' report, which states in part:

---

[56]As noted in Chapter 13, the name of this committee has been changed to the Auditing Standards Board. However, the former name of this group will be used in connection with the appropriate Statements on Auditing Standards as discussed in the text.

[57]AICPA, *Professional Standards, U.S. Auditing Standards/Attestation Standards,* Vol. 1 (New York: AICPA, 2003), AU Sec. 110.03.

Report of Management

Management of Wal-Mart Stores Inc. is responsible for the integrity and objectivity of the financial statements and other information presented in this report. These financial statements have been prepared in conformity with accounting principles generally accepted in the United States. The preparation of financial statements requires certain estimates and judgments, which are based upon currently available information and management's view of current conditions and circumstances.

Management has developed and maintains a system of internal and disclosure controls, including an extensive internal audit program. These controls are designed to provide reasonable assurance that the Company's assets are protected from improper use and that Wal-Mart's accounting records provide a reliable basis for the preparation of financial statements. We continually review, improve and modify these systems and programs in response to changes in business conditions and operations and the recommendations made by Wal-Mart's internal and external auditors. We believe that the system of internal and disclosure controls provides reasonable assurance that Wal-Mart's assets are safeguarded and that the financial information disclosed is reliable.

Our Company was founded on the belief that open communications and the highest standard of ethics are necessary to be successful. Our long-standing "open door" communication policy helps management be aware of and deal with issues in a timely and effective manner. Through the open door policy all Associates are encouraged to inform management at the appropriate level when they are concerned about any matter pertaining to the Company.

Wal-Mart has adopted a Statement of Ethics to guide our Associates in the continued observance of high ethical standards such as honesty, integrity and compliance with the law in the conduct of the Company's business. Familiarity and compliance with the Statement of Ethics is periodically reviewed and acknowledged in writing by all management Associates. The Company also has in place a Related Party Transaction Policy. This policy applies to all Officers and Directors of the Company and requires material related party transactions to be reviewed by the Audit Committee of the Board of Directors. Annually, the Company's Officers and Directors report material related party transactions to the Company and Officers acknowledge their familiarity and compliance with the policy.

We retain Ernst & Young LLP, independent auditors, to audit the Company's financial statements. Their audits are performed in accordance with generally accepted auditing standards. We have made available to Ernst & Young LLP all financial records and related data.

The Board of Directors, through the activities of its Audit Committee consisting solely of outside directors, provides oversight of the process of reporting financial information. The Committee stays informed of the financial condition of the Company and regularly reviews its financial policies and procedures, the independence of the Company's independent auditors, its internal accounting controls and the objectivity of its financial reporting. Both the Company's independent auditors and the internal auditors have free access to the Audit Committee and meet with the Committee periodically, both with and without management present.

H. Lee Scott   Thomas M. Schoewe
President and Chief Executive Officer   Executive Vice President and Chief
                                               Financial Officer[58]

---

[58]Wal-Mart Stores, Inc., *2003 Annual Report,* p. 52.

The audit opinion is presented in the independent auditors' or accountants' report. Such a report may be addressed to the board of directors, to the stockholders, or to both the board and the stockholders. For example, if the independent auditors were employed by the stockholders, then the report would be addressed to them. It should be noted that the report is included in the corporate annual report.

The report consists of three paragraphs. The first is the introductory paragraph, which sets forth the responsibilities of management and the auditors. The second is the scope paragraph, which describes the nature of the audit, and the third paragraph states the opinion. The standard form of an unqualified audit report is as follows:

(Introductory paragraph)

We have audited the accompanying balance sheets of X Company as of December 31, 19X2 and 19X1, and the related statements of income, retained earnings, and cash flows for the years then ended. These financial statements are the responsibility of the Company's management. Our responsibility is to express an opinion on these financial statements based on our audits.

(Scope paragraph)

We conducted our audits in accordance with auditing standards generally accepted in the United States of America. Those standards require that we plan and perform the audit to obtain reasonable assurance about whether the financial statements are free of material misstatement. An audit includes examining, on a test basis, evidence supporting the amounts and disclosures in the financial statements. An audit also includes assessing the accounting principles used and significant estimates made by management, as well as evaluating the overall financial statement presentation. We believe that our audits provide a reasonable basis for our opinion.

(Opinion paragraph)

In our opinion, the financial statements referred to above present fairly, in all material respects, the financial position of X Company as of [at] December 31, 19X2 and 19X1, and the results of its operations and its cash flows for the years then ended in conformity with accounting principles generally accepted in the United States of America.[59]

In the introductory paragraph, the auditors indicate that they are responsible for their audit report and that management has primary responsibility for the financial statements. In regard to the scope of the examination, the auditors state that they have performed not only certain auditing procedures based on their professional judgment but have also conducted their examination within the general guidelines or standards set forth by the AICPA. This scope paragraph communicates to the reader of the financial statements that the auditors' compliance with auditing standards provides reasonable assurance that such statements are free of material misstatements and/or omitted material facts. Furthermore, in the opinion paragraph, the auditors state that the financial statements have been prepared in accordance with accounting principles that are widely accepted in the practice of accounting and, therefore, that such statements are fairly presented. An illustration of the auditors' report follows.

---

[59]"Reports on Audited Financial Statements," *Statement on Auditing Standards No. 58* (New York: AICPA, 1988), par. 8, as amended by ASB interpretation.

Report of Independent Auditors

The Board of Directors and Shareholders,
Wal-Mart Stores, Inc.

We have audited the accompanying consolidated balance sheets of Wal-Mart Stores, Inc. as of January 31, 2003 and 2002, and the related consolidated statements of income, shareholders' equity and cash flows for each of the three years in the period ended January 31, 2003. These financial statements are the responsibility of the Company's management. Our responsibility is to express an opinion on these financial statements based on our audits.

We conducted our audits in accordance with auditing standards generally accepted in the United States. Those standards require that we plan and perform the audit to obtain reasonable assurance about whether the financial statements are free of material misstatement. An audit includes examining, on a test basis, evidence supporting the amounts and disclosures in the financial statements. An audit also includes assessing the accounting principles used and significant estimates made by management, as well as evaluating the overall financial statement presentation. We believe that our audits provide a reasonable basis for our opinion.

In our opinion, the financial statements referred to above present fairly, in all material respects, the consolidated financial position of Wal-Mart Stores, Inc. at January 31, 2003 and 2002, and the consolidated results of its operations and its cash flows for each of the three years in the period ended January 31, 2003, in conformity with accounting principles generally accepted in the United States.

As discussed in Note 1 to the consolidated financial statements, effective February 1, 2002, the Company adopted the provisions of Statement of Financial Accounting Standards No. 142, Goodwill and Other Intangible Assets.[60]

Ernst & Young LLP

Tulsa, Oklahoma
March 19, 2003

Role of the Audit Committee   The work of the audit committee and the independent auditors is very closely related because both groups have common objectives regarding the financial affairs. The audit committee members are responsible for overseeing the independent audit examination as well as the recommendations of the independent auditors. The audit committee members must assure themselves that the financial statements and the system of internal accounting controls are based on acceptable accounting principles and procedures. Moreover, they need assurance that the executives and their staff are reasonably competent and trustworthy.

Although the extent of the audit committee's activities has led to some controversy, it is clearly evident that its effectiveness has been increased by the U.S. Securities and Exchange Commission, the U.S. Congress (FDICIA) (Sarbanes-Oxley Act of 2002), and other private-sector initiatives (National Commission on Fraudulent Financial Reporting, the MacDonald Commission (Canada), and the Cadbury Committee, Hampel Committee, and Committee on Corporate Governance (UK) as well as self-regulatory organizations. The reality of the situation is that the Foreign Corrupt Practices Act, the Private Securities Litigation Reform

---

[60]Ibid., p. 51.

Act, and the aforementioned initiatives place greater responsibilities on the audit committee. Thus, it is critically important that the committee keep a perspective and focus on its oversight role for the system of internal control and financial reporting areas of the company. If the audit committee becomes too deeply involved in management's operational activities, its effectiveness will be diluted. As Ray Groves, E&Y former managing partner, has indicated:

> This does not mean a committee cannot rely on management and the internal and external auditors to see that controls are in good order. The committee's responsibility is to satisfy itself that these groups are performing and the necessary documentation exists.[61]

The audit committee members are in an excellent position to contribute to the external auditing process. For example, the independence of the auditing firm is enhanced because the independent auditors establish a line of communication to the board of directors through the audit committee. In addition, since the audit committee members nominate and select the auditing firm, they are in a position to examine the qualifications of this firm as well as to assess the results of the audit examination.[62]

In a survey of 34 publicly held companies dealing with the effectiveness of audit committees as perceived by both external auditors and audit committee members of those companies, Lawrence P. Kalbers found that practicing audit committees are not uniformly effective and that the auditors rate committee members significantly lower than do members on responsibilities, attributes, and effectiveness. He concludes that the audit committee, management, and auditors need to work toward the right balance of the committee's involvement with audit fees, audit scope, audit results, and internal controls. He believes that training and educating the committee members can help them meet their responsibilities.[63]

The Nature of Internal Auditing

As defined by the Institute of Internal Auditors:

> Internal auditing is an independent, objective assurance and consulting activity designed to add value and improve an organization's operations. It helps an organization accomplish its objectives by bringing a systematic, disciplined approach to evaluate and improve the effectiveness of risk management, control, and governance processes.[64]

For example, internal auditors may evaluate the internal control of a company as well as review management's adherence to the company's policies. They can also help the audit committee with special investigations and compliance audits.

---

[61]Ernst & Whinney, *E&W People*, p. 7.

[62]For further discussion on communication with audit committees, see Chapter 5.

[63]Lawrence P. Kalbers, "An Examination of the Relationship Between Audit Committees and External Auditors," *Ohio CPA Journal* 51, No. 6 (December 1992), p. 27. Similarly, Price Waterhouse noted that: "The single most important findings, and the key to audit committee effectiveness, is: background information and training." See Price Waterhouse, *Improving Audit Committee Performance: What Works Best* (Altamonte Springs, FL: IIA, 1993), p. 2. For further discussion on training and educating audit committee members, see Chapter 5 and Chapter 7 of the second edition, 2000.

[64]Institute of Internal Auditors, *The Professional Practice Framework* (Altamonte Springs, FL: IIA, 2002), p. 3.

However, it is important to recognize that the internal auditing group is not completely independent from corporate management, because the members of the group are employees of the company. To enhance their independence and objectivity, the Institute of Internal Auditors recommends that the chief audit executive should be responsible to an individual whose authority is sufficient to promote independence and provide the necessary internal auditing coverage.[65] Thus, the chief audit executive should report not only to a senior executive, such as the chief financial officer with access to the chief executive officer, but also to the independent audit committee. To ensure the independence of the internal auditing group, the chief audit executive must have free access to meeting regularly with the committee. The internal audit function is discussed more extensively in Chapter 9.

Role of the Audit Committee   The interface between the audit committee and the internal auditing group provides a logical relationship because these groups have common goals.[66] It is important that both groups establish a working relationship which is not counterproductive. More specifically, to maximize the productivity of the internal auditing group, the audit committee should:

- Assist in the overall internal auditing policy determination and approve such policies to ensure that the internal auditing group has authority that is commensurate with its responsibilities
- Review the coordination of the work and schedules of the internal and external auditing groups
- Review not only the qualifications of the chief audit executive and his or her support staff but also the professional development activities of the group
- Review the copies of the internal auditing reports and critically evaluate findings, recommendations, and management's response

As noted in Chapter 1, audit committees have become a key institution in the corporate accountability process. Given the congressional enactment of the Sarbanes-Oxley Act of 2002, many of the past guidelines of the professional and regulatory organizations regarding audit committees have become law. Thus the role and responsibilities of audit committees have become a federal statute by which such committees measure their performance.

To assist audit committees with their new roles and responsibilities, Exhibit 2.4 contains a summary of the sections of the Sarbanes-Oxley Act, and SRO's listing standards, and SEC final rules on audit committee disclosures. Clearly, boards of directors and their audit committees need to reexamine and update their charters to reflect the laws and regulations. Exhibit 2.5 discusses an approach to continuous improvement for audit committees.

---

[65]Institute of Internal Auditors, *The Professional Practice Framework*, p. 7.
[66]For further discussion of the audit committee's role, see *Internal Auditing and the Audit Committee: Working Together Toward Common Goals* (Altamonte Springs, FL: IIA, 1987); and Barbara A. Apostolou and Raymond Jeffords, *Working with the Audit Committee* (Altamonte Springs, FL: IIA, 1990). Also see the video, *Audit Committees and Internal Auditing: An Essential Alliance for Effective Governance* (Altamonte Springs, Fla.: IIA, 1994).

Exhibit 2.4 Audit Committees: Roles and Responsibilities under the Sarbanes-Oxley Act of 2002, SROs, and SEC

Audit Committee Practice Area	Section[a]	Applicability		
		SOA[a]	SROs[b]	SEC[c]
Organization of the Audit Committee				
• Charter			✔	✔
• Membership			✔	✔
• Meetings			✔	
• Independence	301	✔	✔	✔
• Financial Literacy/Expertise	407	✔	✔[f]	✔[f]
Activities				
Internal Control	404	✔	✔[d]	✔
Annual and Interim Financial Statements, CEO/CFO Certification	302/906	✔	✔[d]	✔
Loans to Directors or Offices	402	✔		
Corporate Code of Conduct			✔	
Code of Ethics for CFOs	406	✔		
Auditors				
Internal Auditors			✔[d]	
External Auditors				
• Retention and Fees	301	✔	✔	
• Hiring	206	✔	✔[d]	
• Non-Audit Services	202	✔	✔	
• Auditor Rotation	203/207	✔	✔[d]	
• Disagreements	301	✔	✔[d]	
• Critical Accounting Policies and Disclosures	204, 401, 409	✔	✔	
Communication				
• Opinions from Legal Counsel and Other Advisers	301, 307	✔	✔	
• Whistleblowing Protection	301, 307, 806	✔	✔[e]	
• Stock Exchange Listing Requirements (annual certification)			✔[d]	
• Stock Exchange Listing Requirements (one-time certification)			✔	
• Education and Training			✔	

[a] Sarbanes-Oxley Act of 2002.
[b] NYSE, Nasdaq, AMEX Listing Standards.
[c] SEC Final Rules, Audit Committee Disclosures.
[d] NYSE Listing Standards only; see also SEC Release No. 34-47672.
[e] Nasdaq Listing Standards only.
[f] At least one member must have accounting or related financial management expertise.

Exhibit 2.5   Corporate Audit Committees: An Approach to Continuous
Improvement

CORPORATE AUDIT COMMITTEES:
AN APPROACH TO CONTINUOUS IMPROVEMENT

Audit committees today are faced with the sizable task of overseeing both the auditing and financial reporting processes. The final rules of the SEC, national stock exchanges, and the AICPA's Auditing Standards Board cover corporate governance of audit committees, including independence, qualifications, charters, external auditor involvement, and reports

Nonetheless, it remains up to audit committees to ensure that they continuously improve their oversight role. Continuous improvement requires a constructive relationship between audit committees and management, internal auditors, external auditors, and legal counsel. Audit committees should function as team members and be empowered by their boards to ask tough-minded questions about the audit and financial reporting processes as well as to probe into the entity's affairs. Continuous improvement helps minimize the costs of achieving quality in both financial management services and audit services. Thus, boards of directors are assured that such resources are allocated efficiently and effectively to prevent the costs of poor quality in the board's corporate accountability process.

Continuous improvement approach   To achieve continuous improvement, audit committees should consider the following three-step approach:

- Complete a profile worksheet with details of the committee's role, responsibilities, and organization;
- Develop a customized review and action plan to achieve the committee's goals in the board-approved charter; and
- Develop a quality assurance review based on the elements that guide the committee in adopting quality assurance policies and procedures.

Audit Committee's Profile Worksheet

Audit committees are now required to disclose their written charter in the entity's annual proxy statement. This document provides a clear presentation of the committee's oversight role, responsibilities, and organization. It defines the jurisdictional charge to the committee, minimizing potential litigation risk as well as avoiding the dilution of the committee's activities. See *Exhibit 1* for a suggested format for a profile worksheet.

Audit committees need knowledge about—

- the entity's business and industry,
- significant risks,
- internal control concepts,
- industry accounting practices, and
- complex business transactions.

Likewise, audit committees need to review the following:

- Industry and business data in terms of vulnerability of the industry to changing economic conditions and operating characteristics of the business. Such a review would usually include the annual stockholders' report, SEC filings, (10Qs, 10Ks, annual proxy statement), the entity's website, analytical review procedures, absolute data comparisons, and financial ratio data.
- Management's risk assessment process
- The components of COSO's Internal Control-Integrated Framework (control environment, risk assessment, information and communication, control activities, and monitoring)

(continued)

Exhibit 2.5   *(Continued)*

EXHIBIT 1
AUDIT COMMITTEE'S PROFILE WORKSHEET

Audit Committee Practice Area	Services available from:	Management	Internal Auditors	External Auditors	Legal Counsel	Board of Directors	Compliance with SEC, SROs, ASB	Comments:
Organizational Structure and Composition								
Formation*								
Membership								
Number of members (size)						✔	✔	
Appointments						✔		
Term of Service						✔		
Qualification						✔	✔	
Composition						✔	✔	
Meetings								
Frequency						✔		
Type						✔		
Knowledge Areas								
Type of business and industry		✔						
Internal audit process			✔					
External audit process			✔	✔				
Internal control concepts			✔	✔				
Management's risk assessment		✔	✔	✔				
Industry accounting practices		✔	✔	✔				
Complex business transactions		✔	✔	✔	✔			
Financial reporting process		✔	✔	✔				
Internal communication process**		✔	✔	✔	✔	✔	✔	
External communication process						✔	✔	

*Board resolution or corporate by-laws and a formal written charter
**Related to the above areas

- Industry accounting practices, with particular emphasis on the appropriateness of accounting principles
- Complex business transactions (e.g., restructuring charges and pre-acquisition audits).

Additionally, audit committees should perform a review in connection with other matters, such as—

- code of conduct;
- conflict of interest statements (related party transactions);
- corporate perquisites;
- computer security, business continuity plan, and planned systems modifications; and
- biographical information on senior management and financial management.

Audit Committee's Action Plan

Based on the audit committee's profile worksheet, the chair can develop a customized review and action plan (*Exhibit 2*). This plan serves as an oversight compass for the financial management, audit, legal, and communication process.

Financial management. Responsibility for the integrity and objectivity of the information in financial reports rests with the entity's management. Audit committees should review background information on the competence and integrity of important members of the financial management group.

EXHIBIT 2
AUDIT COMMITTEE'S REVIEW AND ACTION PLAN

Audit Committee Practice Area	Services available from:	Management	Internal Auditors	External Auditors	Legal Counsel	Board of Directors	Compliance with SEC, SROs, ASB	Comments:
Agendas								
Pre-audit Meeting (Audit Scope)								
Audit plan		✔	✔	✔				
Analytical review				✔				
Accounting and auditing developments		✔	✔	✔				
Financial reporting matters		✔	✔	✔				
Risk assessment		✔	✔	✔				
Risk control processes		✔	✔	✔				
Interim meeting (optional)								
Problem areas		✔	✔	✔				
Audit progress				✔				
Post-audit Meeting								
Audit findings			✔	✔				
Analytical review								
Annual financial statements		✔		✔				
SEC Form 10-K Report		✔		✔				
Other Concerns								
Unresolved matters		✔	✔	✔	✔			
Disagreements with management			✔	✔				
Significant audit adjustments			✔	✔				
Completeness of disclosure and risks and uncertainties		✔	✔	✔	✔			
Appropriateness of accounting policies		✔	✔	✔				
Management's representations (client representation letter)		✔				✔		
Lawyer's letter				✔	✔			

(*continued*)

Exhibit 2.5   *(Continued)*

Services available from:	Management	Internal Auditors	External Auditors	Legal Counsel	Board of Directors	Compliance with SEC, SROs, ASB	
Follow-up Meeting							
Management letter	✔	✔	✔				
Evaluation of the external auditors	✔	✔					
Appointment of the external auditors					✔		
Audit and nonaudit fees			✔		✔	✔	
Auditor's independence letter			✔			✔	
Evaluation of the internal auditors and selection or reappointment	✔		✔				
Internal audit plan for the next fiscal year		✔					
Outsourcing activities		✔	✔				
Evaluation of financial management		✔	✔				
Compliance with laws and regulations (disclosure matters)			✔	✔			
Impact of proposed legislation on the financial statements			✔	✔			
Other Matters							
Special investigations				✔	✔		
Information technology (computer security, EDI, business continuity plan)	✔	✔	✔				
Conflict of Interest							
Corporate perquisites (officers' expense accounts, etc.)		✔	✔	✔			
Corporate contributions	✔	✔	✔	✔			
Code of conduct	✔	✔	✔	✔			
Related party transactions	✔	✔	✔	✔			
Illegal, improper or sensitive payments			✔	✔	✔		
Quarterly Reporting Process							
Quality of earnings and disclosures	✔		✔				
Income tax assessments			✔				
Pre-acquisition audits	✔		✔				
Material transactions and contracts (e.g., restructuring charges, etc.)	✔		✔				
Reporting to the Board of Directors							
Formal report					✔		
Reporting to the Stockholders							
Proxy-statement disclosures				✔		✔	
Reporting to the national stock exchange(s)				✔		✔	

Likewise, management is responsible for a system of internal control. Audit committees may request management and auditors to present a review of the COSO components of internal control in order to ensure that internal controls provide a reasonable assurance that the financial accounts are maintained and accounted for under the entity's policies. For financial reporting purposes, audit committees need assurance that management is managing identified risks so that financial statement assertions will not be misstated.

Internal auditing. As part of the monitoring component of the entity's system of internal control, the scope of the internal audit effort extends to several types of audits: financial, operational, compliance, ethics and fraud, systems, and risk audits. Audit committees should review the internal audit plan as well as the organizational structure and composition of the internal audit group. Audit committees want assurance that the entity's comprehensive internal audit program evaluates the adherence to management's policies and procedures.

External auditing. The audit committee's meetings and agendas should be directly linked to the auditing cycle, consisting of a pre-audit interview, an optional interim audit interview, a post-audit interview, and a follow-up interview.

During the pre-audit interview, the agenda ordinarily includes a review and discussion of matters such as the audit plan, accounting and auditing developments that impact the financial statements, risk assessment and related risk control processes, an analytical review, the personnel assigned to the audit team, an internal financial audit plan, and estimated audit and nonaudit fees.

Audit committees or external auditors might request an interim audit interview to address problem areas and discuss the progress of the audit.

The major objective of the post-audit interview is to review the audit findings and the draft of the annual stockholders' report. Typically, audit committees focus on deviations from the audit plan, the analytical review, significant discoveries, resolved and unresolved matters, and disagreements with management, and material audit adjustments as well as immaterial uncorrected misstatements. Additionally, audit committees should review the appropriateness of accounting policies (e.g., conformity with industry practice and alternative accounting principles) and any changes in accounting principle.

During the follow-up interview, audit committees generally focus on recommendations for improvement in internal control, approving the internal audit plan for the following year, and recommending the appointment of the external auditors. They might also engage in a performance review of management, the internal audit group, or the external auditors. Audit committees might also review the external audit and nonaudit fees that must now be disclosed in the annual proxy statement.

Legal process. Both in-house general counsel and outside legal counsel interact with audit committees on various issues:

- The standard of independence for the audit committee members
- The committee's written charter, as described in the entity's annual proxy statement
- Significant litigation, claims, and assessments against the entity
- Any pending litigation against the external auditors, as well as any impairment of their independence
- Compliance with key legislative acts (e.g., the Foreign Corrupt Practices Act, the Private Securities Litigation Reform Act)
- Proposed special investigations
- Material contracts, related party transactions, and contingencies
- Compliance with the entity's code of conduct and conflict of interest statements.

Communications. During the audit committee's audit cycle interviews, the internal communication process consists of both executive and joint sessions. Executive sessions may be used for the audit committee's performance reviews of management, the internal

(continued)

Exhibit 2.5   *(Continued)*

auditing group, and the external auditors, as well as a discussion of external audit and nonaudit fees, and any disagreements with management.

With respect to external communications, audit committees are required to disclose the following items in the entity's annual proxy statement:

- A review and discussion of the entity's consolidated financial statements with management and the independent auditors
- A review of management's representations that the consolidated financial statements were prepared in accordance with GAAP
- Discussion with the independent auditors about SAS 61 matters
- Written disclosures and the ISB 1 letter from the external auditor regarding their independence from the entity
- A consideration of whether the external auditors' provision of nonaudit services is consistent with independence
- A recommendation of whether the audited financial statements should be included in SEC filings
- A recommendation as to the selection of the audit firm
- Presentation of an audit committee charter
- A letter to the appropriate stock exchange certifying the number and qualifications of independent audit committee members.

Audit Committee's Quality Assurance Review

The major objective of this third step in the evaluative process is to effectively strive for zero defects in performing the first two steps. The audit committee's oversight role is to ensure efficiency and effectiveness in these processes, which, in turn, should lead to a high level of assurance of the board's corporate accountability. Given the demand for strong boards and audit committees, the audit committee should reflect and assess their overall operating performance and that of each committee member. This assessment process may be accomplished through a series of targeted questions that effectively address financial accounting and auditing issues affecting the financial statements. For example, audit committees might benchmark their performance review against their formal written charter. *Exhibit 3* contains six quality assurance elements that enable the committee to develop an effective oversight strategy. Comprehensive reporting, combined with an ongoing dialogue between audit committee members and all interested parties, is the key to effective performance.

**EXHIBIT 3
AUDIT COMMITTEE'S QUALITY ASSURANCE
ELEMENTS, POLICIES, AND PROCEDURES**

Quality Assurance Elements	Purpose	Quality Assurance Policies & Procedures
Independence	Avoid a relationship with the entity that would interfere with the director's exercise of independent judgment.	A
Financial knowledge	Directors need to be financially literate.	B
Written charter	Provides a clear understanding of the committee's oversight role, responsibilities, and organization.	C
Performance review	Work performed meets the audit committee's charter.	D
Continuing education	Directors need an ongoing program of additional courses.	E
Monitoring	Annual review for each of the above elements.	F

Examples of related policies and procedures that an audit committee might implement include:

A: Provide for legal counsel's monitoring compliance with independent rules.
B: Establish review procedures for information about new accounting and auditing standards.
C: Communicate the scope of oversight responsibilities to audit committee members.
D: Establish procedures for benchmarking the audit committee's performance review.
E: Establish review procedures for a continuing education program.
F: Provide for reporting monitoring activities to the full board of directors.

Source: This discussion is adapted from an article by Louis Braiotta, Jr., "Corporate Audit Committees: An Approach to Continuous Improvement," *CPA Journal* 72, No. 7 (July 2002), pp. 48–51. Reprinted with permission from CPA Journal, Copyright © 2002, New York State Society of Certified Public Accountants, 530 Fifth Avenue, New York, NY 10036-5101. All rights reserved.

In this overview of the audit committee's role in the auditing process, it is interesting to note some general observations:

- The audit committee has become an integral part of the corporate framework to help fulfill the board of directors' stewardship accountability to its outside constituencies.

- The work of the audit committee is dynamic since the accounting and auditing processes are subject to change.

- Authoritative bodies at home and abroad, such as the U.S. Congress, the national stock exchanges, the Cadbury Committee, the Hampel Committee, and the Committee on Corporate Governance (UK), have established standards for both the board of directors and the auditors to improve the financial reporting process. (See Appendix D on this book's website.)

- The audit committee is fundamental to the concept of corporate accountability.

SOURCES AND SUGGESTED READINGS

American Bar Association, *Corporate Director's Guidebook* (Chicago: ABA, 1978).

American Bar Association, *Corporate Director's Guidebook* (Chicago: ABA, 1994).

American Institute of Certified Public Accountants, *Audit Committees, Answers to Typical Questions about Their Organization and Operations* (New York: AICPA, 1978).

American Institute of Certified Public Accountants, Professional Standards, U.S. Auditing Standards/Attestation Standards, Volume 1. New York, 2003.

American Society of Secretaries, *Current Board Practices* (New York: ASCD, 1996).

American Society of Corporate Secretaries, *Current Board Practices,* 2nd Study (New York: ASCD, 1998).

Atkins, Paul S., "The Sarbanes-Oxley Act of 2002: Goals, Content, and Status of Implementation." (Washington, DC: SEC, February 5, 2003).

Bacon, Jeremy, *The Audit Committee: A Broader Mandate,* Report No. 914 (New York: The Conference Board, Inc., 1988).

Barlas, Stephen, "Auditors Must State Independence." *Management Accounting* 80, No. 7 (January 1999), p. 10.

Bass, Bernard M., *Leadership and Performance Beyond Expectations* (New York: Free Press, 1985).

The Business Roundtable, *The Role and Composition of the Board of Directors of the Large Publicly Owned Corporation* (New York: The Business Roundtable, January 1978).

Carcello, Joseph V., Dana R. Hermanson, and Terry L. Neal, "Disclosure in Audit Committee Charters and Reports." *Accounting Horizons* 16, No. 4, (December 2002), pp. 291–304.

Committee of Sponsoring Organizations of the Treadway Commission, *Internal Control-Integrated Framework* (New York: AICPA, 1992).

Ernst & Whinney, *E&W People,* Booklet No. 46302.

Ferrara, Ralph C., and Philip S. Khinda, "A Workable Audit Committee Charter." *Directors and Boards* 25, No. 1 (Fall 2000), p. 14.

Fleming, John M., "Audit Committees: Roles, Responsibilities, and Performance." *Pennsylvania CPA Journal* 73, No. 2 (Summer 2002), pp. 29–32.

Goodman, Amy L., and Michael J. Scanlon, "Survey of Audit Committee Charters and Audit Committee Reports." *Insights: The Corporate & Securities Law Advisor* 15, No. 8 (August 2001), pp. 13–18.

Hoffman, Ralph and Ray Bromark, "An Audit Committee for Dynamic Times." *Directors & Boards,* **16,** No. 3 (Spring 1992), pp. 51–53, 60.

Institute of Internal Auditors, *The Professional Practice Framework* (Altamonte Springs, FL: IIA, 2002).

Kalbers, Wayne P., "An Examination of the Relationship Between Audit Committees and External Auditors." *The Ohio CPA Journal,* **51,** No. 6 (December 1992), pp. 19–27.

Katz, Eugene M., "Keys to an Effective Audit Committee." *Credit World* 86, No. 4 (March/April 1998), pp. 21–23.

Korn/Ferry International, *Twentieth Annual Board of Directors Study* (New York: Korn/Ferry International, 1993).

Korn/Ferry International, *25th Annual Board of Directors Study* (New York: Korn/Ferry International, 1998).

Leanby, Bruce A., Paul R. Grazina, and John D. Zook, "Improving the Effectiveness of Corporate Audit Committees." *Pennsylvania CPA Journal* 70, No. 2 (Summer 1999), pp. 37–40.

Livingston, Philip, "Financial Experts on Audit Committees—An Overdue Implementation." *Financial Executive* 19, No. 1 (January/February 2003), pp. 6–7.

Livingston, Philip, "Test From Financial Literacy." *Directors and Boards* 26, No. 2 (Winter 2002), pp. 21–23.

National Commission on Fraudulent Financial Reporting, *Report of the National Commission on Fraudulent Financial Reporting* (Washington, DC: NCFFR, 1987).

Olson, John F., "How to Really Make Audit Committees More Effective." *Business Lawyer* 54, No. 3 (May 1999), pp. 1097–1111.

Price Waterhouse, *Improving Audit Committee Performance: What Works Best* (Altamonte Springs, FL: IAA, 1993).

Quinn, Lawrence Richber, "Strengthening the Role of the Audit Committee." *Strategic Finance* 84, No. 6 (December 2002), pp. 42–47.

Richardson, Robert C., and Charles P. Baril, "Can Your Audit Committee Withstand the Market's Scrutiny of Independence?" *Financial Executive* 19, No. 1 (January/February 2003), pp. 35–38.

Sarbanes-Oxley Act of 2002, H.R. Rep. No. 107-610, July 25, 2002.

Securities and Exchange Commission, Release No. 34-47672, File No. SR-NYSE-2002-33, *Proposed Rule Change Relating to Corporate Governance* (April 11, 2003).

Spangler, William D. and Louis Braiotta, Jr., "Leadership and Audit Committee Effectiveness." *Group and Organization Studies* 15, No. 2 (June 1990), pp. 134–157.

Statement on Auditing Standards No. 58, "Reports on Audited Financial Statements" (New York: AICPA, 1988).

Sweeney, Paul, and Cynthia Wallace Vallario, "NYSE Sets Audit Committees on New Road." *Journal of Accountancy* 194, No. 5 (November 2002), pp. 51–59.

Title 1 of Public Law No. 107-204, July 30, 2002.

Verschoor, Curtis C., Michael Barry, and Larry E. Rittenberg, "Reflections on the Audit Committee's Role." *Internal Auditor* 59, No. 2 (April 2002), pp. 26–35.

Vicknair, David, Kent Hickman, and Kay C. Carnes, "A Note on Audit Committee Independence: Evidence from the NYSE on 'Grey' Area Directors." *Accounting Horizons* 7, No. 1 (March 1993), pp. 53–57.

Wal-Mart Stores, Inc. 2003 *Annual Report*.

Wal-Mart Stores, Inc., 2003 Notice of Annual Meeting of Shareholders.

Zetzman, Wayne, "How to Organize and Use the Audit Committee." *Financial Executive* 15, No. 4 (July/August 1989), pp. 54–57.

Chapter 3

The External Users of Accounting Information

The objective of this chapter is to provide a broad perspective on the importance of the enterprise's outside constituencies as well as their need for accounting information. In addition, this chapter will examine the role of audit committees and the ways in which their work is affected by these external groups.

INTRODUCTION

Since the board of directors, through the audit committee, is responsible for assuring that management fulfills its financial reporting obligations, audit committees have an indirect accountability to the external users of accounting information. According to the Financial Accounting Standards Board (FASB):

> Members and potential members of some groups—such as owners, creditors, and employees—have or contemplate having direct economic interests in particular business enterprises. . . . Members of other groups—such as financial analysts and advisors, regulatory authorities, and labor unions—have derived or indirect interests because they advise or represent those who have or contemplate having direct interests.[1]

To respond to the needs of these groups as well as to formulate a basis for financial accounting and reporting standards, the FASB has developed a conceptual framework that consists of six Statements of Financial Accounting Concepts (SFAC) relative to financial reporting for business enterprises:

SFAC No. 1	"Objectives of Financial Reporting by Business Enterprises" (November 1978)
SFAC No. 2	"Qualitative Characteristics of Accounting Information" (May 1980)
SFAC No. 3	"Elements of Financial Statements of Business Enterprises" (December 1980)
SFAC No. 5	"Recognition and Measurement in Financial Statements of Business Enterprises" (December 1984)
SFAC No. 6	"Elements of Financial Statements" (December 1985)[2]

---

[1]Financial Accounting Standards Board, *Statement of Financial Accounting Concepts, No. 1* (Stamford, CT.: FASB, 1978), p. 11.
[2]SFAC No. 4, "Objectives of Financial Reporting by Nonbusiness Organizations," December 1980. It should be noted that SFACs No. 2 and No. 6 apply to nonbusiness enterprises.

SFAC No. 7   "Using cash flow Information and Present Value in Accounting Measurements" (February 2000)

The accounting profession has developed and continues to promulgate accounting standards based on a prescribed set of objectives, definitions, and principles, as set forth in the conceptual framework that is discussed in Chapter 5.[3] Notwithstanding the objectives of complete and accurate information in the financial accounting process, it should be noted that both internal accountants and external auditors exercise judgment in the selection of accounting standards for a fair presentation of the financial statements. Thus, if management has presented the financial statements in conformity with generally accepted accounting principles, then such statements are fairly presented. However, the Auditing Standards Board states in part:

> 11. In connection with each SEC engagement . . . , the auditor should discuss with the audit committee the auditor's judgments about the quality, not just the acceptability, of the entity's accounting principles as applied in its financial reporting. Since the primary responsibility for establishing an entity's accounting principles rests with management, the discussion generally would include management as an active participant. The discussion should be open and frank and generally should include such matters as the consistency of the entity's accounting policies and their application, and the clarity and completeness of the entity's financial statements, which include related disclosures. The discussion should also include items that have a significant impact on the representational faithfulness, verifiability, and neutrality of the accounting information included in the financial statements.[6] Examples of items that may have such an impact are the following:
>
> • Selection of new or changes to accounting policies
>
> • Estimates, judgments, and uncertainties
>
> • Unusual transactions
>
> • Accounting policies relating to significant financial statement items, including the timing of transactions and the period in which they are recorded
>
> Objective criteria have not been developed to aid in the consistent evaluation of the quality of an entity's accounting principles as applied in its financial statements. The discussion should be tailored to the entity's specific circumstances, including accounting applications and practices not explicitly addressed in the accounting literature, for example, those that may be unique to an industry.[4]

---

[6]These characteristics of accounting information are discussed in the Financial Accounting Standards Board (FASB) Statement of Financial Accounting Concepts No. 2, Qualitative characteristics of Accounting Information. FASB Concepts Statement No. 2 notes that consistently understating results or overly optimistic estimates of realization are inconsistent with these characteristics.

---

[3]The terms *standards* and *principles* are used interchangeably in practice and throughout this book.
[4]Statement on Auditing Standards, No. 90, "Audit Committee Communications" (New York: AICPA, 1999), par. 1.

Moreover, in the absence of more authoritative accounting literature concerning the accounting treatment of a particular item, account, or transaction, practitioners can use the conceptual framework to solve the problem.[5] In an article dealing with the subjects of minority interest, stock issues, and legally enforceable contracts, Steven Rubin indicated how the conceptual framework could be used for the appropriate accounting treatment, and he concluded that:

> Concepts statements can provide helpful guidance in resolving knotty practice problems involving liabilities and other matters. Consult them as you would other sources of established accounting principles. You may be surprised to find that these basic statements will provide the help you need.[6]

One way of classifying the external users is to divide them into groups of investors, credit grantors, regulatory agencies, and other outside constituencies. Such classification is useful from the audit committee's point of view, because each constituent has different informational needs and objectives. Thus, the four-way classification of the users is a useful framework for discharging the board of directors' financial accountability. To the extent that the audit committee can monitor the accounting information as well as understand the perceived needs of the outside constituencies, it can provide a balance in the corporate financial reporting process.

THE INVESTORS

Importance of the Investors

Investors are the largest users of accounting information. As a group, investors include not only potential investors but also the stockholders. As the American Assembly indicates:

> Shareholders are among the major groups in the community to which the corporation must respond. As the undisputed owners of the corporation, they possess great potential influence. Vocal shareholders, even if a minority, should be heard. Shareholders can sensitize management and directors to social as well as economic issues and should exercise this power.[7]

---

[5]*Statement on Auditing Standards, No. 69,* "The Meaning of Present Fairly in Conformity with Generally Accepted Accounting Principles in the Independent Auditor's Report" (New York: AICPA, 1992), par. 11.

[6]Steven Rubin, "How Concepts Statements Can Solve Practice Problems," *Journal of Accountancy* 166, No. 4 (October 1988), p. 126. Two authors have developed a flow chart, "An Overview of FASB's Concepts Statements." See Gwen Richardson Pate and Keith G. Stanga, "A Guide to the FASB's Concepts Statements," *Journal of Accountancy* 168, No. 2 (August 1989), pp. 28–31.

[7]The American Assembly, *Corporate Governance in America,* Pamphlet 56 (New York: Columbia University, April 1978), p. 5. The American Assembly convenes annually and has a national session at the Arden House in Harriman, New York. The Assembly conducts forums on national and multinational issues. See *The American Assembly Report 1991–1992* (New York: Columbia University, 1992).

The *New York Stock Exchange Fact Book* in 2001 reported that institutional investors held 46.7 percent, or $6.4 trillion, which represents the market value of 13.6 trillion of all New York Stock Exchange (NYSE) listed stock at the end of the third quarter 2001.[8] In addition, the *American Stock Exchange Fact Book* reported that institutional activity was 74.7 percent of $162.2 billion, which is the value of all stock listed on the American Stock Exchange (AMEX) in 1997.[9] Although the individual investors held 40 percent and others held 13.3 percent of the dollar value of the NYSE stock and 25.3 percent of the dollar value of the AMEX stock for the respective years, the equity investments of institutional investors cannot be overlooked because of their market impact on the volume of trading. These investors represent a dominant force in daily stock trading. Their influential role is important, because they can concentrate their investments in large corporations and, thus, increase their market power.

Furthermore, the SEC reported that "the total dollar amount of securities filed for registration with the SEC during 2002 reached a record of 2.0 trillion"[10] Thus, the investing public is of paramount importance to the nation's capital market as well as to the international marketplace, and corporate management must appraise its position regarding the investor's interests.

The Business Roundtable concluded that:

> Corporations are chartered to serve both their shareholders and society as a whole. The interests of the shareholders are primarily measured in terms of economic return over time. The interests of others in society (other stakeholders) are defined by their relationship to the corporation.
>
> The other stakeholders in the corporation are its employees, customers, suppliers, creditors, the communities where the corporation does business, and society as a whole. The duties and responsibilities of the corporation to the stakeholders are expressed in various laws, regulations, contracts, and custom and practice.[11]

In addition to their significance concerning capital markets, investors have an impact on corporate policies. For example, stockholders can influence corporate policies through their votes at the annual stockholders' meeting. They can vote on such issues as:

- The election and removal of the board of directors
- Amendments to the corporate charter and bylaws
- Proposals of the stockholders to corporate management

---

[8]New York Stock Exchange, *New York Stock Exchange Fact Book* 2001 (New York: NYSE, 2001), p. 61. Visit the web site at *www.nyse.com/marketinfo/shareownersurvey.html*.

[9]American Stock Exchange, *American Stock Exchange Fact Book* 1998 (New York: ASE, 1998), p. 15, and *Security Industry Automation Corporation* database, 1998. More recent information was not available at the time of this writing.

[10]Securities and Exchange Commission, *2002 Annual Report* (Washington, DC: U.S. Government Printing Office, 2002), p. 80.

[11]The Business Roundtable, *Corporate Governance and American Competitiveness* (New York: The Business Roundtable, 1990), p. 4.

- The board of directors' proposals
- The authorization of a new stock or bond issue
- Corporate management's conduct with respect to corporate affairs
- The selection of the independent auditing firm

As a result of the stockholders' voting power, it is essential that the audit committee develop stockholder profiles. For example, committee members should identify the number of stockholders and their related stockholdings in order to isolate the degree of voting power. Voting power may be concentrated in a family group. Such a group can greatly influence corporate policies due to its percentage of stock ownership. Although the board has other demands from its outside constituencies, the audit committee can aid the board through its understanding and familiarity with investors' interests and investments in the corporation. In short, the primary concern of the committee is to give consideration to the stockholders' interests because of their relationship to corporate policy decisions.

In 1992, Richard C. Breeden, former chairman of the SEC, stated in his annual report to Congress:

> The Commission adopted significant revisions of the proxy rules to facilitate effective communications among shareholders and between shareholders and their corporations. The reforms will encourage greater participation by shareholders in corporate governance by removing unnecessary regulatory barriers, reducing the costs of complying with the proxy rules and improving disclosure.

> In addition, the Commission revised its rules to ensure that shareholders receive better information about executive compensation. Among other things, the new executive compensation disclosure rules require new tables that will disclose clearly and concisely the compensation received by a corporation's highest paid executives.[12]

> The Commission adopted important amendments to its executive compensation disclosure requirements. The amendments are designed to (1) ensure that shareholders receive comprehensible, relevant, and complete information about compensation paid to executives upon which to base their voting and investment decisions; and (2) foster accountability of directors to shareholders by permitting shareholders to vote on the proposals of other shareholders with regard to executive and director compensation, and thereby advise the board of directors of the shareholders' assessment of the compensation policies and practices applied by the board.

> After three years of study, two releases for public comment, a two-day public conference, and more than 1,700 public comment letters, the Commission substantially revised its rules governing proxy solicitations. The revisions were adopted to (1) facilitate effective communications among shareholders and between shareholders and their corporations, as well as participation by shareholders in corporate governance, by removing unnecessary regulatory barriers, (2) reduce the costs of complying with the proxy rules, (3) improve disclosures to shareholders, and (4) restore a balance between the free speech rights of shareholders and Congress' concern that solicitation of proxy voting authority be conducted on a fair, honest and informed basis.[13]

---

[12]Securities and Exchange Commission, *1992 Annual Report,* p. viii.
[13]Ibid., p. 53.

Recognizing the significance of the financial reporting process and demands for full disclosure, several investor associations, such as the Investor Responsibility Research Center (IRRC), the National Investor Relations Institute, and the Association for Investment Management and Research, have conducted annual forums dealing with various issues related to the investing public. For example, Maryellen F. Andersen, former chair of the board, and Margaret Carroll, former executive director, of the IRRC, note:

> Increasing numbers of corporate officers and directors looked to IRRC to help inform their policies and decisions on such diverse questions as assessing environmental liability (through our Environmental Information Service); anticipating questions at annual meetings, challenging shareholder proposals at the SEC, preparing responses for the proxy statement, gauging levels of institutional investor interest in key issues and their likely reaction when those issues are raised (through our Proxy Information Service); and deciding whether or when to enter or re-enter South Africa (through our South Africa Review Package). Corporations in other countries, too, began to look to IRRC for many of the same kinds of information.[14]

In 1998, Arthur Levitt, former SEC chairman, reported that:

> [a]n area of great concern to the Commission is inappropriate earnings management. While this is not a new problem, it has risen in a market unforgiving of companies that miss Wall Street's estimates. During the year, our staff issued guidance on various issues relating to the presentation of earnings per share."[15]

Likewise, in 1999, Levitt stated that:

> [a]n area of continued concern to the Commission is inappropriate earnings management. Abusive earnings management involves the use of various forms of gimmickry to distort a company's true financial performance in order to achieve a desired result. Staff Accounting Bulletin 99 reemphasizes that the exclusive reliance on any percentage or numerical threshold in assessing materiality for financial reporting has no basis in the accounting literature or in the law. The staff also issued two other bulletins to provide guidance on the criteria necessary to recognize restructuring liabilities and asset impairments and the conditions prerequisite to recognizing revenue.[16]

More recently, the SEC reported the initiation of these enforcement actions:[17]

---

[14]Investor Responsibility Research Center, *Annual Report 1992* (Washington, DC:IRRC, 1992), p. 3.

[15]Securities and Exchange Commission, *1998 Annual Report* (Washington, DC: U.S. Government Printing Office, 1998), p. vi.

[16]Securities and Exchange Commission, *1999 Annual Report* (Washington, DC: U.S. Government Printing Office, 1999), p. vi. For further discussion, see Chapter 5.

[17]Securities and Exchange Commission, *2002 Annual Report* (Washington, DC: U.S. Government Printing Office, 2002), p.2.

	FY98	**FY99**	**FY00**	**FY01**	**FY02**
Civil Injunctive Actions	214	198	223	205	270
Administrative Proceedings	248	298	244	248	280
Contempt Proceedings	15	29	36	31	47
Reports of Investigation	0	0	0	0	1
Total	477	525	503	484	598

Recall in Chapter 1 the discussion about the erosion of the quality of financial reporting and the quality of earnings. Stockholders and potential investors realize that if a company does not meet or beat Wall Street expectations, then investors will punish the market price of company's stock. Consequently, management has an incentive to manage current and expected earnings because net income is used to measure earnings per share and return on equity as well as the value of management's stock options. Therefore, the quality of earnings may be affected by management's choice of accounting methods and estimates, including nonoperating items on the income statement.

For further discussion, the reader may wish to revisit Arthur Levitt's nine-point action plan in Chapter 1.

As a case in point, the SEC reported:

> *In the Matter of W.R. Grace & Co.* Former senior management of W.R. Grace & Co. and its main health care subsidiary, National Medical Care, Inc., falsely reported results of operations and made false and misleading statements in press releases and at teleconferences with analysts. The managers deferred reporting income, by improperly increasing or establishing reserves, to bring reported earnings into line with targeted earnings. Grace consented to the entry of a cease and desist order, and agreed to establish a $1 million fund for programs to further awareness and education about financial statements and generally accepted accounting principles.[18]

This case illustrates management's use of "cookie jar reserves" whereby management makes unrealistic assumptions to estimate liabilities, which in turn can be reduced in the future to increase net income.

The Need for Accounting Information

As the principal constituency of the corporation, investors make decisions based on financial accounting information. Such data is essentially discretionary, since it is predicated on management's judgment. Although regulatory agencies, such as the SEC, can dictate the form and content of their reports, the investors must rely on corporate management. Moreover, investors must not only evaluate the effectiveness of management but also decide whether to increase or decrease their stockholding based on management's financial accounting representations.

---

[18]Securities and Exchange Commission, *1999 Annual Report*, p. 5. For further discussion, see Securities and Exchange Commission, In the Matter of W.R. Grace & Co., Release No. 34-41578, Accounting and Auditing Enforcement Release No. 1140 (June 30, 1999). See also Ann Davis, "SEC Case Claims Profit 'Management' by Grace, *Wall Street Journal*. April 7, 1999, p. C1.

More important, because of its stewardship accountability, corporate management must periodically communicate its financial accounting information to its constituencies. The corporate financial statements are the principal reports that are used to communicate accounting data. In November 1978, the FASB released its first statement as part of its conceptual framework project for financial accounting and reporting. As a *Statement of Financial Accounting Concepts,* the board concluded the following on objectives of financial reporting:

> Financial reporting should provide information that is useful to present and potential investors and creditors and other users in making rational investment, credit, and similar decisions. The information should be comprehensible to those who have a reasonable understanding of business and economic activities and are willing to study the information with reasonable diligence.
>
> Financial reporting should provide information to help present and potential investors and creditors and other users in assessing the amounts, timing, and uncertainty of prospective cash receipts from dividends or interest and the proceeds from the sale, redemption, or maturity of securities or loans. Since investors' and creditors' cash flows are related to enterprise cash flows, financial reporting should provide information to help investors, creditors, and others assess the amounts, timing, and uncertainty of prospective net cash inflows to the related enterprise.
>
> Financial reporting should provide information about the economic resources of an enterprise, the claims to those resources (obligations of the enterprise to transfer resources to other entities and owners' equity), and the effects of transactions, events, and circumstances that change its resources and claims to those resources.[19]

With respect to the first objective of financial reporting, it is apparent that investors need useful information for investment decisions. However, one must address the usefulness of the financial statements to the users. To resolve this controversy in financial reporting, Kenneth S. Most and Lucia S. Chang found that:

> [t]he accounting contents of the corporate annual report are regarded as its most important contents, and conversely that the president's letter to the stockholders and the pictorial material presented are viewed as relatively unimportant.[20] . . . The authors believe that the results of their research indicate strongly that investors regard financial statement information as useful for their decisions.[21]

The second objective of financial reporting means that the investors need financial information in order to evaluate their investment objectives. Obviously, investors wish to safeguard the principal amount of their investment and maximize the income and capital appreciation. Furthermore, investors must assess their willingness and ability to accept risk. Similarly, management must effectively use the economic resources of the enterprise in order to generate a monetary return to its

---

[19]Financial Accounting Standards Board, *Statement of Financial Accounting Concepts, No. 1,* p. viii.
[20]Kenneth S. Most and Lucia S. Chang, "An Empirical Study of Investor Views Concerning Financial Statements and Investment Decisions," *Collected Papers of the American Accounting Association's Annual Meeting* (Sarasota, FL:AAA, August 1978), pp. 245–246.
[21]Ibid., p. 249.

investors. Thus, "since an enterprise's ability to generate favorable cash flows affects both its ability to pay dividends and interest and the market prices of its securities, expected cash flows to investors and creditors are related to expected cash flows to the enterprise."[22]

Finally, the third objective of financial reporting relates to the enterprise's financial condition and operating performance. Investors need information on the current and future financial strength of the corporation to appraise the soundness of their investment. Such information is critical. Not only does it indicate the ability of the enterprise to meet its short-term and long-term financial commitments, but it allows investors to evaluate their risk and return on investment. Furthermore, investors need information regarding the uses of economic resources in the operations. Although the enterprise may have an adequate financial position, such a position may deteriorate because of poor operational performance. In short, investors want financial information on the use and disposition of the enterprise's economic resources in order to assess their investment policy.[23] More recent developments regarding investors' need for financial information are discussed later in this chapter.

Role of the Audit Committee

In order to discharge their responsibilities in the area of financial reporting effectively, the audit committee should establish operational objectives.[24] The operational objectives should be based on the investor's need for financial accounting information, which is manifested in the board of directors' stewardship accountability. Such operational objectives should be consistent with the FASB's objectives of financial reporting, because the primary purpose of the committee is to provide assurance regarding the usefulness of the accounting information in the financial statements.

Moreover, in addition to the quantitative representations in the financial statements, the committee should use the following qualitative characteristics to assess the financial reporting policies and practices of the corporation:

> The qualitative characteristics of financial statements, like objectives, should be based largely upon the needs of users of the statements. Information is useless unless it is relevant and material to a user's decision. Information should be as free as possible from any biases of the preparer. In making decisions, users should not only understand the information presented, but also should be able to assess its reliability and compare it with information about alternative opportunities and previous experience. In all cases, information is more useful if it stresses economic substance rather than technical form.[25]

---

[22]Financial Accounting Standards Board, *Statement on Financial Accounting Concepts, No. 1*, p. 19.

[23]For further discussion, see SRI International, *Investor Informational Needs and the Annual Report* (Morristown, NJ: Financial Executive Research Foundation, 1987).

[24]For further discussion on the director's role in reviewing financial information and management's statements, see Chapters 10, 13, and 14.

[25]American Institute of Certified Public Accountants, *Report of the Study Group on the Objectives of Financial Statements* (New York: AICPA, 1973), p. 60. For further discussion, see Financial Accounting Standards Board, *Statement of Financial Accounting Concepts No. 2*, "Qualitative Characteristics of Accounting" (Stamford, CT: FASB, May 1980).

The preceding discussions on the operational objectives and the criteria for evaluating the usefulness of the financial statements provide the necessary guidelines for evaluating management's responsibilities in the preparation of the financial statements. In addition, the audit committee should give consideration to the following criteria, which were used by the Financial Analysts Federation in its Awards for Excellence in Corporate Reporting program:

1. Responsiveness of management to analysts' and investors' desire for information prerequisite to real understanding of companies and their problems.

2. Efforts by companies to supply financial and other information going well beyond the level of disclosure required by the SEC, the exchanges, and the FASB.

3. A coordinated and consistent program of personal contact with investors and their representatives—both through provision of experienced and helpful officials in the investor relations function and via regular management presentations to analyst groups, company-sponsored field trips, and so on.

4. A high "candor quotient" in both oral and written communications to the investment community. Too many managements prejudice an otherwise creditable information program by ignoring or glossing over unfavorable developments with a thick patina of corporate optimism.[26]

Subsequently, the Association for Investment Management and Research issued its *Corporate Information Committee Report* (1995–1996). A checklist of criteria for evaluating financial communications effort stated in part:

Annual Published Information

A. Annual Report
 1. Financial Highlights: Are they clear and unambiguous?
 2. President's Letter Review: Does it hit the highlights of the year in an objective manner? Is it relevant to the company's results and candid in appraising problems? It should include:
  a. Review of the year.
  b. Insights into operating rates, unit production levels, and selling prices.
  c. Acquisitions and divestments, if any.
  d. Government business, if material.
  e. Capital expenditures program; start-up expenses.
  f. Research and development efforts.
  g. Employment costs, labor relations, union contracts.
  h. Energy cost and availability.
  i. Environmental and OSHA costs.
  j. Backlogs.
  k. New products.
  l. Legislative and regulatory developments.
  m. Outlook.
  n. Unusual income or expense.
 3. Officers and Directors:
  a. Age, background, and responsibilities.

---

[26]Financial Analysts Federation, "Awards for Excellence in Corporate Reporting," *Financial Analysts Federation News Release* (New York: FAF, January 1978), p. 1.

    b. Description of company organization.

    c. Outside affiliations of directors.

    d. Principal personnel changes.

4. Statement of Corporate Goals:

   What are the short-term and long-term corporate goals, and how and when does management expect to achieve them? (This section could be included in several areas of the report, but separate treatment is preferred.)

5. Discussions of Divisional and/or Segment Operations:

    a. How complete is the breakdown of sales, materials, costs, overhead, and earnings?

    b. Are the segments logical for analytical purposes? Do they parallel lines of business?

    c. Are unusual developments explained, and do the explanations include management's response?

    d. Comparisons with relevant industry developments should include:

       i. Market size and growth.

       ii. Market penetration.

       iii. Geographical divergencies.

    e. Foreign operations:

       i. Revenues, including export sales.

       ii. Consolidated foreign earnings versus equity interest.

       iii. Market and/or regional trends.

       iv. Tax status.

6. Financial Summary and Footnotes:

    a. Statement of accounting principles, including explanation of changes and their effects.

    b. Adjustments to EPS for dilution.

    c. Affiliates' operating information.

    d. Consolidated finance subsidiary's disclosure of separate balance sheet information and operating results.

    e. Cash flow statement (FAS No. 95).

    f. Tax accounting investment tax credits identified, breakdown of current and deferred taxes for U.S. and non-U.S. tax jurisdictions, reconciliation of effective and statutory tax rates, impact of changes in tax law, early application of FAS No. 96.

    g. Clarity of explanation of currency exchange rate accounting:

       i. Impact on earnings from Balance Sheet translation, if any.

       ii. Indication of "Operating" or Income Statement Effect of exchange rate fluctuations.

    h. Property accounts and depreciation policies:

       i. Methods and asset lives used for tax and for financial reporting.

       ii. Quantification of effect on reported earnings of use of different method and/or asset lives for tax purposes.

    i. Investments: composition and market values disclosed.

    j. Inventories: method of valuation and identifying different methods for various product or geographic segments.

    k. Leases and rentals: terms and liability.

    l. Debt repayment schedules.

    m. Pension funds: costs charged to income, interest rate, and wage-inflation assumptions; amount of any unfunded past service liability; amortization period for unfunded liability (FAS No. 87).

    n. Other postemployment benefits: pay-as-you-go amount, discussion of potential liability, impact of FAS No. 106, including plans to fund or amend, and impact of FAS No. 112.

    o. Capital expenditure programs and forecasts, including costs for environmental purposes.

    p. Acquisitions and divestitures (if material):

       i. Description of activity and operating results.

          ii. Type of financial transaction.

          iii. Effect on reported sales and earnings.

          iv. Quantification of purchase acquisitions or small poolings that do not require restatement of prior years' results. (When restating for pooling, both old and new data are useful for comparison.)

    q. Year-end adjustments.

    r. Restatement of quarterly reports to year-end accounting basis.

    s. Research and development and new products; amount and types of outlays and forecasts.

    t. Contingent liabilities, particularly environmental.

    u. Derivation of number of shares used for calculating primary and fully diluted earnings per share.

    v. Disclosures of the fair values of financial instruments (FAS No. 107).

    w. Goodwill amount being amortized and number of years.

    x. Ten-year statistical summary:

          i. Adequacy of income statement and balance sheet detail.

          ii. Helpfulness of "nonstatement" data (e.g., number of employees, adjusted number of shares, price of stock, capital expenditures, etc.)

B. 10-Ks, 10-Qs, and Other Required Published Information

Quarterly and Other Published Information Not Required

A. Quarterly Reports

    1. Depth of commentary on operating results and developments.

    2. Discussion of new products, management changes, and problem areas.

    3. Degree of detail of profit and loss statement, including divisional or segmental breakdown.

    4. Inclusion of a balance sheet and cash flow statement.

    5. Restatement of all prior- and current-year quarters for major pooling acquisitions and quantification of effect of purchase acquisitions and/or disposals.

    6. Breakout of nonrecurring or exceptional income or expense items, including effects from inventory valuation and foreign currency translation factors.

    7. Explicit statement of accounting principles underlying quarterly statements.

    8. Timeliness of reports.

    9. Separate fourth quarter report.

B. Other Published Material

    1. Availability of proxy statements (even though this is required public information).

    2. Annual meeting report; available with questions and answers and identity of those posing questions.

    3. Addresses to analysts' groups: available with questions and answers.

    4. Statistical supplements and fact books.

    5. Company magazines, newsletters, and explanatory pamphlets.

    6. Press releases: Are they sent to shareholders and analysts? Are they timely? Do they include earnings numbers?

    7. How are documents filed with public agencies (SEC, Federal Trade Commission, Department of Labor, court cases, etc.) made available? Does the company disseminate all material information in 10-K, 10-Q, and similar reports?

Other Aspects

A. Is there a designated and advertised individual (or individuals) for shareholder and analyst contacts?

B. Interviews

    1. Knowledgeability and responsiveness of company contact.
    2. Access to policymakers and operational people.
    3. Candor in discussing negative developments.
C. Presentations to analyst groups: frequency and content
D. Company-sponsored field trips and meetings
E. Annual meetings
    1. Accessibility.
    2. Worthwhile to shareholders and analysts.[27]

Finally, the audit committee should be aware of the independent auditing firm's quality control policies and procedures, which provide reasonable assurance that the firm has followed professional standards.[28] The Auditing Standards Board has issued the *Statements on Quality Control Standards,* which identifies five elements of quality control:

1. Independence, integrity, and objectivity
2. Personnel management
3. Acceptance and continuance of clients and engagements
4. Engagement performance
5. Monitoring

Such quality control standards provide a framework for the firm's quality review program. For example, member firms of the SEC Practice Section are required to rotate engagement partners at least every seven years, and audit engagements are subject to a second-partner review process. As noted in Chapter 2, Section 203 of the Sarbanes-Oxley Act limits both the lead partner and concurring partners to a maximum of five consecutive years of service with a five-year time-out.

In an article dealing with the subject of quality review by independent auditors, Brian H. MacIver, James Welch, and Priscilla A. Burnaby report that three of the previous nine quality control standards—namely, independence, supervision, and consultation—are misunderstood or inadequately addressed. The authors note, "The most common inadequacies cited by the team captain in review reports included inadequate and deficient financial statement disclosures, inadequate checklists or failure to prepare checklists properly, and too many hours of continuing professional education in the tax area rather than in the audit area."[29]

---

[27]Association for Investment Management and Research, *Corporate Information Committee Report 1995–96* (Charlottesville, VA: AIMR, 1997), pp. 75–77. Also see Association for Investment Management and Research, *Financial Reporting in the 1990s and Beyond* (Charlottesville, VA: AIMR, 1993).

[28]*Statement on Auditing Standards No. 25,* "The Relationship of Generally Accepted Auditing Standards to Quality Control Standards" (New York: AICPA, 1979). For further discussion, see *Statement on Quality Control Standards No. 2,* "System of Quality Control for a CPA Firm's Accounting and Auditing Practice"; *Statement on Quality Control Standards No. 3,* "Monitoring a CPA Firm's Accounting and Auditing Practice"; AICPA Peer Review Board, *Standards for Performing and Reporting on Peer Reviews* (New York: AICPA, 1996). The audit committee's knowledge and understanding of the independent accounting firm's quality control policies and procedures is important to provide assurance to the full board of directors that the independent auditors are discharging their responsibilities to the client company and the general public.

[29]Brian H. MacIver, James Welch, and Priscilla A. Burnaby, "Quality Review—Observations of a Team Captain," *Ohio CPA Journal* 50, No. 1 (January–April 1991), pp. 54–55.

In their survey of 42 audit partners and managers, Ganesh Krishnamoorthy, Arnie Wright, and Jeffrey Cohen concluded that:

> [o]ne must go beyond just determining whether the committees comply with existing regulations. In fact, 81% of the respondents believe that you need to look at the substance (the actual effectiveness of the audit committee) and not just the form of audit committees. Thus, an audit committee might comply with all existing regulations, but if they are not providing active oversight to the quality and integrity of the financial reporting process, they cannot be relied upon.[30]

An example of the audit committee's role and responsibilities in the financial statement and disclosure matters of Wal-Mart Stores follows.

1. Review and discuss with management, and to the extent the audit Committee deems necessary or appropriate, the Internal Auditors and the Outside Auditors, the Company's disclosure controls and procedures that are designed to ensure that the reports the Company files with the Commission comply with the Commission's rules and forms.

2. Review and discuss with management, the Internal Auditors and the Outside Auditor the annual audited financial statement, including disclosures made in management's discussion and analysis, and recommended to the Board whether the audited financial statements should be included in the Company's Form 10-K.

3. Review and discuss with management, the Internal Auditors and the Outside Auditor the Company's quarterly financial statements, including disclosures made in management's discussion and analysis, prior to the filing of its Form 10-Q, including the results of the Outside Auditor's reviews of the quarterly financial statements.

4. Review and discuss quarterly reports from the Outside Auditor on:

   (a) All critical accounting policies and practices to be used;

   (b) All alternative treatments within GAAP [generally accepted accounting principles] for policies and practices related to material items that have been discussed with management, including ramifications of the use of such alternative disclosures and treatments and the treatment preferred by the Outside Auditor;

   (c) The internal controls adhered to by the Company, management, and the Company's financial, accounting and internal auditing personnel, and the impact of each on the quality and reliability of the Company's financial reporting; and

   (d) Other material written communications between the Outside Auditor and management, such as any management letter or schedule of unadjusted differences.

5. Discuss in advance with management the Company's practice with respect to the types of information to be disclosed and the types of presentations to be made in earnings press releases, including the use, if any, of "pro forma" or "adjusted" non-GAAP information, as well as financial information and earnings guidance provided to analysts and rating agencies.

---

[30]Ganesh Krishnamoorthy, Arnie Wright, and Jeffrey Cohen. "Auditors' Views on Audit Committees and Financial Reporting Quality," *CPA Journal* 75, No. 10, (October 2002), p. 56.

6. Review and discuss with management, the Internal Auditors and the Outside Auditor:

    (a) Significant financial reporting issues and judgments made in connection with the preparation of the Company's financial statements;

    (b) The clarity of the financial disclosures made by the Company;

    (c) The development, selection, and disclosure of critical accounting estimates and the analyses of alternative assumptions or estimates, and the effect of such estimates on the Company's financial statements;

    (d) Potential changes in GAAP and the effect such changes would have on the Company's financial statements;

    (e) Significant changes in accounting principles, financial reporting policies and internal controls implemented by the Company;

    (f) Significant litigation, contingencies and claims against the Company and material accounting issues that require disclosure in the Company's financial statements;

    (g) Information regarding any "second" opinions sought by management from an independent auditor with respect to the accounting treatment of a particular event or transaction;

    (h) Management's compliance with the company's internal accounting and financial controls and the recommendations of management, the Internal Auditors and the Outside Auditor for the improvement of accounting practices and internal controls; and

    (i) The adequacy and effectiveness of the Company's internal accounting nd financial controls and the recommendations of management, the Internal Auditors and the Outside Auditor for the improvement of accounting practices and internal controls; and

    (j) Any difficulties encountered by the Outside Auditor or the Internal Auditors in the course of their audit work, including any restrictions on the scope of activities or access to requested information, and any significant disagreements with management.

7. Discuss with management and the Outside Auditor the effect of regulatory and accounting initiatives as well as off-balance sheet structures and aggregate contractual obligations on the Company's financial statements.

8. Discuss with management the company's major financial risk exposures and the steps management has taken to monitor and control such exposures, including the Company's risk assessment and risk management policies.

9. Discuss with the Outside Auditor the matters required to be discussed by Statement on Auditing Standards ("SAS") No. 61 relating to the conduct of the audit. In particular, discuss:

    (a) The adoption of, or changes to, the Company's significant internal auditing and accounting principles and practices as suggested by the Outside Auditor, Internal Auditors or management; and

    (b) The management letter provided by the Outside Auditor and the Company's response to that letter

10. Receive and review disclosures made to the Audit Committee by the Company's Chief Executive Officer and Chief Financial Officer during their certification process for the Company's Form 10-K and Form 10-Q about (a) any significant deficiencies in the design or operation of internal controls or material weakness therein, (b) any fraud involving management or other associates who have a significant role in the Company's internal controls and (c) any ignificant changes in internal controls or in other factors that could significantly affect internal controls subsequent to the date of their evaluation. [31]

CREDIT GRANTORS

Importance of the Credit Grantors

Obviously, credit grantors are a significant group since they are a source of funds to the enterprise. The group consists of both short-term and long-term lenders of credit, such as banks, insurance companies, trade creditors, and bondholders. Short-term creditors are concerned principally with the corporation's ability to maintain an adequate cash position because they expect to be paid in a short period of time. Hence they focus their attention on the working capital position of the enterprise, which represents the relationship between cash and near-cash assets, such as short-term securities, receivables, inventories, and short-term liabilities. Such information is central to this group's decision-making process because the particular assets may be converted readily into cash. Conversely, long-term creditors are concerned not only with the corporation's ability to generate cash but also with its potential profitability. For example, they are interested in the ability of the enterprise to secure a loan with the necessary assets in relationship to its commitments and contingencies, such as a pending lawsuit. Thus credit grantors are primarily interested in the current solvency position of the corporation and its adherence to the loan covenants. In short, the major objective of the creditors is not only to safeguard their claim against the assets of the enterprise but also to obtain assurance with respect to the debt-paying ability of the corporation.

The Need for Accounting Information

Credit grantors need information on the financial and operational conditions of the enterprise. To judge a credit risk or establish a line of credit, they focus their attention on the financial statements as well as other sources of information, such as Dun & Bradstreet or National Credit Office credit reports.

In a study of June 1978, Keith G. Stanga and James J. Benjamin concluded that:

1. Bankers assign considerable importance to the basic historical financial statements as information sources for making term loan decisions. The comparative income statement is ranked as the most important information item.

2. Bankers attribute a fairly high degree of importance to forecast information. This suggests that accountants should continue striving to improve reporting standards in this area.

3. In general, bankers assign a fairly high degree of importance to information regarding executory contracts. This suggests that the accounting profession should

---

[31]Wal-Mart Stores, Inc., Audit Committee Charter, 2003 (*www.walmartstores.com*), pp. 3–5.

concern itself not only with the accounting and reporting problems associated with leases, but also with other types of executory contracts, such as major purchase commitments, labor contracts, and order backlogs.

4. Bankers consider general purchasing power financial statements as relatively unimportant. As noted earlier, other studies have found that security analysts also attribute little, if any, importance to these statements. Given the paramount nature of user needs in financial accounting, it would seem that the FASB should carefully reconsider the usefulness of price-level statements before making this information mandatory in the future.

5. Bankers assign relatively little value to information on corporate social responsibility and to financial breakdowns of amounts relating to human resources. These feelings are present despite the tremendous interest shown by many accountants in these areas in recent years.[32]

More recently, George Cox and associates report that "the recent spate of corporate disasters almost defies understanding." Such companies have "credit lines with premier lending institutions and yet, disaster struck without much warning to investors, creditors, or employees." They believe that "the audit committee should meet with investment and commercial bankers, as well as rating agency personnel, about the health of the organization." For example, "are bank loans and credit lines competitive, meeting ordinary and customary market terms? Strong oversight and control are the best prescription for company health."[33]

Role of the Audit Committee

Although the finance committee is responsible for the financial policies and program, the audit committee should give attention to the financial reporting matters concerning the credit lenders. The audit committee members are in a unique position because they must monitor the accounting information that is related to the corporation's financial policies. In approaching the financial reporting task, the committee should consult with the chairperson of the finance committee as well as the chief financial officer. For example, the committee's review of the loan agreements and other commitments should be made in view of the preceding discussion of the objectives of financial reporting and the information needs of the credit grantors. Thus the audit committee should be concerned primarily with such matters as:

- The proper disclosure of the short-term and long-term obligations and any outstanding commitments of the corporation
- The adherence to the loan covenants regarding the necessary working capital ratios
- A summary of the sources of creditors' equity and the related cost of debt

---

[32]Keith G. Stanga and James J. Benjamin, "Information Needs of Bankers," *Management Accounting* 59, No. 12 (June 1978), p. 21. FASB No. 33 was rescinded in 1986 by FASB No. 89, which encourages disclosure on a voluntary basis.
[33]George Cox, H. Stephen Grace, Jr., John E. Haupert, Peter Howell, and Ronald H. Wilcomes, "A Prescription for Company Health," *CPA Journal* 72, No. 7 (July 2002), pp. 62–63.

- A forecast of the proposed debt financing activities and repayment schedule and its relationship to the stockholders' equity

As William H. Dougherty, former president of NCNB Corporation, suggests:

> The concern of all involved parties should be with the quality of disclosure—not its quantity, and involved parties should be more vigorous than anyone else in cost/benefit evaluations. . . . The increasing cost of audit and compliance is important because it raises corporate prices.[34]

In his article entitled "The Enron Affair from a Lender's View," Neville Grusd, executive vice president of Merchant Factors, points out that "no one has mentioned the loss sustained by the creditors of Enron." He notes that "most credit grantors, however, rely upon the very financial statements" that the parties in the public sector (the President, SEC, and Congress) are worrying about.[35]

Grusd suggests the following to credit grantors:

- "Become more active in accounting rule making through the American Bankers Association and Commercial Finance Association."
- "If a lender knows the client is a major account of the CPA firm issuing its financials, the lender should take the necessary steps to ensure the quality of the financial reporting."
- With respect to review engagements, "lenders and accountants should discuss the accountant's procedures, then decide the extent to which the lender's own field exam should be extended to cover weak areas."
- Lenders should insist that the financial statements are prepared by "competent and independent CPAs."[36]

In addition to the issues already discussed, several Financial Accounting Standards Board Statements are relevant to credit grantors:

SFAS No. 95	"Statement of Cash Flows" (November 1987)
SFAS No. 105	"Disclosure of Information about Financial Instruments with Off-Balance Sheet Risk and Financial Instruments with Concentration of Credit Risk" (March 1990)
SFAS No. 107	"Disclosure About Fair Value of Financial Instruments" (December 1991)
SFAS No. 133	"Accounting for Derivative Instruments and Hedging Activities" (June 1998)

---

[34]William H. Dougherty, "Financial Reporting—A Banker Looks at the Scene," *Financial Executive* 46, No. 12 (December 1978), p. 53.
[35]Neville Grusd, "The Enron Affair from a Lender's View," *CPA Journal* 72, No. 12 (December 2002), p. 8.
[36]Ibid., pp. 8–10.

These accounting standards are summarized in the following paragraphs.

Reporting Cash Flows In November 1987, the FASB issued SFAS No. 95, "Statement of Cash Flows." The board recognized that a presentation of a company's cash flows is a better measure of liquidity by the users of financial statements. Prior to the issuance of SFAS No. 95, companies could present their funds flow statement on either a working capital or a cash basis. Under the new accounting standard, companies are required to classify cash flows as operating, investing, or financial activities.[37] Management is required to provide additional information on cash flows in its presentation of management's discussion and analysis of financial condition and results of operations. Although the FASB has encouraged management to report cash flows from operating activities by the direct method, which consists of classes of cash transactions, the indirect method is commonly used. For example, *Accounting Trends and Techniques—1990* disclosed that in 1989, 583 companies out of 600 used the indirect method.[38] Under this method, the net income is reconciled to net cash flow from operating activities by adjusting for deferrals, accrual, and noncash charges.

Financial Instruments In the late 1980s, the accounting treatment associated with financial instruments and transactions received a great deal of attention because of the lack of financial accounting and disclosure standards. Typically, such financial instruments were treated as off-balance-sheet financing arrangements or unaccrued loss recognition in the financial statements. In March 1990, the FASB issued SFAS No. 105, which deals with disclosures about off-balance-sheet risk, credit risks, interest rates, and current market values of financial instruments.[39] For example, SFAS No. 105 requires companies to disclose concentrations of credit risk from accounts receivable financing arrangements and other financial instruments. In the event that there is nonperformance by the parties to the financing arrangement, management is required to disclose the dollar amount of the loss resulting from credit risk.[40]

Subsequent to the issuance of SFAS No. 105, in December 1991 the FASB issued SFAS No. 107, which requires all financial and nonfinancial institutions to disclose the fair value of financial instruments whether recognized in the balance sheet or not. If management is unable to obtain the quoted market price of a financial instrument, then it may use the quoted market price of a similar instrument or use a valuation technique, such as estimated future cash flows. Fair value disclosure

---

[37]Financial Accounting Standards Board, *Statement of Financial Accounting Standards No. 95,* "Statement of Cash Flows" (Stamford, CT.: FASB, 1987). See SFAS Nos. 102 and 104 for amendments.
[38]American Institute of Certified Public Accountants, *Accounting Trends and Techniques—1990* (New York: AICPA, 1990).
[39]Financial Accounting Standards Board, *Statement of Financial Accounting Standards, No. 105,* "Disclosure of Information About Financial Instruments with Off-Balance Sheet Risk and Financial Instruments with Concentrations of Credit Risk" (Norwalk, CT.: FASB, 1990).
[40]For further review and discussion, see Chad F. Coben, "Implementing SFAS No. 105's Disclosure Requirements," *Journal of Commercial Lending* 74, No. 7 (March 1992), pp. 13–23; and Nathan M. Lubow, "New Disclosures FASB No. 105," *Secured Lender* 48, No. 6 (November/December 1992), pp. 112, 114.

is required for financial instruments such as accounts and notes receivable and payable, investment securities, options, future contracts, and interest rate swaps.[41]

In June 1998, the Financial Accounting Standards Board issued SFAS No. 133, "Accounting for Derivative Instruments and Hedging Activities," which supersedes SFAS No. 105 and 119 and amends SFAS No. 107. In summary, this new accounting standard requires that:

- All derivatives must be measured at fair value and recognized in the balance sheet as assets or liabilities.
- With the exception for derivatives that qualify as hedges (fair value hedge, cash-flow hedge, and foreign currency hedge), changes in the fair value of derivatives must be recognized in income.

  With respect to derivatives that qualify as hedges, management may elect to use hedge accounting to defer gains or losses; however, it should be noted that the deferral of such gains or losses depends on the effectiveness of the derivative in offsetting changes in the fair value of the hedged item or changes in future cash flows. In addition, the changes in the fair value of asset, liability, or firm commitment being hedged must be recognized in income to the extent of offsetting gains or losses on the hedged instrument.[42]

The use of market value accounting and the estimate of fair values may cause positive or negative variability in income because of changes in the market values and inaccurate estimates of fair values of financial instruments.

The 2002 annual report of a publicly held bank and the 2003 annual report of the largest retailer included the following footnote disclosures.

Financial Instruments

In the normal course of business, the Company is a party to certain financial instruments with off-balance-sheet risk, such as commitments to extend credit, unused lines of credit and standby letters of credit. The Company's policy is to record such instruments when funded.

Fair Value of Financial Instruments

The following methods and assumptions were used by the company in estimating its fair values for financial instruments for purposes of disclosure:

Cash and cash equivalents and accrued interest receivable/payable: The carrying amounts reported in the consolidated statements of condition for these instruments approximate fair value.

---

[41]Financial Accounting Standards Board, *Statement of Financial Accounting Standards No. 107*, "Disclosures About Fair Value of Financial Instruments" (Norwalk, CT.: FASB, 1991). In October 1994, the FASB issued SFAS No. 119, "Disclosure about Derivative Financial Instruments and Fair Value Instruments."

[42]Financial Accounting Standards Board, *Statement of Financial Accounting Standards No. 133*, "Accounting for Derivatives Instruments and Hedging Activities" (Norwalk, CT.: FASB, 1998). With respect to the different types of hedges, disclosure, and transition requirements, see SFAS No. 133. This statement is effective for all fiscal quarters of fiscal years beginning after June 15, 1999. Also see SFAS Nos. 138, 149, and 150 for amendments.

Investment securities and FHLB stock: Fair values for investment securities are based on quoted market prices or dealer quotes. The fair value of FHLB stock is assumed to equal the carrying value since the stock is non-marketable but redeemable at its par value.

Loans and loans held for sale: Fair values for loans are estimated using a discounted cash flow analysis, based on interest rates approximating those currently being offered for loans with similar terms and credit quality.

Deposits: The fair values disclosed for non-interest-bearing accounts and accounts with no stated maturities are, by definition, equal to the amount payable on demand at the reporting date. The fair value of time deposits was estimated by discounting expected monthly maturities at interest rates approximating those currently being offered on time deposits of similar terms.

Borrowings and trust preferred securities: the carrying amounts of repurchase agreements and FHLB line of credit advances approximate fair value. Fair values for FHLB term advances, other borrowings and trust preferred securities are estimated using discounted cash flows, based on current market rates for similar borrowings.

Off-balance-sheet instruments: Off-balance-sheet financial instruments consist of letters of credit and commitments to extend credit. Letters of credit and commitments to extend credit are fair valued based on fees and interest rates currently charged to enter into agreements with similar terms and credit quality.

Note 10: Derivative Financial Instruments

The Company has used interest rate swap agreements ("swaps") from time to time as a part of its overall interest rate risk management strategy. At December 31, 2002, and during the year then ended, the Company had no swaps outstanding. In 2001 and 2000, the swaps modified the repricing characteristics of certain brokered time deposit liabilities. Under the terms of the swaps, the Company received a fixed rate of interest and paid a variable rate of interest. He swaps were entered into with a counterparty that met the Company's established credit standards and the agreements contained collateral provisions protecting the at-risk party. The company considered the credit risk inherent in these contracts to be negligible. The swaps matched the related brokered time deposits in notional/face amount, fixed interest rate, interest payment date and maturity date.

Effective January 1, 2001, the Company adopted SFAS No. 133, "Accounting for Derivative Instruments and Hedging Activities." Under SFAS No. 133, the swaps were accounted for as fair value hedges of the brokered time deposit liabilities. The swaps and the brokered time deposits were recorded at fair value on the consolidated statement of condition. The adoption of SFAS No. 133 had no material impact on net income or shareholders' equity.[43]

Financial Instruments

The company uses derivative financial instruments for hedging and non-trading purposes to manage its exposure to interest and foreign exchange rates. Use of derivative financial instruments in hedging programs subjects the Company to certain risks, such as market and credit risks. Market risk represents the possibility that the value of the derivative instrument will change. In a hedging relationship, the change in the value of the derivative is offset to a great extent by the change in the value of the

---

[43]BSB Bancorp, Inc., *2002 Annual Report,* pp. 32, 39.

underlying hedged item. Credit risk related to derivatives represents the possibility that the counterparty will not fulfill the terms of the contract. Credit risk is monitored through established approval procedures, including setting concentration limits by counterparty, reviewing credit ratings and requiring collateral (generally cash) when appropriate. The majority of the Company's transactions are with counterparties rated A or better by nationally recognized credit rating agencies.

Adoption of FASB 133

On February 1, 2001, the Company adopted Financial Accounting Standards Board Statement No. 133, "Accounting for Derivative and Hedging Activities" (FAS 133) as amended. Because most of the derivatives used by the company at the date of adoption were designated as net investment hedges, the fair value of these instruments was included in the balance sheet prior to adoption of the standard. As a result, the adoption of this standard did not have a significant effect on the consolidation financial statements of the Company.

Fair Value Instruments

The Company enters into interest rate swaps to minimize the risks and costs associated with its financing activities. Under the swap agreements, the company pays variable rate interest and receives fixed interest rate payments periodically over the life of the instruments. The notional amounts are used to measure interest to be paid or received and do not represent the exposure due to credit loss. All of the Company's interest rate swaps are designated as fair value hedges. In a fair value hedge, the gain or loss on the derivative instrument as well as the offsetting gain or loss on the hedged item attributable to the hedged risk are recognized in earnings in the current period. Ineffectiveness results when gains and losses on the hedged item are not completely offset by gains and losses in the hedged instrument. No ineffectiveness was recognized in fiscal 2003 related to these instruments. The fair value of these contracts is included in the balance sheet in the line titled "Other assets and deferred charges."

Net Investment Instruments

At January 31, 2003, the company is a party to cross-currency interest rate swaps that hedge its net investment in the United Kingdom. The agreements are contracts to exchange fixed rate payments in one currency for fixed rate payments in another currency. The Company also holds approximately GBP 1 billion of debt that is designated as hedges of net investment.

During the fourth quarter of fiscal 2002, the Company terminated or sold cross-country instruments that hedged portions of the Company's investments in Canada, Germany and the United Kingdom. These instruments had notional amounts of $6.7 billion. The Company received $1.1 billion in cash related to the fair value of the instruments at the time of the terminations. Prior to the terminations, these instruments were classified as net investment hedges and had been recorded at fair value as current assets on the balance sheet with a like amount recorded on the balance sheet shareholders' equity section in the line "other accumulated comprehensive income." No gain related to the terminations was recorded in the Company's income statement. The fair value of these contracts is included in the balance sheet in the line titled "Other assets and deferred charges."

Cash Flow Hedge

The Company entered into a cross-currency interest rate swap to hedge the foreign currency risk of certain yen denominated intercompany debt. The company has entered into a cross-currency interest rate swap related to U.S. dollar denominated debt securities issued by a Canadian subsidiary of the Company. These swaps are designated as cash flow hedges of foreign currency exchange risk. No ineffectiveness was recognized during fiscal 2003 related to these instruments. The Company expects that the amount of gain existing in other comprehensive income that is expected to be reclassified into earnings within the next 12 months will not be significant. Changes in the foreign currency spot exchange rate result in reclassification of amounts from other comprehensive income to earnings to offset transaction gains or losses on foreign denominated debt. The fair value of these hedges are included in the balance sheet in the line titled "Other assets and deferred charges."

Instrument Not Designated for Hedging

The Company enters into forward currency exchange contracts in the regular course of business to manage its exposure against foreign currency fluctuations on cross-border purchases of inventory. These contracts are generally for short durations of six months or less. Although these instruments are economic hedges, the Company did not designate these contracts as hedges as required in order to obtain hedge accounting. As a result, the Company marks the contracts to market through earnings. The fair value of these contracts is included in the balance sheet in the line titled "Prepaid expenses and other."

Fair Value of Financial Instruments

Instrument	Notional Amount		Fair Value	
(amounts in millions)	**1/31/2003**	1/31/2002	**1/31/2003**	1/31/2002
Derivative financial instruments designated for hedging:				
Receive fixed rate, pay floating rate interest rate swaps designated as fair value hedges	**$8,292**	$3,792	**$803**	$172
Receive fixed rate, pay fixed rate cross-currency interest rate swaps designated as net investment hedges (FX notional amount: GBP 795 at 1/31/2003 and 2002)	**1,250**	1,250	**126**	192
Receive fixed rate, pay fixed rate cross-currency interest rate swap designated as cash flow hedge (FX notional amount: CAD 503 at 1/31/2003 and 2002)	**325**	325	**8**	8
Receive fixed rate, pay fixed rate cross-currency interest rate swap designated as cash flow hedge (FX notional amount: JPY 52,056 at 1/31/2003 and 2002)	**432**	—	**2**	—
	10,299	5,367	**939**	372

Instrument	Notional Amount		Fair Value	
(amounts in millions)	**1/31/2003**	1/31/2002	**1/31/2003**	1/31/2002
Derivative financial instruments not designated for hedging:				
Foreign currency exchange forward contracts (various currencies)	**185**	117	—	—
Basis swap	**500**	500	**2**	1
	685	617	**2**	1
Non-derivative financial instruments:				
Long-term debt	**21,145**	17,944	**20,464**	18,919

Cash and cash equivalents: The carrying amount approximates fair value due to the short maturity of these instruments.

Long term debt: Fair value is based on the Company's current incremental borrowing rate for similar types of borrowing arrangements.

Interest rate instruments and net investment instruments: The fair values are estimated amounts the company would receive or pay to terminate the agreements as of the reporting dates.

Foreign currency contracts: The fair value of foreign currency contracts are estimated by obtaining quotes from external sources.[44]

REGULATORY AGENCIES

Importance of Regulatory Agencies

In a private enterprise economy, the corporation is a productive resource whereby corporate management is engaged in the ultimate economic decisions regarding the use of the enterprise's economic resources. Such economic decisions are influenced by the various regulatory agencies, such as the Securities and Exchange Commission (SEC) and the Federal Trade Commission (FTC), so that management is not totally independent. Moreover, regulatory agencies provide a comprehensive set of rules and regulations in order to control the enterprise as well as to safeguard the interests of investors and the general public. For example, the objective of the Federal Trade Commission is to prevent monopolistic practices and price discrimination in American industry. Also, several commissions supervise certain industries, such as the utility and transportation industries, as well as the area of labor-management relations. Particularly important is the government's regulation of the securities market and the taxation process. Such regulation is essential to the economy to eliminate financial abuses and unfair practices in the private sector. Thus the audit committee should be concerned with the reporting requirements of the governmental regulatory agencies.

---

[44]Wal-Mart Stores, Inc., *2003 Annual Report*, pp. 40–42.

The Need for Accounting Information

In order to formulate sound public policies, the regulatory commissions need accounting information concerning the economic activities of the enterprise. In addition, they need accounting information to monitor the corporation's compliance with the governmental rules and regulations. Although there are many regulatory agencies, of particular importance are the Securities and Exchange Commission and the Federal Trade Commission.

Securities and Exchange Commission The principal purpose of the SEC laws is to provide public disclosure of the relevant facts with respect to new securities and securities listed on the stock exchanges.[45] In particular, the SEC requires a registration statement that contains background information, such as the size and competitive position of the corporation. Moreover, a prospective investor must be furnished a prospectus, which is a summary of the registration statement. For example, the prospectus will contain such matters as the offering price of the securities, the use of the proceeds by the registrant, and the financial statements.[46] Furthermore, the SEC requires periodic reports from the corporations in order to update its files on each corporation. Such periodic reports include the annual report (10-K) and interim reports (10-Q and 8-K).[47]

The SEC annual Form 10-K report is used to update the information that is included in the registration statement. This report must be filed within 90 days of the end of a registrant's fiscal year. The report contains this information:

Part I—Item
1. Business
2. Properties
3. Legal proceedings
4. Submission of matters to a note of security holders

Part II—Item
5. Market for the registrant's common stock and related stockholder matters
6. Selected financial data
7. Management's discussion and analysis of financial condition and results of operations
7a. Quantitative and qualitative disclosure about market risk
8. Financial statements and supplementary data
9. Changes in and disagreements with accountants on accounting and financial disclosure

---

[45]Such rules of law are contained in the Accounting Series Releases, Staff Accounting Bulletins, and Financial Reporting Releases of the SEC.
[46]For a complete description of all the items in the prospectus, see Part I of Form S-1, which is the registration statement.
[47]See Appendix C on this book's website for further information. For further details and description of all forms, see Regulation S-X and Regulation S-K. Copies may be obtained from the U.S. Government Printing Office.

Part III—Item
10. Directors and executive officers of the registrant
11. Executive compensation
12. Security ownership of certain beneficial owners and management
13. Certain relationships and related transactions
14. Controls and procedures

Part IV—Item
15. Exhibits, financial statement schedules, and reports on Form 8-K

Signatures
Certification (Sarbanes-Oxley Act, Section 302)
Certification (Sarbanes-Oxley Act, Section 906)

The SEC quarterly Form 10-Q report is used to report interim changes in the financial position and the results of operating the corporation. This particular report must be filed within 45 days after the close of each of the first three quarters for nonaccelerated filers (market capitalization of $75 million or less).

Accelerated filers are required to file their annual report on Form 10-K within 60 days of their fiscal year-end and their quarterly report on Form 10-Q within 35 days of their quarter-end. The new SEC requirement allows for a three-year phase-in of the new rules.[48]

With respect to the financial information, the report contains information on the preparation of financial information, reviews by the independent public accountants, and other financial information. Concerning other information, the report discloses information on such matters as legal proceedings, changes in securities, and other materially important events.

The SEC Form 8-K report is an interim or current report that contains information with respect to certain significant special events. For example, a change in the independent accounting firm must be reported within two business days subsequent to the change. Other events include such items as a change in control of the registrant or significant legal proceedings. This report is particularly important since it provides timely information regarding the disclosure of material events. Consequently, the SEC needs accounting information not only to monitor management's compliance with its rules but also to protect the investing public.

SEC Topical Developments

The SEC has focused on a number of financial reporting areas that relate to the audit committee's oversight responsibility. The more significant developments in these reporting areas are discussed in the next paragraphs.

---

[48]For further information on additional reportable events, see Securities and Exchange Commission, *Acceleration of Periodic Report Filing Dates and Disclosure Concerning Website Access to Reports,* August 27, 2002, *www.sec.gov.*

Management's Discussion and Analysis   The quality of information reported to the SEC concerning Management's Discussion and Analysis (MD&A) of Financial Condition and Results of Operations in the registrant's filings has been of major concern to the investing public and to the SEC. In response, the SEC issued Financial Reporting Release No. 36, which is an interpretive release regarding disclosures required by Item 303 of Regulation S-K with respect to the registrants' filings containing Management's Discussion and Analysis of Financial Condition and Results of Operations.[49] Based on a review project of such filings, the Commission found that several key disclosure matters, namely, prospective information, liquidity and capital resources analysis, material changes in financial statement line items, and business segment analysis, should be considered by registrants in preparing MD&A disclosures. Apparently the SEC determined that interpretive guidance is needed for disclosures concerning the aforementioned matters.

The SEC requires management to discuss favorable or unfavorable trends, significant events, and uncertainties that impact the various reporting areas. Given that MD&A reporting is highly subjective and that management must comply with Item 303 of Regulation S-K, the question is frequently asked: Is the objective of the MD&A disclosure requirement being accomplished? Clearly, the MD&A narrative discussion is the appropriate vehicle to provide early warning signals or red flags to the investing public. As a case in point, *Management Accounting* recently observed that the SEC issued an order complaining about a registrant's MD&A reporting that did not tell investors that nearly 23 percent of its 1989 earnings came from a foreign subsidiary unit—a situation that would not recur. James Adelman of the SEC's Enforcement Division stated, "It will no longer be acceptable for companies to use 'boilerplate' language in MD&As when they know unfolding developments will have an effect on corporate earnings in the future."[50]

In addition to management's involvement with the preparation of MD&A, independent auditors must review this information to ensure that the narrative discussion is not inconsistent with their findings and conclusions regarding their audit report. For example, if management knows of events, trends, or uncertainties that are reasonably likely to occur, then such information should be reported under prospective information. Conversely, if management concludes that events, trends, or uncertainties are not reasonably likely to occur, then no disclosure is required.

---

[49]Securities and Exchange Commission, "Management's Discussion and Analysis of Financial Condition and Results of Operations; Interpretive Release," Title 17, *Code of Federal Regulations,* Secs. 211, 231, 241, and 271 (June 1989), pp. 1–44. *See* Chapter 10 for additional discussion about the application of critical accounting policies.

[50]Stephen Barlas, "SEC Cracks Down on MD&A Sections," *Management Accounting* 73, No. 12 (June 1992), p. 8. See *Accounting and Auditing Enforcement Release No. 363* (March 31, 1992), 51 SEC Docket 300. Also see *Statement on Standards for Attestation Engagements No. 8,* "Management's Discussion and Analysis" (New York: AICPA, 1998), which provides guidance to independent accountants engaged to examine or review MD&A as well as the use of agreed-on procedures; Reva B. Steinberg and Judith Fellner Weiss, "New Rules on Disclosure of Certain Significant Risks and Uncertainties," *CPA Journal* 65, No. 3 (March 1995), pp. 16–20; SEC's interpretation on year 2000 entitled, *Disclosure of Year 2000 Issues and Consequences by Public Companies, Investment Advisers, Investment Companies, and Municipal Securities Issues* (Washington, DC: SEC, 1998).

Thus the reasonably likely standard, and whether management knows of the trends, events, or uncertainties, determines whether such information is disclosed. If management anticipates such trends, events, or uncertainties, then disclosure is optional under prospective information. Professional auditing standards, in particular SAS No. 59, "The Auditor's Consideration of an Entity's Ability to Continue as a Going Concern," dictate that the independent auditors do have the power to issue an unqualified audit report with an explanatory paragraph describing the material uncertainty.[51] This type of audit report gives a warning signal or a red flag to the investing public with respect to the financial condition of the company. Anthony B. Billings and Larry D. Crumbley assert that auditors have a role in signaling a going concern problem. Their role is governed by SAS No. 59, which advances categories of conditions that may arise, including adverse financial ratios, negative trends, and loan defaults.[52] Moreover, John E. Ellingsen, Kurt Pany, and Peg Fagan point out that "an auditor may have designed and performed audit procedures—such as analyzing liquidity ratios—to ascertain whether the entity is complying with certain loan covenants. Evaluation of the liquidity ratios not only assists the auditor vis-à-vis the loan covenants but also helps the auditor evaluate whether the ratios raise doubt about the company's ability to continue as a going concern."[53] Of course, the auditor must consider the conditions and events in the aggregate, so that unfavorable liquidity ratios coupled with declining profitability ratios and increased debt-solvency ratios may cause substantial doubt about the entity's going concern ability. Accordingly, SAS No. 59 requires that the independent auditors evaluate, in every audit engagement, whether there is substantial doubt about the entity's ability to continue as a going concern.

Given the continuing debate over business failure versus audit failure and the continued number of lawsuits against well-known publicly held companies and public accounting firms, it is imperative that the audit committee focus its attention on MD&A disclosures in the financial reporting process. The committee should (1) review and discuss the SEC's mandate concerning MD&A reporting and (2) evaluate management's compliance with the SEC's mandated disclosures and its interpretive release. Clearly, one would expect the audit committee to help improve the quality of MD&A disclosures in light of the SEC's interpretive release. This subject is further discussed in Chapter 10.

An example of disclosure of critical accounting policies of Wal-Mart Stores, Inc. is as follows:

Summary of Critical Accounting Policies

Management strives to report the financial results of the Company in a clear and understandable manner, even though in some cases accounting and disclosure rules are complex and require us to use technical terminology. We follow generally accepted accounting principles in the U.S. in preparing our consolidated financial statements.

---

[51]*Statement of Auditing Standards, No. 59,* "The Auditor's Consideration of an Entity's Ability to Continue as a Going Concern" (New York: AICPA, 1988).

[52]Anthony B. Billings and Larry D. Crumbley, "Financial Difficulties of Governmental Units," *CPA Journal* 58, No. 7 (October 1988), p. 52.

[53]John E. Ellingsen, Kurt Pany, and Peg Fagan, "SAS No. 59: How to Evaluate Going Concern," *Journal of Accountancy* 168, No. 1 (January 1989), p. 27.

These principles require us to make certain estimates and apply judgments that affect our financial position and results of operations. Management continually reviews its accounting policies, how they are applied and how they are reported and disclosed in our financial statements. Following is a summary of our more significant accounting policies and how they are applied in preparation of the financial statements.

Inventories

We use the retail last-in, first -out (LIFO) inventory accounting method for the Wal-Mart Stores segment, cost LIFO for the SAM'S CLUB segment and other cost measures, including the retail first-in, first-out (FIFO) and average cost methods, for the international segment. Inventories are not recorded in excess of market value. Historically, we have rarely experienced significant occurrences of obsolescence or slow-moving inventory. However, future changes in circumstances, such as changes in customer merchandise preference or unseasonable weather patterns, could cause the company's inventory to be exposed to obsolescence or be slow-moving.

Financial Instruments

We use derivative financial instruments for purposes other than trading to reduce our exposure to fluctuations in foreign currencies and to minimize the risk and cost associated with financial and global operating activities. Generally, the contract terms of hedge instruments closely mirror those of the item being hedged, providing a high degree of risk reduction and correlation. Contracts that are highly effective at meeting the risk reduction and correlation criteria are recorded using hedge accounting. On February 1, 2001, we adopted financial Accounting Standards Board (FASB) Statements No. 133, 137, and 138 (collectively "FAS 133") pertaining to the accounting or derivatives and hedging activities. FAS 133 requires all derivatives, which are financial instruments used by the Company to protect (hedge) itself from certain risks, to be recorded on the balance sheet at fair value and establishes accounting treatment for hedges. If a derivative instrument is a hedge, depending on the nature of the hedge, changes in the fair value of the instrument will either be offset against the change in fair value of the hedged assets, liabilities, or firm commitment through earnings or recognized in other comprehensive income until the hedged item is recognized in earnings. The ineffective portion of an instrument's change in fair value will be immediately recognized in earnings. Most of the company's interest rate hedges qualify for the use of the "short-cut" method of accounting to assess hedge effectiveness. The Company uses the hypothetical derivative method to assess the effectiveness of certain of its net investments and cash flow hedges. Instruments that do not meet the criteria for hedge accounting or contracts for which we have not elected hedge accounting are marked to fair value with unrealized gains or losses reported currently in earnings. Fair values are based upon management's expectation of future interest rate curves and may change based upon changes in those expectations.

Impairment of Assets

We periodically evaluate long-lived assets other than goodwill for indicators of impairment and test goodwill for impairment annually. Management's judgments regarding the existence of impairment indicators are based on market conditions and operational performance. Future events could cause management to conclude that impairment indicators exist and that the value of long-lived assets and goodwill associated with acquired businesses is impaired. Goodwill is evaluated for impairment annually under the provisions of FAS 142 which requires us to make judgments relating to future cash flows and growth rates as well as economic and market conditions.

Revenue Recognition

We recognize sales revenue at the time a sale is made to the customer, except for the following types of transactions. Layaway transactions are recognized when the customer satisfies all payment obligations and takes possession of the merchandise. We recognize SAM'S CLUB membership fee revenue over the 12-month term of the membership. Customer purchases of Wal-Mart/SAM'S CLUB shopping cards are not recognized until the card is redeemed and the customer purchases merchandise using the shopping card. Defective merchandise returned by customers is either returned to the supplier or is destroyed and reimbursement is sought from the supplier.

Insurance/Self-Insurance

We use a combination of insurance, self-insured retention, and/or self-insurance for a number of risks including workers' compensation, general liability, vehicle liability and employee-related health care benefits, a portion of which is paid by the Associates. Liabilities associated with the risks that we retain are estimated in part by considering historical claims experience, demographic factors, severity factors and other actuarial assumptions. The estimated accruals for these liabilities could be significantly affected if future occurrences and claims differ from these assumptions and historical trends.

For a complete listing of our accounting policies, please see Note 1 to our consolidated financial statements that appear after this discussion.[54]

Disagreements with the Independent Auditors[55]   As noted in Part II, Item 9, of the SEC annual 10-K report, a registrant is required to disclose disagreements on accounting and financial disclosure between management and the independent auditors. In addition, the SEC requires a registrant to file a Form 8-K and the independent auditors' response with respect to reporting the reasons for changes in independent auditors. This action on the part of the SEC, coupled with Statement on Auditing Standards No. 50, "Reports on the Application of Accounting Principles," is designed to restrict management from audit opinion shopping. Thus, when the principal auditor's client company requests a report on the application of an accounting principle from another accounting firm, the reporting auditor is required to consult with the principal auditor.[56] Such an auditing standard helps ensure the independent auditor's independence.

Environmental Liabilities[57]   The board of directors has oversight responsibility to determine that management is complying with environmental laws. In some industries with significant environmental exposure, board committees may be

---

[54]Wal-Mart Stores, Inc., *2003 Annual Report*, pp. 22–23.

[55]See Jerry E. Serlin, "Shopping Around: A Closer Look at Opinion Shopping," *Journal of Accounting, Auditing & Finance* 9, No. 1 (Fall 1985), pp. 74–80.

[56]*Statement on Auditing Standards, No. 50,* "Reports on the Application of Accounting Principles" (New York: AICPA, 1986), par 1.

[57]A National Priority List of potentially responsible parties (PRPs) is issued by the U.S. Environmental Protection Agency on an annual basis. See also the SEC's SAB No. 92, "Accounting and Disclosures Relating to Loss Contingencies," and the AICPA's Accounting Standard Executive Committee, *Statement of Position (SOP) No. 96-1,* "Environmental Remediation Liabilities" (New York: AICPA, 1996).

appointed to deal with the issue. Whether the full board or a committee is assigned this responsibility, the audit committee should determine that environmental costs and liabilities are properly reflected in the financial statements and related disclosure.

The committee may recommend to the board the establishment and monitoring of an environmental auditing program. See Chapter 10 for further discussion of this subject.

Executive Compensation Disclosure   On October 15, 1992, the SEC adopted amendments to the executive officer and director compensation disclosure requirements applicable to proxy statements, registration statements, and periodic reports (e.g., 10-Qs and 10-K) under the Securities Act of 1933 and the Securities Exchange Act of 1934 (Release Nos. 33-6962, 34-31327, and IC-19032 applicable to Regulation S-K).[58] In sum, executive compensation disclosures for the chief executive officer and the four other highest-paid executives are now required.

Although the compensation committee of the board of directors has oversight responsibility for executive compensation plans, the audit committee should be assured that management has complied with the SEC's new disclosure requirements. The National Association of Corporate Directors has issued the *Report of the NACD Blue Ribbon Commission on Executive Compensation: Guidelines for Corporate Directors*. The disclosure requirements are summarized as follows:

> A summary table containing detailed information on the total compensation for the last three years of the CEO and the four other most highly paid executives (whose annual compensation exceeds $100,000—up from the $60,000 in effect since 1983).

> A compensation committee report describing the factors affecting the committee's decisions regarding executive compensation, and the rationale for CEO compensation.

> A performance graph comparing the company's five-year shareholder returns with those of other companies.

> Option/SAR tables disclosing various information regarding stock options and stock appreciation rights (SARs) including potential appreciation rates and the unrealized gains on outstanding options.

> Other revisions require expanded disclosure of beneficial ownership of a registrant's securities by its executives, incentive stock option repricing, potential lack of independence of compensation committee members, and details of new compensation plans subject to shareholder approval. Required tables and graphs are included in the Appendices of this report.[59]

---

[58]Securities and Exchange Commission, "Executive Compensation Disclosure," Title 17, *Code of Federal Regulations,* Parts 228, 299, 240, and 249 (October 1992). In November 1993, the SEC amended its executive compensation disclosure rules to address such matters as executives covered, restricted stock holdings, option valuations, and peer group index. See the *Federal Register* 58, No. 227 (November 29, 1993), pp. 63010 and 63017, for further details.

[59]National Association of Corporate Directors, *Report of the NACD Blue Ribbon Commission on Executive Compensation: Guidelines for Corporate Directors* (Washington, DC: NACD, 1993), p. 21. See also Report of the NACD Blue Ribbon Commission Executive Compensation: Guidelines for Corporate Directors (Washington DC: NACD, 2000); the NASD's Compensation Committee Manual (Washington DC: NACD, 2002); and James Redda, The Compensation Committee Handbook (New York: John Wiley & Sons, 2000).

Federal Trade Commission   The major objective of the FTC is to police the business community to eliminate unfair methods of competition. Essentially, the FTC is involved with the enforcement of the antitrust laws, such as the Sherman and Clayton acts. Furthermore, the FTC administers the laws concerning the Robinson-Patman Act. The Robinson-Patman Act prohibits big businesses from exploiting their small competitors through price discrimination and quantity discounts. Thus the FTC needs accounting information regarding distribution costs and related prices to ensure that the corporation is not engaged in unlawful pricing practices.

Role of the Audit Committee

Since the corporate annual report and the SEC annual 10-K report must be examined by the independent public accountants, the audit committee should review these reports with the accountants from a compliance perspective. For example, the audit committee should be concerned with the protection of the corporation's interest against penalties or fines regarding any noncompliance with the laws, such as environmental protection laws. Such penalties can be very costly and reduce the earnings performance of the enterprise. Indeed, there are a myriad of complex laws and regulations affecting the corporation. The members of the committee may not have the necessary legal expertise to determine if the firm is complying with the laws. Accordingly, it may be advisable for the committee to retain the corporation's in-house counsel or outside legal counsel to gain assurance regarding management's compliance. Such assistance will enable the committee to be aware of the effect of certain laws on the corporation and thus avoid expensive or embarrassing fines or penalties. More specifically, the audit committee must make an informed judgment on management's efforts to comply with the laws through a review of the corporation's history of compliance and the necessary managerial corrective actions. Thus the committee can minimize the firm's noncompliance liability based on the above procedures.

OTHER OUTSIDE CONSTITUENCIES

Importance of Other Outside Constituencies

With respect to the significance of the other external users of accounting information, the American Assembly concluded that:

> [e]mployees should be regarded as a crucial part of the constituency of the corporation. Employee interests will be better served by various means, such as collective bargaining, direct communications, and participative management approaches rather than by direct employee representation on boards of directors
>
> Consumers have large roles to play. They act as advance guideposts to the needs and expectations of the marketplace. Corporations which enhance their long-term profitability should build relationships with future customers.[60]

---

[60]The American Assembly, *Corporate Governance in America,* Pamphlet 54 (New York: The American Assembly, 1978), p. 6.

Thus it may be appropriate for corporate management to share the accounting information with the above groups, since such groups not only provide services but also receive the goods and services from the enterprise. Because such groups are vital to the successful operation of the corporation, management should consider sharing its accounting information concerning the economic performance of the enterprise. Although there is no uniform pattern in communicating financial accounting information to employees, it may be desirable to consider a special annual report for employees. Similarly, some managements may consider making available a copy of the annual report to special consumer interest groups.

Through an overview of the importance and the need for accounting information, the audit directors can contribute to improving the effectiveness of the audit function in society. Moreover, the Business Roundtable noted that:

> The central corporate governance point to be made about a corporation's stakeholders beyond the shareholder is that they are vital to the long-term successful economic performance of the corporation. Some argue that only the interests of the shareholders should be considered by directors. The thrust of history and law strongly supports the broader view of the directors' responsibility to carefully weigh the interests of all stakeholders as part of their responsibility to the corporation or to the long-term interests of its shareholders.
>
> Resolving the potentially differing interests of various stakeholders and the best long-term interest of the corporation and its shareholders involves compromises and tradeoffs which often must be made rapidly. It is important that all stakeholder interests be considered, but impossible to assure that all will be satisfied because competing claims may be mutually exclusive.[61]

The Need for Accounting Information

A corporation's stakeholders need accounting information in order to judge management's economic decisions and performance. For example, employees are interested in the solvency position of the corporation since they expect to receive wages in return for their services. Moreover, they are interested in the enterprise's image as a corporate citizen of society. Similarly, consumers need accounting information regarding the present and future economic status of the corporation because they rely on the enterprise to provide the necessary goods and services to the community.

Role of the Audit Committee

To enhance the communication process between the enterprise and stakeholder groups, the committee should consult with the executive in charge of the public relations program. For example, the audit directors should satisfy themselves that the information in any special annual reports to employees is consistent with the financial information in the annual or quarterly reports. In addition, the audit committee should review management's commentary in the special reports in view of

---

[61]The Business Roundtable, *Corporate Governance and American Competitiveness,* p. 4.

the quantitative characteristics of financial reporting. As a participative management approach, the committee may suggest an employee report whereby the financial information is related to each employee. Such reports enhance not only the employee's perception of the organization but also his or her work attitude since both corporate management and the employees are contributing to the organizational goals.

Furthermore, the audit directors should determine that adequate management controls exist with respect to the release of special financial reports to the general public, such as newspaper and other releases, to ensure that such releases are appropriate and consistent with the company's policies and plans. In some instances, it may be desirable to clear such distribution of financial information with the audit committee.

AICPA Position

The board of directors of the American Institute of Certified Public Accountants reported a strategy for making financial reports more useful:

> Financial decision-makers confront change on a daily basis. The integration of financial markets, the impact of technology, the entry of new competitors, the introduction of new and more complex financial products—all of these have made investing a different business than it was just a few years ago. These innovations automatically bring with them changes in the kind of financial information needed. If the accounting profession is to fulfill its obligation to the public, it must not remain static.

> The AICPA has launched an effort to ensure that financial reporting moves with the times. Our Special Committee on Financial Reporting is looking at far-reaching ways to make financial reports more relevant to the realities of today's marketplace by anticipating the financial information needs of the 21st century. This is a wide-ranging and intensive effort. We are ruling out no possibilities as we examine what changes to the existing accounting model should be made to meet user needs in the short and long term. We expect the Special Committee to complete its work within a year.

> In the interim, we are taking more immediate steps to improve the utility of financial reports. In this fast-changing economic environment, investors can't afford to look only backwards. They need to anticipate. To serve this need, the AICPA's Accounting Standards Executive Committee, consistent with a recommendation by the POB [Public Oversight Board], has issued a proposal to require management to disclose risks and uncertainties that could significantly affect the company's operations or financial condition. We urge AcSEC [Accounting Standards Executive Committee] to complete its work with all deliberate speed.

> To provide further assurance to the investing public, we join the POB in calling for a statement by management, to be included in the annual report, on the effectiveness of the company's internal controls over financial reporting, accompanied by an auditor's report on management's assertions. An assessment by the independent auditor will provide greater assurance to investors as to management's statement. The internal control system is the main line of defense against fraudulent financial reporting. The investing public deserves an independent assessment of that line of defense, and management should benefit from the auditor's perspective and insights. We urge the SEC to establish this requirement.

Finally, the SEC should require audit committees to include a statement in the annual report describing their responsibilities and how these responsibilities were discharged. This will increase the attention that audit committee members give their crucial responsibilities. It will also increase the attention paid to their views by management and other directors.[62]

IMPORTANT DEVELOPMENTS IN BUSINESS REPORTING AND ASSURANCE SERVICES

This section briefly highlights and discusses the findings and conclusions of two major studies conducted by the AICPA Special Committee on Financial Reporting (Jenkins Committee) and the AICPA Special Committee on Assurance Services (Elliott Committee). The major objective of this review discussion is to provide an understanding of the issues and emerging trends impacting the public accounting profession that, in turn, are of particular concern to audit committees in the latter half of the 1990s.

In 1991, a Special Committee on Financial Reporting (Jenkins Committee) was established by the AICPA to study the need for a new financial reporting model in response to the information needs of users. After completing a three-year study of the financial reporting system in the United States, in 1994 the AICPA Special Committee on Financial Reporting issued its final comprehensive report (202 pages) and summary report (20 pages), entitled *Improving Business Reporting—A Customer Focus: Meeting the Information Needs of Investors and Creditors*. As part of the AICPA's broad initiative to improve the value of business information and the public's confidence in the financial reporting process, the study examined the relevance and usefulness of business reporting and the independent auditors' association with that type of reporting. The Committee set forth these recommendations with respect to four broad categories:

1. Improving the Types of Information in Business Reporting

   Recommendation 1: Standard setters should develop a comprehensive model of business reporting indicating the types and timing of information that users need to value and assess the risk of their investments.

   Recommendation 2: Improve understanding of costs and benefits of business reporting, recognizing that definitive quantification of costs and benefits is not possible.

2. Financial Statements and Related Disclosures

   Recommendation 1: Improve disclosure of business segment information.

   Recommendation 2: Address the disclosures and accounting for innovative financial instruments.

---

[62]American Institute of Certified Public Accountants, *Meeting the Financial Reporting Needs of the Future: A Public Commitment from the Public Accounting Profession* (New York: AICPA, 1993), pp. 3–4. Also see the AICPA Special Committee on Financial Reporting report, *The Information Needs of Investors and Creditors* (New York: AICPA, 1993).

Recommendation 3: Improve disclosures about the identity, opportunities, and risks of off-balance-sheet financing arrangements and reconsider the accounting for those arrangements.

Recommendation 4: Report separately the effects of core and non-core activities and events, and measure at fair value non-core assets and liabilities.

Recommendation 5: Improve disclosures about the uncertainty of measurements of certain assets and liabilities.

Recommendation 6: Improve quarterly reporting by reporting on the fourth quarter separately and including business segment data.

Recommendation 7: Standard setters should search for and eliminate less relevant disclosures.

3. Auditor Association with Business Reporting

Recommendation 1: Allow for flexible auditor association with business reporting, whereby the elements of information on which auditors report and the level of auditor involvement with those elements are decided by agreement between a company and the users of its business reporting.

Recommendation 2: The auditing profession should prepare to be involved with all the information in the comprehensive model, so companies and users can call on it to provide assurance on any of the model's elements.

Recommendation 3: The newly formed AICPA Special Committee on Assurance Services should research and formulate conclusions on analytical commentary in auditors' reports within the context of the Committee's model, focusing on users' needs for information.

Recommendation 4: The profession should continue its projects on other matters related to auditor association with business reporting.

4. Facilitating Change in Business Reporting

Recommendation 1: National and international standard setters and regulators should increase their focus on the information needs of users, and users should be encouraged to work with standard setters to increase the level of their involvement in the standard-setting process.

Recommendation 2: U.S. standard setters and regulators should continue to work with their non-U.S. counterparts and international standard setters to develop international accounting standards, provided the resulting standards meet users' needs for information.

Recommendation 3: Lawmakers, regulators, and standard setters should develop more effective deterrents to unwarranted litigation that discourages companies from disclosing forward-looking information.

Recommendation 4: Companies should be encouraged to experiment voluntarily with ways to improve the usefulness of reporting consistent with the Committee's model. Standard setters and regulators should consider allowing companies that experiment to substitute information specified by the model for information currently required.

---

[63]American Institute of Certified Public Accountants, *Improving Business Reporting—A Customer Focus, Meeting the Information Needs of Investors and Creditors* (New York: AICPA, 1994), 123–127.

Recommendation 5: Standard setters should adopt a longer term focus by developing a vision of the future business environment and users' needs for information in that environment. Standards should be consistent directionally with that long-term vision.

Recommendation 6: Regulators should consider whether there are any alternatives to the current requirement that public companies make all disclosures publicly available.

Recommendation 7: The AICPA should establish a Coordinating Committee charged to ensure that the recommendations in this report are given adequate consideration by those who can act on them.[63]

As a result of the Special Committee's report, standard setters, regulators, professional organizations, professional practitioners, and academicians need to focus their attention on the points of view on the Committee's recommendations. This report has a wealth of information concerning the business reporting model and a comprehensive illustration of the Committee's recommendations. Audit committees should review these recommendations, with particular emphasis on the elements of the Committee's model of business reporting relative to the current model of financial reporting. Additionally, they should discuss the implications for independent auditors.

Recognizing that audit committees have oversight responsibilities for the external audit process, it is desirable to review the Special Committee's form of report that would be issued by the independent auditors. To improve the independent auditors' communications about their role and responsibility, the Committee attempted to articulate an illustrative audit report. This type of report is shown in Exhibit 3.1.

The Committee's proposed audit report is different in several ways from the standard independent auditors' report. First, the introductory paragraph mentions "core earnings" and the audit of the five-year summary of business data and other descriptions. Additionally, the auditors are expressing their opinion on these presentations as opposed to only financial statements. Second, the auditors would be required to substitute the word *presentation* for *financial statement* in the scope paragraph. Finally, the auditors would be required to express two opinions with respect to both financial and nonfinancial data.

Notwithstanding the FASB's current model of financial reporting, the Special Committee has offered 20 recommendations and a comprehensive model of business reporting. In fact, the Committee goes beyond the full disclosure principle with a requirement for disclosure of nonfinancial data. Of course, the major objective is to minimize information overload within the cost-benefit constraint. Moreover, the Committee has broadened the attest function with respect to seven sections of the annual report, as noted in the proposed auditors' report. Regarding flexible auditors' association with business reporting, the Special Committee recommends that the AICPA Special Committee on Assurance Services and the Auditing Standards Board pursue the subject of alternative levels of assurance within the Committee's reporting framework. In sum, the Committee's report is a significant step in the continuous process of improving financial reporting; however, many preparers of financial statements would argue that the cost of implementing

Exhibit 3.1   Report of Independent Accountants

This example illustrates the form of report that would be issued if the independent accountant had been engaged to render an opinion on the entire FauxCom annual report, although this may not always be the case.

We have audited the accompanying consolidated balance sheet of FauxCom, Inc. as of December 31, 1993, and 1992, and the related consolidated statements of core earnings and net income, cash flows, and stockholders' equity for each of the two years in the period ended December 31, 1993. We also audited the five-year summary of business data, the description of information about management and shareholders, and the scope and description of the Company's businesses accompanying the financial statements. These financial statements, five-year summary and descriptions are the responsibility of the Company's management. Our responsibility is to express an opinion on these presentations based on our audits.

We conducted our audits in accordance with generally accepted auditing standards. Those standards require that we plan and perform the audit to obtain reasonable assurance about whether the information presented is free of material misstatement. An audit includes examining, on a test basis, evidence supporting the amounts and disclosures presented. An audit also includes assessing the accounting principles used and significant estimates made by management, as well as evaluating the overall presentation. We believe that our audits provide a reasonable basis for our opinion.

In our opinion, the financial statements referred to above present fairly, in all material respects, the financial position of FauxCom, Inc. as of December 31, 1993, and 1992, and the results of its operations and its cash flows for each of the two years in the period ended December 31, 1993, in conformity with generally accepted accounting principles. It is also our opinion that the five-year summary and descriptions referred to above are fairly presented, in all material respects, in conformity with the applicable standards.

As part of the audit, we also performed such audit procedures as we considered necessary to evaluate management's assumptions and analyses and the preparation and presentation of the information in the following sections of the annual report:

- Current year review
- Management's analysis of financial and non-financial data
- Opportunities and risks, including those resulting from key trends
- Management's plans, including critical success factors
- Comparison of actual business performance to previously disclosed forward-looking information
- Broad objectives and strategies
- Impact of industry structure on the Company

In our opinion, the accompanying sections described above are presented in conformity with the respective standards of presentation, and management has a reasonable basis for the underlying assumptions and analyses reflected in the aforementioned sections.

February 15, 1994
Boston, Massachusetts

Source: American Institute of Certified Public Accountants, *Comprehensive Report of the Special Committee on Financial Reporting* (New York: AICPA, 1994), p. 184.

the recommendations would be prohibitive. Moreover, it is reasonable to expect that many nonpublic companies, particularly small companies, would have difficulty with the Committee's proposals.

In 1995, the AICPA established the Financial Reporting Coordinating Committee to coordinate actions taken on the recommendations made by the Jenkins Committee. Although the Coordinating Committee held a symposium (fall 1996) to continue the discussion of Jenkins Committee's Comprehensive Model for Business Reporting, the debate between the financial statement preparers and users about the aforementioned recommendations continues. However, the Auditing Standards Board has issued a Statement on Standards for Attestation Engagements (SSAE) No. 8, *Management's Discussion and Analysis* (March 1998), in response to the Jenkins Committee's recommendations. Therefore, financial statement preparers and users can engage the accounting profession to provide assurance on the elements of the Comprehensive Model for Business Reporting.[64]

In 1994, a Special Committee on Assurance Services (Elliott Committee) was established by the AICPA to study and report on the current and future assurance needs of all users of both financial statements and nonfinancial information for decision making. After completing a three-year study of the attestation and assurance processes in the United States, this Special Committee completed its work at the end of December 1996. Similar to the previously mentioned Financial Reporting Coordinating Committee, an Assurance Services Committee was formed by the AICPA to follow up on the findings and conclusions made by the Elliott Committee and communicate new assurance opportunities for AICPA members. The concept of assurance services includes all attestation services with a particular emphasis on enhancing the quality of information through individualized services for decision-making purposes.

As a basis for developing the new concept of assurance services, the Elliott Committee studied such research areas as users' needs for information, megatrends impacting such needs for information, information technology affecting the use of information, and practitioner competencies needed to provide the necessary assurance on the aforementioned information.

Based on the above research areas, the Elliott Committee developed business plans for six initial assurance services, including:

- *Risk Assessment.* This service assures that an entity's profile of business risks is comprehensive and evaluates whether the entity has appropriate systems in place to manage those risks effectively.

- *Business Performance Measurement.* This service evaluates whether an entity's performance measurement system contains relevant and reliable measures for assessing the degree to which the entity's goals and objectives are achieved or how its performance compares to its competitors.

---

[64]For further discussion regarding an examination, review, or an agreed-on procedure engagement, see SSAE No. 8. Also see James L. Craig, "The CPA Journal Symposium on Recommendations for Improving Business Reporting," *CPA Journal* 65, No. 1 (January 1995), pp. 18–27; Daniel J. Noll and Jerry J. Weygandt, "Business Reporting: What Comes Next?" *Journal of Accountancy* 183, No. 2 (February 1997), p. 59.

- *Information Systems Reliability.* This service assesses whether an entity's internal information systems (financial and nonfinancial) provide reliable information for operating and financial decisions.

- *Electronic Commerce.* This service assesses whether systems and tools used in electronic commerce provide appropriate data integrity, security, privacy, and reliability.

- *Health Care Performance Measurement.* This service provides assurance about the effectiveness of health care services provided by health maintenance organizations (HMOs), hospitals, doctors, and other providers.

- *Elder Care Plus.* This service assesses whether specified goals regarding care for the elderly are being met by various caregivers.[65]

Finally, audit committee members should be aware that, in September 1997, the AICPA and the Canadian Institute of Chartered Accountants implemented an electronic commerce service called the CPA Web Trust (a seal of assurance for on-line customers that a business adheres to standards for disclosure, transaction integrity, and information protection). See the AICPA web site, *www.aicpa.org*, or the Committee's report, which is available on CD-ROM.[66]

Indeed, there is little doubt that the AICPA's call for action will further impact on the duties and responsibilities of audit committee members.

In October 2002, the General Accounting Office (GAO) issued a report entitled *Financial Statement Restatements: Trends, Market Impacts, Regulatory Responses, and Remaining Challenges.* The GAO reported that a number of well-publicized announcements about financial statements restatements by large, well-known public companies have erased billions of dollars of previously reported earnings and raised questions about the credibility of accounting practices and the quality of corporate final disclosure and oversight in the United States.[67]

In sum, the GAO's principal findings were:

- The number of restatements due to accounting irregularities grew significantly—by 145 percent—from January 1997 through June 2002.

- The 845 restating companies identified by the GAO had restated their financial statements to adjust revenues, costs, or expenses or to address securities-related issues.

- Issues involving revenue recognition accounted for almost 38 percent of the restatements.

---

[65]American Institute of Certified Public Accountants, *Special Committee on Assurance Services, www.aicpa.org*, 1996.

[66]Also see Robert K. Elliott, "The Future of Assurance Services: Implications for Academia," *Accounting Horizons* 9, No. 4 (December 1995), pp. 118–127; Robert K. Elliott and Donald M. Pallais, four-part series dealing with the future of Assurance Services, *Journal of Accountancy* 183, Nos. 6, 7, 8, 9 (June, July, August, September 1997).

[67]U.S. General Accounting Office, *Financial Statement Restatements: Trends, Market Impact, Regulatory Responses, and Remaining Challenges* GAO-03-138, October 4, 2002, *www.gao.gov/gao-03-138.*

- Of the 845 restating companies, 689 companies lost billions of dollars in market capitalization in the days around the initial reinstatement announcement.[68]

Recognizing that these losses have shaken investors' confidence in the nation's financial reporting system, the GAO believes that the Sarbanes-Oxley Act of 2002 addresses the financial statement restatements concerns, including strengthening corporate governance and improving transparency and accountability to help ensure the accuracy and integrity of its financial reporting system.

Given the recent failures of major corporations, such as Enron, WorldCom, Adelphia, and Global Crossing, the government's increased scrutiny of the accounting profession and the enactment of the Sarbanes-Oxley Act of 2002 have triggered many new legal and regulatory reforms, as discussed in Chapter 1 and Chapter 2. Notwithstanding the demise of the AICPA's Independence Standards Board, Public Oversight Board, and the Auditing Standards Board, for publicly held companies the new Public Company Accounting Oversight Board not only will have oversight and enforcement authority, but also will promulgate auditing, quality control, and independence standards for the accounting profession. Historically, many of the AICPA's Special Committees on financial reporting and POB's blue ribbon panels and committees have served as platforms for the issuance of standards and rules.

It is not known to what extent the new PCAOB will promulgate standards and rules to close the expectations gap. However, the need for reliable and relevant financial information remains of utmost importance to ensure an efficient capital market system.

In an effort to enhance financial reporting and provide guidance for the participants in the financial reporting process (financial statement preparers, auditors, and audit committees), the five largest accounting firms in he United States and the American Institute of Certified Public Accountants set forth these recommended actions as common goals:

Management

- Ensure the proper tone at the top and an expectation that only the highest-quality financial reporting is acceptable.
- Review all elements of the company's internal control—control environment, risk assessment, control activities, information and communication, and monitoring—in light of changes in the company's business environment and with particular attention to significant financial statement areas.
- Ensure the appropriate levels of management involvement and review exist over key accounting policy and financial reporting decisions.
- Establish a framework for open, timely communication with the auditors and the audit committee on all significant matters.
- Strive for the highest quality, most transparent accounting and disclosure—not just what is acceptable—in both financial statements and MD&A.

---

[68]Ibid., p. 1.

- Make sure estimates and judgments are supported by reliable information and the most reasonable assumptions in the circumstances, and that processes are in place to ensure consistent application from period to period.
- Record identified audit differences.
- Base business decisions on economic reality rather than accounting goals.
- Expand the depth and disclosure surrounding subjective measurements used in preparing the financial statements, including the likelihood and ramifications of subsequent changes.
- When faced with a "gray" area, consult with others, consider the need for SEC pre-clearance, and focus on the transparency of financial reporting.

Auditors

- Understand how a company is affected by changes in the current business environment.
- Understand the stresses on the company's internal control over financial reporting, and how they may impact its effectiveness.
- Identify key risk areas, particularly those involving significant estimates and judgments.
- Approach the audit with objectivity and skepticism, notwithstanding prior experiences with or belief in management's integrity.
- Pay special attention to complex transactions, especially those presenting difficult issues of form versus substance.
- Consider whether additional specialized knowledge is needed on the audit team.
- Make management aware of identified audit differences on a timely basis.
- Question the unusual and challenge anything that doesn't make sense.
- Foster open, ongoing communications with management and the audit committee, including discussions about the quality of financial reporting and any pressure to accept less than high-quality financial reporting.
- When faced with a "gray" area, perform appropriate procedures to test and corroborate management's explanations and representations, and consult with others as needed.

Audit Committees

- Evaluate whether management exhibits the proper tone at the top and fosters a culture and environment that promotes high-quality financial reporting, including addressing internal control issues.
- Question management and auditors about how they assess the risk of material misstatement, what the major risk areas are, and how they respond to identified risks.
- Challenge management and the auditors to identify the difficult areas (e,g., significant estimates and judgments) and explain fully how they each made their judgments in those areas.
- Probe how management and the auditors have reacted to changes in the company's business environment.

- Understand why critical accounting principles were chosen and how they were applied and changed, and consider the quality of financial reporting and the transparency of disclosures about accounting principles.

- Challenge management for explanations of any identified audit differences not recorded.

- Understand the extent to which related parties exist and consider the transparency of the related disclosures.

- Read the financial statements and MD&A to see if anything is inconsistent with your own knowledge.

- Consider whether the readers of the financial statements and the MD&A will be able to understand the disclosures and the risks of the company without the access to management that the committee enjoys.

- Ask the auditors about pressure by management to accept less than high-quality financial reporting.

- When faced with a "gray" area, increase the level of communication with management and the auditors.

Management, auditors, and audit committees each must diligently fulfill its own role and effectively work together with the others through proactive communication and information sharing. In working together, we can collectively improve the financial reporting process. This requires renewed commitment by each of the parties to the needs of financial statement users.[69]

SOURCES AND SUGGESTED READINGS

The American Assembly, *Corporate Governance in America,* Pamphlet 54 (New York: Columbia University, April 1978).

The American Assembly, *The American Assembly Report 1991–1992* (New York: The American Assembly, 1992).

American Institute of Certified Public Accountants, *Report of the Study Group on the Objectives of Financial Statements* (New York: AICPA, 1973).

American Institute of Certified Public Accountants, *Accounting Trends and Techniques— 1990* (New York: AICPA, 1990).

American Institute of Certified Public Accountants, *Improving Business Reporting—A Customer Focus, Meeting the Information Needs of Investors and Creditors* (New York: AICPA, 1994).

American Institute of Certified Public Accountants, "Impact of the Current Economic and Business Environment on Financial Reporting" (2000), pp. 1–11, *www.aicpa.org.*

American Stock Exchange, *American Stock Exchange Fact Book 1991* (New York: ASE, 1991).

---

[69]American Institute of Certified Public Accountants, "Impact of the Current Economic and Business Environment on Financial Reporting" (2000), pp. 10–11, *www.aicpa.org.*

Association for Investment Management and Research, *Corporate Information Committee Report 1995–1996* (New York: Association for Investment Management and Research, 1997).

Barlas, Stephen, "SEC Cracks Down on MD&A Sections." *Management Accounting* 73, No. 12 (June 1992), p. 8.

Billings, Anthony B., and Larry D. Crumbley, "Financial Difficulties of Governmental Units." *CPA Journal* 58, No. 7 (October 1988), pp. 52–61.

BSB Bancorp, Inc. *2002 Annual Report.*

The Business Roundtable, *Corporate Governance and American Competitiveness* (New York: The Business Roundtable, 1990).

Coben, Chad F., "Implementing SFAS No. 105's Disclosure Requirements." *Journal of Commercial Landing* 74, No. 7 (March 1992), pp. 13–23.

Cox, George, H. Stephen Grace Jr., John E. Haupert, Peter Howell, and Ronald H. Wilcomes, "A Prescription for Company Health." *CPA Journal* 72, No. 7 (July 2002), pp. 62–63.

Davis, Ann, "SEC Case Claims Profit 'Management' by Grace." *Wall Street Journal* (April 7, 1999), p. C1.

Dougherty, William H., "Financial Reporting—A Banker Looks at the Scene." *Financial Executive*, 46, No. 12 (December 1978), pp. 47–53.

Ellingsen, John E., Kurt Pany, and Peg Fagan, "SAS No. 59: How to Evaluate Going Concern." *Journal of Accountancy* 168, No. 1 (January 1989), p. 27.

Financial Accounting Standards Board, *Statement of Financial Accounting Concepts No. 1* (Stamford, CT.: FASB, 1978).

Financial Accounting Standards Board, *Statement of Financial Accounting Standards, No. 95,* "Statement of Cash Flows" (Stamford,CT.: FASB, 1987).

Financial Accounting Standards Board, *Statement of Financial Accounting Standards, No. 105,* "Disclosure of Information About Financial Instruments with Off-Balance Sheet Risk and Financial Instruments with Concentrations of Credit Risk" (Norwalk, CT.: FASB, 1990).

Financial Accounting Standards Board, *Statement of Financial Accounting Standards No. 107,* "Disclosures About Fair Value of Financial Instruments" (Norwalk, CT.: FASB, 1991).

Financial Accounting Standards Board, *Statement of Financial Accounting Standards, No. 133,* "Accounting for Derivative Instruments and Hedging Activities" (Norwalk, CT.: FASB, 1998).

Financial Accounting Standards Board, *Statement of Financial Accounting Concepts No. 7,* "Using Cash Flow Information and Present Value in Accounting Measurement," (Stamford, CT.: FASB, 2000).

Financial Analysts Federation, "Awards for Excellence in Corporate Reporting," *Financial Analysts Federation News Release* (January 1978).

Grusd, Neville, "The Enron Affair from a Lender's View." *CPA Journal* 72, No. 12 (December 2002), pp. 8–10.

Investor Responsibility Research Center, *Annual Report 1992* (Washington, DC: Investor Responsibility Research Center, 1992).

Krishnamoorthy, Ganesh, Arnie Wright, and Jeffrey Cohen. "Auditors' Views on Audit Committees and Financial Reporting Quality." *CPA Journal, 72* No. 10, (October 2002), pp. 56–57.

Lubow, Nathan M., "New Disclosures FASB No. 105." *Secured Lender* 48, No. 6 (November/December 1992), pp. 112, 114.

MacIver, Brian H., James Welch, and Priscilla A. Burnaby, "Quality Review—Observations of a Team Captain." *Ohio CPA Journal* 50, No. 1 (January–April 1991), pp. 54–55.

Most, Kenneth S., and Lucia S. Chang, "An Empirical Study of Investor Views Concerning Financial Statements and Investment Decisions," *Collected Papers of the American Accounting Association's Annual Meeting* (Sarasota, FL.: American Accounting Association, August 20–23, 1978), pp. 241–260.

National Association of Corporate Directors, *Report of the NACD Blue Ribbon Commission on Executive Compensation: Guidelines for Corporate Directors* (Washington, DC: NACD, 1993).

New York Stock Exchange, *New York Stock Exchange Fact Book 1992* (New York: NYSE, 1992).

Pate, Gwen Richardson, and Keith G. Stanga, "A Guide to the FASB's Concepts Statements." *Journal of Accountancy* 168, No. 2 (August 1989), pp. 28–31.

Rubin, Steven, "How Concepts Statements Can Solve Practice Problems." *Journal of Accountancy* 166, No. 4 (October 1988), pp. 123–124, 126.

Securities and Exchange Commission, "Management's Discussion and Analysis of Financial Condition and Results of Operations; Interpretive Release," Title 17 *Code of Federal Regulations,* Sec. 211, 231, 241, and 271 (June 1989), pp. 1–44.

Securities and Exchange Commission, *Accounting and Auditing Enforcement Release No. 363* (March 31, 1992), 51 SEC Docket 300.

Securities and Exchange Commission, "Executive Compensation Disclosure," Title 17 *Code of Federal Regulations,* Parts 228, 229, 240, and 249 (October 1989). See Rules and Regulations, *Federal Register,* 57, No. 204 (October 21, 1992), pp. 48126–48159.

Securities and Exchange Commission, *1992 Annual Report* (Washington, DC: U.S. Government Printing Office, 1992).

Securities and Exchange Commission, *1997 Annual Report* (Washington, DC: U.S. Government Printing Office, 1997).

Securities and Exchange Commission, *1998 Annual Report* (Washington, DC: U.S. Government Printing Office, 1998).

Securities and Exchange Commission, *1999 Annual Report* (Washington, DC: U.S. Government Printing Office, 1999).

Securities and Exchange Commission, *In the Matter of W.R. Grace & Co., Release No. 34-41578.* Accounting and Auditing Enforcement Release No. 1140 (June 30, 1999).

Securities and Exchange Commission, *2002 Annual Report* (Washington, DC: U.S. Government Printing Office, 2002).

Securities and Exchange Commission, *Acceleration of Periodic Report Filing Dates and Disclosure Concerning Website Access to Reports* (August 27, 2002), *www.sec.gov.*

Serlin, Jerry E., "Shopping Around: A Closer Look at Opinion Shopping." *Journal of Accounting, Auditing & Finance 9,* No. 1 (Fall 1985), pp. 74–80.

SRI International, *Investor Informational Needs and the Annual Report,* Financial Executive Research Foundation (Morristown, NJ: Financial Executive Institute, 1987).

Stanga, Keith G., and James J. Benjamin, "Information Needs of Bankers." *Management Accounting* 59, No. 12 (June 1978), pp. 17–21.

Statement on Auditing Standards No. 25, "The Relationship of Generally Accepted Auditing Standards to Quality Control Standards" (New York: AICPA, 1979).

Statement on Auditing Standards No. 50, "Reports on the Application of Accounting Principles" (New York: AICPA, 1986).

Statement on Auditing Standards No. 59, "The Auditor's Consideration of an Entity's Ability to Continue as a Going Concern" (New York: AICPA, 1988).

Statement on Auditing Standards No. 69, "The Meaning of Present Fairly in Conformity with Generally Accepted Accounting Principles in the Independent Auditor's Report" (New York: AICPA, 1992).

Statement on Auditing Standards No. 90, "Audit Committee Communications" (New York: AICPA, 1999).

U.S. General Accounting Office, *Financial Statement Restatements: Trends, Market Impacts, Regulatory Responses, and Remaining Challenges GAO-03-138* (October 4, 2002), *www.gao.gov/gao-03-138.*

Wal-Mart Stores, Inc., Audit Committee Charter 2003 *www.walmartstores.com*, pp. 1–7.

Wal-Mart Stores, Inc., *2003 Annual Report.*

Chapter 4

The Legal Position of the Audit Committee

Recall from the discussion in Chapter 2 that the Sarbanes-Oxley Act of 2002 and the SEC final rules regarding the composition, roles, and responsibilities of audit committees have established a specific body of law that governs audit committees. Likewise, the legal obligations of audit committee members are manifested in state corporation laws and certain other federal statutes regarding directorate responsibilities. The purpose of this chapter is to review the general legal responsibilities of the committee as well as several legal cases involving the committee. In addition, securities litigation (see Exhibit 4.1) and the guidelines for minimizing the committee's possible legal liability are presented to put the legal position of the audit directors in proper perspective.[1]

The latter portion of Chapter 2 described the legal environment of audit committees under the federal statute and amendments to the federal securities laws. Although the legal provisions are not repeated in this chapter, these three points are reemphasized:

1. The Sarbanes-Oxley Act significantly increases the audit committee's responsibilities, including the cost of directors and officers liability insurance.
2. To help the boards of directors fulfill their fiduciary responsibilities to the stockholders, audit committees should consider their use of authority under Section 301 of the act to engage independent counsel and other advisers. In contrast, the audit committee's legal responsibilities under general corporate law are similar because they may rely on accounting, legal, or other experts when acting in good faith. Such action could be considered an act of due diligence. Such inaction could be considered an act of malfeasance.
3. Finally, the roles, responsibilities, and functions of audit committees should be specific and in compliance with the laws and regulations. The major objective is to avoid additional responsibilities that make the audit committee members vulnerable to claims of a breach of fiduciary responsibilities. (For further information regarding such matters as the business judgment rule, see the Delaware Court of Chancery, *In Re Caremark International Inc. Derivative Litigation*, 698 A. 2d 959 (Del. Ch. 1996) and the section on legal cases in this chapter. Also see William C. Powers, *Report of Investigation by the Special Investigative Committee of the Board of Directors of Enron Corporation* (February 1, 2002) at *www.news.findlaw.com/hdocs/docs/enron/sicreport/*).

---

[1] Although reference is made to both the federal and state statutes, such references provide only a description of the law. One should have recourse to legal counsel for the appropriate legal interpretation.

GENERAL LEGAL RESPONSIBILITIES

State Statutes

Although the board of directors has the statutory power to establish standing committees of the board, several state corporation laws limit the board's powers to delegate authority and responsibility. For example, the New York statute provides that:

> . . . No such committee shall have authority as to the following matters:
>
> 1. The submission to shareholders of any action that needs shareholder's authorization under this chapter
> 2. The filling of vacancies in the board of directors or in any committee
> 3. The fixing of compensation of the directors for serving on the board or on any committee
> 4. The amendment or repeal of the bylaws, or the adoption of new bylaws
> 5. The amendment or repeal of any resolution of the board which by its terms shall not be so amendable or repealable[2]

Thus the audit committee has limited authority; however, such authority is discretionary because the audit directors can exercise their own judgment in the interest of the board. Moreover, the audit committee, since it is formally constituted, is free to meet in between the board meetings.

More important, each member of the board of directors and the standing committees has a statutory duty of care because of the fiduciary relationship between the directors and the corporation. With respect to the duties of the directors and officers, the New York statute indicates:

> Directors and officers shall discharge the duties of their respective positions in good faith and with that degree of diligence, care and skill which ordinarily prudent men would exercise under similar circumstances in like positions. In discharging their duties, directors and officers, when acting in good faith, may rely upon financial statements of the corporation represented to them to be correct by the president or the officer of the corporation having charge of its books of accounts, or stated in a written report by an independent public or certified public accountant or firm of such accountants fairly to reflect the financial condition of such corporations.[3]

Furthermore, since the directors serve the corporation in a fiduciary capacity, their statutory duty of care cannot be delegated because of the personal nature of the director's relationship with the corporation. Hence although the audit committee can make recommendations to the entire board, the final decisions are made by the board because it has overall responsibility for the committee's actions. In short, the standing committees of the board cannot eliminate each director's duties and obligations because of the fiduciary principle.

---

[2]New York Business Corporation Law, Sec. 712, *McKinney's Consolidated Laws of New York Annotated*, Book 6 (Brooklyn, NY: Edward Thompson Company, 1963).
[3]Ibid., Sec. 717.

Particularly important to the concept of the duty of care is the degree of care. To measure its reasonableness, several state corporation laws provide a business judgment rule. Such a rule protects the directors against personal liability on the presumption that they acted not only in good faith but also exercised reasonable care and prudence regarding their decisions. Thus, in the absence of fraud, bad faith, or negligence, a director cannot be held personally liable concerning matters of corporate policy and business judgment.[4]

Furthermore, the directors may be personally liable for negligence with respect to losses suffered by the corporation.[5] The directors can be held jointly and severally liable to the corporation whereby an injured stockholder or creditor can recover a loss from the individual director, several directors, or the full board. For example, if the directors vote to declare dividends from the corporation's capital rather than from its retained earnings, then they are liable because their actions constitute an unauthorized dividend distribution.[6]

Equally important, directors have a duty of loyalty regarding their activities with the corporation. They cannot exploit the corporation for personal gain because of their fiduciary relationship. For example, if a director has a personal interest in a particular corporate transaction, then the director should disassociate him- or herself from the transaction because of the apparent conflict of interest. Thus, each director has an "undivided loyalty and an allegiance" with respect to the interests of the corporation and stockholders.[7]

Moreover, in 1978 the American Bar Association amended Section 35 of its Model Business Corporation Act, which, if adopted as part of the state corporation statutes, increases a director's reliance on the board's standing committees. Specifically, the amendment provides that a director may rely on the information that is presented by a committee although the director is not a member of this group. Such reliance on the board committee is based on the director's confidence in the committee. However, when relying on the committee, the director must adhere to the duty-of-care principle whereby the director should be familiar with the committee's activities. In short, the amendment allows a director to rely on the work of a committee that has an oversight or supervisory responsibility, such as the audit committee. Accordingly, the amendment poses certain questions regarding the legal implications of the committee since it appears that a noncommittee director may be exonerated from any potential liability provided that he or she has exercised his or her duty of care.[8]

---

[4]Ibid.

[5]For example, if it can be proven that a director has breached his or her fiduciary duty to the corporation, then the director may be held personally liable for the losses suffered by the corporation.

[6]New York Business Corporation Law, Sec. 719.

[7]Ibid., Sec. 717.

[8]American Bar Association, *Corporate Director's Guidebook* (Chicago: ABA, 1978), p. 42. Also see American Bar Association, *Corporate Director's Guidebook,* 2nd ed. (Chicago: ABA, 1994). Finally, the reader may wish to review the *Escott v. BarChris Construction Corp.* case, 283 F, Supp. 643 (S.D.N.Y. 1968), which deals with the standard of differential liability. In short, the court states that a director with a particular expertise and access to information may be held to a higher standard of liability. Of course, the performance of individual audit committee members is based on their skills and qualifications and access to information. Thus a member with an accounting background would be more aware of the accounting and auditing implications than would be a member without this expertise.

The state of Connecticut has enacted legislation that requires companies incorporated with at least 100 stockholders to establish an audit committee. In Sections 33-318(b)(1) and 33-318(b)(2), the statute defines the standard of independence and the functions of the audit committee. See the Connecticut General Statutes Annotated in West 1960 and Supplement 1985 (Eagan, MN.: West Publishing Corporation) for further details.

In 1984, the American Bar Association adopted a Revised Model Business Corporation Act. In 1998, the American Bar Association adopted the Model Business Corporate Act. Section 8.25 of the act stipulates that a board of directors may create standing committees, such as an audit committee. This stipulation is consistent with the statutory provisions at the state level. In addition, Section 8.3(0), which deals with the standards of conduct for directors, indicates that a director is entitled to rely on information, opinions, reports, or statements—including financial statements—prepared by officers of the corporation and public accountants. A director is also entitled to rely on the opinions of legal counsel as well as on the work of a standing committee of the board of which he or she is not a member. Thus the American Bar Association has reaffirmed its position with respect to good-faith reliance on officers, public accountants, legal counsel, and committee members of the board. (See Appendix F on this book's website.)

Federal Statutes—Key Sections

In addition to their legal responsibilities at the state level, the directors have a legal liability at the federal level. The federal statutes that are particularly important are summarized below.

Securities Act of 1933   Although this particular act provides financial information regarding the public sale of securities, it is needed "to prohibit misrepresentation, deceit, and other fraudulent acts and practices in the sale of securities."[9] In particular, this act provides for civil liability of the directors with respect to fraud in the registration statement. Section 11(a) of the act provides that:

(1) In case any part of the registration statement, when such part became effective, contained an untrue statement of a material fact or omitted to state a material fact required to be stated therein or necessary to make the statement therein not misleading, any person acquiring such security (unless it is proved that at the time of such acquisition he knew of such untruth or omission) may, either at law or in equity, in any court of competent jurisdiction, sue—

(2) Every person who was a director of . . . the issuer at the time of the filing of the part of the registration statement . . .[10]

---

[9]Securities and Exchange Commission, *The Work of the Securities and Exchange Commission* (Washington, DC: U.S. Government Printing Office, 1974), p. 1.
[10]U.S. Code, Title 15, Sec. 77k.

In order to avoid any liability, Sections 11(b) and 11(c) of the act provide:

Notwithstanding the provisions of subsection (a) of this section no person, other than the issuer, shall be liable as provided therein who shall sustain the burden of proof

(1) that before the effective date of the part of the registration statement with respect to which his liability is asserted (A) he had resigned from or had taken such steps as are permitted by law to resign from, or ceased or refused to act in, every office, capacity, or relationship in which he was described in the registration statement as acting or agreeing to act, and (B) he had advised the Commission and the issuer in writing that he had taken such action and that he would not be responsible for such part of the registration statement; or

(2) that if such part of the registration statement became effective without his knowledge, upon becoming aware of such fact he forthwith acted and advised the Commission, in accordance with paragraph (1) of this subsection, and, in addition, gave reasonable public notice that such part of the registration statement had become effective without his knowledge, or

(3) that (A) as regards any part of the registration statement not purporting to be made on the authority of an expert, and not purporting to be a copy of or extract from a report or valuation of an expert, and not purporting to be made on the authority of a public official document or statement, he had, after reasonable investigation, reasonable ground to believe and did believe, at the time such part of the registration statement became effective, that the statements therein were true and that there was no omission to state a material fact required to be stated therein or necessary to make the statements therein not misleading; and (B) as regards any part of the registration statement purporting to be made upon his authority as an expert or purporting to be a copy of or extract from a report or valuation of himself as an expert, (i) he had, after reasonable investigation, reasonable ground to believe and did believe at the time such part of the registration statement became effective, that the statements therein were true and that there was no omission to state a material fact required to be stated therein or necessary to make the statements therein not misleading, or (ii) such part of the registration statement did not fairly represent his statement as an expert or was not a fair copy of or extract from his report or valuation as an expert; and (C) as regards any part of the registration statement purporting to be made on the authority of an expert (other than himself) or purporting to be a copy of or extract from a report or valuation of an expert (other than himself), he had no reasonable ground to believe and did not believe, at the time such part of the registration statement became effective, that the statements therein were untrue or that there was an omission to state a material fact required to be stated therein or necessary to make the statements therein not misleading, or that such part of the registration statement did not fairly represent the statement of the expert or was not a fair copy of or extract from the report of valuation of the expert; and (D) as regards any part of the registration statement purporting to be a statement made by an official person or purporting to be a copy of or extract from a public official document, he had no reasonable ground to believe and did not believe, at the time such part of the registration statement became effective, that the statements therein were untrue, or that there was an omission to state a material fact required to be stated therein or necessary to make the statements therein not misleading, or that such part of the registration

statement did not fairly represent the statement made by the official person or was not a fair copy of or extract from the public official document.

In determining, for the purpose of paragraph (3) of subsection (b) of this section, what constitutes reasonable investigation and reasonable ground for belief, the standard of reasonableness shall be that required of a prudent man in the management of his property.[11]

Furthermore, Section 12 of the act provides additional liability regarding any transactions that are false or misleading in connection with the issuance of the securities. Thus a director has not only a potential liability with respect to the registration statement but also a liability concerning the written and/or oral representations in the offering prospectus.[12]

Section 13 of the act establishes a limitation in order to enforce a civil action against the wrongdoers.

No action shall be maintained to enforce any liability created under section 77k or 77l (2) of this title unless brought within one year after the discovery of the untrue statement or the omission, or after such discovery should have been made by the exercise of reasonable diligence, or, if the action is to enforce a liability created under section 77l (1) of this title, unless brought within one year after the violation upon which it is based. In no event shall any such action be brought to enforce a liability created under section 77k or 77l (1) of this title more than three years after the security was bona fide offered to the public, or under section 77l (2) of this title more than three years after the sale.[13]

Finally, these penalties may be assessed under the Securities Act of 1933.

Any person who willfully violates any of the provisions of this subchapter, or the rules and regulations promulgated by the Commission under authority thereof, or any person who willfully, in a registration statement filed under this subchapter, makes any untrue statement of a material fact or omits to state any material fact required to be stated therein or necessary to make the statements therein not misleading, shall upon conviction be fined not more than $5,000 or imprisoned not more than five years, or both.[14]

Securities Exchange Act of 1934   The primary purpose of this act is to regulate the public sales of the securities through the securities exchanges or brokers after the original sale of the securities. This act also provides the impetus for the Securities and Exchange Commission. More specifically, Section 18 of the act provides this liability for misleading statements:

(a) Any person who shall make or cause to be made any statement in any application, report, or document filed pursuant to this chapter or any rule or regulation thereunder or any undertaking contained in a registration statement as provided

---

[11]Ibid., Sec. 77 k.
[12]U.S. Code, Title 15, Sec. 77l.
[13]U.S. Code, Title 15, Sec. 77m.
[14]U.S. Code, Title 15, Sec. 77x.

in subsection (d) of section 78o of this title, which statement was at the time and in the light of the circumstances under which it was made false or misleading with respect to any material fact, shall be liable to any person (not knowing that such statement was false or misleading) who, in reliance upon such statement, shall have purchased or sold a security at a price which was affected by such statement, for damages caused by such reliance, unless the person sued shall prove that he acted in good faith and had no knowledge that such statement was false or misleading. A person seeking to enforce such liability may sue at law or in equity in any court of competent jurisdiction. In any such suit the court may, in its discretion, require an undertaking for the payment of the costs of such suit, and assess reasonable costs, including reasonable attorney's fees, against either party litigant.

(c) No action shall be maintained to enforce any liability created under this section unless brought within one year after the discovery of the facts constituting the cause of action and within three years after such cause of action accrued.[15]

In contrast to the 1933 act, a plaintiff must prove that he or she relied on a misstatement of fact or omission of fact in the financial statements and as a result suffered a loss.

Furthermore, Section 10(b) of the act establishes an antifraud provision, which indicates that it is illegal "to use or employ . . . any manipulative or deceptive devices" regarding the security transactions.[16] Equally important, the SEC enacted Rule 10 (b)-5, which provides the following:

It shall be unlawful for any person, directly or indirectly, by the use of any means . . .

(a) to employ any device, scheme, or artifice to defraud,

(b) to make any untrue statement of a material fact or to omit to state a material fact necessary in order to make the statements made, in the light of the circumstances under which they were made, not misleading, or,

(c) to engage in any act, practice, or course of business which operates or would operate as a fraud or deceit upon any person, in connection with purchase or sale of any security.[17]

Thus Rule 10 (b)-5 can hold directors liable primarily because of clause (b). In short, this particular rule increases the director's liability, which did not exist under the provisions of the act.

In addition, the 1934 act provides these penalties:

(a) Any person who willfully violates any provision of this chapter, or any rule or regulation thereunder the violation of which is made unlawful or the observance of which is required under the terms of this chapter, or any person who willfully and knowingly makes, or causes to be made, any statement in any application, report, or document required to be filed under this chapter or any rule or

---

[15]U.S. Code, Title 15, Sec. 78r.
[16]U.S. Code, Title 15, Sec. 78j.
[17]Code of Federal Regulations, Sec. 240, 10(b)-5.

regulation thereunder or any undertaking contained in a registration statement as provided in subsection (d) of section 78o of this title, which statement was false or misleading with respect to any material fact, shall upon conviction be fined not more than $10,000, or imprisoned not more than two years, or both, except that when such person is an exchange, a fine not exceeding $500,000 may be imposed; but no person shall be subject to imprisonment under this section for the violation of any rule or regulation if he proves that he had no knowledge of such rule or regulation.[18]

Several additional federal acts are briefly set forth below. (See Chapter 1 for other congressional legislation and Appendixes E and F for the Foreign Corrupt Practices Act with amendments and the Federal Deposit Insurance Corporation Improvement Act of 1991 on this book's website.)

The Private Securities Reform Act of 1995

During the latter half of 1995, Congress enacted the Private Securities Litigation Reform Act of 1995 based on House bill 1058 and Senate bill 240. The major objective of this reform legislation was to curb the number of abusive securities class action suits. Of particular interest to audit committees is Section 301, "Fraud Detection and Disclosure," and Section 10A, "Audit Requirements." While Section 10A does not expand the auditors' responsibility to detect fraud or illegal acts, it does require auditors who detect illegal acts to report their findings to the Securities and Exchange Commission if the client company fails to take appropriate remedial action on such acts that have a material effect on the financial statements. If the necessary remedial action has not been taken, the auditors are required to notify the board of directors in writing. Based on these events, the board is required to submit the report to the SEC within one business day. If the board fails to notify the SEC, then the auditors are required to submit their report to the SEC the next business day.[19]

Fraud and False Statements Act

Whoever, in any matter within the jurisdiction of any department or agency of the United States knowingly and willfully falsifies, conceals or covers up by any trick, scheme, or device a material fact, or makes any false, fictitious or fraudulent statements or representations, or makes or uses any false writing or document knowing the same to contain any false, fictitious or fraudulent statement or entry, shall be fined not more than $10,000 or imprisoned not more than five years, or both.[20]

---

[18]U.S. Code, Title 15, Sec. 78ff.

[19]The act is contained in Title 1 of Public Law No. 104-67, December 22, 1995. Sections 301 and 10A are contained in Title 3 of Public Law No. 104-67, December 22, 1995. For further discussion, see the act with respect to such matters as proportionate liability, safe harbor for forward-looking statements, and loss causation principle. Also see the U.S. Federal Sentencing Commission's Federal Sentencing Guidelines for Organizations (Washington, DC: U.S. Federal Sentencing Commission, 1990) for an expanded discussion on encouraging effective programs to prevent and detect violations of law; Edward J. Boyle and Fred N. Knopf, "The Private Securities Litigation Reform Act of 1995, *CPA Journal* 66, No. 4 (April 1996), pp. 44–47; and Daniel L. Goldwasser, "The Private Securities Act of 1995: Impact on Accountants," *CPA Journal* 67, No. 6 (June 1997), pp. 72–75.

Mail Fraud Act

Whoever, having devised or intending to devise any scheme or artifice to defraud, or for obtaining money or property by means of false or fraudulent pretenses, representations, or promises, or to sell, dispose of, loan, exchange, alter, give away, distribute, supply, or furnish or produce for unlawful use any counterfeit or spurious coin, obligation, security, or other article, or anything represented to be or intimated to or held out to be such counterfeit or spurious articles, for the purpose of executing such scheme or artifice or attempting so to do, places in any post office or authorized depository for mail matter, any matter or thing whatever to be sent or delivered by the Postal Service, or takes or receives therefrom, any such matter or thing, or knowingly causes to be delivered by mail according to the direction thereon, or at the place at which it is directed to be delivered by the person to whom it is addressed, any such matter or thing, shall be fined not more than $1,000 or imprisoned not more than five years, or both.[21]

Whoever, having devised or intending to devise any scheme or artifice to defraud, or for obtaining money or property by means of false or fraudulent pretenses, representations, or promises, transmits or causes to be transmitted by means of wire, radio, or television communication in interstate or foreign commerce, any writings, signs, signals, pictures, or sounds for the purpose of executing such scheme or artifice, shall be fined not more than $1,000 or imprisoned not more than five years, or both.[22]

Conspiracy Act

If two or more persons conspire to commit any offense against the United States, or to defraud the United States, or any agency thereof in any manner or for any purpose, and one or more of such persons do any act to effect the object of the conspiracy, each shall be fined not more than $10,000 or imprisoned not more than five years, or both.

If, however, the offense, the commission of which is the object of the conspiracy, is a misdemeanor only, the punishment for such conspiracy shall not exceed the maximum punishment provided for such misdemeanor.[23]

Income Taxes[24]

Any person who:

1. *Declaration under penalties of perjury.* Willfully makes and subscribes any return, statement or other document, which contains or is verified by a written declaration that it is made under the penalties of perjury, and which he does not believe to be true and correct as to every material matter; or

2. *Aid or assistance.* Willfully aids or assists in, or procures, counsels or advises the preparation or presentation under, or in connection with any matter arising under, the internal revenue laws, of a return, affidavit, claim or other document,

---

[20]U.S. Code, Title 18, Sec. 1001.

[21] Ibid., Sec. 1341.

[22]Ibid., Sec. 1343.

[23] Ibid., Sec. 371.

[24]It may be advisable to request the outside auditors to remind executives that tax returns must be filed. The audit committee should make certain that the returns were filed appropriately through discussions with the auditors.

which is fraudulent or is false as to any material matter, whether or not such falsity or fraud is with the knowledge or consent of the person authorized or required to present such return, affidavit, claim or document; or

3. *Fraudulent bonds, permits, and entries.*   Simulates or falsely or fraudulently executes or signs any bond, permit, entry, or other document required by the provisions of the internal revenue laws, or by any regulation made in pursuance thereof, or procures the same to be falsely or fraudulently executed or advises, aids in, or connives at such execution thereof; or

4. *Removal or concealment with intent to defraud.*   Removes, deposits, or conceals, or is concerned in removing, depositing, or concealing any goods or commodities for or in respect whereof any tax is or shall be imposed, or any property upon which levy is authorized by section 6331, with intent to evade or defeat the assessment or collection of any tax imposed by this title; or

5. *Compromises and closing agreements.*   In connection with any compromise under section 7122, or offer of such compromise, or in connection with any closing agreement under section 7121, or offer to enter into any such agreement, willfully—

A. *Concealment of property.*   Conceals from any officer or employee of the United States any property belonging to the estate of a taxpayer or other person liable in respect of the tax, or

B. *Withholding, falsifying, and destroying records.*   Receives, withholds, destroys, mutilates, or falsifies any book, document, or record, or makes any false statement, relating to the estate or financial condition of the taxpayer or other person liable in respect of the tax; shall be guilty of a felony and, upon conviction thereof, shall be fined not more than $5,000, or imprisoned not more than 3 years, or both, together with the cost of prosecution.[25]

Any person who willfully delivers or discloses to the Secretary or his delegate any list, return, account, statement, or other document, known by him to be fraudulent or to be false as to any material matter, shall be fined not more than $1,000, or imprisoned not more than 1 year, or both. Any person required pursuant to sections 6047 (b) or (c), 6056, or 6104 (d) to furnish any information to the Secretary or any other person who willfully furnishes to the Secretary or such other person any information known by him to be fraudulent or to be false as to any material matter shall be fined not more than $1,000, or imprisoned not more than 1 year, or both.[26]

LEGAL CASES INVOLVING THE AUDIT COMMITTEE

During the 1970s and 1980s, litigation involving the audit committee exemplified the significance of the audit director's role. The Securities and Exchange Commission's increased enforcement of the provisions of the federal securities laws has imposed greater professional responsibilities on the committee. As one notable conservative columnist and editor stated, "The evolution of the director's responsibility is running ahead of inflation. . . . The contemporary director is supposed to know more about accounting . . . and more about the law."[27] Several legal cases are

---

[25]Internal Revenue Code, Sec. 7206.
[26]Ibid., Sec. 7207.
[27]"Firing Line," *Time* (February 19, 1979), p. 51.

briefly reviewed in order to demonstrate the philosophy of the courts and the SEC with respect to the audit committee.

The Penn Central Case

On August 3, 1972, the SEC released its study regarding the financial collapse of the Penn Central Company to a Special Subcommittee on Investigations of the House of Representatives. With respect to the role of the directors, the SEC found that the directors had a passive role in company affairs. They avoided confrontation with management on issues that were critical to testing the integrity of management and to providing adequate disclosure to the stockholders. For example, the company's CFO was involved in a lawsuit that claimed improper, unlawful conduct in connection with a subsidiary and a private investment club. Although the board authorized an investigation, it later cancelled the investigation because the CFO threatened to resign. As a result, the financial management was permitted to operate without any effective review of control by the board.[28] In particular, the Commission noted that the directors have a responsibility to obtain from management information that is adequate in both "quantity and quality" in order to discharge their state corporate legal liability. For example, a new director indicated that "lists of new equipment did not particularly help him discharge his responsibilities and thus information regarding the corporate objectives and plans was necessary to do the job."[29] Furthermore, the Commission emphasized the "critical importance" of the director's responsibility as well as "greater utilization of public and independent directors." Such independent directors should be judged on the "reasonableness of their judgment."[30] Thus the Commission's findings and conclusions point toward the need for an advisory committee of outside directors. The audit committee would fulfill this particular purpose.

Lum's, Inc. Case

On April 11, 1974, the SEC obtained a consent injunction from the U.S. District Court against Lum's, Inc. whereby the registrant "agreed not to employ any manipulative scheme to defraud and not to commit any proxy fraud in connection with future acquisitions of businesses or business assets." More specifically, the court ordered that the registrant had to include this information in its registration or proxy statement:

1. The identity of the individuals who control the acquired business
2. Any material consideration to be paid for the acquiring business in addition to the purchase price
3. Any material information known indicating that the earnings of an acquired business were affected by the failure of management to maintain proper accounting records and internal controls

---

[28]Commerce Clearing House, *Federal Securities Law Reporter,* par. 78,931.
[29]Ibid.
[30]Ibid.

Furthermore, the registrant had to establish a standing audit committee to review the accountant's evaluations of the system of internal controls and to review other casino activities in terms of personnel and security. The court required that the audit committee consist of two or more members of the board of directors who are not officers or employees of the company.[31] The Lum's consent injunction is of particular importance because it was the impetus toward the establishment of a standing audit committee through court action.

Mattel, Inc. Case

In the Mattel case of *SEC v. Mattel, Inc.* (October 1, 1974), the Commission sought a consent injunction against the registrant for false financial reporting. The Commission charged not only that the registrant's financial statements for 1971 were overstated by $14 million in sales that were subject to customer cancellation but also that the pretax income was overstated by $10.5 million due to inadequate accounting provisions. As a result, the U.S. District Court ordered Mattel to establish and maintain a financial controls and audit committee whereby three of the four members must be unaffiliated directors. In particular, the court required that the committee have these five duties and functions:

1. Review the financial controls and accounting procedures and recommend improvements to management.
2. Review the quarterly financial statements to determine whether such reports are in conformity with generally accepted accounting principles.
3. Review all releases and other information to the news media, general public, and stockholders with respect to the financial condition of the company and approve or disapprove such dissemination.
4. Review the results of the independent audit examination of the financial statements.
5. Approve or disapprove any change of the independent auditors.[32]

Thus, through a consent injunction against Mattel, it is clearly evident that the SEC continued to rely more heavily on the independent audit committee to review and monitor the company's financial controls, accounting procedures, and financial statements. Also, this particular legal action provided an initial framework for the duties and functions of the committee. Indeed, the question of what constitutes proper standards and practices for the committee was emerging through a court settlement; as a consequence the court was dictating the responsibilities of the audit directors. Such an approach is further evidenced by the results of the Killearn Properties case.

Killearn Properties, Inc. Case

In the *SEC v. Killearn Properties, Inc.* case (May 1977), the SEC outlined its directives concerning the audit committee as part of a consent judgment. The de-

---

[31] Ibid., par. 94,504.
[32] Ibid., par. 94,807.

fendants were enjoined from directly or indirectly making use of the mails or other communication to transmit any prospectus regarding the stock since the prospectus must meet the requirement of the securities laws. More specifically, the court ordered the defendants to observe the following policies and practices with respect to the audit committee:

B. The Board of Directors shall continue to maintain an Audit Committee ("Committee") of the Board consisting of at least Three (3) persons who shall be members of the Board and outside directors of Killearn. The Committee shall assume, upon the entering of this Order, the following duties, functions and responsibilities:

i. It should review the engagement of the independent accountants, including the scope and general extent of their review, the audit procedures which will be utilized, and the compensation to be paid.

ii. It should review with the independent accountants, and with the company's chief financial officer (as well as with other appropriate company personnel) the general policies and procedures utilized by the company with respect to internal auditing, accounting, and financial controls. The members of the committee should have at least general familiarity with the accounting and reporting principles and practices applied by the company in preparing its financial statements.

iii. It should review with the independent accountants, upon completion of their audit, (a) any report or opinion proposed to be rendered in connection therewith; (b) the independent accountants' perceptions of the company's financial and accounting personnel; (c) the cooperation which the independent accountants received during the course of their review; (d) the extent to which the resources of the company were and should be utilized to minimize time spent by the outside auditors; (e) any significant transactions which are not a normal part of the company's business; (f) any change in accounting principles; (g) all significant adjustments proposed by the auditor; (h) any recommendations which the independent accountants may have with respect to improving internal financial controls, choice of accounting principles, or management reporting systems.

iv. It should inquire of the appropriate company personnel and the independent auditors as to any instances of deviations from established codes of conduct of the company and periodically review such policies.

v. It should meet with the company's financial staff at least twice a year to review and discuss with them the scope of internal accounting and auditing procedures then in effect; and the extent to which recommendations made by the internal staff or by the independent accountants have been implemented.

vi. It should prepare and present to the company's board of directors a report summarizing its recommendation with respect to the retention (or discharge) of the independent accountants for the ensuing year.

vii. It should have a power to direct and supervise an investigation into any matter brought to its attention within the scope of its duties (including the power to retain outside counsel in connection with any such investigation).

In addition, the Audit Committee shall have the following special duties, functions and responsibilities:

viii. review, either by the Committee as a whole or by a designated member, all releases and other information to be disseminated by Killearn to press media, the public, or shareholders of Killearn which concern disclosure of financial conditions of and projections of financial conditions of Killearn and its subsidiaries;

ix. review of the activities of the officers and directors of Killearn as to their future dealing with the company and take any action the Committee may deem appropriate with regard to such activities;

x. approve any settlement or disposition of any claims or actions from causes of action arising after the date hereof or any litigation now pending which Killearn may have against any past or present officers, directors, employees or controlling persons.[33]

U.S. Surgical Corporation

In February 1984, the SEC filed an action against U.S. Surgical Corporation and six of its senior executives, alleging numerous improper financial reporting practices from 1979 to 1981. The corporation's pretax earnings were overstated by more than $18 million. This overstatement amounted to 56 percent of the pretax earnings reported during 1979 and 1981. In addition, the improper accounting practices continued during 1982 and 1983. In the final consent order, the corporation agreed to appoint two new independent directors to the audit committee and define new responsibilities of the audit committee. In particular, the committee was required to:

Review for a period of at least five years, prior to release, all earnings reports and the financial statements that accompany the annual audit and quarterly review reports of the external auditors and reports of the internal audit department;

Engage the external auditors to review and report to the committee on accounting policies concerning review recognition, capitalization of certain costs, inventories, R&D expenses, and accruals; and

Engage an accounting firm (advisory accountants) for a period of three years to review the services performed by the external auditors, and to assist the committee on other matters as requested[34]

This case demonstrated the need for the board of directors through its audit committee to exercise its oversight responsibility for the internal and external auditing processes and financial reporting disclosures.

Based on a review of the court actions, it is apparent that the audit committee has been established to oversee and monitor the conduct of the corporate officials. Although the committee is not directly involved with the day-to-day management affairs, the SEC and the courts forced the registrants to establish committees in order to comply with the requirements of the federal securities laws. Such legal enforcement of the courts has augmented not only the audit directors' legal obligations but also their standard of duty and loyalty to the enterprise.

The critical involvement of audit committees is highlighted by such companies as California Life Corporation, Playboy Enterprises, Inc., and H.J. Heinz Co. Some of the excerpts from The *Wall Street Journal* involving these companies are used to illustrate the audit committee's involvement.

---

[33] Ibid., par. 96,256.
[34] Ibid., par. 105,124.

California Life Corporation

When the audit committee learned that Cal Life was late in filing its 1978 annual financial statements with the SEC, the committee began an investigation. The late filing was the result of a dispute between management and its independent auditors. As Lancaster reported: "Certainly, the committee had some mitigating problems: a new, inexperienced committee chairman, a chief executive who was hard to deal with, and complex and unanticipated accounting issues." With a high expected loss rate on insurance premiums, the auditors lacked confidence that the deferred costs related to new policies could be recovered from future profits. As a result of this disagreement, the company reported a $3.2 million loss rather than an anticipated $2.6 million profit. Given the situation at Cal Life, a number of actions were taken to improve the financial reporting process. In particular, the senior executives of the firm were replaced and the membership of the audit committee increased to five from three. The committee had convened six times as opposed to two meetings and assumed an active role in overseeing the audit processes.[35]

Clearly, this case demonstrated that the audit committee is a viable mechanism in helping boards of directors discharge their oversight responsibilities for the financial reporting process. There is little question that the committee has assumed greater responsibilities.

Playboy Enterprises, Inc.

In the Playboy Enterprises case, the audit committee requested that Hugh Hefner, chief executive officer of Playboy, and four other executives return to the company more than $900,000. The amounts owed by these parties involved perquisites (perks), such as the use of the DC-9 plane and the value of benefits (lodging, meals, valet, etc.) received from the company. As a result, the aforementioned parties repaid their perks and the board also established a compensation committee.[36] Thus the audit committee's close scrutiny of these activities did unearth a significant problem area before it impaired the integrity of the company.

H.J. Heinz

From 1972 to 1979, Heinz was involved in profit-juggling practices at several divisions. More specifically, the audit committee reported that "the practices, designed to give the appearance of smooth profit growth of the divisions, stemmed partly from inadequate internal accounting controls, poor internal communications, the autonomy of division accountants and careless review of division reports by the Heinz corporate staff."[37] To correct these practices, the audit committee recommended more internal auditors, more corporate supervision of division accountants, and a tougher corporate code of conduct. In addition, the audit committee recommended changing the outside auditing firm, and, as a result,

---

[35]Hal Lancaster, "Fuss at Cal Life Shows Audit Committee Role Is Critical," *Wall Street Journal* (March 17, 1980), p. 1.
[36]Wall Street Journal Staff Reporter, "Playboy Audit Committee Bares Details of Hefner's High Living on Firm's Tab," *Wall Street Journal* (April 4, 1980), p. 6.

another multinational accounting firm is now the auditor. Furthermore, the company hired an outside law firm and another large accounting firm to assist in the special investigation.[38] Clearly, Heinz's audit committee proved to be a very strong and effective operating tool of the company. Its involvement established a high degree of confidence in the quality of the financial reports and disclosures to stockholders, underwriters, and financial analysts. Exhibits 4.1, 4.2, and 4.3 contain a discussion of possible warning signals and "red flags."

As Hugh L. Marsh and Thomas E. Powell assert:

> It would be a misconception to believe the possibility of fraud is the only reason for establishing a chartered audit committee. While the primary role has been to oversee management's financial and reporting responsibilities, the Treadway Commission's investigations indicated that audit committees could serve very effectively to reduce the incidence of fraud.[39]

Livent, Inc.

This case relates to securities class actions brought by investors against Livent and associated individuals and entities. In addition to other defendants, three directors who served on Livent's audit committee were named as defendants. The audit committee members were charged with violating federal securities laws, namely Section 10(b), and Section 20(a) claims of the 1934 act. The case involved fraudulent revenue-generating transactions and manipulation of books and records. The shareholders alleged that the audit committee failed to discover the aforementioned schemes. In the decision, the judge dismissed the Section 10(a) and Section 20(a) violations since the audit committee was not a culpable participant in the fraud schemes. Likewise, the Section 10(a) and Section 20(a) violations were not sufficient to plead scienter as well as the criteria for control person liability.[40]

Manzo v. Rite Aid Corporation

The plaintiffs brought a class action lawsuit against the officers, directors, and outside accounting firm. With respect to the audit committee, they alleged a breach of fiduciary duty with respect to fraudulent financial statements during the class period. The defendants asserted that they deny any wrongdoing with regard to misleading financial statements. They contend good faith reliance on the officers' reports. The court ruled for the defendants, saying that the complaint failed to adequately allege reliance and damages and failed to establish a direct claim and a derivative claim. [41]

---

[37]Thomas Petziner, Jr., "Heinz Senior Officials Didn't Participate in Profit-Juggling Practices, Panel Says," *Wall Street Journal* (May 9, 1980), p. 2.
[38]Ibid.
[39]Hugh L. Marsh and Thomas E. Powell, "The Audit Committee Charter: Rx for Fraud Prevention," *Journal of Accountancy* 167, No. 2 (February 1989), p. 56.
[40]*In Re Livent, Inc. Securities Litigation*, 148 F. Supp. 2d 331 (S.D.N.Y. 2001). For additional court cases, see *Haltman, et al. v. Aura Systems, Inc., et al.*, 844 F. Supp. 544 (C.D. C.A. 1993); and *Bomarko, Inc. v. Hemodynamics, Inc.*, 848 F. Supp. 1335 (W.D. M.I. 1993).
[41]*Manzo v. Rite Aid Corporation*, C.A. No. 18451-NC (Del. Ch. 2002)

Guttman v. Nvidia Corporation

In this case, the plaintiffs alleged that the defendants issued materially misstated financial statements. They contend the defendants used "cookie jar reserves" to smooth earnings in bad times. The court ruled in favor of the defendants because the audit committee did not commit any culpable failure of oversight under the Caremark standard. [42]

As William T. Allen, chancellor of the Court of Chancery of Delaware stated in his decision:

> In order to show that the Caremark directors breached their duty of care by failing adequately to control Caremark's employees, plaintiffs would have to show either (1) that the directors knew or (2) should have known that violations of law were occurring and, in either event, (3) that the directors took no steps in a good faith effort to prevent or remedy that situation, and (4) that such failure proximately resulted in the losses complained of, although under *Cede & Co. v. Technicolor, Inc.*, Del. Supr., 636 A.2d 956 (1994) this last element may be thought to constitute n affirmative defense.

> 1. Knowing violation for statute: Concerning the possibility that the Caremark directors knew of violations of law, none of the documents submitted for review, nor any of the position transcripts appear to provide evidence of it. Certainly the board understood that the company had entered into a variety of contracts with physicians, researchers, and health care providers and it was understood that some of these contracts were with persons who had prescribed treatments that Caremark participated in providing. The board was informed that the Company's reimbursement for patient care was frequently from government funded sources and that such services were subject to the ARPL. But the Board appears to have been informed by experts that the company's practices while contestable, were lawful. There is no evidence that reliance on such reports was not reasonable. Thus, this case presents no occasion to apply a principle to the effect that knowingly causing the corporation to violate a criminal statute constitutes a breach of a director's fuduciary duty. See *Roth v. Robertson*, N.Y. Sup. Ct., 64 Misc. 343, 18 N.Y. 351 (1909); *Miller v. American Tel. & Tel. Co.*, 507 F.2d 759 (3rd ci. 1974). It is not clear that the Board knew the detail found, for example, in the indictments arising from the Company's payments. But, of course, the duty to act in good faith to be informed cannot be thought to require directors to possess detailed infomation about all aspects of the operation of the enterprise. Such a requirement would simply be inconsistent with the scale and scope of efficient organization size in this technological age.

> 2. Failure to monitor: Since it does appears that the Board was to some extent unaware of the activities that led to liability, I turn to a consideration of the potential avenue to director liability that the pleadings take: director inattention or "negligence." Generally where a claim of directorial liability for corporate loss is predicated upon ignorance of liability creating activities within the corporation, as in Graham or in this case, in my opinion only a sustained or systematic failure of the board to exercise oversight—such as an utter failure to attempt to assure a reasonable information and reporting system exists—will establish the lack of good faith that is a necessary condition to liability. Such a test of liability—lack of good faith as evidenced by sustained or systematic failure of a director to exercise reasonable oversight—is quite

---

[42]*Guttman v. Jen-Hsun Huang et al. Nvidia Corporation,* C.A. No. 19571-N.C. (Del. Ch. 2003).

Exhibit 4.1   Securities Litigation and Preventing Fraudulent Reporting

When Kirschner Medical Corp., a Baltimore-based manufacturer of orthopedic equipment, went public in 1986, President Bruce Hegstad planned to go from $6.5 million to $100 million in revenues. They did indeed skyrocket, reaching $55 million in 1989. Naturally, stock prices soared as well.

But the investors who flocked to Kirschner now claim that the company duped them. During the third quarter of 1989, the company lost $488,000. Despite its assurances of a quick rebound, Kirschner lost $2.5 million in the next quarter and wrote off an additional $13.2 million in losses.

During this time, the company allegedly failed to disclose information about defective products, obsolete inventories and an unprofitable European plant. When the bad news finally came out, stock prices dove $17 a share, causing a lost market value of $35.7 million. Claiming fraudulent financial reporting, over 1,000 investors have filed a class-action suit against Kirschner and three of its executives in the U.S. District Court in Baltimore.

In recent years, corporate boards of directors and their audit committees have faced great vulnerability to such litigation.

According to William R. McLucas, the Security and Exchange Commission's enforcement director, "The agency has a hefty backlog of cases, many focusing on financial fraud and accounting problems."

In 1989, the SEC filed enforcement actions against the officers and directors of 30 public companies and 12 public accounting firms, alleging improper financial reporting practices.[a]

Two years earlier, the National Commission on Fraudulent Financial Reporting, established by accounting associations and chaired by former SEC Commissioner James Treadway, reported that it had "reviewed 119 enforcement actions against public companies and 42 cases against independent public accounting firms by the SEC from 1981–1986."

The commission asserted that "public companies should maintain internal controls that provide reasonable assurance that fraudulent financial reporting will be prevented or subject to early detection."

What is fraudulent financial reporting? The commission defines it "as intentional or reckless conduct, whether act or omission, that results in materially misleading financial statements."

Generally speaking, fraudulent reporting occurs when management intentionally overstates assets and improperly recognizes revenue. These actions clearly differ from unintentional errors.

The irregularities are shown by the misapplication of generally accepted accounting principles, inappropriate valuations, and/or omissions of material information from financial statements. For example, the deliberate distortion of accounting records to overstate inventory, along with falsified transactions to increase sales and overstate earnings, is clearly fraudulent financial reporting.

These activities, often referred to as "cooked books" and "cute accounting," cause management to restate the financial statements, which, in turn, causes a decrease in the market price of the stock. Such misleading representations in the company's annual and quarterly figures can be the basis of a class-action lawsuit.

Typically in this type of litigation, a class of stockholders alleges that the board of directors, the officers and the independent auditing firm have prepared and distributed materially false and misleading financial statements and reports to existing stockholders and potential investors.

Plaintiffs accuse defendants of violating Section 10(b) of the Securities Exchange Act, SEC Rule 10(b)-5 and common law. Relief claims are based on fraud, deceit and negligence by the directors, officers, employees and the independent auditors.

Questions of law and fact commonly arising in these cases are:

- Whether defendants knowingly or recklessly disseminated untrue statements of material fact and/or omitted material facts relating to the sales and earnings during the class period;
- Whether the market prices of securities were artificially inflated by reason of the defendants' conduct, constituting a fraud on the market;
- Whether defendants violated Section 10(b) of the 1934 Act and Rule 10(b)-5 and/or perpetrated common law fraud or negligent misrepresentations upon the members of the class;
- Whether the defendant's SEC Form 10-Q, 10K, annual and quarterly reports, and public announcements of expected earnings and growth during the class period were materially false and misleading.

Failure on the part of the audit committee to review and evaluate the financial statements and related accounting policies in accordance with generally accepted accounting principles is clearly malfeasance.

A case in point is Crazy Eddie Inc., which, like many public companies, had audit committees. According to the SEC, Eddie Antar, founder and former chairman of the East Coast electronics chain, directed activities that resulted in overstating the company's 1985 pretax income by $2 million, or 18.9 percent; by approximately $6.7 million, or 33.8 percent, in 1986; and by "tens of millions of dollars" in 1987.

Peter Martosella, who was brought in to run Crazy Eddie after the fraudulent reporting was discovered, told *Forbes* magazine, "You have to be careful how much you expect of the audit committee. You're talking about people brought in by the CEO, and you're telling them they shouldn't necessarily listen to him. It's not realistic, especially when the chief executive is a charismatic person, a darling of the securities world, like Eddie Antar was."

Antar allegedly made $60 million from the sale of his Crazy Eddie stock; investors allegedly lost $200 million. In 1989 the SEC filed a complaint against Antar and other company officials and employees. Last summer the U.S. District Court for New Jersey entered a $73.5 million judgment against Antar, who is currently a fugitive. (It should be noted that Antar was recently apprehended by the authorities.)

Moreover, a group of about 10,000 shareholders have filed a lawsuit in the federal district court in New York against Crazy Eddie's former officers and directors, as well as its external auditor and several Wall Street brokerage firms.

In another case, Sundstrand Corp. pleaded guilty to a criminal defense procurement fraud of overbilling the Defense Department. Sundstrand agreed to pay a $115 million settlement to the federal government. In addition, the liability insurance carrier for Sundstrand's board of directors and officers agreed to pay $15 million to settle shareholder litigation.

An academic research study found that Sundstrand's audit committee was ineffective since it had too few meetings and too many changes in membership.[b]

As a result of the committee's performance, there were management-imposed scope limitations on the internal audit department, which ultimately caused the company to defraud the federal government.

As the Crazy Eddie and Sundstrand cases demonstrate, merely having an audit committee isn't always enough. So what exactly is this committee supposed to do?

The major impetus for establishing and maintaining audit committees occurred in 1978 when the New York Stock Exchange adopted a policy requiring all of its listed companies to have such a committee, composed solely of independent outside directors. Of course, the NYSE's intent was to increase the investing public's confidence in the quality of financial reporting.

(continued)

Exhibit 4.1   *(Continued)*

Before the NYSE's mandate, the SEC required companies to establish and maintain independent audit committees.

Thus, a consent injunction and ancillary relief against respondents charged with fraudulent financial reporting issues—for example, in cases against Lum's Inc. and Mattel Inc. in 1974—provided a framework for defining the duties and functions of audit committees.

Lum's agreed not to commit any proxy fraud in connection with future acquisitions of businesses or business assets. Mattel was charged with overstating sales by $14 million. These sales were subject to customer cancellation.

The question of what constitutes proper standards and practices for the audit committee has emerged through settlements, with the courts dictating the audit committee's responsibilities. In particular, the courts in Lum's and Mattel required the following general responsibilities:

- Recommend or approve appointment or independent auditors.
- Review internal accounting control policies and procedures.
- Oversee the duties and results of the internal audit department.
- Review with the independent auditors the proposed scope and general extent of their audit.
- Review, prior to issuance, financial statements and significant press releases concerning financial results.
- Act as a mediator between management and the independent auditors for any disagreements over accounting issues.

Recognizing the SEC enforcement actions, court decisions and the national stock exchange listing requirements for audit committees, the National Commission on Fraudulent Financial Reporting has fully supported and endorsed implementation of audit committees.

In particular, the commission recommended that "the boards of directors of all public companies should be required by SEC rule to establish audit committees composed solely of independent directors. Such committees should be informed, vigilant, and effective overseers of the financial reporting process and the company's internal controls."

Today, both the American Stock Exchange and the National Association of Securities Dealers have listing requirements for audit committees that are modeled after the NYSE's requirements. The U.S. House of Representatives is currently considering legislation, sponsored by Rep. John Dingell, D-Mich., requiring all public companies to create audit committees.

Given that the audit committee is a part-time operation, the commission's call for vigilance requires committee members to be willing to make a significant commitment of their time.

The audit committee should be informed about the financial and operational aspects of the company and, therefore, should receive sufficient and timely information. If the audit committee meeting is scheduled to coincide with the regular full board meetings, then the committee must receive written information well in advance of the meetings.

To be vigilant, the audit committee should ask probing questions about the propriety of the company's financial reporting process and the quality of its internal controls. This task requires the committee to keep abreast of financial reporting developments affecting the company.

To be an effective independent overseer, the audit committee must be positioned between senior management and the external auditors. This organizational structure allows the audit committee to question management's judgments about financial reporting matters and to suggest improvements in the internal control systems. Finally, the committee should develop a charter that defines its mission, duties and responsibilities; plans its annual agenda; and documents its findings and conclusions.

Through audit committees, boards of directors can meet their oversight responsibilities in the internal and external auditing processes and the financial reporting process.

And, since inhouse legal counsel and outside counsel frequently interact with audit committees, these lawyers are in an excellent position to help the committees develop a constructive relationship between their function and the activities of the full board and, ultimately, minimize the potential for class-action suits by recognizing the warning signals that lead to fraudulent reporting.[c]

For example, corporate legal counsel can assist the audit committees with the following matters:

- Review and approve the standard of independence for the audit committee members as required by the national stock exchanges and the SEC.
- Review the audit committee's charter, which is disclosed in part in the company's annual proxy statement.
- Review significant litigation, claims and assessments with both in-house and outside legal counsel.
- Advise the committee with respect to any pending litigation against the external auditors and any impairment of their independence.
- Advise the committee on proposed investigations and compliance with regulations.

Of course, outside legal counsel may be asked to serve on the audit committee, in which case he or she would address the warning signals directly.

Given the audit committee's critical role in the company's internal control structure, the committee must obtain reasonable assurances from the internal and external auditors that management's assertions in the financial statements are fairly presented. Moreover, the external auditors are required by generally accepted auditing standards to communicate certain matters to the audit committee.

In particular, the auditors are required to report material misstatements in the financial statements or omissions of material information.

It should be emphasized that audit committees should be highly attuned to potential situations of fraudulent financial reporting.

Failure on the part of an audit committee to question management's representations may be the basis for audit committee malfeasance, since the audit committee and the board may be held liable for their failure to know what they were responsible for recognizing.

Source: This discussion is adapted from an article by Louis Braiotta, Jr., "Auditing for Honesty," *American Bar Association Journal* 78, No. 5 (May 1992), pp. 76–79. Copyright (c) 1992 by Louis Braiotta, Jr.

[a]More recently, the SEC has filed actions against the officers and directors and accounting firms, respectively: 1993 (36, 17); 1994 (78, 31); 1995 (71, 11); 1996 (59, 20); 1997 (90, 22), 1998 (64, 15); 1999 (81, 13); 2000 (78, 25); 2001 (92, 20); 2002 (138, 25). For additional reading, see a Best Practices Council of the National Association of Corporate Directors report entitled, *Coping with Fraud and Other Illegal Activity* (Washington, DC: National Association of Corporate Directors, 1998); Committee of Sponsoring Organizations of the Treadway Commission, *Fraudulent Financial Reporting: 1987–1997 An Analysis of U.S. Public Companies* (New York: Committee of Sponsoring Organizations of the Treadway Commission, 1999). See the SEC *Annual Reports* for further information on enforcement proceedings and related cases and Exhibit 4.3.

[b]For further reading, see Curtis C. Verschoor, "A Case Study of Audit Committee Effectiveness at Sundstrand," *Internal Auditing* 4, No. 4 (Spring 1989), pp. 11–19. Also see Verschoor's article, "Miniscribe: A New Example of Audit Committee Ineffectiveness," *Internal Auditing* 5, No. 4 (Spring 1990), pp. 13–19.

[c]See Exhibit 4.2 for further details.

Exhibit 4.2 Warning Signals of the Possible Existence of Fraudulent Financial Reporting

Symptom	Problem	Solution
I. Industry Matters		
Competitive and economic conditions	Overoptimistic news releases with respect to earnings. Capital investment in a rapidly changing industry.	Analyze annual and interim earnings trends to avoid increased opportunities for managing earnings.
Competitive foreign businesses	Foreign competitors have significant advantages.	Discuss management's strategy as it relates to financial matters.
Government regulations	The industry is subject to new regulations that increase the cost of compliance.	Obtain assurance on the entity's compliance affecting financial matters.
Industry accounting practices	Unusual revenue recognition policies and/or deferred expenses to increase earnings.	Access significant accounting policies that are industry-specific from the NAARS data base, and review and discuss this information with the independent auditors.
II. Entity's Business Matters		
Organizational structure	High turnover in key accounting personnel (e.g., controller). Complex corporate structure that is not warranted.	Determine the reasons for such personnel turnover.
Lines of business and product segments	Rapid expansion of business lines in excess of industry averages.	Investigate the reasons for this rapid expansion.
Lack of security over computer operations	Control procedures over computer are weak.	Inquire of management key security problems.

Accounting policies	Significant changes in accounting practices and estimates by management with an excessive interest in earnings. Unusual year-end transactions that increase earnings. Inconsistencies between financial statements, MDA, and the president's letter.	Compare the entity's policies with the industry norms and determine the reasons for the changes. Raise questions on issues that support these transactions; determine the reasons for the inconsistent disclosures.
Conflict-of-interest	Significant contracts that affect financial statements. Frequent related-party transactions. Failure to enforce the corporate code of conduct.	Determine management intent to disclose such contracts; determine how the company addresses possible conflict-of-interest situations; determine how management monitors compliance with the code.
Frequent change of legal counsel	Disagreements on asserted or unasserted claims and contingencies.	Discuss disclosures with general counsel and outside counsel.
Unexplained significant fluctuations in account balances	Material physical inventory variances.	Focus on the analytical review procedures.
III. External Auditing Matters		
Frequent change of auditors	Disagreement on GAAP, which causes opinion shopping.	Investigate the reasons for frequent changes in auditors.
Quantity of lawsuits against the CPA firm	Firm has violated the securities laws.	Review the latest peer review report and the number of lawsuits against the firm.
Nonacceptance of recommendations in the management letter	Breakdowns in the internal control structures.	Obtain assurance from the auditors that management has evaluated the weaknesses and that corrective action has been taken.
IV. Internal Auditing Matters		
Departmental organization	The size of the internal audit department is not compatible with the size of the company.	Discuss this matter with chief internal auditor and independent auditor.
Reporting responsibility	Scope restrictions.	Direct access to the audit committee.

Exhibit 4.3   Unethical Practices in Financial Reporting

SEC Enforcement Division[a]
*Summary of Selected Cases and Alleged Violations—Financial Disclosures
Fiscal Year ended 1989–1997*

Date Filed	Release No.	Nature of Alleged Violations
11/1/88	AAER—208	SEC alleged improper accounting practices (e.g., holding quarterly financial records open to record additional sales; preparing invoices for orders that had not been shipped; and delaying the issuance of credit memos for orders that had been returned). The company and seven officers and employees consented to the entry of the Commission's orders against them.
1/9/89	AAER—212	The registrant had overstated earnings and inventory by inflating quantity and cost figures on inventory count sheets and arranged for the supplier to send a false confirmation to the auditors. The company, its officers, its supplier, and the supplier's president all consented to entry of permanent injunctions.
2/8/89	AAER—215	SEC alleged the improper recognition of revenue. The alleged scheme involved failure to record at least $13 million of product returns and the recording of more than $5 million of fictitious revenue from false invoices. Two defendants consented to the entry of injunctions against them.
6/6/89	LR—12119	The company had overstated revenues by prematurely recording a total of 20 transactions as sales even though the sales have not been completed.
9/6/89	AAER—247	SEC filed an action against officers, directors, and employees. Commission alleged the company falsified financial records to overstate pretax income of $20.6 million instead of a loss in 1987. Defendants sold over $60 million of stock that did not reflect the value of the company. Three defendants consented to the entry of injunctions against them.
5/24/90	AAER—258	The registrant recorded unsupported adjustments to revenue. The Commission alleged the company filed materially false and misleading financial statements.
10/11/90	AAER—279	SEC alleged that former officers engaged in improper revenue recognition practices. They are: (1) recorded transactions as sales when customers had not agreed to purchase the equipment and the equipment was not delivered; (2) recorded trials as sales transactions; and (3) removing inventory to simulate delivery of goods sold. The defendants consented to the entry of injunctions.
10/26/90	AAER—282	The CEO directed officers and employees to engage in a scheme to inflate accounts receivable and inventory. The perpetration created phony invoices to generate sales. Also, the CEO and two other defendants sold common stock when they knew that the market price was based on

Date Filed	Release No.	Nature of Alleged Violations
		materially false representations. Two of the defendants consented to the entry of injunctions.
8/20/91	AAER—311	The corporation used improper revenue recognition practices by recording sales at the time a purchaser agreed verbally to purchase equipment. Also, the client misled the auditors by falsely indicating that certain tractors were loaded for shipment and that risk of loss had passed to the purchaser. The company and two of the individual defendants consented to the entry of injunction.
3/31/92	AAER—363	SEC alleged that the company failed to disclose the importance of its subsidiary's 1989 earnings in the MD&A section of the Form 10-K. The subsidiary accounted for about 23 percent of the parent company's net profit of $497 million. Much of the gain resulted from the country's hyperinflation and a favorable exchange rate. The parent company consented to a cease and desist order.
9/30/93	LR—13813	The Commission alleged that the company made misrepresentations and omissions regarding the deterioration in sales of software and the shipment of $5.2 million of products to certain customers as conditional or fictitious sales. Individual defendants consented to the entry of orders requiring them to disgorge over $2 million and one consented to the entry of a bar from acting as an officer or director of a publicly held company.
3/29/94	EAR—33829	The Commission alleged that, as a result of a fraudulent accounting scheme implemented by three members of the company's senior management, the company reported materially overstated sales, net income, and assets in periodic filings between 1989 and 1992. The inflated sales and earnings enabled the company to falsely report continued growth in revenue and earnings when the company was not profitable. Overall, the company reported nearly $38 million in sales between 1989–1992 that had not taken place.
1/4/95	LR—14375	The company improperly recognized revenue on several transactions. The company's false claims of having sold simulators to customers resulted in income statements in which total revenue was inflated by 46 percent to 93 percent.
9/19/96	R—34-37701	The company filed a 10Q that contained financial statements which materially overstated revenue and materially understated losses by improperly recognizing revenue from purported bill and hold transactions.
2/18/97	LR—15260	The company materially overstated earnings and profitability prior to a convertible debt offering. The company consented to entry of an injunction and an order requiring the payment of $3.28 million in disgorgement.
8/5/98	LR-15832	The registrant consented to the issuing of a cease-and-desist order in which the SEC found that the company

(continued)

Exhibit 4.3   (*Continued*)

Date Filed	Release No.	Nature of Alleged Violations
		violated the periodic reporting provisions. The SEC found that during the four months preceding the company's writedown of $2.7 billion of goodwill, the company made inadequate disclosures about the nature and extent of its net losses.
1/13/99	AAER-1095	The SEC alleged that the registrant made at least 17 false filings in which the company materially overstated its results of operations and financial condition. Four of the defendants consented to the entry of injunction.
10/28/99	LR-16344	The SEC alleged that the defendants engaged in a fraudulent scheme to recognize millions of dollars of revenue prematurely by improperly recording purported "bill and hold" sales to meet sales projections.
9/28/00	EAR-43372	The SEC settled civil administrative fraud charges against a foreign issues for issuing materially false denials concerning merger negotiations. The registrant consented to an entry of a cease and desist order.
5/15/01	LR-17001	The Commission alleged that the defendants engaged in a scheme to fraudulently misrepresent the company's results of operations through the creation of inappropriate accounting reserves—"cookie jar reserves." The scheme was used to purport a rapid turnaround. As a result, at least $60 million of the company's reported earnings came from the accounting fraud.
9/12/01	LR-17126	The SEC instituted a settled administrative proceeding against the registrant for books and records violations associated with illegal payments to foreign officials. The $75,000 illegal payment was made in violation of the Foreign Corrupt Practices Act. This was the first joint action that the SEC and the Department of Justice filed under the Act.
8/21/02	AAER-1617	The SEC filed and settled a civil action against a former officer alleging that he used complex structures, strawmen, hidden payments, and secret loans to create the appearance that such entities were independent from the company. In fact, such entities were used as off-balance sheet financing arrangements inappropriately secured by debt rather than equity securities. The defendant agree to disgorge and forfeit approximately $12 million as well as submit a guilty plea in related criminal proceedings with the U.S. Department of Justice.

Source: The Securities and Exchange Commission *Annual Reports* (Washington, DC: U.S. Government Printing Office, 1990–1997 and 1998–2002).

high. But, a demanding test of liability in the oversight context is probably beneficial to corporate shareholders as a class, as it is in the board decision context, since it makes board service by qualified persons more likely, while continuing to act as a stimulus to good faith performance of duty by such directors.

Here the record supplies essentially no evidence that the director defendants were guilty of a sustained failure to exercise their oversight function. To the contrary, insofar as I am able to tell on this record, the corporation's information systems appear to have represented a good faith attempt to be informed of the relevant facts. If the directors did not know the specifics of the activities that lead to the indictments, they cannot be faulted.

The liability that eventuated in this instance was huge. But the fact that it resulted from a violation of criminal law alone does not create a breach of fiduciary duty by directors. The record at this stage does not support the conclusion that the defendants either lacked good faith in the exercise of their monitoring responsibilities or conscientiously permitted a known violation of law by the corporation to occur. The claims asserted against them must be viewed at this stage as extremely weak.[43]

Recent Developments

Section 307 of the Sarbanes-Oxley Act of 2002 mandates that the Securities and Exchange Commission:

> shall issue rules, in the public interest and for the protection of investors, setting forth minimum standards of professional conduct for attorneys appearing and practicing before the commission in any way in the representation of issuers, including a rule—
>
> (1) requiring an attorney to report evidence of a material violation of securities law or breach of fiduciary duty or similar violation by the company or any agent thereof, to the chief legal counsel or the chief executive officer of the company (or the equivalent thereof); and
>
> (2) if the counsel or officer does not appropriately respond to the evidence (adopting, as necessary, appropriate remedial measures or sanctions with respect to the violation), requiring the attorney to report the evidence to the audit committee of the board of directors of the issuer or to another committee of the board of directors comprised solely of directors not employed directly or indirectly by the issuer, or to the board of directors.[44]

Furthermore, the American Bar Association Task Force on Corporate Responsibility recommended adoption of these governance policies as ABA policy:

> 1. The board of directors of a public corporation must engage in active, independent and informed oversight of the corporation's business and affairs, including its senior management.

---

[43]*See In Re Caremark International Inc. Derivative Litigation,* 698 A. 2d 959 (Del. Ch. 1996).
[44]Sarbanes-Oxley Act of 2002, Section 307, *Rules of Professional Responsibility for Attorneys,* H.R. Rep. No. 107-610 (2002). For further information regarding the standards for professional conduct of attorneys, see Securities and Exchange Commission, *Release No. 33-8155, Implementation of Standards of Professional Conduct for Attorneys* (January 29, 2003).

2. In order to improve the effectiveness of such oversight, the board of directors of a public corporation should adopt governance principles (more fully specified in Part VI of this Report) that (a) establish and preserve the independence and objectivity of directors by eliminating disabling conflicts of interest and undue influence or control by the senior management of the corporation and (b) provide the directors with timely and sufficient information and analysis necessary to the discharge of their oversight responsibilities.

3. The directors should recognize and fulfill an obligation to disclose to the board of directors information and analysis known to them that is relevant to the board's decision making and oversight responsibilities. Senior executive officers should recognize and fulfill an obligation to disclose, to a supervising officer, the general counsel, or the board of directors or committees of the board, information and analysis relevant to such persons' decision making and oversight responsibilities.

4. Providing information and analysis necessary for the directors to discharge their oversight responsibilities, particularly as they relate to legal compliance matters, requires the active involvement of general counsel for the public corporation. (If a public corporation has no internal general counsel, it should identify and designate a lawyer or law firm to act as general counsel. The responsibility for implementing these recommended policies may necessarily be delegated to some extent by the general counsel to subordinate lawyers.)

5. A lawyer representing public corporation shall serve the interests of the entity, independent of the personal interests of any particular director, officer, employee or shareholder.

6. The general counsel of a public corporation should have primary responsibility for assuring the implementation of an effective legal compliance system under the oversight of the board of directors.

7. Public corporations should adopt practices in which:

   a. The selection, retention, and compensation of the corporation's general counsel are approved by the board of directors.

   b. General counsel meets regularly and in executive session with a committee of independent directors to communicate concerns regarding legal compliance matters, including potential or ongoing material violations of law by, and breaches of fiduciary duty to, the corporation.

   c. All reporting relationships of internal and outside lawyers for a public corporation establish at the outset a direct line of communication with general counsel through which these lawyers are to inform the general counsel of material potential or ongoing violations of law by, and breaches of fiduciary duty to, the corporation.

8. The model Business Corporation Act and the general corporation laws of the states, and the courts interpreting and applying the duties of directors, should more clearly delineate the oversight responsibility of directors generally, and the unique role that independent directors play in discharging that responsibility in public company settings. (Among the specific oversight matters that should be considered in relation to the Model Business Corporation Act or its commentary and the state corporate laws as well as in relation to important guidance such as the *Corporate Director's Guidebook* are at least the following: selecting, evaluating, and compensating the chief executive officer and other members of senior management; reviewing, approving, and monitoring

fundamental financial and business strategies and the performance of the company relative to those strategies; assessing major risks facing the company; and ensuring that reasonable processes are in place to maintain the integrity of the company and the corresponding accountability of senior management, including processes relating to integrity of financial reporting, compliance with law and corporate codes of legal and ethical conduct, and processes designed to prevent improper related party transactions. Federal law [particularly the securities law, including the rules and regulations adopted by the SEC] also plays a significant role in affecting and promoting corporate responsibility.)

9. Engagements of counsel by the board of directors, or by a committee of the board, for special investigations or independent advice should be structured to assure independence and direct reporting to the board of directors or the committee.

10. The SEC and the state attorney disciplinary authorities should cooperate in sharing information in order to promote effective and appropriate enforcement of rules of conduct applicable to counsel to public corporations.

11. The courts, law schools and lawyer professional organizations such as the ABA should promote awareness of, and adherence to, the professional responsibilities of lawyers in their representation of public corporations.

12. Law firms and law departments should adopt procedures to facilitate and promote compliance with rules of professional conduct governing the representation of public corporations. (In its Preliminary Report [at 43], the task force stated its intention to consider issues involving potential conflicts of interest arising out of lawyers' business and investment relationships with clients. The testimony submitted to the Task Force, however, did not significantly focus on such issues, and the Task Force therefore recommends that further review of the issues be taken by interested professional organizations, including the appropriate ABA entities.)[45]

With respect to audit committees, the ABA Task Force recommended these corporate governance practices:

The board of directors should establish an audit committee, composed exclusively of independent directors.

a. The audit committee should meet regularly outside the presence of any senior executive officer.

b. The audit committee should be:

i. authorized to engage and remove the corporation's outside auditor (or if legally permissible, to recommend such engagement or removal to the Board), and to determine the terms of the engagement of the outside auditor;

ii. authorized and afforded resources sufficient to engage independent accounting and legal advisers when determined by the committee to be necessary or appropriate; and

---

[45]American Bar Association, *Report of the American Bar Association Task Force on Corporate Responsibility* (Chicago, ABA, 2003), pp. 31–33.

      iii. responsible for recommending or establishing policies relating to non-audit services provided by the corporation's outside auditor to the Corporation and other aspects of the Corporation's relationship with the outside auditor that may adversely affect that firm's independence.

    c. The resolution of the board of directors creating the committee should specify whether the foregoing decisions are to be made exclusively by the audit committee, or (where legally permissible) by the full board of directors (or by the independent directors) upon the recommendation of the committee.

Section 301 of the Sarbanes-Oxley Act of 2002 requires the SEC to adopt rules requiring the national securities exchanges and national securities associations to adopt listing standards providing, among other things, that (i) each member of the audit committee be independent, (ii) the audit committee be "directly responsible for the appointment, compensation, and oversight of the work of any registered public accounting firm employed" by the company, and (iii) the audit committee have authority to engage independent counsel and other advisers. On January 8, 2003 the SEC proposed rules to implement these statutory requirements. (Proposed Exchange Act rule 10A-3, at *www.sec.gov/rules/proposed/34-47137.htm*.)

The Sarbanes-Oxley Act (§201, adding Section 10A(h) of the Exchange Act) also requires that public company auditing firms perform permitted non-audit services only upon advance approval by the audit committee.

The listing standards prescribed by Section 301 of the Sarbanes-Oxley Act of 2002 appear to require that the board of directors delegate to the audit committee direct and exclusive responsibility for the matters specified in the statute. The Task Forces's recommendations differ in that they would allow the full board of directors (or all of the independent directors) to act on such matters, upon recommendation of the audit committee acting pursuant to the recommended procedures. The Task Force prefers this approach because of the potential benefits of information and insight that may be gained from other independent directors and even from directors who do not meet prevailing standards of independence.[46]

GUIDELINES FOR MINIMIZING LEGAL LIABILITY

Obviously, the audit directors wish to avoid potential legal liability. To achieve this objective, the directors should conduct their activities in a manner above reproach. As evidenced by the statutory laws and court cases, their posture is critically important in the corporate environment. Hence they should not only exercise the required standards of care and loyalty in their positions but foster the professionalism regarding their directorship.

    To assist the members of the audit committee in minimizing their possible legal liability, the following guidelines are provided. Such guidelines do not purport to be all-inclusive and are not intended to preclude the insertion of additional matters. Also, it should be noted that the guidelines are presented in view of the oversight and advisory capacity of the committee.

---

[46]Ibid., pp. 65–66.

Minimizing the Audit Committee's Legal Liability: A Checklist

I. The Independent Auditors

  A. Have we inquired about the qualifications of the personnel whom we engaged in the audit?

    1. Review the backgrounds of the executive partner and auditing personnel.

    2. Inquire about the auditing firm's registration with the SEC practice division of the AICPA.

    3. Inquire about the CPA firm's participation in the voluntary peer review professional practice programs.

  B. Have we reviewed their engagement letter?

    The auditor's engagement letter sets forth the nature and scope of the audit engagement in order to avoid any misunderstanding between the auditing firm and the client. This letter constitutes a contract regarding the professional services of the CPA firm.

  C. Is there evidence that the audit examination was properly planned, supervised, and reviewed?

    1. Inquire about the overall audit plan concerning the scope, conduct, and timing of the audit examination.

    2. Discuss the level of knowledge which is required for the corporation and the industry.

    3. Discuss the ratio of staff assistants to supervisors in connection with the level of responsibilities for the audit.

    4. Review or request an outline of the supervisory review procedures of the staff assistant's work and note any disagreements among the audit personnel.

  D. Does the corporate annual report contain a fair and meaningful presentation of the information concerning the financial statements, footnotes, and supplementary information?

    Significant changes in the external reporting practices of the corporation should be discussed (e.g., departures from generally accepted accounting principles, exceptions to the consistent application of accounting principles, and the alternative applications of generally accepted accounting principles).

  E. Have we reviewed the recommendations made in their management letter to assure the auditors' objectivity?

    1. The management letter contains the auditors' recommendations as a result of their evaluation of the system of internal control. Any matters regarding the material weaknesses in the system of internal control should be discussed as well as full compliance with the provisions of the Foreign Corrupt Practices Act.

    2. Discuss the implementation of the recommendations in the current and prior years' management letters as well as causes of management disagreement with the auditors.

  F. Have we reviewed the lawyer's letter concerning litigations, claims, and assessments?

1. The lawyer's letter contains the opinion of legal counsel with respect to potential litigation, such as a pending lawsuit. Such information is provided to the CPA firms for possible disclosure in the financial statements.
2. Discuss the accounting treatment concerning the contingency losses and effect on the financial statements.

G. Have we reviewed the letter of management's representation?
The chief financial officer and chief executive officer will furnish a letter to the auditing firm with respect to the corporation's representations concerning the financial position and the results of operations. This letter should be examined in view of the facts in the letter and in the financial statements. This letter is particularly important since it confirms management's responsibilities for the financial statements.

H. Have we reviewed:
1. Any amendments to the bylaws or corporate charter?
2. The minutes of the meetings of the board of directors, directors' committees, and stockholders (e.g., compensation committee or finance committees)?

I. Have we reviewed the corporation's compliance with the auditors and legal counsel concerning the:
1. Securities statutes?
2. Antitrust laws?
3. Income tax laws?
4. Labor laws?
5. Regulatory laws applicable to the industry?

J. Have we made an evaluation of any material non–arm's-length transactions, such as loans to officers?

K. Have we reviewed:
1. Results of peer review?
2. Litigation against the CPA firm?
3. Adequacy of professional liability insurance?
4. Independence issues as required by ISB Standard No. 1?
5. Required disclosures to the audit committee as required by SAS #61?
6. Extent of management services provided by CPA firm and impact on independence?

II. The Internal Auditors[47]

A. Have we reviewed the qualifications of the internal audit staff?
1. Review the backgrounds of the director of internal auditing and the internal auditing group.
2. Inquire about the internal audit staff's participation in the programs of the Institute of Internal Auditors and other professional societies.
3. Discuss their qualifications with the independent auditing firm.

B. Have we reviewed their charter or audit plan?

---

[47]For further reference, see Exhibit 9.11 in Chapter 9, "Vital Checkpoints: Internal Audit Questions for the Audit Committee," prepared by Richard Hickok and Jules Zimmerman.

C. Have we considered the reporting responsibility of the internal audit staff?

D. Is there evidence that the work of the internal audit staff was properly planned, supervised, and reviewed?
See item number C under "The Independent Auditors."

E. Have we reviewed:
1. Reports on compliance audits?
2. Reports on operational audits?
3. Reports on financial audits?
4. Reports on the system of internal accounting and administrative controls?
   - Have we reviewed the recommendations made in their reports with respect to objectivity?
   - Have we considered the possibility of a long-form report from the Director of Internal Auditing?

F. Have the internal auditors' recommendations in connection with the prior years' internal audit been implemented?

G. Have we scrutinized cases of management disagreements with the internal auditors?

H. Have we reexamined the relationship of the internal audit function to the other departments?

I. How are activities of the internal audit staff and the independent auditors interrelated?

J. If the corporation has an electronic data processing installation, have we considered the use of independent EDP consultants to audit the installation?

III. The Representatives of Management (Chief Executive Officer, Chief Financial Officer, Treasurer, and Controller)

A. Are the qualifications of the representatives of management consistent with the corporate bylaws?

B. Have we reviewed their administrative functions in relationship to the present financial and accounting policies? (See company's organization chart.)

C. Have these individuals exercised their authority in accordance with the corporate bylaws?

D. Have we reviewed the minutes of the meeting of the board of directors concerning their compensation?

E. Have we reviewed their written reports concerning their responses to the deficiencies noted in the internal audit reports?

F. Are all employees who handle cash, securities, and other valuables bonded?

G. Are the financial and accounting policies and procedures set forth in manuals?

H. Are interim financial reports prepared for submission to management on a timely basis?

I. Is the quality and quantity of information in the interim reports adequate?

J. Have we discussed cases of management disagreements with the auditors?

K. Have we discussed:

    1. The engagement letter?

    2. The management letter from the independent auditors?

    3. The letter of management's representations?

    4. The lawyer's letter?

L. Have we discussed the periodic filings with the various regulatory agencies?

Signed by: _____ Date _____

[Should be signed by the chairman of the audit committee][48]

In view of the preceding discussions on the legal position of the audit committee, it is important that the audit directors fully understand the nature and scope of their legal responsibilities concerning the corporation's outside constituencies and the securities markets. However, they should keep their legal obligations in proper perspective. Such obligations should be integrated and balanced with the committee's functions so that the committee's purpose is not defeated. In short, the directors should discharge their responsibilities in a professional manner and not become totally preoccupied with the legal rules and regulations.

SOURCES AND SUGGESTED READINGS

American Bar Association, *Corporate Director's Guidebook* (Chicago: ABA, 1978).

American Bar Association, *Corporate Director's Guidebook* (Chicago: ABA, 1994).

American Bar Association, *Report of The American Bar Association Task Force on Corporate Responsibility* (Chicago, ILL: American Bar Association, 2003), pp. 1–89.

Bomark, Inc. v. Hemodynamics, Inc., 848 F. Supp. 1335 (W.D.M.I. 1993).

Braiotta, Louis, "Auditing for Honesty." *American Bar Association Journal,* 78, No. 5 (May 1992), pp. 76–79.

Commerce Clearing House, *Federal Securities Law Reporter* (Chicago: Commerce Clearing House, 1972–73, 1974–75, 1977–78 Transfer binder).

Commerce Clearing House, *Federal Securities Law Reporter* (Chicago: Commerce Clearing House, 1984–1985 Transfer binder).

Committee on Corporate Laws, Section of Corporation, Banking and Business Law of the American Bar Association, *Revised Model Business Corporation Act—Chapter 8: Directors and Officers* (Chicago, Ill.: American Bar Association, 1984).

Committee on Corporate Laws of the Section of Business Law, *Model Business Corporation Act—Chapter 8: Directors and Officers* (Chicago, Ill.: American Bar Association, 1998).

---

[48]It is advisable that the audit committee document its activities and have in-house counsel or outside legal counsel review documentation for content and use prior to adoption. Such procedures will help protect the audit committee in cases of possible litigation.

Connecticut General Statutes Annotated, Sections 33-318(b)(1) and (2), West 1960 and Supplement 1985.

"Firing Line," *Time* (February 19, 1979), p. 51.

Guttman v. Jen-Hsun Huang et al. Nvidia Corporation, C.A. No. 19571-N.C. (Del. Ch. 2003).

Internal Revenue Code Chapter 75A, Crimes (1954).

Haltman, et al. v. Aura Systems, Inc., et al., 844 F. Supp. 544 (C.D.C.A. 1993).

In re Caremark, Derivative Litigation Delaware Court of Chancery, 1996 698 A. 2d 959.

In re Livent, Inc. Securities Litigation, 148 F. Supp. 2d 331 (S.D.N.Y. 2001).

International, Inc. Derivative Litigation, 698 A. 2d 959 (Del. Ch. 1996).

Manzo v. Rite Aid Corporation, C.A. No. 18451-N.C. (Del. Ch. 2002).

Lancaster, Hal, "Fuss at Cal Life Shows Audit Committee Role is Crucial, Experts Say." *The Wall Street Journal* (March 17, 1980). p. 1.

Marsh, Hugh L., and Thomas E. Powell, "The Audit Committee Charter: Rx for Fraud Prevention." *Journal of Accountancy,* 167, No. 2 (February 1989), pp. 55–57.

New York Business Corporation Law, *McKinney's Consolidated Laws of New York Annotated* (Brooklyn, N.Y.: Edward Thompson Company, 1963, Book 6).

Petziner, Thomas, Jr., "Heinz Senior Officials Didn't Participate in Profit-Juggling Practices, Panel Says." *The Wall Street Journal* (May 9, 1980), p. 2.

Powers, William C., Report of Investigation by the Special Investigative Committee of the Board of Directors of Enron Corporation (February 1, 2002), *http://news.findlaw.com/hdocs/docs/enron/sicreport/*

Sarbanes-Oxley Act of 2002, Section 307, Rules of Professional Responsibility for Attorneys, H.R. Rep. No. 107-610 (2002).

Securities and Exchange Commission, 1993, 1994, 1995, 1996, 1997 *Annual Reports* (Washington, DC: U.S. Government Printing Office).

Securities and Exchange Commission, Release No. 33-8155, Implementation of Standards of Professional Conduct for Attorneys (January 29, 2003).

Securities Exchange Act Rule 10(b)-5, Title 17, Code of Federal Regulations, Sec. 240 (1974).

Securities and Exchange Commission, *The Work of the Securities and Exchange Commission* (Washington, DC: U.S. Government Printing Office, 1974).

United States Code, Titles 15 and 18 (1970).

Verschoor, Curtis C., "Miniscribe: A New Example of Audit Committee Ineffectiveness." *Internal Auditing* 5, No. 4 (Spring 1990), pp. 13–19.

Verschoor, Curtis C., "A Case Study of Audit Committee Effectiveness at Sundstrand," *Internal Auditing* 4, No. 4 (Spring 1989), pp. 11–19.

The Wall Street Journal Staff Reporter, "Playboy Audit Committee Bares Details of Hefner's High Living on Firm's Tab." *The Wall Street Journal* (April 4, 1980), p. 6.

Chapter 5

Rules of the Road— Auditing and Related Accounting Standards

The purpose of this chapter is to introduce the broad framework of generally accepted auditing standards and the integration of such standards with their respective generally accepted financial accounting standards. The integration of auditing and accounting standards will enhance the audit committee's understanding of the application of accounting standards in the preparation of the financial statements. Moreover, the audit committee will acquire not only a broad perspective on the essential purpose of the audit examination, but also the salient points concerning the auditors' report. In succeeding chapters, additional financial accounting standards will be discussed in more detail.

AN OVERVIEW OF GENERALLY ACCEPTED AUDITING STANDARDS

Nature of Generally Accepted Auditing Standards

In Chapter 2, reference was made to the auditing standards concerning the scope paragraph of the auditors' report. More specifically, the auditors state:

> We conducted our audit in accordance with auditing standards generally accepted in the United States of America. Those standards require that we plan and perform the audit to obtain reasonable assurance about whether the financial statements are free of material misstatement. An audit includes examining, on a test basis, evidence supporting the amounts and disclosures in the financial statements. An audit also includes assessing the accounting principles used and significant estimates made by management, as well as evaluating the overall financial statement presentation. We believe that our audit provides a reasonable basis for our opinion.

Explicit in the preceding sentence is the auditors' representation that the audit examination has been conducted based not only on authoritative guidelines or rules as established by the American Institute of Certified Public Accountants but also on their professional judgment in the application of auditing procedures. As approved and adopted by the membership of the AICPA, generally accepted auditing standards are as follows:

General Standards

1. The audit is to be performed by a person or persons having adequate technical training and proficiency as an auditor.

2. In all matters relating to the assignment, an independence in mental attitude is to be maintained by the auditor or auditors.

3. Due professional care is to be exercised in the performance of the audit and the preparation of the report.

Standards of Field Work

1. The work is to be adequately planned and assistants, if any, are to be properly supervised.

2. A sufficient understanding of the internal control structure is to be obtained to plan the audit and to determine the nature, timing, and extent of tests to be performed.

3. Sufficient competent evidential matter is to be obtained through inspection, observation, inquiries, and confirmations to afford a reasonable basis for an opinion regarding the financial statements under audit.

Standards of Reporting

1. The report shall state whether the financial statements are presented in accordance with generally accepted accounting principles.

2. The report shall identify those circumstances in which such principles have not been consistently observed in the current period in relation to the preceding period.

3. Informative disclosures in the financial statements are to be regarded as reasonably adequate unless otherwise stated in the report.

4. The report shall either contain an expression of opinion regarding the financial statements taken as a whole or an assertion to the effect that an opinion cannot be expressed. When an overall opinion cannot be expressed, the reasons therefore should be stated. In all cases where an auditor's name is associated with financial statements, the report should contain a clear-cut indication of the character of the auditor's work, if any, and the degree of responsibility the auditor is taking.[1]

These auditing standards provide a useful framework for measuring the quality of the auditors' professional performance concerning the audit examination and the audit report. Such standards are totally inflexible because the public accountancy profession wishes to maintain high standards and uniformity in the practice of auditing. However, auditing procedures are flexible since the auditors use various methods based upon their professional judgment to perform the audit. Furthermore, the Auditing Standards Board of the AICPA periodically issues pronouncements on auditing matters that represent the board's interpretations of generally accepted auditing standards. These pronouncements provide the auditors with guidance and direction regarding various auditing procedures in a particular auditing situation. (See Appendix A.)

---

[1]American Institute of Certified Public Accountants, *Professional Standards, U.S. Auditing Standards/Attestation Standards,* Vol. 1 (Copyright © 2003 by the AICPA, Inc.), AU Sec. 150.03.

AN ANALYSIS OF THE AUDITING STANDARDS

General Auditing Standards

With respect to the general standards, adequate technical training and proficiency as an auditor implies that the individuals who are performing the audit are professional accountants (certified public accountants). Certified public accountants are requisite to the audit function since their major objective is to express an independent opinion on the financial statements. Their professional opinion is critically important to the users of the financial statements because such users need assurance on corporate management's financial accounting representations. Moreover, independent auditors have a duty of professional care whereby they must exercise their professional judgment with reasonable care and diligence. (Visit *www.aicpa.org*, Code of Professional Conduct.)

Auditing Standards of Fieldwork   The first standard of fieldwork centers around the auditors' objectives, plans, and procedures concerning the particular audit engagement. For example, the Auditing Standards Executive Committee points out:

> Audit planning involves developing an overall strategy for the expected conduct and scope of the examination. The nature, extent, and timing of planning vary with the size and complexity of the entity, experience with the entity, and knowledge of the entity's business.[2]
>
> Supervision involves directing the efforts of assistants who are involved in accomplishing the objectives of the examination and determining whether those objectives were accomplished.[3]

Thus the first standard of fieldwork requires that the auditors plan their necessary auditing procedures subsequent to their review of such matters as the corporation's accounting policies and procedures and the industry practices of the particular entity. Also, they are required to develop and administer the necessary levels of proper supervision regarding the audit examination.[4]

The second standard of fieldwork requires that the auditors obtain a sufficient understanding of the internal control structure. (See Chapter 8.) Their evaluation of the system of internal control is necessary in order to determine how much reliance can be placed on the entity's financial accounting system. Since the financial statements are the product of the accounting system, the auditors must examine the internal controls and the related recordings of various business transactions. Furthermore, the auditors evaluate the system of internal control to determine the extent of their tests of the accounting records as well as their auditing procedures.

As the third standard of fieldwork, sufficient competent evidential matter means that the auditors must obtain and examine internal and external documentation that

---

[2]*Statement on Auditing Standards No. 22,* "Planning and Supervision" (New York: AICPA, 1978), par. 3.
[3]Ibid., par. 9.
[4]For a complete description of the organizational and operational aspects of a public accounting firm, see any standard auditing textbook.

supports the financial accounting representations in the financial statements. For example, the auditors will examine not only sales invoices and other documentations but also correspondence from various parties outside the entity, such as banks and customers. The amount of evidential matter to be examined is based on the auditors' professional judgment. Obviously, the auditors' major objective is to examine sufficient evidence to enable them to express their opinion on the fairness of the presentations in the financial statements.

The standards of fieldwork are directly related to the scope of the auditors' examination. The scope of the audit is critically important because the auditors may not express an unqualified opinion on the financial statements if their scope is limited. As the Auditing Standards Executive Committee states:

> Restrictions on the scope of his examination, whether imposed by the client or by circumstances such as the timing of his work, the inability to obtain sufficient competent evidential matter, or an inadequacy in the accounting records, may require him to qualify his opinion or to disclaim an opinion.[5]

Thus it is imperative that the audit committee examine those situations that may preclude the issuance of an unqualified opinion as a result of a limitation on the auditors' scope. For example, a limitation on the auditors' observation of physical inventories or the confirmation of accounts receivable would be considered a restriction on the scope.[6]

In March 2002, the Auditing Standards Board issued a hierarchy of generally accepted auditing standards in order to realign and clarify the authority and guidance in the myriad of auditing literature. Exhibit 5.1 contains the three levels in the hierarchy of generally accepted auditing standards. Given this hierarchy of auditing standards, it is reasonable to expect that audit committees should have a systematic process in place to ensure that they are informed about current authoritative auditing literature.

Since the standards of reporting are closely associated with an understanding of generally accepted accounting principles, such standards are discussed in the next section of this chapter.

INTEGRATION OF AUDITING AND RELATED ACCOUNTING STANDARDS

As discussed in Chapter 2, the auditors state in the third paragraph of their report that they are expressing an opinion on the fair presentation of the financial statements. Also, their opinion gives assurance to the users of the statements that management has presented the financial statements in conformity with generally accepted accounting principles.

---

[5]AICPA, *Professional Standards, U.S. Auditing Standards/Attestation Standards*, Vol. 1, AU Sec. 508.22. See Chapter 13 for a discussion on the various types of auditing reports.
[6]AICPA, *Professional Standards, U.S. Auditing Standards/Attestation Standards*, Vol. 1, AU Sec. 508.24.

Exhibit 5.1   GAAS Hierarchy Summary

Level of Authority

Level 1: Auditing Standards[a] (included the 10 generally accepted auditing standards and the Statements on Auditing Standards).

Level 2: Interpretive Publications[b] (includes Interpretations of the SASs, auditing guidance in AICPA Audit and Accounting Guides, and AICPA auditing Statements of Position).

Level 3: Other Auditing Publications[c] (includes other AICPA publications not mentioned above; auditing articles in professional journals, including the AICPA's CPA Letter; continuing professional education programs and other instructional materials, textbooks, guide books, audit programs, and checklists; and other auditing publications from state CPA societies, other organizations, and individuals).

Source: Statement on Auditing Standards No. 95, "Generally Accepted Auditing Standards" (New York: AICPA, 2002) pars. 1–7.

[a]The auditor should be prepared to justify departures from the SASs.

[b]The auditor should be aware of and consider interpretive publications applicable to his or her audit, and if not applied the auditor should be prepared to explain how he or she complied with the SAS provisions.

[c]The third-level publications have no authoritative status; however, they may help the auditor understand and apply the SASs.

If there are no exceptions noted by the auditors with respect to the consistent application of generally accepted accounting principles and adequate informative disclosure in the financial statements, then the users can assume that such statements are fairly presented. The following discussion provides an analysis of the four auditing standards of reporting and the opinion paragraph of the auditors' report.

Nature of Generally Accepted Accounting Principles

The first auditing standard of reporting requires the auditors to make a statement in their report on whether the financial statements are presented in accordance with generally accepted accounting principles. In contrast with the 10 generally accepted auditing standards, an authoritative list of generally accepted accounting principles or standards has not been established by any one authoritative source. However, the official pronouncements of several authoritative bodies have been recognized as generally accepted accounting principles. (See Appendix A.) Exhibit 5.2 contains a hierarchy of generally accepted accounting principles.

In addition, several other organizations have influenced modern accounting thought (see Appendix B), such as:

- American Accounting Association
- Institute of Management Accountants
- Financial Executives International
- Institute of Internal Auditors

Exhibit 5.2 GAAP Hierarchy Summary

Nongovernmental Entities	State and Local Governments

Established Accounting Principles

10a. FASB Statements and Interpretations, APB Opinions, and AICPA Accounting Research Bulletins

10b. FASB Technical Bulletins, AICPA Industry Audit and Accounting Guides, and AICPA Statements of Position

10c. Consensus positions of the FASB Emerging Issues Task Force and AICPA Practice Bulletins

10d. AICPA accounting interpretations, "Qs and As" published by the FASB staff, as well as industry practices widely recognized and prevalent

12a. GASB Statements and Interpretations, plus AICPA and FASB pronouncements if made applicable to state and local governments by a GASB Statement or Interpretation

12b. GASB Technical Bulletins, and the following pronouncements if specifically made applicable to state and local governments by the AICPA: AICPA Industry Audit and Accounting Guides and AICPA Statements of Position

12c. Consensus positions of the GASB Emerging Issues Task Force and AICPA Practice Bulletins if specifically made applicable to state and local governments by the AICPA

12d. "Qs and As" published by the GASB staff, as well as industry practices widely recognized and prevalent

Other Accounting Literature

11. Other accounting literature, including FASB Concepts Statements; APB Statements; AICPA Issues Papers; International Accounting Standards Committee Statements; GASB Statements, Interpretations, and Technical Bulletins; pronouncements of other professional associations or regulatory agencies; AICPA *Technical Practice Aids*; and accounting textbooks, handbooks, and articles

13. Other accounting literature, including GASB Concepts Statements; pronouncements in categories (*a*) through (*d*) of the hierarchy for nongovernmental entities when not specifically made applicable to state and local governments; APB Statements; FASB Concepts Statements; AICPA Issues Papers; International Accounting Standards Committee Statements; pronouncements of other professional associations or regulatory agencies: AICPA *Technical Practice Aids*; and accounting textbooks, handbooks, and articles

---

Source: Statement on Auditing Standards No. 69, "The Meaning of Present Fairly in Conformity with Generally Accepted Accounting Principles in the Independent Auditor's Report" (New York: AICPA, 1992), par. 15.

- Cost Accounting Standard Board
- Other regulatory agencies (e.g., Securities and Exchange Commission)

According to the Accounting Principles Board, accounting principles are described in this way:

> Generally accepted accounting principles incorporate the consensus at a particular time as to which economic resources and obligations should be recorded as assets and liabilities by financial accounting. . . .

> Generally accepted accounting principles encompass the conventions, rules, and procedures necessary to define accepted accounting practice at a particular time. The standard of generally accepted accounting principles includes not only broad guidelines of general application, but also detailed practices and procedures.[7]

Since the publication of APB No. 4, the Financial Accounting Standards Board has issued six Statements of Financial Accounting Concepts relative to business organizations and one statement with respect to financial reporting by nonbusiness organizations. In Chapter 3, these statements were identified and their implementation discussed.

Management's selection of accounting principles, methods, or procedures should be based on those principles of accounting that have general acceptance among the public accounting profession. Adoption of such principles is particularly important because it affects the auditors' opinion on the financial statements. If management applies significant accounting principles that lack general acceptance, then the auditors cannot express an unqualified opinion on the statements.[8] Moreover, Rule 203 of the AICPA Rules of Conduct of the Code of Professional Ethics states:

> A member shall not (1) express an opinion or state affirmatively that the financial statements or other financial data of any entity are presented in conformity with generally accepted accounting principles or (2) state that he or she is not aware of any material modifications that should be made to such statements or data in order for them to be in conformity with generally accepted accounting principles, if such statements or data contain any departure from an accounting principle promulgated by bodies designated by Council[9] to establish such principles that have a material effect on the statements or data taken as a whole. If, however, the statements or data contain such a departure and the member can demonstrate that due to unusual circumstances the financial statements or data would otherwise have been misleading, the member can comply with the rule by describing the departure, its approximate effects, if practicable, and the reasons why compliance with the principle would result in a misleading statement.[10]

---

[7]*Statement of the Accounting Principles Board No. 4,* "Basic Concepts and Accounting Principles Underlying Financial Statements of Business Enterprises" (New York: AICPA, 1970), pars. 137–138.
[8]*AICPA Professional Standards, U.S. Auditing Standards/Attestation Standards,* Vol. 1, AU Sec. 508.35.
[9]See the bodies designated by Council to promulgate technical standards in the Code of Professional Conduct at *www.aicpa.org.*
[10]AICPA, *Rules of Conduct of the Code of Professional Conduct* Visit *www.aicpa.org.*

Thus the auditors may express an unqualified opinion; however, their audit report should be modified to describe the circumstances.

Consistency   With respect to the third standard of reporting, the auditors are not required to state in their report whether the accounting principles have been consistently applied in the current and preceding periods. However, as previously mentioned, consistency in the application of accounting principles and adequate informative disclosure in the financial statements can be assumed by the users unless the auditors take exception in their audit report. As the APB pointed out:

> Consistency is an important factor in comparability within a single enterprise. Although financial accounting practices and procedures are largely conventional, consistency in their use permits comparison over time.[11]

The FASB reaffirmed its predecessor's position in SFAC No. 2, which states:

> Information about a particular enterprise gains greatly in usefulness if it can be compared with similar information about other enterprises and with similar information about the same enterprise for some other period or some other point in time. Comparability between enterprises and consistency in the application of methods over time increases the informational value of comparisons of relative economic opportunities or performance. The significance of information, especially quantitative information, depends to a great extent on the user's ability to relate it to some benchmark.[12]

Such a requirement is necessary because management has flexibility in the selection of accounting methods or procedures. In the practice of accounting, several alternative accounting methods are available to management for financial reporting. For example, the annual depreciation charges on the entity's plant and equipment may be computed on the basis of several acceptable depreciation methods. As a result, the auditors must satisfy themselves that management has applied the alternative accounting methods on a consistent basis from period to period in order to enhance the comparability of the financial statements. The comparability of financial statements is essential since the users of the statements make economic decisions and thus need financial accounting information that is meaningful.

However, management can make changes in the application of alternative accounting methods. Changes in the economic conditions that affect a particular enterprise may require a change in the application of an accounting method. For example, a corporation may change its method of pricing inventory items because of the inflationary conditions in the economy and the effects on the financial statements. It is incumbent upon management to justify the change in the accounting methods whereby a particular change enhances a fairer presentation in the financial statements. Such an accounting change should be disclosed in the financial

---

[11]*Statement of the Accounting Principles Board, No. 4,* par. 98.

[12]Financial Accounting Standards Board, *Statement of Financial Accounting Concepts No. 2,* "Qualitative Characteristics of Accounting Information" (Stamford, CT: FASB, May 1980), p. 2. See paras. 120–122 for additional emphasis.

statements in order to indicate the effects of the change on the statements.[13] Moreover, the auditors are required to point out the change in the application of the accounting methods by modifying their report with an additional paragraph following the opinion paragraph.[14] (See Chapter 10.)

Disclosure   The third reporting standard regarding informative disclosures implies that the information in the financial statements should be relevant to the users of accounting information. The information in the body of the statements, footnotes, and supplementary materials should be pertinent to the informational needs of the users. The accounting principle related to this particular auditing standard is known as the full disclosure principle. Under this principle, management has a reporting responsibility to its constituencies to disclose financial information that is necessary for a proper understanding of the financial statements. Such disclosure of information is based on management's judgment. Furthermore, the auditors have a professional obligation to ensure reasonably adequate informative disclosures in the statements.

The fundamental recognition criteria are set forth by the FASB:

> An item and information about it should meet four fundamental recognition criteria to be recognized and should be recognized when the criteria are met, subject to a cost-benefit constraint and a materiality threshold. Those criteria are:
>
> *Definitions*—The item meets the definition of an element of financial statements.
>
> *Measurability*—It has a relevant attribute measurable with sufficient reliability.
>
> *Relevance*—The information about it is capable of making a difference in user decisions.
>
> *Reliability*—The information is representationally faithful, verifiable, and neutral.
>
> All four criteria are subject to a pervasive cost-benefit constraint: the expected benefits from recognizing a particular item should justify perceived costs of providing and using the information. Recognition is also subject to a materiality threshold: an item and information about it need not be recognized in a set of financial statements if the item is not large enough to be material and the aggregate of individually immaterial items is not large enough to be material to those financial statements.[15]

However, management may not disclose certain information because such disclosure may injure the entity's competitive position.

Materiality   With respect to materiality, the FASB indicates:

> Individual judgments are required to assess materiality in the absence of authoritative criteria or to decide that minimum quantitative criteria are not appropriate in

---

[13]*Opinions of the Accounting Principles Board No. 20,* "Accounting Changes" (New York: AICPA, 1971), par. 17.

[14]AICPA, *Professional Standards, U.S. Auditing Standards/Attestation Standards,* Vol. 1, AU Sec. 508.16.

[15]Financial Accounting Standards Board, *Statement of Financial Accounting Concepts No. 5,* "Recognition and Measurement in Financial Statements of Business Enterprises" (Stamford, CT: FASB, 1984), par. 63.

particular situations. The essence of the materiality concept is clear. The omission or misstatement of an item in a financial report is material if, in the light of surrounding circumstances, the magnitude of the item is such that it is probable that the judgment of a reasonable person relying upon the report would have been changed or influenced by the inclusion or correction of the item.[16]

The Auditing Standards Board has reaffirmed the FASB position on materiality as mentioned in SAS No. 47, "Audit Risk and Materiality in Conducting an Audit."

Implicit in the preceding narrative is the pervasive influence of the materiality principle on the financial statements. Although the materiality of a particular financial fact is a matter of professional judgment, consideration should be given to the significance of the information in relationship to the users' information needs. Such consideration may include the effect of the financial item on the entity's net income or financial condition. For example, an inventory loss of $10,000 would be a material item in the financial statements of a small trading or manufacturing concern because such a loss may represent 5 to 10 percent of the company's assets. However, in a large conglomerate enterprise with billions of dollars in assets, inventory loss of $10,000 would be an immaterial item in the financial statements. Thus the nature and size of the financial item and its relative importance to the financial statements determine the materiality of the item. In short, no definitive rules or criteria are used to judge materiality since the circumstances regarding each audit examination vary.

In 1999, Arthur Levitt, former SEC chairman, reported that: "Staff Accounting Bulletin 99 reemphasizes that the exclusive reliance on any percentage or numerical threshold in assessing materiality for financial reporting has no basis in the accounting literature or in the law."[17] As a result, independent auditors are required to assess both quantitative and qualitative factors in their determination of whether an item is material. Likewise, independent auditors are required to obtain an acknowledgment from management of uncorrected misstatements and discuss these misstatements with the audit committee.

To enhance the usefulness of the financial statements, the APB has adopted a rule with respect to the disclosure of accounting policies. In particular, "the Board believes that the disclosure is particularly useful if given in a separate 'Summary of Significant Accounting Policies' preceding the notes to the financial statements or as the initial note."[18] For example, the disclosures would include, among others, the basis of consolidation, depreciation methods, inventory pricing methods, accounting for research and development costs, and translation of foreign currencies.[19]

---

[16]Financial Accounting Standards Board, *Statement of Financial Accounting Concepts No. 2,* par. 132.
[17]Securities and Exchange Commission, *1999 Annual Report* (Washington, DC: U.S. Government Printing Office), p. 84. For examples of qualitative factors, see SEC Staff Accounting Bulletin No. 99, "Materiality" (August 12, 1999). Also see *Statement on Auditing Standards No. 89,* "Audit Adjustments," and *Statement on Auditing Standards No. 90,* "Audit Committee Communications" (New York: AICPA, 1999).
[18]*Opinions of the Accounting Principles Board No. 22,* "Disclosure of Accounting Policies" (New York: AICPA, 1972), par. 15.
[19]Ibid., par. 13.

The disclosure principle is particularly important because if the auditors do not concur with the adequacy of management's disclosures, then they cannot express an unqualified opinion. Such inadequate disclosures should be stated in their audit report. For further information or additional disclosure matters, see Chapter 10.

Fairness   The fourth auditing standard of reporting requires that the independent auditors express their opinion on the fairness of the financial presentation in the financial statements. However, if the auditors cannot express an opinion, then they are required to acknowledge this fact and the related reasons. Moreover, the auditors are required to disclose the nature of their association and responsibility with the financial statements when their names are associated with the statements. Their professional opinion is based on their informed judgment as a result of the audit. Their opinion should not be construed as an absolute guarantee regarding the accuracy of the financial statements. Furthermore, the Auditing Standards Board points out the following with respect to the term *fairness*:

> The independent auditor's judgment concerning the "fairness" of the overall presentation of financial statements should be applied within the framework of generally accepted accounting principles. Without that framework the auditor would have no uniform standard for judging the presentation of financial position, results of operations, and cash flows in financial statements.[20]

In summary, the auditors should base their judgment on matters such as:

- Whether the accounting principles selected and applied have general acceptance
- Whether the accounting principles are appropriate in the circumstances
- Whether the financial statements, including the related notes, are informative of matters that may affect their use, understanding, and interpretation
- Whether the information presented in the financial statements is classified and summarized in a reasonable manner
- Whether the financial statements reflect the underlying events and transactions in a manner that presents the statements within limits that are reasonable and practicable to attain in financial statements[21]

The preceding discussions of an overview of auditing standards and their integration with related accounting standards indicate the need for a framework of acceptable guidelines in order to meet the demand for financial accounting information. Particularly important is the judgment and discretion of management

---

[20]*Statement on Auditing Standards No. 69,* par. 3.

[21]Ibid., par. 4. With respect to current Securities and Exchange initiatives dealing with such matters as materiality, revenue recognition, in-process research and development, reserves, and audit adjustments, the reader should visit Arthur Levitt's speech, *www.sec.gov/news/speeches/spch220.txt*. For additional information regarding the guidance on the criteria necessary to recognize restructuring liabilities and asset impairments and the criteria to recognizing revenue, see *Staff Accounting Bulletin No. 100,* "Restructuring Charges and Asset Impairment" (November 24, 1999) and *Staff Accounting Bulletin No. 101* "Revenue Recognition" (December 3, 1999) (Washington, DC: SEC, 1999).

and the independent auditors. Management's involvement in the application of acceptable accounting standards and the auditors' attestation of their financial judgments enhances the usefulness of the financial statements. More important, it is incumbent on the audit committee to understand the causes or reasons for the auditors' inability to express an unqualified opinion on the financial statements.

Whereas the preceding discussion focuses on the basic framework of auditing standards and the relationship to accounting standards, Exhibit 5.3 is a summary of the more significant auditing standards and related topical areas of interest to audit committees.

ATTESTATION ENGAGEMENTS

In addition to the generally accepted auditing standards associated with the annual audit of financial statements, the Auditing Standards Board and the Accounting and Review Services Committee have issued a codification of four statements on Standards for Attestation Engagements (SSAEs) and two SSAEs in response to the banking reform legislation (FDICIA). The basic framework for these standards is shown in Exhibit 5.4. The auditor's responsibility for attestation engagements with respect to special reports, reviews, and agreed-upon procedures is discussed in Chapter 13.

Exhibit 5.5 lists the attestation standards and related topical areas of concern to audit committees. The reader may wish to consult other AICPA statements such as Statements on Standards for Accounting and Review Services, Statements on Standards for Management Consulting Services, Statements on Quality Control Standards, Standards for Performing and Reporting on Quality Reviews, Statements on Responsibilities in Tax Practices, and Statements on Standards for Accountants' Services on Prospective Financial Information.

INTERNATIONAL AUDITING STANDARDS

Recognizing that there is a movement toward the "globalization" of the world's securities markets, the International Organization of Securities Commission (IOSCO)[22] has been working with the International Accounting Standards Committee (IASC) (renamed International Auditing and Assurance Standards Board [IAASB])[23] and the International Federation of Accountants (IFAC) to develop harmonized accounting and auditing standards. The objective of the initiatives is to enable a company that has complied with these international standards in its equity securities offering documents, to raise capital in a global capital marketplace.

In response to the demand for international auditing standards, the IFAC established an International Auditing and Assurance Standards Board. This board has issued a number of pronouncements and related statements, as shown in Exhibit 5.6. Although such standards are adopted on a voluntary basis, the goal of

---

[22]International Federation of Accountants, *1992 Annual Report,* p. 3.
[23]See American Institute of Certified Public Accountants, *Professional Standards,* Vol. 2, Sec. AC 9000 for the International Accounting Standards, New York, June 1, 2003.

Exhibit 5.3   Summary of Significant Auditing Standards

Auditing Pronouncements	Topical Area

Statements on Auditing Standards:

No. 12, "Inquiry of a Client's Lawyer Concerning Litigation, Claims, and Assessments"	Accounting for contingencies (see SFAS No. 5 and Interpretation No. 14)
No. 22, "Planning and Supervision"	Audit plans and execution
No. 31, "Evidential Matter"	Management's assertions
No. 45, "Omnibus Statement on Auditing Standards—1983"	Related party disclosures (see SFAS No. 57)
No. 47, "Audit Risk and Materiality in Conducting an Audit"	Inherent and control risks (see SFAC No. 2)
No. 50, "Reports on the Application of Accounting Principles"	Other auditors' opinions
No. 54, "Illegal Acts by Clients"	Violations of laws and regulations that have a material direct effect on financial statements
No. 55, "Consideration of the Internal Control Structure in a Financial Statement Audit"	Quality of the control environment and level of control risk
No. 56, "Analytical Procedures"	Analysis and evaluation of financial statement information
No. 57, "Auditing Accounting Estimates"	Reasonableness of estimates
No. 58, "Reports on Audited Financial Statements"	Types of auditor's reports
No. 59, "The Auditor's Consideration of an Entity's Ability to Continue as a Going Concern"	Violation of the going-concern assumption
No. 60, "Communication of Control-Structure Related Matters Noted in an Audit"	Reportable conditions (deficiencies in the internal control structure) as noted in the management letter
No. 61, "Communication with Audit Committees"	Selection of significant accounting policies and discussion of the auditor's disagreement with management
No. 62, "Special Reports"	Attestation of other historical financial information
No. 65, "The Auditor's Consideration of the Internal Audit Function in an Audit of Financial Statements"	Internal control and the quality of the internal audit function
No. 72, "Letters for Underwriters and Certain Other Requesting Parties" (See also SAS No. 76 and No. 86 for amendments.)	Comfort letters to investment banking firms
No. 73, "Using the Work of a Specialist"	Expert opinions (e.g., environmental liabilities)
No. 78, "Consideration of Internal Control in a Financial Statement Audit: An Amendment to SAS No. 55"	Revises the definition and description of internal control
No. 79, "Amendment to SAS No. 58, Reports on Audited Financial Statements"	Eliminated the requirement that auditors modify their reports for a significant uncertainty

Auditing Pronouncements	Topical Area
No. 83, "Establishing an Understanding with the Client"	Communicates the objectives of the engagement, responsibilities of management and the auditors, and any limitations of the engagement
No. 84, "Communications Between Predecessor and Successor Auditors"	Auditor changes (SEC 8-K Report)
No. 85, "Management Representations"	Audit evidence acknowledging management's responsibility for the financial statements
No. 87, "Restricting the Use of an Auditor's Report"	Auditor's reports intended only for use by certain parties
No. 89, "Audit Adjustments"	Acknowledges to the auditors that the effects of any uncorrected misstatements brought to management by the auditors are not material, both individually and in the aggregate. Communicates the aforementioned misstatements to the audit committee.
No. 90, "Audit Committee Communications"	Discussions about the quality, not just the acceptability, of accounting principles for financial reporting as well as communications of matters related to interim financial information.
No. 92, "Auditing Derivative Instruments, Hedging Activities, and Investments in Securities"	Auditing financial statement assertions about derivative instruments, hedging activities, and investment securities. (see SFAS No. 133)
No. 93, "Omnibus Statement on Auditing Standards—2000"	Withdraws SAS No. 75; amends SAS No. 58; amends SAS No. 84.
No. 94, "The Effect of Information Technology on the Auditor's Consideration of Internal Control in a Financial Statement Audit"	The effect of IT on internal control and assessment of control risk.
No. 95, "Generally Accepted Auditing Standards"	Establishes an authoritative hierarchy for GAAS
No. 96, "Audit Documentation"	Revises SAS No. 41, "Working Papers," and requires greater audit documentation.
No. 97, "Amendment to SAS No. 50, Reports on the Application of Accounting Principles"	Prohibits an accountant from providing a written report on the application of accounting principles not involving facts and circumstances of a specific entity
No. 98, "Omnibus SAS—2000"	Provides clarifying guidance to SAS Nos. 95, 25, 47, 70, 58, 8, 52, 29, 1.
No. 99, "Consideration of Fraud in a Financial Statement Audit"	Revises SAS No. 82, "Consideration of Fraud in a Financial Statement Audit" assessing the risk of material misstatement of the financial statements

(continued)

Exhibit 5.3   *(Continued)*

Auditing Pronouncements	Topical Area
No. 100, "Interim Financial Information"	Revises SAS No. 71, "Interim Financial Information Quarterly Reports—SEC 10Q Reports" (see APB No. 28)
No. 101, "Auditing Fair Value Measurements and Disclosures"	Accounting basis for measurement or disclosure of a financial statement item is fair value.

Note: The Auditing Standards Board has rescinded SAS No. 21 "Segment Information." The Board's Audit Issues Task Force has issued an interpretation "Applying Audit Procedures to Segment Disclosures in Financial Statements" of SAS No. 31, "Evidential Matter." Also see SAS No. 86, "Amendment to SAS No. 72, Letters for Underwriters and Certain Other Requesting Parties."

Exhibit 5.4   Standards for Attestation Engagements

General Standards

1. The engagement shall be performed by a practitioner having adequate technical training and proficiency in the attest function.
2. The engagement shall be performed by a practitioner having adequate knowledge in the subject matter.
3. The practitioner shall perform the engagement only if he or she has reason to believe that the subject matter is capable of evaluation or measurement against criteria standards or benchmarks that are available to users.
4. In all matters relating to the engagement, an independence in mental attitude shall be maintained by the practitioner.
5. Due professional care shall be exercised in the performance of the engagement.

Standards of Fieldwork

1. The work shall be adequately planned and assistants, if any, shall be properly supervised.
2. Sufficient evidence shall be obtained to provide a reasonable basis for the conclusion that is expressed in the report.

Standards of Reporting

1. The report shall identify the subject matter or the assertion being reported on and state the character of the engagement.
2. The report shall state the practitioner's conclusion about the subject matter or the assertion based on the criteria against which the subject matter was measured.
3. The report shall state all of the practitioner's significant reservations about the engagement.
4. The report on an engagement to evaluate subject matter that has been prepared based on agreed-upon criteria or an assertion related thereto or on an engagement to apply agreed-upon procedures should contain a statement restricting its use to the parties who have agreed upon such criteria or procedures.

Source: Statement on Standards for Attestation Engagements No. 9, "Amendments to Statement on Standards for Attestation Engagements Nos. 1, 2, and 3" (New York: AICPA, 1999), p. 2. Reprinted with permission. Copyright 1999 by The American Institute of Certified Public Accountants, Inc.

Exhibit 5.5   Summary of Significant Standards for Attestation Engagements

Statements on Standards for Attestation Engagements		Topical Area
Codification of SSAE No. 1	"Attestation Standards"	Framework for attestation engagements
Codification of SSAE No. 1	"Attest Services Related to MAS Engagements"	Part of a management advisory services engagement
Codification of SSAE No. 1	"Statements on Standards for Accountants' Services on Prospective Financial Information, Financial Information, Financial Forecasts and Projections"	Financial information about the company's expected financial position, results of operations, and cash flows
Codification of SSAE No. 1	"Reporting on Pro Forma Financial Information"	Pro forma adjustments derived from audited or unaudited historical financial statements
SSAE No. 2	"Reporting on an Entity's Internal Control Structure over Financial Reporting"	Management's assertion about the effectiveness of internal control environment
SSAE No. 3	"Compliance Attestation"	Management's assertion on compliance with specified laws and regulations
SSAE No. 4	"Agreed-upon Procedures Engagements"	Used for engagements other than SAS No. 75 engagements
SSAE No. 5	"Amendment to SSAE No. 1"	Working papers
SSAE No. 6	"Reporting on an Entity's Internal Control Over Financial Reporting: An Amendment to SSAE No. 2"	Internal control
SSAE No. 7	"Establishing an Understanding with the Client"	Communicates the objecives of the engagement
SSAE No. 8	"Management's Discussion and Analysis"	Disclosure and compliance with SEC rules
SSAE No. 9	"Amendments to SSAE Nos. 1, 2, and 3"	
SSAE No. 10	"Attestation Standards: Revision and Recodification"	Codification of SSAE Nos. 1–9
SSAE No. 11	"Audit Documentation"	Renames working papers
SSAE No. 12	"Amendment to SSAE 10"	

Exhibit 5.6   International Auditing Pronouncements

International Standards on Auditing

AU   International Standards on Auditing—Introduction
AU 8000   International Standards on Auditing
            8012—Preface to International Standards on Auditing and Related Services
            8020—Glossary of Terms
            8025—IT Glossary of Terms
            8100—Assurance Engagements
            8120—Framework of International Standards on Auditing
            8200—Objective and General Principles Governing on Audit of Financial Statements
            8210—Terms of Audit Engagements
            8220—Quality Control for Audit Work
            8230—Documentation
            8240—The Auditor's Responsibility to Consider Fraud and Error in an Audit of Financial Statements
            8240A—Fraud and Error
            8250—Consideration of Laws and Regulations in an Audit of Financial Statements
            8260—Communications of Audit Matters with those Charged with Governance
            8300—Planning
            8310—Knowledge of the Business
            8320—Audit Materiality
            8400—Risk Assessments and Internal Control
            8401—Auditing in a Computer Information Systems Environment
            8402—Audit Considerations Relating to Entities Using Service Organizations
            8500—Audit Evidence
            8501—Audit Evidence—Additional Considerations for Specific Items
            8505—External Confirmations
            8510—Initial Engagements—Opening Balances
            8520—Analytical Procedures
            8530—Audit Sampling and Other Selective Testing Procedures
            8540—Audit of Accounting Estimates
            8545—Auditing Fair Value Measurements and Disclosures
            8550—Related Parties
            8560—Subsequent Events
            8570—Going Concern
            8580—Management Representations
            8600—Using the Work of Another Auditor
            8610—Considering the Work of Internal Auditing
            8620—Using the Work of an Expert
            8700—The Auditor's Report on Financial Statements
            8700A—The Auditor's Report on Financial Statements
            8710—Comparatives
            8720—Other Information in Documents Containing Audited Financial Statements
            8800—The Auditor's Report on Special Purpose Audit Engagements
            8810—The Examination of Prospective Financial Information
            8910—Engagements to Review Financial Statements

Exhibit 5.6   *(Continued)*

        8920—Engagements to Perform Agreed-upon Procedures Regarding
             Financial Information
        8930—Engagements to Compile Financial Information

International Auditing Practice Statements

AU 10,000   International Auditing Practice Statements
        10,001—Inter-Bank Confirmation Procedures
        10,010—IT Environments—Stand-Alone Microcomputers
        10,020—IT Environments—On-Line Computer Systems
        10,030—IT Environments—Database Systems
        10,040—The Relationship Between Banking Supervisors and Bank's
             External Auditors
        10,050—The Special Considerations in the Audit of Small Entities
        10,060—Audits of the Financial Statements of Banks
        10,080—Risk Assessments and Internal Control—CIS Characteristics
             and Considerations
        10,090—Computer-Assisted Audit Techniques
        10,100—The Consideration of Environmental Matters in the Audit of
             Financial Statements
        10,120—Auditing Derivative Financial Instruments
        10,130—Electronic Commerce—Effect on the Audit of Financial
             Statements

Source: Reprinted with permission from the American Institute of Certified Public Accountants, *Professional Standards International Auditing,* Vol. 2 (Copyright © 2003 by the AICPA).

---

these international organizations and boards is to foster harmonized standards on an international basis. Given the audit committee's oversight responsibility for financial reporting, these standards may have an impact on companies at home and abroad. More recently, the IAASB issued an International Standard on Auditing (ISA) entitled "Communications to Those Charged with Governance." In short, the IAPC, the board's predecessor, indicated that such an ISA is needed for these reasons:

> It recognizes the need to provide standards and guidance on the auditor's responsibility to communicate matters of governance interest, arising from the audit of financial statements, to those charged with governance of an entity. Although the structures of governance vary from country to country reflecting cultural and legal background, in many jurisdictions the auditor is required to communicate matters of governance interest, arising from the audit of financial statements, to those charged with governance of an entity. Furthermore, the communication of these matters is part of a mechanism by which the external auditors can add value to the role of those responsible for the governance of the entity.[24]

---

[24]International Auditing Practices Committee, "Communications to Those Charged with Governance," Exposure Draft (New York: IFA, August 1998), pp. 2–3.

Thus the IAASB has recognized the benefits of a corporate governance approach to the audit process as a requisite for harmonizing the international accounting and auditing standards. The Public Oversight Board has argued that the auditing profession shift its focus from a compliance and rule-oriented audit to a corporate governance approach.

SOURCES AND SUGGESTED READINGS

American Institute of Certified Public Accountants, *Rules of Conduct of the Code of Professional Ethics* (New York: AICPA, 1997).

American Institute of Certified Public Accountants, *Professional Standards, International Auditing,* Vol. 2 (New York: AICPA, 2003).

American Institute of Certified Public Accountants, *Professional Standards, U.S. Auditing Standards/Attestation Standards,* Vol. 1 (New York: AICPA, 2003).

Financial Accounting Standards Board, *Statement of Financial Accounting Concepts No. 2,* "Qualitative Characteristics of Accounting Information" (Stamford, CT: FASB, 1980).

Financial Accounting Standards Board, *Statement of Financial Accounting Concepts No. 5,* "Recognition and Measurement in Financial Statements of Business Enterprises" (Stamford, CT: FASB, 1984).

International Auditing Practices Committee, "Communications to Those Charged with Governance," Exposure Draft (New York: IFA, 1998).

International Federation of Accountants, *1992 Annual Report* (New York: IFA, 1992).

Opinions of the Accounting Principles Board, No. 20, "Accounting Changes" (New York: AICPA, 1971).

Opinions of Accounting Principles Board No. 22, "Disclosure of Accounting Policies" (New York: AICPA, 1972).

Securities and Exchange Commission, *1999 Annual Report* (Washington, DC: U.S. Government Printing Office).

Securities and Exchange Commission, "Materiality," *Staff Accounting Bulletin No. 99* (Washington, DC: SEC, August 12, 1999).

Securities and Exchange Commission, "Restructuring Charges and Asset Impairment," *Staff Accounting Bulletin No. 100* (Washington, DC: SEC, November 24, 1999).

Securities and Exchange Commission, "Revenue Recognition," *Staff Accounting Bulletin No. 101* (Washington, DC: SEC, December 3, 1999).

Statement of the Accounting Principles Board, No. 4, "Basic Concepts and Accounting Principles Underlying Financial Statements of Business Enterprises" (New York: AICPA, 1970).

Statement on Auditing Standards No. 22, "Planning and Supervision" (New York: AICPA, 1978).

Statement on Auditing Standards No. 69, "The Meaning of Present Fairly in Conformity with Generally Accepted Accounting Principles in the Independent Auditor's Report" (New York: AICPA, 1992).

Statement on Auditing Standards No. 89, "Audit Adjustments" (New York: AICPA, 1999).

Statement on Auditing Standards No. 99, "Audit Committee Communications" (New York: AICPA, 1999).

Statement on Standards of Attestation Engagements No. 9 "Amendments to Statement on Standards for Attestation Engagements Nos. 1, 2, and 3" (New York: AICPA, 1999).

Part Two

The Planning Function of the Audit Committee

Chapter 6

An Overview of
Audit Planning

The auditing needs and goals of the enterprise are dynamic since they change as the responsibilities of the corporate directors become more complex. Thus the demands on the quality and quantity of auditing services change. To achieve an effective and efficient auditing process, audit planning is essential to meet the fluctuating auditing needs of the enterprise.

Since the audit committee has an oversight responsibility for the overall audit plan, it is essential that it understand not only the purpose of audit planning but also its usefulness in ensuring an effective and efficient auditing process. Although the process of audit planning is an amalgamation of the internal managerial talents as well as the external auditing talents, the audit committee should review the overall audit plan and recommend it to the board of directors for its approval.[1] Therefore, the purpose of this chapter is to introduce the meaning and benefits of audit planning and the broad segments of the overall audit plan. The role of the audit committee in overseeing the entity's audit plan is discussed in Chapter 7.

MEANING OF AUDIT PLANNING

As discussed in the preceding chapter, adequate audit planning is one of the tenets of the generally accepted auditing standards of fieldwork. To indicate its significance, the Auditing Standards Executive Committee's definition is restated:

> Audit planning involves developing an overall strategy for the expected conduct and scope of the examination. The nature, extent, and timing of planning vary with the size and complexity of the entity, experience with the entity, and knowledge of the entity's business.[2]

Furthermore, " 'materiality' and 'audit risk' underlie the application of all the standards, particularly the standards of field work and reporting."[3] Thus implicit in the auditors' planning efforts is their concern with particular financial accounts and locations, such as subsidiaries or divisions that are subject to a high exposure of risk. For example, since "cash transactions are more susceptible to fraud than inventories," the audit work should be "more conclusive."[4] Moreover, the quality of

---

[1]Such board approval is desirable in order to establish a formal corporate audit policy statement in accordance with the charter for the audit committee.

[2]*Statement on Auditing Standards No. 22,* "Planning and Supervision" (New York: AICPA, 1978), par. 3.

[3]American Institute of Certified Public Accountants, Professional Standards, *U.S. Auditing Standards/Attestation Standards,* Vol. 1 (New York: AICPA, 2003), AU Sec. 150.03.

[4]Ibid., AU Sec. 150.05.

the system of internal control is important because "of the influence on auditing procedures of a greater or lesser degree of misstatement; i.e., the more effective the internal control, the less degree of control risk."[5] A summary by the AICPA Control Risk Audit Guide Revision Task Force of some examples of both inherent and control risk attributes that the auditor might consider and the audit decisions that might be affected is presented in Exhibit 6.1. (See Chapter 8.)

Although the definition of audit planning applies to the independent auditors, it correlates closely with the audit committee's planning efforts. An analysis of the definition will be useful to the audit committee regarding its responsibilities in the audit planning function.

ANALYSIS OF AUDIT PLANNING AND THE COMMITTEE

Overview of the Audit Committee's Strategy[6]

To review the entity's audit plan effectively, the audit committee members need their own plan of action. Their plan should be integrated with the annual auditing cycle, which consists of: (1) initial planning segment, (2) preaudit segment, and (3) postaudit segment. Thus they will engage in audit planning at several different times during the auditing cycle. The typical steps in the auditing cycle are illustrated in Exhibit 6.2.

For example, during the preaudit segment, James K. Loebbecke, former partner of Touche Ross (now Deloitte & Touche), points out:

> Experience suggests . . . that both auditors and their clients—either management and/or audit committee members—should formally discuss not only the auditor's general methodology but also his specific approach in the client's own situation. This, indeed, should be a regular and early part of every audit examination.[7]

---

[5]Ibid.

[6]The reader may wish to review the list of auditing pronouncements mentioned in Chapter 5. For example, SAS Nos. 22, 47, 84, and 50 are all relative to the initial planning segment and SAS Nos. 22, 45, 47, 55, 56, 60, 61, 73, 90, 93, 94, 97, and 99 are applicable to the preaudit segment. Of course, the audit committee should review and discuss the decision factors regarding the acceptance and continuance with the independent auditors as well as the engagement letter with the independent auditors. (See SAS No. 83.)

[7]James K. Loebbecke, "Audit Planning and Company Assistance," *CPA Journal* 47, No. 11 (November 1977), p. 34. Also see Douglas R. Carmichael, "The Annual Audit Tune-up," *CPA Journal* 67, No. 12 (December 1997), pp. 24–29. Moreover, independent accounting firms have implemented a new approach to the annual audit engagement in order to provide more value by identifying performance improvement opportunities for clients. For example, KPMG Peat Marwick (1995) has a Business Measurement Process for identifying and assessing the client's business risk through the audit process.

This process has drawn the attention of CEOs and audit committee members. In particular, Kathryn D. Wriston responds to the question of what the board of directors and its audit committee expect and concludes: "The financial vitality of the organization and its long-term strategies to enhance shareholder value includes an assessment of various risks the company faces. Audit involvement in these areas has struck me as being potentially very beneficial to directors" (p. 18). See Kathryn Wriston, "The CPA Journal Symposium on the Future of Assurance Services," *CPA Journal* 66, No. 5 (May 1996), pp. 15–18.

Auditors explicitly address certain business risks in a financial statement audit. For example, environmental risks, such as legal and regulatory risks, are addressed in the annual audit, whereas competitor and sovereign/political risks are not addressed by the auditors. For further discussion, see KPMG Peat Marwick, *Business Measurement Process* (New York: Montvale, NJ: KPMG Peat Marwick, 1995); PricewaterhouseCoopers, *ABAS Audit Approach Team Asset* (New York: PricewaterhouseCoopers, 1999).

Exhibit 6.1 Illustration of the Audit Risk Concept

	Example Attributes Considered by the Auditor		Responses by the Auditor
	Inherent Risk	Control Risk	Detection Risk
Matters Pervasive to Many Account Balances or Transaction Classes	• Profitability relative to the industry • Sensitivity of operating results to economic factors • Going concern problems • Nature, cause, and number of known and likely misstatements detected in the prior audit • Management turnover • Management reputation • Management accounting skills	• Business planning, budgeting, and monitoring of performance • Management attitude and actions regarding financial reporting • Management consultation with auditors • Management concern about external influences • Audit committee • Internal audit function • Personnel policies and practices	• Overall audit strategy • Number of locations • Significant balances or transaction classes • Degree of professional skepticism • Staffing • Levels of supervision and review
Matters Pertaining to Specific Account Balances or Transaction Classes	• Difficult to audit accounts or transactions • Contentious or difficult accounting issues • Susceptibility to misappropriation • Complexity of calculations • Extent of judgment related to assertions • Sensitivity of valuations to economic factors • Nature, cause, and number of known and likely misstatements detected in the prior audit	• Effectiveness of the accounting system • Personnel policies and practices • Adequacy of accounting records • Segregation of duties • Adequacy of safeguards over assets and records (including software)	• Substantive analytical procedures and tests of details • Nature of tests • Timing of tests • Extent of tests

Auditors consider the types of factors presented above; however, it is not necessary to categorize such factors by type of risk.

Source: AICPA, *Audit Guide for Consideration of Internal Control in a Financial Statement Audit* (1996), p. 223. Reprinted with permission from the American Institute of Certified Public Accountants, Inc.

Exhibit 6.2   Example: Auditing Cycle

Example: Auditing Cycle (12/31/03 year end)

	Pre-Audit Meeting *(May or June)*	Audit scope
	Interim Audit Meeting *(October or November)*	Audit progress
Completion of field work January 20, 2004	**Post-Audit Meeting** *(early February)*	Review/approve drafts of 10-K annual report
March 15, 2004 Date of annual meeting and proxy statements	**Follow-up Meeting** *(late February or early March)* *(Hold prior to mailing proxy solicitation materials.)*	Recommendations in management letter

Note: The dates in the auditing cycle would be adjusted for the SEC rule on accelerated filers for the three-year phase-in of the new requirements.

In SAS No. 61, the Auditing Standards Board stated, "This statement requires the auditor to ensure that the audit committee receives additional information regarding the scope and results of the audit that may assist the audit committee in overseeing the financial reporting and disclosure process for which management is responsible."[8] For example, the independent auditors will discuss such matters as the audit approach and related threshold of materiality and levels of audit risk, anticipated changes in accounting policies and new accounting pronouncements, and special areas that need attention.

With respect to audit risk, the independent auditors attempt to minimize the risk that they have possibly issued an unqualified auditor's report with respect to financial statements that are materially misstated. In addition to following the guidance in SAS No. 47, "Audit Risk and Materiality," in conducting an audit, the auditors have to be aware of intentional misstatements or omissions of information in the financial statements. To assist them in this area of audit risk, the Auditing Standards Board has issued SAS No. 99, "Consideration of Fraud in a Financial Statement Audit." The Board has identified warning signals, or "red flags," for the auditors in assessing the risk of materially misstated financial statements due to fraud. The fraud risk factors considered in assessing this type of risk during the

---

[8]*Statement on Auditing Standards No. 61,* "Communication with Audit Committees" (New York: AICPA, 1988), par. 2.

planning phase and other conditions that may indicate evidence of fraud during the audit are presented in Exhibits 6.3 and 6.4.[9]

In addition to the guidance for the independent auditor's assessment of audit risk, the Auditing Standards Board has issued SAS No. 56, "Analytical Procedures." This statement "requires the use of analytical procedures in the planning and overall review stages of all audits."[10] The Board states:

> Analytical procedures involve comparisons of recorded amounts, or ratios developed from recorded amounts, to expectations developed by the auditor. The auditor develops such expectations by identifying and using plausible relationships that are reasonably expected to exist based on the auditor's understanding of the client and of the industry in which the client operates. Following are examples of sources of information for developing expectations:
>
> > Financial information for comparable prior period(s) giving consideration to known changes
> >
> > Anticipated results—for example, budgets, or forecasts including extrapolations from interim or annual data
> >
> > Relationships among elements of financial information within the period
> >
> > Information regarding the industry in which the client operates—for example, gross margin information
> >
> > Relationships of financial information with relevant nonfinancial information[11]

Given the accrued benefits from the use of analytical procedures by independent auditors, the results of comparative financial statement balances and financial ratios should alert the audit committee to high-risk areas that may have a significant impact on the financial statements. Recall the discussion in Chapter 4 with respect to "cooked books" and "cute accounting," which produce fraudulent financial statements. For example, the audit committee should be alert to improper revenue recognition methods, such as a "bill and hold" arrangement between the company and a customer. Here the company records a sale that increases earnings, but the customer is not obligated to take delivery of the products.[12]

Furthermore, the audit committee will be discussing other aspects of the audit with the senior management representatives—for example, the chief financial

---

[9]For a further discussion of fraud risk factors, see Howard Groveman, "How Auditors Can Detect Financial Statement Misstatement," *Journal of Accountancy* 180, No. 4 (October 1995), pp. 83–86; Vicky B. Heiman-Hoffman, Kimberly P. Morgan, and James M. Patton, "The Warning Signs of Fraudulent Financial Reporting," *Journal of Accounting* 182, No. 10 (October 1996), pp. 75–77. Also visit *www.aicpa.org/antifraud/management* for *Management Antifraud Programs and Controls* (New York: AICPA, 2002).

[10]*Statement on Auditing Standards No. 56,* "Analytical Procedures" (New York: AICPA, 1988), par. 1.

[11]Ibid., par. 5. Also see Patrick S. Callahan, Henry R. Jaenicke, and Donald L. Neebes, "SAS 56 and 57: Increasing Audit Effectiveness," *Journal of Accountancy* 165, No. 10 (October 1988), pp. 56–68; and Walter K. Kunitake, Andrew D. Luzi, and William G. Glezen, "Analytical Review in Audit and Review Engagements," *CPA Journal* 55, No. 4 (April 1985), pp. 18–26.

[12]For additional reading, see *SEC v. Barry J. Minkow, Litigation Release* No. 12579 (August 15, 1990), 46 SEC Docket 1777, and *SEC v. Donald D. Sheelen et al., Accounting and Auditing Enforcement Release No. 215* (February 8, 1989), 42 SEC Docket 1562.

Exhibit 6.3   Risk Factors Relating to Misstatements Arising from Fraudulent
Financial Reporting

Risk factors that relate to misstatements arising from fraudulent financial reporting may
be grouped in the following three categories:

Incentives/Pressures
A. Financial stability or profitability is threatened by economic, industry, or entity
    operating conditions, such as (or as indicated by):
    • High degree of competition or market saturation, accompanied by declining
      margins
    • High vulnerability to rapid changes, such as changes in technology, product
      obsolescence, or interest rates
    • Significant declines in customer demand and increasing business failures in either
      the industry or overall economy
    • Operating losses making the threat of bankruptcy, foreclosure, or hostile imminent
    • Recurring negative cash flows from operations or an inability to generate cash
      flows from operations while reporting earnings and earnings growth
    • Rapid growth or unusual profitability, especially compared to that of other
      companies in the same industry
    • New accounting, statutory, or regulatory requirements
B. Excessive pressure exists for management to meet the requirements or expectations
    of third parties due to the following:
    • Profitability or trend level expectations of investment analysts, institutional
      investors, significant creditors, or other external parties (particularly expectations
      that are unduly aggressive or unrealistic), including expectations created by
      management in, for example, overly optimistic press releases or annual report
      messages
    • Need to obtain additional debt or equity financing to stay competitive—including
      financing of major research and development or capital expenditures
    • Marginal ability to meet exchange listing requirements or debt repayment or other
      debt covenant requirements
    • Perceived or real adverse effects of reporting poor financial results on significant
      pending transactions, such as business combinations or contract awards
C. Information available indicates that management or the board of directors' personal
    financial situation is threatened by the entity's financial performance arising from the
    following:
    • Significant financial interest in the entity
    • Significant portions of their compensation (for example, bonuses, stock options,
      and earn-out arrangements) being contingent upon achieving aggressive targets for
      stock price, operating results, financial position, or cash flow
    • Personal guarantees of debts of the entity
D. There is excessive pressure on management or operating personnel to meet financial
    targets set up by the board of directors or management, including sales or
    profitability incentive goals.

Opportunities
A. The nature of the industry or the entity's operation provides opportunities to engage
    in fraudulent financial reporting that can arise from the following:
    • Significant related-party transactions not in the ordinary course of business or with
      related entities not audited or audited by another firm

- A strong financial presence or ability to dominate a certain industry sector that allows the entity to dictate terms or conditions to suppliers or customers that may result in inappropriate or non-arm's-length transaction
- Assets, liabilities, revenues, or expenses based on significant estimates that involve subjective judgments or uncertainties that are difficult to corroborate
- Significant, unusual or highly complex transactions, especially those close to period end that pose difficult "substance over form" questions
- Significant operations located or conducted across international borders in jurisdictions where differing business environments and cultures exist
- Significant bank accounts or subsidiary or branch operations in tax-haven jurisdictions for which there appears to be no clear business justification

B. There is ineffective monitoring of management as a result of the following:
- Domination of management by a single person or small group (in a nonowner-managed business) without compensating controls
- Ineffective board of directors or audit committee ovesight over the financial reporting process and internal control

C. There is a complex or unstable organizational structure, as evidenced by the following:
- Difficulty in determining the organization or individuals that have controlling interest in the entity
- Overly complex organizational structure involving unusual legal entities or managerial lines of authority
- High turnover of senior management, counsel, or board members

D. Internal control components are deficient as a result of the following:
- Inadequate monitoring of controls, including automated controls and controls over interim financial reporting (where external reporting is required)
- High turnover rates or employment of ineffective accounting, internal audit, or information technology staff
- Ineffective accounting and information systems, including situations involving reportable conditions

Attitudes/Rationalizations

Risk factors reflective of attitudes/rationalizations by board members, management, or employees, that allow them to engage in and/or justify fraudulent financial reporting, may not be susceptible to observation by the auditor. Nevertheless, the auditor who becomes aware of the existence of such information should consider it in identifying the risks of material misstatement arising from fraudulent financial reporting. For example, auditors may become aware of the following information that may indicate a risk factor:

- Ineffective communication, implementation, support, or enforcement of the entity's values or ethical standards by management or the communication of inappropriate values or ethical standards
- Nonfinancial management's excessive participation in or preoccupation with the selection of accounting principles or the determination of significant estimates
- Known history of violations of securities laws or other laws and regulations, or claims against the entity, its senior management, or board members alleging fraud or violations of laws and regulations
- Excessive interest by management in maintaining or increasing the entity's stock price or earnings trend
- A practice by management of committing to analysts, creditors, and other third parties to achieve aggressive or unrealistic forecasts
- Management failing to correct known reportable conditions on a timely basis

(continued)

Exhibit 6.3   *(Continued)*

- An interest by management in employing inappropriate means to minimize reported earnings for tax motivated reasons
- Recurring attempts by management to justify marginal or inappropriate accounting on the basis of materiality
- The relationship between management and the current or predecessor auditor is strained, as exhibited by the following:
  - Frequent disputes with the current predecessor auditor on accounting, auditing, or reporting matters
  - Unreasonable demands on the auditor, such as unreasonable time constraints regarding the completion of the audit or the issuance of the auditor's report
  - Formal or informal restrictions on the auditor that inappropriately limit access to people or information or the ability to communicate effectively with the board of directors or audit committee
  - Domineering management behavior in dealing with the auditor, especially involving attempts to influence the scope of the auditor's work or the selection or continuance of personnel assigned to or consulted on the audit engagement

---

Source: Reprinted with permission from *Statement on Auditing Standards No. 99*, "Consideration of Fraud in a Financial Statement Audit" (New York: AICPA, 2002, Appendix to SAS No. 99).

---

officer and the director of internal auditing. Thus the overall planning strategy of the directors will be based on their conference with these parties.

More specifically, these steps provide a framework for the committee's strategy:

1. *Develop an understanding of the entity's business and its industry.*[13] This step is particularly important because the audit committee should understand the external and internal environment within which the entity must operate. Such an understanding of the environmental characteristics will provide all members of the committee with the knowledge to assess the overall audit plan effectively. To accomplish this step, the audit directors should develop a macroapproach supplemented with the suggested professional development course as discussed in Chapter 7.
2. *Review the following with respect to each segment of the corporate audit plan as discussed in the succeeding section of this chapter:*
   a. Purpose and objectives of each audit plan

---

[13]The AICPA publishes *Audit and Accounting Guides* and *Industry Risk Alerts*. The audit committee may wish to consult these publications (e.g., *Consideration of the Internal Control Structure in a Financial Statement Audit*) to obtain an orientation to the entity's industry. Also see Robert Walker, "Know Your Client's Business," *CA Magazine* 124, No. 6 (June 1991), pp. 49–52; John P. McAllister and Mark W. Dirsmith, "How the Client's Business Environment Affects the Audit," *Journal of Accountancy* 59, No. 2 (February 1982), pp. 68–74; Donald N. Wolfe and Gerald Smith, "Planning the Audit in a Distressed Industry," *CPA Journal* 58, No. 10 (October 1988), pp. 46–50; and John W. Hardy and Larry A. Deppe, "Client Acceptance: What to Look For and Why," *CPA Journal* 62, No. 5 (May 1992), pp. 20–27.

Exhibit 6.4   Risk Factors Relating to Misstatements Arising from Misappropriation of Assets

---

Incentives/Pressures

A. Personal financial obligations may create pressure on management or employees with access to cash or other assets susceptible to theft to misappropriate those assets.

B. Adverse relations between the entity and the employees with access to cash or other assets susceptible to theft may motivate those employees to misappropriate those assets. For example, adverse relationships may be created by the following:
- Known or anticipated future employee layoffs
- Recent or anticipated changes to employee compensation or benefit plans
- Promotions, compensation, or other rewards inconsistent with expectations

Opportunities

A. Certain characteristics or circumstances may increase the susceptibility of assets to misappropriation. For example, opportunities to misappropriate assets increase when there are the following:
- Large amounts of cash on hand or processed
- Inventory items that are small in size, of high value, or in high demand
- Easily convertible assets, such as bearer bonds, diamonds, or computer chips
- Fixed assets that are small in size, marketable, or lacking observable identification of ownership

B. Inadequate internal control over assets may increase the susceptibility for misappropriation of those assets. For example, misappropriation of assets may occur because there is the following:
- Inadequate segregation of duties or independent checks
- Inadequate management oversight of employees responsible for asstes, for example, inadequate supervision or monitoring of remote locations
- Inadequate job applicant screening of employees with access to assets
- Inadequate recordkeeping with respect to assets
- Inadequate system of authorization and approval of transactions (for example, in purchasing)
- Inadequate physical safeguards over cash, investments, inventory, or fixed assets
- Lack of complete and timely reconciliations of assets
- Lack of timely and appropriate documentation of transactions, for example credits for merchandise returns
- Lack of mandatory vacations for employees performing key control functions
- Inadequate management understanding of information technology, which enables information technology employees to perpetrate a misappropriation
- Inadequate access controls over automated records, including controls over and review of computer systems event logs.

Attitudes/Rationalizations

Risk actors reflective of employee attitudes/rationalizations that allow them to justify misappropriations of assets are generally not susceptible to observation by the auditor. Nevertheless, the auditor who becomes aware of the existence of such information should consider it in identifying the risks of material misstatement arising from misappropriations of assets. For example, auditors may become aware of the following attitudes or behavior of employees who have access to assets susceptible to misappropriation:

- Disregard for the need for monitoring or reducing risks related to misappropriations of assets.

(continued)

Exhibit 6.4   *(Continued)*

- Disregard for internal control over misappropriations of assets by overriding existing controls or by failing to correct known internal control deficiencies
- Behavior indicating displeasure or dissatisfaction with the company or its treatment of the employee
- Changes in behavior or lifestyle that may indicate assets have been misappropriated

---

[1]Management incentive plans may be contingent upon achieving targets relating only to certain accounts or selected activities of the entity, even though the related accounts or activities may not be material to the entity as a whole.

Source: Reprinted with permission from *Statement on Auditing Standards No. 99,* "Consideration of Fraud in a Financial Statement Audit." Copyright (c) 2002 by the American Institute of Certified Public Accountants, Inc.

---

    b. Resources available for each plan

      Based on their discussions with the independent auditors, the director of internal auditing, and other senior management officers, the audit directors should be familiar with the overall purpose and objectives of each audit segment of the total corporate audit plan. Of particular importance to the committee is assurance of a coordinated plan consistent with the overall auditing goals of the organization. Such assurance may be obtained through a well defined and documented general statement of auditing objectives. Subsequent to the committee's review, the audit objectives and any other relevant information should be formalized into a written corporate document. This corporate document, along with the audit committee's recommendations, should be presented to the board of directors for its approval. Such board approval establishes a formal audit policy.

3. *Based on the audit policy, the internal and external auditing groups should develop appropriate audit plans that are consistent with the entity's auditing goals.* Obviously, the audit directors are not responsible for the preparation of the comprehensive corporate audit plan. However, they must assure themselves that the plan is consistent with the organization's policy. Thus the appropriate internal and external auditing plans will be consolidated into the overall corporate audit plan. Subsequent to the committee's review, the corporate audit plan should be formalized into a written document. This particular document will be used as a reference guide for future audits.

4. *Review and appraise the corporate audit policy and plan annually.* In order to guard against obsolescence, the audit committee should review and revise the audit policy and plan on a regular periodic basis.

Chapter 7 discusses the preceding steps along with other aspects of the committee's role.

BENEFITS OF AUDIT PLANNING

Assurance of an Effective Audit Plan

Clearly, the audit committee wishes to obtain maximum auditing services at a reasonable cost. William S. Albrecht observes that one large accounting firm reported that its audit fees have increased "over 50 percent in the last four years" and another firm's increased "40 percent."[14] Consequently, a sound corporate audit plan coupled with the committee's auditing strategy enhances the entity's opportunity to minimize audit costs and maximize on auditing services. Audit planning realizes a number of benefits:

1. It facilitates the effective allocation of resources to the audit function.
2. Inherent in the audit planning process is the psychological benefit of inducing the parties involved to think ahead and thus anticipate potential problems or opportunities.
3. Communication and cooperation among the auditing groups and management is enhanced since the audit committee coordinates their efforts toward the goals of the audit.
4. Since the board of directors expects the audit committee to monitor the audit function, audit planning provides assistance to the committee in accomplishing its task.
5. The audit committee can assess the effectiveness of the audits since the preaudit plan can be compared with the actual results of the audits.
6. Through a review of the audit plan, the committee develops confidence in handling problem areas.

Furthermore, the audit committee's review of the overall plan of the audit provides valuable information, such as:

- A summary of the company's financial reporting requirements and the timetable for meeting those requirements
- An understanding of the relationship between the company's system of internal accounting control and the scope of the audit
- The effect of accounting and auditing pronouncements and of SEC and other regulatory requirements on the scope of the audit

---

[14]William S. Albrecht, "Toward Better and More Efficient Audits," *Journal of Accountancy* 144, No. 6 (December 1977), p. 48. With respect to audit costs, "The audit committee should consider whether, and the extent to which, the actual costs of an audit exceed the estimated costs. When cost overruns are significant, the committee should seek satisfactory explanations for the variance. The committee might also wish to consider whether the presently engaged auditors have offered suggestions for management action that can reduce audit costs without diminishing audit effectiveness" (p. A-25). See Daniel J. McCauley and John C. Burton, *Audit Committees* 49 (Washington, DC: C.P.S., Bureau of National Affairs, 1986).

Also see Glenn E. Sumners and Barbara Apostolou, "Preparation Can Cut Audit Fees," *Financial Manager* 3, No. 1 (January/February 1990), pp. 46–49. The reader may wish to consult Chapter 4, which discusses the legal position of the audit committee and fraudulent financial reporting.

- The extent to which the external auditor uses the work of internal auditors in establishing the scope of his or her examination
- Changes in the company's organization, operations, or controls that have caused the external auditor to change the scope of his or her examination
- The degree of audit coverage, such as locations to be visited and the extent of procedures such as inventory observation, receivable confirmation, and so on
- The extent to which auditors other than the principal auditor are used
- Any potential problems that might cause the auditor to qualify his or her opinion
- Accounting principles management has selected for new transactions and the auditor's evaluation of those principles[15]

COMPONENTS OF THE CORPORATE AUDIT PLAN

An Overview

The corporate audit plan should be designed to give consideration to these factors: (1) financial disclosures, (2) operational efficiency, (3) compliance with corporate policies, and (4) compliance with laws. Thus the overall audit plan should include:

1. Statement of the proposed year-end and interim financial audits (see Exhibit 6.5).
2. Statement of the proposed operational audits
3. Statement of the proposed internal compliance audits
4. Statement on the status of the external compliance audits

To develop these statements effectively, it is necessary to review the essential segments of the overall audit plan. Because such a plan should be comprehensive, the following segments provide a useful framework:

- Financial audit segment
- Operational audit segment
- External compliance audit segment
- Internal compliance audit segment

The next discussion elaborates on each type of nongovernment audit within each auditing segment.

Financial Audits   The financial audit is concerned principally with the audit of the entity's financial statements. Such an audit is conducted by the independent auditors who express their opinion on the fairness of the financial statements. As discussed in Chapter 5, the independent auditors conduct their examination in ac-

---

[15]American Institute of Certified Public Accountants, *Audit Committees, Answers to Typical Questions About Their Organization and Operations* (New York: AICPA, 1978), pp. 15–16.

Exhibit 6.5   Types of Government Audits and Attestation Engagements

Introduction

2.01   This chapter describes the types of audits and attestation engagements that audit organizations perform, or arrange to have performed, of government entities, programs, and federal awards administered by contractors, nonprofit entities, and other nongovernment entities. This description is not intended to limit or require the types of audits or attestation engagements that may be performed or arranged to be performed. In performing work described below in accordance with generally accepted government auditing standards (GAGAS), auditors should follow the applicable standards included and incorporated in chapters 3 through 8. This chapter also describes nonaudit services that audit organizations may provide, although these services are not covered by GAGAS.

2.02   All engagements begin with objectives, and those objectives determine the type of work to be performed and the auditing standards to be followed. The types of work, as defined by their objectives that are covered by GAGAS, are classified in this document as financial audits, attestation engagements, and performance audits.

2.03   Engagements may have a combination of objectives that include more than one type of work described in this chapter or may have objectives limited to only some aspects of one type of work. Auditors should follow the standards that are applicable to the individual objectives of the audit or attestation engagement.

2.04   In some engagements, the applicable standards that apply to the specific audit objective will be apparent. For example, if the audit objective is to express an opinion on financial statements, the standards for financial audits apply. However, for some engagements, there may be overlap between the applicable objectives. For example, if the objectives are to determine the reliability of performance measures, this work can be done in accordance with either the standards for attestation engagements or for performance audits. In cases where there is a choice between applicable standards, auditors should consider users' needs and the auditors' knowledge, skills, and experience in deciding which standards to follow. Auditors should apply the standards that are applicable to the type of assignment conducted (the financial audit standards, the attestation engagement standards, or the performance auditing standards).

Financial Audits

2.05   Financial audits are primarily concerned with providing reasonable assurance about whether financial statements are presented fairly in all material respects in conformity with generally accepted accounting principles (GAAP),[a] or with a comprehensive basis of accounting other than GAAP. Other objectives of financial audits, which provide for different levels of assurance and entail various scopes of work, may include:

a. providing special reports for specified elements, accounts, or items of a financial statement; [b]
b. reviewing interim financial information;
c. issuing letters for underwriters and certain other requesting parties;
d. reporting on the processing of transactions by service organizations; and:
e. auditing compliance with regulations relating to federal award expenditures and other governmental financial assistance in conjunction with or as a by-product of a financial statement audit.

2.06   Financial audits are performed under the American Institute of Certified Public Accountants' (AICPA) generally accepted auditing standards for field work and

(continued)

Exhibit 6.5 *(Continued)*

---

reporting, as well as the related AICPA Statements on Auditing Standards (SAS). GAGAS prescribe general standards and additional field work and reporting standards beyond those provided by the AICPA when performing financial audits. (See chapters 3, 4, and 5 for standards and guidance for auditors performing a financial audit in accordance with GAGAS.):

Attestation Engagements

2.07   Attestation engagements[c] concern examining, reviewing, or performing agreed-upon procedures on a subject matter or an assertion[d] about a subject matter and reporting on the results. The subject matter of an attestation engagement may take many forms, including historical or prospective performance or condition, physical characteristics, historical events, analyses, systems and processes, or behavior. Attestation engagements can cover a broad range of financial or nonfinancial subjects and can be part of a financial audit or performance audit. Possible subjects of attestation engagements could include reporting on:

a. an entity's internal control over financial reporting;
b. an entity's compliance with requirements of specified laws, regulations, rules, contracts, or grants;
c. the effectiveness of an entity's internal control over compliance with specified requirements, such as those governing the bidding for, accounting for, and reporting on grants and contracts;
d. management's discussion and analysis (MD&A) presentation;
e. prospective financial statements or pro-forma financial information;
f. the reliability of performance measures;
g. final contract cost;
h. allowability and reasonableness of proposed contract amounts; and:
i. specific procedures performed on a subject matter (agreed-upon procedures).

2.08   Attestation engagements are performed under the AICPA's attestation standards, as well as the related AICPA Statements on Standards for Attestation Engagements (SSAE). GAGAS prescribe general standards and additional field work and reporting standards beyond those provided by the AICPA for attestation engagements. (See chapters 3 and 6 for standards and guidance for auditors performing an attestation engagement in accordance with GAGAS.)

Performance Audits

2.09   Performance audits entail an objective and systematic examination of evidence to provide an independent assessment of the performance and management of a program against objective criteria as well as assessments that provide a prospective focus or that synthesize information on best practices or cross-cutting issues. Performance audits provide information to improve program operations and facilitate decision making by parties with responsibility to oversee or initiate corrective action, and improve public accountability. Performance audits encompass a wide variety of objectives, including objectives related to assessing program effectiveness and results; economy and efficiency; internal control;[e] compliance with legal or other requirements; and objectives related to providing prospective analyses, guidance, or summary information. Performance audits may entail a broad or narrow scope of work and apply a variety of methodologies; involve various levels of analysis, research, or evaluation; generally provide findings, conclusions, and recommendations; and result in the issuance of a report. (See chapters 3, 7, and 8 for standards and guidance for auditors performing a performance audit in accordance with GAGAS.)

2.10 Program effectiveness and results audit objectives address the effectiveness of a program and typically measure the extent to which a program is achieving its goals and objectives. Economy and efficiency audit objectives concern whether an entity is acquiring, protecting, and using its resources in the most productive manner to achieve program objectives. Program effectiveness and results audit objectives and economy and efficiency audit objectives are often interrelated and may be concurrently addressed in a performance audit. Examples of these audit objectives include assessing

   a. the extent to which legislative, regulatory, or organizational goals and objectives are being achieved;
   b. the relative ability of alternative approaches to yield better program performance or eliminate factors that inhibit program effectiveness;
   c. the relative cost and benefits or cost effectiveness of program performance;[f]
   d. whether a program produced intended results or produced effects that were not intended by the program's objectives;
   e. the extent to which programs duplicate, overlap, or conflict with other related programs;
   f. whether the audited entity is following sound procurement practices;
   g. the validity and reliability of performance measures concerning program effectiveness and results, or economy and efficiency; and:
   h. the reliability, validity, or relevance of financial information related to the performance of a program.

2.11 Internal control audit objectives relate to management's plans, methods, and procedures used to meet its mission, goals, and objectives. Internal control includes the processes and procedures for planning, organizing, directing, and controlling program operations, and the system put in place for measuring, reporting, and monitoring program performance. Examples of audit objectives related to internal control include the extent that internal control of a program provides reasonable assurance that

   a. organizational missions, goals, and objectives are achieved effectively and efficiently;
   b. resources are used in compliance with laws, regulations, or other requirements;
   c. resources are safeguarded against unauthorized acquisition, use, or disposition;
   d. management information and public reports that are produced, such as performance measures, are complete, accurate, and consistent to support performance and decision making;
   e. security over computerized information systems will prevent or timely detect unauthorized access; and
   f. contingency planning for information systems provides essential back-up to prevent unwarranted disruption of activities and functions the systems support.

2.12 Compliance audit objectives relate to compliance criteria established by laws, regulations, contract provisions, grant agreements, and other requirements[g] that could affect the acquisition, protection, and use of the entity's resources and the quantity, quality, timeliness, and cost of services the entity produces and delivers. Compliance objectives also concern the purpose of the program, the manner in which it is to be conducted and services delivered, and the population it serves.

(continued)

Exhibit 6.5 (*Continued*)

2.13   Audit organizations also undertake work that provides a prospective focus or may provide guidance, best practice information, and information that cuts across program or organizational lines, or summary information on issues already studied or under study by an audit organization. Examples of objectives pertaining to this work include

    a. assessing program or policy alternatives, including forecasting program outcomes under various assumptions;

    b. assessing the advantages and disadvantages of legislative proposals;

    c. analyzing views of stakeholders on policy proposals for decision makers;

    d. analyzing budget proposals or budget requests to assist legislatures in the budget process;

    e. identifying best practices for users in evaluating program or management system approaches, including financial and information management systems; and

    f. producing a high-level summary or a report that affects multiple programs or entities on issues studied or under study by the audit organization.

Nonaudit Services Provided by Audit Organizations:

2.14   Audit organizations may also provide nonaudit services that are not covered by GAGAS.[h] Nonaudit services generally differ from financial audits, attestation engagements, and performance audits in that auditors may (1) perform tasks requested by management that directly support the entity's operations, such as developing or implementing accounting systems; determining account balances; developing internal control systems; establishing capitalization criteria; processing payroll; posting transactions; evaluating assets; designing or implementing information technology or other systems; or performing actuarial studies or (2) provide information or data to a requesting party without providing verification, analysis, or evaluation of the information or data, and, therefore, the work does not usually provide a basis for conclusions, recommendations, or opinions on the information or data. These services may or may not result in the issuance of a report. In the case of nongovernment auditors who conduct audits under GAGAS, the term nonaudit services is synonymous with consulting services.

2.15   GAGAS do not cover nonaudit services described in this chapter since such services are not audits or attestation engagements. Therefore, auditors should not report that nonaudit services were conducted in accordance with GAGAS. However, audit organizations are encouraged to establish policies for maintaining the quality of this type of work, and may wish to disclose such policies in any product resulting from this work, any other professional standards followed, and the quality control steps taken.

2.16   Importantly, although GAGAS do not provide standards for conducting nonaudit services, auditors providing such services need to ensure that their independence to provide audit services is not impaired by providing nonaudit services. (See chapter 3, general standards on independence.)

---

[a]The three authoritative bodies for establishing accounting principles and financial reporting standards are the Federal Accounting Standards Advisory Board (federal government), the Governmental Accounting Standards Board (state and local governments), and the Financial Accounting Standards Board (nongovernmental entities).

[b]Special reports apply to auditors' reports issued in connection with the following: (1) financial statements that are prepared in conformity with a comprehensive basis of accounting other than generally accepted accounting principles; (2) specified elements, accounts, or items of a financial statement; (3) compliance with aspects of contractual agreements or regulatory requirements related to audited financial statements; (4) financial presentations to comply with contractual agreements or regulatory requirements; or (5) financial information presented in prescribed forms or schedules that require a prescribed form of auditors' report.

[c]For consistency within GAGAS, the word "auditor" is used to describe individuals conducting and reporting on attestation engagements.

[d]An assertion is any declaration or set of declarations made by management about whether the subject matter is based on or in conformity with the criteria selected.

[e]The term "internal control" in this document is synonymous with the term management control and, unless otherwise stated, covers all aspects of an entity's operations (programmatic, financial, and compliance).

[f]These objectives focus on combining cost information with information about outputs or the benefit provided and outcomes or the results achieved.

[g]Compliance requirements can be either financial or nonfinancial in nature.

[h]If audit organizations provide nonaudit services, audit organizations need to consider whether providing these services creates a personal impairment either in fact of appearance that adversely affects their independence for conducting audits.

Source: Comptroller General of the United States, *Government Auditing Standards 1994 Revision* (Washington, D.C.: U.S. General Accounting Office, 2003), pars. 2.01 to 2.16.

cordance with generally accepted auditing standards and determine whether the financial statements are presented in conformity with generally accepted accounting principles. For example, the external auditors will examine the entity's statement of income, balance sheet, statement of cash flows, and the notes to the financial statements. Moreover, the auditors' examination will include a review of the system of internal controls (tests of controls) and substantive testing of transactions and records based on their professional judgment. The independent auditors must plan their audit engagement and document their audit plan. The audit plan in Exhibit 6.6 is an example. Note that the audit plan will vary from company to company; thus it may require expansion or contraction of certain areas in actual practice.[16]

Although the year-end financial audit is associated with the independent accounting firm, management may request interim financial audits from the internal auditing group. For example, management may request an internal financial audit of the financial statements at the end of a specified period, such as a month or quarter of the year. Internal auditors will conduct their examination and express their opinion on the statements. Such statements will be used within the entity, not distributed to the external users of accounting information. Furthermore, the internal auditors may conduct a review of the system of internal control to determine their effectiveness. Also, they may review management's actions toward the protection and security of the entity's assets. Finally, as a result of their financial audit, the internal auditors may be requested to engage in special assignments, such as the implementation of a fraud prevention program involving various branches or warehouse locations.

---

[16]Exhibit 6.6 is a simplified version intended to stress the time budget aspects of the audit plan.

Exhibit 6.6 Financial Audit Plan

Time Summary Form

Client: _____   Financial Statement Date: _____

	Budgeted Time					
	Asst.	I/C	Mngr.	Ptnr.	Tot.	Assist.
Planning & administration						
Internal control structure						
Cash						
Investments						
Receivables						
Inventories						
Other assets						
Property & equipment						
Notes & loans payable						
Payables & accruals						
Income taxes						
Other liabilities						
Equity						
Revenues						
Expenses						
Commitments, contingencies, & subsequent events						
Related parties						
Trial balance & adjustments						
Supervision & review						
Management letter						
Report preparation						
Totals						

Source: George Marthinuss and Larry L. Perry, *Comprehensive Engagement Manual*, Vol. 3, Chapter. 11 (New York: AICPA, 1992), pp. 11–14. Copyright (c) 1992 by the American Institute of Certified Public Accountants, Inc. Reprinted with permission.
*Attach memorandum explaining significant variances.

Operational Audits   Operational audits are usually performed by the internal auditing staff. The primary purpose of such audits is to review and appraise the activities of a certain function of the enterprise. For example, the internal auditors may review the operating efficiency and the effectiveness of the internal controls of a department. Such a review is essentially a service to management since the auditors generally make recommendations for operational improvements. In addition, the internal auditors may be requested not only to evaluate the managerial performance of the individual managers but to implement fraud prevention measures within the organization. Consequently, the internal auditing group is a critically important auditing resource since such a group can serve management on a company-wide basis.

Although operational auditing is associated with the internal auditors, management may request the services of the management advisory staff of the independent accounting firm. This particular arrangement is known as a management audit. For example, management may request an overall review of a particular function, such as purchasing of materials. Obviously, before such professional services are requested, management should weigh the costs against the benefits of the audit.

The operational audit plan may be similar to the financial audit plan; however, the functional units of the entity will be substituted for the financial accounts, as shown in Exhibit 6.6. Furthermore, the plan should be modified to include nonfinancial matters, such as conflicts of interests.

Compliance Audits   In contrast to operational audits, compliance audits are oriented primarily not only toward internal adherence to managerial policies but toward the entity's compliance with the various rules and regulations of the regulatory agencies. (See Chapter 4.) For example, the internal auditors may be requested to review the policies and procedures with the traffic and transportation department to determine whether their personnel are adhering to the entity's policies. Conversely, the chief financial officer or legal counsel may be involved with a compliance audit regarding an SEC or internal revenue service review.

The internal compliance audit plan may be structured on the same basis as the operational audit plan. However, the external compliance audit segment should disclose the status of legal compliance matters. Such a status should be a summary of the committee's discussions with the independent auditors and legal counsel. For example, the summary may include abstracts of the lawyer's letter as well as any other correspondence concerning legal compliance. The major objective is to review and inquire about the significance and implications of the entity's legal requirements and contractual obligations.

SOURCES AND SUGGESTED READINGS

Albrecht, William S. "Toward Better and More Efficient Audits." *Journal of Accountancy* 144, No. 6 (December 1977), pp. 48–50.

American Institute of Certified Public Accountants, *Audit Committees, Answers to Typical Questions About Their Organization and Operations* (New York: AICPA, 1978).

American Institute of Certified Public Accountants, *Professional Standards, U.S. Auditing Standards/Attestation Standards,* Vol. 1 (New York: AICPA, 2003).

American Institute of Certified Public Accountants, *Audit Guide, Consideration of Internal Control in a Financial Statement Audit* (New York: AICPA, 1996).

Callahan, Patrick S., Henry R. Jaenicke, and Donald L. Neebes, "SAS 56 and 57: Increasing Audit Effectiveness." *Journal of Accountancy* 165, No. 10 (October 1988), pp. 56–68.

Hardy, John W., and Larry A. Deppe, "Client Acceptance: What to Look For and Why." *CPA Journal* 62, No. 5 (May 1992), pp. 20–27.

Kunitake, Walter K., Andrew D. Luzi, and William G. Glezen, "Analytical Review in Audit and Review Engagements." *CPA Journal* 55, No. 4 (April 1985), pp. 18–26.

Loebbecke, James K., "Audit Planning and Company Assistance." *CPA Journal* 47, No. 11 (November 1977), pp. 31–34.

McAllister, John P., and Mark W. Dirsmith, "How the Client's Business Environment Affects the Audit." *Journal of Accountancy* 59, No. 2 (February 1982), pp. 68–74.

McCauley, Daniel J., and John C. Burton, *Audit Committees* 49 (Washington, DC: CPS Bureau of National Affairs, 1986).

Securities and Exchange Commission, *Accounting and Auditing Enforcement Release No. 215,* SEC v. Donald D. Sheelen, et al. (February 8, 1989), 42 SEC Docket 1562.

Securities and Exchange Commission, *Litigation Release No. 12579,* SEC v. Barry J. Minkow (August 15, 1990), 46 SEC Docket 1777.

Statement on Auditing Standards No. 22, "Planning and Supervision" (New York: AICPA, 1978).

Statement on Auditing Standards No. 56, "Analytical Procedures" (New York: AICPA, 1988).

Statement on Auditing Standards No. 61, "Communication with Audit Committees" (New York: AICPA, 1988).

Statement on Auditing Standards No. 99, "Consideration of Fraud in a Financial Statement Audit" (New York: AICPA, 2002).

Sumners, Glenn E., and Barbara Apostolou, "Preparation Can Cut Audit Fees." *Financial Manager* 3, No. 1 (January/February 1990), pp. 46–49.

U.S. General Accounting Office, *Government Auditing Standards, Standards for Audit of Government Organizations, Programs, Activities and Functions* (Washington, DC: U.S. Government Printing Office, 2003).

Walker, Robert, "Know Your Client's Business." *CA Magazine* 124, No. 6 (June 1991), pp. 49–52.

Wolfe, Donald N., and Gerald Smith, "Planning the Audit in a Distressed Industry." *CPA Journal* 58, No. 10 (October 1988), pp. 46–50.

Video

American Institute of Certified Public Accountants, *Fraud and the Financial Statement Audits: Auditor Responsibilities Under SAS No. 99.* (New York: 2003). Length of video: 135 minutes

Audit Committee's Role in Planning the Audit

Chapter 6 discussed the meaning and benefits of audit planning as well as the overall segments of the corporate audit plan. This chapter will enhance the audit committee members' skills and ability to appraise the entity's audit plan effectively. In particular, they will learn the basic steps of planning a strategy toward their review of the audit plan. Such steps will serve as a practical guide to review the coordination of the overall audit plan by the internal and external auditors.

THE COMMITTEE'S PLANNING FUNCTION

Introduction

The planning function of the committee centers on the purpose for which it was organized. The primary purpose of the committee is to provide assurance to the full board of directors that the internal and external resources allocated to the audit function are used effectively to accomplish the goals and objectives of the overall audit plan. To allocate resources to the audit processes effectively, the committee should adopt its own plan of action. In formulating the plan for accomplishing its objective, the committee should consider an integrated approach. Such an approach should be oriented toward the segments of the auditing cycle, which are: (1) initial planning segments, (2) preaudit segment, and (3) postaudit segment. The four steps in planning the committee's approach may be summarized as follows[1]:

1. Develop an understanding of the entity's business and its industry.
2. Review the overall purpose, objectives, and resources available for the corporate audit plan and recommend the auditing goals and objectives for approval by the full board of directors.
3. Review the audit plans of the internal and external auditing groups.
4. Appraise the corporate audit plan annually.

---

[1]The reader may wish to review the highlights of these steps in Chapter 6. It should be reemphasized that the audit committee is not responsible for the preparation of the comprehensive audit plan, since this is done by the internal and external auditing groups.

DEVELOPING AN INTEGRATED PLANNING APPROACH

Initial Planning Segment

Although the audit committee is removed from the entity's day-to-day operating activities, it should be oriented primarily toward the qualitative characteristics of the enterprise and its industry through a macroapproach. This approach is designed to give the audit committee a sense of the entity's existence and how it must interact with its environment. The underlying rationale for this approach may be stated in this way. If the audit committee members have not only a basic understanding of the entity's position in the industry as well as other environmental considerations, such as the economic conditions, but also an understanding of the operational characteristics of the business, then they can discharge their committee responsibilities more effectively. Thus before focusing their attention on the major aspects of the audit plan, the directors should engage in a study and review of the functional aspects of the enterprise. In obtaining this effective overview of the business, the directors should:

> [o]btain a knowledge of matters that relate to the nature of the entity's business, its organization, and its operating characteristics. . . . For example, the type of business, type of products and services, capital structure, related parties, locations, and production, distribution, and compensation methods. . . . Also, consider matters affecting the industry in which the entity operates, such as economic conditions, government regulations, and changes in technology. . . . Accounting practices common to the industry, competitive conditions, and, if available, financial trends and ratios should also be considered.[2]

Obviously, their orientation toward the entity is a substantial undertaking since the directors have limited time to contribute. An example of board and committee meetings is that of the Wal-Mart Stores, Inc.[3] (see Exhibit 7.1). Korn/Ferry International reported in its annual survey of 327 companies that 48 percent of the directors in 1992 spent annually 40 to 100 hours on board matters, including review and preparation time, meeting attendance, and travel.[4]

Although the audit committee members may be oriented toward the corporation through management presentations and plant visits, it may be advisable to formalize a program for educating them. In light of an action-oriented SEC, the enactment of the Foreign Corrupt Practices Act, the Sarbanes-Oxley Act, SROs listing standard litigation against directors, the Treadway report, and the COSO report,[5] such a program is desirable in meeting the dynamic changes in corporate governance and accountability.

---

[2]*Statement on Auditing Standards No. 22,* "Planning and Supervision" (New York: AICPA, 1978), par. 7.
[3]Wal-Mart Stores, Inc., *Notice of 2003 Annual Meeting of Shareholders Proxy Statement,* p. 4.
[4]Korn/Ferry International, *Twentieth Annual Board of Directors Study* (New York: Korn/Ferry International, 1993), p. 19. Subsequently, Korn/Ferry International reported in its survey of 903 companies (1,020 directors) that "[t]he average number of hours required annually to serve on a board continues to run about 150, a serious limit for busy people" (p. 7). See Korn/Ferry International, *25th Annual Board of Directors Study* (New York: Korn/Ferry International, 1998).
[5]See Appendix I on this book's website.

Exhibit 7.1   Sample of Board Committee Functions and Meetings

Board Committees			
Committee	Members	Functions and Additional Information[b]	Number of Meetings
Audit	Stanley C. Gault Roland A. Hernandez[a] J. Paul Reason	• Reviews financial reporting, policies, procedures, and internal controls of Wal-Mart • Recommends appointment of outside auditors • Reviews related party transactions • The Board has determined that the members are "independent" as defined by the current listing standards of the New York Stock Exchange and • The Board has adopted a written charter for the Audit Committee	8
Compensation, Nominating and Governance[c]	James W. Breyer Dawn G. Lepore Elizabeth A. Sanders Jose H. Villarreal[a]	• Administers Wal-Mart's Stock Incentive Plan of 1998 for executive officers • Sets interest rate applicable to Wal-Mart's Officer Deferred Compensation Plan • Sets and verifies attainment of goals under Wal-Mart's Management Incentive Plan, as amended • Reviews salary and benefits issues • Reviews and provides guidance regarding the Company's image • Responsible for corporate governance issues and • Recommends candidates to the Board for Nomination to the Board	6
Executive	Thomas M. Coughlin David D. Glass[a] H. Lee Scott, Jr. S. Robson Walton	• Implements policy decisions of the Board and • Acts on the Board's behalf between Board meetings • Administers Wal-Mart's Stock Incentive Plan of 1998 for associates who are not	2 (4)

(continued)

Exhibit 7.1 *(Continued)*

Stock Option	Thomas M. Coughlin David D. Glass H. Lee Scott, J.[a] S. Robson Walton	directors or officers subject to subsection 16(a) of the Securities and Exchange Act of 1934, as amended	4
Strategic Planning and Finance	John T. Chambers Jack C. Shewmaker[a] John T. Walton	• Reviews important financial decisions and • Advises regarding long-range strategic planning	4

[a]Committee Chairperson
[b]On March 6, 2003, the Board adopted revised written charters for each Board Committee. The revised charters are available at *www.walmartstores.com*.
[c]On March 6, 2003, the Board changed this Committee's name to the "Compensation, Nominating and Governance Committee" to reflect its responsibility for corporate governance issues.
[d]The Executive Committee met twice and acted by unanimous written consent nineteen times during the fiscal year.

To educate the directors effectively so that audit committee members can have productive meetings and contribute to the board of directors, they should consider the adoption of the audit director's professional development program shown in Exhibit 7.2. Such a program should be instituted on the basis that it will enhance the audit director's ability to serve effectively on the committee.

Exhibit 7.2 Professional Development Program

Description	Presentation *(Estimated)*
I. Industry Matters Discussions with executive management on the external environmental matters, such as: 1. Competitive and economic conditions 2. Government regulations 3. Foreign operations 4. New technological advancements 5. Industry accounting practices 6. Changes in social attitudes 7. Management's risk assessment process	One day, group discussion
II. Entity's Business Matters Discussions with key executives on the internal environmental matters, such as: 1. Historical perspective of the business a. Organizational structure	Two days, group discussion

  b. Lines of business and product segments
2. Company objectives and policies, particularly
  financial accounting policies, controls, and
  procedures
3. Summary of the entity's principles of operations*
4. Legal obligations of the enterprise
5. Significant documentation, such as the
  corporate charter and bylaws
6. Management's risk assessment process

III. Internal Auditing Matters   One day, presentation and
Review and discuss with the internal auditing   group discussion
executive such matters as:
1. The nature and functions of the internal
  auditing group
2. Organizational characteristics of the staff
3. Representative audit programs and reports
4. The interface between the staff and the
  independent auditors
5. The monitoring activities of the staff

IV. External Auditing Matters   One day, presentation and
Review and discuss with the executive partner group discussion
matters such as:
1. The nature and overall purpose of the audit
2. Organizational characteristics of the firm
  and biographical data regarding the auditing
  personnel assigned to the audit, including
  rotations of staff
3. Prior year's annual reports, Form 10-K
  report, interim financial reports (10Qs),
  and any 8K reports
4. Key documentation, such as the engagement
  letter, management letter, client representation letter, and the lawyer's letter
5. Role of the CPA in matters such as:
a. Internal controls, audit risk assessment, fraud
  risk assessment, business risk assessment,
  materiality, computer security, and legal
  compliance with the Foreign Corrupt
  Practices Act
b. Internal auditing evaluation and peer reviews
c. Financial reporting disclosures, audited and
  unaudited statements (e.g., management's
  discussion and analysis, environmental liabilities)
d. Conflicts of interest advisement
e. Filings with various regulatory agencies
6. Other services of the firm, such as tax
  services

---

*Tour a selected plant location and/or sales location to understand the cost accounting system.

Implementation of the program may be coordinated through an executive who is responsible for the corporate human resources or the in-house development and training programs. Clearly, each entity can establish a development program to meet its own needs.

With respect to the adoption of the program, several key points should be noted:

- The duration of the program will vary since it is contingent on the size and complexity of the entity. The directors should participate in the program for a reasonable period of time each year.

- Each director should be required to complete a reasonable number of hours of advance preparation.

- The coordinator of the program should be responsible for the necessary reading materials and conference schedules. Therefore, he or she should consult with the appropriate information sources, such as the internal and external auditing group, in order to obtain the necessary literature.

- The directors should be given an opportunity to critique the program in order to enhance the quality and viability of the conference program.

Phase 1: Preaudit Planning Segment

During this segment of the auditing cycle, the committee should review and appraise: (1) the goals and objectives of the audit function and (2) the resources available for the audit processes. Subsequent to its review, the committee should recommend that the goals and objectives developed are in accordance with the charter for the audit committee, which is approved by the board of directors.[6] The major objective of the committee is to gain assurance that the goals and objectives are well defined and explicit. Such a step is necessary because the objectives will become the basis for the conduct of the entity's auditing activities. Thus a general statement of auditing policy will provide a course of action for the parties who are responsible for the entity's audit processes. Moreover, auditing policies not only provide an established framework for the internal and external auditing activities but also identify the type and quality of auditing services to be rendered.

In view of the audit committee's oversight and advisory capacity, the auditing objectives and resource requirements should be defined by the executive auditing personnel. For example, the executive partner of the independent accounting firm will formulate the audit objectives based on his or her discussion with the corporate management accounting executives. Generally speaking, the objectives will relate to the annual financial audit, which includes the annual audit of the financial statements and SEC filings. However, the accounting firm may be requested to render other services, such as tax and management advisory services. The objectives of the external audit ultimately will be spelled out in the independent auditor's engagement letter. Consequently, the audit committee should review and discuss the engagement letter with the executive partner.

---

[6]The overall audit plan refers to the charter for the audit committee, which requires full board approval. The annual audit plan does not require full board approval.

Although the financial audit is a major part of the overall audit plan, there are collateral objectives with respect to the operational and compliance audits. Accordingly, the internal auditing executive should define the objectives for the entity's operational and compliance auditing plans. In particular, the broad objectives of such plans should include a provision to maximize the organization's economic resources and minimize the causes of inefficiencies or uneconomical practices.

For example, the objectives may include a provision for performance auditing as well as special-purpose audits. Obviously, such objectives vary with the size and complexity of the entity and the professional judgment of the executive internal auditor. Accordingly, the audit committee should request a written general statement of the corporate internal auditing objectives and should review and discuss this corporate document with the internal auditing executive. It is imperative that the objective be documented in order to avoid any misunderstanding among the committee members and the internal auditing group. Furthermore, to achieve an effective review posture, the audit committee should also discuss the corporate auditing goals with the chief financial officer and the controller. The major objective of this interview is to determine that the overall auditing goals satisfy the needs of the organization.

In addition to the preceding approach, the audit committee should give consideration to these points:

- Are the general auditing objectives for the entity well defined?
- Do the auditing goals appear to be workable or realistic in relation to the auditing resources? For example, is the structure and organization of the internal audit staff conducive to the auditing needs and objectives of the entity?
- Do all the executives who participate in the audit process understand the overall goals and objectives?
- Do the independent auditors and the internal auditors have any conflicting objectives?
- What is the independent auditor's assessment of the objectives of the internal audit staff?
- Do the objectives allow the entity to maximize on the auditing services at a reasonable cost?

Although audit committee members are not accounting and auditing experts, they should challenge the objectives and request possible modifications, if necessary. Subsequent to their review, the general auditing objectives should be recommended to the board of directors in order to establish a formal auditing policy statement. Once approved, the auditing policy will serve as a blueprint of the entity's audit processes.

Phase 2: Preaudit Planning Segment

The major role of the audit committee members is to review the corporate audit plan. Since the audit policy has been established, their task is to ensure that the entity's auditing plan is consistent with the audit policy. Thus the planning process of the audit requires the support of the independent auditors, internal auditors, and senior accounting executives. The audit committee essentially reviews the coordination of the plans and schedules from the preceding parties. The parties involved in the planning process should work together to ensure that they are working toward their goals as indicated in the policy statement.

For example, the audit plan of the independent auditors may include such matters as:

- Background information on the client, general information disclosed in the early sections of the SEC form 10-K report (e.g., organization data, business operations and products, audit risk assessment, etc.).
- The purpose and objectives of the audit and the nature, extent, and timing of the audit work, information disclosed in the auditor's engagement letter.
- Assignment and scheduling of audit personnel.
- Preaudit work to be performed by the client's staff. Obviously, the independent auditors will modify their plan, if necessary, during the course of their audit examination.

In view of the working relationship between the work of the independent auditors and the internal auditors, the external auditors may take an active role in formulating the audit plan of the internal auditing group. However, each group has its own auditing goals and responsibilities. The internal auditors cannot assume the role of the external auditors. For example, the internal auditors are concerned primarily with the operational and compliance auditing functions, whereas the independent auditors are concerned with the financial audit activities. According to the Auditing Standards Board:

> Even though the internal auditors' work may affect the auditor's procedures, the auditor should perform procedures to obtain sufficient, competent, evidential matter to support the auditor's report. Evidence obtained through the auditor's direct personal knowledge, including physical examination, observation, computation, and inspection, is generally more persuasive than information obtained indirectly.
>
> The responsibility to report on the financial statements rests solely with the auditor. Unlike the situation in which the auditor uses the work of other independent auditors, this responsibility cannot be shared with the internal auditors. Because the auditor has the ultimate responsibility to express an opinion on the financial statements, judgments about assessments of inherent and control risks, the materiality of misstatements, the sufficiency of tests performed, the evaluation of significant accounting estimates, and other matters affecting the auditor's report should always be those of the auditor.[7]

Moreover, the independent auditor must not only assess the competence and objectivity of the internal auditors but also supervise and test their work if they

---

[7]*Statement on Auditing Standards No. 65,* "The Auditor's Consideration of the Internal Audit Function in an Audit of Financial Statements" (New York: AICPA, 1991), pars. 18 and 19.

provide direct assistance in performing the independent auditor's work.[8] Thus based on the independent auditor's judgment, the internal auditing staff may offer valuable assistance during the audit.

In order to appraise the corporate audit plan effectively, the audit committee should give consideration to the following criteria[9]:

- The authority and responsibility for each segment of the corporate audit plan should be clearly defined.
- The chief financial officer should acknowledge his or her general support for the plan to avoid opposition during the course of the internal and external auditing engagements.
- The internal and external resources available for the audit function should be adequate and properly allocated.
- The plan should be realistic against the conditions of the business and its industry.
- The plan should be realistic and consistent with the goals and objectives as expressed in the corporate audit policy statement.
- The scope of the audit plans should be defined and explicit to avoid any duplication of auditing effort.
- The general criteria used to identify areas subject to audit should be explicit (e.g., What is the auditing firm's policy on materiality?).
- The plan should incorporate any applicable resolutions as a result of the board of directors' and stockholders' meetings as well as take into account related matters of the other standing committees, such as the finance committee.
- The extent of auditing work should be reasonable in relationship to the quality of the internal control system. Also, the time associated with each audit plan should be reasonable in relation to the size and complexity of the entity's operations and organizational structure.
- An analysis of the costs and benefits of the auditing resources should be made (e.g., What is the desirability of allocating more financial auditing work to the internal audit staff and reducing the audit time of the independent auditors?).

Postaudit Segment

In the preceding discussion, the committee reviewed and appraised the audit planning activities of the auditors and corporate accounting management officers. Such a review related to the initial planning segment of the auditing cycle. However, this final step should be accomplished during the postaudit segment of the auditing cycle whereby the audit directors should reassess the corporate audit plan. On the basis of their reassessments, the directors should assure themselves that the auditing policy and preaudit plans were effective in order to provide the assurances required by the board of directors.

---

[8]Ibid., par. 27.
[9]This list is not all-inclusive and is not intended to preclude the insertion of additional criteria.

To provide such assurances to the board, these three general comments are applicable for related auditing and attestation standards (see Chapter 5):

1. The audit committee should inquire into the degree of cooperation received from the entity's personnel who are involved in the auditing process. Also, it should be satisfied that the audit examination was conducted in an impartial and objective manner.
2. Based on a review of the preaudit plan criteria, the committee should assess the results of the audit and inquire into the reasons for any differences (e.g., Are there any problems that preclude the independent auditors from complying with the generally accepted auditing standards?). Such inquiries should be made in relation to the independent auditor's management letter, which discloses their reportable conditions and recommendations for improving the entity's system of internal control. Also, the committee should review progress reports or correspondence regarding the results of the audit (e.g., internal audit reports and financial management correspondence).
3. The committee should inquire into additional matters such as:
   a. The qualitative aspects of the manpower resources allocated to the auditing function (e.g., the quality of the internal auditing group).
   b. The entity's policy and programs concerning general business practices (e.g., corporate conduct, sensitive payments, management perquisites, and conflicts of interest).
   c. The financial reporting disclosure practices of the entity (e.g., accounting policies and SEC disclosure requirements).

RECOMMENDING THE APPOINTMENT OF THE INDEPENDENT AUDITORS

A Synopsis

Based on a review of the independent auditors' report in the annual report, the addressee of their report is ordinarily the board of directors and the shareholders, since the board approves the selection or reappointment and recommends the firm to the shareholders. Selection or reappointment of the auditors is within the province of the audit committee and is required by the Sarbanes-Oxley Act of 2002, as discussed in Chapter 2. For example, the Wal-Mart audit committee:

- Reviews financial reporting, policies, procedures, and internal controls of Wal-Mart
- Recommends appointment of outside auditors
- Reviews related party transactions
- The Board has determined that the members are "independent" as defined by the current listing standards of the New York Stock Exchange and
- The Board has adopted a written charter for the Audit Committee[10]

---

[10]Wal-Mart Stores, Inc., *Notice of 2003 Annual Meeting of Shareholders Proxy Statement,* p. 4.

Refer to the discussion in Appendix D on this book's website regarding the Independence Standards Board's requirement that independent auditors issue an annual independence confirmation. Thus the committee should address this question: What criteria should be used in the selection and reappointment of the independent auditors?

According to the American Institute of Certified Public Accountants, the committee should give consideration to these five points[11]:

1. *Executive auditing personnel*[12] What has been the company's past experience with the personnel assigned to the audit? Do they convey the impression that they value the company as a client? Do they seem able to work compatibly, but efficiently and independently, with management and the audit committee? Do they demonstrate an understanding of the company's business problems? Do they anticipate problems and advise the company of new accounting tax or SEC developments?

2. *Quality of professional services* Can the firm supply the professional services the company needs? For example, does the firm have access to individuals skilled in matters affecting the company (i.e., industry and SEC specialists or specialists in the problems of smaller companies), and are their skills made available to the company? Does the firm have the capability to serve the company efficiently?

3. *Firm's policies* What are the firm's quality control policies, including its training policies? What is the firm's policy on rotation of the personnel assigned to the audit? On acceptance of clients? On recruitment of personnel? On growth?[13]

4. *Audit fees* Has the firm satisfactorily explained significant variances in actual fees from estimate? Have suggestions been made for management actions that might reduce fees?

    With respect to ways for reducing audit fees, management should:
    a. Develop and maintain an accounting policies and procedures manual
    b. Develop an internal auditing group if the costs and potential benefits warrant such a group
    c. Ensure that significant and/or unusual transaction cycles are properly documented and approved
    d. Discuss changes in the system of internal control with the independent auditors prior to implementation to ensure cost-effectiveness
    e. Follow up on the recommendations noted in the independent auditor's management letter to correct deficiencies

---

[11]American Institute of Certified Public Accountants, *Audit Committees, Answers to Typical Questions about Their Organization and Operations* (New York: AICPA, 1978), p. 15. For more information on the relationship between the independent auditors and boards of directors, see the related sections of the Sarbanes-Oxley Act in Chapter 2 and at the end of this chapter.

[12]Visit the American Institute of Certified Public Accountants, Code of Professional Conduct, at *www.aicpa.org*.

[13]Cindy H. Nance and William W. Holder, "Planning for the Audit: Logical Steps Towards Cost Containment." *Financial Executive* 45 (May 1977), pp. 48–49.

    f. Discuss with the auditors significant accounting transactions and their implications during the preaudit planning segment of the auditing cycle (e.g., the impact of new accounting and auditing pronouncements on the audit)

    g. Request a summary of auditing schedules to be prepared by the client's staff

    h. Decide on the desirability of an audit coordinator in order to expedite the audit process[14]

5. *Nonaudit fees*   Independent auditing firms of the AICPA/SEC Practice Section are required to report to the audit committee or to the board of directors total fees received for management advisory services and a description of the services rendered during the year.[15] In addition, the National Commission on Fraudulent Financial Reporting recommended that the audit committee "review management's plan to engage the independent public accountant to perform management advisory services during the coming year."[16] Such reporting requirements give assurance to the audit committee and the full board of directors that the independence of the auditing firm is not compromised. These requirements became law under Sections 201, 202, and 301 of the Sarbanes-Oxley Act of 2002.

In summary, as Adolph G. Lurie pointed out:

> Management should review the company's operations and determine what services it needs from an independent certified public accountant.
>
> In addition to contemplating its needs, management should consider the cost of an auditor's services in relation to its requirements. . . . All things being equal, the lowest fee may not obtain the type and quality of service needed to meet the particular situation.[17]

The Sarbanes-Oxley Act of 2002 provides certain sections related to audit planning for all engagements. These sections were presented in detail in Chapter 2; Exhibit 7.3 shows only the titles of each section for convenience. Therefore, audit committee members should revisit Chapter 2 during their review and discussion of the agenda for the audit committee meetings. Of course, the audit committee members also should review the provisions of the SEC final rules and SRO's listing standards, where appropriate.

---

[14]The audit committee also may wish to consider other matters, such as the independent auditors' professional indemnity insurance and past and pending litigation.

[15]American Institute of Certified Public Accountants, Membership Requirement Regarding Communications with Audit Committees or Boards of Directors of SEC Clients. In the Division for CPA Firms, SEC Practice Section *Peer Review Manual:* Update 3-B (New York: AICPA, 1987).

[16]National Commission on Fraudulent Financial Reporting, *Report of the National Commission on Fraudulent Financial Reporting* (Washington, DC: National Commission on Fraudulent Financial Reporting, 1987), p. 44.

[17]Adolph G. Lurie, *Working with the Public Accountant* (New York: McGraw-Hill, 1977), pp. 15–16.

Exhibit 7.3   Sarbanes-Oxley Act of 2002: Checklist Reminder of Key Sections for
Audit Committees

TITLE II—AUDITOR INDEPENDENCE
Sec. 201. Services outside the scope of practice of auditors.
Sec. 202. Preapproval requirements.
Sec. 203. Audit partner rotation.
Sec. 204. Auditor reports to audit committees.
Sec. 205. Conforming amendments.
Sec. 206. Conflicts of interest.
Sec. 207. Study of mandatory rotation of registered public accounting firms.
Sec. 208. Commission authority.
Sec. 209. Considerations by appropriate State regulatory authorities.
TITLE III—CORPORATE RESPONSIBILITY
Sec. 301. Public company audit committees.
Sec. 302. Corporate responsibility for financial reports.
Sec. 303. Improper influence on conduct of audits.
Sec. 304. Forfeiture of certain bonuses and profits.
Sec. 305. Officer and director bars and penalties.
Sec. 306. Insider trades during pension fund blackout periods.
Sec. 307. Rules of professional responsibility for attorneys.
Sec. 308. Fair funds for investors.
TITLE IV—ENHANCED FINANCIAL DISCLOSURES
Sec. 401. Disclosures in periodic reports.
Sec. 402. Enhanced conflict of interest provisions.
Sec. 403. Disclosures of transactions involving management and principal stockholders.
Sec. 404. Management assessment of internal controls.
Sec. 405. Exemption.
Sec. 406. Code of ethics for senior financial officers.
Sec. 407. Disclosure of audit committee financial expert.
Sec. 408. Enhanced review of periodic disclosures by issuers.
Sec. 409. Real time issuer disclosures.
TITLE VIII—CORPORATE AND CRIMINAL FRAUD ACCOUNTABILITY
Sec. 801. Short title.
Sec. 802. Criminal penalties for altering documents.
Sec. 803. Debts nondischargeable if incurred in violation of securities fraud laws.
Sec. 804. Statute of limitations for securities fraud.
Sec. 805. Review of Federal Sentencing Guidelines for obstruction of justice and
extensive criminal fraud.
Sec. 806. Protection for employees of publicly traded companies who provide evidence
of fraud.
Sec. 807. Criminal penalties for defrauding shareholders of publicly traded companies.
TITLE IX—WHITE-COLLAR CRIME PENALTY ENHANCEMENTS
Sec. 901. Short title.
Sec. 902. Attempts and conspiracies to commit criminal fraud offenses.
Sec. 903. Criminal penalties for mail and wire fraud.
Sec. 904. Criminal penalties for violations of the Employee Retirement Income
Security Act of 1974.
Sec. 905. Amendment to sentencing guidelines relation to certain white-collar offenses.
Sec. 906. Corporate responsibility for financial reports.

Source: Sarbanes-Oxley Act of 2002, H.R. Rep. 107-610 (2002). The material contained in this text
excludes Section 1, Titles I, V, VI, VII, X, and XI, and Sections 2 and 3.

SOURCES AND SUGGESTED READINGS

American Institute of Certified Public Accountants, *Audit Committees, Answers to Typical Questions About Their Organization and Operations* (New York: AICPA, 1978).

American Institute of Certified Public Accountants, Membership Requirement Regarding Communication with Audit Committees or Boards of Directors of SEC Clients. In the Division for CPA Firms SEC Practice Section *Peer Review Manual:* Update 3-B (New York: AICPA, 1987).

Korn/Ferry International, *Twentieth Annual Boards of Directors Study* (New York: Korn/Ferry International, 1993).

Korn/Ferry International, *25th Annual Board of Directors Study* (New York: Korn/Ferry International, 1998).

Lurie, Adolph G., *Working with the Public Accountant* (New York: McGraw-Hill, 1977).

McKesson Corporation, *1992 Annual Report.*

Nance, Cindy H., and William W. Holder, "Planning for the Audit: Logical Steps Towards Cost Containment." *Financial Executive* 45 (May 1977), pp. 46–50.

National Commission on Fraudulent Financial Reporting, *Report of the National Commission on Fraudulent Financial Reporting* (Washington, DC: NCFFR, 1987).

Sarbanes-Oxley Act of 2002, H. R., Rep 107-610 (2002).

Statement on Auditing Standards No. 22, "Planning and Supervision" (New York: AICPA, 1978).

Statement on Auditing Standards No. 65, "The Auditor's Consideration of the Internal Audit Function of Financial Statements" (New York: AICPA, 1991).

Wal-Mart Stores, Inc., *Notice of 2003 Annual Meeting of Shareholders Proxy Statement.*

Part Three

The Monitoring and Reviewing Functions of the Audit Committee

Chapter 8

Monitoring the System of Internal Control

In view of legislative action—for example, the Foreign Corrupt Practices Act, the Federal Deposit Insurance Corporation Improvement Act, the Sarbanes-Oxley Act, the Securities and Exchange Commission final rules, and private sector initiatives of the self-regulatory organizations—the board of directors will rely increasingly on the audit committee for assurance that management is complying with the internal accounting control provisions of the act, and the New York Stock Exchange listing standards. To assist the committee with its task, this chapter examines the meaning of internal control, the recent developments regarding the responsibilities for such controls, and the role of the audit committee.

MEANING OF INTERNAL CONTROL

Definition and Basic Concepts

In October 1987, the National Commission on Fraudulent Financial Reporting concluded:

> An element within the company of overriding importance in preventing fraudulent financial reporting is the tone set by top management that influences the corporate environment within which financial reporting occurs. To set the right tone, top management must identify and assess the factors that could lead to fraudulent financial reporting; all public companies should maintain internal controls that provide reasonable assurance that fraudulent financial reporting will be prevented or subject to early detection—this is a broader concept than internal accounting controls—and all public companies should develop and enforce effective, written codes of corporate conduct. As a part of its ongoing assessment of the effectiveness of internal controls, a company's audit committee should annually review the program that management establishes to monitor compliance with the code. The Commission also recommends that its sponsoring organizations cooperate in developing additional, integrated guidance on internal controls.[1]

---

[1]National Commission on Fraudulent Financial Reporting, *Report of the National Commission on Fraudulent Financial Reporting* (Washington, DC: NCFFR, 1987), p. 11.

Such recommendations reaffirm the congressional legislation dealing with the internal accounting control provision of the Foreign Corrupt Practices Act, which is designed to reduce the incidence of fraudulent financial reporting.

In April 1988, the Auditing Standards Board of the AICPA published its definition of internal control structure:

> An entity's internal control structure consists of the policies and procedures established to provide reasonable assurance that specific entity objectives will be achieved. Although the internal control structure may include a wide variety of objectives and related policies and procedures, only some of these may be relevant to an audit of the entity's financial statements. Generally, the policies and procedures that are relevant to an audit pertain to the entity's ability to record, process, summarize, and report financial data consistent with the assertions embodied in the financial statements. Other policies and procedures, however, may be relevant if they pertain to data the auditor uses to apply auditing procedures. For example, policies and procedures pertaining to nonfinancial data that the auditor uses in analytical procedures, such as production statistics, may be relevant in an audit.[2]

Furthermore, the Auditing Standards Board stated that an entity's internal control structure consists of these elements:

- The control environment
- The accounting system
- Control procedures[3]

The Board defined these three elements in this way:

> *Control environment* The collective effect of various factors on establishing, enhancing, or mitigating the effectiveness of specific policies and procedures. Such factors include (1) management philosophy and operating style, (2) organizational structure, (3) the function of the board of directors and its committees, (4) methods of assigning authority and responsibility, (5) management control methods, (6) the internal audit function, (7) personnel policies and practices, and (8) external influences concerning the entity.

> *Accounting system* The methods and records established to identify, assemble, analyze, classify, record, and report an entity's transactions and to maintain accountability for the related assets and liabilities.

> *Control procedures* The policies and procedures in addition to the control environment and accounting system that management has established to provide reasonable assurance that specific entity objectives will be achieved.[4]

---

[2]*Statement on Auditing Standards No. 55,* "Consideration of the Internal Control Structure in a Financial Statement Audit" (New York: AICPA, 1988), par. 6.
[3]Ibid., par. 8.
[4]Ibid., par. 67.

In September 1992, the Committee of Sponsoring Organizations (COSO) of the Treadway Commission issued its final report, *Internal Control-Integrated Framework*. COSO defines and describes internal control as functioning to:

1. Establish a common definition serving the needs of different parties.

2. Provide a standard against which business and other entities—large or small, in the public or private sector, for profit or not—can assess their control systems and determine how to improve them.

   Internal control is broadly defined as a process, effected by an entity's board of directors, management and other personnel, designed to provide reasonable assurance regarding the achievement of objectives in the following categories:

   Effectiveness and efficiency of operations

   Reliability of financial reporting

   Compliance with applicable laws and regulations[5]

An executive summary of COSO's four-volume report is presented in Appendix I on this book's website, which contains the five interrelated components of internal control.

In June 1994, COSO published an addendum, which stated in part: The new addendum "encourages managements that report to external parties on controls over financial reporting to also cover controls over safeguarding of assets against unauthorized acquisition, use or disposition." Those controls, according to the addendum, should be "designed to provide reasonable assurance regarding prevention or timely detection of unauthorized acquisition, use or disposition of the entity's assets that could have a material effect on the financial statements."[6]

COSO provided the illustrative report shown in Exhibit 8.1.

As discussed in Appendix F on this book's website, the Federal Deposit Insurance Corporation Improvement Act of 1991 requires that management and the independent auditors report on the internal control structure over financial reporting and compliance with specified laws and regulations. In response, the Auditing Standards Board has issued two Statements on Standards for Attestation Engagements: SSAE No. 2, "Reporting on an Entity's Internal Control Structure over Financial Reporting," and SSAE No. 3, "Compliance Attestation." More specifically, SSAE No. 2 deals with the independent auditor's report on management's

---

[5]Committee of Sponsoring Organizations of the Treadway Commission, *Internal Control-Integrated Framework* (New York: AICPA, 1992), p. 1. For additional reading, see *Statement on Auditing Standards No. 78*, "Consideration of Internal Control in a Financial Statement Audit: An Amendment to SAS No. 55" (New York: AICPA, 1995) and copies of the four-volume COSO report, which may be obtained from the AICPA. Also see Thomas P. Kelley, "The COSO Report: Challenge and Counter-challenge," *Journal of Accountancy* 175, No. 2 (February 1993), pp. 10–18. For a good discussion on internal control, see Wanda A. Wallace, *Handbook of Internal Accounting Controls,* 2nd ed. (Englewood Cliffs, NJ: Prentice-Hall, 1991); and Michael W. Maher, David W. Wright, and William R. Kinney, Jr., "Assertions-Based Standards for Integrated Internal Control," *Accounting Horizons* 4, No. 4 (December 1990), pp. 1–8.
[6]Committee of Sponsoring Organizations of the Treadway Commission, *Addendum to "Reporting to External Parties"* (New York: AICPA, 1994), p. 1.

Exhibit 8.1   Illustrative Report: Reporting to External Parties

---

XYZ Company maintains a system of internal control over financial reporting and[a] over safeguarding of assets against unauthorized acquisition, use or disposition which is designed to provide reasonable assurance to the Company's management and board of directors regarding the preparation of reliable published financial statements and such asset safeguarding. The system contains self-monitoring mechanisms, and actions are taken to correct deficiencies as they are identified. Even an effective internal control system, no matter how well designed, has inherent limitations—including the possibility of the circumvention or overriding of controls—and therefore can provide only reasonable assurance with respect to financial statement preparation and such asset safeguarding. Further, because of changes in conditions, internal control system effectiveness may vary over time.

The Company assessed its internal control system as of December 31, 20XX in relation to criteria for effective internal control over financial reporting described in "Internal Control—Integrated Framework" issued by the Committee of Sponsoring Organizations of the Treadway Commission. Based on this assessment, the Company believes that, as of December 31, 20XX, its system of internal control over financial reporting and[a] over safeguarding of assets against unauthorized acquisition, use or disposition met those criteria.

Source: Committee of Sponsoring Organizations of the Treadway Commission, Addendum to "Reporting to External Parties" (New York: AICPA, 1994), p. 7. Copyright (c) 1994 by the American Institute of Certified Public Accountants, Inc. Reprinted with permission.
[a]In circumstances where all controls over safeguarding of assets against unauthorized acquisition, use or disposition fall within the category of controls over financial reporting, "and" may be changed to "including."

---

assertion regarding the effectiveness of the entity's internal control structure. When management presents its assertion in a separate report that will accompany the independent auditor's report, the form of report is as shown in Exhibit 8.2.

With respect to SSAE No. 3 and management's assertion in a separate report that will accompany the independent auditor's report, the form of the report is illustrated in Exhibit 8.3.

RESPONSIBILITY FOR THE SYSTEM OF INTERNAL CONTROL

Management Certification

As described in Chapter 2, Section 302(a) of the Sarbanes-Oxley Act of 2002 and the SEC's final rule requires a registrant's chief executive officer (CEO) and chief financial officer (CFO) to certify each quarterly and annual report. Moreover, the SEC rule requires registrants to maintain disclosure controls and procedures and assess their effectiveness; included are internal controls over financial reporting and compliance controls to ensure adherence to SEC disclosure requirements.[7]

---

[7]This CEO and CFO certification is in addition to the certification required under Section 906(a) of the Act. This criminal provision requires that the CEO and CFO certification accompany each periodic report that includes financial statements.

Exhibit 8.2 Independent Accountant's Report, SSAE No. 2

[*Introductory paragraph*]

We have examined management's assertion [*identify management's assertion, for example, that W Company maintained an effective internal control over financial reporting as of December 31, 20XX*] included in the accompanying [*title of management report*].

[*Scope paragraph*]

Our examination was made in accordance with standards established by the American Institute of Certified Public Accountants and, accordingly, included obtaining an understanding of the internal control over financial reporting, testing, and evaluating the design and operating effectiveness of the internal control and such other procedures as we considered necessary in the circumstances. We believe that our examination provides a reasonable basis for our opinion.

[*Inherent limitations paragraph*]

Because of inherent limitations in any internal control, misstatements due to error or fraud may occur and not be detected. Also, projections of any evaluation of the internal control over financial reporting to future periods are subject to the risk that the internal control may become inadequate because of changes in conditions, or that the degree of compliance with the policies or procedures may deteriorate.

[*Opinion paragraph*]

In our opinion, management's assertion [*identify management's assertion, for example, that W Company maintained an effective internal control over financial reporting as of December 31, 20XX*] is fairly stated, in all material respects, based upon [*identify stated or established criteria*]

Source: Statement on Standards for Attestation Engagements No. 2, "Reporting on an Entity's Internal Control Structure Over Financial Reporting" (New York: AICPA, 1993), par. 51. See also *Professional Standards, U.S. Auditing Standards/Attestation Standards,* Vol. 1, AT Sec. 400.46. For further reference, see Joseph Takacs, "Attestation Engagements on Internal Control Structure over Financial Reporting," *CPA Journal* 63, No. 8 (August 1993), pp. 48–53. This standard has been recodified as Section 501 of SSAE No. 10.

Internal Control Reporting

As noted in Chapter 2, Section 404(a) of the Sarbanes-Oxley Act requires the SEC to issue rules requiring annual reports to contain an assessment of the effectiveness of internal control over financial reporting. Additionally, Section 404(b) of the act requires the Public Company Accounting Oversight Board to issue standards for independent auditors to attest to management's report on internal control. Recognizing that the Federal Deposit Insurance Corporation Improvement Act of 1991 requires managements of many insured depository institutions to report on the effectiveness of internal control over financial reporting as well as the independent auditors' report on management's assertions, the forthcoming standards are more likely to reflect the current auditing standards, which are consistent with the COSO report.

Exhibit 8.3   Independent Accountant's Report, SSAE No. 3

[Introductory paragraph]

We have examined management's assertion about *[name of entity]*'s compliance with *[list specific compliance requirements]* during the *[period]* ended *[date]* included in the accompanying *[title of management report]*. Management is responsible for *[name of entity]*'s compliance with those requirements. Our responsibility is to express an opinion on management's assertion about the entity's compliance based on our examination.

[Scope paragraph]

Our examination was made in accordance with standards established by the American Institute of Certified Public Accountants and, accordingly, included examining, on a test basis, evidence about *[name of entity]*'s compliance with those requirements and performing such other procedures as we considered necessary in the circumstances. We believe that our examination provides a reasonable basis for our opinion. Our examination does not provide a legal determination on *[name of entity]*'s compliance with specified requirements.

[Opinion paragraph]

In our opinion, management's assertion *[identify management's assertion—for example, that Z Company complied with the aforementioned requirements for the year ended December 31, 20X1]* is fairly stated in all material respects.

Source: Statement on Standards for Attestation Engagements No. 3, "Compliance Attestation" (New York: AICPA, 1993), par. 55. It should be observed that few, if any, companies to date have made such management assertions along with the independent auditors' report thereon. This standard has been recodified as Section 601 of SSAE No. 10.

In June 2003, the Securities and Exchange Commission adopted a final rule, "Management Reports on Internal Control Over Financial Reporting and Certification of Disclosure in Exchange Act Period Reports," which requires registrants, other than registered investment companies, to include in their annual reports a report by management on the company's internal control over financial reporting. More specifically, the internal control report must include:

- A statement of management's responsibility for establishing and maintaining adequate internal control over financial reporting for the company
- Management's assessment of the effectiveness of the company's internal control over financial reporting as of the end of the company's most recent fiscal year
- A statement identifying the framework used by management to evaluate the effectiveness of the company's internal control over financial reporting
- A statement that the registered public accounting firm that audited the company's financial statements included in the annual report has issued an attestation report on management's assessment of the company's internal control over financial reporting[8]

[8]Securities and Exchange Commission, Release No. 33-8238 (Washington, DC: SEC, June 5, 2003), *www.sec.gov/rules/final/33-8238.htm*, p. 1.

Additionally, management is required to evaluate any material change in the company's internal control during a fiscal quarter, including certifications to certain periodic reports.[9]

The Independent Auditors

According to one former executive audit partner, "the independent auditor's external review is an indispensable supplement" to a corporate system of internal controls, but it is no substitute for it."[10] As indicated in Chapter 5, the independent auditors are required to study and evaluate the system of internal control. The study and evaluation is performed during their interim-period work, ordinarily a predetermined period prior to the date of the financial statements.

The independent auditors' major objective is to determine whether the internal control is adequate so that the financial accounting transactions are recorded properly and presented fairly in the financial statements. Furthermore, they must evaluate the controls in order to determine not only how much reliance can be placed on such controls but also the extensiveness of their auditing procedures. Obviously, if the internal control structure is weak, then the assessment of control risk is high; thus the auditors must extend their auditing procedures to minimize the risk of errors in the financial statements and limit the level of detection risk. During the audit engagement, the auditors test the accounting system through verification tests. For example, tests of controls consist of the auditors' selection of several transactions whereby such transactions are traced through the accounting system. Such tests allow the auditors to determine the degree of reliance they can place on the internal control structure. However, the auditors' examination of the cancelled checks in connection with the bank reconciliation and the examination of the vendors' invoices in support of account balances are substantive tests of transactions.

Since the auditors are required to communicate to senior management and the board of directors or its audit committee reportable conditions in internal control, the following form of report is recommended.[11]

In planning and performing our audit of the financial statements of the ABC Corporation for the year ended December 31, 19XX, we considered its internal control in order to determine our auditing procedures for the purpose of expressing our opinion on the financial statements and not to provide assurance on the internal control. However, we noted certain matters involving the internal control and its operation that we consider to be reportable conditions under standards established by the American

---

[9]Ibid., p. 1. For additional information, visit the web site and note the SEC's particular rule that states: "auditors may assist management in documenting internal controls. When the auditor is engaged to assist management in documenting internal controls, management must be actively involved in the process." The audit committee may wish to have discussions with the internal chief audit executive regarding the extent to which the independent auditors participate in documenting internal controls over financial reporting in the context of auditor independence and management's assertion about internal controls.

[10]John C. Biegler, "Rebuilding Public Trust in Business," *Financial Executive* 45 (June 1977), p. 30.

[11]*Statement on Auditing Standards No. 60*, "Communication of Internal Control Related Matters Noted in an Audit" (New York: AICPA, 1988), pars. 2 and 12. See also *Professional Standards, U.S. Auditing Standards/Attestation Standards*, Vol. 1, AU Sec. 325.02 and 325.12. A reportable condition may be of such magnitude as to be considered a material weakness in internal control.

Institute of Certified Public Accountants. Reportable conditions involve matters coming to our attention relating to significant deficiencies in the design or operation of the internal control that, in our judgment, could adversely affect the organization's ability to record, process, summarize, and report financial data consistent with the assertions of management in the financial statements.

(Include paragraphs to describe the reportable conditions noted.)

This report is intended solely for the information and use of the audit committee (board of directors, board of trustees, or owners in owner-managed enterprises), management, and others within the organization (or specified regulatory agency or other specified third party).[12]

Although the independent auditors may communicate improvements for the system of internal control, they cannot opine on the company's compliance with the Foreign Corrupt Practices Act, because that is a legal matter. In short, although the independent auditors cannot express a legal opinion on the entity's compliance with the act, management should give strong consideration to their recommendations in order to indicate its intent to comply with the law.

The Auditing Standards Board's position in the compliance attestation standard, specifically states:

A report issued in accordance with the provisions of this Statement does not provide a legal determination on an entity's compliance with specified requirements. However, such a report may be useful to management, legal counsel, or third parties in making such determinations.[13]

Another important element of the internal control environment is the internal audit function. As discussed in Chapter 2, the internal auditing group plays a significant part in establishing and maintaining the internal control structure. Although its members are engaged principally in compliance and operational auditing, which deals with the efficiency of the various operating units, they make an important contribution to the financial audit engagements. The independent auditors' consideration and use of the work of internal auditors is discussed in Chapter 9.

THE ROLE OF THE AUDIT COMMITTEE

General Considerations

According to the Committee of Sponsoring Organizations of the Treadway Commission, everyone in an organization has responsibility for internal control. Their roles and responsibilities are characterized in this way:

- *Management*—The chief executive officer is ultimately responsible and should assume "ownership" of the system. More than any other individual, the chief ex-

---

[12]The audit committee may wish to discuss the independent auditor's findings and conclusions with respect to their assessment of internal accounting controls at service organizations. See Chapter 5 for the applicable auditing standards. The committee also may wish to consult the AICPA's auditing guide and auditing procedures study, which deals with internal control.

[13]*Statement on Standards for Attestation Engagements No. 3,* par. 3.

ecutive sets the "tone at the top" that affects integrity and ethics and other factors of a positive control environment. In a large company, the chief executive fulfills this duty by providing leadership and direction to senior managers and reviewing the way they're controlling the business. Senior managers, in turn, assign responsibility for establishment of more specific internal control policies and procedures to personnel responsible for the unit's functions. In a smaller entity, the influence of the chief executive, often an owner-manager, is usually more direct. In any event, in a cascading responsibility, a manager is effectively a chief executive of his or her sphere of responsibility. Of particular significance are financial officers and their staffs, whose control activities cut across, as well as up and down, the operating and other units of an enterprise.

- *Board of Directors*—Management is accountable to the board of directors, which provides governance, guidance and oversight. Effective board members are objective, capable and inquisitive. They also have a knowledge of the entity's activities and environment, and commit the time necessary to fulfill their board responsibilities. Management may be in a position to override controls and ignore or stifle communications from subordinates, enabling a dishonest management which intentionally misrepresents results to cover its tracks. A strong, active board, particularly when coupled with effective upward communications channels and capable financial, legal and internal audit functions, is often best able to identify and correct such a problem.

- *Internal Auditors*—Internal auditors play an important role in evaluating the effectiveness of control systems, and contribute to ongoing effectiveness. Because of organizational position and authority in an entity, an internal audit function often plays a significant monitoring role.

- *Other Personnel*—Internal control is, to some degree, the responsibility of everyone in an organization and therefore should be an explicit or implicit part of everyone's job description. Virtually all employees produce information used in the internal control system or take other actions needed to effect control. Also, all personnel should be responsible for communicating upward problems in operations, noncompliance with the code of conduct, or other policy violations or illegal actions.[14]

A number of external parties often contribute to achievement of an entity's objectives. External auditors, bringing an independent and objective view, contribute directly through the financial statement audit and indirectly by providing information useful to management and the board in carrying out their responsibilities. Others providing information to the entity useful in effecting internal control are legislators and regulators, customers and others transacting business with the enterprise, financial analysts, bond raters, and the news media. External parties, however, are not responsible for, nor are they a part of, the entity's internal control system.

Moreover, the Auditing Standards Board has issued *Statement on Auditing Standards No. 60*, "Communication of Internal Control Related Matters Noted in an Audit," which requires the external auditor to communicate reportable conditions to the audit committee. Reportable conditions are matters that "represent

---

[14]COSO, *Internal Control—Integrated Frameworks, Executive Summary* (New York: AICPA, 1992), pp. 5–6.

significant deficiencies in the design or operation of the internal control structure, which could adversely affect the organization's ability to record, process, summarize, and report financial data consistent with the assertions of management in the financial standards."[15]

Finally, the New York Stock Exchange has proposed a rule change to Section 303A of its Corporate Governance Standards, which states, in part:

(viii) report regularly to the board of directors.

Commentary: The audit committee should review with the full board any issues that arise with respect to the quality or integrity of the company's financial statements, the company's compliance with legal or regulatory requirements, the performance and independence of the company's independent auditors, or the performance of the internal audit function.

General Commentary to Section 303A(7)(d): While the fundamental responsibility for the company's financial statements and disclosures rests with management and the independent auditor, the audit committee must review: (A) major issues regarding accounting principles and financial statement presentations, including any significant changes in the company's selection or application of accounting principles, and major issues as to the adequacy of the company's internal controls and any special audit steps adopted in light of material control deficiencies; (B) analyses prepared by management and/or the independent auditor setting forth significant financial reporting issues and judgments made in connection with the preparation of the financial statements, including analyses of the effects of alternative GAAP methods on the financial statements; (C) the effect of regulatory and accounting initiatives, as well as off-balance sheet structures, on the financial statements of the company; and (D) the type and presentation of information to be included in earnings press releases (paying particular attention to any use of "pro forma," or "adjusted" non-GAAP, information), as well as review any financial information and earnings guidance provided to analysts and rating agencies.

General Commentary to Section 303A(7): To avoid any confusion, note that the audit committee functions specified in Section 303A(7) are the sole responsibility of the audit committee and may not be allocated to a different committee.[16]

Although the involvement of the committee is clearly evident, it is obvious that management faces a difficult task of implementing and for monitoring the recommendations as set forth by COSO in its four-volume report. The absence of definitive criteria for evaluating the adequacy of the system of internal control no longer exists. Clearly management has a standard against which it can measure the effectiveness of the company's internal control.

---

[15]American Institute of Certified Public Accountants, *U.S. Auditing Standards/Attestation Standards*, Vol. 1 (New York: AICPA, 2003), AU Sec. 325.02.

Although the preparation of a management letter is not required by generally accepted auditing standards, many accounting firms issue such a letter, which contains recommendations for improving the efficiency and effectiveness of the company's operations.

[16]Securities and Exchange Commission, Release No. 34-47672 (Washington, DC: Securities and Exchange Commission, April 11, 2003, *www.sec.gov/rules/sro/34-47672.htm*), Section 303A (7)(d) (viii).

With respect to annual reporting and the 2003 proxy statement season, an illustration from Wal-Mart Stores, Inc., discloses these statements on internal control:

> Management has developed and maintains a system of internal and disclosure controls, including an extensive internal audit program. These controls are designed to provide reasonable assurance that the Company's assets are protected from improper use and that Wal-Mart's accounting records provide a reliable basis for the preparation of financial statements. We continually review, improve and modify these systems and programs in response to changes in business conditions and operations and the recommendations made by Wal-Mart's internal and external auditors. We believe that the system of internal and disclosure controls provides reasonable assurance that Wal-Mart's assets are safeguarded and that the financial information disclosed is reliable.[17]

2003 Annual Proxy Statement
Audit Committee Report

Wal-Mart's management is responsible for Wal-Mart's internal controls and financial reporting, including the preparation of Wal-Mart's consolidated financial statements. Wal-Mart's independent auditors are responsible for auditing Wal-Mart's annual consolidated financial statements in accordance with generally accepted auditing standards and ensuring that the financial statements fairly present Wal-Mart's results of operations and financial position. The independent auditors also are responsible for issuing a report on those financial statements. The Audit Committee annually recommends to the Board for its approval an independent accounting firm to be Wal-Mart's independent auditors. Beginning with the June 6, 2003 shareholders' meeting, ratification of the Board's approval of the independent auditors is being sought. Ernst & Young LLP is Wal-Mart's current independent auditor.[18]

4. Review and discuss quarterly reports from the Outside Auditor on:

   (c) The internal controls adhered to by the Company, management, and the Company's financial, accounting and internal auditing personnel, and the impact of each on the quality and reliability of the Company's financial reporting; and

6. Review and discuss with management, the Internal Auditors and the Outside Auditor:

   (e) Significant changes in accounting principles, financial reporting policies and internal controls implemented by the Company;

9. Discuss with the Outside Auditor the matters required to be discussed by Statement on Auditing Standards ("SAS") No 61 relating to the conduct of the audit. In particular, discuss:

   (a) The adoption of, or changes to, the Company's significant internal auditing and accounting principles and practices as suggested by the Outside Auditor, Internal Auditors or management; and

---

[17]Wal-Mart Stores, Inc., *2003 Annual Report*, p. 52.
[18]Wal-Mart Stores, Inc., *2003 Notice of Annual Meeting of Shareholders and Proxy Statement*, pp. 5–6

(b) The management letter provided by the Outside Auditor and the Company's response to that letter.

Oversight of the Company's Internal Audit Function

24. Communicate with management and the Internal Auditors to obtain information concerning internal audits, accounting principles adopted by the Company, internal controls of the Company, management, and the Company's financial and accounting personnel, and review the impact of each on the quality and reliability of the Company's financial statements.

25. Evaluate the internal auditing department and its impact on the accounting practices, internal controls and financial reporting of the Company.

Compliance Oversight Responsibilities

28. Obtain reports from management, the Company's senior internal auditing executive and the Outside Auditor concerning whether the Company and its subsidiary/foreign affiliated entities are in compliance with applicable legal requirements and the Statement of Ethics. Obtain and review reports and disclosures of insider and affiliated party transactions. Advise the Board with respect to the Company's policies and procedures regarding compliance with applicable laws and regulations and the Statement of Ethics.[19]

Accordingly, the audit committee should give consideration to these points:

1. Has management devised and implemented a plan of action in order to demonstrate its compliance with applicable legislative action, such as the Foreign Corrupt Practices Act (FCPA); the Federal Deposit Insurance Corporation Improvement Act (FDICIA), the Sarbanes-Oxley Act, including the SEC final rules and the self-regulatory listing standards? (See Appendixes E and F on the book's website).
   a. Does management understand the accounting control provisions of the acts? Is such an understanding documented?
   b. Has management documented (e.g., accounting policies and procedures manual) the present system of internal control in view of the COSO report and SEC final rule and Section 404 of the Sarbanes-Oxley Act?
2. Based on the independent auditor's management letter, has management implemented its recommendations for improving the system of internal control? (For example, the chief audit executive may submit a summary report on the follow-up action taken by management.)
3. Have the independent auditors discussed with legal counsel any reportable conditions that are a violation of the acts? (The committee should discuss the lawyer's letter and the client's letter of management representations with the independent auditor.)
4. Has the chief audit executive supplied the necessary special reports regarding the scope of study and evaluation of administrative controls?

---

[19]Wal-Mart Stores, Inc., *Audit Committee Charter, www.walmartstores.com.* pp. 3–7.

In retrospect, the Public Oversight Board issued these recommendations on reporting on internal control:

Recommendation V-12

The SEC should require registrants to include in a document containing the annual financial statements: (a) a report by management on the effectiveness of the entity's internal control system relating to financial reporting; and (b) a report by the registrant's independent accountant on the entity's internal control system relating to financial reporting.

Recommendation V-13

The Auditing Standards Board should establish standards that require clear communication of the limits of the assurances being provided to third parties when auditors report on the adequacy of client internal control systems.[20]

SOURCES AND SUGGESTED READINGS

American Institute of Certified Public Accountants, *Considerations of the Internal Control Structure in a Computer Environment: A Case Study* (New York: AICPA, 1991).

American Institute of Certified Public Accountants, *Audit Guide for Consideration of the Internal Control Structure in a Financial Statement Audit* (New York: AICPA, 1996).

American Institute of Certified Public Accountants, *U.S. Auditing Standards/Attestation Standards,* Vol. 1 (New York: AICPA, 2003).

Biegler, John C., "Rebuilding Public Trust in Business." *Financial Executive* 45, No. 6 (June 1977), pp. 28–31.

Committee of Sponsoring Organizations of the Treadway Commission, *Internal Control—Integrated Framework* (New York: AICPA, 1992).

Committee of Sponsoring Organizations of the Treadway Commission, *Addendum to* "Reporting to External Parties" (New York: AICPA, 1994).

DeZoort, F. Todd, "An Analysis of Experience Effects on Audit Committee Members' Oversight Judgments." *Accounting, Organizations and Society* 23, No. 1 (January 1998), pp. 1–21.

Kelley, Thomas P., "The COSO Report: Challenge and Counterchallenge." *Journal of Accountancy* 175, No. 2 (February 1993), pp. 10–18.

Maher, Michael W., David W. Wright, and William R. Kinney, Jr., "Assertions-Based Standards for Integrated Internal Control." *Accounting Horizons* 4, No. 4 (December 1990), pp. 1–8.

National Commission on Fraudulent Financial Reporting, *Report of the National Commission on Fraudulent Financial Reporting* (Washington, DC: NCFFR, 1987).

---

[20]Public Oversight Board, *A Special Report by the Public Oversight Board of the SEC Practice Section, AICPA* (Stamford, CT: POB, 1993), p. 54. As previously mentioned, the Auditing Standards Board has issued two attestation standards that address the Public Oversight Board's recommendation.

For an interesting discussion on the audit committee's experience with respect to internal controls oversight tasks, see F. Todd Dezoort, "An Analysis of Experience Effects on Audit Committee Members' Oversight Judgments," *Accounting, Organizations and Society* 23, No. 1 (January 1998), pp. 1–21.

Public Oversight Board, *A Special Report by the Public Oversight Board of the SEC Practice Section, AICPA* (Stamford, CT: POB, 1993).

Sarbanes-Oxley Act of 2002, H.R. Rep. No. 107-610 (2002).

Securities and Exchange Commission, Release No. 33-8238 (Washington, DC: SEC, June 5, 2003, *www.sec.gov/rules/final/33-82.htm.*)

Securities and Exchange Commission, Release No. 34-47672 (Washington, DC: SEC, April 11, 2003, *www.sec.gov/rules/sro/34-47672.htm*), Section 303A(7)(d)(viii).

Statement on Auditing Standards No. 60, "Communication of Internal Control Structure Related Matters Noted in an Audit" (New York: AICPA, 1988).

Statement on Auditing Standards No. 78, "Consideration of Internal Control in a Financial Statement Audit: An Amendment to SAS No. 55" (New York: AICPA, 1995).

Statement on Standards for Attestation Engagements No. 2, "Reporting on an Entity's Internal Control Structure Over Financial Reporting" (New York: AICPA, 1993).

Statement on Standards for Attestation Engagements No. 3, "Compliance Attestation" (New York: AICPA, 1993).

Takacs, Joseph, "Attestation Engagements on Internal Control Structure over Financial Reporting." *CPA Journal* 63, No. 8 (August 1993), pp. 48–53.

Wallace, Wanda, A., *Handbook of Internal Accounting Controls,* 2nd ed. (Englewood Cliffs, NJ: Prentice Hall, 1991).

Wal-Mart Stores, Inc., *2003 Annual Report.*

Wal-Mart Stores, Inc., *2003 Notice of Annual Meeting of Shareholders and Proxy Statement.*

Wal-Mart Stores, Inc., *Audit Committee Charter, www.walmartstores.com.*

Chapter 9

Monitoring the Internal Audit Function

Although references have been made to the internal audit function in the preceding chapters, the major objective of this chapter is to provide guidance for the audit committee's ongoing appraisal of the effectiveness of the entity's corporate auditing staff. In this chapter, the audit committee will examine such matters as the structure and organization of the auditing staff, their organizational independence, logistical staff matters, and the quality of personnel and training. In addition, a recapitulation of the salient points concerning the committee's review of this function is provided. Also, the reader should visit the Institute of Internal Auditors at *www.theiia.org* for further information regarding the professional standards and ethics of the internal auditors as well as practice advisories.

PURPOSE AND NEED FOR MONITORING THE INTERNAL AUDIT FUNCTION

General Matters

The Institute of Internal Auditors (IIA) defines internal auditing as:

> an independent, objective assurance and consulting activity designed to add value and improve an organization's operations. It helps an organization accomplish its objectives by bringing a systematic, disciplined approach to evaluate and improve the effectiveness of risk management, control, and governance processes.[1]

As discussed in Chapter 2, the audit committee and the internal auditing group have a logical interface, since both groups have common goals. For example, the audit committee members are a service to the board of directors, and the internal auditors are a service to the operating management. Both groups are engaged in an independent assessment of the internal control, as discussed in Chapter 8 as well as risk management and internal governance. Implicit in their ongoing appraisal of the system of internal control is the audit committee's monitoring of the internal audit function. This monitoring is extremely beneficial to the board and its operating management for the following reasons. First, the committee's review of the internal auditing staff not only enhances the staff's independence but also strengthens its

---

[1]Institute of Internal Auditors, *The Professional Practices Framework* (Altamonte Springs, FL: IIA, 2002), p. 3.

image in the corporate structure. Second, through the committee's review of the organizational structure and scope of the entity's internal audit function, the external auditing fees can be minimized since the coordination of both auditing activities reduces the potential of either groups to be counterproductive. Third, an effective internal auditing group assists the audit committee in discharging its responsibilities because of its limited time and oversight capacity. Thus it is evident that the committee's oversight responsibility for the internal auditing function is within its province to ensure that such a corporate resource is used effectively and efficiently.

Moreover, the National Commission on Fraudulent Financial Reporting has strongly endorsed the concept of internal auditing to reduce the incidence of fraudulent financial reporting:

> All public companies must have an effective and objective internal audit function. The internal auditor's qualifications, staff, status within the company, reporting lines, and relationship with the audit committee of the board of directors must be adequate to ensure the internal audit function's effectiveness and objectivity. The internal auditor should consider his audit findings in the context of the company's financial statements and should, to the extent appropriate, coordinate his activities with the activities of the independent public accountant.[2]

As the Auditing Standards Board notes:

> Monitoring is a process that assesses the quality of internal control performance over time. It involves assessing the design and operation of controls on a timely basis and taking necessary corrective actions. This process is accomplished through ongoing activities, separate evaluations, or by various combinations of the two. In many entities, internal auditors or personnel performing similar functions contribute to the monitoring of an entity's activities. Monitoring activities may include using information from communications from external parties such as customer complaints and regulator comments that may indicate problems or highlight areas in need of improvement.

> The auditor should obtain sufficient knowledge of the major types of activities the entity uses to monitor internal control over financial reporting, including how those activities are used to initiate corrective actions. When obtaining an understanding of the internal audit function, the auditor should follow the guidance in paragraphs 4 through 8 of SAS No. 65, The Auditor's Consideration of the Internal Audit Function in an Audit of Financial Statements.[3]

As Curtis C. Verschoor and Joseph P. Liotta conclude:

> Internal auditors should place a high priority on an in-depth review of their relationships with the board of their organization. Internal auditors must not only evaluate whether or not they are in full compliance with the recommendations of *SIAS No. 7*; they should also consider ways of enhancing the quality of their relationships with the board. Copies of *SIAS No. 7* should be furnished to senior management, members

---

[2]*Report of the National Commission on Fraudulent Financial Reporting* (Washington, DC: NCFFR, 1987), pp. 11–12. For further discussion of the internal audit function and chief internal auditor, see pp. 37–39 of the Commission's report.

[3]*Statement on Auditing Standards No. 78,* "Consideration of Internal Control in a Financial Statement Audit: An Amendment to SAS No. 55" (New York: AICPA, 1995), pars. 38, 39.

of the board, and external auditors, to inform them of the new IIA reporting guidelines. In view of the trend toward increased communication between external auditors and the board, internal auditors may well wish to reexamine the reporting threshold they use to inform the board of their activities. The public is demanding more effective performance by internal auditors, thereby offering the profession an even greater opportunity for service.[4]

Finally, the Committee of Sponsoring Organizations of the Treadway Commission stated:

> Internal auditors play an important role in evaluating the effectiveness of control systems, and contribute to ongoing effectiveness. Because of organizational position and authority in an entity, an internal audit function often plays a significant monitoring role.[5]

Karen N. Horn, former chairman and CEO of Bank One and a member of several audit committees, summarizes the relationship between the audit committee and internal auditors:

> Our joint responsibilities to our companies are now defined much more broadly. Any type of change this far reaching must become part of the corporate culture. As a senior manager and director, my obligation is to provide you with what the Committee of Sponsoring Organizations calls integrity, ethical values, a control environment, and clear management objectives—in short, to nurture a culture that allows you to do the things described in this article. Internal auditors are then the champions of this new control culture.

> The activities are as complex and changing as our organizations; and I believe they have never been more important.[6]

---

[4]Curtis C. Verschoor and Joseph P. Liotta, "Communication with Audit Committees," *Internal Auditor* 47, No. 2 (April 1990), p. 47. *Statement on Internal Auditing Standards No. 7,* "Communications with the Board of Directors," is now codefaced in *The Professional Practices Framework* and discussed in the corporate auditing independence section of this chapter. For an interesting discussion on the perceptions of audit committee members and chief internal auditors, see Lawrence P. Kalbers, "Audit Committees and Internal Auditors," *Internal Auditor* 49, No. 6 (December 1992), pp. 37–44. See also Jerry Strawser and Barbara Apostolou, "The Role of Internal Auditor Communication with the Audit Committee," *Internal Auditing* 6, No. 2 (Fall 1990), pp. 35–42; and Curtis Verschoor, "Internal Auditing Interactions with the Audit Committee," *Internal Auditing* 7, No. 4 (Spring 1992), pp. 20–23.

[5]Committee of Sponsoring Organizations of the Treadway Commission, *Internal Control-Integrated Framework* (New York: AICPA, 1992), p. 5. For additional emphasis, see pp. 84–85 of the "Framework" volume.

[6]Karen N. Horn, "An Audit Committee Member Looks at Internal Auditing," *Internal Auditor* 49, No. 6 (December 1992), p. 36. For an expanded discussion of the relationship between the audit committee and internal auditors, see William E. Chadwick, "Tough Questions, Tough Answers," *Internal Auditor* 52, No. 6 (December 1995), pp. 63–65; Dwight L. Allison, Jr., "Internal Auditors and Audit Committees," *Internal Auditor* 51, No. 1 (February 1994), pp. 50–55. A recent study of chief internal auditors of 72 Canadian manufacturing companies (sales > $50 million), found that "while there were no significant differences with respect to involvement in decisions to dismiss the chief internal auditor, audit committees consisting of solely nonemployee directors were more likely, than audit committees with one or more insiders, to (1) have frequent meetings with the chief internal auditor, and (2) review the internal auditing program and results of internal auditing" (p. 51). See D. Paul Scarbrough, Dasaratha V. Rama, and K. Raghunandan, "Audit Committee Composition and Interaction with Internal Auditing: Canadian Evidence," *Accounting Horizons* 12, No. 1 (March 1998), pp. 51–62.

More recently, the New York Stock Exchange proposed an amendment to its *Listed Company Manual* to implement a listing standard, Section 303A(7)(e), which states:

(e) Each listed company must have an internal audit function.

Commentary: Listed companies must maintain an internal audit function to provide management and the audit committee with ongoing assessments of the company's risk management processes and system of internal control. A company may choose to outsource this function to a firm other than its independent auditor.[7]

In an effort to close the gap between available guidance and current practice, the Institute of Internal Auditors has issued *Standards for the Professional Practice of Internal Auditing*, which are contained in *The Professional Practices Framework*. These standards are shown in Exhibit 9.1.

In order to monitor the internal audit function effectively, the agenda for the audit committee should include a review of:

• The objectives, plans, and policy of the corporate internal auditing group (discussed in Chapters 6 and 7 in relation to the planning activities of both the committee and the internal audit group)
• The organization of the internal auditing group
• The quality of the auditing personnel and training as well as the use of outside service providers
• The operational activities of the staff in the context of achieving their goals and objectives (see Chapters 2 and 3)

Such an approach to the monitoring function of the committee enhances its ability to meet the expectations of the board of directors. As discussed in Chapter 1, the audit committee has a critical role in helping the board fulfill its corporate stewardship accountability.

REVIEWING THE ORGANIZATION OF THE CORPORATE AUDIT STAFF

Organizational Structure

Of particular importance to the audit committee is the organizational status of the internal auditing staff in the corporate structure. Structure and organization should be designed to carry out effectively an independent appraisal of management's activities. In view of the Foreign Corrupt Practices Act and the Sarbanes-Oxley Act of 2002, an effective and efficient internal auditing staff can assist management with its implementation of a sound system of internal control. Thus it behooves the audit committee to monitor the organizational framework of the corporate auditing group to ensure a comprehensive scope.

---

[7]Securities and Exchange Commission, Release No. 34-47672, *Self-Regulatory Organizations; Notice of Filing of Proposed Rule Change and Amendment No. 1 Thereto by the New York Stock Exchange, Inc. Relating to Corporate Governance* (Washington, DC: SEC, April 11, 2003), p. 12.

Exhibit 9.1   Standards for the Professional Practice of Internal Auditing

---

Attribute Standards

1000 Purpose, Authority, and Responsibility
The purpose, authority, and responsibility of the internal audit activity should be formally defined in a charter, consistent with the Standards, and approved by the board.[1]

    1000.A1 The nature of assurance services provided to the organization should be defined in the audit charter. If assurances are to be provided to parties outside the organization, the nature of these assurances should also be defined in the charter.

    1000.C1 The nature of consulting services should be defined in the audit charter.

1100 Independence and Objectivity
The internal audit activity should be independent, and internal auditors should be objective in performing their work.

    1110 Organizational Independence

    The chief audit executive should report to a level within the organization that allows the internal audit activity to fulfill its responsibilities.

        1110.A1 The internal audit activity should be free from interference in determining the scope of internal auditing, performing work, and communicating results.

    1120 Individual Objectivity

    Internal auditors should have an impartial, unbiased attitude and avoid conflicts of interest.

    1130 Impairments to Independence or Objectivity

    If independence or objectivity is impaired in fact or appearance, the details of the impairment should be disclosed to appropriate parties. The nature of the disclosure will depend upon the impairment.

        1130.A1 Internal auditors should refrain from assessing specific operations for which they were previously responsible. Objectivity is presumed to be impaired if an auditor provides assurance services for an activity for which the auditor had responsibility within the previous year.

        1130.A2 Assurance engagements for functions over which the chief audit executive has responsibility should be overseen by a party outside the internal audit activity.

        1130.C1 Internal auditors may provide consulting services relating to operations for which they had previous responsibilities.

        1130.C2 If internal auditors have potential impairments to independence or objectivity relating to proposed consulting services, disclosure should be made to the engagement client prior to accepting the engagement.

1200 Proficiency and Due Professional Care
Engagements should be performed with proficiency and due professional care.

    1210 Proficiency

    Internal auditors should possess the knowledge, skills, and other competencies needed to perform their individual responsibilities. The internal audit activity collectively should possess or obtain the knowledge, skills, and other competencies needed to perform its responsibilities.

        1210.A1 The chief audit executive should obtain competent advice and assistance if the internal audit staff lacks the knowledge, skills, or other competencies needed to perform all or part of the engagement.

        1210.A2 The internal auditor should have sufficient knowledge to identify the indicators of fraud but is not expected to have the expertise of a person whose primary responsibility is detecting and investigating fraud.

(continued)

Exhibit 9.1   *(Continued)*

    1210.C1 The chief audit executive should decline the consulting engagement or obtain competent advice and assistance if the internal audit staff lacks the knowledge, skills, or other competencies needed to perform all or part of the engagement.

1220 Due Professional Care

Internal auditors should apply the care and skill expected of a reasonably prudent and competent internal auditor. Due professional care does not imply infallibility.

    1220.A1 The internal auditor should exercise due professional care by considering the:

- Extent of work needed to achieve the engagement's objectives.
- Relative complexity, materiality, or significance of matters to which assurance procedures are applied.
- Adequacy and effectiveness of risk management, control, and governance processes.
- Probability of significant errors, irregularities, or noncompliance.
- Cost of assurance in relation to potential benefits.

    1220.A2 The internal auditor should be alert to the significant risks that might affect objectives, operations, or resources. However, assurance procedures alone, even when performed with due professional care, do not guarantee that all significant risks will be identified.

    1220.C1 The internal auditor should exercise due professional care during a consulting engagement by considering the:

- Needs and expectations of clients, including the nature, timing, and communication of engagement results.
- Relative complexity and extent of work needed to achieve the engagement's objectives.
- Cost of the consulting engagement in relation to potential benefits.

1230 Continuing Professional Development

Internal auditors should enhance their knowledge, skills, and other competencies through continuing professional development.

1300 Quality Assurance and Improvement Program

The chief audit executive should develop and maintain a quality assurance and improvement program that covers all aspects of the internal audit activity and continuously monitors its effectiveness. The program should be designed to help the internal audit activity add value and improve the organization's operations and to provide assurance that the internal audit activity is in conformity with the Standards and the Code of Ethics.

1310 Quality Program Assessments

The internal audit activity should adopt a process to monitor and assess the overall effectiveness of the quality program. The process should include both internal and external assessments.

1311 Internal Assessments

Internal assessments should include:

- Ongoing reviews of the performance of the internal audit activity; and
- Periodic reviews performed through self-assessment or by other persons within the organization, with knowledge of internal audit practices and the Standards.

1312 External Assessments

External assessments, such as quality assurance reviews, should be conducted at least once every five years by a qualified, independent reviewer or review team from outside the organization.

1320 Reporting on the Quality Program
The chief audit executive should communicate the results of external assessments to the board.

1330 Use of "Conducted in Accordance with the Standards"
Internal auditors are encouraged to report that their activities are "conducted in accordance with the Standards for the Professional Practice of Internal Auditing." However internal auditors may use the statement only if assessments of the quality improvement program demonstrate that the internal audit activity is in compliance with the Standards.

1340 Disclosure of Noncompliance
Although the internal audit activity should achieve full compliance with the Standards and internal auditors with the Code of Ethics, there may be instances in which full compliance is not achieved. When noncompliance impacts the overall scope or operation of the internal audit activity, disclosure should be made to senior management and the board.

Performance Standards

2000 Managing the Internal Audit Activity
The chief audit executive should effectively manage the internal audit activity to ensure it adds value to the organization.

2010 Planning
The chief audit executive should establish risk-based plans to determine the priorities of the internal audit activity, consistent with the organization's goals.

2010.A1 The internal audit activity's plan of engagements should be based on a risk assessment, undertaken at least annually. The input of senior management and the board should be considered in this process.

2010.C1 The chief audit executive should consider accepting proposed consulting engagements based on the engagement's potential to improve management of risks, add value, and improve the organization's operations. Those engagements that have been accepted should be included in the plan.

2020 Communication and Approval
The chief audit executive should communicate the internal audit activity's plans and resource requirements, including significant interim changes, to senior management and to the board for review and approval. The chief audit executive should also communicate the impact of resource limitations.

2030 Resource Management
The chief audit executive should ensure that internal audit resources are appropriate, sufficient, and effectively deployed to achieve the approved plan.

2040 Policies and Procedures
The chief audit executive should establish policies and procedures to guide the internal audit activity.

2050 Coordination
The chief audit executive should share information and coordinate activities with other internal and external providers of relevant assurance and consulting services to ensure proper coverage and minimize duplication of efforts.

2060 Reporting to the Board and Senior Management
The chief audit executive should report periodically to the board and senior management on the internal audit activity's purpose, authority, responsibility, and performance relative to its plan. Reporting should also include significant risk exposures and control issues, corporate governance issues, and other matters needed or requested by the board and senior management.

(continued)

Exhibit 9.1   (*Continued*)

2100 Nature of Work

The internal audit activity evaluates and contributes to the improvement of risk management, control, and governance systems.

2110 Risk Management

The internal audit activity should assist the organization by identifying and evaluating significant exposures to risk and contributing to the improvement of risk management and control systems.

2110 A1 Internal audit activity should monitor and evaluate the effectiveness of the organization's risk management system.

2110.A2 The internal audit activity should evaluate risk exposures relating to the organization's governance, operations, and information systems regarding the:
• Reliability and integrity of financial and operational information.
• Effectiveness and efficiency of operations.
• Safeguarding of assets.
• Compliance with laws, regulations, and contracts.

2110.C1 During consulting engagements, internal auditors should address risk consistent with the engagement's objectives and should be alert to the existence of other significant risks.

2110.C2 Internal auditors should incorporate knowledge of risks gained from consulting engagements into the process of identifying and evaluating significant risk exposures of the organization.

2120 Control

The internal audit activity should assist the organization in maintaining effective controls by evaluating their effectiveness and efficiency and by promoting continuous improvement.

2120.A1 Based on the results of the risk assessment, the internal audit activity should evaluate the adequacy and effectiveness of controls encompassing the organization's governance, operations, and information systems. This should include:
• Reliability and integrity of financial and operational information.
• Effectiveness and efficiency of operations.
• Safeguarding of assets.
• Compliance with laws, regulations, and contracts.

2120.A2 Internal auditors should ascertain the extent to which operating and program goals and objectives have been established and conform to those of the organization.

2120.A3 Internal auditors should review operations and programs to ascertain the extent to which results are consistent with established goals and objectives to determine whether operations and programs are being implemented or performed as intended.

2120.A4 Adequate criteria are needed to evaluate controls. Internal auditors should ascertain the extent to which management has established adequate criteria to determine whether objectives and goals have been accomplished. If adequate, internal auditors should use such criteria in their evaluation. If inadequate, internal auditors should work with management to develop appropriate evaluation criteria.

2120.C1 During consulting engagements, internal auditors should address controls consistent with the engagement's objectives and should be alert to the existence of any significant control weaknesses.

2120.C2 Internal auditors should incorporate knowledge of controls gained from consulting engagements into the process of identifying and evaluating significant risk exposures of the organization.

2130 Governance

The internal audit activity should contribute to the organization's governance process by evaluating and improving the process through which (1) values and goals are established and communicated, (2) the accomplishment of goals is monitored, (3) accountability is ensured, and (4) values are preserved.

2130.A1 Internal auditors should review operations and programs to ensure consistency with organizational values.

2130.C1 Consulting engagement objectives should be consistent with the overall values and goals of the organization.

2200 Engagement Planning

Internal auditors should develop and record a plan for each engagement.

2201 Planning Considerations

In planning the engagement, internal auditors should consider:

- The objectives of the activity being reviewed and the means by which the activity controls its performance.
- The significant risks to the activity, its objectives, resources, and operations and the means by which the potential impact of risk is kept to an acceptable level.
- The adequacy and effectiveness of the activity's risk management and control systems compared to a relevant control framework or model.
- The opportunities for making significant improvements to the activity's risk management and control systems.

2201.C1 Internal auditors should establish an understanding with consulting engagement clients about objectives, scope, respective responsibilities, and other client expectations. For significant engagements, this understanding should be documented.

2210 Engagement Objectives

The engagement's objectives should address the risks, controls, and governance processes associated with the activities under review.

2210.A1 When planning the engagement, the internal auditor should identify and assess risks relevant to the activity under review. The engagement objectives should reflect the results of the risk assessment.

2210.A2 The internal auditor should consider the probability of significant errors, irregularities, noncompliance, and other exposures when developing the engagement objectives.

2210.C1 Consulting engagement objectives should address risks, controls, and governance processes to the extent agreed upon with the client.

2220 Engagement Scope

The established scope should be sufficient to satisfy the objectives of the engagement.

2220.A1 The scope of the engagement should include consideration of relevant systems, records, personnel, and physical properties, including those under the control of third parties.

2220.C1 In performing consulting engagements, internal auditors should ensure that the scope of the engagement is sufficient to address the agreed-upon objectives. If internal auditors develop reservations about the scope during the engagement, these reservations should be discussed with the client to determine whether to continue with the engagement.

2230 Engagement Resource Allocation

Internal auditors should determine appropriate resources to achieve engagement

(continued)

Exhibit 9.1   (*Continued*)

objectives. Staffing should be based on an evaluation of the nature and complexity of each engagement, time constraints, and available resources.

2240 Engagement Work Program

Internal auditors should develop work programs that achieve the engagement objectives. These work programs should be recorded.

2240.A1 Work programs should establish the procedures for identifying, analyzing, evaluating, and recording information during the engagement. The work program should be approved prior to the commencement of work, and any adjustments approved promptly.

2240.C1 Work programs for consulting engagements may vary in form and content depending upon the nature of the engagement.

2300 Performing the Engagement

Internal auditors should identify, analyze, evaluate, and record sufficient information to achieve the engagement's objectives.

2310 Identifying Information

Internal auditors should identify sufficient, reliable, relevant, and useful information to achieve the engagement's objectives.

2320 Analysis and Evaluation

Internal auditors should base conclusions and engagement results on appropriate analyses and evaluations.

2330 Recording Information

Internal auditors should record relevant information to support the conclusions and engagement results.

2330.A1 The chief audit executive should control access to engagement records. The chief audit executive should obtain the approval of senior management and/or legal counsel prior to releasing such records to external parties, as appropriate.

2330.A2 The chief audit executive should develop retention requirements for engagement records. These retention requirements should be consistent with the organization's guidelines and any pertinent regulatory or other requirements.

2330.C1 The chief audit executive should develop policies governing the custody and retention of engagement records, as well as their release to internal and external parties. These policies should be consistent with the organization's guidelines and any pertinent regulatory or other requirements.

2340 Engagement Supervision

Engagements should be properly supervised to ensure objectives are achieved, quality is assured, and staff is developed.

2400 Communicating Results

Internal auditors should communicate the engagement results promptly.

2410 Criteria for Communicating

Communications should include the engagement's objectives and scope as well as applicable conclusions, recommendations, and action plans.

2410.A1 The final communication of results should, where appropriate, contain the internal auditor's overall opinion.

2410.A2 Engagement communications should acknowledge satisfactory performance.

2410.C1 Communication of the progress and results of consulting engagements will vary in form and content depending upon the nature of the engagement and the needs of the client.

2420 Quality of Communications

Communications should be accurate, objective, clear, concise, constructive, complete, and timely.

2421 Errors and Omissions

If a final communication contains a significant error or omission, the chief
audit executive should communicate corrected information to all individuals
who received the original communication.

2430 Engagement Disclosure of Noncompliance with the Standards

When noncompliance with the Standards impacts a specific engagement, communication of the results should disclose the:

• Standard(s) with which full compliance was not achieved,
• Reason(s) for noncompliance, and
• Impact of noncompliance on the engagement.

2440 Disseminating Results

The chief audit executive should disseminate results to the appropriate individuals.

2440.A1 The chief audit executive is responsible for communicating the final
results to individuals who can ensure that the results are given due
consideration.

2440.C1 The chief audit executive is responsible for communicating the final
results of consulting engagements to clients.

2440.C2 During consulting engagements, risk management, control, and
governance issues may be identified. Whenever these issues are significant to
the organization, they should be communicated to senior management and the
board.

2500 Monitoring Progress

The chief audit executive should establish and maintain a system to monitor the disposition of results communicated to management.

2500.A1 The chief audit executive should establish a follow-up process to monitor
and ensure that management actions have been effectively implemented or that
senior management has accepted the risk of not taking action.

2500.C1 The internal audit activity should monitor the disposition of results of
consulting engagements to the extent agreed upon with the client.

2600 Management's Acceptance of Risks

When the chief audit executive believes that senior management has accepted a level of
residual risk that is unacceptable to the organization, the chief audit executive should
discuss the matter with senior management. If the decision regarding residual risk is not
resolved, the chief audit executive and senior management should report the matter to
the board for resolution.

---

[1]When used in these Standards, the term "board" is defined as a board of directors, audit committee
of such boards, head of an agency or legislative body to whom internal auditors report, board of
governors or trustees of a nonprofit organization, or any other designated governing bodies of an
organization.

Source: Institute of Internal Auditors, *The Professional Practices Framework* (Altamonte Springs,
FL: IIA, 2002), pp. 7–22.

In retrospect, Michael J. Barrett and P. Tiessen set forth these proposed recommendations with respect to organizational support for the internal audit group.

Senior Management

Internal audit must be provided with adequate resources and personnel to perform audit examinations with appropriate frequency at all organizational levels, areas, and activities.

Internal audit director's reporting position should be at an administrative level that will ensure independence.

Internal audit director's salary and promotion possibilities should be commensurate with his or her administrative reporting level.

Internal audit director should be free of undue influence to limit the scope of the department's audit scope and audit assignment schedule.

All organizational levels, areas, and activities should be subject to internal audit examination. Those performed by senior management should comply with the Corporate Code of Conduct.

Internal audit recommendations should receive strong mandated attention, and there should be appropriate follow-up to better ensure that management has taken appropriate remedial action.

Audit Committee

Audit committee should be composed entirely of external members of the board of directors who are not affiliated with the company in any other capacity.

Director of internal audit should communicate directly and regularly to the audit committee.

Audit committee should play a significant role in concurring with the salary and promotion judgments of senior management for the internal audit director.

Reports or report summaries should be communicated to the audit committee on a regular basis.

Director should meet regularly and privately with the audit committee with no other members of management present.

Requests from the audit committee for special assignments should be considered to be a normal and routine part of the internal audit department's responsibilities.

Director should feel no obligation to immediately report audit committee special assignment requests to senior management.

Director should have the right and responsibility to communicate specific matters directly to the audit committee, and internal audit should be actively encouraged to do so. A communication policy for internal audit should be established to indicate items and reports that should be directly communicated to the audit committee.

A cordial, informal, routine, and trusting relationship should be established and fostered between the director and the audit committee.[8]

---

[8]Michael J. Barrett and P. Tiessen, "Organizational Support for Internal Auditing," *Internal Auditing* 5, No. 2 (Fall 1989), pp. 52–53.

Finally, Joseph Castellano, Harper Roehm, and John P. Walker used a "focus-group approach" to explore the relationship between external auditors (EA) and internal auditors (IA). Their objective was to study the implications of the Treadway Commission's recommendation "that the audit committee meet with the external auditors to discuss the performance of the internal auditors and vice versa." They concluded:

> While many companies have already implemented this recommendation, this study shows that external and internal auditors do not believe that audit committees give their respective inputs equal weight. External auditors tended to be more concerned about what the CFO reported to the committee about their performance than what the internal auditor reported. However, the IA group indicated that they believed the EA input to the audit committee was very important, more so than the CFO's input. These relative differences appear to be related to the audit committee's perceived organizational status of the IA.

> The Director of Internal Auditing should be elevated in the organizational hierarchy to a level consistent with the CFO. This would minimize board discounting of IA input, enhance the quality of audits, and meet the spirit of the Treadway recommendation.[9]

Thus it is important to recognize that the framework for the internal auditing function should be established so that it correlates closely with the auditing segments of the corporate audit plan discussed in Chapter 6. This broad framework also should incorporate the nature and scope of the entity's operational activities. For example, it is obvious that if the enterprise is operating on a multinational basis, then the framework for the internal auditing function should be designed to address the auditing needs of the entity in both the domestic and international arenas. Consequently, the organizational structure of this auditing group should be balanced in order to provide assurance to the board that the internal auditing resources are allocated properly.

Exhibit 9.2 presents the Institute of Internal Auditors' guidance on the organizational structure.

To ensure that the organizational framework for the internal auditing function is comprehensive and balanced, the audit committee should give consideration to:

- Corporate auditing philosophy
- Corporate auditing independence
- Logistical matters, such as the size and geographic location of staff

Corporate Auditing Philosophy

Continuing developments in corporate accountability and governance necessitate an ongoing appraisal of the entity's auditing philosophy. The audit committee's approach to a reexamination of such a philosophy should be based on its understanding of the auditing group's approaches to the internal auditing function.

---

[9]Joseph Castellano, Harper Roehm, and John P. Walker, "Status & Quality," *Internal Auditor* 49, No. 3 (June 1992), p. 52.

Exhibit 9.2   Practice Advisory 1000-1: Internal Audit Charter

Related Standard

1000 Purpose, Authority, and Responsibility

The purpose, authority, and responsibility of the internal audit activity should be formally defined in a charter, consistent with the Standards, and approved by the board.

Nature of this Practice Advisory: *Internal auditors should consider the following suggestions when adopting an internal audit charter. This guidance is not intended to represent all the considerations that may be necessary when adopting a charter, but simply a recommended set of items that should be addressed. Compliance with Practice Advisories is optional.*

1. The purpose, authority, and responsibility of the internal audit activity should be defined in a charter. The chief audit executive should seek approval of the charter by senior management as well as acceptance by the board, audit committee, or appropriate governing authority. The charter should (a) establish the internal audit activity's position within the organization; (b) authorize access to records, personnel, and physical properties relevant to the performance of engagements; and (c) define the scope of internal audit activities.

2. The internal audit activity's charter should be in writing. A written statement provides formal communication for review and approval by management and for acceptance by the board. It also facilitates a periodic assessment of the adequacy of the internal audit activity s purpose, authority, and responsibility. Providing a formal, written document containing the charter of the internal audit activity is critical in managing the audit function within the organization. The purpose, authority, and responsibility should be defined and communicated to establish the role of the internal audit activity and to provide a basis for management and the board to use in evaluating the operations of the function. If a question should arise, the charter also provides a formal, written agreement with management and the board about the role and responsibilities of the internal audit activity within the organization.

3. The chief audit executive should periodically assess whether the purpose, authority, and responsibility, as defined in the charter, continue to be adequate to enable the internal audit activity to accomplish its objectives. The result of this periodic assessment should be communicated to senior management and the board.

Source: Institute of Internal Auditors, *The Professional Practice Framework* (Altamonte Springs, FL: Institute of Internal Auditors, 2002), pp. 35–36.

For example, the auditing approaches may be traditional and therefore not totally conducive to the entity's auditing needs. Such an approach is evidenced by the group's preoccupation with the traditional internal financial auditing activities. Although such auditing activities may reduce the outside auditing costs, it is essential that the audit committee review the auditing approaches in the operational and compliance areas. As indicated in Chapter 6, the committee's review of the scope of the entity's internal audit plans should enable it to ensure that adequate coverage is given to the auditing segments of the corporate audit plan. Furthermore, the audit committee should be satisfied that the internal auditing philosophy is supported by modern approaches to the internal auditing function. For example, if the entity has a strong computer environment, then the committee should be satisfied that the internal auditing group has the necessary information technology expertise. Also, since the independent auditors are required to study and evaluate the entity's internal audit function as part of their review of the internal accounting controls, the committee should request a written opinion of their assessment of the internal auditing philosophy and the organizational structure. Obviously, the committee should give strong consideration to the recommendations made by the independent auditors. Many of the salient points discussed in this text will assist the audit committee in its assessment of the entity's internal auditing philosophy.

Corporate Auditing Independence

Fundamental to the structure and organization of the corporate auditing staff is their independence within the corporate framework. While it is obvious that the members of this group are employees of the corporation, their reporting relationship should be established so that the chief audit executive is responsible to an executive with enough authority to provide the necessary internal auditing coverage. Such a reporting relationship has been ruled as mandatory guidance by the Institute of Internal Auditors. Historically, the Conference Board, in a 1978 study on internal auditing, surveyed 274 companies and reported that 76 percent of the internal audit managers report to a vice presidential level or higher, whereas only 40 percent of them reported to such a level in 1963.[10] Moreover, "fifteen percent of the respondents (as against 9 percent in 1963) report to one of the top three officers (chairman, vice chairman, president) or to a board committee."[11]

In 1988, the Conference Board found in a survey of 692 companies that the audit committee has closer ties to internal auditing. The Board reported:

> The survey produced further evidence of the closer working relationship between audit committees and the internal audit function. Just as access to the audit committee by the outside auditing firm has been strengthened, so too has access by the chief internal auditor. It is more common now for charters to require the committee to meet in private with the internal auditor (with no members of management present), or to state that the committee will be available to the internal auditor when necessary, or both.

> Another way companies support the independent status of the internal auditing function is to specify in writing that the audit committee must have a say—or, at a minimum, must be consulted and thoroughly informed—when there is to be a change in internal auditors. Some committees are also charged with monitoring the pay level of the head of internal auditing. These links give the internal auditor an ally in high places and presumably discourage management from trying to undermine or compromise his/her sense of independence.

---

[10]Paul Macchiaverna, *Internal Auditing,* Report No. 748 (New York: The Conference Board, 1978), p. 53.
[11]Ibid., p. 54.

Another major trend is the increasing extent to which internal auditors formally report to the audit committee. In the 1978 survey, 25 percent of participating firms engaged in this practice. By 1987, this was true of almost *half* (47 percent).[12]

It is apparent that the trend over the years has been to enhance the independence and objectivity of the internal auditing staff. Although some corporate auditing executives are reporting to the chairman of the board or the president, Edward G. Jepsen, former partner of Price Waterhouse & Company (now PricewaterhouseCoopers), points out:

> As a practical matter, such a person (chairman or president) may not be able to give the department the attention it needs—and thus there is a danger that it would become isolated from top management. A common organizational structure is for the department to report directly on a day-to-day basis to the company's senior financial officer and have a dotted-line relationship (implying less frequent contact but clear access) to the chairman or president.[13]

Also, Jepsen states that a "logical development" of the formation of the audit committee is having the corporate auditing executive meet periodically with the committee to discuss the corporate auditing function.[14] For example, the Conference Board's "survey shows that more than seven out of ten auditing staffs are meeting regularly with their committees (audit) to discuss auditing affairs."[15] More specifically, of the 258 internal auditing staffs surveyed, 55 percent discuss the internal auditing organization.[16] It is clearly evident that the internal audit staff must be "free of organizational pressures" that restrict their independence and objectivity in "selecting areas to be examined or in evaluating those areas."[17] Also, as discussed in Chapter 2, the director of internal auditing must be able to meet regularly with the audit committee.

More recently, the Institute of Internal Auditors has issued several Practice Advisories dealing with organization independence and boards of directors and audit committees: They are:

PA 1110-1   "Organizational Independence"

PA 1110-2   "Chief Audit Executive (CAE) Reporting Lines"

PA 2060-1   "Reporting to the Board and Senior Management"

PA 2060-2   "Relationship with the Audit Committee"

Exhibits 9.3, 9.4, 9.5, and 9.6 contain information about these Practice Advisories.

---

[12]Jeremy Bacon, *The Audit Committee: A Broader Mandate,* Report No. 914 (New York: The Conference Board, 1988), pp. 20–21.
[13]Edward G. Jepsen, "Internal Auditors Move into the Spotlight," *Internal Auditor* 36, No. 2 (April 1979), pp. 27–28.
[14]Ibid.
[15]Macchiaverna, *Internal Auditing,* p. 55.
[16]Ibid., p. 57.
[17]Jepsen, "Internal Auditors," p. 27.

Logistical Matters

Depending on the nature, size, and complexity of the entity, management will have different corporate auditing needs. Thus the particular circumstances of the entity will govern the organizational structure of the internal auditing staff. For example, the Conference Board reports that "corporate audit staffs are either centralized at corporate headquarters or are decentralized, with some members

---

Exhibit 9.3   Practice Advisory 1110-1: Organizational Independence

Related Standard

1110 Organizational Independence
The chief audit executive should report to a level within the organization that allows the internal audit activity to accomplish its responsibilities.

Nature of this Practice Advisory: *Internal auditors should consider the following Suggestions when evaluating organizational independence. This guidance is not intended to represent all the considerations that may be necessary during such an evaluation, but simply a recommended set of items that should be addressed. Compliance with Practice Advisories is optional.*

1. Internal auditors should have the support of senior management and of the board so that they can gain the cooperation of engagement clients and perform their work free from interference.

2. The chief audit executive should be responsible to an individual in the organization with sufficient authority to promote independence and to ensure broad audit coverage, adequate consideration of engagement communications, and appropriate action on engagement recommendations.

3. Ideally, the chief audit executive should report functionally to the audit committee, board of directors, or other appropriate governing authority, and administratively to the chief executive officer of the organization.

4. The chief audit executive should have direct communication with the board, audit committee, or other appropriate governing authority. Regular communication with the board helps assure independence and provides a means for the board and the chief audit executive to keep each other informed on matters of mutual interest.

5. Direct communication occurs when the chief audit executive regularly attends and participates in meetings of the board, audit committee, or other appropriate governing authority which relate to its oversight responsibilities for auditing, financial reporting, organizational governance, and control. The chief audit executive's attendance and participation at these meetings provide an opportunity to exchange information concerning the plans and activities of the internal audit activity. The chief audit executive should meet privately with the board, audit committee, or other appropriate governing authority at least annually.

6. Independence is enhanced when the board concurs in the appointment or removal of the chief audit executive.

Source: Institute of Internal Auditors, *The Professional Practice Framework* (Altamonte Springs, FL: IIA, 2002), pp. 53–54.

Exhibit 9.4   Practice Advisory 1110-2: Chief Audit Executive Reporting Lines

Related Standard:

1110—Organizational Independence	**Nature of This Practice Advisory**
The chief audit executive should report to a level within the organization that allows the internal audit activity to accomplish its responsibilities.	Internal auditors should consider the following guidance when establishing or evaluating the reporting lines and relationships with organizational officials to whom the CAE reports. This guidance is not intended to represent all the considerations that may be necessary during such an evaluation, but simply a recommended set of items that should be considered. **Compliance with Practice Advisories is optional.**

1. The IIA's *Standards for the Professional Practice of Internal Auditing (Standards)* require that the chief audit executive (CAE) report to a level within the organization that allows the internal audit activity to fulfill its responsibilities. The Institute believes strongly that to achieve necessary independence, the CAE should report functionally to the audit committee or its equivalent. For administrative purposes, in most circumstances, the CAE should report directly to the chief executive officer of the organization. The following descriptions of what The IIA considers "functional reporting" and "administrative reporting" are provided to help focus the discussion in this practice advisory.
   - Functional Reporting—The functional reporting line for the internal audit function is the ultimate source of its independence and authority. As such, The IIA recommends that the CAE report functionally to the audit committee, board of directors, or other appropriate governing authority. In this context, report functionally means that the governing authority would—
   - approve the overall charter of the internal audit function.
   - approve the internal audit risk assessment and related audit plan.
   - receive communications from the CAE on the results of the internal audit activities or other matters that the CAE determines are necessary, including private meetings with the CAE without management present
   - approve all decisions regarding the appointment or removal of the CAE.
   - approve the annual compensation and salary adjustment of the CAE.
   - make appropriate inquiries of management and the CAE to determine whether there are scope or budgetary limitations that impede the ability of the internal audit function to execute its responsibilities.
   - Administrative Reporting—Administrative Reporting is the reporting relationship within the organization's management structure that facilitates the day-to-day operations of the internal audit function. Administrative reporting typically includes:
   - budgeting and management accounting.
   - human resource administration including personnel evaluations and compensation.
   - internal communications and information flows.
   - administration of the organization's internal policies and procedures.

2. This advisory focuses on considerations in establishing or evaluating CAE reporting lines. Appropriate reporting lines are critical to achieve the independence, objectivity, and organizational stature for an internal audit function necessary to effectively fulfill its obligations. CAE reporting lines are also critical to ensuring the appropriate flow

of information and access to key executives and managers that are the foundations of risk assessment and reporting of results of audit activities. Conversely, any reporting relationship that impedes the independence and effective operations of the internal audit function should be viewed by the CAE as a serious scope limitation, which should be brought to the attention of the audit committee or its equivalent.

3. This advisory also recognizes that CAE reporting lines are impacted by the nature of the organization (public or private as well as relative size); common practices of each country; growing complexity of organizations (joint ventures, multinational corporations with subsidiaries); and the trend towards internal audit groups providing value-added services with increased collaboration on priorities and scope with their clients. Accordingly, while the IIA believes that there is an ideal reporting structure with functional reporting to the Audit Committee and administrative reporting to the CEO, other relationships can be effective if there are clear distinctions between the functional and administrative reporting lines and appropriate activities are in each line to ensure that the independence and scope of activities is maintained. Internal auditors are expected to use professional judgement to determine the extent to which the guidance provided in this advisory should be applied in each given situation.

4. The *Standards* stress the importance of the chief audit executive reporting to an individual with sufficient authority to promote independence and to ensure broad audit coverage. The *Standards* are purposely somewhat generic about reporting relationships, however, because they are designed to be applicable at all organizations regardless of size or any other factors. Factors that make "one size fits all" unattainable include organization size, and type of organization (private, governmental, corporate). Accordingly, the CAE should consider the following attributes in evaluating the appropriateness of the administrative reporting line.
   - Does the individual have sufficient authority and stature to ensure the effectiveness of the function?
   - Does the individual have an appropriate control and governance mindset to assist the CAE in their role?
   - Does the individual have the time and interest to actively support the CAE on audit issues?
   - Does the individual understand the functional reporting relationship and support it?

5. The CAE should also ensure that appropriate independence is maintained if the individual responsible for the administrative reporting line is also responsible for other activities in the organization, which are subject to internal audit. For example, some CAEs report administratively to the Chief Financial Officer, who is also responsible for the organization's accounting functions. The internal audit function should be free to audit and report on any activity that also reports to its administrative head if it deems that coverage appropriate for its audit plan. Any limitation in scope or reporting of results of these activities should be brought to the attention of the audit committee.

6. Under the recent move to a stricter legislative and regulatory climate regarding financial reporting around the globe, the CAE's reporting lines should be appropriate to enable the internal audit activity to meet any increased needs of the audit committee or other significant stakeholders. Increasingly, the CAE is being asked to take a more significant role in the organization's governance and risk management activities. The reporting lines of the CAE should facilitate the ability of the internal audit activity to meet these expectations.

(continued)

Exhibit 9.4 (*Continued*)

7. Regardless of which reporting relationship the organization chooses, several key
   actions can help assure that the reporting lines support and enable the effectiveness
   and independence of the internal auditing activity.
   • Functional Reporting:
     • The functional reporting line should go directly to the Audit Committee or its
       equivalent to ensure the appropriate level of independence and communication.
     • The CAE should meet privately with the audit committee or its equivalent, with-
       out management present, to reinforce the independence and nature of this report-
       ing relationship.
     • The audit committee should have the final authority to review and approve the
       annual audit plan and all major changes to the plan.
     • At all times, the CAE should have open and direct access to the chair of the audit
       committee and its members; or the chair of the board or full board if appropriate.
     • At least once a year, the audit committee should review the performance of the
       CAE and approve the annual compensation and salary adjustment.
     • The charter for the internal audit function should clearly articulate both the
       functional and administrative reporting lines for the function as well as the princi-
       ple activities directed up each line.
   • Administrative Reporting:
     • The administrative reporting line of the CAE should be to the CEO or another
       executive with sufficient authority to afford it appropriate support to accomplish
       its day-to day activities. This support should include positioning the function and
       the CAE in the organization's structure in a manner that affords appropriate
       stature for the function within the organization. Reporting too low in an organiza-
       tion can negatively impact the stature and effectiveness of the internal audit
       function.
     • The administrative reporting line should not have ultimate authority over the
       scope or reporting of results of the internal audit activity.
     • The administrative reporting line should facilitate open and direct communica-
       tions with executive and line management. The CAE should be able to communi-
       cate directly with any level of management including the CEO.
     • The administrative reporting line should enable adequate communications and
       information flow such that the CAE and the internal audit function have an
       adequate and timely flow of information concerning the activates, plans and
       business initiatives of the organization.
     • Budgetary controls and considerations imposed by the administrative reporting
       line should not impede the ability of the internal audit function to accomplish its
       mission.

8. CAEs should also consider their relationships with other control and monitoring
   functions (risk management, compliance, security, legal, ethics, environmental,
   external audit) and facilitate the reporting of material risk and control issues to the
   audit committee.

Source: Institute of Internal Auditors, visit the web site at www.theiia.org.

Exhibit 9.5   Practice Advisory 2060-1: Reporting to the Board and Senior Management

---

Related Standard

B2060 Reporting to Board and Senior Management
The chief audit executive should report periodically to the board and senior management on the internal audit activity's purpose, authority, responsibility, and performance relative to its plan. Reporting should also include significant risk exposures and control issues, corporate governance issues, and other matters needed or requested by the board and senior management.

Nature of This Practice Advisory: *Internal auditors should consider the following suggestions when reporting to the board and senior management. This guidance is not intended to represent all the considerations that may be necessary, but simply a recommended set of items that should be addressed. Compliance with Practice Advisories is optional.*

1. The chief audit executive should submit activity reports to senior management and to the board at least annually. Activity reports should highlight significant engagement observations and recommendations and should inform senior management and the board of any significant deviations from approved engagement work schedules, staffing plans, and financial budgets, and the reasons for them.

2. Significant engagement observations are those conditions that, in the judgment of the chief audit executive, could adversely affect the organization. Significant engagement observations may include conditions dealing with irregularities, illegal acts, errors, inefficiency, waste, ineffectiveness, conflicts of interest, and control weaknesses. After reviewing such conditions with senior management, the chief audit executive should communicate significant engagement observations and recommendations to the board, whether or not they have been satisfactorily resolved.

3. Management's responsibility is to make decisions on the appropriate action to be taken regarding significant engagement observations and recommendations. Senior management may decide to assume the risk of not correcting the reported condition because of cost or other considerations. The board should be informed of senior management's decisions on all significant observations and recommendations.

4. The chief audit executive should consider whether it is appropriate to inform the board regarding previously reported, significant observations and recommendations in those instances when senior management and the board assumed the risk of not correcting the reported condition. This may be particularly necessary when there have been organization, board, senior management, or other changes.

5. In addition to subjects covered above, activity reports should also compare (a) actual performance with the internal audit activity's goals and audit work schedules, and (b) expenditures with financial budgets. Reports should explain the reason for major variances and indicate any action taken or needed.

Source: Institute of Internal Auditors, *The Professional Practices Framework* (Altamonte Springs, FL: IIA, 2002), pp. 135–136.

Exhibit 9.6 Practice Advisory 2060-2: Relationship with the Audit Committee

Related Standard:

2060—Independence and Objectivity	Nature of this Practice Advisory
The chief audit executive should report periodically to the board and senior management on the internal audit activity's purpose, authority, responsibility, and performance relative to its plan. Reporting should also include significant risk exposures and control issues, corporate governance issues, and other matters needed or requested by the board and senior management.	Internal auditors should consider the following suggestions regarding the relationship between the internal audit activity and the audit committee of the governing body. This guidance is not intended to represent all necessary considerations, but merely summarizes key information concerning appropriate relationships between audit committees and internal auditing. **Compliance with Practice Advisories is optional.**

1. The term "audit committee," as used in this document, refers to the governance body that is charged with oversight of the organization's audit and control functions. Although these fiduciary duties are often delegated to an audit committee of the board of directors, the information in this Practice Advisory is also intended to apply to other oversight groups with equivalent authority and responsibility, such as trustees, legislative bodies, owners of an owner-managed entity, internal control committees, or full boards of directors.

2. The Institute of Internal Auditors recognizes that audit committees and internal auditors have interlocking goals. A strong working relationship with the audit committee is essential for each to fulfill its responsibilities to senior management, board of directors, shareholders, and other outside parties. This Practice Advisory summarizes The Institute's views concerning the aspects and attributes of an appropriate relationship between an audit committee and the internal audit function. The Institute acknowledges that audit committee responsibilities encompass activities that are beyond the scope of this advisory, and in no way intends it to be a comprehensive description of audit committee responsibilities.

3. There are three areas of activities that are key to an effective relationship between the audit committee and the internal audit function, chiefly through the Chief Audit Executive (CAE):
   - Assisting the audit committee to ensure that its charter, activities, and processes are appropriate to fulfill its responsibilities.
   - Ensuring that the charter, role, and activities of internal audit are clearly understood and responsive to the needs of the audit committee and the board.
   - Maintaining open and effective communications with the audit committee and the chairperson.

Audit Committee Responsibilities

4. The CAE should assist the committee in ensuring that the charter, role and activities of the committee are appropriate for it to achieve its responsibilities. The CAE can play an important role by assisting the committee to periodically review its activities and suggesting enhancements. In this way, the CAE serves as a valued advisor to the committee on audit committee and regulatory practices. Examples of activities that the CAE can undertake are:

- Review the charter for the audit committee at least annually and advise the committee whether the charter addresses all responsibilities directed to the committee in any terms of reference or mandates from the board of directors.
- Review or maintain a planning agenda for the audit committee's meeting that details all required activities to ascertain whether they are completed and that assists the committee in reporting to the board annually that it has completed all assigned duties.
- Draft the audit committee's meeting agenda for the chairman's review and facilitate the distribution of the material to the audit committee members and write up the minutes of the audit committee meetings.
- Encourage the audit committee to conduct periodic reviews of its activities and practices compared with current best practices to ensure that its activities are consistent with leading practices.
- Meet periodically with the chairperson to discuss whether the materials and information being furnished to the committee are meeting their needs.
- Inquire from the audit committee if any educational or informational sessions or presentations would be helpful, such as training new committee members on risk and controls.
- Inquire from the committee whether the frequency and time allotted to the committee are sufficient.

Internal Audit Activity's Role

5. The CAE's relationship to the audit committee should revolve around a core role of the CAE ensuring that the audit committee understands, supports, and receives all assistance needed from the internal audit function. The IIA supports the concept that sound governance is dependent on the synergy generated among the four principal components of effective corporate governance systems: boards of directors, management, internal auditors, and external auditors. In that structure, internal auditors and audit committees are mutually supportive. Consideration of the work of internal auditors is essential for the audit committee to gain a complete understanding of an organization's operations. A primary component of the CAE's role with the committee is to ensure this objective is accomplished and the committee views the CAE as their trusted advisor. The chief audit executive can perform a number of activities to accomplish this role:
   - Request that the committee review and approve the internal audit charter on an annual basis. (A model internal audit department charter is available on The Institute's Web site at *http://www.theiiaorg/ecm/guide-ia.cfm?doc_id=383*)
   - Review with the audit committee the functional and administrative reporting lines of internal audit to ensure that the organizational structure in place allows adequate independence for internal auditors. (Practice Advisory 1110-2: Chief Audit Executive (CAE) Reporting Lines)
   - Incorporate in the charter for the audit committee the review of hiring decisions, including appointment, compensation, evaluation, retention, and dismissal of the CAE.
   - Incorporate in the charter for the audit committee to review and approve proposals to outsource any internal audit activities.
   - Assist the audit committee in evaluating the adequacy of the personnel and budget, and the scope and results of the internal audit activities, to ensure that there are no budgetary or scope limitations that impede the ability of the internal audit function to execute its responsibilities.
   - Provide information on the coordination with and oversight of other control and monitoring functions (e.g. risk management, compliance, security, business continuity, legal, ethics, environmental, external audit).

(continued)

Exhibit 9.6   (*Continued*)

- Report significant issues related to the processes for controlling the activities of the organization and its affiliates, including potential improvements to those processes, and provide information concerning such issues through resolution.
- Provide information on the status and results of the annual audit plan and the sufficiency of department resources to senior management and the audit committee.
- Develop a flexible annual audit plan using an appropriate risk-based methodology, including any risks or control concerns identified by management, and submit that plan to the audit committee for review and approval as well as periodic updates.
- Report on the implementation of the annual audit plan, as approved, including as appropriate any special tasks or projects requested by management and the audit committee.
- Incorporate into the internal audit charter the responsibility for the internal audit department to report to the audit committee on a timely basis any suspected fraud involving management or employees who are significantly involved in the internal controls of the company. Assist in the investigation of significant suspected fraudulent activities within the organization and notify management and the audit committee of the results.
- Audit committees should be made aware that quality assessment reviews of the internal audit activity be done every five years in order for the audit activity to declare that it meets The IIA's *Standards for the Professional Practice of Internal Auditing (Standards)*. Regular quality assessment reviews will provide assurance to the audit committee and to management that internal auditing activities conform to *Standards*.

Communications with the Audit Committee

6. While not to diminish any of the activities noted above, in a large part the overall effectiveness of the CAE and audit committee relationship will revolve around the communications between the parties. Today's audit committees expect a high level of open and candid communications. If the CAE is to be viewed as a trusted advisor by the committee, communications is the key element. Internal auditing, by definition, can help the audit committee accomplish its objectives by bringing a systematic, disciplined approach to its activities, but unless there is appropriate communications, it is not possible for the committee to determine this. The chief audit executive should consider providing communications to the audit committee in the following areas.
   - Audit committees should meet privately with the CAE on a regular basis to discuss sensitive issues.
   - Provide an annual summary report or assessment on the results of the audit activities relating to the defined mission and scope of audit work.
   - Issue periodic reports to the audit committee and management summarizing results of audit activities.
   - Keep the audit committee informed of emerging trends and successful practices in internal auditing.
   - Together with external auditors, discuss fulfillment of committee information needs.
   - Review information submitted to the audit committee for completeness and accuracy.
   - Confirm there is effective and efficient work coordination of activities between internal and external auditors. Determine if there is any duplication between the work of the internal and external auditors and give the reasons for such duplication.

Source: Institute of Internal Auditors, visit the web site at *www.theiia.org*.

permanently located at various subsidiaries or divisions."[18] Furthermore, the Board's study disclosed a number of internal auditing staffs have made changes in their organizational structure. They are:

> Reporting of subsidiary and divisional audit staffs in some companies has been centralized. These units now report to corporate auditing, instead of to subsidiary or division management. Typically, this has been due to bolster the independence of resident audit staffs, and to increase corporate control over decentralized operations.
>
> Decentralizing audit operations on a geographical basis—moving auditors formerly based at corporate headquarters to other company locations. This has been done so that auditing can better cover far-flung company operations. It also reduces the amount of travel required of auditors—a major cause of dissatisfaction which can result in high staff turnover.
>
> Creating special sections—to focus on individual corporate functions, or specialist groups, which assist the main audit group. For example, most EDP audit sections perform specialized data processing audits, as well as assist financial or operational auditors in their duties.[19]

Moreover, Jepsen notes that although there is no definitive criterion for relating the size of the staff with "corporate sales or total assets," consideration should be given to the quality of the system of internal control.[20] Clearly, the size and location of the internal auditing staff should be a function of the adequacy of the internal accounting and administrative controls. Thus the committee should assess the potential opportunity cost and related degree of risk management is willing to assume. For example, the committee should discuss with both the internal and independent auditing executives the potential opportunity cost of not auditing specific locations in light of the internal control conditions. One large corporation reported that "15 major locations are audited once a year, while the remaining 185 minor locations are scheduled for visits once every two years."[21] The selection of the major areas is ordinarily based on the concept of materiality and relative risk (discussed in Chapter 5) for the financial audit. Conversely, in connection with the operational audits, "it should be possible to develop some estimates of the profit contribution resulting from the operational audits compared to the related audit costs."[22] Consequently, the committee should review the budget of the internal auditing staff as well as the outside auditing fees in relation to the entity's auditing needs and potential auditing benefits. Obviously, if the system of internal control is strong, based on the opinions of both the independent and internal auditors, then the high costs of such auditing services should be curtailed.

Equally important, the committee should review the organization chart of the internal auditing function to determine that it is balanced in accordance with the corporate audit plan. An illustrative organization chart in Exhibit 9.7 shows how

---

[18]Macchiaverna, *Internal Auditing*, p. 68.
[19]Ibid., pp. 68–69.
[20]Jepsen, "Internal Auditors," p. 28.
[21]Macchiaverna, *Internal Auditing*, p. 71.
[22]Jepsen, "Internal Auditors," p. 31.

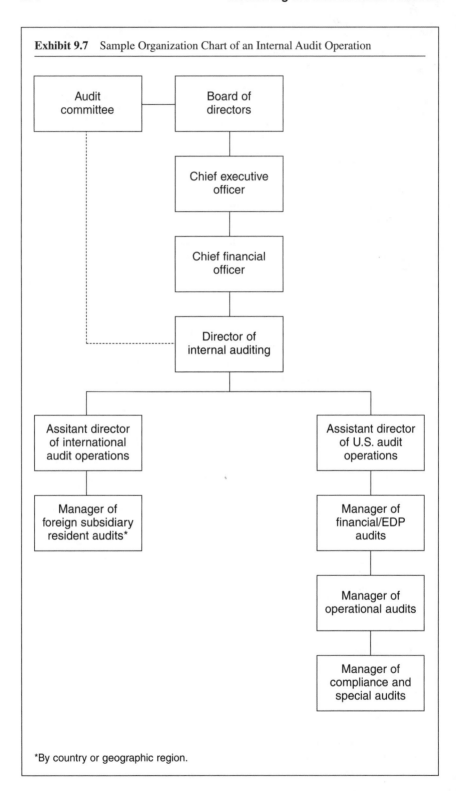

Exhibit 9.7 Sample Organization Chart of an Internal Audit Operation

*By country or geographic region.

the internal audit function might be organized on a centralized basis for a multinational enterprise. Because the chart is simplified, the organizational arrangements will vary and contain more detail in actual practice. The major objective is to show the reporting and functional relationships of the internal auditing function. Moreover, the scope of the international auditing operations also will involve financial, operational, and compliance audits at the resident audit staff level. For example, the Conference Board found that the organizational arrangements regarding the international auditing operations vary whereby "some companies base their international auditors at corporate headquarters in the U.S.," and others are centrally located overseas.[23] If the enterprise is highly diversified, it may decide to decentralize its internal auditing function for such reasons as "increased travel costs," increased "staff dissatisfaction" with traveling, and "more frequent audit coverage."[24] In short, the organizational arrangement should be designed to maximize the corporate auditing services and minimize the economic cost of such services without sacrificing the quality of the auditing work.

In performing a review of the logistical matters, the audit committee should discuss with the chief audit executive the performance standards of the *Standards for the Professional Practice of Internal Auditing*. The objective of the audit committee is to ensure that the internal audit group is positioned to provide the requisite auditing coverage. Such professional standards enable boards of directors and their audit committees to benchmark and align the wide range of internal audit services that encompasses both financial and nonfinancial control areas, including risk management and internal governance.

In addition to logistical matters, Anthony J. Ridley, retired general auditor of the Ford Motor Company and past chairman of the Institute of Internal Auditors, recommends that chief audit executives consider an audit committee event matrix for important events that occur outside regularly scheduled meetings. Ridley points out: "The easiest way to resolve this quandary is to ask your audit committee in advance about the things they want to know—and when—and then capture their preferences in an event matrix for ongoing use. The matrix can eliminate much of the guesswork related to providing information to your audit committee."[25] Some of the generic events are:

- Defalcations and ethics violations
- Litigation
- Regulatory concerns and adverse publicity
- Financial reporting
- Independence and effectiveness of auditors[26]

---

[23]Macchiaverna, *Internal Auditing,* p. 71.
[24]Ibid., pp. 72–73.
[25]Anthony J. Ridley, "An Audit Committee Event Matrix," *Internal Auditor* 57, No. 2 (April 2000), p. 54.
[26]Ibid., p. 54.

APPRAISING THE QUALITY OF THE AUDITING STAFF

The Corporate Auditing Staff

The quality and training of the auditing personnel have an important influence on the performance of the staff. If the auditing personnel's training, skills, and education are not compatible to their broadened responsibilities, they become preoccupied with the routine checking of the accounting transactions and records. As a result, management becomes more susceptible to unfavorable developments, such as deficiencies in the system of internal control and potential fraudulent practices.

It is imperative that the audit committee review the selection process for the corporate auditing personnel. In reviewing the selection process, the committee should consult sections 1200 and 1300 of the *Standards for the Professional Practice of Internal Auditing*, including the related *Practice Advisories*. These guidelines enable the audit committee to review and discuss with the chief audit executive the knowledge, skills, and other competencies collectively needed by the internal audit group to perform its responsibilities. Likewise, the audit committee needs assurance that the internal audit group has established policies and procedures for adequate staffing, levels of supervision, and continuing education programs.

As mentioned in Chapter 2, Section 201 of the Sarbanes-Oxley Act of 2002 prohibits a registered public accounting firm from providing internal audit outsourcing services for an SEC audit client.[27]

With respect to the selection of outside service providers by the chief audit executive, the Institute of Internal Auditors has issued a Practice Advisory as shown in Exhibit 9.8.

In order to facilitate discussion, the audit committee should review the independent auditor's comments regarding the quality of auditing personnel in relation to these three considerations:

1. The professional qualifications and educational backgrounds of the staff. For example, the Conference Board found that audit managers are attempting to "elevate the professionalism" of the internal audit staff by employing "more CPA's, certified internal auditors or MBA's."[28]

2. Professional training and development programs for the corporate audit staff are available through several professional accounting societies and especially the Institute of Internal Auditors. Also, in-house professional development programs of the independent accounting firm may be a possible source of training. For example, to increase the professionalism of the internal audit staff, the Institute of Internal Auditors sponsors the Certified Internal Auditor (CIA) Program. As John D. Marquardt and John F. Bussman report, "The number of candidates sitting for the CIA Exam has increased from 654 in 1974, the year

---

[27]Sarbanes-Oxley Act of 2002, H.R. Rep. No. 107-610 (2002). For an expanded discussion, see Anthony J. Ridley and Lew Burnham, "Where Are the Auditors?" *Directors and Boards* 22, No. 2 (Winter 1998), pp. 61–63.

[28]Macchiaverna, *Internal Auditing*, p. 75.

Exhibit 9.8 Practice Advisory 1210.A-1: Obtaining Services to Support or Complement the Internal Audit Activity

Related Standard

1210.A1 The chief audit executive should obtain competent advice and assistance if the internal audit staff lacks the knowledge, skills, or other competencies needed to perform all or part of the engagement.

Nature of This Practice Advisory: *Internal auditors should consider the following suggestions when contemplating acquiring additional services to support the internal audit activity. This guidance is not intended to represent all the considerations that may be necessary, but simply a recommended set of items that should be addressed. Compliance with Practice Advisories is optional.*

1. The internal audit activity should have employees or use outside service providers who are qualified in disciplines such as accounting, auditing, economics, finance, statistics, information technology, engineering, taxation, law, environmental affairs, and such other areas as needed to meet the internal audit activity's responsibilities. Each member of the internal audit activity, however, need not be qualified in all disciplines.

2. An outside service provider is a person or firm, independent of the organization, who has special knowledge, skill, and experience in a particular discipline. Outside service providers include, among others, actuaries, accountants, appraisers, environmental specialists, fraud investigators, lawyers, engineers, geologists, security specialists, statisticians, information technology specialists, the organization's external auditors, and other audit organizations. An outside service provider may be engaged by the board, senior management, or the chief audit executive.

3. Outside service providers may be used by the internal audit activity in connection with, among other things:
   - Audit activities where a specialized skill and knowledge are required such as information technology, statistics, taxes, language translations, or to achieve the objectives in the engagement work schedule.
   - Valuations of assets such as land and buildings, works of art, precious gems, investments, and complex financial instruments.
   - Determination of quantities or physical condition of certain assets such as mineral and petroleum reserves.
   - Measuring the work completed and to be completed on contracts in progress.
   - Fraud and security investigations.
   - Determination of amounts by using specialized methods such as actuarial determinations of employee benefit obligations.
   - Interpretation of legal, technical, and regulatory requirements.
   - Evaluating the internal audit activity's quality improvement program in accordance with Section 1300 of the Standards.
   - Mergers and acquisitions.

4. When the chief audit executive intends to use and rely on the work of an outside service provider, the chief audit executive should assess the competency, independence, and objectivity of the outside service provider as it relates to the particular assignment to be performed. This assessment should also be made when the outside service provider is selected by senior management or the board, and the chief audit executive intends to use and rely on the outside service provider's work. When the

(continued)

Exhibit 9.8   (*Continued*)

---

selection is made by others and the chief audit executive's assessment determines that he or she should not use and rely on the work of an outside service provider, the results of the assessment should be communicated to senior management or the board, as appropriate.

5. The chief audit executive should determine that the outside service provider possesses the necessary knowledge, skills, and other competencies to perform the engagement. When assessing competency, the chief audit executive should consider the following:
   • Professional certification, license, or other recognition of the outside service provider's competency in the relevant discipline.
   • Membership of the outside service provider in an appropriate professional organization and adherence to that organization's code of ethics.
   • The reputation of the outside service provider. This may include contacting others familiar with the outside service provider's work.
   • The outside service provider's experience in the type of work being considered.
   • The extent of education and training received by the outside service provider in disciplines that pertain to the particular engagement.
   • The outside service provider's knowledge and experience in the industry in which the organization operates.

6. The chief audit executive should assess the relationship of the outside service provider to the organization and to the internal audit activity to ensure that independence and objectivity are maintained throughout the engagement. In performing the assessment, the chief audit executive should determine that there are no financial, organizational, or personal relationships that will prevent the outside service provider from rendering impartial and unbiased judgments and opinions when performing or reporting on the engagement.

7. In assessing the independence and objectivity of the outside service provider, the chief audit executive should consider:
   • The financial interest the provider may have in the organization.
   • The personal or professional affiliation the provider may have to the board, senior management, or others within the organization.
   • The relationship the provider may have had with the organization or the activities being reviewed.
   • The extent of other ongoing services the provider may be performing for the organization.
   • Compensation or other incentives that the provider may have.

8. If the outside service provider is also the organization's external auditor and the nature of the engagement is extended audit services, the chief audit executive should ascertain that work performed does not impair the external auditor's independence. Extended audit services refers to those services beyond the requirements of audit standards generally accepted by external auditors. If the organization's external auditors act or appear to act as members of senior management, management, or as employees of the organization, then their independence is impaired. Additionally, external auditors may provide the organization with other services such as tax and consulting. Independence, however, should be assessed in relation to the full range of services provided to the organization.

9. The chief audit executive should obtain sufficient information regarding the scope of the outside service provider's work. This is necessary in order to ascertain that the

scope of work is adequate for the purposes of the internal audit activity. It may be prudent to have these and other matters documented in an engagement letter or contract. The chief audit executive should review with the outside service provider:
- Objectives and scope of work.
- Specific matters expected to be covered in the engagement communications.
- Access to relevant records, personnel, and physical properties.
- Information regarding assumptions and procedures to be employed.
- Ownership and custody of engagement working papers, if applicable.
- Confidentiality and restrictions on information obtained during the engagement.

10. Where the outside service provider performs internal audit activities, the chief audit executive should specify and ensure that the work complies with the Standards for the Professional Practice of Internal Auditing. In reviewing the work of an outside service provider, the chief audit executive should evaluate the adequacy of work performed. This evaluation should include sufficiency of information obtained to afford a reasonable basis for the conclusions reached and the resolution of significant exceptions or other unusual matters.

11. When the chief audit executive issues engagement communications, and an outside service provider was used, the chief audit executive may, as appropriate, refer to such services provided. The outside service provider should be informed and, if appropriate, concurrence should be obtained prior to such reference being made in engagement communications.

Source: Institute of Internal Auditors, *The Professional Practice Framework* (Altamonte Springs, FL: IIA, 2002), pp. 71–75.

it was first offered, to 2,091 in 1978."[29] More recently, according to the Certification Department of the Institute of Internal Auditors, as of November 1992, the number of certified internal auditors has increased to 19,264. Clearly, the trend is toward professionalizing the internal audit staff in order to enhance their professional auditing integrity and objectivity in the corporate structure.

3. The performance appraisal and evaluation system. "These typically evaluate: (1) an auditor's technical knowledge; (2) compliance with audit policies and procedures; (3) administrative skills and work habits; and (4) effectiveness in interpersonal relationships."[30]

The audit committee's appraisal of the quality and training of the corporate auditing staff provides assurance to the board of directors that the internal auditing function is adequately staffed. Such assurance to the board indicates that this auditing staff is used wisely and responsibly in the interests of the board's outside constituencies.

As previously noted, the Auditing Standards Board has issued SAS No. 65, "The Auditor's Consideration of the Internal Audit Function in an Audit of Financial Statements." This auditing standard is designed to provide expanded guidance

---

[29]John D. Marquardt and John F. Bussman, "The CIA Examination: A Topical Profile and Index Update," *The Internal Auditor* 36, No. 2 (April 1979), p. 41.
[30]Macchiaverna, *Internal Auditing,* p. 89.

to independent auditors when considering the work performed by internal auditors. Recognizing that both the audit committee and the independent auditors have cross-purposes in understanding and assessing the internal audit functions, Exhibits 9.9 and 9.10 compare the SAS No. 65 requirements with a model response from the director of internal auditing. These responses are not intended to be all-inclusive. However, such model responses will enable the audit committee to gain reasonable assurance on the effective interaction between the internal audit group and the independent auditors.

In addition to the model responses in Exhibits 9.9 and 9.10, the reader may wish to review Exhibit 9.11, which contains a list of questions dealing with internal auditing activities, as well as Exhibit 9.12, regarding quality program assessments.

Exhibit 9.9 Representative Responses for Understanding the Internal Audit Function

SAS No. 65 Requirements	Internal Auditors' Documented Response
• Organizational status with the entity	• Presentation and discussion of a written charter or mission statement of the internal audit function and free access to the entity's audit committee.
• Application of professional standards	• Adherence to high professional standards as promulgated by the IIA's *Standards for the Professional Practice of Internal Auditing,* official pronouncements, and *Code of Ethics.*
• Audit plans	• Discussion, coordination, and implementation of the planned external and internal audit scope and related joint planning memos relative to audit risk assessment (e.g., small divisions and subsidiaries that have undergone recent management changes or other material changes in their business activities may need additional audit work). • Discussion of proposed scope of any special investigations relative to the potential impact on the financial statements and the opinion of general counsel. • Review on the follow-up of the external auditor's management letter and nonaudit services.
• Access to records and any scope limitations on activities	• Review of unrestricted access to records and departments as disclosed in the written charter of the internal audit function and approved by the audit committee.

Source: Louis Braiotta, Jr., and Hugh L. Marsh, "Developing a Constructive Relationship Under the Guidance of SAS No. 65," *Internal Auditing* 8, No. 2 (Fall 1992), p. 7. Reprinted with permission from *Internal Auditing,* copyright © 1992, Warren Gorham Lamont, 31 St. James Avenue, Boston, MA 02116. All rights reserved.

Exhibit 9.10 Representative Responses for Assessing Competency and Objectivity of the Internal Auditors

SAS No. 65 Requirements	Internal Auditors' Documented Response
• Educational level and professional experience of internal auditors	• Presentation and discussion of the current vitas of the internal audit group and their organization and composition (e.g., generalists with operational backgrounds versus financial auditing personnel). Demonstrate a mix of auditing skills and education.
• Professional certification and continuing education	• Advisement of the number of CIAs, MBAs, CPAs, CMAs, and CISAs on the staff • Advisement of the number of professional training and development opportunities for the staff and the budgeted dollar amount.
• Audit policies, programs, and procedures	• Presentation of audit policies and procedures relative to financial, operational, and compliance audits, including quality control, rotation practices, and corporate conduct.
• Practices regarding assignment of internal auditors	• Discussion of work schedules, time budgets, and costs.
• Supervision and review of internal auditors' activities	• Discussion of the level of knowledge required for the entity and the industry. • Review of the ratio of staff assistants to supervisors relative to the scope and responsibilities for the audit. • Discussion of supervisory review procedures of staff assistants' work and note disagreements. • Review of audit risk assessment methodologies.
• Quality of working-paper documentation, reports, and recommendations	• Review of the reports issued with a response from the auditee and reasons for management disagreements, including the timeliness of both. • Review of the timetable for implementing recommendations.
• Evaluation of internal auditors' performance relative to SAS No. 65 requirements	• Discussion of the most recent peer review reports on the internal audit function. • Discussion of prior year's review of the internal audit function by the external auditors and any response or changes made as a result.

Exhibit 9.11 Vital Checkpoints: Internal Audit Questions for the Audit Committee

Mission Statement. Each company should develop and disseminate an annual policy statement re the objectives of internal audit.

- ✓ Does a mission statement exist for the internal audit function?
- ✓ Is this mission statement approved by the chief executive officer or senior management?
- ✓ Are the internal audit objectives known and understood by all levels of management?

Annual Internal Audit Plan. The senior internal auditor should prepare an annual plan setting forth goals and objectives such as:

- Planned level of audit coverage
- Staffing
- Areas of audit risk
- Degree of coordination with external audit function
- Special projects
- Annual cost
- Compliance with corporate codes of conduct
- ✓ Is this plan reviewed and approved by appropriate levels of management?
- ✓ Was this plan reviewed with the external auditors?
- ✓ Were their comments and/or recommendations incorporated in the plan?
- ✓ Did they note any deficiencies in the plan that were not incorporated in the final plan?
- ✓ Has management placed any scope restrictions on the extent of audit coverage?
- ✓ Does the plan provide coverage of the Company's computer control functions?
- ✓ Do you have the necessary human resources in terms of trained experienced staff to achieve the annual plan?

Progress Reports. The internal auditor should report annually on progress in meeting the previously approved annual plan:

- ✓ Has management adequately addressed the comments and recommendations set forth in your reports?
- ✓ Who receives copies of your reports?
- ✓ Are copies of your recent reports made available to the external auditor?
- ✓ Do they receive appropriate management support?
- ✓ Were there any significant recommendations relating to control weaknesses or company policy that have not been adequately addressed and corrected?
- ✓ Do you monitor that the necessary corrective action has in fact been implemented?
- ✓ Did your audit procedures uncover any instances of employee fraud, questionable or illegal payments, or violations of laws or regulations? (Follow-up questions, as appropriate).
- ✓ Were any limitations placed on the phase of your audit plan during this period?

✓ Did you receive appropriate management support and cooperation?

✓ In connection with the audit functions completed during this period, did you review all the related computer control functions? Were they deemed adequate?

✓ Is the computer security system reviewed in connection with these audit procedures? Are they adequate?

✓ Does each computer system reviewed have an adequate backup system and disaster contingency plan?

Other Areas. Additional areas can be covered in private meetings with internal auditors as appropriate:

✓ Are you satisfied with the adequacy and competence of financial management in the areas subject to audit review?

✓ Does the internal audit function receive the appropriate level of support from senior management and operating management?

✓ Are you satisfied with the level of cooperation and support from the external auditors?

✓ Are the internal and external audit functions coordinated to maximize the effectiveness of both groups and to minimize any unnecessary duplication of effort?

✓ Have there been any material changes in the internal audit staff that would adversely impact your ability to complete your objective for the current period?

✓ To what extent, if any, have you been assigned special projects that have adversely impacted your ability to achieve your goals?

✓ Are you satisfied that the "tone at the top" is appropriate?

✓ Has the company taken the appropriate action with respect to management comments submitted by the external auditors?

Further Questions. Additional internal auditing questions can be addressed privately to financial personnel, senior management, or the external auditor, as appropriate:

✓ Are you satisfied with respect to the level of performance of the internal audit function?

✓ Do the internal auditors perform their duties and responsibilities objectively and professionally?

✓ Do they perform their audits effectively?

✓ Are they considered constructive and effective by operating management?

✓ Do they receive the appropriate level of management support and cooperation?

✓ Does an appropriate degree of mutual respect exist between the internal and external auditors?

✓ Is there an effective working relationship between the internal and external auditors to maximize effectiveness and minimize cost?

Source: Richard S. Hickok and Jules Zimmerman, *Vital Checkpoints: Internal Audit Questions for the Audit Committee* (New York: Hickok Associates, Inc., 1990). Copyright © 1990 by Hickok Associates, Inc. Reprinted with permission.

Exhibit 9.12   Practice Advisory 1310-1: Quality Programs Assessments; Practice Advisory 1311-1: Internal Assessments; and Practice Advisory 1312-1: External Assessments

---

Related Standard

1310 Quality Program Assessments
The internal audit activity should adopt a process to monitor and assess the overall effectiveness of the quality program. The process should include both internal and external assessments.

Nature of this Practice Advisory: *Internal auditors should consider these suggestions when implementing and assessing quality programs within the internal audit activity. This guidance is not intended to represent all the procedures necessary for comprehensive quality programs or their assessment, but simply is a recommended set of quality assessment practices. Compliance with Practice Advisories is optional.*

1. **Implementing Quality Programs:** The chief audit executive (CAE) should be accountable for implementing processes that are designed to provide reasonable assurance to the various stakeholders of the internal audit activity that it:
   - Performs in accordance with its charter, which should be consistent with the Standards for the Professional Practice of Internal Auditing and Code of Ethics,
   - Operates in an effective and efficient manner, and
   - Is perceived by those stakeholders as adding value and improving the organization's operations.

   These processes should include appropriate supervision, periodic internal assessment and ongoing monitoring of quality assurance, and periodic external assessments.

2. **Monitoring Quality Programs:** Monitoring should include ongoing measurements and analyses of performance metrics, e.g., cycle time and recommendations accepted.

3. **Assessing Quality Programs:** Assessments should evaluate and conclude on the quality of the internal audit activity and lead to recommendations for appropriate improvements. Assessments of quality programs should include evaluation of:
   - Compliance with the Standards and Code of Ethics,
   - Adequacy of the internal audit activity's charter, goals, objectives, policies, and procedures,
   - Contribution to the organization's risk management, governance, and control processes,
   - Compliance with applicable laws, regulations, and government or industry standards,
   - Effectiveness of continuous improvement activities and adoption of best practices, and
   - Whether the audit activity adds value and improves the organization's operations.

4. **Continuous Improvement:** All quality improvement efforts should include a communication process designed to facilitate appropriate modification of resources, technology, processes, and procedures as indicated by monitoring and assessment activities.

5. **Communicating Results:** To provide accountability, the CAE should share the results of external, and, as appropriate, internal quality program assessments with the various stakeholders of the activity, such as senior management, the board, and external auditors.

Related Standard

1311 Internal Assessments
Internal assessments should include:
   - Ongoing reviews of the performance of the internal audit activity; and

- Periodic reviews performed through self-assessment or by other persons within the organization, with knowledge of internal audit practices and the Standards.

Nature of this Practice Advisory: *Internal auditors should consider these suggestions when performing internal assessments within the internal audit activity. This guidance is not intended to represent all the procedures necessary for comprehensive internal assessments, but is simply a recommended set of internal assessment practices. Compliance with Practice Advisories is optional.*

1. **Ongoing Renews:** Ongoing assessments may be conducted through:
   - Engagement supervision as described in Practice Advisory 2340-1: Engagement Supervision,
   - Checklists and other means to provide assurance that processes adopted by the audit activity (e.g., in an audit and procedures manual) are being followed,
   - Feedback from audit customers and other stakeholders, and
   - Analyses of performance metrics, (e.g., cycle time and recommendations accepted),
   - Project budgets, time keeping systems, audit plan completion, cost recoveries, and so forth.

2. Conclusions should be developed as to the quality of ongoing performance, and follow-up action should be taken to assure appropriate improvements are implemented.

3. **Periodic Reviews:** Periodic assessments should be designed to assess compliance with the activity's charter, the Standards for the Professional Practice of Internal Auditing, the Code of Ethics, and the efficiency and effectiveness of the activity in meeting the needs of its various stakeholders. The IIA's *Quality Assessment Manual* includes guidance and tools for internal reviews.

4. Periodic assessments may:
   - Include more in-depth interviews and surveys of stakeholder groups,
   - Be performed by members of the internal audit activity (self-assessment),
   - Be performed by CIAs, or other competent audit professionals, currently assigned elsewhere in the organization,
   - Encompass a combination of self-assessment and preparation of materials subsequently reviewed by CIAs, or other competent audit professionals, from elsewhere in the organization, and
   - Include benchmarking of the internal audit activity's practices and performance metrics against relevant best practices of the internal audit profession.

5. Conclusions should be developed as to the quality of performance and appropriate action initiated to achieve improvements and conformity to the Standards, as necessary.

6. The chief audit executive (CAE) should establish a structure for reporting results of periodic reviews that maintains appropriate credibility and objectivity. Generally, those assigned responsibility for conducting ongoing and periodic reviews should report to the CAE while performing the reviews and should communicate their results directly to the CAE.

7. Communicating Results: The CAE should share the results of internal assessments and necessary action plans with appropriate persons outside the activity, such as senior management, the board, and external auditors.

(continued)

Exhibit 9.12 *(Continued)*

Related Standard

1312 External Assessments

External assessments, such as quality assurance reviews, should be conducted at least once every five years by a qualified, independent reviewer or review team from outside the organization.

Nature of This Practice Advisory: *Internal auditors should consider these suggestions when planning and contracting for an external assessment of their internal audit activity. This guidance is not intended to represent all the considerations necessary for an external assessment but simply a recommended set of high-level considerations with respect to the external assessment. Compliance with Practice Advisories is optional.*

1. **General Considerations:** External assessments of an internal audit activity should appraise and express an opinion as to the internal audit activity's compliance with the Standards for the Professional Practice of Internal Auditing and, as appropriate, should include recommendations for improvement. These reviews can have considerable value to the chief audit executive (CAE) and other members of the internal audit activity. Only qualified persons (paragraph 4 below) should perform such reviews.

2. An external assessment is required within five years of January 1, 2002. Earlier adoption of the new Standard requiring an external assessment is highly recommended. Organizations that have had external reviews are encouraged to have their next external review within five years of their last review.

3. On completion of the review, a formal communication should be provided to the board (as defined in the Glossary to the Standards) and to senior management.

4. **Qualifications for External Reviewers:** External reviewers, including those who validate self-assessments (paragraph 13 below), should be independent of the organization and of the internal audit activity. The review team should consist of individuals who are competent in the professional practice of internal auditing and the external assessment process. To be considered as external assessment candidates, qualified individuals could include IIA Quality Assurance reviewers, regulatory examiners, consultants, external auditors, other professional service providers, and internal auditors from outside the organization.

5. **Independence:** The organization that is performing the external assessment, the members of the review team, and any other individuals who participate on the assessment should be free from any obligation to, or interest in, the organization that is the subject of the review or its personnel. Individuals who are in another department of that organization, although organizationally separate from the internal audit activity, are not considered independent for purposes of conducting an external assessment.

6. Reciprocal peer review arrangements between three or more organizations can be structured in a manner that alleviates independence concerns. Reciprocal peer reviews between two organizations generally should not be performed.

7. External assessments should be performed by qualified individuals who are independent of the organization and who do not have either a real or apparent conflict of interest. "Independent of the organization" means not a part of, or under the control of, the organization to which the internal audit activity belongs. In the

selection of an external reviewer, consideration should be given to a possible real or apparent conflict of interest that the reviewer may have due to present or past relationships with the organization or its internal audit activity.

8. **Integrity and Objectivity:** Integrity requires the review team to be honest and candid within the constraints of confidentiality. Service and the public trust should not be subordinated to personal gain and advantage. Objectivity is a state of mind and a quality that lends value to a review team's services. The principle of objectivity imposes the obligation to be impartial, intellectually honest, and free of conflicts of interest.

9. **Competence:** Performing and communicating the results of an external assessment requires the exercise of professional judgment. Accordingly, an individual serving as a reviewer should:
   - Be a competent, certified audit professional, e.g., CIA, CPA, CA, or CISA, who possesses current knowledge of the Standards,
   - Be well versed in the best practices of the profession, and
   - Have at least three years of recent experience in the practice of internal auditing at a management level.

10. The review team should include members with information technology expertise and relevant industry experience. Individuals with expertise in other specialized areas may assist the external review team. For example, statistical sampling specialists or experts in control self-assessment may participate in certain segments of the review.

11. **Approval by Management and the Board:** The CAE should involve senior management and the board in the selection process for an external reviewer and obtain their approval.

12. **Scope of External Assessments:** The external assessment should consist of a broad scope of coverage that includes the following elements of the internal audit activity:
    - Compliance with the *Standards*, the IIA's *Code of Ethics*, and the internal audit activity's charter, plans, policies, procedures, practices, and applicable legislative and regulatory requirements,
    - The expectations of the internal audit activity expressed by the board, executive management and operational managers,
    - The integration of the internal audit activity into the organization's governance process, including the attendant relationships between and among the key groups involved in that process,
    - The tools and techniques employed by the internal audit activity,
    - The mix of knowledge, experience, and disciplines within the staff, including staff focus on process improvement, and
    - The determination whether the audit activity adds value and improves the organization's operations.

13. **Self-assessment with Independent Validation:** An alternative process is for the CAE to undertake a self-assessment with independent external validation with the following features:
    - A comprehensive and fully documented self-assessment process.
    - An independent on-site validation by a qualified reviewer (paragraph 4 above).
    - Economical time and resource requirements.

14. A team under the direction of the CAE should perform the self-assessment process. The IIA's *Quality Assessment Manual* contains an example of the process, including

(continued)

Exhibit 9.12   *(Continued)*

---

guidance and tools for the self-assessment. A qualified, independent reviewer should perform limited tests of the self-assessment to validate the results and express an opinion about the indicated level of the activity's conformity to the Standards.

15. Communicating the results of the self-assessment should follow the process outlined below (paragraph 17).

16. While a full external review achieves maximum benefit for the activity and should be included in the activity's quality program, the self-assessment with independent validation provides an alternative means of complying with this Standard 1312.

17. **Communicating Results:** The preliminary results of the review should be discussed with the CAE during and at the conclusion of the assessment process. Final results should be communicated to the CAE or other official who authorized the review for the organization.

18. The communication should include the following:
    • An opinion on the internal audit activity's compliance with the Standards based on a structured rating process. The term "compliance" means that the practices of the internal audit activity, taken as a whole, satisfy the requirements of the Standards. Similarly, "noncompliance" means that the impact and severity of the deficiency in the practices of the internal audit activity are so significant that it impairs the internal audit activity's ability to discharge its responsibilities. The expression of an opinion on the results of the external assessment requires the application of sound business judgment, integrity, and due professional care.
    • An assessment and evaluation of the use of best practices, both those observed during the assessment and others potentially applicable to the activity.
    • Recommendations for improvement, where appropriate.
    • Responses from the CAE that include an action plan and implementation dates.

19. The CAE should communicate the results of the review and necessary action plan to senior management, as appropriate, and to the board.

Source: Institute of Internal Auditors, *The Professional Practice Framework* (Altamonte Springs, FL: IIA, 2002), pp. 89–99.

While each audit committee may develop its own approach to monitoring the activities of the corporate auditing staff, the following recapitulation of the seven salient points should be helpful.[31]

1. Assist in the overall internal auditing policy determination, and approve such policies to ensure that the staff has authority commensurate with their responsibilities.

---

[31]The reader should review the questions in the checklist in Chapter 3. It should be reemphasized that the audit directors are reviewing and assessing this function in their oversight and advisory capacity. They are *not* assuming the day-to-day operations of this particular group. For additional discussion, see Joseph Mchugh and K. Raghunandan, "Hiring & Firing the Chief Internal Auditor," *Internal Auditor* 54, No. 4 (August 1994), pp. 34–39; Wanda A. Wallace and G. Thomas White, "Reporting on Internal Control," *Internal Auditor* 51, No. 4 (August 1994), pp. 40–42.

2. Review the scope of the internal and external auditing plans to maximize on the resources allocated to the audit function and minimize the outside auditing fees.
3. Review copies of the internal auditing reports and critically evaluate the findings, recommendations, management's response, and courses of action taken. Also, review the disposition of the recommendations in the independent auditor's management letter.
4. Review and appraise the staff's organization regarding their auditing philosophy, independence, and logistical operations.
5. Assess the quality of the auditing personnel and training to ensure that the internal auditing function is adequately staffed. Also, the auditing work should be properly planned, supervised, and reviewed.
6. Assure the director of internal auditing that the committee supports his or her function in the corporate structure and the director has access to the committee and the functional areas within the entity. Also, obtain assurance that the staff is receiving the proper cooperation from management.
7. Determine the need for special assignments, such as investigating computer security and other methods for the protection of the assets (e.g., cases of management disagreements with the auditors).

An example of the audit committee's oversight involvement is reflected in the Audit Committee Charter of Wal-Mart's Stores.

Oversight of the Company's Internal Audit Function

- Ensure that the Company has an internal audit function.
- Review and concur in the appointment, replacement, reassignment or dismissal of the senior internal auditing executive, and the compensation package for such person.
- Review the significant reports to management prepared by the internal auditing department and management's responses.
- Communicate with management and the Internal Auditors to obtain information concerning internal audits, accounting principles adopted by the Company, internal controls of the Company, management, and the Company's financial and accounting personnel, and review the impact of each on the quality and reliability of the Company's financial statements.
- Evaluate the internal auditing department and its impact on the accounting practices, internal controls and financial reporting of the Company.
- Discuss with the Outside Auditor the internal audit department's responsibilities, budget and staffing and any recommended changes in the planned scope of the internal audit.[32]

It is evident that the internal audit function is extremely important in the corporate structure because it assists corporate management, including the board and its audit committee, in fulfilling its responsibilities for corporate accountability. The audit directors have a critical role in monitoring the activities of the internal

---

[32]Wal-Mart Stores, Inc., *Audit Committee Charter, www.walmartstores.com*, p. 6.

auditing staff as well as preserving the board's independence in the corporate auditing process.

SOURCES AND SUGGESTED READINGS

Bacon, Jeremy, *The Audit Committee: A Broader Mandate,* Report No. 914 (New York: The Conference Board, Inc., 1988).

Barrett, Michael J., and P. Tiessen, "Organizational Support for Internal Auditing." *Internal Auditor* 5, No. 2 (Fall 1989), pp. 39–53.

Braiotta, Louis, Jr., and Hugh L. Marsh, "Developing a Constructive Relationship Under the Guidance of SAS No. 65." *Internal Auditing* 8, No. 2 (Fall 1992), pp. 3–11.

Castellano, Joseph, Harper Roehm, and John P. Walker, "Status & Quality." *Internal Auditor* 49, No. 3 (June 1992), pp. 49–52.

Committee of Sponsoring Organizations of the Treadway Commission, *Internal Control-Integrated Framework* (New York: AICPA, 1992).

Horn, Karen N., "An Audit Committee Member Looks at Internal Auditing." *Internal Auditor* 49, No. 6 (December 1992), pp. 32–36.

Institute of Internal Auditors, *The Professional Practices Framework* (Altamonte Springs, FL: IIA, 2002).

Jepsen, Edward G., "Internal Auditors Move into the Spotlight." *Internal Auditor* 36, No. 2 (April 1979), pp. 26–32.

Kalbers, Lawrence P., "Audit Committees and Internal Auditors." *Internal Auditor* 49, No. 6 (December 1992), pp. 37–44.

Macchiaverna, Paul, *Internal Auditing,* Report No. 748 (New York: The Conference Board, Inc., 1978).

Marquardt, John D., and John F. Bussman, "The CIA Examination: A Topical Profile and Index Update." *Internal Auditor* 36, No. 2 (April 1979), pp. 41–47.

National Commission on Fraudulent Financial Reporting, *Report of the National Commission on Fraudulent Financial Reporting* (Washington, D.C.: National Commission on Fraudulent Financial Reporting, 1987).

Ridley, Anthony J., "An Audit Committee Event Matrix," *Internal Auditor* 57, No. 2 (April 2000), pp. 53–56.

Sarbanes-Oxley Act of 2002, H.R. Rep. No. 107-610 (2002).

Statement on Auditing Standards No. 65, "The Auditor's Consideration of the Internal Audit Function in an Audit of Financial Statements" (New York: AICPA, 1991).

Statement on Auditing Standards No. 78, "Consideration of Internal Control in a Financial Statement Audit: An Amendment to SAS No. 55" (New York: AICPA, 1995).

Strawser, Jerry, and Barbara Apostolou, "The Role of Internal Auditor Communication with the Audit Committee." *Internal Auditing* 6, No. 2 (Fall 1990), pp. 35–42.

Verschoor, Curtis, "Internal Auditing Interactions with the Audit Committee." *Internal Auditing* 7, No. 4 (Spring 1992), pp. 20–23.

Verschoor, Curtis, and Joseph P. Liotta, "Communication with Audit Committees." *Internal Auditor* 47, No. 2 (April 1990), pp. 42–47.

Wal-Mart Stores, Inc., *Audit Committee Charter, www.walmartstores.com.*

Chapter 10

Reviewing Accounting Policy Disclosures

The purpose of this chapter is to introduce accounting policy disclosures in the financial statements. Through a review of the significant accounting policies and critical accounting policies and estimates, the audit committee can obtain assurance on behalf of the board of directors that management is fulfilling its financial accounting reporting responsibilities. Such a review will be conducted with the independent public accountants in order to determine the integrity and objectivity of the financial statements based on management's formulation and implementation of the corporate accounting policies. Although this chapter will discuss accounting pronouncements concerning accounting disclosures (APB No. 22) and accounting changes (APB No. 20), it makes no attempt to discuss in detail the technical pronouncements applicable to APB No. 22, since such a discussion is beyond the scope of the text. As indicated in Chapter 2, the purpose of the audit committee is to oversee and monitor the accounting and auditing processes; technical accounting matters are management's responsibility. The reader may wish to consult any standard accounting text for detailed information regarding the technical subjects as outlined in APB No. 22.

AUDIT COMMITTEE'S REVIEW OBJECTIVE

A Look Back and an Overview

As indicated in Chapters 1 and 3, the audit committee has a critical role in reviewing the disclosures in the financial statements. The committee represents an independent check on corporate management with respect to its responsibilities for reporting its stewardship accountability to the outside constituencies. In particular, the audit committee is responsible for assuring that management has prepared the financial statements in conformity with generally accepted accounting principles (GAAP). Thus it must assess not only management's judgment regarding the application of accounting principles but also the adequacy of the disclosures in the financial statements.[1] According to the American Institute of Certified Public Accountants, the committee's review objective may be summarized in this way:

---

[1]For a more detailed discussion of accounting principles, see Chapter 5.

The audit committee should meet with management and the external auditor to review the financial statements and the audit results. This is an especially important function of the audit committee.

Some audit committees confine their review of the financial statements to major or critical items, while others examine the statements in considerable detail. The scope of the review is something each audit committee must set forth for itself, bearing in mind that at the conclusion of the meeting the members should have a comprehensive understanding of any major financial reporting problems encountered, how they were resolved, and whether the resolution is satisfactory. Factors affecting the extent of the review include the committee's confidence in management, the system of internal accounting control, and the external auditor; the existence of any unresolved differences between the auditor and management; the extent of adjustments or additional disclosures, if any, proposed by the auditor; and any unusual occurrences during the year. The committee's major concern throughout the review should be whether the financial statements fairly present the company's financial results in conformity with generally accepted accounting principles.[2]

In addition, it is important that audit committee members be aware that the Public Oversight Board has issued these recommendations with respect to determination of accounting treatment in the financial reporting process:

Recommendation V-6

The following recommendation of the Macdonald Commission should be adopted by the Auditing Standards Board in the United States:

> When new accounting policies are adopted in response to new types of transactions or new kinds of assets or obligations, the auditor should be satisfied that the accounting policies adopted properly reflect the economic substance of the transaction, asset, or liability in accordance with the broad theory governing present-day financial reporting and the established concept of conservatism in the face of uncertainty.

Recommendation V-7

Peer reviewers should evaluate the consultation process by which specific accounting conclusions are reached, as they do now, and should also inquire whether that process leads to accounting that is appropriate in the circumstances. In testing compliance with the consultation policies and procedures in a firm, the peer review team should evaluate the quality of the conclusions reached.

Recommendation V-8

The concurring partner, whose participation in an audit is a membership requirement of the SEC Practice Section, should be responsible for assuring that those consulted on accounting matters are aware of all of the relevant facts and circumstances, including an understanding of the financial statements in whose context the accounting policy is being considered. The concurring and consulting partners should know enough about the client to ensure that all of the relevant facts and circumstances are marshalled, and also possess the increased detachment that comes from not having

---

[2]American Institute of Certified Public Accountants, *Audit Committees, Answers to Typical Questions About Their Organization and Operations* (New York: AICPA, 1978), pp. 16–17.

to face the client on an ongoing basis. The concurring partner should have the responsibility to conclude whether the accounting treatment applied is consistent with the objectives of Recommendation V-6.[3]

The American Institute of Certified Public Accountants has set forth the following to further ensure the independent auditor's integrity and objectivity in the financial reporting process:

> The credibility of the independent audit is essential to public trust, the keystone of the financial reporting system. The accounting profession prides itself on the integrity and objectivity of its members. The future of our profession, not to mention our livelihood, rests on this reputation.

> A few recent high-profile financial scandals have, however, called auditors' independence into question. Neither the accounting profession nor the financial markets can afford an erosion of public confidence. For that reason, auditors must scrupulously preserve their objectivity, in reality and appearance. We therefore call on the SEC and other regulatory bodies to prohibit public companies and other organizations with public accountability from hiring the partner responsible for their audit for one year after the partner ceases to serve that client.

> Additional steps can be taken, with the support of the business community, to secure public confidence in the independent audit and the financial reporting system. SEC registrants and other publicly accountable organizations should be required to have audit committees composed entirely of independent directors whenever practicable. The audit committee members should be charged with specific responsibilities, including overseeing the financial reporting process, and recommending appointment of the entity's auditors.[4]

The reader may wish to revisit Chapter 1 and Chapter 3 to review the key discussion points made by several key organizations about the financial reporting process. While the preceding review objective is broad based, it is important to reemphasize the audit committee's position regarding such review activities. As John J. Schornack, former partner of Arthur Young & Co. (now Ernst & Young), points out:

> Audit committee members are not omniscient. . . . Matters of compliance with professional reporting standards and technical disclosures are the responsibilities of corporate management and the professional experts such as the outside auditor and legal counsel. . . . The primary purpose of the audit committee is oversight of the financial reporting.[5]

James Gerson et al., partners of Coopers & Lybrand (now PricewaterhouseCoopers), note that "to effectively review financial statements, the audit committee

---

[3]Public Oversight Board, A Special Report by the Public Oversight Board of the SEC Practice Section, AICPA (Stamford, CT: POB, 1993), pp. 48–49.
[4]American Institute of Certified Public Accountants, *Meeting the Financial Reporting Needs of the Future: A Public Commitment from the Public Accounting Profession* (New York: AICPA, 1993), p. 4.
[5]John J. Schornack, "The Audit Committee—A Public Accountant's View," Journal of Accountancy 147, No. 4 (April 1979), p. 74.

must understand the company's business and industry, and the attendant risks. The committee should be satisfied that the key financial systems and the procedures and controls that support them will generate information necessary to manage and properly report on the operations of the company."[6] The authors further state:

> Typically, the committee meets with management and the independent auditors to review the financial statements for the year and the results of the annual audit. The nature of this review depends on the complexity of the company, its industry, and the committee's confidence in company management. When performing this review, the committee should pay particular attention to judgmental areas, such as those involving valuation of assets and liabilities. The committee should be sensitive to areas where different assumptions and judgments could have a significant effect on the statements. These areas could include accounting and disclosure for obsolete or slow-moving inventory; the allowance for doubtful accounts; warranty, product liability and litigation reserves; and commitments and contingencies.[7]

In January 2003, the Securities and Exchange Commission issued rules that require independent auditors to report on a timely basis certain information to the audit committee. These rules are pursuant to Section 204, Auditor Reports to Audit Committees, under the Sarbanes-Oxley Act of 2002, which state:

> In particular, the Sarbanes-Oxley Act requires that the auditor report to the audit committee on a timely basis (a) all critical accounting policies used by the registrant, (b) alternative accounting treatments that have been discussed with management along with the potential ramifications of using those alternatives, and (c) other written communications provided by the auditor to management, including a schedule of unadjusted audit differences. These rules strengthen the relationship between the audit committee and the auditor.[8]

These rules are presented in the next section of this chapter.

Such oversight responsibility of the audit committee is evidenced in Wal-Mart's annual report, as presented in Exhibit 10.1.

Thus, in order to discharge its oversight responsibility concerning financial reporting, the committee's agenda should include a review of the significant accounting policies and their related disclosure requirements as well as critical

---

[6]James S. Gerson, J. Robert Mooney, Donald F. Moran, and Robert K. Waters, "Oversight of the Financial Reporting Process—Part I," *CPA Journal* 59, No. 7 (July 1989), p. 28.

[7]James S. Gerson, J. Robert Mooney, Donald F. Moran, and Robert K. Waters, "Oversight of the Financial Reporting Process—Part II," *CPA Journal* 59, No. 8 (August 1989), p. 40. A study on the association between audit committee formation and the quality of accounting earnings found "a significant increase in the market's reaction to earnings reports subsequent to the formation of the audit committee" (p. 1). See John J. Wild, "The Audit Committee and Earnings Quality," *Journal of Accounting, Auditing & Finance* 11, No. 2 (Spring 1996), pp. 247–276. Also, the reader should visit the AICPA's SEC Practice Section web site at *www.aicpa.org/members/div/secps/index.htm* for the Practice Alert 2000-2, "Quality of Accounting Principles-Guidance for Discussions with Audit Committees."

[8]Securities and Exchange Commission, Release No. 33-8183, "Strengthening the Commission's Requirements Regarding Auditor Independence," January 28, 2003, *www.sec.gov/rules/final/33-8183.htm*, p. 3.

Exhibit 10.1 Illustrative Management Report

Report of Management

Management of Wal-Mart Stores Inc. is responsible for the integrity and objectivity of the financial statements and other information presented in this report. These financial statements have been prepared in conformity with accounting principles generally accepted in the United States. The preparation of financial statements requires certain estimates and judgments, which are based upon currently available information and management's view of current conditions and circumstances.

Management has developed and maintains a system of internal and disclosure controls, including an extensive internal audit program. These controls are designed to provide reasonable assurance that the Company's assets are protected from improper use and that Wal-Mart's accounting records provide a reliable basis for the preparation of financial statements. We continually review, improve and modify these systems and programs in response to changes in business conditions and operations and the recommendations made by Wal-Mart's internal and external auditors. We believe that the system of internal and disclosure controls provides reasonable assurance that Wal-Mart's assets are safeguarded and that the financial information disclosed is reliable.

Our Company was founded on the belief that open communications and the highest standard of ethics are necessary to be successful. Our long-standing "open door" communication policy helps management be aware of and deal with issues in a timely and effective manner. Through the open door policy all Associates are encouraged to inform management at the appropriate level when they are concerned about any matter pertaining to the Company.

Wal-Mart has adopted a Statement of Ethics to guide our Associates in the continued observance of high ethical standards such as honesty, integrity and compliance with the law in the conduct of the Company's business. Familiarity and compliance with the Statement of Ethics is periodically reviewed and acknowledged in writing by all management Associates. The Company also has in place a Related Party Transaction Policy. This policy applies to all Officers and Directors of the Company and requires material related party transactions to be reviewed by the Audit Committee of the Board of Directors. Annually, the Company's Officers and Directors report material related party transactions to the Company and Officers acknowledge their familiarity and compliance with the policy.

We retain Ernst & Young LLP, independent auditors, to audit the Company's financial statements. Their audits are performed in accordance with generally accepted auditing standards. We have made available to Ernst & Young LLP all financial records and related data.

The Board of Directors, through the activities of its Audit Committee consisting solely of outside directors, provides oversight of the process of reporting financial information. The Committee stays informed of the financial condition of the Company and regularly reviews its financial policies and procedures, the independence of the Company's independent auditors, its internal accounting controls and the objectivity of its financial reporting. Both the Company's independent auditors and the internal auditors have free access to the Audit Committee and meet with the Committee periodically, both with and without management present.

H. Lee Scott
President and Chief Executive
Officer

Thomas M. Schoewe
Executive Vice President and Chief
Financial Officer

Source: Wal-Mart Stores, Inc., *2003 Annual Report*, p. 52.

accounting policies. Such a review will enable the committee to obtain assurance that management is fulfilling its financial accounting and reporting responsibilities. Furthermore, since the board of directors is concerned primarily with corporate policies, the committee can ensure that major changes in accounting policies are brought before the board in a timely manner. Therefore, the remainder of this chapter will discuss the committee's role in reviewing accounting policy disclosures.[9]

ACCOUNTING POLICY DISCLOSURES

Accounting Policies

As noted in Chapter 4, the Securities and Exchange Commission in the Killearn Properties case indicated that the audit committee should have at least general familiarity with accounting and reporting principles and practices in preparing its financial statements. Thus the committee members should have a broad overview of the significant accounting policies. Such a task is a critical undertaking since it requires the committee to judge management's formulation and implementation of such policies. The committee will look to the independent public accountants' professional assessment of the entity's accounting policies in accordance with the disclosure requirements, discussed in Chapter 5. For example, the audit committee's understanding of the information in the financial statement and significant accounting policies is evidenced by the data included in the Report of Management, as illustrated by Wal-Mart Stores, Inc., in Exhibit 10.1.

The independent auditors must be satisfied that management is complying with the disclosure requirements as outlined by the Accounting Principles Board.[10] For example, management must present a summary of the significant accounting policies as part of the financial statements in the annual report. Such disclosure of significant accounting policies sets forth the accounting principles and methods used to prepare the financial statements. A summary of significant accounting policies frequently includes:[11]

*   Basis of consolidation and use of estimates and assumptions
*   Depreciation methods
*   Financial instruments
*   Inventory pricing methods
*   Accounting for research and development costs
*   Basis for foreign currency translation

---

[9]For a more detailed discussion of reporting publicly on internal control, see Curtis C. Verschoor, "Reporting on Internal Control: An Analysis of Empirical Evidence," *Internal Auditing* 12, No. 1 (Summer 1996), pp. 43–45; Frank R. Urbanic, "A Content Analysis of Audit Committee Reports," *Internal Auditing* 12, No. 1 (Summer 1996), pp. 36–42; and Chapter 8 of this book.

[10]See Opinions of the Accounting Principles Board, No. 22, "Disclosure of Accounting Policies" (New York: AICPA, 1972), par. 15.

[11]As previously noted, the reader may wish to consult a standard accounting text. Also see Appendix A for further reference information.

- Accounting treatment for:

  Pension plans

  Intangible assets, such as goodwill

  Income taxes and investment credits

  Revenue recognition on long-term construction contracts

- Accounting changes

A summary of significant accounting policies of Wal-Mart Stores, Inc., is illustrated in Exhibit 10.2.

Obviously, the disclosure of the key accounting policies will vary from company to company; however, it is incumbent on the independent auditors to concur with management on the adequacy of such policy disclosures. If management's disclosures are inadequate, the independent auditors cannot express an unqualified opinion on the financial statements.

Therefore, as part of its financial review responsibilities, the committee should discuss "any significant disagreement between management and the independent accountants and whether such disagreement has been resolved to the satisfaction of both."[12] Concerning the resolution of such disagreements, the committee should stress the overall objectives of financial reporting as discussed in Chapter 3.

Critical Accounting Policies

Recall in Chapters 5, 6, 7, and 8 that generally accepted auditing standards require the independent auditors to communicate certain matters to the audit committee. The reader may wish to revisit these chapters at this point. As previously noted, Section 204 of the Sarbanes-Oxley Act requires the independent auditors to make certain timely communications to the audit committee. Therefore, prior to the filing of the auditors' report, the Securities and Commission requires the independent auditors to communicate this information:

Background Information

1. Critical Accounting Policies and Practices

Consistent with our proposal, we are establishing rules requiring communication by accountants to audit committees of all critical accounting policies and practices. In December 2001, we issued cautionary advice regarding each issuer disclosing in the Management's Discussion and Analysis section of its annual report those accounting policies that management believes are most critical to the preparation of the issuer's financial statements. The cautionary advice indicated that "critical" accounting policies are those that are both most important to the portrayal of the company's financial condition and results and require management's most difficult, subjective or complex judgments, often as a result of the need to make estimates about the effect of matters that are inherently uncertain. As part of that cautionary advice, we stated:

the selection, application and disclosure of critical accounting policies. Consistent with auditing standards, audit committees should be apprised of the evaluative

---

[12]Schornack, "The Audit Committee," p. 76.

Exhibit 10.2 Significant Accounting Policies

1 Summary of Significant Accounting Policies

Consolidation

The consolidated financial statements include the accounts of subsidiaries. Significant intercompany transactions have been eliminated in consolidation.

Cash and Cash Equivalents

The Company considers investments with a maturity of three months or less when purchased to be cash equivalents. The majority of payments due from banks for customer credit card transactions process within 24–48 hours. All credit card transaction that process in less than seven days are classified as cash and cash equivalents. Amounts due from banks for credit card transactions that were classified as cash totaled $276 million and $173 million at January 31, 2003 and 2002, respectively.

Receivables

Accounts receivable consist primarily of trade receivables from customers of our McLane subsidiary, receivables from insurance companies generated by our pharmacy sales, receivables from real estate transactions and receivables from suppliers for marketing or incentive programs. Additionally, amounts due from banks for customer credit card transactions that take in excess of seven days to process are classified as accounts receivable.

Inventories

The Company uses the retail last-in, first-out (LIFO) method for general merchandise within the Wal-Mart Stores segment, cost LIFO for the SAM'S CLUB segment and grocery items within the Wal-Mart Stores segment, and other cost methods, including the retail first-in, first-out (FIFO) and average cost methods, for the International segment. Inventories are not recorded in excess of market value.

Financial Instruments

The Company uses derivative financial instruments for purposes other than trading to reduce its exposure to fluctuations in foreign currencies and to minimize the risk and cost associated with financial and global operating activities. Generally, contract terms of a hedge instrument closely mirror those of the hedged item providing a high degree of risk reduction and correlation. Contracts that are highly effective at meeting the risk reduction and correlation criteria are recorded using hedge accounting. On February 1, 2001, the Company adopted Financial Accounting Standards Board (FASB) Statements No. 133, 137 and 138 (collectively "FAS 133") pertaining to the accounting for derivatives and hedging activities. FAS 133 requires all derivatives to be recorded on the balance sheet at fair value and establishes accounting treatment for three types of hedges. If a derivative instrument is a hedge, depending on the nature of the hedge, changes in the fair value of the instrument will either be offset against the change in fair value of the hedged assets, liabilities, or firm commitments through earnings or recognized in other comprehensive income until the hedged item is recognized in earnings. The ineffective portion of an instrument's change in fair value will be immediately recognized in earnings. Instruments that do not meet the criteria for hedge accounting or contracts for which the Company has not elected hedge accounting, are marked to fair value with unrealized gains or losses reported currently in earnings. At January 31, 2001, the majority of the Company's derivatives were hedges of net investments in foreign operations, and as such, the fair value of these derivatives had already been recorded on the balance sheet as either assets or liabilities and in other comprehensive income under the current accounting guidance. As the majority of the Company's derivative portfolio was already recorded on the balance sheet, the adoption of FAS 133 did not have a material impact on the Company's consolidated financial statements taken as a whole.

Interest During Construction
For interest costs to properly reflect only that portion relating to current operations, interest on borrowed funds during the construction of property, plant and equipment is capitalized. Interest costs capitalized were $124 million, $130 million, and $93 million in 2003, 2002 and 2001, respectively.

Long-lived Assets
The Company periodically reviews long-lived assets, if indicators of impairments exist and if the value of the assets is impaired, an impairment loss would be recognized.

Goodwill and Other Acquired Intangible Assets
Following the adoption of FAS 142, see the new accounting pronouncements section of this note, goodwill is not amortized, instead it is evaluated for impairment annually. Other acquired intangible assets are amortized on a straight-line basis over the periods that expected economic benefits will be provided. The realizability of other intangible assets is evaluated periodically when events or circumstances indicate a possible inability to recover the carrying amount. These evaluations are based on undiscounted cash flow and profitability projections that incorporate the impact of existing Company businesses. The analyses require significant management judgment to evaluate the capacity of an acquired business to perform within projections. Historically, the Company has generated sufficient returns from acquired businesses to recover the cost of the goodwill and other intangible assets.

Goodwill is recorded on the balance sheet in the operating segments as follows (in millions):

	January 31, 2003	January 31, 2002
International	**$8,985**	$8,028
SAM'S CLUB	**305**	305
Other	**231**	233
Total Goodwill	**$9,521**	$8,566

Changes in International segment goodwill are the result of foreign currency exchange rate fluctuations and the addition of $197 million of goodwill resulting from the Company's Amigo acquisition. See Note 6.

Foreign Currency Translation
The assets and liabilities of all foreign subsidiaries are translated at current exchange rates. Related translation adjustments are recorded as a component of other accumulated comprehensive income.

Revenue Recognition
The Company recognizes sales revenue at the time it sells merchandise to the customer, except for layaway transactions. The Company recognizes layaway transactions when the customer satisfies all payment obligations and takes possession of the merchandise. The Company recognizes SAM'S CLUB membership fee revenue over the twelve-month term of the membership. Customer purchases of Wal-Mart/SAM'S CLUB shopping cards are not recognized until the card is redeemed and the customer purchases merchandise by using the shopping card.

SAM'S CLUB Membership Revenue Recognition
The Company recognizes SAM'S CLUB membership fee revenues both domestically and internationally over the term of the membership, which is 12 months. The following table

(continued)

Exhibit 10.2   *(Continued)*

provides unearned revenues, membership fees received from members and the amount of revenues recognized in earnings for each of the fiscal years 2001, 2002 and 2003:

Deferred revenue January 31, 2000	$337
Membership fees received	706
Membership revenue recognized	(674)
Deferred revenue January 31, 2001	369
Membership fees received	748
Membership revenue recognized	(730)
Deferred revenue January 31, 2002	387
Membership fees received	834
Membership revenue recognized	(784)
Deferred revenue January 31, 2003	$437

SAM'S CLUB membership revenue is included in the other income line in the revenues section of the consolidated statements of income.

The Company's deferred revenue is included in accrued liabilities in the consolidated balance sheet. The Company's analysis of historical membership fee refunds indicates that such refunds have been insignificant. Accordingly, no reserve exists for membership fee refunds at January 31, 2003.

Cost of Sales

Cost of sales includes actual product cost, change in inventory, buying allowances received from our suppliers, the cost of transportation to the Company's warehouses from suppliers and the cost of transportation from the Company's warehouses to the stores and Clubs and the cost of warehousing for our SAM'S CLUB segment.

Payments from Suppliers

Wal-Mart receives money from suppliers for various reasons, the most common of which are as follows:

Warehousing allowances - allowances provided by suppliers to compensate the Company for distributing their product through our distribution systems which are more efficient than most other available supply chains. These allowances are reflected in cost of sales when earned.

Volume discounts - certain suppliers provide incentives for purchasing certain volumes of merchandise. These funds are recognized as a reduction of cost of sales at the time the incentive target is earned.

Other reimbursements and promotional allowances - suppliers may provide funds for specific programs including markdown protection, margin protection, new product lines, special promotions, specific advertising and other specified programs. These funds are recognized at the time the program occurs and the funds are earned.

At January 31, 2003 and 2002, the Company had $286 million and $279 million respectively, in accounts receivable associated with supplier funded programs. Further, the Company had $185 million and $178 million in unearned revenue included in accrued liabilities for unearned vendor programs at January 31, 2003 and 2002, respectively.

Operating, Selling and General and Administrative Expenses

Operating, selling and general and administrative expenses include all operating costs of the Company that are not related to the transportation of products from the supplier to the warehouse or from the warehouse to the store. Additionally, the cost of warehousing and occupancy for our Wal-Mart segment distribution facilities are included in operating, selling and general and administrative expenses. Because we do not include the cost of our Wal-Mart segment distribution facilities in cost of sales, our gross profit and gross margin may not be comparable to those of other retailers that may include all costs related to their distribution facilities in costs of sales and in the calculation of gross profit and gross margin.

Advertising Costs

Advertising costs are expensed as incurred and were $676 million, $618 million and $574 million in 2003, 2002 and 2001, respectively. Advertising cost consists primarily of print and television advertisements.

Pre-opening Costs

The costs of start-up activities, including organization costs and new store openings, are expensed as incurred.

Insurance/Self-Insurance

The Company uses a combination of insurance, self-insured retention, and self-insurance for a number of risks including workers' compensation, general liability, vehicle liability and employee related health care benefits, a portion of which is paid by the Associates. Liabilities associated with these risks are estimated in part by considering historical claims experience, demographic factors, severity factors and other actuarial assumptions.

Depreciation and Amortization

Depreciation and amortization for financial statement purposes are provided on the straight-line method over the estimated useful lives of the various assets. Depreciation expense, including amortization of property under capital lease, for the years 2003, 2002 and 2001 was $3.1 billion, $2.7 billion and $2.4 billion, respectively. For income tax purposes, accelerated methods are used with recognition of deferred income taxes for the resulting temporary differences. Estimated useful lives for financial statements purposes are as follows:

Building and improvements	5–50 years
Fixtures and equipment	5–12 years
Transportation equipment	2–5 years
Internally developed software	3 years

Net Income Per Share

Basic net income per share is based on the weighted average outstanding common shares. Diluted net income per share is based on the weighted average outstanding shares adjusted for the dilutive effect of stock options and restricted stock grants (16 million, 16 million and 19 million shares in 2003, 2002 and 2001, respectively). The Company had approximately 10.0 million, 3.5 million and 2.0 million option shares outstanding at January 31, 2003, 2002 and 2001, respectively, that were not included

(continued)

Exhibit 10.2   *(Continued)*

in the dilutive earnings per share calculation because the effect would have been antidilutive.

Estimates and Assumptions

The preparation of consolidated financial statements in conformity with generally accepted accounting principles requires management to make estimates and assumptions. These estimates and assumptions affect the reported amounts of assets and liabilities. They also affect the disclosure of contingent assets and liabilities at the date of the consolidated financial statements and the reported amounts of revenues and expenses during the reporting period. Actual results may differ from those estimates.

Stock-based Compensation

The Company has various stock option compensation plans for Associates. The Company currently accounts for those plans under the recognition and measurement provisions of APB Opinion No. 25, "Accounting for Stock Issued to Employees," and related interpretations. Historically, no significant stock-based employee compensation has been recognized under APB Opinion No. 25. In August 2002, the Company announced that on February 1, 2003, it will adopt the expense recognition provisions of the Financial Accounting Standards Board Statement No. 123, "Accounting and Disclosure of Stock-Based Compensation" ("FAS 123"). Under FAS 123, compensation expense is recognized based on the fair value of stock options granted. The Company has chosen to retroactively restate its results of operations for this accounting change. The adoption of the fair value method will result in a reduction of retained earnings at that date of $348 million, representing the cumulative stock option compensation recorded for prior years net of the tax effect. The Company's estimates that the impact of changing the accounting method for the adoption of FAS 123 will have an impact of $0.02 to $0.03 per share in the year of adoption.

Pro forma information, regarding net income and income per share is required by FAS Statement 123, "Accounting for Stock-Based Compensation," (FAS No. 123) and has been determined as if the Company had accounted for its employee stock option plans granted since February 1, 1995 under the fair value method of that statement.

The effect of applying the fair value method of FAS No. 123 to the stock option grants subsequent to February 1, 1995, results in the following net income and net income per share (amounts in millions except per share data):

Fiscal Years Ended January 31,	**2003**	2002	2001
Net income as reported	**$8,039**	$6,671	$6,295
Less total stock-based employee compensation expense determined under fair value based method for all awards, net of related tax effects	**(84)**	(79)	(60)
Pro forma net income	**7,955**	6,592	6,235
Pro forma earnings per share—basic	**$1.80**	$1.48	$1.40
Pro forma earnings per share—dilutive	**$1.79**	$1.47	$1.39

The fair value of these options was estimated at the date of the grant using the Black-Scholes option pricing model with the following assumption ranges: risk-free interest rates between 2.5% and 7.2%, dividend yields between 0.4% and 1.3%, volatility factors between 0.23 and 0.41, and an expected life of the option of 7.4 years for the options issued prior to November 17, 1995, and 3 to 7 years for options issued thereafter.

The Black-Scholes option valuation model was developed for use in estimating the fair value of traded options, which have no vesting restrictions and are fully transferable. In addition, option valuation methods require the input of highly subjective assumptions including the expected stock price volatility. Using the Black-Scholes option evaluation model, the weighted average value of options granted during the years ended January 31, 2003, 2002, and 2001, were $18, $24, and $22, per option, respectively.

New Accounting Pronouncements

On February 1, 2002, the Company adopted Financial Accounting Standards Board Statements of Financial Accounting Standards No. 141, "Business Combinations" ("FAS 141"), and No. 142, "Goodwill and Other Intangible Assets" ("FAS 142"). Under FAS 142, goodwill and intangible assets deemed to have indefinite lives are no longer amortized but are subject to annual impairment reviews. The following tables adjust certain information for fiscal 2002 and 2001, as if the non-amortization provisions of FAS 142 had been in place at that time and compares that adjusted information to the comparable information for fiscal 2003:

	Net Income (in Millions)			Basic Earnings Per Share			Diluted Earnings Per Share		
	2003	2002	2001	**2003**	2002	2001	**2003**	2002	2001
As reported	**$8,039**	$6,671	$6,295	**$1.81**	$1.49	$1.41	**$1.81**	$1.49	$1.40
Add back: Goodwill amortization (net of $11 million tax impact in each of fiscal 2002 and 2001)	—	235	235	—	0.06	0.05	—	0.05	0.05
As adjusted	**$8,039**	$6,906	$6,530	**$1.81**	$1.55	$1.46	**$1.81**	$1.54	$1.45

During fiscal 2003, the Company adopted FAS No. 144, "Accounting for the Impairment or Disposal of Long-Lived Assets." FAS No. 144 develops an accounting model, based upon the framework established in FAS No. 121, for long-lived assets to be disposed by sales. The accounting model applies to all long-lived assets, including discontinued operations, and it replaces the provisions of ABP Opinion No. 30, "Reporting Results of Operations - Reporting the Effects of Disposal of a Segment of a Business and Extraordinary, Unusual and Infrequently Occurring Events and Transactions," for disposal of segments of a business. FAS No. 144 requires long-lived assets held for disposal to be measured at the lower of carrying amount or fair values less costs to sell, whether reported in continuing operations or in discontinued operations. The adoption of FAS No. 144 did not have a material impact on the Company's financial position or results of operations.

In August 2001, the FASB issued FAS No. 143, "Accounting for Asset Retirement Obligations." This statement requires the Company to recognize the fair value of a liability associated with the cost the Company would be obligated to incur in order to retire an asset at some point in the future. The liability would be recognized in the period in which it is incurred and can be reasonably estimated. The standard is effective for fiscal years beginning after June 15, 2002. The Company will adopt this standard at the

(continued)

beginning of its fiscal 2004. The Company believes the adoption of FAS No. 143 will not have a material impact on its financial position or results of operations.

In July 2002, the FASB issued FAS No. 146, "Accounting for Costs Associated with Exit or Disposal Activities." FAS No. 146 addresses financial accounting and reporting for costs associated with exit or disposal activities and replaces EITF Issue No. 94-3, "Liability Recognition for Certain Employee Termination Benefits and Other Costs to Exit an Activity (including Certain Costs Incurred in a Restructuring)." FAS No. 146 requires that a liability for a cost associated with an exit or disposal activity be recognized when the liability is incurred. FAS No. 146 also establishes that fair value is the objective for initial measurement of the liability. The statement is effective for exit or disposal activities initiated after December 31, 2002. The Company believes the adoption of FAS No. 146, which will occur in fiscal 2004, will not have a material impact on its financial position or results of operations.

In November 2002, the FASB's Emerging Issues Task Force (EITF) reached a consensus on EITF 02-16 "Accounting by a Reseller for Cash Consideration Received from a Vendor," which addresses the accounting for 'Cash Consideration' (which includes slotting fees, cooperative advertising payments etc.) and 'Rebates or Refunds' from a vendor that are payable only if the merchant completes a specified cumulative level of purchases or remains a customer of the vendor for a specified period of time. With regards to the 'cash considerations,' the EITF agreed that the consideration should be treated as a reduction of the prices of the vendor products or services and should therefore be included as a reduction of cost of sales unless the vendor receives, or will receive, an identifiable benefit in exchange for the consideration. With respect to the accounting for a rebate or refund again, the EITF agreed that such refunds or rebates should be recognized as a reduction of the cost of sales based on a systematic and rational allocation of the consideration to be received. This guidance should be applied prospectively to arrangements entered into after December 15, 2002. The Company is currently evaluating the impact of this new guidance which will be applied in the first quarter of fiscal 2004.

Reclassifications

Certain reclassifications have been made to prior periods to conform to current presentations.

Source: Wal-Mart Stores, Inc., *2003 Annual Report*, pp. 34–38.

criteria used by management in their selection of the accounting principles and methods. Proactive discussions between the audit committee and the company's senior management and auditor about critical accounting policies are appropriate.

In May 2002, the Commission proposed rules to require disclosures that would enhance investors' understanding of the application of companies' critical accounting policies. The May 2002 proposed rules cover (1) accounting estimates a company makes in applying its accounting policies and (2) the initial adoption by a company of an accounting policy that has a material impact on its financial presentation. Under the first part of those proposed rules, a "critical accounting estimate" is defined as an accounting estimate recognized in the financial statements (1) that requires the registrant to make assumptions about matters that are highly uncertain at the time the accounting estimate is made and (2) for which different estimates that the company reasonably could have used in the current period, or changes in the accounting estimate that are reasonably likely to occur from period to period, would have a material impact on the presentation of the registrant's financial condition, changes in financial condition or results of operations. The May 2002 proposed rules outline certain disclosures that a company would be required to make about its critical accounting estimates. In addition, under the second part of the May 2002 proposed rules, a company would be required to make certain disclosures about its initial adoption of accounting policies, including the choices the company had among accounting principles.

Accountants and issuers should read and refer to the December 2001 Cautionary Guidance to determine the types of matters that should be communicated to the audit committee under this rule. We are not requiring that those discussions follow a specific form or manner, but we expect, at a minimum, that the discussion of critical accounting estimates and the selection of initial accounting policies will include the reasons why estimates or policies meeting the criteria in the Guidance are or are not considered critical and how current and anticipated future events impact those determinations. In addition, we anticipate that the communications regarding critical accounting policies will include an assessment of management's disclosures along with any significant proposed modifications by the accountants that were not included.

2. Alternative Accounting Treatments

We recognize that the complexity of financial transactions results in accounting answers that are often the subject of significant debate between management and the accountants. Some commenters to the proposed rules suggested that this rule be restricted to material accounting alternatives. These commenters indicated that restricting these communications will assist audit committee members by focusing their attention on important accounting alternatives. One commenter believes that only alternative treatments under GAAP that were the subject of serious consideration and debate by the accountant and management should be communicated to the audit committee.

We understand the concerns expressed and, accordingly, we have clarified the final rule. Providing audit committees with information on material accounting alternatives is consistent with the objectives of the Act and will minimize the risk that audit committee members will be distracted from material accounting policy matters by the numerous discussions between the accountant and management on the application of accounting principles to relatively small transactions or events. Therefore, these rules require communication, either orally or in writing, by accountants to audit committees of all alternative treatments within GAAP for policies and practices related to material items that have been discussed with management, including the ramifications of the use of such alternative treatments and disclosures and the treatment preferred by the accounting firm. This rule is intended to cover recognition, measurement, and disclosure considerations related to the accounting for specific transactions as well as general accounting policies.

We believe that communications regarding specific transactions should identify, at a minimum, the underlying facts, financial statement accounts impacted, and applicability of existing corporate accounting policies to the transaction. In addition, if the accounting treatment proposed does not comply with existing corporate accounting policies, or if an existing corporate accounting policy is not applicable, then an explanation of why the existing policy was not appropriate or applicable and the basis for the selection of the alternative policy should be discussed. Regardless of whether the accounting policy selected preexists or is new, the entire range of alternatives available under GAAP that were discussed by management and the accountants should be communicated along with the reasons for not selecting those alternatives. If the accounting treatment selected is not, in the accountant's view, the preferred method, we expect that the reasons why the accountant's preferred method was not selected by management also will be discussed.

Communications regarding general accounting policies should focus on the initial selection of and changes in significant accounting policies, as required by GAAS, and should include the impact of management's judgments and accounting estimates, as well as the accountant's judgments about the quality of the entity's accounting principles. The discussion of general accounting policies should include the range of alternatives available under GAAP that were discussed by management and the accountants along with the reasons for selecting the chosen policy. If an existing accounting policy is being modified, then the reasons for the change also should be communicated. If the accounting policy selected is not the accountant's preferred policy, then we expect the discussions to include the reasons why the accountant considered one policy to be preferred but that policy was not selected by management.

The separate discussion of critical accounting policies and practices is not considered a substitute for communications regarding general accounting policies, since the discussion about critical accounting policies and practices might not encompass any new or changed general accounting policies and practices. Likewise, this discussion of general accounting policies and practices is not intended to dilute the communications related to critical accounting policies and practices, since the issues affecting critical accounting policies and practices, such as sensitivities of assumptions and others, may be tailored specifically to events in the current year, and the selection of general accounting policies and practices should consider a broad range of transactions over time.

3. Other Material Written Communications

We understand written communications between accountants and management range from formal documents, such as engagement letters, to informal correspondence, such as administrative items. We also acknowledge that historically not all forms of written communications provided to management have been provided to the audit committee. Our rule is intended to implement Section 205 of the Sarbanes-Oxley Act, which clarified the substance of information that should be provided by accountants to audit committees to facilitate accountant and management oversight by those committees.

The Sarbanes-Oxley Act specifically cites the management letter and schedules of unadjusted differences as examples of material written communications to be provided to audit committees. Examples of additional written communications that we expect will be considered material to an issuer include:

- Management representation letter;
- Reports on observations and recommendations on internal controls;
- Schedule of unadjusted audit differences, and a listing of adjustments and reclassifications not recorded, if any;

- Engagement letter, and
- Independence letter.

These examples are not exhaustive, and accountants are encouraged to critically consider what additional written communications should be provided to audit committees.[13]

The Securities and Exchange Commission amended Regulation S-X in this way:

> [E]ach public accounting firm registered with the Board that audits an issuer's financial statements must report to the issuer's audit committee (1) all critical accounting policies and practices used by the issuer, (2) all material alternative accounting treatments within GAAP that have been discussed with management, including the ramifications of the use of the alternative treatments and the treatment preferred by the accounting firm, (3) other material written communications between the accounting firm and management of the issuer such as any management letter or schedule of "unadjusted differences," and (4) in the case of registered investment companies, all non-audit services provided to entities in the investment company complex that were not pre-approved by the investment company's audit committee. The required reports need not be in writing, but must be provided to the audit committee before the auditor's report on the financial statements is filed with the Commission.[14]

Exhibit 10.3 presents Wal-Mart's summary of critical accounting policies.

Accounting Changes

Of particular importance to the audit committee are the changes in accounting during the fiscal period. According to the Accounting Principles Board:

> A change in accounting by a reporting entity may significantly affect the presentation of both financial position and results of operations for an accounting period and the trends shown in comparative financial statements and historical summaries. The change should therefore be reported in a manner which will facilitate analysis and understanding of the financial statements.[15]

In order to familiarize the committee with the accounting changes, the types of changes are briefly set forth at this point.

Change in Accounting Principle A change in accounting principle results from the adoption of a generally accepted accounting principle different from the one used previously for reporting purposes. For example, a change in the method of inventory pricing is a common change in accounting principles. Although there

---

[13] Securities and Exchange Commission, Release No. 33-8183, "Strengthening the Commission's Requirements Regarding Auditor Independence," January 28, 2003, *www.sec.gov/rules/final/33-8183.htm*, pp. 33–38.

[14] Ibid., p. 45.

[15]*Opinions of the Accounting Principles Board No. 20*, "Accounting Changes" (New York: AICPA, 1971), para. 1.

Exhibit 10.3   Critical Accounting Policies at Wal-Mart Stores, Inc.

Summary of Critical Accounting Policies

Management strives to report the financial results of the Company in a clear and under-standable manner, even though in some cases accounting and disclosure rules are complex and require us to use technical terminology. We follow generally accepted accounting principles in the U.S. in preparing our consolidated financial statements. These principles require us to make certain estimates and apply judgments that affect our financial position and results of operations. Management continually reviews its accounting policies, how they are applied and how they are reported and disclosed in our financial statements. Fol-lowing is a summary of our more significant accounting policies and how they are applied in preparation of the financial statements.

Inventories

We use the retail last-in, first-out (LIFO) inventory accounting method for the Wal-Mart Stores segment, cost LIFO for the SAM'S CLUB segment and other cost methods, in-cluding the retail first-in, first-out (FIFO) and average cost methods, for the International segment. Inventories are not recorded in excess of market value. Historically, we have rarely experienced significant occurrences of obsolescence or slow moving inventory. However, future changes in circumstances, such as changes in customer merchandise pref-erence or unseasonable weather patterns, could cause the Company's inventory to be ex-posed to obsolescence or be slow moving.

Financial Instruments

We use derivative financial instruments for purposes other than trading to reduce our ex-posure to fluctuations in foreign currencies and to minimize the risk and cost associated with financial and global operating activities. Generally, the contract terms of hedge in-struments closely mirror those of the item being hedged, providing a high degree of risk reduction and correlation. Contracts that are highly effective at meeting the risk reduction and correlation criteria are recorded using hedge accounting. On February 1, 2001, we adopted Financial Accounting Standards Board (FASB) Statements No. 133, 137 and 138 (collectively "FAS 133") pertaining to the accounting for derivatives and hedging activi-ties. FAS 133 requires all derivatives, which are financial instruments used by the Com-pany to protect (hedge) itself from certain risks, to be recorded on the balance sheet at fair value and establishes accounting treatment for hedges. If a derivative instrument is a hedge, depending on the nature of the hedge, changes in the fair value of the instrument will either be offset against the change in fair value of the hedged assets, liabilities, or firm commitment through earnings or recognized in other comprehensive income until the hedged item is recognized in earnings. The ineffective portion of an instrument's change in fair value will be immediately recognized in earnings. Most of the Company's interest rate hedges qualify for the use of the "short-cut" method of accounting to assess hedge ef-fectiveness. The Company uses the hypothetical derivative method to assess the effective-ness of certain of its net investment and cash flow hedges. Instruments that do not meet the criteria for hedge accounting or contracts for which we have not elected hedge accounting are marked to fair value with unrealized gains or losses reported currently in earnings. Fair values are based upon management's expectation of future interest rate curves and may change based upon changes in those expectations.

Impairment of Assets

We periodically evaluate long-lived assets other than goodwill for indicators of impairment and test goodwill for impairment annually. Management's judgments regarding the existence of impairment indicators are based on market conditions and operational performance. Future events could cause management to conclude that impairment indicators exist and that the value of long-lived assets and goodwill associated with acquired businesses is impaired. Goodwill is evaluated for impairment annually under the provisions of FAS 142 which requires us to make judgments relating to future cash flows and growth rates as well as economic and market conditions.

Revenue Recognition

We recognize sales revenue at the time a sale is made to the customer, except for the following types of transactions. Layaway transactions are recognized when the customer satisfies all payment obligations and takes possession of the merchandise. We recognize SAM'S CLUB membership fee revenue over the 12-month term of the membership. Customer purchases of Wal-Mart/SAM'S CLUB shopping cards are not recognized until the card is redeemed and the customer purchases merchandise using the shopping card. Defective merchandise returned by customers is either returned to the supplier or is destroyed and reimbursement is sought from the supplier.

Insurance/Self-Insurance

We use a combination of insurance, self-insured retention, and/or self-insurance for a number of risks including workers' compensation, general liability, vehicle liability and employee-related health care benefits, a portion of which is paid by the Associates. Liabilities associated with the risks that we retain are estimated in part by considering historical claims experience, demographic factors, severity factors and other actuarial assumptions. The estimated accruals for these liabilities could be significantly affected if future occurrences and claims differ from these assumptions and historical trends.

For a complete listing of our accounting policies, please see Note 1 to our consolidated financial statements that appear after this discussion.

Source: Wal-Mart Stores, Inc., *2003 Annual Report*, pp. 22–23.

---

is a presumption that an accounting principle, once adopted, should not be changed, management may overcome this presumption if it justifies the use of an alternative acceptable accounting principle. For example, management may justify the change in accounting principle on the basis of the issuance of a new FASB accounting standard. Moreover, management may justify the change on the basis that such a change in accounting method enhances the fairness in the presentation of the financial statements.

With respect to the disclosure of a change in accounting principle, the Board stated:

> The nature of and justification for a change in accounting principle and its effect on income should be disclosed in the financial statements of the period in which the change is made. The justification for the change should explain clearly why the newly adopted accounting principle is preferable.[16]

---

[16]Ibid., par. 17. Additional reporting matters should be discussed with the chief financial officer and/or the external auditor.

Exhibit 10.4   Illustrative Accounting Changes

Accounting Changes

Statement of Financial Accounting Standards No. 106, "Employers' Accounting for Postretirement Benefits Other Than Pensions," and No. 109, "Accounting for Income Taxes," were implemented in the fourth quarter of 1992, effective as of January 1, 1992. The cumulative effect of these accounting changes on years prior to 1992, as shown below, has been reflected in the first quarter of 1992.

	(millions of dollars)
SFAS No. 106 (net of $408 million income tax effect)	$(800)
SFAS No. 109	760
Net charge	$(40)

The cumulative effect per share was $(0.64) and $0.61 for SFAS No. 106 and No. 109, respectively, resulting in a net change of $(0.03).

Neither standard had a material effect on 1992 income before the cumulative effect of the accounting changes.

Source: Exxon Corporation, *1992 Annual Report*, p. F12.

An example of a change in accounting principle is disclosed in the 1992 annual report of Exxon Corporation, presented in Exhibit 10.4.

Change in Accounting Estimate   Certain accounting actions are based on management's judgment regarding the use of estimates. Accounting estimates are required because of the matching principle of accounting that revenues and their related costs must be properly matched in the same accounting period to determine a fair measurement of the net income or loss of the entity. Thus as management acquires additional information and more experience concerning such matters as the economic life of plant and equipment assets and probable uncollectible receivables, a change in accounting estimate may occur.

Concerning the disclosure of changes in accounting estimates, Ford Motor Company reported:

> Depreciation and Amortization—Automotive. Depreciation is computed using an accelerated method that results in accumulated depreciation of approximately two-thirds of asset cost during the first half of the asset's estimated useful life. On average, buildings and land improvements are depreciated based on a 30-year life; automotive machinery and equipment are depreciated based on a $14\frac{1}{2}$-year life.
>
> It is the company's policy to review periodically fixed asset lives. A study completed during 1990 indicated that actual lives for certain asset categories generally were longer than the useful lives used for depreciation purposes in the company's financial statements. Therefore, during the third quarter of 1990, the company revised the

estimated useful lives of certain categories of property, retroactive to January 1, 1990. The effect of this change in estimate was to reduce 1990 depreciation expense by $211 million and increase 1990 net income, principally in the U.S., by $135 million or $0.29 per share.

When plant and equipment are retired, the general policy is to charge the cost of such assets, reduced by net salvage proceeds, to accumulated depreciation. All maintenance, repairs and rearrangement expenses are expensed as incurred. Expenditures that increase the value or productive capacity of assets are capitalized. The cost of special tools is amortized over periods of time representing the productive use of such tools. Preproduction costs incurred in connection with new facilities are expensed as incurred.[17]

Change in the Reporting Entity   This particular change occurs when the reporting entity changes its reporting as a result of a change in its composition, such as a merger. As the Board points out:

> One special type of change in accounting principle results in financial statements which, in effect, are those of a different reporting entity. This type is limited mainly to (a) presenting consolidated or combined statements in place of statements of individual companies, (b) changing specific subsidiaries comprising the group of companies for which consolidated financial statements are presented, and (c) changing the companies included in combined financial statements. A different group of companies comprise the reporting entity after each change. A business combination accounted for by the pooling of interests method also results in a different reporting entity.[18]

For example, Bristol-Myers Squibb reported:

Business Combination

On October 4, 1989, Squibb Corporation merged with a subsidiary of Bristol-Myers Company, and Bristol-Myers Company changed its name to Bristol-Myers Squibb Company. As a result, 97.4 million shares of Squibb common stock became entitled to be exchanged at a ratio of one share of Squibb for 2.4 Bristol-Myers Squibb shares, and 9.8 million shares of Squibb common stock owned by Squibb as treasury stock were retired. The merger has been accounted for as a pooling-of-interests.

In connection with the merger, a charge of $740 million was recorded in the fourth quarter of 1989 to integrate the operations of Bristol-Myers and Squibb and to organize its businesses on a global basis. The fourth quarter of 1989 also included an additional $115 million charge for the costs of professional fees and other expenses related to the merger. The after-tax effect of both charges was $693 million, or $1.32 per share.[19]

Thus it is apparent that management has "choices among accounting principles or procedures" and that such choices affect "the major areas in the financial state-

---

[17]Ford Motor Company, *1990 Annual Report*, p. 26.
[18]*Opinions of the Accounting Principles Board No. 20*, para. 12.
[19]Bristol-Myers Squibb Company, *1990 Annual Report*, p. 56.

ments requiring subjective determinations."[20] Hence the major objective of the committee is to review management's choices of accounting principles and methods with the external auditor in order to obtain assurance that its choices not only are in compliance with the current accounting standards but also are properly disclosed.

GUIDELINES FOR REVIEWING ACCOUNTING POLICY DISCLOSURES

General Approach

In reviewing the accounting policy disclosures, the audit committee should adopt a systematic review approach. Such an approach should include:

1. *Preliminary review*   Before meeting with management and the external auditors, the committee should be familiar with such matters as:
   a. The nature of the accounting practices of the business and its industry. It should request a summary of the entity's financial reporting requirements. If necessary the committee may wish to review the accounting policies and procedures manual and other documented information regarding the relationship between the accounting system and internal accounting controls. Are such accounting practices in line with the industry practices?
   b. A summary of the minutes of the meetings of the stockholders, board of directors, and other standing committees of the board, particularly the finance committee. The accounting policies should reflect the board's authorization regarding the financial accounting affairs of the entity.
   c. The prior year's financial statements and audit reports and a summary of the effect of accounting pronouncements of the FASB, AICPA, and SEC on the statements. Are there any trends that have a disproportionate effect on the financial status of the entity?
   d. The impact of accounting changes and the rationale for such changes in the previous accounting periods.
   e. The prior years' government reports, such as the SEC and IRS report filings. The committee may wish to engage the services of tax counsel or legal counsel concerning such matters.

   In addition to the preceding matters, the committee should request a written summary of an annual review of the accounting policy disclosures from the chief financial officer, executive audit partner, and executive internal auditor. Such a summary review will enable the committee to identify major financial reporting problems that affect the accounting policies. Obviously, the committee can expedite its review through the use of such summaries and thus maximize its review

---

[20]Schornack, "The Audit Committee," pp. 75–76.

time. Much of the preliminary review activities can occur during the initial and preaudit segments of the auditing cycle, as discussed in Chapters 6 and 7.

2. *Postaudit review*   During the committee's review of the drafts of the financial statements, it should give consideration to the following matters with the aforementioned parties:

   a. Proposed management changes in accounting policies, such as a change in the inventory pricing methods and the external auditor's concurrence. Also, proposed changes in such policies concerning the new reporting requirements of the FASB, SEC, and other regulatory agencies.[21]

   b. Changes in the entity's operations, such as a merger with an acquisition of another entity and the related effects on the existing accounting policies. Certain accounting standards govern the accounting treatment for the basis of valuing such investments (e.g., equity versus cost method of accounting). In view of the recommendations of the other standing committees and the approval of the board, the accounting policies should reflect such resolutions. An example of the committee's involvement and a change in accounting policy is reflected in the Bristol-Myers Squibb Annual Report shown in Exhibits 10.5 and 10.6.

   c. The committee should judge the existing accounting policies in light of the objectives of financial reporting discussed in Chapter 3. Such financial reporting objectives serve as a criterion for judging management's selection of accounting methods.[22]

   d. Since many independent accounting firms engaged in auditing publicly held corporations implement quality control review programs, the committee should ask the external auditor to review the disclosure checklist items applicable to the significant accounting policies. As a basis for discussion, the committee can use the auditor's summary review memo, previously requested, in order to reconcile significant disclosure matters. Moreover, the committee may wish to request a copy of the accounting firm's disclosure checklist concerning the financial statements. Such disclosure checklists are usually cross-referenced to the disclosure requirements in the accounting pronouncements. An illustrative accounting policy disclosure checklist in Exhibit 10.7 shows how the audit committee might document its review.[23]

In summary, as Russell E. Palmer, former managing partner of Touche Ross and Co. (now Deloitte & Touche), points out, "Committee members need not be auditors, or even accountants, but they must understand the financial reporting

---

[21]SEC matters regarding proxy materials should be discussed at this point, particularly compliance with the rules of the AICPA's SEC Practice Section. See Chapter 7.

[22]The reader should review in Chapter 5 such concepts as consistency, full disclosure, materiality, and fairness in financial statement presentation as well as certain enhanced financial disclosures sections of the Sarbanes-Oxley Act in Chapter 2.

[23]This checklist is not all-inclusive; and additional matters may be inserted based on the committee's judgment.

Exhibit 10.5   Illustrative Disclosure of Management's Financial Reporting Responsibility

---

Report of Management

Management is responsible for the preparation, presentation and integrity of the financial information presented in this Report. The accompanying consolidated financial statements have been prepared in conformity with accounting principles generally accepted in the United States of America, applying certain estimates and judgments as required. In management's opinion, the consolidated financial statements present fairly the Company's financial position, results of operations and cash flows.

The Company maintains a system of internal controls and procedures to provide reasonable assurance that transactions are properly authorized and that they are appropriately recorded and reported in the financial statements and that Company assets are adequately safeguarded. The system consists, in part, of the careful selection, training and development of financial managers, the dissemination of written internal accounting policies and an organizational structure that segregates responsibilities. The Company's internal auditors continually evaluate the adequacy and effectiveness of this system of internal accounting, policies, procedures and controls, and actions are taken to correct deficiencies as they are identified. As set forth in the Company's Standards of Business Conduct and Ethics and in the Company's Pledge, the Company is committed to adhering to the highest standards of moral and ethical behavior in all of its business activities.

PricewaterhouseCoopers LLP, the Company's independent accountants, have audited the annual financial statements in accordance with auditing standards generally accepted in the United States of America. Their report appears on this page.

The Audit Committee of the Board of Directors, composed solely of outside directors, meets regularly with the internal auditors, the independent accountants and management to review accounting, auditing, internal control structure and financial reporting matters. The internal auditors and independent accountants have full and free access to the Audit Committee.

Peter R. Dolan
Chairman of the Board and
Chief Executive Officer

Andrew R.J. Bonfield
Senior Vice President and
Chief Financial Officer

March 26, 2003

Source: Bristol-Myers Squibb, *2002 Annual Report*, p. 58.

Exhibit 10.6   Illustrative Changes in Accounting Policy

Impairment of Long-Lived Assets

Effective January 1, 2002, the Company adopted the provisions of SFAS No. 144, *Accounting for the Impairment of Long-Lived Assets*. The adoption of SFAS No. 144 did not have a material effect on the consolidated financial statements of the Company. SFAS No. 144 establishes the accounting for impairment of long-lived tangible and intangible assets other than goodwill and for the disposal of a segment of a business. Pursuant to SFAS No. 144, the Company periodically evaluates whether current facts or circumstances indicate that the carrying value of its depreciable assets to be held and used may not be recoverable. If such circumstances are determined to exist, an estimate of undiscounted future cash flows produced by the long-lived asset, or the appropriate grouping of assets, is compared to the carrying value to determine whether an impairment exists. If an asset is determined to be impaired, the loss is measured based on quoted market prices in active markets, if available. If quoted market prices are not available, the estimate of fair value is based on various valuation techniques, including a discounted value of estimated future cash flows. The Company reports an asset to be disposed of at the lower of its carrying value or its estimated net realizable value.

Capitalized Software

Certain costs to obtain internal use software for significant systems projects are capitalized and amortized over the estimated useful life of the software, which ranges from four to ten years. Costs to obtain software for projects that are not significant are expensed as incurred. Capitalized software, net of accumulated amortization, as of December 31, 2002 and 2001 was $370 million and $333 million, respectively.

Acquisitions

The Company adopted SFAS No. 141, *Business Combinations*, in 2001. SFAS No. 141 requires that companies use the purchase method of accounting for all business combinations initiated after June 30, 2001.

Investments

The Company consolidates all majority (more than 50%) owned subsidiaries where it has the ability to exercise control. The Company accounts for 50% or less owned companies over which it has the ability to exercise significant influence using the equity method of accounting. The Company's share of net income or losses of equity investments is included in minority interest in the consolidated statement of earnings. The Company periodically reviews these equity investments for impairment and adjusts these investments to their fair value when a decline in market value is deemed to be other than temporary. During 2002, the Company recorded an asset impairment charge of $379 million for an other than temporary decline in the market value of ImClone Systems Incorporated (ImClone).

Long-term investments in securities, which comprises marketable equity securities and other securities and investments for which market values are not readily available, are included in other assets. Marketable equity securities are classified as available-for-sale and reported at fair value. Fair value is based on quoted market prices as of the end of the reporting period. Other securities and investments for which market values are not readily available are carried at cost. Unrealized gains and losses are reported, net of their related tax effects, as a component of accumulated other comprehensive income (loss) in stockholders' equity until sold. At the time of sale, any gains or losses calculated by the specific

---

(continued)

Exhibit 10.6   *(Continued)*

---

identification method are recognized in other (income)/expense. Losses are also recognized in income when a decline in market value is deemed to be other than temporary.

Goodwill

The Company adopted SFAS No. 142, *Goodwill and Other Intangible Assets*, on January 1, 2002, with certain provisions adopted as of July 1, 2001 with respect to amortization of goodwill arising from acquisitions made after June 30, 2001. SFAS No. 142 addresses the initial recognition and measurement of intangible assets acquired outside a business combination and the recognition and measurement of goodwill and other intangible assets subsequent to their acquisition. Under the new rules, goodwill is no longer amortized but is subject to annual impairment tests. In connection with this accounting change, the goodwill resulting from the Company's acquisition of the DuPont pharmaceuticals business and investment in ImClone is not amortized.

The goodwill arising from business acquisitions prior to July 1, 2001 was amortized on a straight-line basis over periods ranging from 15 to 40 years. This goodwill is not amortized effective January 1, 2002. In each of 2001 and 2000, goodwill amortization expense was $75 million.

In accordance with SFAS No. 142, goodwill is tested for impairment upon adoption of the new standard and annually thereafter. SFAS No. 142 requires that goodwill be tested for impairment using a two-step process. The first step is to identify a potential impairment and the second step measures the amount of the impairment loss, if any. Goodwill is deemed to be impaired if the carrying amount of a reporting unit's goodwill exceeds its estimated fair value. The Company has completed its goodwill impairment assessment which indicated no impairment of goodwill.

Intangible Assets

Intangible assets, consisting of patents, technology and licenses, are amortized on a straight-line basis over periods ranging from 3 to 17 years, representing the remaining life of the assets. SFAS No. 142 requires that indefinite-lived intangible assets be tested for impairment using a one-step process which consists of a comparison of the fair value to the carrying value of the intangible asset. Intangible assets are deemed to be impaired if the net book value exceeds the estimated fair value. All other intangible assets are evaluated for impairment in accordance with SFAS No. 144 as described above.

Product Liability

Accruals for product liability are recorded, on an undiscounted basis, when it is probable that a liability has been incurred and the amount of the liability can be reasonably estimated, based on existing information. These accruals are adjusted periodically as assessment efforts progress or as additional information becomes available. Receivables for related insurance or other third-party recoveries for product liabilities are recorded, on an undiscounted basis, when it is probable that a recovery will be realized. Insurance recoverable recorded on the balance sheet has, in general, payment terms of two years or less. Amounts of receivables recognized, not in excess of related liabilities, as of December 31, 2002 and 2001 were $1 million and $158 million, respectively.

Contingencies

In the normal course of business, the Company is subject to contingencies, such as legal proceedings and claims arising out of its business, that cover a wide range of matters, including, among others, product liability, environmental liability and tax matters. In accordance with SFAS No. 5, *Accounting for Contingencies*, the Company records accruals for such contingencies when it is probable that a liability will be incurred and the amount of loss can be reasonably estimated. For a discussion of contingencies, reference is made to Note 8, Income Taxes, and Note 22, Litigation Matters, to these consolidated financial statements.

Source: Bristol-Myers Squibb, *2002 Annual Report*, p. 39.

---

process."[24] Thus while each member of the committee may not possess the requisite accounting knowledge, they should approach their review task with imagination, perceptiveness, and resourcefulness in order to assure themselves that the policies are reasonable and consistent with the financial reporting requirements of the FASB, AICPA, SEC, and other regulatory agencies. Furthermore, the committee should exercise judgment regarding the need for the use of specialists in areas of complex accounting, tax, and legal matters. For example, several independent consultants, who are retired partners of CPA firms, sit on the corporate audit committee to assist the committee with complex accounting issues.[25] In short, the primary objective of the committee's review should be to scrutinize management's judgment in selecting the accounting principles and methods used in the preparation of the financial statements and to recommend the statements for the approval of the board of directors.

---

[24]Russell E. Palmer, "Audit Committees—Are They Effective? An Auditor's View," *Journal of Accountancy* 144, No. 3 (September 1977), p. 78.

[25]Obviously, a retired partner would not sit on the audit committee of a corporation that is a client of his or her former firm. As two commentators point out: "[A]nalysts, stakeholders, the press, juries and jurists, and the public would not be persuaded that a retired partner of an audit firm could perform effectively as a member of the audit committee of a client of the partner's firm." Dan M. Guy and Stephen A. Zeff, "Independence and Objectivity: Retired Partners on Audit Committees," *CPA Journal* 72, No. 7 (July 2002), p. 34.

Exhibit 10.7   Accounting Policy Disclosures: A Checklist

	Yes	No	Remarks
1. Summary of the significant accounting policies reviewed by the external auditor, chief financial officer, and internal auditor. Summaries obtained.	_____	_____	
2. Accounting policies are consistent in relationship to the industry practices (conservative or liberal).	_____	_____	
3. Current reporting requirements are reflected in the accounting policies.	_____	_____	
4. Accounting changes reviewed and the external auditor's concurrence obtained.	_____	_____	
5. Disclosure of significant accounting policies is adequate to support the auditor's unqualified opinion.	_____	_____	
6. Major financial reporting problems resolved satisfactorily.	_____	_____	
7. Unresolved differences between the auditor and management reviewed.	_____	_____	
8. Additional disclosures reviewed.	_____	_____	
9. Unusual occurrences during the year, such as a disposal of a segment of the business properly disclosed in the financial statements.	_____	_____	
10. Accounting policies are consistent with a fair presentation of the financial statement in conformity with generally accepted accounting principles.	_____	_____	
11. Accounting policies reflect the board's authorization regarding financial and accounting matters.	_____	_____	

Signed by: _____ Date _____

(Should be signed by the chairman of the audit committee)*

———————

*See Chapter 4 with respect to procedures to document audit committee activities.

SOURCES AND SUGGESTED READINGS

American Institute of Certified Public Accountants, *Audit Committees, Answers to Typical Questions about Their Organization and Operations* (New York: AICPA, 1978).

American Institute of Certified Public Accountants, *Meeting the Financial Reporting Needs of the Future: A Public Commitment from the Public Accounting Profession* (New York: AICPA, 1993).

American Institute of Certified Public Accountants, *Practice Alert 2000-2* "Quality of Accounting Principles-Guidelines for Discussions with Audit Committees," *www.aicpa .org/members/div/secps/index.htm.*

Bristol-Myers Squibb Company, *2002 Annual Report.*

Exxon Corporation, *1992 Annual Report.*

Ford Motor Company, *1990 Annual Report.*

Gerson, James S., J. Robert Mooney, Donald F. Moran, and Robert K. Waters, "Oversight of the Financial Reporting Process—Part I." *CPA Journal* 59, No. 7 (July 1989), pp. 22–28.

Gerson, James S., J. Robert Mooney, Donald F. Moran, and Robert K. Waters, "Oversight of the Financial Reporting Process—Part II." *CPA Journal* 59, No. 8 (August 1989), pp. 40, 42–47.

Guy, Dan M., and Stephen A. Zeff, "Independence and Objectivity: Retired Partners on Audit Committees." *CPA Journal* 72, No. 7 (July 2002), pp. 30–34.

McKesson Corporation, *1998 Annual Report.*

Opinions of the Accounting Principles Board, No. 20. "Accounting Changes" (New York: American Institute of Certified Public Accountants, 1971).

Opinions of the Accounting Principles Board, No. 22, "Disclosure of Accounting Policies" (New York: American Institute of Certified Public Accountants, 1972).

Palmer, Russell, E., "Audit Committees—Are They Effective? An Auditor's View," *Journal of Accountancy* 144, No. 3 (September 1977), pp. 76–79.

Public Oversight Board, *A Special Report by the Public Oversight Board of the SEC Practice Section,* AICPA (Stamford, Conn.: Public Oversight Board, 1993).

Schornack, John J., "The Audit Committee—A Public Accountant's View," *Journal of Accountancy* 147, No. 4 (April 1979), pp. 73–77.

Securities and Exchange Commission, *Release No. 33-8183*, "Strengthening the Commission's Requirements Regarding Auditor Independence," January 28, 2003, *www.sec.gov/ rules/final/33-8183.htm.*

Wal-Mart Stores, Inc., *2003 Annual Report.*

Chapter 11

A Perspective on Fraud and the Auditor

In view of the general misconception concerning the auditor's responsibility for the detection of fraud, the purpose of this chapter is to examine the implications of management fraud as it relates to the external auditor and the audit committee. Moreover, audit committee members will not only examine the meaning and rationale for management fraud but also explore ways to safeguard the entity against such fraud. The committee's monitoring of certain general business practices, such as conflicts of interest, will be discussed in Chapter 12.

MEANING OF FRAUD IN A FINANCIAL STATEMENT AUDIT

According to the Auditing Standards Board of the AICPA, fraud and its characteristics are described in this way:

> Fraud is a broad legal concept and auditors do not make legal determinations of whether fraud has occurred. Rather, the auditor's interest specifically relates to acts that result in a material misstatement of the financial statements. The primary factor that distinguishes fraud from error is whether the underlying action that results in the misstatement of the financial statements is intentional or unintentional. For purposes of the Statement, *fraud* is an intentional act that results in a material misstatement in financial statements that are the subject of an audit.[1]

The Board describes the types of misstatements as follows:

- *Misstatements arising from fraudulent financial reporting* are intentional misstatements or omissions of amounts or disclosures in financial statements designed to deceive financial statement users where the effect causes the financial statements not to be presented, in all material respects, in conformity with generally accepted accounting principles (GAAP). Fraudulent financial reporting may be accomplished by the following:
  - Manipulation, falsification, or alteration of accounting records or supporting documents from which financial statements are prepared
  - Misrepresentation in or intentional omission from the financial statements of events, transactions, or other significant information
  - Intentional misapplication of accounting principles relating to amounts, classification, manner of presentation, or disclosure

---

[1] *Statement on Auditing Standards No. 99*, "Consideration of Fraud in a Financial Statement Audit" (New York: AICPA, 2002), par. 5.

Fraudulent financial reporting need not be the result of a grand plan or conspiracy. It may be that management representatives rationalize the appropriateness of a material misstatement, for example, as an aggressive rather than indefensible interpretation of complex accounting rules, or as a temporary misstatement of financial statements, including interim statements, expected to be corrected later when operational results improve.

- *Misstatements arising from misappropriation of assets* (sometimes referred to as theft or defalcation) involve the theft of an entity's assets where the effect of the theft causes the financial statements not to be presented, in all material respects, in conformity with GAAP. Misappropriation of assets can be accomplished in various ways, including embezzling receipts, stealing assets, or causing an entity to pay for goods or services that have not been received. Misappropriation of assets may be accompanied by false or misleading records or documents, possibly created by circumventing controls. The scope of this Statement includes only those misappropriations of assets for which the effect of the misappropriation causes the financial statements not to be fairly presented, in all material respects, in conformity with GAAP.[2]

In addition, the Institute of Internal Auditors defines fraud as:

Any illegal acts characterized by deceit, concealment or violation of trust. These acts are not dependent upon the application of threat of violence or of physical force. Frauds are perpetrated by individuals and organizations to obtain money, property or services; to avoid payment or loss of services; or to secure personal or business advantages.[3]

With respect to the identification of fraud, the Institute's *Standards for the Professional Practice of Internal Auditing* indicate:

The internal auditor should have sufficient knowledge to identify the indicators of fraud but is not expected to have the expertise of a person whose primary responsibility is detecting and investigating fraud.[4]

With respect to fraudulent financial reporting, the National Commission on Fraudulent Financial Reporting defined such reporting as:

intentional or reckless conduct, whether act or omission, that results in materially misleading financial statements. Fraudulent financial reporting can involve many factors and take many forms. It may entail gross and deliberate distortion of corporate records, such as inventory count tags, or falsified transactions, such as fictitious sales or orders. It may entail the misapplication of accounting principles. Company employees at any level may be involved, from top to middle management to lower-level personnel. If the conduct is intentional, or so reckless that it is the legal equivalent of intentional conduct, and results in fraudulent financial statements, it comes

---

[2]Ibid., par. 6.

[3]Institute of Internal Auditors, *The Professional Practices Framework* (Altamonte Springs, FL: IIA, 2002), p. 26.

[4]Ibid., section 1210. A2., p. 9 For further information regarding the identification of fraud and the internal auditor's responsibility for detection, see Practice Advisory 1210. A2-1 and 1210.A2-2.

within the Commission's operating definition of the term *fraudulent financial reporting*.

Fraudulent financial reporting differs from other causes of materially misleading financial statements, such as unintentional errors. The Commission also distinguished fraudulent financial reporting from other corporate improprieties, such as employee embezzlements, violations of environmental or product safety regulations, and tax fraud, which do not necessarily cause the financial statements to be materially inaccurate.[5]

Although there is a distinction between fraudulent financial reporting and misappropriation of assets, this chapter addresses both types of fraud.

Although both the private sector and public sector have initiated action, particularly the Foreign Corrupt Practices Act of 1977 and Sections 301 and 302 of the Sarbanes-Oxley Act of 2002 (discussed in Chapter 1), to protect the business community against management fraud, it is apparent that such positive actions will not completely eliminate this corporate problem. Since the passage of the acts, management fraud cases continue to be discussed in the news media. The cost of management fraud to the business community is indeterminable, primarily because many cases are not revealed or not discovered. Furthermore, the cost of compliance to safeguard the entity from management fraud is increasing. For example, see the reports by the Association of Certified Fraud Examiners in Exhibits 11.1 and 11.2.[6]

Consequently, the cost in money and time to businesses and consumers to reform corporate behavior, as well as the cost of liability insurance, is constantly increasing.

In October 1997, Ernst & Young's Fraud Investigative Group in the United Kingdom surveyed senior executives in 11,000 major organizations in 32 countries. Based on 1,205 responses, Ernst & Young reported these findings:

- The experience of organisations participating in our surveys shows that the curse of fraud continues. More than half had been defrauded in the last 12 months. 30% had suffered more than five frauds in the last five years.

- 84% of the worst frauds were committed by employees, nearly half of whom had been with the organisation for over 5 years.

- Most of the worst frauds were committed by management.

- 87% of respondents thought the incidence of fraud would increase, or at best remain static, over the next 5 years. Yet less than half of these organisations had done as much as they cost effectively could to protect their business against fraud.

- Only 13% of fraud losses had been recovered—including insurance recoveries.

---

[5]National Commission on Fraudulent Financial Reporting, *Report of the National Commission on Fraudulent Financial Reporting* (Washington, DC: NCFFR, 1987), p. 2.

[6]In an article entitled "Six Common Myths about Fraud," Joseph T. Wells, chairman of the Association of Certified Fraud Examiners, identifies such myths as: (1) Most people will not commit fraud; (2) Fraud is not material; (3) Most fraud goes undetected; (4) Fraud is usually well concealed; (5) The auditor can't do a better job in detecting fraud; and (6) Prosecuting fraud perpetrators deters others. For further discussion, see *Journal of Accountancy* 169, No. 2 (February 1990), pp. 82–88. Also see Joseph T. Wells, "Occupational Fraud: The Audit as Deterrent," *Journal of Accountancy* 193, No. 4 (April 2002), pp. 24–28.

Exhibit 11.1 Association of Certified Fraud Examiners, 2002 Report to the Nation, Occupational Fraud and Abuse, Executive Summary

---

- This study covers 663 occupational fraud cases that caused over $7 billion in losses.
- Certified fraud examiners estimate that six percent of revenues will be lost in 2002 as a result of occupational fraud and abuse. Applied to the U.S. Gross Domestic Product, this translates to losses of approximately $600 billion, or about $4,500 per employee.
- Over half of the frauds in this study caused losses of at least $100,000 and nearly one in six caused losses in excess of $1 million.
- All occupational frauds fall into one of three categories: asset misappropriations, corruption, or fraudulent statements.
  - Over 80% of occupational frauds involve asset misappropriations. Cash is the targeted asset 90% of the time.
  - Corruption schemes account for 13% of all occupational frauds and they cause over $500,000 in losses, on average.
  - Fraudulent statements are the most costly form of occupational fraud with median losses of $4.25 million per scheme.
- The average scheme in this study lasted 18 months before it was detected.
- The most common method for detecting occupational fraud is by a tip from an employee, customer, vendor or anonymous source. The second most common method is by accident.
- Organizations with fraud hotlines cut their fraud losses by approximately 50% per scheme. Internal audits, external audits, and background checks also significantly reduce fraud losses.
- The typical perpetrator is a first-time offender. Only seven percent of occupational fraudsters in this study were known to have prior convictions for fraud-related offenses.
- Small businesses are the most vulnerable to occupational fraud and abuse. The average scheme in a small business causes $127,500 in losses. The average scheme in the largest companies costs $97,000.

Source: Association of Certified Fraud Examiners, *2002 Report to the Nation Occupational Fraud and Abuse* (Austin, TX: ACFE, 2002) p. ii.

- Respondents' replies indicated that the better the directors' understanding of the business as a whole, the lower the incidence of fraud they suffered.
- However, less than half the respondents believed that their directors had a good understanding of areas outside their core business, including remote and overseas operations.
- Less than a quarter of the respondents believed their directors had a good understanding of electronic communication or information technology.
- With the millennium approaching fast, three in four organisations had failed to include within their Year 2000 projects an assessment of the vulnerability of their computer systems to fraud.
- The proportion of organisations with fraud reporting policies was higher than in our last survey, but communication of these to the workforce was still poor.[7]

---

[7]Ernst & Young, *Fraud: The Unmanaged Risk, An International Survey of the Effect of Fraud on Business* (London: Ernst & Young, 1998), p. 1.

Exhibit 11.2   Detecting and Preventing Fraud

Obviously, a key to dealing with fraud is detecting it when it occurs. Respondents were asked how the frauds they investigated were initially discovered. There were 532 responses to this question, the results of which are summarized below. The most common method of detection was a tip from an employee, which occurred in over a quarter of the cases reviewed. This data suggests that effective reporting mechanisms and open channels of communication from employees to management can have a positive effect on fraud detection and mitigation.

INITIAL DETECTION OF FRAUDS

METHOD/PERCENT OF CASES[a]

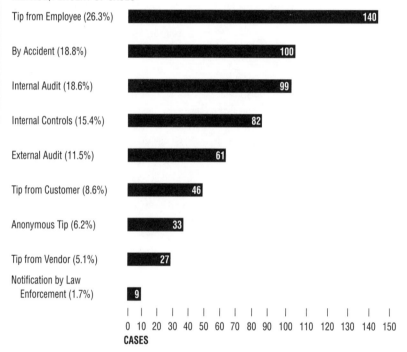

Respondents were asked, based on their own expertise, which of the following eight measures are most helpful in preventing fraud against organizations. Each participant ranked the following measures in order of their perceived effectiveness, assigning a "1" to the measure that is most effective, a "2" to the measure that is next most effective, and so on. Thus, the most effective anti-fraud measures would have the lowest average scores.

A strong system of internal controls was viewed as the most effective anti-fraud measure by a wide margin. Detailed background checks on new employees were thought to be the next most important measure, followed by regular fraud audits.

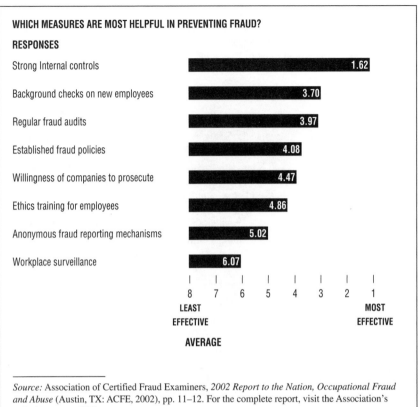

WHICH MEASURES ARE MOST HELPFUL IN PREVENTING FRAUD?

RESPONSES

Strong Internal controls	1.62
Background checks on new employees	3.70
Regular fraud audits	3.97
Established fraud policies	4.08
Willingness of companies to prosecute	4.47
Ethics training for employees	4.86
Anonymous fraud reporting mechanisms	5.02
Workplace surveillance	6.07

8   7   6   5   4   3   2   1

LEAST   MOST
EFFECTIVE   EFFECTIVE

AVERAGE

Source: Association of Certified Fraud Examiners, *2002 Report to the Nation, Occupational Fraud and Abuse* (Austin, TX: ACFE, 2002), pp. 11–12. For the complete report, visit the Association's web site at *www.CFEnet.com.*
[a]Total exceeds 100% because some participants cited more than one method for initial discovery of the frauds.

As David Sherwin, head of Ernst & Young's Fraud Investigation Group, asserts:

Companies need to act positively to prevent fraud from happening in the first place. They should ensure all the simple steps are conscientiously applied.

Areas of neglect include:

- *Lack of knowledge of the workings of remote sites and overseas operations.* Senior management reveals that it still doesn't make regular visits to remote locations in order to ensure that adequate controls are in place—placing too much reliance, instead, on local management.

- *Poor understanding by directors of electronic communications and IT.* Although computer systems are being widely reviewed to eliminate "millennium bomb" problems, the vulnerability of these systems to fraud was checked by only one in four companies surveyed.

- *Inadequate fraud-reporting policies for staff.* While most companies are developing such policies, communication remains poor. Over half the companies said they were opposed to hotlines to enable staff to report fraud. Such opposition was lowest in the U.S. and greatest in continental Europe.[8]

Intentional Distortions of Financial Statements

Concerning management's deliberate misrepresentations in the entity's financial position and results of operations, L. B. Sawyer, A. A. Murphy, and M. Crossley report:

> Management fraud has been found in overstatements of inventory to show healthy assets which are, in truth, sickly . . . the acceptance of inferior goods to conceal a tottering cash position . . . delayed key expenditures to increase current profits to the detriment of the long-range survival of the company . . . overstatements of receivables to puff both assets and sales . . . fictitious sales which construct a facade of vigorous business volume . . . and understatements of liabilities to gloss over the financial picture.[9]

With respect to legal cases concerning management fraud and the audit committee, the reader should review several cases in Chapter 4. Such a review indicates that the SEC and the courts have ruled on the establishment of the audit committee by the registrant in order to comply with the provisions of the federal securities laws. As a result, the legal obligations of audit committee members have intensified because their standard duty of care and loyalty to the entity has increased in light of the management fraud activities. Consequently, the audit committee will look to the internal and external auditing executives as well as legal counsel for assistance in preventing management fraud. In short, since management fraud is perpetrated by the top executives of the entity, ordinarily it is conducted on a sophisticated basis and thus requires the professional expertise of auditors, legal counsel, or special investigators.

The rationale for management fraud is essentially attributable to "different pressures" that force management into deliberate misrepresentations of accounting information as well as the misappropriations of assets.[10] Sawyer, Murphy, and Crossley summarize the reasons:

- "Executives sometimes take rash steps from which they cannot retreat," such as setting unattainable objectives regarding the earnings per share figure. Such rash actions may involve actually lying to the external auditors in order to inflate the bottom line of the entity.
- "Profit centers may distort facts to hold off divestments," whereby management of a subsidiary will deliberately manipulate transactions and alter documents and records to falsify its profitability performance.

---

[8]Ernst & Young, *Ernst's & Young's Business Upshot* (Cleveland, OH) (July/August 1998), p. 3.
[9]Lawrence B. Sawyer, Albert A. Murphy, and Michael Crossley, "Management Fraud: The Insidious Specter," *Internal Auditor* 36, No. 2 (April 1979), pp. 12–13.
[10]Ibid., p. 17.

- "Incompetent managers may deceive in order to survive," based on their actual performance versus their reported results.
- "Performance may be distorted to warrant larger bonuses," through the manipulation of the reported figures regarding the company's incentive plans.
- "The need to succeed can turn managers to deception," whereby such individuals place personal gains and self-interest before their stewardship accountability to their constituencies (discussed in Chapter 2).
- "Unscrupulous managers may serve interests which conflict," as discussed in Chapter 4 in relation to the state and federal statutory laws covering the directors and officers. Such laws provide a standard duty of care and loyalty to the entity.
- "Profits may be inflated to obtain advantages in the marketplace," whereby the perpetrators are confident that "their own abilities transcend any fear of detection."
- "People who control both the assets and their records are in a perfect position to falsify the latter." Thus a sound system of internal control, discussed in Chapter 8, is essential.[11]

Expanding on the aforementioned rationale and motivation for fraudulent financial reporting, the National Commission on Fraudulent Financial Reporting characterized various situations and opportunities:

Fraudulent financial reporting usually occurs as the result of certain environmental, institutional, or individual forces and opportunities. These forces and opportunities add pressures and incentives that encourage individuals and companies to engage in fraudulent financial reporting and are present to some degree in all companies. If the right combustible mixture of forces and opportunities is present, fraudulent financial reporting may occur.

A frequent incentive for fraudulent financial reporting that improves the company's financial appearance is the desire to obtain a higher price from a stock or debt offering or to meet the expectations of investors. Another incentive may be the desire to postpone dealing with financial difficulties and thus avoid, for example, violating a restrictive debt covenant. Other times the incentive is personal gain: additional compensation, promotion, or escape from penalty for poor performance.

Situational pressures on the company or an individual manager also may lead to fraudulent financial reporting. Examples of these situational pressures include:

Sudden decreases in revenue or market share. A single company or an entire industry can experience these decreases.

Unrealistic budget pressures, particularly for short-term results. These pressures may occur when headquarters arbitrarily determines profit objectives and budgets without taking actual conditions into account.

Financial pressure resulting from bonus plans that depend on short-term economic performance. This pressure is particularly acute when the bonus is a significant component of the individual's total compensation.

---

[11]Ibid., pp. 17–19.

Opportunities for fraudulent financial reporting are present when the fraud is easier to commit and when detection is less likely. Frequently these opportunities arise from:

The absence of a board of directors or audit committee that vigilantly oversees the financial reporting process.

Weak or nonexistent internal accounting controls. This situation can occur, for example, when a company's revenue system is overloaded from a rapid expansion of sales, an acquisition of a new division, or the entry into a new, unfamiliar line of business.

Unusual or complex transactions. Examples include the consolidation of two companies, the divestiture or closing of a specific operation, and agreements to buy or sell government securities under a repurchase agreement.

Accounting estimates requiring significant subjective judgment by company management. Examples include reserves for loan losses and the yearly provision for warranty expense.

Ineffective internal audit staffs. This situation may result from inadequate staff size and severely limited audit scope.

A weak corporate ethical climate exacerbates these situations. Opportunities for fraudulent financial reporting also increase dramatically when the accounting principles for transactions are nonexistent, evolving, or subject to varying interpretations.[12]

The rationale for management fraud is based on the various pressures that emanate from the internal and external environment of the corporation. Moreover, such frauds are augmented by the economic motives of the perpetrator as well as the organizational structure of the entity.

Computer Fraud

In addition to management fraud, computer fraud has been a major constant problem of the business community. In 1987, the National Commission on Fraudulent Financial Reporting concluded:

The increasing power and sophistication of computers and computer-based information systems may contribute even more to the changing nature of fraudulent financial reporting. The last decade has seen the decentralization and the proliferation of computers and information systems into almost every part of the company. This

---

[12]National Commission on Fraudulent Financial Reporting, *Report of the National Commission on Fraudulent Financial Reporting,* pp. 23–24. For a good discussion, see James D. Stice, W. Steve Albrecht, and Leslie M. Brown, "Lessons to be Learned—ZZZZ Best, Regina, and Lincoln Savings," *CPA Journal* 61, No. 4 (April 1991), pp. 52–53. A recent study of 75 fraud and 75 no-fraud firms noted that no-fraud firms with outside members on the board of directors significantly reduce the likelihood of financial statement fraud. See Mark S. Beasley, "An Empirical Analysis of the Relation between the Board of Director Composition and Financial Statement Fraud," *Accounting Review* 71, No. 4 (October 1996), pp. 443–465. For additional reading, see a Best Practices Council of the National Association of Corporate Directors report, *Coping with Fraud and Other Illegal Activity* (Washington, D.C.: National Association of Corporate Directors, 1998); Mark S. Beasley, Joseph V. Carcello, and Dana R. Hermanson, *Fraudulent Financial Reporting: 1987–1997 An Analysis of U.S. Public Companies* (New York: COSO of the Treadway Commission, 1999).

development has enabled management to make decisions more quickly and on the basis of more timely and accurate information. Yet by doing what they do best—placing vast quantities of data within easy reach—computers multiply the potential for misusing or manipulating information, increasing the risk of fraudulent financial reporting.[13]

As defined by Brandt Allen:

Computer fraud is . . . any defalcation or embezzlement accomplished by tampering with computer programs, data files, operations, equipment or media and resulting in losses sustained by the organization whose computer system was manipulated.[14]

For an expanded discussion of computer fraud, see *The Computer and Internet Fraud Manual* published by the Association of Certified Fraud Examiners.

THE EXTERNAL AUDITOR'S RESPONSIBILITY

An Overview[15]

As discussed in Chapter 6 dealing with audit planning, the Auditing Standards Board of the AICPA issued a standard that requires independent auditors to assess the risk of materially misstated financial statements due to fraud.

The AICPA's new fraud standard (SAS No. 99, "Consideration of Fraud in a Financial Statement Audit," effective for audits beginning on or after December 15, 2002, supersedes the previous SAS No. 82 fraud standard) will have new implications for audit committees. Although the new fraud standard provides external auditors with revised and expanded guidelines on consideration of fraud during an audit engagement, their responsibility to plan and perform the audit to obtain reasonable assurance about whether the financial statements are free of material misstatements, whether caused by error or fraud, has not changed. However, external auditors are required to give consideration of fraud throughout the audit and place increased emphasis on the need for heightened professional skepticism.

SAS No. 99 retains the two types of fraud as noted in SAS No. 82: (1) fraudulent financial reporting, involving intentional material misstatements or omissions of material amounts or disclosures in the financial statements, and (2) misappropriation of assets, involving the theft of an entity's assets.

---

[13]National Commission on Fraudulent Financial Reporting, *Report of the National Commission on Fraudulent Financial Reporting,* p. 28. The reader may wish to review the Equity Funding Corporation of America case, which illustrates the use of computers to create fictitious insurance policies and, in turn, overstate assets by more than $120 million and overstate the corporation's earnings. See *United States v. Weiner,* 578 F. 2d 757 (9th Cir.), cert. denied, 439 U.S. 981 (1978).
[14]Brandt Allen, "The Biggest Computer Frauds: Lessons for CPA's," *Journal of Accountancy* 143, No. 5 (May 1977), 52.
[15]In addition to the external auditor's role and responsibility for detecting fraud and illegal acts, the reader may wish to consult other auditing standards with respect to the internal auditor, fraud examiner, and government auditors. See the bibliography for the applicable reference.

The new standard requires the external auditors to identify and document fraud risks rather than fraud risk factors (e.g., risk of misappropriation of inventory). Additionally, the news standard renames the categories of fraud risk factors: (1) incentive/pressure, (2) opportunity, and (3) attitudes/rationalization. (For additional information, see appendix to SAS No. 99 as well as Chapter 6.)

SAS No. 99 establishes the following process to address the potential for intentional material misstatements in the financial statements. The standard requires the auditors to:

- Gather information necessary to identify the risks of material misstatements
- Identify risks of material misstatements
- Assess identified risks
- Respond to the results of the assessment
- Evaluate audit evidence
- Communicate fraud to interested parties
- Document the auditors' consideration of fraud[16]

With respect to the effect of fraud on the auditor's report, the Board states:

> The auditor should evaluate whether identified risks of material misstatement due to fraud can be related to specific financial-statement account balances or classes of transactions and related assertions, or whether they relate more pervasively to the financial statements as a whole. Relating the risks of material misstatement due to fraud to the individual accounts, classes of transactions, and assertions will assist the auditor in subsequently designing appropriate auditing procedures.
>
> Certain accounts, classes of transactions, and assertions that have high inherent risk because they involve a high degree of management judgment and subjectivity also may present risks of material misstatement due to fraud because they are susceptible to manipulation by management. For example, liabilities resulting from a restructuring may be deemed to have high inherent risk because of the high degree of subjectivity and management judgment involved in their estimation. Similarly, revenues for software developers may be deemed to have high inherent risk because of the complex accounting principles applicable to the recognition and measurement of software revenue transactions. Assets resulting from investing activities may be deemed to have high inherent risk because of the subjectivity and management judgment involved in estimating fair values of those investments.
>
> In summary, the identification of a risk of material misstatement due to fraud involves the application of professional judgment and includes the consideration of the attributes of the risk, including:
>
> - The *type* of risk that may exist, that is, whether it involves fraudulent financial reporting or misappropriation of assets

---

[16]Statement on Auditing Standards No. 99, "Consideration of Fraud in a Financial Statement Audit," par. 2. For further reference, see Douglas R. Carmichael, "The Auditor's New Guide to Errors, Irregularities and Illegal Acts," *Journal of Accountancy* 166, No. 3 (September 1988), pp. 40–48.

- The *significance* of the risk, that is, whether it is of a magnitude that could lead to result in a possible material misstatement of the financial statements

- The *likelihood* of the risk, that is, the likelihood that it will result in a material misstatement in the financial statements[a]

- The *pervasiveness* of the risk, that is, whether the potential risk is pervasive to the financial statements as a whole or specifically related to a particular assertion, account, or class of transactions.[17]

---

[a]The occurrence of material misstatements of financial statements due to fraud is relatively infrequent in relation to the total population of published financial statements. However, the auditor should not use this as a basis to conclude that one or more risks of a material misstatement due to fraud are not present in a particular entity.

Finally, the external auditor has a responsibility to communicate fraud to the audit committee or board of directors. More specifically:

Whenever the auditor has determined that there is evidence that fraud may exist, that matter should be brought to the attention of an appropriate level of management. This is appropriate even if the matter might be considered inconsequential, such as a minor defalcation by an employee at a low level in the entity's organization. Fraud involving senior management and fraud (whether caused by senior management or other employees) that causes a material misstatement of the financial statements should be reported directly to the audit committee. In addition, the auditor should reach an understanding with the audit committee regarding the nature and extent of communications with the committee about misappropriations perpetrated by lower-level employees.

If the auditor, as a result of the assessment of the risks of material misstatement, has identified risks of material misstatement due to fraud that have continuing control implications (whether or not transactions or adjustments that could be the result of fraud have been detected), the auditor should consider whether these risks represent reportable conditions relating to the entity's internal control that should be communicated to senior management and the audit committee. (See SAS No. 60, *Communication of Internal Control Related Matters Noted in an Audit* {AICPA, *Professional Standards*, vol. 1, AU sec. 325.04]). The auditor also should consider whether the absence of or deficiencies in programs and controls to mitigate specific risks of fraud or to otherwise help prevent, deter, and detect fraud represent reportable conditions that should be communicated to senior management and the audit committee.

The auditor also may wish to communicate other risks of fraud identified as a result of the assessment of the risks of material misstatements due to fraud. Such a communication may be a part of an overall communication to the audit committee of business and financial statement risks affecting the entity and/or in conjunction with the auditor communication about the quality of the entity's accounting principles (see SAS No. 61, AU sec. 380.11).

The disclosure of possible fraud to parties other than the client's senior management and its audit committee ordinarily is not part of the auditor's responsibility and ordinarily would be precluded by the auditor's ethical or legal obligations of

---

[17]Ibid., pars. 38, 39, 40.

confidentiality unless the matter is reflected in the auditor's report. The auditor should recognize, however, that in the following circumstances a duty to disclose to parties outside the entity may exist:

a. To comply with certain legal and regulatory requirements[a]

b. To a successor auditor when the successor makes inquiries in accordance with SAS No. 84, *Communications Between Predecessor and Successor Auditors*[b] (AICPA, *Professional Standards*, vol. 1, AU sec. 315)

c. In response to a subpoena

d. To a funding agency or other specified agency in accordance with requirements for the auditors of entities that receive governmental financial assistance[c]

Because potential conflicts between the auditor's ethical and legal obligations for confidentiality of client matters may be complex, the auditor may wish to consult with legal counsel before discussing matters covered by paragraphs 79 through 81 with parties outside the client.[18]

---

[a]These requirements include reports in connection with the termination of the engagement, such as when the entity reports an auditor change on Form 8-K and the fraud or related risk factors constitute a *reportable event* or is the source of a *disagreement*, as these terms are defined in Item 304 of Regulation S-K. These requirements also include reports that may be required, under certain circumstances, pursuant to Section 10A(b)1 of the Securities Exchange Act of 1934 relating to an illegal act that has a material effect on the financial statements.
[b]SAS No. 84 requires the specific permission of the client.
[c]For example, *Government Auditing Standards* (the Yellow Book) require auditors to report fraud or illegal acts directly to parties outside the audited entity in certain circumstances.

In addition to fraud in a financial statement audit, the external auditor has a responsibility for detecting illegal acts by client companies. As defined by the Auditing Standards Board:

> The term *illegal acts,* for purposes of this Statement, refers to violations of laws or governmental regulations. Illegal acts by clients are acts attributable to the entity whose financial statements are under audit or acts by management or employees acting on behalf of the entity. Illegal acts by clients do not include personal misconduct by the entity's personnel unrelated to their business activities.[19]

Although the external auditor may recognize that the client has committed an illegal act, the determination of whether the act is illegal is dependent on legal judgment. Therefore, the auditor would consult with legal counsel or await a court ruling, depending on the circumstances.

In view of the fact that illegal acts vary in their relation to the financial statements, the Auditing Standards Board makes this distinction between direct and indirect effects:

> The auditor considers laws and regulations that are generally recognized by auditors to have a direct and material effect on the determination of financial statement

---

[18]Ibid., pars. 79, 80, 81, 82.
[19]*Statement on Auditing Standards, No. 54,* "Illegal Acts by Clients" (New York: AICPA, 1988), par. 2. For further discussion, see Donald L. Neebes, Dan M. Guy, and O. Ray Whittington, "Illegal Acts: What Are the Auditor's Responsibilities?" *Journal of Accountancy* 171, No. 1 (January 1991), pp. 82–84, 86, 88, 90–93.

amounts. For example, tax laws affect accruals and the amount recognized as expense in the accounting period; applicable laws and regulations may affect the amount of revenue accrued under government contracts. However, the auditor considers such laws or regulations from the perspective of their known relation to audit objectives derived from financial statement assertions rather than from the perspective of legality *per se*. The auditor's responsibility to detect and report misstatements resulting from illegal acts having a direct and material effect on the determination of financial statement amounts is the same as that for fraud as described in SAS No. 82, "Consideration of Fraud in a Financial Statement Audit."

Entities may be affected by many other laws or regulations, including those related to securities trading, occupational safety and health, food and drug administration, environmental protection, equal employment, and price-fixing or other antitrust violations. Generally, these laws and regulations relate more to an entity's operating aspects than to its financial and accounting aspects, and their financial statement effect is indirect. An auditor ordinarily does not have sufficient basis for recognizing possible violations of such laws and regulations. Their indirect effect is normally the result of the need to disclose a contingent liability because of the allegation or determination of illegality. For example, securities may be purchased or sold based on inside information. While the direct effects of the purchase or sale may be recorded appropriately, their indirect effect, the possible contingent liability for violating securities laws, may not be appropriately disclosed. Even when violations of such laws and regulations can have consequences material to the financial statements, the auditor may not become aware of the existence of the illegal act unless he is informed by the client, or there is evidence of a governmental agency investigation or enforcement proceeding in the records, documents, or other information normally inspected in an audit of financial statements.[20]

Warning signals for possible illegal acts are presented in Exhibit 11.3.

Finally, the auditor is required to communicate with the audit committee in this way:

> The auditor should assure himself that the audit committee, or others with equivalent authority and responsibility, is adequately informed with respect to illegal acts that come to the auditor's attention. The auditor need not communicate matters that are clearly inconsequential and may reach agreement in advance with the audit committee on the nature of such matters to be communicated. The communication should describe the act, the circumstances of its occurrence, and the effect on the financial statements. Senior management may wish to have its remedial actions communicated to the audit committee simultaneously. Possible remedial actions include disciplinary action against involved personnel, seeking restitution, adoption of preventive or corrective company policies, and modifications of specific control procedures. If senior management is involved in an illegal act, the auditor should communicate directly with the audit committee. The communication may be oral or written. If the communication is oral, the auditor should document it.[21]

With respect to detection of management fraud and reporting illegal acts, the Public Oversight Board set forth these recommendations.

---

[20]Ibid., pars. 5, 6.

[21]*Statement on Auditing Standards, No. 54,* "Illegal Acts by Clients," par. 17.

Exhibit 11.3 Warning Signals of Possible Illegal Acts

- Unauthorized transactions, improperly recorded transactions, or transactions not recorded in a complete or timely manner in order to maintain accountability for assets

- Investigation by a governmental agency, an enforcement proceeding, or payment of unusual fines or penalties

- Violations of laws or regulations cited in reports of examinations by regulatory agencies that have been made available to the auditor

- Large payments for unspecified services to consultants, affiliates, or employees

- Sales commissions or agents' fees that appear excessive in relation to those normally paid by the client or to the services actually received

- Unusually large payments in cash, purchases of bank cashiers' checks in large amounts payable to bearer, transfers to numbered bank accounts, or similar transactions

- Unexplained payments made to government officials of employees

- Failure to file tax returns or pay government duties or similar fees that are common to the entity's industry or the nature of its business

Source: Statement on Auditing Standards No. 54, "Illegal Acts by Clients," par. 9.

Recommendation V-1

Accounting firms should assure that auditors more consistently implement, and be more sensitive to the need to exercise the professional skepticism required by, the auditing standard that provides guidance on the auditor's responsibility to detect and report errors and irregularities.

Recommendation V-2

The Auditing Standards Board, the Executive Committee of the SEC Practice Section or some other appropriate body should develop guidelines to assist auditors in assessing the likelihood that management fraud which may affect financial information may be occurring and to specify additional auditing procedures when there is a heightened likelihood of management fraud.[22]

Recommendation V-14

The accounting profession should support carefully drafted legislation requiring auditors to report to the appropriate authorities, including the SEC, suspected illegalities discovered by the auditor in the course of an audit if the client's management or board of directors fails to take necessary action with respect to such suspected ille-

[22]Public Oversight Board, *A Special Report by the Public Oversight Board of the SEC Practice Section, AICPA* (Stamford, CT: POB, 1993), p. 43.

galities and the auditor believes that they are or may be significant to the entity. The profession should seek adequate guidance as to the types of illegalities that would be encompassed by this requirement.[23]

It is reemphasized that the auditor's purpose is to express an objective opinion on the fairness of the presentation in the financial statements. A review of the scope paragraph of the external auditor's standard report explicitly indicates that he or she should plan and perform the audit to obtain reasonable assurance about whether the financial statements are free of material misstatement. Such a statement is also acknowledged to the client company in the engagement letter, whereby the auditor explicitly states that the audit may not detect all material irregularities. Accordingly, if the auditor conducts his or her examination in accordance with generally accepted auditing standards, then he or she is not responsible for the detection of fraud. It should be recognized that the auditor's examination in full compliance with the promulgated auditing standards is not a guarantee that fraud is totally nonexistent. As noted in the preceding discussion on computer fraud, a sophisticated scheme along with collusion may go undetected by the independent auditor. As a result, it is incumbent on the audit committee to obtain reasonable assurance from the external auditors that management has taken the necessary actions to protect the assets of the entity. Such assurance is obtained through the committee's review of the auditor's management letter regarding management's responsibility for the financial accounting system and the related internal controls as well as appropriate fidelity bond insurance coverage.

In view of the nature and complex problems of management fraud, the AICPA's standing committee on methods, perpetration, and detection of fraud has provided a preliminary list of warning signals of the possible existence of fraud. (See Exhibit 11.4.)

This checklist of warning signals is particularly important as a guide to the audit committee in its inquiries of the audit partner to identify the auditor's alertness to the possibility of fraud. For example, the committee may wish to correlate the checklist of warning signals with the auditor's management letter in order to identify potential problem areas. The major objective is to determine whether the auditor is taking a fresh look at the current year's audit examination as opposed to merely rolling over previous years' examinations. Furthermore, the committee's review of the checklist will enable it to create an environment "that fosters morality and high business ethics."[24] "The systems should provide checks and balances and reports that cause flares to streak across the corporate sky if improprieties are practiced."[25]

---

[23]Ibid., p. 55.
[24]Sawyer, Murphy, and Crossley, "Management Fraud," p. 24.
[25]Ibid.

Exhibit 11.4 Warning Signals of the Possible Existence of Fraud

1. Highly domineering senior management and one or more of the following, or similar, conditions are present:
   - An ineffective board of directors and/or audit committee.
   - Indications of management override of significant internal accounting controls.
   - Compensation or significant stock options tied to reported performance or to a specific transaction over which senior management has actual or implied control.
   - Indications of personal financial difficulties of senior management.
   - Proxy contests involving control of the company or senior management's continuance, compensation, or status.

2. Deterioration of quality of earnings evidenced by:
   - Decline in the volume or quality of sales (e.g., increased credit risk or sales at or below cost).
   - Significant changes in business practices.
   - Excessive interest by senior management in the earnings per share effect of accounting alternatives.

3. Business conditions that may create unusual pressures:
   - Inadequate working capital.
   - Little flexibility in debt restrictions such as working capital ratios and limitations on additional borrowings.
   - Rapid expansion of a product or business line markedly in excess of industry averages.
   - A major investment of the company's resources in an industry noted for rapid change, such as a high technology industry.

4. A complex corporate structure where the complexity does not appear to be warranted by the company's operations or size.

5. Widely dispersed business locations accompanied by highly decentralized management with inadequate responsibility reporting system.

6. Understaffing which appears to require certain employees to work unusual hours, to forego vacations, and/or to put in substantial overtime.

7. High turnover rate in key financial positions such as treasurer or controller.

8. Frequent change of auditors or legal counsel.

9. Known material weaknesses in internal control which could practically be corrected but remain uncorrected, such as:
   - Access to computer equipment or electronic data entry devices is not adequately controlled.
   - Incompatible duties remain combined.

10. Material transactions with related parties exist or there are transactions that may involve conflicts of interest.

11. Premature announcements of operating results or future (positive) expectations.

12. Analytical review procedures disclosing significant fluctuations which cannot be reasonably explained, for example:
    - Material account balances.
    - Financial or operational interrelationships.

- Physical inventory variances.
- Inventory turnover rates.

13. Large or unusual transactions, particularly at year-end, with material effect on earnings.

14. Unusually large payments in relation to services provided in the ordinary course of business by lawyers, consultants, agents, and others (including employees).

15. Difficulty in obtaining audit evidence with respect to:

- Unusual or unexplained entries.
- Incomplete or missing documentation and/or authorization.
- Alterations in documentation or accounts.

16. In the performance of an examination of financial statements unforeseen problems are encountered, for instance:

- Client pressures to complete audit in an unusually short time or under difficult conditions.
- Sudden delay situations.
- Evasive or unreasonable responses of management to audit inquiries.

Source: American Institute of Certified Public Accountants, *CPA Letter* 59, No. 5 (March 12, 1979), p. 4

INVESTIGATING KNOWN FRAUD[26]

Summary Guidelines

As previously noted, the annual audit examination does not guarantee the nonexistence of fraud. However, through a sound system of internal control, adequate fidelity bond insurance, and effective internal and external audits, the entity is afforded reasonable protection against fraud. Nevertheless, on the discovery of fraud, it is essential that the board of directors call for a careful and competent investigation of the situation. While such an investigation is a burden on the entity, "corporate heads, including the boards of directors, should regard the occurrence as a business problem, not a legal problem."[27] Hence the board, through its audit committee, should demonstrate that it has taken the necessary course of action to properly uncover the fraud in order to maximize on its recovery from the fidelity bond insurance company.

Although the approach to an investigation may vary, Sawyer, Murphy, and Crossley point out that "an executive should be assigned to coordinate . . . the investigation."[28] Ordinarily the executive is the director of internal auditing.

---

[26]For further reference, see Denzil Y. Causey, "The CPA Guide to Whistle Blowing," *CPA Journal* 58, No. 8 (August 1988), pp. 26–37; Timothy L. Williams and W. Steve Albrecht, "Understanding Reactions to Fraud," *Internal Auditor* 47, No. 4 (August 1990), pp. 45–51. As discussed in Chapter 2, the reader should review Section 806 dealing with whistle-blowing protection for employees.

[27]Sawyer, Murphy, and Crossley, "Management Fraud," p. 20.

[28]Ibid.

However, the audit committee may wish to engage special investigators and/or external auditors whereby both groups will coordinate their efforts with the internal auditors. Moreover, the surety company usually makes its own investigation because it must attest to the validity of the entity's claim. However, it is important to recognize that such an investigation should not be made solely by the surety company because its objective is to minimize the claim for the loss. Thus the audit committee should ensure that the investigation is properly coordinated with the auditors or the special investigators and the surety company. In particular, the committee should be assured that: (1) the suspect has not been notified of the present investigation; (2) the investigation has been properly planned in advance and will be conducted expeditiously to prevent covering up the evidence; (3) all corporate transactions involving the suspect and the methods used to perpetrate the fraud have been properly investigated and documented; (4) the existence of possible collusion has been carefully considered; (5) the dollar amount of the defalcation has been properly ascertained and the amount of the funds recovered; and (6) any legal action, if appropriate, has been taken against the perpetrator(s). Such assurance is obtained through the committee's review of the reports from the auditors, legal counsel, and the surety company as well as its consultation with the external audit partner regarding disclosure matters in the financial statements.

From the preceding discussion, it is evident that the audit committee should recognize not only the primary purpose of the annual audit examination but also the implications of the auditor's responsibility for the detection of fraud. The committee will look primarily to the internal and external auditors for assistance concerning the necessary measures for the prevention of fraud. For example, it may request a periodic survey of the fraud prevention measures within the entity. Such a survey may be done by the internal audit group to determine the soundness of the system of internal control. Consequently, during its review of the audit plans discussed in Chapters 6 and 7, the committee should address the need for a survey of the fraud prevention measures. When such a survey is conducted, the committee should review the internal auditor's report with the outside audit partner to obtain the partner's assessment of the entity's fraud prevention activities. The committee should be satisfied that there is adequate follow-up regarding the internal auditor's recommendations so that if and when fraud should occur, it can be confident that the cause of the fraud was not related to recommendations that were overlooked. Such an oversight on the part of the committee may be a cause for an unrecovered insurance claim. It is obvious that the audit committee must be alert not only to the possibility of fraud but also to the steps necessary to safeguard the entity from such fraud.

As Hugh L. Marsh and Thomas E. Powell conclude:

> It would be a misconception to believe the possibility of fraud is the only reason for establishing a chartered audit committee. While the primary role has been to oversee management's financial and reporting responsibilities, it is only one task. Nevertheless, the Treadway Commission's investigations indicated that audit committees could serve very effectively to reduce the incidence of fraud. When fraudulent financial reporting did occur despite the existence of an audit committee, the following important points in the audit committee's charter often had been omitted:

Authorization for resources. As noted by the Treadway Commission, only in unusual circumstances would an audit committee need a separate staff, but the means for accomplishing this should be addressed.

Issues related to CPAs' independence. The press has made much ado about the practice of some CPAs of using audit services as a "loss leader" for management advisory services. Strong opinions have been expressed on both sides of this issue, but it would seem prudent for the audit committee to oversee management's judgments about the independence of its CPAs.

Seeking a second opinion. Some observers speak of it disparagingly as "opinion shopping"; others refer to it as seeking a technically correct opinion. But any time a second opinion is sought, the audit committee should know what the issues were and how they were resolved.

Preservation of internal auditor independence. Internal auditors occupy the unique position of "independent" staff members. This independence is strengthened and ensured through audit committee action. Direct and unrestricted access to records is essential and the audit committee should concur with the appointment and discharge of the director of internal audit.[29]

THE AUDIT COMMITTEE'S OVERSIGHT APPROACH TO FRAUD RISK ASSESSMENT

As part of their oversight of the audit process and the SAS No. 99 requirements, audit committees need to assure the full board of directors of any indications of possible fraud and illegal acts, including management's remedial actions. More specifically, audit committees can expect to have discussions with their external auditors regarding fraud risk areas during the information-gathering phase. Likewise, audit committees will be notified about fraud findings and reportable conditions during the communication phase.

To achieve effective oversight responsibility for fraud risk areas, audit committees should consider this two-step approach:

1. Complete a profile worksheet with the details of the entity's potential fraud risk area.
2. Address a set of representative questions for the preaudit and postaudit meetings.

Audit Committee's Profile Worksheet—Fraud Risk Areas

Given the thrust of the new fraud standard, it is reasonable to expect that audit committees will include a statement regarding their fraud risk discussions in their written charter, which is disclosed in the entity's annual proxy statement. Exhibit 11.5 shows a suggested format for a profile worksheet.

---

[29]Hugh L. Marsh and Thomas E. Powell, "The Audit Committee Charter: Rx for Fraud Prevention," *Journal of Accountancy* 167, No. 2 (February 1989), pp. 55–57.

Exhibit 11.5 Audit Committee's Profile Worksheet of the Entity's Fraud Risk Areas

Audit Committee Practice Area	Services Available from:						
	Management	Internal Auditors	External Auditors	Legal Counsel	Board of Directors	Compliance with SEC, SROs, ASB, or Sarbanes-Oxley Act	Comments:
Knowledge Areas							
Industry Matters							
Competition	✓	✓	✓				
Economic conditions	✓	✓	✓				
Technology	✓	✓	✓				
Government regulations	✓	✓	✓	✓			
Industry accounting practices	✓	✓	✓				
Entity's Business Matters							
Organizational structure (management integrity)			✓		✓		
Business and product segments (Business model profile)	✓	✓	✓				
Policies and procedures for detecting fraud, illegal acts, and whistleblower protection (e.g., conflicts-of-interests (related party transactions) monitoring, compliance with the corporate code of conduct, monitoring compliance with laws and regulations, and management override of control(s))	✓	✓	✓	✓	✓	✓	
Management's risk assessment process (business risk profile and internal control concepts)	✓	✓	✓				

	C1	C2	C3	C4	C5	C6
Accounting policies and practices	✓	✓	✓			
Complex business transactions and contracts	✓	✓	✓			
Frequent change of legal counsel				✓	✓	
Financial reporting process (quarterly and annual financial statements)	✓	✓	✓			✓
Internal communication process	✓	✓	✓		✓	✓
External communication process	✓	✓			✓	✓
External Audit Process						
Selection or retention of auditors (terms of service, qualifications, composition, and independence of the audit engagement team)	✓	✓	✓		✓	✓
Frequent change of auditors (disagreement on GAAP, which causes opinion shipping).	✓	✓	✓		✓	✓
Quantity of lawsuits against the CPA firm	✓	✓	✓	✓	✓	
Nonacceptance of recommendations in the management letter (breakdowns in internal controls)	✓	✓	✓			✓
Internal Audit Process						
Approve hiring or termination of the internal auditing executive (term of service, qualifications and composition of the internal audit groups)		✓	✓		✓	
Departmental organization and size		✓	✓			
Reporting responsibility		✓	✓			
Scope restrictions and access to requested information		✓	✓			
Quantity of special projects and investigations dealing with material noncompliance	✓	✓		✓		✓

To adequately plan a review of the fraud risk areas, audit committees need knowledge about the entity's:

- Business model and industry
- Business risks and internal control environment
- Policies and procedures for detecting fraud and illegal acts
- Accounting industry practices
- Complex business transactions and significant contracts
- Financial reporting process

Likewise, audit committees need to review:

- The operational characteristics of the entity and the vulnerability of the industry to changing economic conditions and competitive pressures. Such a review usually would include recent annual and interim financial statements, SEC filings (1O-Qs and 10-Ks), annual proxy statement, the entity's website, and analytical review procedures (e.g., absolute data comparison, financial ratio data) Additionally, an evaluation of management integrity would include biographical information on senior executives and financial management.
- Management's risk assessment process and related internal controls (i.e., the components of COSO's Internal Control—Integrated Framework)
- Management's policies and procedures with respect to:
  - Conflicts-of-interest statements
  - Corporate code of conduct
  - Laws and regulations
  - Management override of controls
- Industry accounting practices, with particular emphasis on the appropriateness of accounting principles
- Complex business transactions (e.g., restructuring charges)
- Financial reporting process at the individual financial account and transaction class level
- Internal and external communication processes
- Internal and external auditing processes

Audit Committee's Meetings and Agendas—Fraud Risk Areas

Based on the profile worksheet, audit committees need to know what questions to ask with respect to the auditors' assessment of fraud risk and their response to the overall audit approach.

During the preaudit meeting, audit committees can elicit information that is helpful in setting objectives and implementation measures related to fraud prevention and detection. For example, audit committees may ask the auditors to expand the scope of their examination with respect to areas of revenue recognition

---

Exhibit 11.6   Representative Questions for Preaudit Meetings—Fraud Risk Planning

- To what extent can the planned audit scope be relied on to detect fraud? (See audit engagement letter for the auditors' responsibilities.)
- What steps were taken by the audit engagement team in assessing the likelihood that fraud which may affect financial information may be occurring?
  - Inquiries of management and employees other than management
  - Observations with regard to preliminary analytical procedures, including procedures related to revenue recognition (i.e., unusual and unexpected results)
  - Consideration of fraud risk factors relative to fraudulent financial reporting and misappropriation of assets (incentives/pressures, opportunities, and attitudes/rationalizations)
  - Consideration of other information (e.g., integrity of management)
  - Identification of fraud risks, including type of risk, significance, likelihood and pervasiveness
  - Assessment of identified fraud risks and consideration of the entity's programs and controls to prevent, detect, and mitigate fraud
  - Response to fraud risk assessment in the overall audit approach, including the nature, timing, and extent of audit procedures as well as additional procedures related to management override of controls
- What areas will be emphasized due to the heightened likelihood of fraud?
- What areas require special attention by the audit committee? (e.g., Sarbanes-Oxley's Corporate and Criminal Fraud Accountability provision, including record retention and destruction procedures as well as whistleblower protection)
- Were there any allegations of unethical behavior in the financial reporting process?

---

or misappropriation of inventory. This information is also useful in setting objectives in areas such as internal audit and special investigations. Exhibits 11.6 and 11.7 provide questions that enable audit committees to establish specific objectives related to fraud risk areas.

During the postaudit meeting, audit committees need answers to questions dealing with fraud detection, illegal acts, and breakdowns in internal control that arose in the audit engagement. Exhibit 11.7 indicates some representative questions.

In reviewing the financial statements, audit committees should request a fraud risk assessment at the financial account and transaction class level. They should be alert to areas that involve judgment in recognition, valuation, measurement, and disclosure as well as management's assertions regarding asset realization and liability measurement.

In addition, audit committees should be alert to situations involving breakdowns in the system of internal control. As previously noted, audit committees should review and study the areas of COSO's Internal Control—Integrated Framework in the context of the auditors' fraud risk assessment.

Finally, audit committees should be concerned with material audit adjustments and immaterial uncorrected misstatements, including aggressive versus conservative accounting policies and any changes in accounting principles.

Exhibit 11.7   Representative Questions for Postaudit Meeting—Fraud Risk Areas

- To what extent did the actual scope of the fraud risk audit findings differ from the preaudit plan? What were the causes for the difference?

- Did management restrict the scope of the audit or access to requested information?

- Were there disagreements with management on accounting policies and practices, including estimates and assumptions?

- What recommendations were made to management to improve the system of internal control?

- What assessment was given to the entity's policies and procedures for detecting conflicts of interests (e.g., related party transactions) and management override of controls, including directives of the board of directors?

- Was there any incidence of noncompliance with laws and regulations, including the provisions of Sarbanes-Oxley?

- Was there any incidence of noncompliance with the corporate code of conduct?

- What were the accounting treatments with respect to complex transactions, unusual transactions, and material contracts?

- Were there any proposed accounting adjustments, including immaterial uncorrected adjustments?

In sum, the new fraud standard will affect the audit committee's pre- and postaudit meetings and related agendas and presumably will help engender a high degree of integrity in both the audit processes and the financial reporting process.

SEC Financial Fraud and Disclosure—Cases in Point

The following summary of selected SEC cases and alleged violations provide illustrations of fraudulent techniques. For additional reading, the reader should review the appropriate SEC Litigation Release or Accounting and Auditing Enforcement Release.

Date Filed	Release No.	Nature of Alleged Violation
10/28/99	LR-16344	The SEC alleged that the defendants engaged in a fraudulent scheme to recognize revenues prematurely by improperly recording purported "bill and hold" sales. The alleged purpose of this activity was to meet sales projections. As a result, the firm overstated accounts receivable, sales, pretax income, net income, and earnings per share.

5/15/01	LR-17001	The Commission alleged that the defendants engaged in a scheme to fraudulently misrepresent the firm's results of operations in connection with a purported "turnaround" of the firm. Inappropriate accounting reserves—"cookie jar reserves"—were created to overstate quarterly income and growth.
3/27/02	AAER-1533	The SEC alleged inaccurate quarterly financial statements (3/31/96 to 3/31/99) and annual financial statements (12/31/95 to 12/31/98). Such inaccuracies arose in connection with $1.44 billion restructuring charges in a postmerger period. The firm materially overstated this restructuring charge by accruing $354 million that did not constitute restructuring liabilities under GAAP. The firm voluntarily restated its financial statements.
7/24/02	AAER-1599	The Commission alleged that the firm fraudulently excluded billions of dollars in liabilities from its consolidated financial statements by hiding them in off-balance sheet affiliates, falsified operations statistics, and inflated earnings to meet Wall Street expectations.
9/12/02	AAER-1627	The SEC filed action against three former top executives, alleging that they failed to disclose the multimillion-dollar, low-interest, and interest-free loans from the firm for personal expenses. Also, they covertly caused the company to forgive tens of millions of dollars in outstanding loans without proper disclosures.

Thus audit committees need to review and discuss with the internal and external auditors and financial management:

1. Premature revenue recognition situations, such as those related to unshipped products and bill and hold sales not at the customer request
2. Unrealistic assumptions related to accounting estimates "cookie jar reserves"
3. Big Bath restructuring charges in which certain expenses belong to future periods
4. The key provisions of the Sarbanes-Oxley Act of 2002 that relate to such matters as personal loans to executives (Section 402) and disclosure of off-balance sheet transactions and other relationships (Section 401).

Exhibit 11.8 shows the number of SEC enforcement cases initiated during the past five years.

Exhibit 11.8   SEC Enforcement Cases

Number of Issuer Financial Statement and Reporting Cases Initiated by the SEC

Issuer	2002	2001	2000	1999	1998
Financial Disclosure	141	103	100	89	75
Reporting Other	22	9	3	5	4
Total	163	112	103	94	79

Source: Securities and Exchange Commission, *Annual Reports* (Washington, DC: U.S. Government Printing Office, 1998–2002).

SOURCES AND SUGGESTED READINGS

American Institute of Certified Public Accountants, *The CPA Letter* 59, No. 5 (March 12, 1979), pp. 1–6.

American Institute of Certified Public Accountants, *Management Antifraud Programs and Controls*. For more information on fraud prevention and deterence, visit the AICPA's Antifraud Resource Center, *www.aicpa.org/antifraud*.

Association of Certified Fraud Examiners, Annual Fraud Conference, *www.CFEnet.com*.

Association of Certified Fraud Examiners, *Fraud Statistics Fact Sheet* (Austin, TX: ACEF, 1993).

Association of Certified Fraud Examiners, *Report to the Nation on Occupational Fraud Abuse* (Austin, TX: ACEF, 1996, 2002).

Beasley, Mark S., "An Empirical Analysis of the Relation Between the Board of Director Composition and Financial Statement Fraud." *Accounting Review* 71, No. 4 (October 1996), pp. 443–465.

Brandt, Allen, "The Biggest Computer Frauds: Lesson for CPA's," *Journal of Accountancy* 143, No. 5 (May 1977), pp. 52–62.

Carmichael, Douglas R., "The Auditor's New Guide to Errors, Irregularities and Illegal Acts," *Journal of Accountancy* 166, No. 3 (September 1988), pp. 40–48.

Causey, Denzil Y., "The CPA Guide to Whistle Blowing." *CPA Journal* 58, No. 8 (August 1988), pp. 26–37.

Ernst & Young, *Fraud: The Unmanaged Risk, An International Survey of the Effect of Fraud on Business* (London: Ernst & Young, 1998).

Institute of Internal Auditors bookstore, visit the web site at *www.theiia.org* for information on fraud, ethics, law.

Marsh, Hugh L., and Thomas E. Powell, "The Audit Committee Charter: Rx for Fraud Prevention." *Journal of Accountancy* 167, No. 2 (February 1989), pp. 55–57.

Menkus, Belden, "Eight Factors Contributing to Computer Fraud." *Internal Auditor* 47, No. 5 (October 1990), pp. 71–73.

National Commission on Fraudulent Financial Reporting, *Report of the National Commission on Fraudulent Financial Reporting* (Washington, DC: NCFFR, 1987).

Neebes, Donald L., Dan M. Guy, and O. Ray Whittington, "Illegal Acts: What Are the Auditor's Responsibilities?" *Journal of Accountancy* 171, No. 1 (January 1991), pp. 82–84, 86, 88, 90–93.

Public Oversight Board, *A Special Report by the Public Oversight Board of the SEC Practice Section, AICPA* (Stamford, CT: POB, 1993).

Sawyer, Lawrence B., Albert A. Murphy, and Michael Crossley, "Management Fraud: The Insidious Specter." *Internal Auditor,* 36, No. 2 (April 1979), pp. 11–25.

Statement on Auditing Standards No. 54, "Illegal Acts by Clients" (New York: AICPA, 1988).

Statement on Auditing Standards No. 55, "Consideration of the Internal Control Structure in a Financial Statement Audit" (New York: AICPA, 1988).

Statement on Auditing Standards No. 99, "Consideration of Fraud in a Financial Statement Audit" (New York: AICPA, 2002).

Stice, James D., W. Steve Albrecht, and Leslie M. Brown, "Lessons to be Learned—ZZZZ Best, Regina, and Lincoln Savings." *CPA Journal* 61, No. 4 (April 1991), pp. 52–53.

United States v. Weiner, 578 F. 2d 757 (9th Cir), cert. denied, 439 U.S. 981 (1978).

Wells, Joseph T., "Six Common Myths About Fraud." *Journal of Accountancy* 169, No. 2 (February 1990), pp. 82–88.

Williams, Timothy L., and W. Steve Albrecht, "Understanding Reactions to Fraud." *Internal Auditor,* No. 4 (August 1990), pp. 45–51.

The reader also may wish to visit the web sites of other organizations as noted in Appendix B.

Additional Suggested Readings

Albrecht, W. S., M. B. Romney, D. J. Cherrington, I. R. Payne, and A. J. Roe, *How to Detect and Prevent Business Fraud* (Englewood Cliffs, NJ: Prentice-Hall, 1982).

American Institute of Certified Public Accountants, "Fraud Beat." *Journal of Accountancy* (published monthly).

Association of Certified Fraud Examiners, *Professional Standards and Practices for Certified Fraud Examiners* (Austin, TX: ACFE, 2002).

Association of Certified Fraud Examiners, *The White Paper* (Austin, TX: ACFE, published bimonthly).

Bloom Becker, Buck, *Spectacular Computer Crimes* (New York: Dow Jones Irwin, 1990).

Bologna, G. Jack, and Robert J. Lindquist, *Fraud Auditing and Forensic Accounting* (New York: John Wiley & Sons, 1987).

Bologna, G. Jack, Robert J. Lindquist, and Joseph Wells, *The Accountant's Handbook of Fraud & Commercial Crime* (New York: John Wiley & Sons, 1992).

Davia, Howard R., Patrick C. Coggins, John C. Wildeman, and Joseph T. Kastantin, *Management Accountants' Guide to Fraud Discovery and Control* (New York: John Wiley & Sons, 1992).

Domanick, Joe, *Faking It in America* (Chicago: Contemporary Books, 1989).

Elliott, Robert K., and John J. Willingham, *Management Fraud: Detection and Deterrence* (New York: Petrocelli Books, 1980).

Glover, Hubert D., and James C. Flagg, *Effective Fraud Detection and Prevention Techniques* (Altamonte Springs, FL: IIA, 1993).

Institute of Internal Auditors, "Fraud Findings." *Internal Auditor* (published monthly).

Institute of Internal Auditors, *The Professional Practice Framework* (Altamonte Springs, FL: IIA, 2002.

Jacobson, Alan, *How to Detect Fraud Through Auditing* (Altamonte Springs, FL: IIA, 1990).

Kellogg, Irving, *Fraud, Window Dressing, and Negligence in Financial Statements* (New York: McGraw-Hill, 1991).

Levy, Marvin M., *Computer Fraud: A Basic Course for Auditors* (New York: AICPA, 1990).

Levy, Marvin M., *Detection of Errors, Fraud, and Illegal Acts* (New York: AICPA, 1990).

Merchant, Kenneth A., *Fraudulent and Questionable Financial Reporting* (Morristown, NJ: Financial Executive Research Foundation, 1987).

Securities and Exchange Commission, *Annual Reports* (Washington, DC: U.S. Government Printing Office, 1998, 1999, 2000, 2001, 2002).

U.S. General Accounting Office, *Government Auditing Standards, Standards for Audit of Governmental Organizations, Programs, Activities, and Functions* (Washington, DC: U.S. Government Printing Office, 1988).

White, Richard, and William G. Bishop, "The Role of the Internal Auditor in the Deterrence, Detection, and Reporting of Fraudulent Financial Reporting," *The Institute of Internal Auditors Reports on Fraud* (Altamonte Springs, FL: IIA, 1986).

Videos

Association of Certified Fraud Examiners, *Cooking the Books: What Every Accountant Should Know About Fraud* (1991); *The Corporate Con: Internal Fraud and the Auditor* (1992); and *Beyond the Numbers: Professional Interview Techniques* (1994) Austin, TX; length of videos: 50 minutes.

Institute of Internal Auditors, *A New Look at Ethics and Fraud.* Altamonte Springs, FL, 1988; length of video: 60 minutes.

For additional videos, visit the Association of Certified Fraud Examiners' web site, *www.cfenet.com.*

Chapter 12

Reviewing Certain General Business Practices

In Chapter 1, it was established that corporate boards of directors and their audit committees have a major role in establishing and maintaining corporate accountability and governance. In addition, it was noted that the boards and their committees have encountered increasing pressure from the SEC and Congress as evidenced particularly by the passage of the Foreign Corrupt Practices Act (See Appendix D on this book's website) and the Sarbanes-Oxley Act. Such pressures have created an environment whereby the audit committee should review and monitor certain corporate policies and practices regarding sensitive payment areas. The purpose of this chapter is to examine those areas, such as questionable foreign payments, conflicts of interest, corporate perquisites, and corporate contributions. This chapter will discuss the nature of these sensitive matters and identify ways to assist the committee with its review.

QUESTIONABLE FOREIGN PAYMENTS

Nature of Questionable Foreign Payments

In view of the Foreign Corrupt Practices Act, many accounting practitioners and corporate executives have been studying the legal and ethical implications of the foreign bribery provision.[1] Their examination of this provision includes not only a definitional analysis of the questionable foreign payments but also corporate policy and compliance matters. As discussed in Appendix D on this book's website, the primary purpose of the bribery provision is to prohibit all U.S. companies, both private and public, foreign companies registered with the SEC, and directors, officers, stockholders, employees, and agents to bribe foreign government officials. Furthermore, the act states that any direct or indirect payment or offer intended to

---

[1]With respect to the antibribery section of the act, the Criminal Division of the Justice Department has adopted review procedures to assist management. In short, the Justice Department will review the proposed transactions only on written request, and it will issue a review letter to determine whether disclosure is required. This matter should be discussed with the executive audit partner, the chief financial officer, and legal counsel. For further reference, see the Department of Justice's "Foreign Corrupt Practices Act Option Procedure," *Code of Federal Regulations,* Sec. 28, Part 77.

promote business constitutes foreign bribery. Equally important, the act prohibits the use of mails or any means or instrumentalities of interstate commerce to make corrupt payments or authorization of the payments regarding "anything of value" to:

1. Any foreign official,
2. Any foreign political party or official thereof, or
3. Any person, while knowing or having reason to know that all or a portion of the payment will be offered to any of the preceding groups or any candidate for foreign political office.[2]

Moreover, it should be noted that certain payments called "facilitating" or "grease" payments are not covered under the act because such payments are ministerial or clerical. However, with respect to disclosure of such payments, the SEC indicates:

> These so-called facilitating payments have been deemed to be material where the payments to particular persons are large in amount or the aggregate amounts are large, or where corporate management has taken steps to conceal them through false entries in corporate books and records.[3]

Thus it is management's responsibility to identify and determine whether payments for customs documents or minor permits, which are essentially facilitating payments, should be disclosed.

As mentioned in Appendix E on this book's website, the Foreign Corrupt Practices Act was amended in August 1988. The amendments not only limited criminal penalties to individuals who knowingly failed to comply with the internal accounting control provision but also clarified the term *bribery* and increased penalties.[4] As Judith L. Roberts reports, the amendments' clarification and restriction of criminal penalties should substantially reduce the compliance burden and anticompetitive impact of the Foreign Corrupt Practices Act.[5] In addition, Marlene C. Piturro observed that since the enactment of the act, the FBI has uncovered "400 cases of misconduct and recouped $300 million in illegal payments."[6] See Appendix E on this book's website, for further discussion of the act.

Triton Energy Corporation, for example, disclosed the following in its annual report to stockholders:

---

[2]The act is contained in Title I of Public Law No. 95-213. (See Appendix E on this book's website.)

[3]Securities and Exchange Commission, "Report of the Securities and Exchange Commission on Questionable and Illegal Corporate Payments and Practices," submitted to the Senate Banking, Housing and Urban Affairs Committee, May 12, 1976, p. 27.

[4]The amendments are contained in The Omnibus Trade and Competitiveness Act, in Title V of Public Law No. 100-418, August 23, 1988. (See Appendix E on this book's website.)

[5]Judith L. Roberts, "Revision of the Foreign Corrupt Practices Act by the 1988 Omnibus Trade Bill: Will It Reduce the Compliance Burdens and Anticompetitive Impact?" *Brigham Young University Law Review,* No. 2 (1989), p. 506.

[6]Marlene C. Piturro, "Just Say . . . Maybe," *World Trade* 5, No. 5 (June 1992), p. 86.

Federal Securities Lawsuits—From May 27, 1992, through June 15, 1992, six separate suits were filed in federal district court in Dallas, Texas, by alleged shareholders against the Company and various present and former directors and officers of the Company. Plaintiffs in all of these cases seek to represent alleged classes of persons and/or entities who purchased the Company's securities. The plaintiffs in five of the six suits allege violations of the Securities Exchange Act of 1934 (the "1934 Act") and Rule 10b-5 promulgated thereunder, common law fraud and statutory fraud and negligent misrepresentation. Among other allegations, the plaintiffs base their claims upon alleged disclosure deficiencies in the Company's reports filed under the 1934 Act with respect to the financial condition of the Company, the Janacek litigation, the Company's Indonesian operations, including certain alleged bribes, violations of Indonesian law and falsified accounting records, and related arbitration and litigation matters. Plaintiffs in these cases seek, among other relief, to recover both actual and exemplary monetary damages in unspecified amounts. The parties to these five lawsuits have agreed, subject to the Court's approval, to consolidate these cases into a single lawsuit. The parties in a sixth lawsuit have not yet agreed to consolidation with the other federal securities lawsuits. Plaintiffs in the sixth case allege violations of Sections 10(b) and 20(a) of the 1934 Act and Rule 10b-5 promulgated thereunder. Among other allegations, the plaintiffs assert claims based upon an alleged conspiracy among the defendants in the case to manipulate the price of the Company's securities and alleged insider trading. Plaintiffs in this case also allege disclosure deficiencies, including failure to disclose material facts about the Company's financial condition. In addition, the plaintiffs in the sixth case have asserted certain claims against the Company's independent auditors. Plaintiffs in this case seek, among other relief, to recover actual and exemplary monetary damages in unspecified amounts and to force the individual defendants to disgorge alleged profits made in certain securities transactions.

These federal securities lawsuits are at a very preliminary stage. Due to the various uncertainties inherent in litigation, no assurance can be given as to the ultimate outcome of this litigation or any effect the litigation may ultimately have on the Company's consolidated financial condition. The Company intends to vigorously defend these lawsuits. Based on knowledge of the facts to date and consultation with its legal advisors, including in-house counsel to the Company, the Company currently believes that the Company's liabilities, if any, with respect to these lawsuits should not have a material adverse effect on the Company's consolidated financial condition.[7]

On May 20, 1993, *the Wall Street Journal* observed:

Triton Energy Corp. acknowledged that the Justice Department is investigating whether the company violated federal law and is most likely focusing on the Foreign Corrupt Practices Act related to Triton's Indonesian operations. The SEC is conducting a similar inquiry and the company is cooperating.[8]

---

[7]Triton Energy Corporation, *1992 Annual Report,* p. 34.
[8]"Triton Energy Corp.: Justice Department Probing for Possible Law Violations," *Wall Street Journal* (May 20, 1993), Sec. A, p. 7, col. 3. See also Andy Zipser, "Crude Grab? How a Tiny Producer Lost Its Indonesian Stake," *Barron's* 72, No. 21 (May 25, 1992), pp. 12–15, and "Triton to Settle SEC's Indonesia Bribery Charges," *Oil and Gas Journal* 95, No. 10 (March 10, 1997), p. 27.

More recently, the SEC continues to enforce the provisions of the Foreign Corrupt Practices Act, as shown in Exhibit 12.1.

Moreover, the Organization of Economic Cooperation and Development (OECD) reached an accord with its member countries to address the problem of bribery in international business. As Donald J. Johnston, secretary-general of the OECD, points out:

> The Convention on Combating Bribery of Foreign Public Officials in International Business Transactions is an instrument which will permit OECD and other countries to move in a co-ordinated manner to adopt national legislation to make it a crime to bribe foreign public officials. The Convention sets a high standard for national laws. It includes a broad, clear definition of bribery; it requires dissuasive penalties; it sets a strong standard for enforcement; and it provides for mutual legal assistance. The

Exhibit 12.1   Selected Cases and Alleged Violations—Foreign Corrupt Practices Act

Date Filed	Release No.	Nature of Alleged Violations
12/21/00	LR-16839	On December 21, 2000, the Commission instituted settled administrative proceedings against a registrant for books and records violations resulting from payments of $22 million to foreign officials by one of the company's wholly owned subsidiaries in Argentina. These improper payments were made in violation of the Foreign Corrupt Practices Act of 1997 (FCPA). The company also consented to the entry of a judgment in U.S. District Court ordering it to pay a $300,000 penalty.
1/15/02	LR-17310	The Commission filed a civil action against two former officers of registrant, alleging that they authorized over $500,000 in bribery payments to Haitian customs officials to reduce the company's import taxes by approximately $1.5 million.
8/1/02	LR-17651	The Commission instituted settled cease-and-desist proceedings against the registrant and obtained an order directing it to pay a $150,000 penalty based on its expansion into Venezuela and Nicaragua.

Source: Securities and Exchange Commission, 2001 and 2002 *Annual Report* (Washington, DC: U.S. Government Printing Office, 2001, 2002).

entry into force provisions are designed to encourage signatories to act quickly and in concert.[9]

The Convention contains 17 articles. Article 8 includes an accounting provision that states:

> 1. In order to combat bribery of foreign public officials effectively, each Party shall take such measures as may be necessary, within the framework of its laws and regulations regarding the maintenance of books and records, financial statement disclosures, and accounting and auditing standards, to prohibit the establishment of off-the-books accounts, the making of off-the-books or inadequately identified transactions, the recording of non-existent expenditures, the entry of liabilities with incorrect identification of their object, as well as the use of false documents, by companies subject to those laws and regulations, for the purpose of bribing foreign public officials or of hiding such bribery.

> 2. Each Party shall provide effective, proportionate and dissuasive civil, administrative or criminal penalties for such omissions and falsifications in respect of the books, records, accounts and financial statements of such companies.[10]

Obviously, the negotiated convention by the OECD with its member nations is a major step toward solving the problem of bribery in international business. Presumably the OECD's convention will be adopted by the individual governments of the member countries.

Summary Guidelines: Historical Perspective

To monitor questionable foreign payments effectively, the audit committee should review the corporate policy and other documentation that supports management's compliance with such policy. Concerning corporate policy, the American Assembly's recommendations regarding the standards of corporate conduct are useful in formulating policy guidelines:

> Although American corporations operating overseas should give due regard to the ethical judgments of other societies, each U.S. corporation can maintain only one set of universal principles that must not be compromised in foreign subsidiaries. Some U.S. practices of a less important nature may be adjusted to custom, practice, and law; such cases should be evaluated before the fact and stated publicly.

> American corporations should proscribe bribery and kickbacks everywhere. . . . American corporations operating in foreign lands should not be prohibited by American law from contributing to political parties when such contributions are legal under that country's laws, expected as part of good corporate responsibility, and are disclosed.[11]

---

[9]Organization of Economic Cooperation and Development, *Convention on Combating Bribery of Foreign Public Officials in International Business Transactions* (Paris: OECD, 1997), p. 3.
[10]Ibid., p. 8.
[11]The American Assembly, *The Ethics of Corporate Conduct,* Pamphlet 52 (New York: Columbia University, April 1977), pp. 6–7.

Such a corporate policy is essential as evidenced by a Conference Board study whereby the Board surveyed 35 firms on their approaches to the improper payments problem and found that "a handful" of companies did not have problems because of their existing corporate policies and practices.[12] Such companies "simply enjoin company employees from any illegal activity or conflicts of interest."[13] However, "many companies reported sharp divisions in their management ranks regarding the types of payments that should be enjoined."[14] Thus it is necessary to define clearly the proper and improper payments within the context of the Foreign Corrupt Practices Act to avoid any misunderstanding among the employees. Furthermore, the justification for such a corporate policy is supportable, as the *Journal of Accountancy* observed in a study of 109 large corporations, which disclosed:

> ... Dozens of corporations maintained more than $63.1 million in off-book bank accounts that were not part of the official corporate books. ... $14.2 million in sensitive payments was financial through overbilling, and $3.3 million was through ... phony invoices ... $2 million was funneled through closely guarded cost funds ... known to just a few top company executives. Inflated expense accounts generated almost $500,000 more—typically for personal political contributions by key management personnel.[15]

Moreover, "such payments are usually concealed by schemes that would be undetectable by auditors, no matter how thorough the audit."[16] Such findings and conclusions totally agree with the discussion in Chapter 11.

Consequently, as Walter E. Hanson, former chairman of Peat, Marwick, Mitchell & Co. (now KPMG Peat Marwick) points out, senior management should establish "clear and unequivocal statements of policy and codes of conduct as well as 'mechanisms,' such as the audit committee, to monitor corporate management's behavior."[17] In short, "self-policing by business is the only alternative ... to increasing government regulation and eventual government takeover."[18] See Appendix J on this book's website for further discussion on business conduct.

With respect to monitoring the improper foreign payments area, former partner Dennis R. Beresford and James D. Bond of Ernst and Whinney (now Ernst & Young) conclude:

> A key element in preventing and detecting illegal foreign bribes is proper supervision of employees in sensitive positions. A formal code of conduct that is appropriately communicated and monitored is a most important step in exercising this proper care.[19]

---

[12]James Greene, "Assuming Ethical Conduct Abroad," *Conference Board Information Bulletin,* No. 12 (November 1976), p. 1.

[13]Ibid., p. 3.

[14]Ibid.

[15]See Charles E. Simon and Company, "An Examination of Questionable Payments and Practices," *Journal of Accountancy* 145, No. 4 (May 1978), p. 7.

[16]Ibid.

[17]Walter E. Hanson, "A Blueprint for Ethical Conduct," Statement in Quotes, *Journal of Accountancy* 145, No. 6 (June 1978), p. 80.

[18]Ibid., p. 82.

[19]Dennis R. Beresford and James D. Bond, "The Foreign Corrupt Practices Act—Its Implications to Financial Management," *Financial Executive* 46, No. 8 (August 1978), p. 32.

Specifically, the Conference Board found that "a heavy majority" of the companies enforce compliance with their policies through a "periodic (usually annual) statement from their managers."[20] An example of such a statement follows:

> Representing my organization, I warrant that, to the best of the my knowledge, none of our employees is in violation of the company's policies and practices with regard to business ethics, offering or accepting gifts and gratuities, contributions, conflict of interest, safeguarding company assets, community and governmental participation, and sales agents, consultants and other professional services, and that these policies and practices are reviewed with key employees annually.[21]

Moreover, several public accounting firms request such statements.[22]

John C. Taylor, partner of Paul, Weiss, Rifkind, Wharton, and Garrison, suggests that the prevention of improper payments can be controlled through proper internal controls:

> The policy must require that every payment and every transaction with outside parties is reflected on the books of the corporation promptly, accurately and in the normal financial reporting channels.
>
> The policy must absolutely prohibit bribes, payments for illegal acts, and legally proscribe political contributions.
>
> The policy must be specific and intelligible to people in the field who will have to operate within its bounds.[23]

Hence the policy must define what are "proper and improper payments at a high corporate level directly responsible to the board.[24]

For example, the policy should include predetermined fixed levels of responsibility regarding the decisions in the sensitive payments area. Thus it is essential that the policy identify those executives in charge of the acceptable arrangements for proper payments as well as their reporting responsibility to the audit committee or the board of directors.[25]

With respect to enforcing such a policy, Taylor indicates that "normal auditing techniques are the best means of uncovering departures from the policy."[26] Such techniques should be coupled with these procedures:

> . . . review of all professional and consulting fees. . . . use of annual representation letters from all personnel in sensitive positions . . . constant review of signatories on all bank accounts world wide. . . . obtain letters from outside professionals, agents, and joint ventures certifying that they are not using corporate funds . . . for improper purposes.[27]

---

[20]Greene, "Assuring Ethical Conduct," p. 17.

[21]Ibid.

[22]Ibid.

[23]John C. Taylor III, "Preventing Improper Payments Through Internal Controls," *Conference Board Record* 13, No. 8 (August 1976), pp. 17–18.

[24]Ibid., p. 18.

[25]Ibid.

[26]Ibid.

[27]Ibid.

Hugh L. Marsh, former general manager of internal auditing for the Aluminum Company of America, points out the compliance of Alcoa with the Foreign Corrupt Practices Act. Such compliance includes:

Policy guidelines for business conduct

Representation letters of compliance with company policy

Conflict of interest surveys at the request of the board of directors

Monitoring and auditing procedures to ensure compliance with company policy and reports to the Audit Committee

Maintaining a corporate Security Department

Circulating a summary of the Foreign Corrupt Practices Act by the chief executive officer to all managers worldwide[28]

Moreover, Marsh continues:

. . . I urge you to sit down with your chief financial officer and legal counsel and obtain a thorough understanding of the implications of this law. I urge you to involve these people as well as your external auditors in assessing the risk within your own business and developing an inventory of control practices. . . . I urge that you consider development of a policy statement for standards of conduct of your business and develop monitoring procedures that are appropriate.[29]

Additional Summary Guidelines

As James S. Gerson et al. point out:

The committee should be aware that the Foreign Corrupt Practices Act (FCPA) requires public companies to keep reasonably detailed records of all transactions and to maintain internal accounting controls that provide reasonable assurance that those transactions are properly authorized and recorded.[30]

With respect to boards of directors and their compliance with applicable laws and regulations, the Business Roundtable states:

Law compliance is a fundamental requirement of both private and corporate persons. Boards of directors participate in a number of different ways. The audit committee of the board of directors, actions of other board committees, the approval and review policies of the board, review by the corporate general counsel, and, where necessary, by outside counsel retained by the general counsel or appointed by the board are all procedures that can be used in fulfilling this function.

---

[28]Hugh L. Marsh, "The Foreign Corrupt Practices Act: A Corporate Plan for Compliance," *Internal Auditor* 36, No. 2 (April 1979), pp. 73–74.

[29]Ibid., p. 76.

[30]James S. Gerson, J. Robert Mooney, Donald F. Moran, and Robert K. Waters, "Oversight of the Financial Reporting Process—Part I," *CPA Journal* 59, No. 7 (July 1989), p. 28.

Legislation and regulation affecting the corporation change frequently. The general counsel of the corporation should regularly brief the board on significant changes in applicable laws, including legal developments affecting the corporation or their duties as directors.[31]

Finally, in an article dealing with compliance with the amended act, Sandra G. Gustavson and Jere W. Morehead suggest the following to help coordinate a company's compliance efforts and loss control program:

- Develop clear, specific policy statements
- Establish and maintain a written code of conduct
- Implement formal approval procedures for payments[32]

The External Auditor's Responsibility

As noted in Chapter 11, the external audit examination cannot guarantee that irregularities or illegal acts are nonexistent. According to the Auditing Standards Board:

> Certain illegal acts have a direct and material effect on the determination of financial statement amounts. Other illegal acts, such as those described,[33] may, in particular circumstances, be regarded as having material but indirect effects on financial statements. The auditor's responsibility with respect to detecting, considering the financial statements effects of, and reporting these other illegal acts is described in this Statement. These other illegal acts are hereinafter referred to simply as *illegal acts*. The auditor should be aware of the possibility that such illegal acts may have occurred. If specific information comes to the auditor's attention that provides evidence concerning the existence of possible illegal acts that could have a material indirect effect on the financial statements, the auditor should apply audit procedures, specifically directed to ascertaining whether an illegal act has occurred. However, because of the characteristics of illegal acts as explained above, an audit made in accordance with generally accepted auditing standards provides no assurance that illegal acts will be detected or that any contingent liabilities that may result will be disclosed.[34]

As a case in point, "When something has come to a director's attention in the area of commercial bribery, what can the auditors do to help directors find out if there is a problem: for example, in a department where there may be a suspicion of a kickback?"[35] According to David L. James, former partner of Arthur Young and Co. (now Ernst & Young), the board member should discuss this matter with "a member of the audit committee, preferably the chairman." Furthermore, James points out:

---

[31]The Business Roundtable, *Corporate Governance and American Competitiveness* (New York: The Business Roundtable, 1990), p. 10.

[32]Sandra G. Gustavson and Jere W. Morehead, "Complying with the Amended Foreign Corrupt Practices Act," *Risk Management* 37, No. 4 (April 1990), p. 5.

[33]See Chapter 11 for additional emphasis.

[34]*Statement on Auditing Standards, No. 54,* "Illegal Acts by Clients" (New York: AICPA, 1988), par. 7.

[35]Gerald F. Boltz, Grover R. Heyler, David L. James, and Francis M. Wheat, "Corporate Directors' Responsibilities," *Financial Executive* 45, No. 1 (January 1977), p. 21.

When we get into the area of irregularities, e.g., fraud, questionable conduct, and the like, we sit down with the audit committee, indicate that this question has been raised, glean as much information from the director as possible, and then figure out how to attack the particular problem.[36]

While the external auditors can assist the audit committee in the sensitive payments area, it is important to recognize that:

[w]ith respect to high level executive conflicts of interest, the Board of Directors has the obligation, in selecting such executives, to make exhaustive background checks of prospective candidates such as are now being followed in filling high U.S. Government posts.[37]

Such investigations of the candidates will not only help curtail the problem of improper payments and conflicts of interest but also will strengthen the board's image in the business community. As a result, the major objective is to review the corporate policy and internal monitoring procedures, as discussed in this chapter and the preceding chapter, with the external auditors.

In short, as Grover R. Heyler, partner of Latham and Watkins, concludes, ". . . directors need to go beyond what the auditors might be able to do."[38] In addition to the annual questionnaires regarding sensitive areas, Heyler suggests that:

- A conflict of interest committee can be established.
- The board can require reports on trading in the company's stock.
- Controls on the disclosure of inside information and press releases can be initiated.
- Provisions can be made for some independent review of relationships between the company and firms affiliated with insiders.[39]

CORPORATE PERQUISITES

Meaning of Corporate Perquisites

During the latter part of the 1970s, the SEC scrutinized the area of perquisites, or "perks," as evidenced by several SEC releases. For example, SEC Release No. 33-5758, issued in November 1976, stated:

. . . it has been suggested that disclosure should be required of the numerous emerging forms of indirect compensation or "perquisites" now given to management personnel.

Furthermore, in April 1977 the SEC asked, in Securities Exchange Act Release No. 13482, "Should the Commission amend its proxy rules . . . to provide for

---

[36]Ibid.
[37]Herbert Robinson and J. Karl Fishbach, "Commercial Bribery—The Corporation as Victim," *Financial Executive* 47, No. 4 (April 1979), p. 16.
[38]Boltz, Heyler, James, and Wheat, "Corporate Directors' Responsibilities," p. 20.
[39]Ibid.

more detailed or comprehensive disclosure of management remuneration?" Finally, in August 1977, the SEC issued Interpretative Release No. 33-5856, "Disclosure of Management Remuneration," whereby it pointed out that the securities acts require not only the disclosure of direct remuneration paid to directors and officers but also personal benefits ". . . sometimes referred to as 'perquisites.' " The Commission believed that certain personal benefits received by management from the corporation should be reported as remuneration:

> Among the benefits received by management which the Commission believes should be reported as remuneration are payments made by registrants for the following purposes: (1) home repairs and improvements; (2) housing and other living expenses (including domestic service) provided at principal and/or vacation residences of management personnel; (3) the personal use of company property such as automobiles, planes, yachts, apartments, hunting lodges, or company vacation houses; (4) personal travel expenses; (5) personal entertainment and related expenses; and (6) legal, accounting, and other professional fees for matters unrelated to the business of the registrant. Other personal benefits which may be forms of remuneration are the following: the ability of management to obtain benefits from third parties, because the corporation compensates, directly or indirectly, the bank or supplier for providing the loan or services to management; and the use of the corporate staff for personal purposes.

> Certain incidental personal benefits which are directly related to job performance may be omitted from aggregate reported remuneration provided they are authorized and properly accounted for by the company. Parking places, meals at company facilities, and office space and furnishings at company-maintained offices are a few examples of personal benefits directly related to job performance.

> In addition, certain incidental benefits received by management which are ordinary and necessary to the conduct of company business may not be forms of remuneration. These job-related benefits are benefits which are available to management employees generally, which do not relieve the individual of expenditures normally considered to be of a personal nature and which are extended to management solely for the purposes of attracting and maintaining qualified personnel, facilitating their conduct of company business, or improving their efficiency in job performance. While itemized expense accounts may be considered job-related benefits whose value would be excluded from the aggregate remuneration reported, some may be forms of remuneration if they are excessive in amount or conferred too frequently. In any case, management is usually in the best position to determine whether a certain benefit should be viewed as a form of remuneration based on the facts and circumstances involved in each situation.

> The value of all forms of remuneration should be included within the appropriate item(s) of disclosure. Nonmonetary forms of remuneration must be valued as accurately as possible. The appropriate valuation may be based upon appraisals, the value of the benefit to the recipient, the valuation assigned for tax purposes, or some other appropriate standard.

Although the SEC release attempted to resolve the disclosure problem of perquisites, many accounting practitioners and corporate executives raised questions regarding the disclosure of certain items. In an attempt to resolve the issues, the SEC issued a second Interpretive Release, No. 33-5904, which contained questions and interpretative responses of the Commission's Division of Corporation Finance. In particular, the questions related to (a) the use of company property; (b) membership in clubs and professional associations; (c) medical, insurance, and other reimbursement plans; (d) payments for living and related expenses; (e) use of corporate staff; (f) benefits from third parties; (g) company products; and (h) business expenses. Specifically, the Commission asserted[40]:

> Corporations make a great variety of expenditures which relate to management, many of which result in benefits to executives. Whether these constitute remuneration usually depends upon the facts and circumstances involved in each situation. In general, expenditures which simply assist an executive in doing his job effectively or which reimburse him for expenses incurred in the performance of his functions are not remuneration, while expenditures made for his personal benefit or for purposes unrelated to the business of the company would constitute remuneration. In some instances, expenditures may serve both purposes, and if neither is predominant, allocation to the extent reasonably feasible may be called for.

> In determining whether the value of specific benefits should be included in aggregate remuneration, registrants should keep in mind that full disclosure of the remuneration received by officers and directors is important to informed voting and investment decisions. In particular, remuneration information is necessary for an informed assessment of management and is significant in maintaining public confidence in the corporate system. Of course, accurate and sufficiently detailed books and records are prerequisites to the appropriate disclosure of remuneration information.[41]

Of particular importance to the audit committee is SEC Release No. 33-6003, issued in December 1978 to amend Regulation S-K. This release affects not only item 4 of the S-K but also proxy materials and other filing forms. For example, this release increases all remuneration paid to or accrued by the corporation's five highest-paid officers or directors whose total remuneration exceeds $50,000 annually.[42]

As mentioned in Chapter 3, in October 1992 the SEC adopted amendments to the executive officer and director compensation disclosure requirements. With respect to perquisites, Release Nos. 33-6962, 34-31327, and 1C-19032 pertaining to Regulation S-K set forth:

> *Perquisites.* Several commenters suggested that, to reflect inflation, the perquisites and other personal benefits reporting threshold should be raised from the lesser of $25,000 or 10% of reported salary and bonus, and that the requirement to itemize each perquisite or benefit in a footnote be eliminated. Given the effect of inflation

---

[40]In addition to the SEC releases cited, the reader should review Release No. 33-5950, "Proposed Amendments to Disclosure Forms Regulations" (July 1978) with the independent auditors.

[41]Although the SEC has stated that perquisites of less than $10,000 per individual may be excluded in the aggregate renumeration, such exclusion should be disclosed in the registrant's transmittal letter.

[42]As of October 21, 1992, this amount was increased to $100,000, as discussed in Chapter 3. For further reference, see Kathleen T. McGahran, "SEC Disclosure Regulation and Management Perquisites," *The Accounting Review* 63, No. 1 (January 1988), pp. 23–41; and Coopers & Lybrand, "Executive Perquisites Study Release: An Overview of the Findings," *Executive Briefing* (May 1992), pp. 1–3.

since the last revision of Item 402 in 1983, which has been taken into account in the Commission's upward adjustment of the dollar benchmark for designating the named executives, the Commission similarly has increased the perks/personal benefits threshold in the final rule to call for disclosure only when the aggregate value of these items exceeds the lesser of either $50,000 or 10% of total salary and bonus disclosed in the Summary Compensation Table.

As proposed, the registrant would have been required to identify each perquisite included in the amount reported in a footnote to the Other Annual Compensation column. The Item has been revised to require footnote or textual narrative disclosure of the nature and value of any particular perquisite or benefit only for those perks valued at more than 25% of the sum of all perquisites reported as Other Annual Compensation for that executive.[43]

In view of these new disclosure requirements in the company's annual proxy statement, the audit committee should ascertain that the compensation committee and management are complying with the compensation and perquisite disclosure requirement. Such information should be reviewed by general counsel and the independent auditors.

Summary Guidelines

In monitoring corporate perquisites, the audit committee should give consideration to these three matters.

1. All perquisites should be formally approved by the board of directors as recommended by the compensation or audit committee. Such approval should be duly noted in the minutes of the board's meetings and the committee's meetings.
2. The perquisites should be clearly defined in view of the SEC releases regarding the nature of such payments or reimbursements. As discussed in this chapter, such SEC releases provide guidance to the auditors and management in connection with the entity's compliance with the securities laws. Such perks should not be excessive or unusual in light of the rulings.
3. The committee should request a report from the internal auditors concerning the status of the entity's perquisites.[44] In reviewing the audit report, the committee should obtain assurance in writing that the internal accounting and administrative controls (discussed in Chapter 8) are effective. Also, the committee

---

[43]Securities and Exchange Commission, "Executive Compensation Disclosure," *Federal Register* 57, No. 204 (October 21, 1992), p. 48131.

[44]It may be advisable to retain the outside auditors to review the travel and entertainment expenses for several of the senior executives each year. It is imperative that the company have an appropriate approval system of expense accounts. In its 1987 report, the National Commission on Fraudulent Financial Reporting recommended that "the committee should review in-house policies and procedures for regular review of officers' expenses and perquisites, including any use of corporate assets, inquire as to the results of the review, and, if appropriate, review a summarization of the expenses and perquisites of the period under review" (Washington, DC: National Commission on Fraudulent Financial Reporting, 1987), p. 180.

should inquire about management's method of valuation of personal benefits and related tax consequences. Thus it is desirable to discuss the tax implications with the corporate tax specialist or outside tax advisor in order to coordinate the income tax and SEC reporting requirements.

CORPORATE CONTRIBUTIONS

In addition to the usual practice of monitoring certain business practices, such as compliance with the Foreign Corrupt Practices Act in regard to perquisites and travel and entertainment, audit committees also may be requested by the board of directors to review other business practices, such as corporate contributions, to ensure compliance with corporate policy.

Nature of Corporate Contributions

According to R. A. Schwartz, corporate contributions or philanthropy may be defined as "a philanthropic transfer of wealth to be a one way flow of resources from a donor to a donee, a flow voluntarily generated by the donor though based on no expectation that a return flow, or economic quid pro quo, will reward the act."[45] Furthermore, as reported by C. Lowell Harriss:

> The interests and kinds of involvement differ enormously from firm to firm, as do the dollar outlays in corporate giving. Deductions on corporate tax returns of contributions have been rising, from $252 million in 1950 to $1,350 million in 1976. But such contributions represent less than 1 percent of profits and less than 5 percent of the community's total philanthropy.[46]

Corporate contributions also consist of nonmonetary giving, which includes:

- Employees' personal time in nonprofit activities
- Company property, such as the firm's auditorium
- Loans at concessionary rates
- Job training for the disadvantaged and disabled.[47]

As Harriss observes in a Conference Board study by James F. Harris and Anne Klepper, "If a price tag were put on all such nonmonetary or indirect aid in 1974, the estimate of corporate contributions would double (to well over $2 billion)."[48]

---

[45]R. A. Schwartz, *Corporate Philanthropic Contributions,* Pamphlet 72 (New York: New York University, 1968), p. 480.
[46]C. Lowell Harriss, "Corporate Giving: Rationale and Issues," *Two Essays on Corporate Philanthropy and Economic Education* (Los Angeles: International Institute for Economic Research, October 1978), p. 2.
[47]Ibid., p. 3.
[48]See James F. Harris and Anne Klepper, "Corporate Philanthropic Public Service Activities" (New York: The Conference Board, 1976).

Business Week observed that "total corporate giving has remained flat at $6.1 billion since 1990." Typically, "corporation donations are usually 1% to 2% of pretax domestic income." For example, more companies have developed a strategic plan and target charities more directly related to their operations.[49]

Concerning the justification of corporate contributions, Schwartz notes that:

• Gifts that will enhance the public image of a corporation can advantageously shift the demand curve for corporation's product.

• The compatibility of corporate giving with monetary profit maximization is further suggested by the benefits a firm can derive from "farming out" research programs to educational institutions, while reaping both the gains of subsequent technological advances and the beneficial publicity with the gift.[50]

Although the Foreign Corrupt Practices Act covers illegal contributions abroad, it is also illegal to make political contribution through the use of corporate funds in U.S. federal elections. As noted by Roderick M. Hills, former chairman of the SEC: "The 'chance' of 'Watergate' gave us the opportunity for better government, and began a series of corporate investigations that already have improved our vision and raised corporate behavioral standards."[51] Thus it is necessary "to create an internal reporting system that will place these rather difficult payment questions squarely before the independent directors, outside auditors, and outside counsel."[52]

Summary Guidelines

Ferdinand K. Levy and Gloria M. Shatto summarize four evaluative principles regarding corporate contributions programs:

1. If the gift is not legal or if it is questionable, don't make it.
2. The contribution should represent the corporation and should not be a personal gift or whim of one executive.
3. Contributions "in kind" or well specified are generally preferable to unrestricted gifts.
4. Each contribution should stand alone and be capable of being justified on the basis of some type of cost-benefit analysis.[53]

---

[49]Lois Therrien, "Corporate Generosity Is Greatly Depreciated," *Business Week* (November 2, 1992), pp. 118–120.

[50]Schwartz, *Corporate Philanthropic Contributions,* p. 480. For further reference, see Harry L. Freeman, "Corporate Strategic Philanthropy," *Vital Speeches* 58, No. 8 (February 1, 1992), pp. 246–250; Betty S. Coffee and Jia Wang, "Board Composition and Corporate Philanthropy," *Journal of Business Ethics* 11, No. 10 (October 1992), pp. 771–778.

[51]Roderick M. Hills, "Views on How Corporations Should Behave," *Financial Executive* 44, No. 11 (November 1976), p. 34.

[52]Ibid., p. 32.

[53]Ferdinand K. Levy and Gloria M. Shatto, "A Common Sense Approach to Corporate Corporations," *Financial Executive* 46, No. 8 (September 1978), p. 37.

Moreover, "the entire corporate giving program . . . must be open to the public and should be capable of both an internal and external audit."[54] Thus it is evident that the audit committee should review the corporation's policy concerning its contributions and adhere to the monitoring practices discussed earlier in this chapter.

James A. Joseph notes that foundations need to:

- Clarify what is private and what is public;
- Reaffirm the moral authority of the traditional notion of public trust;
- Examine whether the enthusiasm with which foundations portray nonprofit voluntary activities as a distinctive sector may contribute to the tendency of critics and supporters to overlook the diversity within that sector;
- Demonstrate to the public that responsible governance and efficient management are all part of the public trust; and
- Reflect, retain, and reaffirm principles and practices that are fundamental to effectiveness in philanthropy.[55]

The following financial statement disclosure regarding this subject is presented to inform the reader of management's representations to the stockholders.

> *Schering-Plough*—Through corporate giving, the Schering-Plough Foundation and employee voluntarism—contributed much in 1992 to the communities where it operates; to health care, educational and arts organizations; and to those in need. The Foundation made grants totalling $2.8 million in 1992, complementing corporate contributions of $1.9 million.[56]

Recent business and audit failures of major corporations highlight the need for the audit committee to monitor and enforce a conflicts-of-interest policy statement to help ensure the integrity of the company as well as to avoid civil or criminal penalties. To assist the audit committee with the review and discussion activity, Exhibit 12.2 contains the overall content of a conflicts-of-interest program. Of course, this program may be modified and therefore is not all-inclusive.

Additionally, Exhibit 12.3 contains a discussion of possible warning signals and "red flags" related to the Enron debacle.

In summary, audit committees have increasingly assumed additional responsibilities such as those discussed in this chapter. Perhaps the most challenging are directing and monitoring special investigations related to management fraud and fraudulent financial reporting, as discussed in Chapters 4 and 11. Based on the ever-increasing duties and responsibilities of the audit committee, the role of monitoring business practices will continue to expand into additional areas in the future.

---

[54]Ibid., p. 38.

[55]James A. Joseph, "Reaffirming Our Public Accountability," *Foundation News* 33, No. 4 (July/August 1992), pp. 44–45.

[56]Schering-Plough, *1992 Annual Report,* p. 4

Exhibit 12.2 Conflicts-of-Interest Program[a]

Description	Presentation (Estimated)
Review and discuss[a] with the business ethics and compliance officer such matters as:	One day, presentation, and group discussion

- Company's conflicts-of-interest policies and prevention and detection procedures in view of the Sarbanes-Oxley Act (Sections 206, 303, 304, 305, 306, 307, 402, 403, 406, 501, 802, 806), SEC rules, and SROs listing standards

- Results of special investigations into conflicts-of-interest situations, corrective action taken, SEC disclosure (Form 8-K), and press releases, if appropriate

- Audit findings of directors, officers, and employees compliance with the company's code of conduct, including the code of ethics for senior financial officers and internal auditors

- Recommended improvements in management controls to mitigate non-compliance with the above activities and related party transactions, including the issuance of both internal or external audit reports as well as the board of directors policy statement

- Changes in the conflicts-of-interest policies and practices in view of company acquisitions, divestitures, and joint ventures

- Compliance with loan covenants and funding of pension plans

- Certification of periodic compliance with the conflicts-of-interest policy statements by appropriate employees
- Provisions for continuous surveillance and enforcement

---

[a]In the absence of a business ethnics and compliance officer, the chief audit executive may present and discuss the program with the audit committee.

Exhibit 12.3   Lessons from the Enron Effect

- The audit committee should be informed about the financial and operational aspects of the company and, therefore, should receive sufficient and timely information. If the audit committee meeting is scheduled to coincide with the regular full board meetings, then the committee must receive written information well in advance of the meetings.

- To be vigilant, the audit committee should ask probing questions about the propriety of the company's financial reporting process and the quality of its internal controls. This task requires the committee to keep abreast of financial reporting developments affecting the company.

- To be an effective independent overseer, the audit committee must be positioned between senior management and the external auditors. This organizational structure allows the audit committee to question management's judgments about financial reporting matters and to suggest improvements in the internal control systems. The committee's charter defines its mission, duties, and responsibilities; plans its annual agenda; and documents its findings and conclusions.

- Failure on the part of the audit committee to review and evaluate the financial statements and related accounting policies in accordance with generally accepted accounting principles is clearly malfeasance.

- One of the conclusions from the Report of the Special Investigation Committee of the Board of directors of Enron Corporation (Powers Report) was:

  "The Board, and in particular the Audit and Compliance Committee, has the duty of ultimate oversight over the Company's financial reporting. While the primary responsibility for financial reporting abuses discussed in the Report lies with management, the participating members of the Committee believe those abuses could and should have been prevented or detected at an earlier time had the Board been more aggressive and vigilant" (p. 24).

  For example, red flags that fraudulent financial reporting may be occurring (and the appropriate action item) include:

  - Overoptimistic news release with respect to earnings. **Action item:** Analyze annual and interim earnings trends to avoid increased opportunities for managing earnings

  - Industry accounting practices in contrast to unusual revenue recognition policies to increase earnings. **Action item:** Access significant accounting policies that are industry-specific from a finncial reporting data base and review this information with both internal and external auditors.

  - Rapid growth of the organization. **Action item:** Investigate reasons for rapid expansion in relationship to both top-line and bottom-line double digit annual growth rates as well as significant increases in year-to-year changes relative to past performance.

  - Significant changes in accounting practices and estimates by management with an excessive interest in earnings. **Action item:** Compare these changes with industry norms and determine the reason for them.

  - Conflict-of-interest and significant contracts that affect financial statements. Frequent related-party transactions and failure to enforce the corporate code of conduct. **Action item:** Determine management's intent to disclose such contracts as well as how the firm addresses conflict-of-interest situations and monitors compliance with the code. If necessary, conduct or authorize a special investigation and retain independent councel and other professionals.

- Unexplained significant fluctuations in account balances. **Action item:** Focus on analytical review procedures and discuss the findings with both internal and external auditors.

- Breakdowns in the system of internal control. **Action item:** Obtain assurance from both the internal and external auditors that management has evaluated the weaknesses and recommendations in the management letter and that corrective action has been taken.

- Scope restrictions placed by management on both the internal and external auditors. **Action item:** Give assurance to the auditors that they have unrestricted and free access to the audit committee.

Audit committee members should be highly attuned to the potential of fraudulent financial reporting. Failure on the part of the audit committee to question management's representations may be the basis for audit committee malfeasance, since the audit committee and the board may be held liable for failure to know what they were responsible for recognizing.

Source: This discussion is adapted from an article by Louis Braiotta, Jr., "Lessons from the Enron Effect," at *www.smartpros.com* (March 2002).

SOURCES AND SUGGESTED READINGS

The American Assembly, *The Ethics of Corporate Conduct*. Pamphlet 52 (New York: Columbia University, April 1977), pp. 1–11.

Beresford, Dennis R., and James D. Bond, "Foreign Corrupt Practices Act—Its Implications to Financial Management." *Financial Executive* 46, No. 8 (August 1978), pp. 26–32.

Braiotta, Louis, Jr., "Lessons from the Enron Effect." March 2002, *www.smartpros.com.*

Boltz, Gerald E., Grover R. Heyler, David L. James, and Francis M. Wheat, "Corporate Directors' Responsibilities." *Financial Executive* 45, No. 1 (January 1977), pp. 12–21.

The Business Roundtable, *Corporate Governance and American Competitiveness* (New York: The Business Roundtable, 1990).

Charles E. Simon and Company, "An Examination of Questionable Payments and Practices." *Journal of Accountancy* 145, No.4 (May 1978), p.7.

Coffee, Betty S., and Jia Wang, "Board Composition and Corporate Philanthropy." *Journal of Business Ethics* 11, No. 10 (October 1992), pp. 771–778.

Coopers & Lybrand, "Executive Perquisites Study Release: An Overview of the Findings." *Executive Briefing* (May 1992).

Department of Justice, "Foreign Corrupt Practices Act Option Procedure." *Code of Federal Regulations,* Sec. 28, Part 77, 1978.

Foreign Corrupt Practices Act, Title I of Public Law No. 95-213, December 19, 1977.

Freeman, Harry L., "Corporate Strategic Philanthropy." *Vital Speeches* 58, No. 8 (February 1, 1992), pp. 246–250.

Gerson, James S., J. Robert Mooney, Donald F. Moran, and Robert K. Waters, "Oversight of the Financial Reporting Process—Part I." *CPA Journal* 59, No. 7 (July 1989), pp. 22–28.

Greene, James, "Assuring Ethical Conduct Abroad." *The Conference Board Information Bulletin No. 2* (November 1976), pp. 1–18.

Gustavson, Sandra G., and Jere W. Morehead. "Complying with the Amended Foreign Corrupt Practices Act." *Risk Management* 37, No. 4 (April 1990), pp. 76–82.

Hanson, Walter E., "A Blueprint for Ethical Conduct." Statement in "Quotes," *Journal of Accountancy* 145, No. 6 (June 1978), pp. 80–84.

Harris, James F., and Anne Klepper, *Corporate Philanthropic Public Service Activities* (New York: The Conference Board, 1976).

Harriss, C. Lowell, "Corporate Giving: Rationale and Issues." *Two Essays on Corporate Philanthropy and Economic Education* (Los Angeles, Calif.: International Institute for Economic Research, October 1978), pp. 1–13.

Hills, Roderick M., "Views on How Corporations Should Behave." *Financial Executive* 44, No. 11 (November 1976), pp. 32–34.

Joseph, James A., "Reaffirming Our Public Accountability." *Foundation News* 33, No. 4 (July/August 1992), pp. 44–45.

Levy, Ferdinand K., and Gloria M. Shatto, "A Common Sense Approach to Corporate Contributions." *Financial Executive* 46, No. 9 (September 1978), pp. 36–40.

Marsh, Hugh L., "The Foreign Corrupt Practices Act: A Corporate Plan for Compliance." *Internal Auditor* 36, No. 2 (April 1979), pp. 72–76.

McGrahan, Kathleen T., "SEC Disclosure Regulation and Management Perquisites." *Accounting Review* 63, No. 1 (January 1988), pp. 23–41.

National Commission on Fraudulent Financial Reporting, *Report of the National Commission on Fraudulent Financial Reporting* (Washington, DC: NCFFR, 1987).

The Omnibus Trade and Competitiveness Act, Title V of Public Law No. 100-418. August 23, 1988.

Organization of Economic Cooperation and Development, *Convention on Combating Bribery of Foreign Public Officials in International Business Transactions* (Paris: OECD, 1997).

Piturro, Marlene C., "Just Say . . . Maybe," *World Trade* 5, No. 5 (June 1992), pp. 86–91.

Roberts, Judith L., "Revision of the Foreign Corrupt Practices Act by the 1988 Omnibus Trade Bill: Will It Reduce the Compliance Burdens and Anticompetitive Impact?" *Brigham Young University Law Review,* No. 2 (1989), pp. 491–506.

Robinson, Herbert, and J. Karl Fishbach, "Commercial Bribery—The Corporation as Victim." *Financial Executive* 47, No. 4 (April 1979), pp. 16–19 and 50–51.

Schering-Plough, *1992 Annual Report.*

Schwartz, R. A. *Corporate Philanthropic Contributions.* Pamphlet 72 (New York: New York University, June 1968), pp. 479–497.

Securities and Exchange Commission, "Report of the Securities and Exchange Commission on Questionable and Illegal Corporate Payments and Practices" (Washington, DC: SEC, May 12, 1976).

Securities and Exchange Commission, "Executive Compensation Disclosure." *Federal Register* 57, No. 204 (October 21, 1992), pp. 48126–48159.

Securities and Exchange Commission, *Annual Reports* (Washington, DC: U.S. Government Printing Office, 2001, 2002).

Statement on Auditing Standards, No. 54, "Illegal Acts by Clients" (New York: AICPA, 1988).

Taylor, John C. III, "Preventing Improper Payments Through Internal Controls." *The Conference Board Record* 13, No. 8 (August 1976), pp. 17–19.

Therrien, Lois, "Corporate Generosity Is Greatly Depreciated." *Business Week* (November 2, 1992), pp. 118–120.

Triton Energy Corporation, *1992 Annual Report.*

"Triton Energy Corp.: Justice Department Probing for Possible Law Violations" *Wall Street Journal,* (May 20, 1993), sec. A, p. 7, col. 3.

Zipser, Andy, "Crude Grab? How a Tiny Producer Lost Its Indonesian Stake." *Barron's* 72, No. 21 (May 25, 1992), pp. 12–15.

Part Four

The Reporting Function and the Audit Committee

Chapter 13

Independent Auditors' Reports

The independent auditors' report is the expression of their professional opinion on the financial statements. As discussed in Chapter 2, although the financial statements are management's responsibility, the independent auditors have a responsibility to attest to the fairness of management's representations in the statements through their audit report.

The purpose of this chapter is to familiarize the audit committee with the different types of audit opinions as well as other audit reports regarding matters such as interim financial information and special reports.[1] An understanding of the audit opinions and other audit reports provides an important opportunity for each audit committee member to obtain additional insight into the nature and importance of the independent auditors' reporting responsibility.

THE AUDITORS' REPORTS ON AUDITED FINANCIAL STATEMENTS

As discussed in Chapters 2 and 5, the independent auditors or accountants report their objective opinion on the fairness of the representations in the financial statements. Such an expression of their opinion is required in accordance with generally accepted auditing standards as promulgated by the Auditing Standards Board (previously Auditing Standards Executive Committee of the AICPA). Moreover, it was indicated that corporate management has full responsibility for the fairness of the representations in the financial statements. Such a distinction concerning the responsibility for the financial statements is particularly important because if the independent auditors do not concur with the fairness of management's representations, then they are required to inform the users of the financial statements of their exceptions. In particular, the fourth auditing standard of reporting is restated for additional emphasis.

---

[1]Attestation engagements with respect to other information, such as reports on internal control and compliance with specified laws and regulations, were discussed in Chapter 5.

The Standard Auditors' Report (Unqualified Opinion)

> The report shall either contain an expression of opinion regarding the financial state-
> ments, taken as a whole,[2] or an assertion to the effect that an opinion cannot be ex-
> pressed. When an overall opinion cannot be expressed, the reasons therefor should
> be stated. In all cases where an auditor's name is associated with financial state-
> ments, the report should contain a clear-cut indication of the character of the audi-
> tor's work, if any, and the degree of responsibility the auditor is taking.[3]

A particular report, the Standard Auditors' Report (Unqualified Opinion), is used
by the auditors when they have no exceptions regarding management's representations in the financial statements. In practice, such a report is often described as a
"clean opinion." An example of this report was illustrated and discussed in Chapter 2. Explicit in the auditors' unqualified report is that their examination has been
performed within the general auditing guidelines or standards as set forth by the
AICPA. Moreover, their unqualified opinion informs the users of the financial statements that such statements have been prepared by management in conformity with generally accepted accounting principles applied on a consistent basis.
Such an unqualified opinion is based not only on their examination of the financial
statements but also on tests of the accounting records that underlie such statements.

While the auditors' report is not explicit with respect to the system of internal
control, it implies that the entity's internal control structure is adequate. However,
since the inception of the Foreign Corrupt Practices Act, this audit report has been
reevaluated in terms of its content because it is argued that the auditors should
make their report explicit with respect to management's adherence to the accounting provision in the act. For example, in April 1979, the SEC in its Release
No. 34-15772 announced its proposed rules for requiring a statement of management on internal accounting control in the annual reports of all publicly held corporations. Such a statement should disclose management's compliance with the
internal accounting control provision of the Foreign Corrupt Practices Act as well
as uncorrected material weaknesses in the controls as reported by the independent
auditors. Furthermore, the Commission's proposal requires the independent auditors to modify their audit report to disclose management's inaction in disclosing or
correcting such material weaknesses. While this proposal is applicable to fiscal
years that end between December 16, 1979, and December 15, 1980, the Commission also proposes that the auditors express an opinion on management's report
on the system of internal accounting control for fiscal years that end after December 15, 1980.[4]

---

[2]According to the Auditing Standards Board, the phrase "taken as a whole" with respect to the financial statements applies to the statements of both the current period and one or more prior periods presented on a comparative basis. See *Statement on Auditing Standards No. 58* "Reports on Audited
Financial Statements" (New York: AICPA, 1988), par. 04.

[3]The reader may wish to review Chapter 5 at this point.

[4]In May 1980, the SEC decided to withdraw this proposed rule; however, it will continue to monitor
private sector initiatives and reconsider the need for new rules over the next three years.

Independent Auditor's Reports

As discussed in Chapter 8, Section 302 of the Sarbanes-Oxley Act of 2002 requires specific representation on the system of internal control. (See Section 302(a)(4) regarding the signing by the officers.)

Additionally, Section 404 of the Sarbanes-Oxley Act requires management to report annually on its assessment of the effectiveness of internal controls. The act also requires the company to file a report from its independent auditors regarding the expression of an opinion as to whether management's assessment is fairly stated. Thus it is evident that the users of the financial statements rely on the auditors' report to determine whether the statements are fairly presented. As a result, the auditors' report must be clear and concise with respect to the findings and results of the audit examination. To achieve this objective, the Auditing Standards Board has developed audit reports or opinions, which are summarized here:

- *Unqualified opinion.* An unqualified opinion states that the financial statements present fairly, in all material respects, the financial position, results of operations, and cash flows of the entity in conformity with generally accepted accounting principles. This is the opinion expressed in the standard report.
- *Explanatory language added to the auditor's standard report.* Certain circumstances, while not affecting the auditor's unqualified opinion on the financial statements, may require that the auditor add an explanatory paragraph (or other explanatory language) to his report.
- *Qualified opinion.* A qualified opinion states that, except for the effects of the matter(s) to which the qualification relates, the financial statements present fairly, in all material respects, the financial position, results of operations, and cash flows of the entity in conformity with generally accepted accounting principles.
- *Adverse opinion.* An adverse opinion states that the financial statements do not present fairly the financial position, results of operations, or cash flows of the entity in conformity with generally accepted accounting principles.
- *Disclaimer of opinion.* A disclaimer of opinion states that the auditor does not express an opinion on the financial statements.[5]

As discussed in Chapter 8, the Auditing Standards Board has issued *Statement on Standards for Attestation Engagements No. 2,* "Reporting on the Entity's Internal Control Structure over Financial Reporting," now recodified in SSAE No. 10. Given the demand from the investing public for management's assertions about the effectiveness of the entity's internal control and the requirements of the

---

[5]*Statement on Auditing Standards No. 58*, "Reports on Audited Financial Statements" (New York: AICPA, 1988), par. 10. For additional reference, see Robert S. Roussey, Ernest L. Ten Eyck, and Mimi Blanco-Best, "Three New SASs: Closing the Communication Gap," *Journal of Accountancy* 166, No. 6 (December 1988), pp. 44–52.

Sarbanes-Oxley Act, it is reasonable to expect that the audit committee understand this type of attestation engagement. Thus it is important for the audit committee to review closely and discuss the recommendations in the annual management letter from the independent auditors.

Explanatory Language with the Auditor's Standard Report

The Auditing Standards Board requires independent auditors to modify their standard audit report under certain circumstances. Such a modification may require the addition of an explanatory paragraph or other explanatory language. More specifically, the circumstances include instances when:

a. The auditor's opinion is based in part on the report of another auditor.

b. To prevent the financial statements from being misleading because of unusual circumstances, the financial statements contain a departure from an accounting principle promulgated by a body designated by the AICPA Council to establish such principles.*

c. There is substantial doubt about the entity's ability to continue as a going concern.

d. There has been a material change between periods in accounting principles or in the method of their application.

e. Certain circumstances relating to reports on comparative financial statements exist.

f. Selected quarterly financial data required by SEC Regulation S-K has been omitted or has not been reviewed.

g. Supplementary information required by the Financial Accounting Standards Board (FASB) or the Governmental Accounting Standards Board (GASB) has been omitted, the presentation of such information departs materially from FASB or GASB guidelines, the auditor is unable to complete prescribed procedures with respect to such information, or the auditor is unable to remove substantial doubts about whether the supplementary information conforms to FASB or GASB guidelines.

h. Other information in a document containing audited financial statements is materially inconsistent with information appearing in the financial statements.[6]

Certain circumstances may arise, for example, when the auditors must rely on the report of another auditor or the auditors may not be independent. With respect to the former, the auditors' reporting obligations are based on their decisions whether to make reference to the other auditors' report. Therefore, if the auditors decide "to make reference to the report of another auditor as a basis, in part," for

---

*For further reference, see "Departures from the New Standard Auditor's Report on Financial Statements of Business Enterprises: A Survey of the Application of Statement on Auditing Standards, No. 58," *Financial Report Survey* (New York: AICPA, 1990).

[6]American Institute of Certified Public Accountants, *Professional Standards, U.S. Auditing Standards/ Attestation Standards,* Vol. 1 (New York: AICPA, 2003), AU Sec. 508.11.

their opinion, their report should disclose this fact.[7] When auditors decide to make no reference to the report of another auditor because of their acceptance of the auditor's independence and reputation, the standard short-form unqualified report is acceptable.

However, when the auditors are not independent—for example, there is a conflict of interest between the public accounting firm and the client—they should "disclaim an opinion with respect to the financial statements and should state specifically" that they are not independent.[8] Such an action is necessary on the part of the auditors, because of the auditing standard of independence discussed in Chapter 5.

Furthermore, in addition to their expression of an unqualified opinion, the auditors may wish to emphasize certain matters regarding the financial statements. For example, they may wish to indicate that the corporation has had "significant transactions with related parties," such as transactions between the entity and the officers or directors.[9] In addition, they may wish to disclose "an unusually important subsequent event" that occurred after the date of the financial statements. Obviously, such matters are disclosed based on the professional judgment of the auditors. However, while the auditors may wish to emphasize certain matters, they can express an unqualified opinion.

To familiarize the audit committee with various examples of the wording in the auditors' modified unqualified report, a model report is presented in Exhibit 13.1.

OTHER AUDITING OPINIONS

The Qualified Opinion

According to the Auditing Standards Board, the auditors may express a qualified opinion that " 'except for' the effects of the matter to which the qualification relates, the financial statements" are presented fairly.[10] Concerning the "exceptions" noted by the auditors, the Board delineated these circumstances:

> There is a lack of sufficient competent evidential matter or there are restrictions on the scope of the audit that have led the auditor to conclude that he cannot express an unqualified opinion and he has concluded not to disclaim an opinion.

> The auditor believes, on the basis of his audit, that the financial statements contain a departure from generally accepted accounting principles, the effect of which is material, and he has concluded not to express an adverse opinion.[11]

With respect to the aforementioned circumstances, an example of the auditors' report is illustrated in Exhibit 13.2.

---

[7]American Institute of Certified Public Accountants, *Professional Standards, U.S. Auditing Standards/Attestation Standards,* Vol. 1 (New York: AICPA, 2003), AU Sec. 508.12.

[8]Ibid., AU Sec. 504.09.

[9]Ibid., AU Sec. 508.19.

[10]Ibid., AU Sec. 508.20.

[11]Ibid., AU Sec. 20.

Exhibit 13.1   Independent Auditor's Report: Example 1

Opinion Based in Part on Report of Another Auditor

We have audited the consolidated balance sheets of ABC Company as of December 31, 20X2 and 20X1, and the related consolidated statements of income, retained earnings, and cash flows for the years then ended. These financial statements are the responsibility of the Company's management. Our responsibility is to express an opinion on these financial statements based on our audits. We did not audit the financial statements of B Company, a wholly-owned subsidiary, which statements reflect total assets of $_____ and $_____ as of December 31, 20X2 and 20X1, respectively, and total revenues of $_____ and $_____ for the years then ended. Those statements were audited by other auditors whose report has been furnished to us, and our opinion, insofar as it relates to the amounts included for B Company, is based solely on the report of the other auditors.

We conducted our audits in accordance with auditing standards generally accepted in the United States of America. Those standards require that we plan and perform the audit to obtain reasonable assurance about whether the financial statements are free of material misstatement. An audit includes examining, on a test basis, evidence supporting the amounts and disclosures in the financial statements. An audit also includes assessing the accounting principles used and significant estimates made by management, as well as evaluating the overall financial statement presentation. We believe that our audits and the report of other auditors provide a reasonable basis for our opinion.

In our opinion, based on our audits and the report of other auditors, the consolidated financial statements referred to above present fairly, in all material respects, the financial position of ABC Company as of December 31, 20X2 and 20X1, and the results of its operations and its cash flows for the years then ended in conformity with accounting principles generally accepted in the United States of America.[a]

Lack of Consistency

As discussed in Note X to the financial statements, the Company changed its method of computing depreciation in 20X2.[b]

An Entity's Ability to Continue as a Going Concern

The accompanying financial statements have been prepared assuming that the Company will continue as a going concern. As discussed in Note X to the financial statements, the Company has suffered recurring losses from operations and has a net capital deficiency that raises substantial doubt about its ability to continue as a going concern. Management's plans in regard to these matters are also described in Note X. The financial statements do not include any adjustments that might result from the outcome of this uncertainty.[c]

---

[a]*Statement on Auditing Standards No. 58,* par. 13, as amended by ASB interpretation.
[b]Professional Standards, *U.S. Auditing Standards/Attestation Standards,* Vol. 1, AU Sec. 508.17.
[c]*Statement on Auditing Standards No. 59,* "The Auditor's Consideration of an Entity's Ability to Continue as a Going Concern" (New York: AICPA, 1988), par. 13. For further discussion, see John E. Ellingsen, Kurt Pany, and Peg Fagan, "SAS No. 59: How to Evaluate Going Concern," *Journal of Accountancy* 168, No. 1 (January 1989), 24–31.

Exhibit 13.2   Independent Auditor's Report: Example 2

Scope Limitations

[Same first paragraph as the standard report]
Except as discussed in the following paragraph, we conducted our audits in accordance with auditing standards generally accepted in the United States of America. Those standards require that we plan and perform the audit to obtain reasonable assurance about whether the financial statements are free of material misstatement. An audit includes examining, on a test basis, evidence supporting the amounts and disclosures in the financial statements. An audit also includes assessing the accounting principles used and significant estimates made by management, as well as evaluating the overall financial statement presentation. We believe that our audits provide a reasonable basis for our opinion.

We were unable to obtain audited financial statements supporting the Company's investment in a foreign affiliate stated at $_____ and $_____ at December 31, 20X2 and 20X1, respectively, or its equity in earnings of that affiliate of $_____ and $_____, which is included in net income for the years then ended as described in Note X to the financial statements; nor were we able to satisfy ourselves as to the carrying value of the investment in the foreign affiliate or the equity in its earnings by other auditing procedures. In our opinion, except for the effects of such adjustments, if any, as might have been determined to be necessary had we been able to examine evidence regarding the foreign affiliate investment and earnings, the financial statements referred to in the first paragraph above present fairly, in all material respects, the financial position of X Company as of December 31, 20X2 and 20X1, and the results of its operations and its cash flows for the years then ended in conformity with accounting principles generally accepted in the United States of America.ᵃ

Departure from a Generally Accepted Accounting Principle

[Same first and second paragraphs as the standard report]
The Company has excluded, from property and debt in the accompanying balance sheets, certain lease obligations that, in our opinion, should be capitalized in order to conform with generally accepted accounting principles. If these lease obligations were capitalized, property would be increased by $_____ and $_____, long-term debt by $_____ and $_____, and retained earnings by $_____ and $_____ as of December 31, 20X2 and 20X1, respectively. Additionally, net income would be increased (decreased) by $_____ and $_____ and earnings per share would be increased (decreased) by $_____ and $_____, respectively, for the years then ended.

In our opinion, except for the effects of not capitalizing certain lease obligations as discussed in the preceding paragraph, the financial statements referred to above present fairly, in all material respects, the financial position of X Company as of December 31, 20X2 and 20X1, and the results of its operations and its cash flows for the years then ended in conformity with accounting principles generally accepted in the United States of America.ᵇ

Inadequate Disclosure

[Same first and second paragraphs as the standard report]
The Company's financial statements do not disclose *[describe the nature of the omitted disclosures]*. In our opinion, disclosure of this information is required by generally accepted accounting principles.

In our opinion, except for the omission of the information discussed in the preceding paragraph, . . .ᶜ

ᵃ*Professional Standards, U.S. Auditing Standards/Attestation Standards*, Vol. 1, AU Sec. 26 (New York: AICPA, 2003).
ᵇIbid., AU Sec. 39.
ᶜIbid., AU Sec. 42. For further reference, see Jack C. Robertson, "Analysts' Reactions to Auditors' Messages in Qualified Reports," *Accounting Horizons* 2, No. 2 (June 1988), pp. 82–89.

The Adverse Opinion

The adverse opinion is expressed by the auditors when, in their judgment, "the financial statements taken as a whole are not presented fairly in conformity with generally accepted accounting principles."[12] The adverse opinion is appropriate where the auditors' exceptions are so material that the statements as a whole are not fairly presented. Thus the distinction between the adverse opinion and qualified opinion is predicated on the concept of materiality discussed in Chapter 5. When the auditors express an adverse opinion, their audit report should disclose "all the substantive reasons" for the opinion as well as "the principal effects of the subject matter" on the financial statements, "if reasonably determinable."[13] "If the effects are not reasonably determinable, the report should so state."[14] If management applies accounting principles that are not in conformity with acceptable principles (discussed in Chapter 5), then the auditors are required to render an adverse opinion. For example, if management refuses to disclose material information in the notes to the statements, such inaction constitutes a violation of the disclosure principle. Thus an adverse opinion is appropriate. Such a violation of the disclosure principle would materially distort the financial statements taken as a whole. However, the expression of an adverse opinion is infrequent in practice because management opts for an unqualified opinion and as a result makes the necessary adjustments.

An example of an adverse opinion is shown in Exhibit 13.3.

Disclaimer of Opinion

When the auditors lack sufficient information to form an opinion regarding the financial statements, their report should indicate that they are unable to express an opinion. For example, it is appropriate to express a disclaimer of opinion when the auditors have not conducted "an examination sufficient in scope" to warrant the expression of an opinion on the statements taken as a whole.[15] In contrast to the qualified opinion, the disclaimer of opinion means that the auditors do not have sufficient knowledge about the fairness of management's representations in the financial statements. Furthermore, the auditors should indicate the reason for the disclaimer of opinion in their report. Thus, although the circumstances regarding the issuance of the qualified opinion may be the same for a disclaimer of opinion, the distinction between the former and the latter is based on the degree of materiality with respect to each circumstance. Such a distinction is contingent on the auditors' professional judgment. Accordingly, the audit committee should inquire about the public accounting firm's criteria for judging materiality as it relates to the financial statements.

An example of a disclaimer of opinion is shown in Exhibit 13.4.

---

[12]Ibid., AU Sec. 58.
[13]Ibid., AU Sec. 59.
[14]Ibid.
[15]Ibid., AU Sec. 62.

Exhibit 13.3   Independent Auditor's Report: Example 3

Adverse Opinion

[Same first and second paragraphs as the standard report]

As discussed in Note X to the financial statements, the Company carries its property, plant, and equipment accounts at appraisal values, and provides depreciation on the basis of such values. Further, the Company does not provide for income taxes with respect to differences between financial income and taxable income arising because of the use, for income tax purposes, of the installment method of reporting gross profit from certain types of sales. Generally accepted accounting principles require that property, plant, and equipment be stated at an amount not in excess of cost, reduced by depreciation based on such amount, and that deferred income taxes be provided.

Because of the departures from generally accepted accounting principles identified above, as of December 31, 20X2 and 20X1, inventories have been increased $_____ and $_____ by inclusion in manufacturing overhead of depreciation in excess of that based on cost; property, plant, and equipment, less accumulated depreciation, is carried at $_____ and $_____ in excess of an amount based on the cost to the Company; and deferred income taxes of $_____ and $_____ have not been recorded; resulting in an increase of $_____ and $_____ in retained earnings and in appraisal surplus of $_____ and $_____, respectively. For the years ended December 31, 20X2 and 20X1, cost of goods sold has been increased $_____ and $_____, respectively, because of the effects of the depreciation accounting referred to above and deferred income taxes of $_____ and $_____ have not been provided, resulting in an increase in net income of $_____ and $_____, respectively.

In our opinion, because of the effects of the matters discussed in the preceding paragraphs, the financial statements referred to above do not present fairly, in conformity with accounting principles generally accepted in the United States of America, the financial position of X Company as of December 31, 20X2 and 20X1, or the results of its operations or its cash flows for the years then ended.

Source: Professional Standards, U.S. Auditing Standards/Attestation Standards, Vol. 1 (New York: AICPA, 2003), AU Sec. 60.

OTHER REPORTS OF THE AUDITORS

Report on Interim Financial Statements

In addition to the auditors' opinion on the annual financial statements, the Auditing Standards Board states:

> The Securities and Exchange Commission (SEC) requires[a] a registrant to engage an independent accountant to review the registrant's interim financial information, in accordance with this Statement, before the registrant files its quarterly report on Form 10-Q or Form 10-QSB. Although this Statement does not require an accountant to issue a written report on a review of interim financial information, the SEC

Exhibit 13.4   Independent Auditor's Report: Example 4

Disclaimer of Opinion

We were engaged to audit the accompanying balance sheets of X Company as of December 31, 20X2 and 20X1, and the related statements of income, retained earnings, and cash flows for the years then ended. These financial statements are the responsibility of the Company's management.

[Second paragraph of standard report should be omitted]

The Company did not make a count of its physical inventory in 20X2 or 20X1, stated in the accompanying financial statements at $_____ as of December 31, 20X2, and at $_____ as of December 31, 20X1. Further, evidence supporting the cost of property and equipment acquired prior to December 31, 20X1, is no longer available. The Company's records do not permit the application of other auditing procedures to inventories or property and equipment.

Since the Company did not take physical inventories and we were not able to apply other auditing procedures to satisfy ourselves as to inventory quantities and the cost of property and equipment, the scope of our work was not sufficient to enable us to express, and we do not express, an opinion on these financial statements.

Source: Professional Standards, U.S. Auditing Standards and Attestation Standards, Vol. 1 (New York: AICPA, 2003), AU Sec. 63.

---

requires that an accountant's review report be filed with the interim financial information if, in any filing, the entity states that the interim financial information has been reviewed by an independent public accountant.

SAS No. 84, *Communications Between Predecessor and Successor Auditors* (AICPA, *Professional Standards*, vol. 1, AU sec. 315), requires a successor auditor to contact the entity's predecessor auditor and make inquiries of the predecessor auditor in deciding whether to accept appointment as an entity's independent auditor. Such inquiries should be completed before accepting an engagement to perform an initial review of an entity's interim financial information.[16]

---

[a]The Securities and Exchange Commission (SEC) requirement is set forth in Rule 10-01(d) of Regulation S-X for Form 10-Q and item 310(b) of Regulation S-B for Form 10-QSB.

With respect to the independent auditors' objective of a review of interim financial statements, the Auditing Standards Board points out:

The objective of a review of interim financial information pursuant to this Statement is to provide the accountant with a basis for communicating whether he or she is aware of any material modifications that should be made to the interim financial in-

---

[16]*Statement on Auditing Standards No. 100,* "Interim Financial Information" (New York: AICPA, 2002), pars. 3 and 4. SAS No. 100 was issued to improve the guidance on performing reviews of interim financial information of public companies. The SEC requires that the registrant submit timely filings of interim financial information. For further information, see the AICPA's Professional Issues Task Force Practice Alert 2000-4, "Quarterly Review Procedures for Public Companies" (New York: AICPA, 2000).

formation for it to conform with generally accepted accounting principles. The objective of a review of interim financial information differs significantly from that of an audit conducted in accordance with generally accepted auditing standards. A review of interim financial information does not provide a basis for expressing an opinion about whether the financial statements are presented fairly, in all material respects, in conformity with generally accepted accounting principles. A review consists principally of performing analytical procedures and making inquiries of persons responsible for financial and accounting matters, and does not contemplate (*a*) tests of accounting records through inspection, observation, or confirmation; (*b*) tests of controls to evaluate their effectiveness; (*c*) obtaining corroborating evidence in response to inquiries; or (*d*) performing certain other procedures ordinarily performed in an audit. A review may bring to the accountant's attention significant matters affecting the interim financial information, but it does not provide assurance that the accountant will become aware of all significant matters that would be identified in an audit. Paragraph 22 of this Statement provides guidance to the accountant if he or she becomes aware of information that leads him or her to believe that the interim financial information may not be in conformity with generally accepted accounting principles.[17]

To achieve their review objective, The independent auditors should apply these topical procedures:

- Establishing an understanding with client regarding the services to be performed in an engagement to review interim financial information (pars. 8–9)
- Obtaining knowledge of the entity's business and its internal control (pars. 10–14)
- Requiring analytical procedures, inquiries, and other review procedures (emphasis added—comparing disaggregated revenue data by month and by product line or operating segment during the current interim period with that of comparable prior periods (pars. 15–23)
- Obtaining written representation from management concerning such matters as management's responsibility for the financial statements (par. 24)
- Evaluating the results of interim review procedures (pars. 25–28)
- Communicating to the management, the Audit Committee, and others (pars. 29–36)
- Reporting on a review of interim financial information (pars. 37–46)
- Obtaining the client's representation concerning the review engagement (pars. 47–50)
- Preparing documentation for the review of interim financial information (pars. 51–52).[18]

The audit committee's review of the reports of the independent auditors' limited reviews of the interim financial statements is an important task, because it can

---

[17]Ibid., par. 7.

[18]Ibid. See paragraphs parenthetically noted above. Also, see the appendices on this book's website for examples of analytical procedures, unusual or complex situations, and illustration representation letters.

alert the board of directors to possible changes in accounting policies in a timely manner and thus minimize unanticipated financial reporting implications at the end of the year.[19]

With respect to communication with audit committees, the Auditing Standards Board requires the following procedures:

> As a result of conducting a review of interim financial information, the accountant may become aware of matters that cause him or her to believe that (a) material modification should be made to the interim financial information for it to conform with generally accepted accounting principles or (b) that the entity filed the Form 10-Q or Form 10-QSB before the completion of the review. In such circumstances, the accountant should communicate the matter(s) to the appropriate level of management as soon as practicable.

> If, in the accountant's judgment, management does not respond appropriately to the accountant's communication within a reasonable period of time, the accountant should inform the audit committee or others with equivalent authority and responsibility (hereafter referred to as the audit committee) of the matters as soon as practicable. This communication may be oral or written. If information is communicated orally, the accountant should document the communication.

> If, in the accountant's judgment, the audit committee does not respond appropriately to the accountant's communication within a reasonable period of time, the accountant should evaluate whether to resign from the engagement to review the interim financial information and as the entity's auditor. The accountant may wish to consult with his or her attorney when making these evaluations.

> When conducting a review of interim financial information, the accountant may become aware of fraud or possible illegal acts. If the matter involves fraud, it should be brought to the attention of the appropriate level of management. If the fraud involves senior management or results in a material misstatement of the financial statements, the accountant should communicate the matter directly to the audit committee as described in SAS No. 99, *Consideration of Fraud in a Financial Statement Audit* (AICPA, *Professional Standards*, vol. 1, AU sec. 316.79–82). If the matter involves possible illegal acts, the accountant should assure himself or herself that the audit committee is adequately informed, unless the matter is clearly inconsequential.[a] (See SAS No. 54, *Illegal Acts by Clients* [AICPA, *Professional Standards*, vol. 1, AU sec. 317.17].)

> When conducting a review of interim financial information, the accountant may become aware of matters relating to internal control that may be of interest to the audit committee. Matters that should be reported to the audit committee are referred to as reportable conditions. Reportable conditions are matters coming to the accountant's attention that, in his or her judgment, should be communicated to the audit committee because they represent significant deficiencies in the design or operation of internal control that could adversely affect the organization's ability to initiate, record,

---

[19]In its 1987 report, the National Commission on Fraudulent Financial Reporting recommended that "the audit committee's oversight responsibilities undertaken on behalf of the board of directors extend to the quarterly reporting process. The audit committee should review the controls that management has established to protect the integrity of the quarterly reporting process. This review should be ongoing" (p. 48). As noted earlier, *SAS No. 100* provides the agenda items for the audit committee's review of quarterly reporting. Such a review will help minimize opportunities for managing earnings through improper revenue recognition or deferred expense recognition.

summarize, and report financial data consistent with management's assertions in the interim financial information. The accountant also may wish to submit recommendations related to other matters that come to the accountant's attention.[b]

When conducting a review of interim financial information, the accountant also should determine whether any of the matters described in SAS No. 61, *Communication With Audit Committees* (AICPA, *Professional Standards*, vol. 1, AU sec. 380), as amended, as they relate to the interim financial information, have been identified. If such matters have been identified, the accountant should communicate them to the audit committee or be satisfied, through discussion with the audit committee, that such matters have been communicated to the audit committee by management. For example, the accountant should determine that the audit committee is informed about the process used by management to formulate particularly sensitive accounting estimates; about a change in a significant accounting policy affecting the interim financial information; about adjustments that, either individually or in the aggregate, could have a significant effect on the entity's financial reporting process; and about uncorrected misstatements aggregated by the accountant that were determined by the management to be immaterial, both individually and in the aggregate, to the interim financial statements taken as a whole.[c]

The objective of a review of interim financial information differs significantly from that of an audit. Therefore, any communication the accountant may make about the quality, not just the acceptability, of the entity's accounting principles as applied to its interim financial reporting generally would be limited to the effect of significant events, transactions, and changes in accounting estimates that the accountant considered when conducting the review of interim financial information. Further, interim review procedures do not provide assurance that the accountant will become aware of all matters that might affect the accountant's judgments about the quality of the entity's accounting principles that would be identified as a result of an audit.

If the accountant has identified matters to be communicated to the audit committee, the accountants should attempt to make such communications with the audit committee, or at least its chair, and a representative of management before the entity files its interim financial information with a regulatory agency (such as the SEC). If such communications cannot be made before the filing, they should be made as soon as practicable in the circumstances. The communications may be oral or written. If information is communicated orally, the accountant should document the communications.[20]

---

[a]The accountant may have additional communication responsibilities pursuant to SAS No. 54, *Illegal Acts by Clients* (AICPA, *Professional Standards*, vol. 1, AU sec. 317); Section 10A of the Securities Exchange Act of 1934; and SAS No. 99, *Consideration of Fraud in a Financial Statement Audit* (AICPA, *Professional Standards*, vol. 1, AU sec. 316).

[b]SAS No. 60, *Communication of Internal Control Related Matters Noted in an Audit* (AICPA, *Professional Standards*, vol. 1, AU sec. 325), provides guidance on communicating reportable conditions related to internal control.

[c]The presentation to the audit committee should be similar to the summary of uncorrected misstatements included in or attached to the management representation letter that is described in paragraph 24(h) of this Statement.

---

[20]*SAS No. 100*, pars. 29–36. More recently, the New York Stock Exchange reaffirmed both the Blue Ribbon Committee on Improving the Effectiveness of Corporate Audit Committees and the National Commission on Fraudulent Financial Reporting position on quarterly reporting. (See SEC Release No. 34-47672, April 11, 2003.)

The two technical accounting pronouncements related to interim financial reports are Accounting Principles Board Opinion No. 28 and Financial Accounting Standards Board Statement No. 3. Audit Committee members may wish to review these pronouncements prior to their meetings with the independent auditors. In particular, they should inquire about the methods of recognizing revenues and expenses and how the annual operating costs are allocated to the interim periods. The major objective is to identify and comprehend management's methods of reporting interim financial information because the stockholders use the information to predict earnings for the year.

An example of a report on reviewed interim financial information presented in a quarterly report is illustrated below.

Independent Accountant's Report

We have reviewed the accompanying [*describe the interim financial information or statements reviewed*] of ABC Company and consolidated subsidiaries as of September 30, 20X1, and for the three-month and nine-month periods then ended. This (These) financial information (statements) is (are) the responsibility of the company's management.

We conducted our review in accordance with standards established by the American Institute of Certified Public Accountants. A review of interim financial information consists principally of applying analytical procedures to financial data and making inquiries of persons responsible for financial and accounting matters. It is substantially less in scope than an audit conducted in accordance with generally accepted auditing standards, the objective of which is the expression of an opinion regarding the financial statements taken as a whole. Accordingly, we do not express such an opinion.

Based on our review, we are not aware of any material modifications that should be made to the accompanying financial information (statements) for it (them) to be in conformity with accounting principles generally accepted in the United States of America.

[*Signature*]

[*Date*][21]

Special Reports

According to the Auditing Standards Board, special reports apply to:

- Financial statements that are prepared in conformity with a comprehensive basis of accounting other than generally accepted accounting principles (e.g., cash-basis statements)
- Specified elements, accounts, or items of a financial statement (e.g., working capital position)

---

[21]Ibid., par. 38.

- Compliance with aspects of contractual agreements or regulatory requirements related to audited financial statements (e.g., restrictions relative to a bond indenture).

- Financial presentations to comply with contractual agreements or regulatory provisions (e.g., restrictions relative to dividend payments, such as maintaining specified financial ratios)

- Financial information presented in prescribed forms or schedules that require a prescribed form of auditor's report (e.g., filings with a regulatory agency)[22]

Of particular importance to the audit committee are the second and fourth items in the preceding list, because the committee may request the auditors to report on royalties, sales for the purpose of computing a rental fee, employee profit participation, or the adequacy of the provision for taxes. Moreover, the auditors may issue a special report in connection with a proposed acquisition, the claims of creditors, or management's compliance with contractual agreements. While such reports may be appropriate under the preceding circumstances, it is suggested that the committee give consideration to the cost/benefit advantages from such reports. As indicated earlier, the committee should give strong consideration to the internal auditing staff regarding its request for special reports.

It is evident that the auditors' professional opinion on the financial statements augments the integrity and objectivity of management's representations in such statements. In addition, the audit committee should be familiar with the auditors' reports because each member has an obligation to provide the impetus to ensure that the proper audit opinion is rendered. Accordingly, the committee should review the audit report during the postaudit review period to determine the audit opinion on the financial statements for the current fiscal period. If an opinion other than an unqualified opinion will be issued, the committee should review and discuss the matters in question with the independent auditors and the senior accounting officers to obtain their concurrence on the auditors' exceptions. Such review meetings may be conducted on a separate or joint basis, depending on the attendant circumstances. The major objective is to identify the particular exceptions and to advise the board of directors in a timely manner of the audit opinion regarding such exceptions so that the board may deal with them.

SOURCES AND SUGGESTED READINGS

American Institute of Certified Public Accountants, *Professional Standards, U.S. Auditing Standards/Attestation Standards,* Vol. 1 (New York: AICPA, 2003).

Ellingsen, John E., Kurt Pany, and Peg Fagan, "SAS No. 59: How to Evaluate Going Concern." *Journal of Accountancy,* 168, No. 1 (January 1989), pp. 24–31.

---

[22]*Statement on Auditing Standards No. 62,* "Special Reports" (New York: AICPA, 1989), par. 1. With respect to agreed-upon procedures engagements, see Section 501 of *Statement of Standards for Attestation Engagement No. 10*" (New York: AICPA, 2001).

National Commission on Fraudulent Financial Reporting, *Report of the National Commission on Fraudulent Financial Reporting* (Washington, DC: NCFFR, 1987).

Robertson, Jack C., "Analysts' Reactions to Auditors' Messages in Qualified Reports." *Accounting Horizons* 2, No. 2 (June 1988), pp. 82–89.

Roussey, Robert S., Ernest L. Ten Eyck, and Mimi Blanco-Best, "Three New SASs: Closing the Communication Gap." *Journal of Accountancy* 166, No. 6, (December 1988), pp. 44–52.

Statement on Auditing Standards No. 58, "Reports on Audited Financial Statements" (New York: AICPA, 1988).

Statement on Auditing Standards No. 59, "The Auditor's Consideration of an Entity's Ability to Continue as a Going Concern" (New York: AICPA, 1988).

Statement on Auditing Standards No. 62, "Special Reports" (New York: AICPA, 1989).

Statement on Auditing Standards No. 100, "Interim Financial Information" (New York: AICPA, 2002).

Chapter 14

The Audit Committee's Report and Concluding Observations

The audit committee of the board of directors is elected by the board in order to allow committee members to focus their attention on corporate accountability matters in greater depth than would be practical for the full board. Furthermore, the board of directors sets forth the duties and responsibilities of the audit committee in the committee's charter. It is therefore incumbent on the committee to report regularly to the board of directors that it is properly performing its responsibilities as set forth in the charter. An illustrative audit committee charter was presented in Chapter 2. At this point, the reader may wish to revisit the components and narrative discussion in charter.

The manner in which audit committees report varies from board to board, but, as noted by The Conference Board,[1] substantially all audit committees report to the board at least annually and often more frequently. In addition, as noted in Chapter 2, the Securities and Exchange Commission has required that registrants provide in their proxy statements a report from the audit committee to the shareholders. Likewise, the New York Stock Exchange has set forth a reporting requirement to the board of directors.

The purpose of this chapter is to provide guidance to the chair and members of the audit committee with respect to their reporting responsibilities to the board, following each committee meeting, or in a written format as outlined herein.

This chapter also presents the author's concluding observations and some perspectives on future developments.

PURPOSE OF THE AUDIT COMMITTEE'S REPORT

The audit committee's report is the basis for reporting on the board of directors' charge to the committee. It should be addressed to the full board of directors and

---

[1]The Conference Board found that "almost every audit committee in the survey (98 percent, or 664 companies) gives a formal accounting of its activities at least once a year," a finding essentially unchanged from the 1978 survey. However, the frequency of reports to the board has risen, from a median of two for all companies in 1978 to three reports in 1987; just 14 percent report only once a year. See Jeremy Bacon, *The Audit Committee: A Broader Mandate,* Report No. 914 (New York: The Conference Board, 1988), p. 17.

explain their findings and recommendations concerning primarily the overall effectiveness of both the internal and external auditing functions and other areas within their original jurisdiction as defined by the board. In addition, the report should be based on their participation in the audit planning process as well as their monitoring activities, discussed in the preceding chapters. Such a report is critically important to the board for these reasons:

- It communicates to the board financial, accounting, and auditing matters of particular interest that were noted in the audit directors' reviews and discussions with the internal and external auditing executives and the senior representatives of management, such as the chief financial officer.

- Their report not only contains an independent and objective appraisal of the audit functions but also provides assurance to the board that management is fulfilling its stewardship accountability to its outside constituencies, particularly the stockholders.

- The report reflects the audit committee members' responsibility to exercise the legal duty of care in view of the fiduciary principle, discussed in Chapter 4. The reader should reread this chapter prior to the preparation of the report. Also, the reader should refer to Appendix H on this book's website.

- It calls the board's attention to nonfinancial accounting matters of significance, such as conflicts of interest and other general business practices.

Audit committee members are in a unique position within the framework of corporate accountability because they provide a constructive dimension to the board in helping the directors discharge their fiduciary responsibility to the stockholders. Through a review of their functions (discussed in Chapter 2), it is clearly evident that the scope of their position is broad based. Such a position enables audit committee members to obtain a broad perspective of the entity's business operations and its industry. As a result of their knowledge and their exposure to the subjects discussed in this text, they are in a position to recognize the auditing needs of the entity as well as to understand compliance matters with corporate policies. Although they are not directly involved in the day-to-day accounting and auditing management activities, their seasoned business experience permits them to monitor the changes in accounting and auditing standards that affect the financial reporting responsibilities of both the board of directors and the officers of the corporation. Furthermore, because of their independent posture in the corporate framework and their broad overview of the entity, they are not restricted to one particular function in the organization. Equally important, they can anticipate potential financial reporting problems as well as communicate management's course of action regarding the solutions to such problems.

In short, audit committee members have a critical role in developing their report for the board because of their responsibility to formulate recommendations based on their meetings with the auditors and senior financial officers. Such recommendations are a result of their review of the coordinated efforts of the above executives and their discussions with those executives. Consequently, it is incumbent on the audit directors to develop a report that is responsive to the needs and interests of the board of directors.

The New York Stock Exchange has issued this directive with respect to the audit committee's assistance with board oversight:

(viii) report regularly to the board of directors.

Commentary: The audit committee should review with the full board any issues that arise with respect to the quality or integrity of the company's financial statements, the company's compliance with legal or regulatory requirements, the performance and independence of the company's independent auditors, or the performance of the internal audit function.

General Commentary to Section 303A(7)(d): While the fundamental responsibility for the company's financial statements and disclosures rests with management and the independent auditor, the audit committee must review: (A) major issues regarding accounting principles and financial statement presentations, including any significant changes in the company's selection or application of accounting principles, and major issues as to the adequacy of the company's internal controls and any special audit steps adopted in light of material control deficiencies; (B) analyses prepared by management and/or the independent auditor setting forth significant financial reporting issues and judgments made in connection with the preparation of the financial statements; (C) the effect of regulatory and accounting initiatives, as well as off-balance sheet structures, on the financial statements of the company; and (D) the type and presentation of information to be included in earnings press releases (paying particular attention to any use of "pro forma," or "adjusted" non-GAAP, information), as well as review any financial information and earnings guidance provided to analysts and rating agencies.

General Commentary to Section 303A(7): To avoid any confusion, note that the audit committee functions specified in Section 303A(7) are the sole responsibility of the audit committee and may not be allocated to a different committee.[2]

GUIDELINES FOR PREPARING THE REPORT

General Comments

In view of their oversight, monitoring, and advisory capacity, it is important to recognize that the audit directors' report should convey this position to the other board members. Moreover, the audit directors should communicate their findings and recommendations and avoid any final decisions, since such decisions are not within the province of the committee. Therefore, it is desirable to reexamine the committee's charge from the board and develop the report in response to this charge. This particular charge has been discussed in Chapter 2, and it is suggested that the reader review the committee's functions at this time.

---

[2]Securities and Exchange Commission, *Release No. 34-47673, Proposed Rule Change Relating to Corporate Governance*, April 11, 2003, *www.sec.gov/ruls/SRO/34-47672.htm.*

In developing their report, the audit directors should be particularly alert to present or potential financial reporting and compliance problems. Such a charge is a difficult task for a member of the committee. However, subsequent to their orientation program as outlined in Chapter 7 along with their continuous committee meetings, each member's ability to recognize such problems will be enhanced. Obviously, such a skill is not acquired as the result of only a few meetings. Nevertheless, through an understanding of the entity's business and other subjects as discussed in this text, each member can assess his or her own strengths and weaknesses and develop the necessary proficiency. Furthermore, the quality of their report will be contingent on not only each member's perceptiveness and inquisitiveness but also their creativity concerning appropriate recommendations to the board. For example, during the committee's preaudit planning segment of the auditing cycle, discussed in Chapters 6 and 7, the committee should inquire and discuss with auditors and management any particular matters they should be aware of regarding the audit examination. Such inquiries will enable the committee to identify potential areas for possible recommendations to the board. For example, in Chapter 10 it was observed that the audit committee of Wal-Mart Stores, Inc. reviews the changes in accounting policy. Thus it can be seen that the committee has a key role in evaluating and understanding the accounting policies of the corporation. Clearly, audit committee members should plan their agenda to allow each member sufficient time to study and review the subjects for the report. In summary, each member should keep the board's expectations in proper perspective during the report development period and realize that fellow board members will be relying on the report regarding the board's overall final decisions.

Sources of Information for the Report

Although the sources of information for the report will vary among different audit committees, the following recapitulation of the common sources discussed in the text is applicable:
1. Independent auditors
   a. Engagement letter and independence confirmation letter
   b. Management letter and audit committee reports
   c. Interim financial audit reports
   d. Annual auditors' report in the corporate annual report
   e. Special audit reports, if applicable
2. Corporate management
   a. Lawyer's letter for the outside auditors
   b. Management's letter of representation to the outside auditors
   c. Minutes of meetings of the board and its other standing committees, such as the audit and finance committees[3]

---

[3]Obviously, the minutes of the audit committee's meetings should be documented. Such a record of the committee's proceedings during the year facilitates the preparation of the report. The chairman of the audit committee should be satisfied that the recorded minutes of each committee meeting are sufficient and adequate in terms of the committee's findings, conclusions, and recommendations.

    d. Minutes of the annual stockholders meeting

    e. The annual corporate report and proxy materials

    f. Compliance reports with the regulatory agencies, particularly the SEC and the IRS

    g. Management report in the annual report

    h. Releases to employees and the general report through the public relations office

3. Internal auditors

Reports on the following:

    a. Compliance audits

    b. Operational audits

    c. Financial audits

    d. Internal control system

    e. Risk management

    f. Governance

    g. Long-form internal audit report, if available

    h. Special survey reports, such as conflicts of interest and fraud prevention measures

4. Other sources of information

    a. Audit committee's professional development program as discussed in Chapter 7

    b. Interviews with the chief executive officer, chief financial officer, and legal counsel

    c. Bulletins within the organization and outside the organization, such as the newsletters from the professional accounting firms

Report Preparation

The audit committee's report is essentially an informational report that contains its overall assessment of the preceding sources of information along with its separate or joint meetings with the auditors and the representatives of management. Ordinarily, such a report will be prepared by the chair of the committee prior to the issuance of the annual corporate report and subsequent to the committee's postaudit conference. However, it may be desirable to issue an interim committee report with respect to special matters, such as interim financial information, so that such matters are communicated to the board in a timely manner. Thus it is highly probable that the audit committee may issue more than one report during the fiscal period.

During the phases of the auditing cycle, discussed in Chapters 6 and 7, the audit committee will have several review meetings concerning the auditing activities and compliance matters. Such review meetings along with the minutes of those meetings assist the committee in the preparation of the report. Although the content of the report may evolve from the transcripts of their meetings, it is important that audit committee members provide sufficient time to develop their report. Moreover, they should be satisfied not only that the facts are properly documented in the minutes but also that their proposal recommendations are practical and reasonable.

In contrast to the independent auditors' report, discussed in Chapter 13, the audit committee's report is not standardized by a professionally recognized accounting organization, such as the AICPA. Nonetheless, the committee's report should describe the activities of their meetings, which consist primarily of their reviews, discussions, findings, and recommendations. In developing the content of the report, the committee's comments should not contradict the audit report opinion of the external auditors or the conclusions of the director of internal auditing. Therefore, subsequent to the preparation of the first draft of the report, the report content should be checked against the sources of information, primarily the audit reports, to avoid potential misunderstandings among the other board members.

While there are no definitive rules on the subjects, length, and format for the internal report to the board of directors, the committee should give consideration to these points[4]:

1. The title of the report should be Audit Committee's Report.
2. The report should be addressed to the board of directors and dated.
3. The charge of the audit committee should be stated in the beginning of the report. Such information should be taken from the corporate bylaws or from a formal resolution passed by the board.
4. The report should contain a statement of the scope of the committee's review. For example, the scope of the report may include the following statement:
    We have made a review of the corporate audit policy statement and related internal and external auditing plans and results for the (period of review) in order to determine whether such functions were being performed in an effective manner. Our review included a discussion of the following: (1) a summary of the entity's financial reporting requirements and the annual report and proxy materials; (2) the system of internal accounting control and the scope of the audit; (3) the coordinated activities between the internal and external auditors regarding the scope of the audit; (4) management's judgment in the selection and application of accounting principles in the preparation of the financial statements; and (5) the entity's compliance with the applicable laws and regulations, particularly the federal securities laws and income tax laws, with the independent auditors and legal counsel.
5. A summary of the committee's review activities and a general discussion of such activities for the current fiscal period. The report should contain a chronological account of the committee's meeting activities. The subjects for the report will consist of the committee's reviews during the phases of the auditing cycle. For example, the committee should describe all significant accounting

---

[4]The author believes it may be desirable to prepare a formal report (as illustrated) in view of not only the potential legal liability of the committee but also the professionalism of the audit committee members.

changes and related accounting policy disclosure matters that were approved during the postaudit review segment of the auditing cycle. For additional guidance on the subjects for the report, the reader should review the check list and other guidelines as discussed in the preceding chapters.

6. A summary of the committee's recommendations regarding such matters as the selection of the public accounting firm and changes in the internal auditing policies. Such recommendations may be incorporated with the preceding step. The reader should review the salient points in Chapter 7 regarding the selection or reappointment of the public accounting firm. Also, the committee will approve certain matters, such as financial statement disclosure matters (e.g., changes in accounting policies) as well as the audit and nonaudit fees.

7. The report should be signed by the chair, and names of other committee members should be disclosed in the report.

8. The committee may wish to provide attachments of principles's reports, such as the independent auditors' management letter, management's letter of representation to the auditors, and other special reports based on its discretion.

A suggested format for the report is presented in Exhibit 14.1. Subsequent to their recommendations, audit committee members may wish to use this paragraph:

Based on our reviews, we are confident that management has fulfilled its reporting stewardship accountability in connection with the financial statements, and we are assured that both the internal and external auditors have properly discharged their appropriate auditing responsibilities.

Finally, publicly held corporations are required by the SEC and self-regulatory organizations to disclose a report of the audit committee's activities in their annual

---

Exhibit 14.1   Illustrative Audit Committee Internal Report

(To Board of Directors)   (Date of Report)

(Charge of the audit committee)

(Scope of committee's reviews)

(Summary of the committee's review activities in chronological order)

(Summary of the committee's recommendations)

                                                   Respectfully Submitted,

                              Signed by: _____

                                                   (Name of chairman)

                                                   (Names of other committee
                                                   members)

(Attachments, if appropriate)

proxy statements. Such action exemplifies the committee's role as representatives of the stockholders. An example of the committee's report of Wal-Mart Stores, Inc., is shown in Exhibit 14.2.[5]

---

[5]In 1987, the National Commission on Fraudulent Financial Reporting recommended that "the Securities and Exchange Commission require all annual reports to stockholders to include a letter from the chairman of the audit committee describing the committee's responsibilities and activities." For further reference, see the *Report of the National Commission on Fraudulent Financial Reporting* (Washington, DC: NCFFR, 1987). In addition, in 1988, the MacDonald Commission in Canada supported the recommendation of the National Commission on Fraudulent Financial Reporting: "Indeed, we would go further. We advocate a publicly stated mandate from the board to the audit committee. The committee's annual reporting to the shareholders would then describe specifically what it did to discharge its mandate." See the *Report of the Commission to Study the Public's Expectations of Audits* (Toronto: Canadian Institute of Chartered Accountants, 1988), p. 36. For further reference, see Marilyn R. Kintzel, "The Use of Audit Committee Reports in Financial Reporting," *Internal Auditing* 6, No. 4 (Spring 1991), pp. 16–24; and Frank Urbancic, "The Usefulness of Audit Committee Reports: Assessments and Perceptions," *Journal of Applied Business Research* 7, No. 3 (Summer 1991), pp. 36–41. As noted in Chapter 10, Exhibit 10.1, the Blue Ribbon Committee on Improving the Effectiveness of Corporate Audit Committees recommends that the SEC require all reporting companies to include a letter from the auditee in the company's annual report to shareholders and Form 10-K Annual Report (see Chapter 2 for further details).

Exhibit 14.2   Audit Committee Report of Wal-Mart Stores, Inc.

Wal-Mart's Audit Committee consists of three directors, each of whom is "independent" as defined by the current listing standards of the New York Stock Exchange. The members of the Committee are Stanley C. Gault, Roland A. Hernandez, who is the Committee's chairperson, and J. Paul Reason. The Audit Committee is governed by a written charter adopted by the Board. Given the current trends in corporate governance, recent legislation by Congress, and the proposed New York Stock Exchange corporate governance listing standards, the Audit Committee and the Board recently adopted a revised Audit Committee charter in March 2003. A copy of the revised charter is available on our website at *www.walmartstores.com*.

   Wal-Mart's management is responsible for Wal-Mart's internal controls and financial reporting, including the preparation of Wal-Mart's consolidated financial statements. Wal-Mart's independent auditors are responsible for auditing Wal-Mart's annual consolidated financial statements in accordance with generally accepted auditing standards and ensuring that the financial statements fairly present Wal-Mart's results of operations and financial position. The independent auditors also are responsible for issuing a report on those financial statements. The Audit Committee monitors and oversees these processes. The Audit Committee annually recommends to the Board for its approval an independent accounting firm to be Wal-Mart's independent auditors. Beginning with the June 6, 2003 shareholders' meeting, ratification of the Board's approval of the independent auditors is being sought. Ernst & Young LLP is Wal-Mart's current independent auditor.

   As part of the oversight process, the Audit Committee regularly meets with management, the outside auditors, and Wal-Mart's internal auditors. The Audit Committee often meets with these groups in closed sessions. Throughout the year, the Audit Committee had full access to management, and the outside and internal auditors for the Company. To fulfill its responsibilities, the Audit Committee did the following:

- reviewed and discussed with Wal-Mart's management and the independent auditors Wal-Mart's consolidated financial statements for the fiscal year ended January 31, 2003;
- reviewed management's representations that those consolidated financial statements were prepared in accordance with generally accepted accounting principles and fairly present the results of operations and financial positions of the Company;
- discussed with the independent auditors the matters required by Statement on Auditing Standards 61, including matters related to the conduct of the audit of Wal-Mart's consolidated financial statements;
- received written disclosures and the letter from the independent auditors required by Independence Standards Board Standard No. 1 relating to their independence from Wal-Mart, and discussed with Ernst & Young LLP their independence from Wal-Mart;
- based on the discussions with management and the independent auditors, the independent auditors' disclosures and letter to the Audit Committee, the representations of management to the Audit Committee and the report of the independent auditors, the Audit Committee recommended to the board that Wal-Mart's audited annual consolidated financial statements for fiscal year 2003 be included in Wal-Mart's Annual Report on Form 10-K for the fiscal year ended January 31, 2003 for filing with the Securities and Exchange Commission;
- reviewed all non-audit services performed for Wal-Mart by Ernst & Young LLP and considered whether Ernst & Young LLP's provision of non-audit services was compatible with maintaining its independence from Wal-Mart;
- recommended that the Board select Ernst & Young LLP as Wal-Mart's independent auditors to audit and report on the annual consolidated financial statements of Wal-Mart filed with the Securities and Exchange Commission prior to Wal-Mart's annual shareholders meeting to be held in calendar year 2004; and
- consulted with advisors regarding the Sarbanes-Oxley Act of 2002, the New York Stock Exchange's proposed corporate governance listing standards and the corporate governance environment in general and considered any additional requirements placed on the Audit Committee as well as additional procedures or matters that the Audit Committee should consider.

The Audit Committee submits this report:

Stanley C. Gault
Roland A. Hernandez, Chairperson
J. Paul Reason

Source: Wal-Mart Stores, Inc. *2003 Annual Meeting and Proxy Statement*, pp. 5–6.

CONCLUDING OBSERVATIONS

Over the past two decades, the audit committee of the board of directors has evolved into a viable mechanism (an independent oversight group) in promoting a high degree of integrity in both the internal and external auditing processes as well as the financial reporting process. While the evolutionary process that created the audit committee was relatively slow, the major impetus toward the mandatory establishment of the committee came from the New York Stock Exchange in June 1978. Its adoption of mandatory audit committees as a listing requirement on the stock exchange has established standards to improve the accountability of corporate boards of directors and managers to their outside constituencies. Since the adoption of the listing requirement, the stock exchange(s) of an increasing number of countries with developed or emerging equity markets have adopted audit committees to increase transparency in their stock exchanges, which, in turn, helps facilitate foreign investment. Indeed, it is reasonable to expect that this trend will continue. The managements of stock exchanges have accepted the audit committee as a key mechanism within the corporate framework to help the board of directors not only address the needs of information users who rely on dependable financial reporting but also properly discharge its financial and fiduciary responsibilities to shareholders and other constituencies. Thus to the extent that the audit committee can monitor the internal and external audit processes and understand the perceived financial accounting information needs of the entity's constituencies, it can provide a balance in the corporate financial reporting process.

As Harold M. Williams, former chairman of the SEC, once stated in an address before the Securities Regulation Institute:

> Although the American Institute of Certified Public Accountants recently concluded that it should not compel public companies to establish audit committees as a precondition to obtaining an independent auditor's certification, it reiterated its support for the audit committee concept. In addition, the Foreign Corrupt Practices Act, and the importance which it places on establishing mechanisms to insure that the company has a functioning system of internal accounting controls, has given added impetus to the audit committee movement.
>
> Thus, at this point, the central task is to define the audit committee's responsibilities and enhance the quality of the committee's work.[6]

In light of Williams's comments, the first edition of this book was written to respond to the central task of clearly defining the audit committee's responsibilities as well as to enhance the quality of the committee's work. The audit committee is fundamental to the improvement of the board of directors' stewardship accountability to its constituencies.

It is clearly evident from the public and private sector initiatives in the 1980s and 1990s as well as the Sarbanes-Oxley Act of 2002 that the concept of audit committees has continued as an integral part of corporate governance and accountability. Both sectors have recognized that audit committees have made important contributions in promoting the investing public's confidence in the integrity of the auditing processes and the financial reporting process. Equally important, audit committees have become a key element in the entity's system of internal control to help engender a high degree of credibility of financial reporting, which, in turn, helps safeguard the securities market. Their independent oversight responsibility in the internal control environment helps to ensure the independence of both internal and external auditors. As a result, the full board of directors is assured of objective financial reporting by management.

---

[6]Harold M. Williams, "Corporate Accountability—One Year Later," address presented at the Sixth Annual Securities Regulation Institute, San Diego, California, January 18, 1979.

Future Perspectives Revisited

The 19 years since the first edition, 10 years since the second edition, and 5 years since the third edition of this book were published have been years of dynamic changes in corporate governance, particularly as it has affected audit committees. In the author's view, the future will continue to bring further changes and added duties and responsibilities for members of audit committees.

The intent here is not to comment fully on each of these possible developments but merely to use a "crystal ball," presenting the views of one informed commentator on audit committee activities since the third edition.

Reporting

- As recommended by the Treadway Report, reports of audit committees will increasingly be included in corporate annual reports.

  Reality Check: The Securities and Exchange Commission and the self-regulatory organizations now require that audit committees's reports be included in the annual proxy statement to shareholders.

- Corporate management will be required to include in its annual report a statement about the adequacy of the company's internal control, and the company's external auditors will be required to comment on that statement.

  Reality Check: The Sarbanes-Oxley Act of 2002 and the SEC rules implementing the act now require that the annual report contain a report on management's responsibility for internal controls and assessment of the effectiveness of internal controls for financial reporting, including the independent auditors' attestation report on management's assertion related to the annual audit.

- Future legislation will require the external auditor to report to appropriate authorities, such as the SEC, suspected illegalities discovered by the auditor if the company's management or board of directors (i.e., audit committee) fails to take appropriate action.

  Reality Check: The Private Securities Litigation Reform Act of 1995 requires external auditors who detect illegal acts to report their findings to the SEC if the client fails to take appropriate action on such acts that have a material effect on the financial statements. The Sarbanes-Oxley Act of 2002 established a whistle-blower communication process.

- The form and content of financial statements will be revised over time, as suggested by the Public Oversight Board. In addition, disclosures relating to business risks and uncertainties will result in further disclosures in financial reports and in modification to the standard auditor's reports. Both of these factors will have future implications for audit committees.

  Reality Check: The Sarbanes-Oxley Act of 2002 replaced the Public Oversight Board with the Public Company Accounting Oversight Board to oversee the accounting profession.

- The Treadway Report included a recommendation that corporate audit committees have additional responsibilities with respect to an entity's unaudited quarterly earnings report. Although this recommendation has not been adopted by many corporations, it is the author's belief that audit committees' oversight in the future will include quarterly reporting to further ensure the integrity of the interim reporting process.

Reality Check: The Sarbanes-Oxley Act of 2002 requires that the CEO and the CFO must certify annual and quarterly reports, including disclosure controls and procedures. The New York Stock Exchange has set forth the requirement that the audit committee members discuss annual and quarterly financial statements with management and the independent auditors.

Other Areas of Future Change

Internal Auditing   As noted in the 1988 Conference Board Research Report ("The Audit Committee: A Broader Mandate"), audit committees are believed to have significantly improved procedures and practices related to the internal auditing function. It is expected that this will continue.

The report of the Treadway Commission recommended that all public companies have an internal audit function. Despite this, many companies, particularly those in the middle and small "cap" range, have not adopted this recommendation for a variety of reasons, including those related to the current economic environment.

It is the author's belief that there will be continued demand to require an internal audit function for all public companies. Furthermore, in those instances in which it may not be economically feasible or practicable to establish a fully staffed internal audit function, this service will be procured from outside firms that specialize in providing such services to the middle and small markets.

Reality Check: The New York Stock Exchange has set forth a requirement that each listed company must have an internal audit function. Additionally, it is unlawful for independent auditors to provide internal audit outsourcing services to SEC audit clients.

Enhanced Audit Committee Liability   The Conference Board Report ("The Audit Committee: A Broader Mandate") indicated that CEOs and CFOs could be deemed to have a special responsibility or knowledge that could increase the possibility of their being sued in a class action. However, most believed that corporate indemnification, D & O insurance, and state statutory protection would be sufficient to offset the additional exposure.

Nevertheless, in view of increasing litigation against members of boards serving on corporate audit committees, it is prudent for audit committee directors to follow the guidance of the Treadway Report and good audit committee practices, as set forth in this book. It is increasingly important from a litigation point of view for an audit committee to do its job well and to document that fact.

Reality Check: As indicated in Chapter 4, the audit committee legal liability exposure is under both state and federal statutory laws. With the enactment of the Sarbanes-Oxley Act, it is reasonable to expect that the committee's enhanced legal liability may be in the area of internal governance. For example, the audit committee should know when to retain the services of independent advisors. However, as evidenced by other cases and in particular the Caremark International case, the audit committee must demonstrate active oversight and due diligence in discharging its responsibilities.

Independent Advisors

The Federal Deposit Insurance Corporation Improvement Act of 1991 (FDICIA) sets forth a number of requirements with respect to audit committees, as noted elsewhere in this book. It further requires larger depository financial institutions to provide independent counsel to audit committees. The Treadway Report also recommended that audit committees have the authority to retain expert consultants or advisors to assist them as needed in meeting their duties and responsibilities, or possibly to evaluate the committee's performance.

In view of the ever-expanding duties and responsibilities of audit committees and, perhaps, increased liability in the future, it is not unreasonable to assume that committees will increasingly seek outside independent advisors to assist them in the effective performance of their charter.

Reality Check: As previously mentioned, the Sarbanes-Oxley Act of 2002 establishes a requirement for the retention of outside independent advisors by the audit committee.

While the dynamic changes in corporate governance and the financial reporting needs of investors continue to impact the role and responsibility of audit committees, to limit the potential litigation risk, the board of directors should consider the overall performance of the committee and reexamine periodically the terms of reference in the committee's charter, as set forth in this book.

Recognizing that audit committees have an independent oversight function and operate on a part-time basis, the board and management should avoid diluting the activities of the committee by inappropriately expanding the scope of its charter. Thus the board should approve any modifications in the terms of reference of the audit committee.

Clearly, the rapidly changing environment in both the corporate and financial communities necessitates the need for a continuing education program for audit committees. Such a program would enable the committee to cope with recent accounting, auditing, and financial reporting developments and thus enable members better to assist their full boards of directors with discharging their fiduciary responsibilities to the shareholders. The self-regulatory organizations (NYSE and Nasdaq) have set forth recommendations regarding continuing education for boards of directors and their standing committees. Professor Jane F. Mutchler has proposed "a more holistic view of auditing." She combines the dictionary definition of auditing and the definition of assurance services from the AICPA Special Committee on Assurance Services (Elliott Committee):

> an independent, methodological examination and review of a situation or condition and a reporting of the results of the examination to improve the quality of information or its context for decision makers.[7]

---

[7]Jane F. Mutchler, "Report of the Chairperson," Auditing Section/American Accounting Association, *Auditor's Report* 20 (Fall 1996), pp. 1–2.

Given this definition, Mutchler concludes:

> If we view auditing in this context, a whole new world beyond financial statement auditing opens up. Now we are talking about systems auditing, operational auditing, ethics auditing, risk auditing, management auditing, business process auditing. This not only provides a vision for new services to be offered but also, and perhaps more important for our organization, provides a whole new vision for curriculum and research issues.[8]

In a study dealing with boards of directors and corporate governance over the next 10 years, Oxford Analytica reported with respect to the oversight function:

> The key question regarding the oversight function of corporate boards concerns their ability to discipline or even replace management for poor performance before a company is overtaken by a crisis. This is no easy task: challenging the management of a company, even if it is not performing well, requires board members to be well-informed and confident. They are also very likely to need the backing of powerful stakeholders as a counterweight to the power of the CEO.
>
> Oversight is thus likely to be most effective where directors:
>
> > Possess and have a reputation for considerable expertise relevant to evaluating the firm's performance; and
> >
> > Respond to the interests of major shareholders, or are individuals who enjoy the backing of major shareholders.
>
> Certain organizational and structural changes may enhance the ability of the board to keep a watchful eye on management's actions. The rise of the audit committee in US, Canadian, and UK corporations is one of the most important such developments and merits careful examination.[9]

Recently, both Corporate America and the accounting profession have come under increased congressional scrutiny because of major accounting scandals that have shaken the global capital markets. Since the Enron and WorldCom fallout, a number of public and private sector institutions have issued reforms with respect to audit committees and corporate governance. Presumably these reforms and the new regulatory and legal framework will provide guidance and assistance to boards of directors and their audit committee in effectively discharging their fiduciary responsibilities to shareholders. Likewise these reforms will enable audit committees to maintain quality in their oversight of the audit processes and financial reporting process to restore investor confidence in the financial reporting system.

---

[8]Ibid., 2.

[9]Oxford Analytica, *Board Directors and Corporate Governance, Trends in the G7 Countries over the Next Ten Years, Executive Report* (Oxford: Oxford Analytica, 1992), p. 7. For an expanded discussion of forward-looking activities of audit committees, see Arthur L. Ruffing, Jr., "The Future Role of the Audit Committee," *Directors & Boards* 18, No. 3 (Spring 1994), pp. 51–54. Also, the reader may wish to review Exhibit D.1 in Appendix D on this book's website to see the rise of audit committees in certain countries and to see the 1998 speeches on the Internet by Lynn Turner, chief accountant of the SEC, that address the role of audit committees: *www.sec.gov/news/speeches/spch226.htm*.

This fourth edition has examined the chronological events and developments in both the public and private sectors associated with audit committees. Such examination is essential in order to enhance their effectiveness. Given the increasing pervasiveness and the number of audit committees, it is reasonable to expect that they will continue to receive a high level of attention from the investing public.

SOURCES AND SUGGESTED READINGS

Bacon, Jeremy, *The Audit Committee: A Broader Mandate,* Report No. 914 (New York: The Conference Board, 1988).

Canadian Institute of Chartered Accountants, *Report of the Commission to Study the Public's Expectations of Audits* (Toronto: CICA, 1988).

Kintzel, Marilyn R., "The Use of Audit Committee Reports in Financial Reporting." *Internal Auditing* 6, No. 4 (Spring 1991), pp. 16–24.

Mutchler, Jane F., "Report of the Chairperson." *The Auditor's Report* 20 (Fall 1996), pp. 1–2.

National Commission on Fraudulent Financial Reporting, *Report of the National Commission on Fraudulent Financial Reporting* (Washington, DC: NCFFR, 1987).

Oxford Analytica, *Board Directors and Corporate Governance, Trends in the G7 Countries over the Next Ten Years, Executive Report* (Oxford: Oxford Analytica, 1992).

Ruffing, Arthur L., Jr., "The Future Role of Audit Committee." *Directors & Boards* 18, No. 3 (Spring 1994), pp. 51–54.

Securities and Exchange Commission, *Release No. 34-47672, Proposed Rule Change Relating to Corporate Governance*, April 11, 2003, *www.sec.gov/ruls/SRO/34-47672.htm.*

Urbancic, Frank, "The Usefulness of Audit Committee Reports: Assessments and Perceptions." *Journal of Applied Business Research* 7, No. 3 (Summer 1991), pp. 36–41.

Wal-Mart Stores, Inc., *2003 Annual Meeting and Proxy Statement.*

Wal-Mart Stores, Inc., *2003 Annual Report.*

Williams, Harold M., "Corporate Accountability—One Year Later," January 18, 1979. Address presented at the Sixth Annual Securities Regulation Institute, San Diego, California.

Accounting, Auditing, and Attestation Standards Topical Index of References to Accounting Principles Board, Financial Accounting Standards Board, Statement on Auditing Standards, Statement on Standards for Attestation Engagements, and Accounting Standards Executive Committee Pronouncements as of June 30, 2003

Accounting/Auditing Topic	APB Reference Number	FASB Standard Reference Number	FASB Interpretation Reference Number	SAS Reference Number	SSAE Reference Number
Accounting changes	20*	32,* 56, 73, 83	1, 20	58	
Accounting estimate	20*			57	
Accounting policies	22*				
Accounts receivable and payable—interest on transfers	21*	77	2	67	
Accounts receivable confirmation				67	
Adequacy of disclosure in financial statements				32	
Agreed-upon procedures					4**
Analytical review procedures				56	
Asset retirement obligations		143			
Attestation standards					1*
Audited financial statements—other information				8	
Audit adjustments				89	
Audit planning and supervision				22	
Audit risk and materiality				47	
Audit sampling				39	
Audits of governmental entities				74	
Auditors' reports				26, 29, 35, 42, 50, 51, 58*, 97, 98, 62, 69, 79, 87, 91, 95	
Business combinations	16*	10, 38, 79, 141	4, 9*		
Business segment report		14,* 18, 21, 24, 30, 131		21	
Capitalization of interest cost		34,* 42, 58, 62	33		

Accounting/Auditing Topic	APB Reference Number	FASB Standard Reference Number	FASB Interpretation Reference Number	SAS Reference Number	SSAE Reference Number
Extraordinary items	30				
Filing under Federal Securities Statutes				37	1*
Financial forecasts and projections					
Financial instruments		105,* 107,* 119,* 126,* 133,* 137, 149, 150	39		
Financial reporting and changing prices		39,* 40, 41, 33,* 46, 54, 82, 89,* 70			
Fair value measurement				101	
Financial statements-not-for-profit		117*			
Foreign currency exchange		8, 20, 52	15, 17, 37		
Franchise fee revenue		45			
Fraud				99	
Future contracts		80			
Guarantor's accounting			45		
Illegal client acts				54	
Impairment of long-lived assets		139, 144			
Income taxes	11,* 23,* 24	9, 31, 37, 109	18, 22, 29		
Inquiry of a client's lawyer				12	
Intangible assets	17*	44,* 72,* 121,* 142			
Interim financial information	28*	3		100	
Internal audit effects on the audit				65	
Internal control—IT				94	
Internal control—communication of weakness				55,* 60	2,** 6**
Investments in common stock	18*	94	35	92	

Topic	(1)	(2)	(3)	(4)	(5)	(6)
Investments in securities	2,* 4					
Investment tax credit		115, 124				8**
Leases		13,* 17,* 22, 23, 26,* 27, 28, 29, 98	25, 32	19, 21, 23, 24, 26, 27		
Letters for underwriters					72, 79, 86	
Loan impairment		114, 118			87	
Management discussion and analysis		134				
Mortgage-backed securities	29					
Nonmonetary transactions	78			30		
Obligations callable by the creditor	8*					
Pension plans		35,* 36, 75,* 87, 88, 110, 132		3		
Postretirement benefits other than pension		81, 106, 112				
Preacquisition contingencies of purchased enterprises		38				
Prior period adjustments		16				
Processing of transactions by service organizations		49			70,* 88	
Product financing arrangements					25	12
Quality control for CPA firms					59	
Question about an entity's continued existence				43		
Real estate sales		6				
Refinancing of expected short-term obligations						
Related-party transactions		57			45	
Reporting on pro forma financial information				41		1**
Repurchase and reverse purchase						
Research and development costs		2, 68				
Reserves		5				
Restricting the use of an auditor's report					87	

Accounting/Auditing Topic	APB Reference Number	FASB Standard Reference Number	FASB Interpretation Reference Number	SAS Reference Number	SSAE Reference Number
Revenue recognition right of return		48			
Special termination benefits paid to employees		74			
Specialized industry areas		50, 51, 53,* 60,* 61, 63,* 65,* 66,* 67, 71,* 90, 91,* 92, 97, 101, 111, 113, 120, 122, 139	36, 40		
Stock-based compensation		123, 148	44		
Subsequent events				1	
Supplementary information required by FASB				52	
Transfers and servicing of financial assets and extinguishment of liabilities		125,* 127, 140			
Transfers of assets		136	42		
Troubled debt restructuring—debtors and creditors		15			
Understanding with the client				83	7**
Using the work of a specialist				73, 76	
Working papers				41	5**
Note: For oil and gas companies see		19,* 25,* 69		45	

*Partially or fully amended.
**Revised and recodified SSAE Nos. 1–9 into SSAE No. 10.

AICPA STATEMENTS OF POSITION (SOPS)

SOP 94-1, Inquiries of State Insurance Regulators

SOP 94-2, The Application of the Requirements of Accounting Research Bulletins, Opinions of the Accounting Principles Board, and Statements and Interpretations of the Financial Accounting Standards Board to Not-for-Profit Organizations

SOP 94-3, Reporting of Related Entities for Not-for-Profit Organizations

SOP 94-4, Reporting of Investment Contracts Held by Health and Welfare Benefit Plans and Defined-Contribution Pension Plans

SOP 94-5, Disclosures of Certain Matters in the Financial Statements of Insurance Enterprises

SOP 94-6, Disclosure of Certain Significant Risks and Uncertainties

SOP 95-1, Accounting for Certain Insurance Activities of Mutual Life Insurance Enterprises

SOP 95-2, Financial Reporting by Nonpublic Investment Partnerships

SOP 95-3, Accounting for Certain Distribution Costs of Investment Companies

SOP 95-4, Letters for State Insurance Regulators to Comply With the NAIC Model Audit Rule

SOP 95-5, Auditors' Reporting on Statutory Financial Statements of Insurance Companies

SOP 96-1, Environmental Remediation Liabilities

SOP 97-1, Accounting by Participating Mortgage Loan Borrowers

SOP 97-2, Software Revenue Recognition—supersedes SOP 91-1

SOP 97-3, Accounting by Insurance and Other Enterprises for Insurance-Related Assessments

SOP 98-1, Accounting for the Costs of Computer Software Developed or Planned for Internal Use

SOP 98-2, Accounting for Costs of Activities of Not-For-Profit Organizations and State and Local Governmental Entities That Include Fund-Raising

SOP 98-3, Audits of States, Local Governments, and Not-For-Profit Organizations Receiving Federal Awards—supersedes SOP 92-9, Audits of Not-For-Profit Organizations Receiving Federal Awards.

SOP 98-4, Deferral of the Effective Date of a Provision of SOP 97-2, Software Revenue Recognition

SOP 98-5, Reporting on the Costs of Start-up Activities

SOP 98-9, Modification of SOP 97-2

SOP 99-1, Guidance to Practitioners in Conducting and Reporting on an Agreed-Upon Procedures Engagement to Assist Management in Evaluating the Effectiveness of Its Corporate Compliance Program

SOP 99-2, Accounting for and Reporting of Postretirement Medical Benefit (401(b)) Features of Defined Benefit Pension Plans

SOP 99-3, Accounting for and Reporting of Certain Defined Contributions Plan Investments and Other Disclosure Matters

SOP 00-1, Auditing Health Care Third-Party Revenue and Related Receivables

SOP 00-2, Accounting by Producers or Distributions of Films

SOP 00-3, Accounting by Insurance Enterprises for Demutualizations and Formations of Mutual Insurance Companies and for Certain Long-Duration Participating Contracts

SOP 01-1, Amendments to Scope of SOP 95-2, Financial Reporting by Nonpublic Investment Partnerships, to Include Commodity Pools

SOP 01-2, Health and Welfare Benefit Plan Accounting

SOP 01-3, Performing Agreed-Upon Procedures Engagements that Address Internal Control Over Derivative Transactions as Required by the New York State Insurance Law

SOP 01-4, Reporting Pursuant to Association for Investment Management and Research Performance Presentation Standards

SOP 01-5, Amendments to Specific AICPA Pronouncements for Changes Related to the NAIC Codification

SOP 01-6, Accounting by Certain Entities (Including Entities with Trade Receivables) That Lend to or Finance the Activities of Others

SOP 02-1, Performing Agreed-Upon Procedures Engagements that Address Annual Claims Prompt Payment Reports as Required by the New Jersey Administrative Code

SOP 02-2, Accounting for Derivative Instruments and Hedging Activities by Not-for-Profit Health Care Organizations, and Clarification of the Performance Indicator

Professional Accounting Associations, Business Organizations, Boards, Commissions, and Directors Publications

The American Assembly
Columbia University
475 Riverside Drive
Suite 456
New York, NY 10115-0456
(212) 870-3500
www.columbia.edu/cu/amassembly

American Accounting Association
5717 Bessie Drive
Sarasota, FL 34233
(813) 921-7747
www.aaahq.org/index.cfm

American Bar Association
750 N. Lake Shore Drive
Chicago, IL 60611
1-800-285-2221
www.abanet.org

American Institute of Certified Public
Accountants
1211 Avenue of the Americas
New York, NY 10036-8775
(212) 596-6200 or 1-888-777-7077
www.aicpa.org

American Law Institute
4025 Chestnut Street
Philadelphia, PA 19104
1-800-253-6397
www.ali-aba.org

American Society of Corporate
Secretaries, Inc.
521 Fifth Avenue
New York, NY 10175
(212) 681-2000
www.ascs.org

Association for Investment
Management and Research
560 Ray C. Hunt Drive
P.O. Box 3668
Charlottesville, VA 22903
(800) 247-8132
www.aimr.org

Association of Certified Fraud
Examiners
The Gregor Building
716 West Avenue
Austin, TX 78701
(512) 478-9070
1-800-245-3321
www.cfenet.com

Association of Government
Accountants
2200 Mount Vernon Avenue
Alexandria, VA 22301
(703) 684-6931
www.rutgers.edu/accounting/raw/aga/
home.htm

Australian Institute of Company
   Director
Company Director House
3rd Floor
71 York Street
Sydney, NSW, Australia
(02) 299-8788

The Business Roundtable
1615 L Street N.W.
Suite 1100
Washington, DC 20036
(202) 872-1260
www.brtable.org

The Canadian Institute of Chartered
   Accountants
277 Wellington Street West
Toronto, Canada M5V 3H2
(416) 977-3222
www.cica.ca

Committee of Sponsoring
   Organizations of the Treadway
   Commission (COSO)
American Institute of Certified Public
   Accountants
1211 Avenue of the Americas
6th Floor
New York, NY 10036-8775
(212) 575-6656
www.aicpa.org

The Conference Board
845 Third Avenue
New York, NY 10022
(212) 339-0345
www.conference-board.org

The Corporate Board
4440 Hagadorn Road
Okemos, MI 48864
(517) 336-1700
www.corporateboard.com

Directorship Search Group
Directorship
8 Sound Shore Drive
Greenwich, CT 06830
(203) 618-7000
www.directorship.com

Directors & Boards
1845 Walnut Street
Philadelphia, PA 19103
(215) 567-3200
www.directorsandboards.com

Financial Accounting Standards
   Board
401 Merritt 7
P.O. Box 5116
Norwalk, CT 06856
(203) 847-0700
www.fasb.org

Financial Executives International
10 Madison Avenue, P.O. Box 1938
Morristown, NJ 07962
(201) 898-4609
www.fei.org

Government Accounting Standards
   Board
401 Merritt 7
P.O. Box 5116
Norwalk, CT 06856
(203) 847-0700
www.fasb.org

Heidrick and Struggles
245 Park Avenue
New York, NY 10167
(212) 867-9876
www.H-S.com

The Institute of Internal Auditors, Inc.
247 Maitland Avenue
Altamonte Springs, FL 32701
(407) 830-7600
www.theiia.org

International Accounting Standards
   Board
30 Cannon Street
London EC4M 6XH
United Kingdom
(44) 713530565
www.iasc.org.uk

International Auditing and Assurance
   Standards Board
545 Fifth Avenue
New York, NY 10017
(212) 471-8702
www.ifac.org

International Federation of
   Accountants (IFAC)
545 Fifth Avenue
New York, NY 10036
(212) 471-8702
www.ifac.org

International Organization of
   Securities Commissions (IOSCO)
C/ Oquendo 12
28006 Madrid
Spain
(34) 914175549
www.iosco.org

Institute of Corporate Directors
277 Wellington Street West
Toronto, Ontario M5V 3H2
(416) 204-3311
www.icd.ca

Institute of Management Accountants
10 Paragon Drive
Montvale, NJ 07645
1-800-638-4427
www.imanet.org

Investor Responsibility Research
   Center
Suite 700
1350 Connecticut Avenue N.W.
Washington, DC 20036
(202) 833-0700
www.irrc.org

Korn/Ferry International
237 Park Avenue
New York, NY 10017
(212) 687-1834
www.kornferry.com

National Association of Corporate
   Directors
1828 L Street N.W.
Suite 801
Washington, DC 20036
(202) 775-0509
www.nacdonline.org

National Association of Securities
   Dealers, Inc.
1735 K Street, NW
Washington, DC 20006
(202) 728-8000
www.nasd.com

National Investor Relations Institute
8020 Towers Crescent Drive
Suite 250
Vienna, VA 22182
(703) 506-3570
www.niri.org

New York State Society of Certified
   Public Accountants
530 Fifth Avenue
New York, NY 10036-5101
1-800-633-6320
www.nysscpa.com

New York Stock Exchange, Inc.
Eleven Wall Street
New York, NY 10005
(212) 656-2017
www.nyse.com

Organization for Economic
    Co-operation and Development
2 Rue André-Pascal
75775 Paris, Cedex 16
France
www.oecd.org

Oxford Analytica, Ltd.
52 New Inn Hall Street
Oxford OX1 2QB, England
(44) 865-244442

Public Company Accounting
    Oversight Board
1666 K Street N.W.
Washington, DC 20006
(202) 207-9100
www.pcaobus.org

Russell Reynolds Associates
200 Park Avenue
New York, NY 10166
(212) 351-2000
www.russreyn.com

U.S. General Accounting Office
Washington, DC 20548
(202) 275-6241
www.gao.gov

U.S. Securities and Exchange
    Commission
450 Fifth Street N.W.
Washington, DC 20549
(202) 942-8088
www.sec.gov

Index

financial statements, 98, 291
organizations influencing, 182, 184
selection of accounting methods, 184
sources of, 182, 183
unqualified opinion of auditors, 184, 185
Generally accepted auditing standards (GAAS),
    80
  and accounting standards, 181–189. *See also*
    Generally accepted accounting
    principles (GAAP)
  and auditing procedures, 179
  auditors' reports, 373
  field work standards, 179–181
    and audit planning, 199
    materiality, 199
  general standards, 179, 180
  reporting standards, 179
    conformance with GAAP, 182–185
    consistency, 185, 186
    disclosures, 186
    fairness, 188, 189
    materiality, 186–188
  scope of report, 178
Gerson, James S., 293, 356
Global Crossing, 137
Going concern evaluation, 124
Government Accounting Standards Board, 414
Government audits, 211–215
"Grease payments," 350
Groves, Ray, 84
Grusd, Neville, 114
Gulf Canada Resources, Ltd., 7
Guttman v. Nvidia Corporation, 159, 169

Hanson, Walter E., 354
Harris, James F., 362
Harriss, C. Lowell, 362
Heidrick and Struggles, 414
Heyler, Grover R., 358
Hickman, Kent, 55
Hills, Roderick M., 363
H.J. Heinz, 157, 158
Hoffman, Ralph, 44
Horn, Karen N., 251

Illegal acts, 399
  board of directors, responsibilities regarding,
    357, 358
  communication with audit committee, 333
  defined, 332
  detection of, 332, 333
  external auditor's responsibilities, 357, 358
  reporting recommendations, 333–335
  warning signs, 334
Independence standard, 43–45, 48, 54–55,
    77–79

Independence Standards Board, 137
Independent auditors
  appointment of, 228
  and audit committee, 83, 84, 384, 385, 392
  and audit planning, 226
  auditors' report. *See* Auditors' report
  change in auditors, 126
  duty of care, 180
  external auditing, nature of, 80–84
  fraud
    communication to audit committee,
      331–333
    detection of, 333–335
    effect of on auditor's report, 330, 331
    and fairness of presentation in financial
      statements, 335
    illegal acts by client companies, 332, 333
    investigation, 338
    standards and responsibilities, 329–330
  illegal acts, responsibilities concerning, 332,
    333, 357, 358
  integrity and objectivity, 293
  and internal controls, 241, 242
  management compliance with disclosure
    requirements, 296
  reporting to audit committee, 306–309
    examples, 378, 379
Institute of Corporate Directors, 415
Institute of Internal Auditors (IIA), 182, 414
  fraud defined, 321
  independence of internal auditors, 263
  internal auditing defined, 84, 249
  Practice Advisories. *See* Practice Advisories
  *Standards for the Professional Practice of
    Internal Auditing,* 252–259
Institute of Management Accountants, 182, 415
Institutional investors, 100
Insurance
  directors and officers liability insurance, 143
  insurance companies as credit grantors. *See*
    Credit grantors
Internal audit group, 249
  assessments, 284–288
  and audit committee, 33, 85, 94, 249–252,
    263, 264
  audit committee event matrix, 275
  and audit planning, 226
  corporate philosophy, 261–263
  and external auditors, 261
  focus-group approach, 261
  future trends, 400
  importance of, 289, 290
  independence, 263, 264
    Practice Advisories, 264–272
  internal auditing defined, 84, 249
  internal control. *See* Internal control